On
Thermonuclear
War

On
Thermonuclear
War

HERMAN KAHN
With a new introduction by Evan Jones

Transaction Publishers
New Brunswick (U.S.A.) and London (U.K.)

Library of Congress Catalog Number: 2006050043
ISBN: 978-1-4128-0664-0
Printed in the United States of America

Library of Congress Cataloging-in-Publication Data

Kahn, Herman, 1922-
   On thermonuclear war / Herman Kahn, with a new introduction by Evan Jones.
      p. cm.
   Includes bibliographical references and index.
   1. Nuclear warfare. I. Title.

U263.K324   2007
355.02'17—dc22   2006050043

CONTENTS

TABLES

PART I

LECTURE I

CHAPTER I

CHAPTER II

CHAPTER III

TABLES

LIST OF FIGURES

INTRODUCTION TO THE TRANSACTION EDITION

On Thermonuclear War was controversial when published and remains so today. It is iconoclastic; worse, it is interdisciplinary. Finally (to the horror of many of its critics), it is calm and compellingly reasonable. This book was widely read on both sides of the Iron Curtain, and the result was serious revision in both Western and Soviet strategy and doctrine. It brought rationality to the public nuclear debate at a time when hysteria on all sides was the norm. As a result, both sides were better able to avoid disaster during the Cold War. Although developed from a Cold War perspective, the strategic concepts still apply: strategic defense, local animosities, and the usual balance-of-power issues are still very much with us.

Kahn's stated purpose in writing this book was simply: "avoiding disaster and buying time, without specifying the use of this time." By the late 1950s, with both sides H-bomb-armed, both reason and time were in short supply. We have all heard the analogies: two scorpions trapped in a bottle; a bee who must die if it stings even once; two men up to their waists in gasoline, arguing over who has the most matches; international suicide. In 1955, fifty-two Nobel laureates signed the Mainu Declaration that any nation unwilling to denounce force as a final resort would "cease to exist." Many thought that further study into the matter was not only counterproductive, but immoral. And, at that, official public policy regarding the use of nuclear weapons left much to be desired: "Nuclear Tripwire," "Massive Retaliation," and what later became known as Mutual Assured Destruction ("MAD").

Kahn, a military analyst at Rand since 1948, understood that a defense based on that sort of inconceivable presumption was morally questionable and not credible. One European critic bitterly observed that in order to defend Europe, America had promised to commit murder-suicide: "We urge you to break this promise." And, partly as a result of this book (and its "sequels"), official policy came to rely more and more on the doctrine of "flexible response." Kahn's "counterforce plus avoidance" theory of threatening military targets while avoiding civilian centers quietly came to reality over the next three decades.

Contemporary critics excoriated *On Thermonuclear War* as a "how-to" book: "how to fight a nuclear war; how to win it; how to get away with it."

Yet it should be obvious to any impartial reader that Kahn is actually demonstrating how to avoid it; how to limit it; how to end it (or win it without firing a shot).

This book was the first to make sense of nuclear weapons. Originally created from a series of lectures, it provides insight into how policymakers consider such issues. One may agree with Kahn or disagree with him on specific issues, but he has clearly defined the terrain of the argument. He also looks at other weapons of mass destruction such as biological and chemical, and the history of its past use.

Kahn has been compared (unfavorably) with Machiavelli, but the Clausewitz analogy is more apt. The problems of defense in the modern world are unprecedentedly complex. He carefully examined the principle of how a nation can take up an essentially defensive posture in an environment dominated by inherently offensive weapons. He reminds us that defense via deterrence can be a subtle notion. Even the *Peace Catalog* (1984 edition) dryly observed that *On Thermonuclear War* is "still the best introduction to the if-we-do-this-they'll-do-that school of strategic analysis."

The Cold War is over. Despite crises ranging from Berlin to Cuba, the West won a decisive victory without the use of a single nuclear weapon on either side. But the nuclear genie is out of the bottle, and the lessons and principles developed in *On Thermonuclear War* apply as much to today's China, Russia, Iran, and North Korea as they did to the Soviets.

Evan Jones

FOREWORD

IN THE ANALYSIS of military problems since the war, the contribution of civilians has been unprecedentedly large in volume and high in quality. Herman Kahn's book clearly demonstrates the chief reason for this phenomenon. The problems of defense have become inordinately complex, and their solution is not susceptible to the rules of thumb, often called principles, which the military derived from past experience. For stating and solving these problems, all the analytical techniques are required which the disciplines of social science, history, and mathematics have evolved. These techniques are not nearly adequate, but they are the best we have, and we must employ them if we do not want to base judgment and policy to an excessive degree on vague reasoning and sheer guesswork. Indeed, *On Thermonuclear War* is as remarkable for its sophisticated exercises in method as it is for the substantive solutions and proposals it offers. Without his masterly command of method, it would have been impossible for Herman Kahn to examine such an extraordinary range of interrelated problems and, compared with the extant literature, do it so exhaustively.

Since these are lectures in book form, some of the informality of the original presentation—of its style and organization—has been preserved. The step-by-step presentation of extremely complex problems will be appreciated by the reader as long as he refrains from evaluating particular points out of the unfolding context. Initially some readers may boggle at the unfamiliar idiom, which is hard-hitting and subtle, colorful and dispassionate, professional and as inevitably personal as are the different styles of, for example, Morgenstern and Brodie. Finally, it may be worth saying that, though the subject matter raises profound moral issues, this is not a book about the moral aspects of military problems.

Most of the research for this book was done at The RAND Corporation. It was written largely while the author was a Visiting Research Associate at the Center of International Studies. We were glad to support this venture and to sponsor its publication. Herman Kahn's presence at the Center was for many of us a great learning experience. This book opens this experience to many others.

KLAUS KNORR

Center of International Studies
Princeton University
May 23, 1960

PREFACE

MEN AND GOVERNMENTS have long lived with the painful problem of choice. Even those with courage to make hard choices and the willingness to choose resolutely between good and evil, redemption and damnation, joy and sorrow, have never been able to insure the final result. The final outcome of benevolent, informed, and intelligent decisions may turn out to be disastrous. But choices must be made; dies must be cast. So it is with the most dramatic "choices" open to the free world in our day: arms control, peaceful coexistence, rearmament, dynamic rollback, appeasement, Soviet domination, thermonuclear war, or whatever shifting alternatives seem most appealing or least unpalatable from year to year.

The above "hard choices" are in sharp contrast to the vision of material progress held everywhere. In the United States and Western Europe poverty as a general economic problem has in the main been eliminated. There remain depressed areas (parts of Italy and Greece, for example), and there are many social and welfare problems (i.e., the Negro or migrant in parts of our nation, or the widowed family, or the aged and the sick), but the basic economic problem of providing the necessities seems to have been largely solved. Of course, people are still interested in improving their lot. In fact, there is much intense debate as to whether we should buckle down and double our wealth every ten years (6 per cent annual increase) or take it easy and double our wealth every twenty or forty years. But the current and future reality of vast military power concentrated in the hands of several unpredictable countries, accompanied by the past reality of expansionist doctrine in the communist nations, has brought Americans and Europeans face to face with the sobering thought that this triumph of material progress and human security may be reversed. We can choose among several courses of action. We have to be resolute and hopeful in our actions. And we have to be prepared for the possibility that we have chosen wrongly or that events may nevertheless continue to unfold in a thoroughly relentless way in spite of our choices.

This book examines the military side of what may be the major problem that faces civilization, comparing some of the alternatives that seem available and some of the implications in these choices. Even here I have not been as comprehensive, for reasons of space, as I would have liked to be. I have mostly restricted the discussion to the deterrence and waging of thermonuclear "Central Wars" between the United States and the Soviet Union, touching only lightly on Limited War and related alliance problems.

The lectures that form the body of the book were initially delivered in March 1959 at Princeton University to acquaint my colleagues at The Center of International Studies and some invited guests with certain aspects of thermonuclear war that are often overlooked. The lectures have been given in eleven other places in substantially the form in which they appear here. Less extensive presentations have also been given in more places and times than I care to remember. More than 5,000 persons with special interest in the subject, some of them highly qualified experts, have heard some portion or other of the material, and many of them have commented on it to the author in public and in correspondence. In spite of the fact that the material has been extensively thought out and talked over, I have approached publication with some hesitation. Much of the material in the lectures came out of "completed" study projects, but this book can be considered to contain more suggestions for work to be done than exposition of work completed.

If the book had had to wait until all the ideas in it could be thought through and set down with the great care that they really deserve, it would have been several years or longer before I could have had it ready for publication—particularly considering the pressure of other work. Barring a large increase in the research effort, it would be even longer before all of the researchable material was investigated. As it was, I kept an anxious publisher waiting almost a year while I carried a draft of the manuscript with me on airplanes and railroads.

I have preserved some of the style of the lectures throughout, at the risk of offending those who dislike occasional verbalisms in print, in order to feel freer in occasionally advancing tentative or speculative notions.

The major quality that distinguishes this book from most of the other works in this field is the adoption of the Systems Analysis point of view—the use of quantitative analysis where possible, and the setting up of a clear line of demarcation showing where quantitative analysis was not found relevant in whole or in part. Where data were not available or where they remain classified, I have tried to set forth the basic formulation of how such calculations are made or could be made. The techniques and philosophy are quite similar to those of the Operations Analyst, but due to the breadth of the problems and the resulting increased uncertainties the role of mathematics and lengthy computations is subordinated almost (but not quite) to the vanishing point, while a careful description of what the world is like gains much attention. For this reason, it has seemed possible to write for an audience that includes laymen without making any important technical concessions.

It is necessary to be quantitative. For example, in describing the aftermath of a war it is not particularly illuminating to use words such as "intolerable," "catastrophic," "total destruction," "annihilating retaliation," and so on. These words might be reasonable if it were really true that in a modern war the *total* target system would be "overkilled" by factors of five or ten. It would then be fruitless to calculate or describe the exact degree of overkill. But as we shall see, the facts do not lead in this direction. It is therefore important to get a "feel" for what the levels of damage might really be under various circumstances.

Some people appear to be very suspicious of calculations—and correctly so. I have written extensively elsewhere * on how quantitative analyses can lead either wittingly or unwittingly to error, but that does not mean that nonquantitative analyses are any less misleading. There is another reason for using numbers. The only way in which we can communicate even intuitive notions with any accuracy is to use quantitative measures. This may have the unfortunate effect of giving an appearance of great certainty, but I have taken care to use such words as "could," "may," "might," "should," "about," "neighborhood of," and so on, with some frequency. More than this I cannot do, for it would be unreasonable to be deliberately vague just because some readers will be vague.

I am convinced that whether or not the book is widely read in the United States and Europe, it will be read by some Russians at least, and it will be taken into account by some Soviet military planners. Whether this is a good or a bad thing I can hardly know, for it *is* important that the United States and Russia have certain views in common about strategic military problems. If this book can contribute to molding and creating a common background, it may be constructive. Nevertheless, a book of this character presents a certain danger. In the present world, where so much depends upon deterrence (which is, after all, a psychological phenomenon), and where

---

* Herman Kahn and Irwin Mann, *Techniques of Systems Analysis,* The Rand Corporation, Research Memorandum RM-1829-1, June 1957; and *Ten Common Pitfalls,* Research Memorandum RM-1937, July 17, 1957.

the Soviets' failure to exploit weaknesses in our posture may be due to inertia or innate conservatism, any book that treats deterrence objectively may encourage the Soviets toward experiment.

On the other hand, it is important for us to realize that certain problems exist, so that we can consider them before they reach the crisis stage; in some cases we must do so years before. *This book is dedicated to the goal of anticipating, avoiding, and alleviating crises.* I hope that it will stimulate interest in this goal among all those who are in a position to contribute to an understanding of the world's military and quasi-military problems. Also, I have long felt that there are many at universities and elsewhere who could contribute but do not, perhaps because they feel the problems are futile or uninteresting or so veiled in classified data that nothing can be done by those who have only the open literature available to them. Perhaps this book will help open some academic doors. I hope so.

There are also untapped intellectual resources among the ranks of those idealists who are deeply concerned but tend resolutely to close their minds to the nature and existence of military problems. I know of few people who believe that Western security problems will be solved by purely military preparations, but I believe that it is equally unlikely that a successful prescription will fail to involve adequate and well-designed military establishments. To the extent that certain idealists are willing to come to grips with the real world, their suggestions and programs are much more likely to prove helpful. To the extent that they are unwilling to do this I would conjecture that they are likely to do as much harm as good, but this kind of judgment is so uncertain that I advance it more as a warning than as a criticism.

I have a firm belief that unless we have more serious and sober thought on various facets of the strategic problem than seems to be typical of most discussion today, both classified and unclassified, we are not going to reach the year 2000—and maybe not even the year 1965—without a cataclysm of some sort, and that this cataclysm will prove a lot more cataclysmic than it needs to be. It is with the hope of decreasing the probability of catastrophe and alleviating the consequences of thermonuclear war if it comes that I offer these pages to all with the interest—and the courage—to read them.

HERMAN KAHN

Princeton, New Jersey
June 10, 1960

ACKNOWLEDGMENTS

THE CONCEPTS on which these three lectures are based originated in work done under the auspices of The RAND Corporation and continued at The Center of International Studies at Princeton University while I was on leave of absence from RAND. While many of the things that I discuss grew out of studies done by The RAND Corporation, the presentation and synthesis are my own. I accept full responsibility for them. However, I owe a tremendous debt to many friends and colleagues—so many that it would be impossible for me to identify them all. I will content myself with mentioning some of the major debts. In particular, I owe a good deal to early work done by E. J. Barlow and J. F. Digby in air defense, by Bernard Brodie in the general field of strategic planning, by Jack Hirshleifer on civil defense, and by Albert Wohlstetter, Frederic Hoffman, and H. S. Rowen on survival of strategic forces. Much of Lecture I, parts of Lecture II, and the Appendix derive from joint effort devoted to a RAND Corporation civil defense study which I led. This study is reported in RAND Report R-322-RC, *A Report on a Study of Non-Military Defense*, July 1, 1958. Because so much of the book is based on the findings of this study, I would like to repeat here some remarks that prefaced the report on that study:

The study . . . [was] supported by The RAND Corporation as part of its program of RAND-sponsored research. In addition to its work for the United States Air Force and other government agencies, the Corporation regularly sponsors, with its own funds, research projects in areas of importance to national security and public welfare. RAND-sponsored research is considered to be fundamentally the responsibility of the individuals involved in the project, and the conclusions of such projects are not necessarily endorsed by the Corporation. Such studies are published in the hope that they may contribute to wider understanding of important national problems.

This study of nonmilitary defense was initiated, directed, and formulated in its central features by Herman Kahn. Particular parts of the study were the responsibility of the following individuals, approximately in the order the subjects are mentioned in this report: Leon Gouré, foreign policy implications; Irwin Mann, improvised fallout shelters and other inexpensive measures; Robert Panero (from the staff of Guy B. Panero Engineers), mines and deep rock shelters; John O'Sullivan, conventional shelters and costs of complete shelter systems; Fred Iklé, strategic evacuation and social problems; Maj. Gen. Frank Ross, USA, ret., tactical evacuation; Leonard Berkovitz, performance of shelter systems under hypothetical attacks; Harold H. Mitchell, M.D., medical effects of radiation; Jerald

Hill, long-term fallout problems; Joseph Carrier, food and agriculture; Paul Clark, economic recuperation after a 50-city attack; Norman Hanunian, heavier attacks and industrial shelters; Col. George Reinhardt, USA, ret., "starter set" and recuperation stockpiles; Harry Rowen, interactions with active offense; Philip Dadant, interactions with active defense; Richard Moorsteen, Soviet nonmilitary defense capabilities. This summary report was drafted by Paul Clark.

A number of people in government agencies have been helpful in furnishing information and orientation. While it would be impossible to list them all, the assistance of the following should be acknowledged: Federal Civil Defense Administration—John Devaney, Gerald Gallagher, Jack Greene, Ralph Spears, Benjamin Taylor; Federal Reserve Board—Roland Robinson; Naval Radiological Defense Laboratory—Walmer Strope, Paul Tompkins; Office of Defense Mobilization—Joseph Coker, Brig. Gen. Harold Huglin, USAF, Burke Horton, Vincent Rock, Charles Sullivan; Science Advisory Committee—Spurgeon Keeney. Of course, none of the above is responsible for any portion of the study.

This report is unclassified, and no part of it depends on the use of classified information. In particular the hypothetical attacks considered in evaluating various nonmilitary defense measures should not be construed as statements of enemy offense capability or of U.S. defense capability. They are simply hypotheses about threats that appear conceivable sometime in the future and that provide a measure of the possible role of nonmilitary defense systems. Moreover, this report has been written as a summary statement for general distribution; technical aspects of the study are not presented in full detail.

I went to the Center of International Studies in February 1959 and spent several months there preparing these lectures. I then spent about half my remaining months at the Center rewriting, revising, and amplifying the lectures for eventual publication and for oral delivery. It would have been impossible for me to have done this task under such pressure of time if I had not had the help, advice, and encouragement of Klaus Knorr, Associate Director of the Center, and I would like to express my gratitude to him at this point.

An early version of the manuscript was read by Bernard Brodie, Daniel Ellsberg, and William Kaufmann—all of whom made helpful comments. Parts of this book (roughly pages 144–153 on "Doomsday Machines," pages 226–231 on the various ways war can start, and some brief excerpts from World Wars III to VII) appeared as an article in a special issue on Arms Control of *Daedalus* (Fall 1960) and benefited greatly from many comments by Donald G. Brennan, the special editor of this issue. I would also like to thank Marvin Lavin, Sidney G. Winter, Jr., and William Bowen for their helpful comments on Lecture I and Gordon A. Craig for his comments on

World Wars I and II in Lecture III. My thanks go also to Robert N. Grosse and his colleagues in the cost analysis section of The RAND Corporation for supplying almost all the statistical data used in the various figures. Lastly, I would like to express my appreciation to Gordon Hubel of Princeton University Press, not only for his essential contribution to the editing of the manuscript, but for possessing the exact mixture of tolerance and stern disciplinarianism that is so helpful in getting a book out of a reluctant author.

Finally and most important, I would like to thank Vaughn D. Bornet for his editing and suggestions on the language and substance of the book and Hubert L. Moshin for handling so many of the administrative and technical details of formulating and presenting the lectures and writing the book.

It should not be necessary for me to state that the discussions in this book do not necessarily reflect the opinions of any of the people or organizations that I have mentioned.

HERMAN KAHN

LECTURE I

THE NATURE AND FEASIBILITY OF
THERMONUCLEAR WAR

CHAPTER I

ALTERNATIVE NATIONAL STRATEGIES

Introduction

ON July 16, 1960 the world entered the sixteenth year of the nuclear era. Yet we are increasingly aware that after living with nuclear bombs for fifteen years we still have a great deal to learn about the possible effects of a nuclear war. We have even more to learn about conducting international relations in a world in which force tends to be both increasingly more available and increasingly more dangerous to use, and therefore in practice increasingly unusable. As a result of this continuous secular change in the basic structure of the international situation, foreign and defense policies formulated early in the nuclear era badly need review and reformulation.

In considering these basic foreign and defense policies it is desirable to distinguish many different military postures and the corresponding possible strategies for both the United States and the Soviet Union. This treatment of thermonuclear warfare will mostly concern itself with four typical possible postures, which I will call Finite Deterrence, Counterforce as Insurance, Preattack Mobilization Base, and Credible First Strike Capability respectively. I will discuss the possibilities and implications of these postures from the point of view of the Soviet Union and the United States. While there is no reason why the two most powerful nations should have similar views, I will not initially dwell on possible asymmetries, deferring discussion of the separate national problems. A number of typical basic postures (important concepts italicized for emphasis) are listed in Table 1, roughly in order of increasing ability to wage general war.

Probably the most valuable thing that the Executive Office could do to improve over-all defense planning would be to select one of these postures and the corresponding strategies, or possibly some clearly defined alternative not on the list, and let the Office of Civil and Defense Mobilization, the Department of Defense, and the Department of State know its decision. The decision could then be debated at the proper level, and it would not be necessary to conduct a philosophical debate at the staff level, on what business the Department of Defense should be in every time somebody brought up a technical question on Air Defense, Command and Control, and so on. National debates should be conducted at the national level where feasibility, desirability, and possible consequences can be discussed responsibly and from proper points of view. It is not possible to do this even at the level of a senior but technical advisory group attached to Departments or even to the

❖❖

TABLE 1

ALTERNATIVE NATIONAL POSTURES [a]

1. Internal Police Force plus "World Government"
2. *Minimum Deterrence* plus *Limited War* plus *Arms Control*
3. Add insurance to the *Minimum Deterrent:*
    (a) for reliability (*Finite Deterrence*)
    (b) against unreliability (*Counterforce as Insurance*)
    (c) against a change in policy (*Preattack Mobilization Base*)
4. Add *Credible First Strike Capability*
5. "Splendid" First Strike and no Limited War Capability
6. Dreams

---

[a] I am indebted to Richard B. Foster of Stanford Research Institute for the suggestion to make a list of this sort. He has used a somewhat different breakdown in some unpublished investigations on the actual strategic views held by U.S. decision makers.

❖❖

Executive Office, much less at lower staff levels. Advisory groups and agency and departmental staffs should be mainly concerned with implementing the general policy and reporting back to their superiors on cost, performance, and feasibility. In actual practice the great national debate on what business the Department of Defense should be in often occurs at the advisory group or relatively low staff levels, and important projects whose approval or disapproval may set crucial constraints on over-all policy are approved or rejected on the basis of some very narrow and parochial views of what this over-all national policy ought to be; sometimes the effects on over-all national policy are not even examined. All of this could be eliminated if the big decisions were consciously formulated, debated, and then decided at the proper level rather than treated as a number of fragmented issues to be treated on an ad hoc basis.

4

In this first chapter I will consider the postures in Table 1 from an over-all point of view, deferring details to later chapters. In this discussion I will define certain widely used terms in a manner that disagrees with some (but not all) usage. In general, I feel it is better to do this than to invent some completely new word or term, and I will normally continue this practice throughout the book. One of the most important things that could be done to facilitate discussion of defense problems would be to create a vocabulary that is both small enough and simple enough to be learned, precise enough to communicate, and large enough so that all of the important ideas that are contending can be comfortably and easily described. One of my major objectives in writing this book is to facilitate the creation of such a vocabulary.

1. Internal Police Force plus "World Government"

There seems to be little point in discussing the view that finds a solution in a totally disarmed world. Neither our own emotional desires nor the fact that there are many earnest proponents for this policy should sway us toward a position that ignores some of the basic realities. It has probably always been impractical to imagine a completely disarmed world, and the introduction of the thermonuclear bomb has added a special dimension to this impracticality. Given the large nuclear stockpiles in the Soviet Union, the United States, and the British Isles, it would be child's play for one of these nations to hide completely hundreds of these bombs. Even if some caches were found, one could not be sure that these were not decoys to allay suspicions, and yet there would be a great loathness to cancel the agreement just because "a few malcontents had conspired against the peace." The violator would then have an incredible advantage if the agreement ever broke down and the arms race started again. This surely means that even if all nations should one day agree to total nuclear disarmament, we must presume that there would be the hiding of some nuclear weapons or components as a hedge against the other side doing so. An international arrangement for banishing war through disarmament will not call for total disarmament but will almost undoubtedly include provisions for enforcement that cannot be successfully overturned by a small, hidden force. Otherwise, it would be hopelessly unstable. Even if the problem of what we may call the "clandestine cache" were solv-

5

THE NATURE AND FEASIBILITY OF WAR

able, the writer still is of the belief that one could not disarm the world totally and expect it to remain disarmed. But the problem of the clandestine nuclear cache in itself makes total disarmament especially infeasible.

While total disarmament can be ruled out as an immediate possibility, one can conceive of some sort of international authority which might have a monopoly of war-making capability. Such a postulated international authority would have to have enough power to be able to overwhelm any nation that had reserved hidden destructive potential. An international agency with a near-monopoly of force might come from any of the following possibilities (listed in order of apparent probability rather than desirability): (1) a Soviet or U.S. dominated world arising most likely out of war; (2) some other kind of postwar organization; (3) an S.U.–U.S. combination which is in effect a world government, though it may not openly be called that; (4) some of the NATO nations and China added to the above combination as influential, if not equal partners; (5) the Haves against the Have Nots, most likely without exploitation, but with stringent arms control in which authority and responsibility are roughly proportioned to military and economic development and, perhaps, with aid to underdeveloped nations; (6) a sort of World Federal state where power is proportioned to sovereignty and population as in the U.S. Congress. However, it is most doubtful in the absence of a crisis or war that a world government can be set up in the next decade. There are to date no serious proposals along such lines.[1] Certainly the official suggestions occasionally put out by the Soviet and U.S. governments are not to be taken seriously as possible solutions.

While it may seem high time to spell out practical proposals for world government, no such attempt will be made in this book. While

---

[1] The most serious recent attempt to describe a possible world government is given in the book, *World Peace Through World Law* (Harvard University Press, Cambridge, 1958), by Grenville Clark and Louis B. Sohn. One problem with proposals such as those in the Clark-Sohn book is the same problem that many of the white colonists in Africa have in trying to deal with African independence movements. If independence is granted, they are not sufficiently protected from the new government; if only limited sovereignty is granted the nonwhite population gets to be very unhappy at the attempt to maintain the unsatisfactory *status quo*. It is worth noting in this connection that it is easier to be a hero than a saint. It really would not be difficult to find thousands of Westerners willing to give up their lives for a world government of a satisfactory sort but one would find very few willing to accept Chinese or Indian standards of living, or any appreciable risk of this occurring, for either themselves or their families. Similarly, the underdeveloped nations are going to resent any real or fancied hindrances to their working out their salvation.

6

I believe that even a poor world government might be preferable to an uncontrolled arms race, I also believe that the practical difficulties are so large that it is a digression to dwell on such possibilities as a possible solution for the problems of the sixties. And the problems of the sixties are important! About the only way "world government" and other long-run considerations affect the kind of analysis done here is the avoidance of otherwise desirable short-term measures that might seriously hinder or foreclose desirable long-term possibilities. Even this modest ambition toward shaping the seventies is difficult to realize because there are controversies over where we want to be, as well as how to get there. However, there seems to be some consensus on what we are trying to avoid even if we cannot agree on what we are for. This book will concentrate on the problem of avoiding disaster and buying time, without specifying the use of this time. This seeming unconcern for long-term objectives will distress some readers, but some of our immediate problems must be understood more clearly than in the past if we are to control the direction in which we are going. It is the hallmark of the amateur and dilettante that he has almost no interest in how to get to his particular utopia. Perhaps this is because the practical job of finding a path may be more difficult than the job of designing the goal.[2] Let us consider, then, some of the practical military alternatives that we face in the 1960–1975 time period.

2. Minimum Deterrence plus Limited War plus Arms Control

This view, or the modest variant of it called Finite Deterrence, is probably the most widely held view in the West of what is a desirable and feasible strategic posture. Among the adherents to this position can be found most intellectuals interested in military affairs, staff people in the federal government, civilians who seek to qualify as "military experts" (including scientists and technicians), many military planners in the three services, and the vast majority of

[2] One of my amateur friends has pointed out that "It is the hallmark of the expert professional that he doesn't care where he is going as long as he proceeds competently." This seems to be a reasonable charge against this book, but I still believe that the limited focus of this book is valuable. Of those readers who are most interested in long-term goals, very few will have ever seen much discussion of the military problem as a "military problem" or the interactions of military calculations, or the lack of them, with policy. Some of these readers will deny the existence of such interactions. Just as it would do the "militarists" some good to be exposed to utopian thinking, it will do the "utopians" even more good to be exposed to some military thinking.

foreign and domestic lay analysts. What, then, is meant by Minimum Deterrence?

The notion is dramatic: It is that no nation whose decision makers are sane would attack another nation which was armed with a sufficiently large number of thermonuclear bombs. Thus all a nation that is so armed has to worry about is insanity, irresponsibility, accident, and miscalculation. Even such a sober expert as General Maxwell Taylor expressed this view as follows:

> The avoidance of deliberate general atomic war should not be too difficult since its unremunerative character must be clear to the potential adversaries. Although actual stockpile sizes are closely guarded secrets, a nation need only feel reasonably sure that an opponent has some high-yield weapons, no matter how indefinite their exact number, to be impressed with the possible consequences of attacking him.[3]

The above was written in 1956 but is quoted in a book he published in 1959. It is only fair to add that General Taylor's views have changed and, as expressed in the book, now show much more concern with the problem of deterring general war than this quotation would indicate. He also mentions that it was very difficult for him to change his views and take the problem of deterrence seriously. It is even more difficult for laymen who do not have access to the same information to achieve this feat.

In general, the believers in Minimum Deterrence seem to view the deterrence of a rational enemy as almost a simple philosophical consequence of the *existence* of thermonuclear bombs. They argue that the decision to initiate thermonuclear war is such a momentous one—the risks are so great—that it is unlikely that such a decision will be affected by the relatively minor details of each side's military posture. One is tempted to call this "the layman's view," since people holding it show only the slightest interest in such matters as the status of the alert forces, holes in the warning networks, the range of the bombers, reliability of missiles, the degree of protection offered by current arrangements for hardening, dispersal, and concealment, and the multitude of other questions that bother sober students of the problem of retaliation. Nevertheless, the Minimum Deterrence view is held by such a surprisingly large number of experts that it may be gratuitously insulting to call it a layman's view.

An extreme form of the Minimum Deterrence theory is the view

---

[3] Maxwell D. Taylor, *The Uncertain Trumpet*, Harper & Brothers, New York, 1959, p. 184.

that the current strategic forces of the United States and the Soviet Union, if used, will automatically result in world annihilation or at least mutual homicide. In 1955, fifty-two Nobel laureates signed a statement (the Mainau Declaration) which included the following: "*All* nations must come to the decision to renounce force as a final resort of policy. If they are not prepared to do this they will *cease to exist.*" There is a beautiful simplicity about this statement. It does not differentiate between attacker and defender, belligerent and neutral, Northern and Southern Hemisphere, but simply says *all* nations. It does not talk about degree of damage but simply says *cease to exist.*

Everybody recognizes that statements such as the above are sometimes no more than rhetoric. If this were all there is to it one would not worry. But belief follows language as much as the other way round. Contemporary phrases, used by both experts and laymen in describing war, expressions like "balance of terror," "thermonuclear stalemate," "suicidal war," "mutual annihilation," "inescapable end of civilization," "destruction of all life," "end of history," "live together or die together," and "nobody wins a suicide pact," indicate a widespread inclination to believe that thermonuclear war would eventuate in mutual annihilation as the result of almost any plausible turn of military events. The view of the phrasemakers is reinforced by the use of deterrence analogies, such as two people on a single keg of dynamite—each with a button, two scorpions in a bottle, two heads on a single chopping block, or the bee that dies when it stings.

Popular literature has picked up the idea of ultimacy. An example is Neville Shute's interesting but badly researched book *On the Beach*, which presumes and describes the total extinction of humanity as a result of all-encompassing and inescapable atmospheric radioactivity coming from a thermonuclear war. Many shorter pieces have been written along similar lines. Western (but not Soviet) reviewers and critics have almost uniformly taken the theme of world destruction seriously. These Westerners and their readers do not consider it a fantastic notion that nuclear war would mean the inevitable end of the world. The world annihilation possibility is considered to be a sober and accurate appraisal of the destructive power of existing weapons systems.

Not all agree, of course. In fact, some "diehards" are tempted to dismiss such a statement as the Mainau Declaration as an extremist expression of some left wing or radical scientists. This is too strong a denial. A cursory examination of the names of the signers indicates that this hypothesis does not seem tenable for a majority of them. The Nobel laureates who authored the "cease to exist" statement probably had more than rhetoric and literature in mind. Many of them had either made calculations or seen calculations (or at least thought they had) which indicated to them that world annihilation or some practical equivalent was a reasonably sober estimate of the results of nuclear war. Most of the signers would be willing to go before a technical audience with a defense of the "end of history" position as a sober estimate—and the believers in recovery and recuperation would often have some difficulty in documenting their side of the case. It is important to realize that there are "experts" who believe in world annihilation and who hold strongly to this view, experts who can and will argue their position vehemently, quantitatively, and often persuasively.

The automatic mutual annihilation view is not unique to the West. As we will see in Lecture III, Malenkov publicly introduced it to the Soviet Union several years ago, apparently arguing in the now-classical fashion that with nuclear war entailing the end of civilization, the capitalists would not attack; the Soviet Union, he said, could afford to reduce investment in heavy industry and military products and concentrate on consumer goods. A different view seems to have been held by Khrushchev and the Soviet military. They agreed that war would be horrible, but at the same time they argued that this was no reason for the Soviet Union to drop its guard; given sufficient preparations only the capitalists would be destroyed. With some important modifications their views seem to have prevailed.

Why do reasonably sober and knowledgeable people hold some version of this view of automatic mutual annihilation? In this first lecture, I will try to describe some of the data and calculations that have given rise to these cataclysmic expectations and explain why the situation is not, at least for the immediate future, as they describe it.

A thermonuclear war is quite likely to be an *unprecedented catastrophe* for the defender. Depending on the military course of events, it may or may not be an unprecedented catastrophe for the attacker, and for some neutrals as well. But an "unprecedented" catastrophe can be a far cry from an "unlimited" one. Most important of all, sober study shows that *the limits on the magnitude of the*

ALTERNATIVE NATIONAL STRATEGIES

catastrophe seem to be closely dependent on what kinds of prepara-tions have been made, and on how the war is started and fought.

While the notions in the above paragraph may strike some readers as being obvious, I must repeat that they are by no means so. The very existence of the irreconcilable group predicting total catastro-phe is proof. One can divide military thinkers into two classes: those who believe that any war would result in no less than mutual annihi-lation, and those who feel this is not necessarily so or even that it is in all likelihood wrong. The latter group is probably correct, at least for the military capabilities that are likely to be available in the next decade or so. Yet on the whole they have not done very much "homework" to prove their point. The total disaster group has done a great deal of homework. This could mean that the first group is likely for a time to win many an argument on this question.

This concept of mutual homicide, sure and certain, has in many ways been peculiarly comforting to those holding it. It makes plausible the conviction that when governments are informed of the terrible consequences of a nuclear war they will realize there could be no victors. There would be no sense to such a war. Would a sane leader ever start such a cataclysm? Of course not. The expected vio-lence of war would deter him. Those who hold this comforting con-cept may even get angry at anyone who ventures to assay estimates of the precise degree of risk which a "successful" attacker might actually face.

The mutual homicide theory yields other comforts. If one grants that each side will utterly destroy the other, one must also grant that expensive preparations to reduce casualties, lessen damage, and facilitate postwar recuperation are useless. Can we not spare our-selves the financial burden of such preparations? The "logic" has sometimes been carried further, some arguing that modern weapons are so enormously destructive that only a few are needed to deter the enemy. Therefore, the argument goes, war can be deterred with much smaller forces than in the past; in any case we certainly do not need more.

The view from this plateau is attractive to many groups who are determined on disarmament and certain types of arms control. For them, the Minimum Deterrence notion implies a certain kind of automatic stability which makes it safe to be casual about both agreements and possible violations. One must concede that the very concept of Minimum Deterrence implies that the two nations involved have in effect signed a reliable nonaggression treaty with their populations as hostages to insure adherence to this treaty; the only strategic problem that seems to be left is an accidental or unauthorized violation of this nonaggression "treaty." It is such possibilities that are the subject of arms control negotiations.

The mutual annihilation view is also comforting to many idealistic individuals, particularly to those who have an intrinsic abhorrence of any use of force. The bizarreness of a war in which both sides expect to get annihilated confirms their intuition that this whole business of military preparations is silly: a stupid and dangerous game which we ought to discourage nations—our own country, at least— from playing. At the same time these idealists can afford to scoff at attempts to reduce casualties from, say, 100 million to 50 million Americans, reflecting that the situation is hopeless anyway and that the only Respectable Cause is the total elimination of war. They regard programs other than their own as foolish or sinister and designed to cause people discomfort by making it sound plausible that there really is a national security problem toward the relief of which considerable amounts of money, energy, and intelligence need to be allocated.

Among those who take the view that Minimum Deterrence is a desirable, feasible, or the only possible strategic goal are many who nevertheless seek to add a Limited War capability. They recognize that *even if the United States and the Soviet Union cannot wage all-out war against each other this does not mean that the role of force will be entirely eliminated.* There may still be many disputes between the two nations—disputes which may tempt one side to use force on a small scale. If the only counter the other nation has is to commit suicide by starting a thermonuclear war, that nation most likely will not act. Therefore, one needs Limited War capabilities to meet limited provocations. Those who adhere to the Minimum Deterrence theory often feel that the "nonaggression treaty" of mutual deterrence is so binding and so stable it is impossible to provoke the other side to violate it by anything less than an all-out attack. Seen in this perspective, cannot one safely use the most extreme forms of violence in a limited war?

We must expand on this point. Some of those who feel strongly that it is easy to make deterrence reliable suggest using the threat of limited or controlled nuclear retaliation to "regulate" Soviet behavior. An extreme form of this notion might go as follows: If the Soviets threaten to take over Berlin, the U.S. could threaten to blow up a major Soviet city in retaliation, perhaps after warning the inhabitants to evacuate it. In their anger and distress the Soviets would then blow up one U.S. city in exchange. We would be enraged in turn, but because we would want to stop the tit-for-tat exchange, we would call a halt after warning the Soviets that any similar aggressions in the future would also result in a city exchange. However angry both of us would be, we would not start an all-out war, according to this argument, because suicide is not a rational way of expressing one's anger. It would be in the interests of both to stop the exchange at this point. By then, from the Soviet point of view, the taking of Berlin would seem unprofitable, since the loss of the Soviet city would appear more costly than the value of Berlin plus the destruction of a U.S. city. We have gained through making it clear to the Soviets that similar future actions would be equally unprofitable. On the other hand, by destroying a U.S. city, the Soviets have made it clear that we should not lightly use controlled thermonuclear retaliation as a tactic. While the whole idea sounds bizarre, concepts like this are bound to be a logical consequence of a world in which all-out war has been made to seem *rationally infeasible,* but one in which we feel it is necessary to punish or limit the other side's provocations. The timid *or sober* may feel that Minimum Deterrence might be strained to the breaking point by such acts; for them there must be caution on the types and levels of violence to accompany limited war or limited provocations.

3. *Three Kinds of Insurance*

The next view of what could result in a satisfactory strategic capability adds several kinds of "insurance" to the simple Minimum Deterrence position.[4] There are at least three kinds of insurance which a survival-conscious person might wish to add, the first being *Insurance for Reliability.* We will label the view that *worries about the details* of obtaining a "punishing" retaliation, but does not want any more strategic capability than this, the *Finite Deterrence*

---

[4] The addition is meant in terms of the capability of the force that is being procured; the entire force may be redesigned to get some appropriately modified version of the original capability (possibly at a reduced level) and the new insurance one.

strategy.[5] In many ways, and with some inconsistencies, this is the official U.S. view. The believers in Finite Deterrence do not quite accept the idea that reliable deterrence can be obtained simply by stocking thermonuclear bombs and having a weapon system which could deliver these bombs in peacetime. They notice that when the problem of retaliation is studied, rather than asserted, it is difficult to retaliate effectively, since the enemy can do many things to prevent, hinder, or negate retaliation. Evaluation of the effectiveness of retaliation must bear in mind that the Russians can strike *at a time and with tactics of their choosing.* We will strike back, no doubt, but with *a damaged and not fully coordinated force* which must conduct its operations in the *postattack environment.* The Soviets may use *blackmail threats to intimidate our postattack tactics.* Under these conditions, the Russian defense system is likely to be *alerted.* Indeed, if the strike has been preceded by a tense period, their active defense forces would long since have been *augmented,* and their cities may be at least partially *evacuated.*

Any of the considerations referred to by italicized words can change the effectiveness of a retaliatory strike by an order of magnitude. Yet almost all of them are ignored in most discussions of the effectiveness of our deterrent force. Sometimes they are even relegated to the position of unimportant "technical details." They are far more than this. The possibilities indicated by the italicized words will be discussed at some length in Lecture II. I only want to mention here that the believer in Finite Deterrence is somewhat aware of these problems; he wants to have ready more than the bare minimum force that *might* be able to retaliate effectively (the Minimum Deterrence position). The advocate of Finite Deterrence wants enough forces to cover *all* contingencies. He may even want mixed forces, considering that it may be possible for a clever enemy to discover an unexpected countermeasure against a single kind of force no matter how large. Thus he may well want different types of missiles, bombers, strategic submarines, aircraft carriers, and so forth. In addition, sober advocates of Finite Deterrence wish to have the various weapons systems so deployed and operated that they will

---

[5] Originally, Minimum Deterrence and Finite Deterrence meant the same thing. The word "Minimum" was coined by some Polaris enthusiasts who argued we needed very little to deter the Soviets. Because the word "Minimum" carried a connotation of gambling with the nation's security for budgetary reasons, it was changed to "Finite" (which had the connotation of wanting enough and no more and also suggested that the opponents wanted an infinite or at least an unreasonable amount).

14

have a guaranteed capability, even in a crisis in which the enemy has taken extraordinary measures to negate the capability. They want these forces dispersed, protected, and alert; the arrangements for command, control, and communications must be able to withstand degradation by both peacetime and wartime tactics of the enemy. These sober believers in Finite Deterrence tend to insist on an objective capability as opposed to one that is only "psychological." And even those believers in Finite Deterrence who would be satisfied with a façade yearn for an impressive-looking façade. One might characterize the Finite Deterrence position as an expert version of the Minimum Deterrence position, held by an expert who wants to look good to other experts.

The notion of Finite Deterrence is therefore not as dramatic as the notion of Minimum Deterrence. The believer in Finite Deterrence is willing to concede that it takes some effort to guarantee Mutual Homicide, that it is not automatic. However, the notion of Finite Deterrence is still dramatic, since most followers of this doctrine believe that *the advent of thermonuclear bombs has changed the character of an all-out war in such a way that if both opponents are prepared the old-fashioned distinctions between victory, stalemate, and defeat no longer have much meaning.* It was once believed that if one country had forces twice as large as those of another country, the first country was the stronger. Those who believe in Finite Deterrence challenge this view. Sometimes they rest their case on this idea: the only purpose of strategic forces is to deter rather than to fight; once one has the ability to damage seriously, say, 10 or 20 enemy cities, this is enough force to deter, and therefore enough force. More often, backers of Finite Deterrence take a more extreme position. They argue that you can do no more than kill somebody once, to overkill by a factor of ten is no more desirable than overkilling by a factor of two—it is simply a waste of effort. They also usually argue that with some thought it should be easy to design strategic systems that can overkill, even in retaliation. Once we procure the limited (i.e., finite) forces required to do this job we have enough strategic forces and do not need any more— no matter what the enemy does.

In the year 1960 I believe that even adherents to an extreme Minimum Deterrence position tended to agree, under pressure, that the nation should buy whatever insurance is needed to make retaliation at least "look" potentially reliable and effective. In this sense,

15

the orthodox Minimum Deterrence School is no longer as respectable as might once have been inferred from the remarks of the most enthusiastic proponents of a defense built solely around small Minuteman and Polaris systems. Most of the more sober analysts have come to talk about *Finite* Deterrence, by which they mean having a generous adequacy for deterrence, but that is all they want for the general war. Specifically, they often tend to be against any counterforce capability, (The word "counterforce" includes not only an active counterforce that can destroy or damage the enemy's force on the ground, but also other methods of countering the opponent's force, such as Active and Passive Defense).[6]

Some believers in Finite Deterrence are against counterforce as a useless diversion of forces; others would not even be interested in having any counterforce even if it were free, because they consider it destabilizing. They notice at least one circumstance in which an enemy is likely to attack even if he is worried about the retaliatory destruction that he will suffer. This circumstance occurs when he believes his attack is pre-emptive, that by striking first he is only forestalling an attack being launched on him. Most believers in Finite Deterrence are so convinced of the efficacy of their deterrence that they believe such an idea could only arise as a result of miscalculation, since no rational man could order an attack against an enemy who has made at least moderate preparations to ward it off. However, they recognize that if both forces are in a condition of super alert it may be easy to have such a misunderstanding. Or equally likely, there is the problem that Thomas Schelling of Harvard (and RAND) has called "the reciprocal fear of surprise attack," where each side imputes to the other aggressive intentions and misreads purely defensive preparations as being offensive. There are unfortunately many postures possible in which a disastrous train of self-confirming actions and counteractions could be set into motion.

---

[6] The word "counterforce" is usually used to apply to an ability to destroy the enemy on the ground. It is true that the best *counter* against an unprotected SAC base is a bomb on the base. But the best counter against a hidden missile may be a shelter; the best counter against a bomber carrying many bombs may be active defense; the best counter against the enemy destroying our cities may be the use of retaliatory threats; the best counter against fallout-type attacks is shelters plus anti-contamination. I will use the term Counterforce as Insurance to cover all of the above —indeed to include anything which might counter the use or effectiveness of the enemy's force. While many of my colleagues object to my using the term counterforce in this manner, the new term has the important virtue of discouraging parochial attitudes. It emphasizes that any method of countering the enemy's force may be useful, and that the allocation between the different methods should be made by objective considerations and not by slogans or outworn doctrine.

16

In order to prevent this from occurring, some believers in Finite Deterrence think it is important for us to disabuse ourselves of the idea that there can be any circumstance in which it makes sense to attack the Soviet Union, and they want us to adopt a posture which makes it clear to the Soviets that we are so disabused. As part of this posture we should make as few preparations as possible to alleviate the effects of the war or protect ourselves from a Soviet retaliatory strike. This will convince the Soviets that we do not intend to attack them except in retaliation; they will then be able to relax and not be trigger-happy. As one (partial) adherent to Finite Deterrence, Oskar Morgenstern, explained: "In order to preserve a nuclear stalemate under conditions of nuclear plenty it is necessary for *both* sides to possess invulnerable retaliatory forces. . . . it is in the interest of the United States for Russia to have an invulnerable retaliatory force and vice versa [i.e., one may wish to strengthen the enemy's retaliatory capability and weaken one's 'Counterforce as Insurance']." [7]

Many who accept the Finite Deterrence view have another reason for not defending or protecting anything but the retaliatory capability; they see no need for programs to protect people and property, because they think it is not feasible to protect either people or property. These people often argue that it does not matter whether one dies immediately from blast, heat, or radiation, or dies later from the effects of radioactivity, disease, or starvation—as long as one is going to die. And they go on to assert that modern war is so horrible that everyone or almost everyone will be killed immediately—or will eventually be destroyed by one of the aftereffects.

A surprisingly large number of official military experts and planners seem to hold views, at least unconsciously, which are really a variation of the Finite Deterrence view that the only purpose of the strategic forces is to deter. This is illustrated by the following apocryphal quotation:

❖❖

TABLE 2

ONE PROFESSIONAL'S VIEW OF HIS PROFESSION

"If these buttons are ever pressed, they have *completely failed* in their purpose! The equipment is useful only if it is not used."

—General Aphorism

❖❖

[7] *The Question of National Defense*, New York, Random House, 1959, pp. 74, 76.

Even though the above statement may be intended to be rhetoric rather than policy, it is far from innocuous. If one were to deduce the beliefs of some policy makers from the decisions they make, he would find that in a rather high percentage of cases the planners seem to care less about what happens after the buttons are pressed than they do about looking "presentable" before the event. They show slight interest in maintaining an appreciable operational capability on the second day of the war; if deterrence should fail, they, as well as many scientists, could not be less interested in the details of what happens—so long as the retaliatory strike is launched.

It is my contention that failure to launch an effective retaliatory attack is only the first of many possible failures. Even if one retaliates successfully, there can ensue significant and meaningful failures. These will occur one after another if the attitude exemplified in the above quotation becomes too universal in either the making or execution of policy. And even Deterrence Only advocates should realize that there are subtle but important differences between a posture which is to be a façade to impress the enemy and one which is supposed to have an objective capability.

Insurance Against Unreliability. Some of the proponents of Finite Deterrence do not have an antipathy toward all forms of counterforce. They are willing to insure against unreliability. That is, even though deterrence has been made as reliable as they think it can be made, they realize that it may still fail; for example, from accident, human irrationality, miscalculation, or unauthorized behavior. Given this nonzero probability of a war, they find it difficult not to go through the motions of doing "something" to mitigate its effects. Even totally convinced "mutual annihilation" decision makers may be unwilling to admit openly that there are no preparations to alleviate the consequences of a war. It is difficult for any government to look at its people and say in effect, "We can no longer protect you in a war. We have no answer to blackmail except a counterblackmail threat, and we have no preparations to deal with accidental war except trying to make it so dreadful that everybody will be careful in advance."

A façade of being able to alleviate may also be useful in international relations. It reassures one's allies about one's resolve and induces uncertainty and (hopefully) fear in the enemy. Even if it were true that both sides in the cold war conflict were unwilling to risk a thermonuclear war over any issue that could arise between them, it would weaken their diplomatic strength to admit this openly since the admitting power would be conceding that the other power could always get its way by staking a little more.

Some decision makers who accept the Finite Deterrence view are willing to pay for insurance against unreliability for more than political or psychological reasons. Even those who hold that war means mutual annihilation are sometimes willing for us to act beyond their beliefs—or fears. While this is inconsistent, it is not necessarily irrational. They understand that paper calculations can be wrong and are willing to hedge against this possibility. Sometimes these decision makers are making a distinction that (rather surprisingly) is not usually made. They may distinguish, for example, between 100 million dead and 50 million dead, and argue that the latter state is better than the former. They may distinguish between war damage which sets the economy of a country back fifty years or only ten years. *Actually, when one examines the possible effects of thermonuclear war carefully, one notices that there are indeed many postwar states that should be distinguished.* If most people do not or cannot distinguish among these states it is because the gradations occur as a result of a totally bizarre circumstance—a thermonuclear war. The mind recoils from thinking hard about that; one prefers to believe it will never happen. If asked, "How does a country look on the day of the war?" the only answer a reasonable person can give is "awful." It takes an act of iron will or an unpleasant degree of detachment or callousness to go about the task of distinguishing among the possible degrees of awfulness.

But surely one can ask a more specific question. For example, *"How does a country look five or ten years after the close of war, as a function of three variables: (1) the preparations made before the war, (2) the way the war started, and (3) the course of military events?"* Both very sensitive and very callous individuals should be able to distinguish (and choose, perhaps) between a country which survives a war with, say, 150 million people and a gross national product (GNP) of $300 billion a year, and a nation which emerges with only 50 million people and a GNP of $10 billion. The former would be the richest and the fourth largest nation in the world, and one which would be able to restore a reasonable facsimile of the prewar society; the latter would be a pitiful remnant that would contain few traces of the prewar way of life. When one asks this kind of question and examines the circumstances and possible outcomes of a future war in some detail, it appears that it is useful and necessary to make many distinctions among the results of thermonuclear war. The figures in Table 3 illustrate some simple distinctions which one may wish to make at the outset of his deliberations in this field.

❖❖❖

TABLE 3
TRAGIC BUT DISTINGUISHABLE POSTWAR STATES

Dead	Economic Recuperation
2,000,000	1 year
5,000,000	2 years
10,000,000	5 years
20,000,000	10 years
40,000,000	20 years
80,000,000	50 years
160,000,000	100 years

Will the survivors envy the dead?

❖❖❖

Here I have tried to make the point that if we have a posture which might result in 40 million dead in a general war, and as a result of poor planning, apathy, or other causes, our posture deteriorates and a war occurs with 80 million dead, we have suffered an additional disaster, an *unnecessary* additional disaster that is almost as bad as the original disaster. If on the contrary, by spending a few billion dollars, or by being more competent or lucky, we can cut the number of dead from 40 to 20 million, we have done something vastly worth doing! The survivors will not dance in the streets or congratulate each other if there have been 20 million men, women, and children killed; yet it would have been a worthwhile achievement to limit casualties to this number. It is very difficult to get this point across to laymen or experts with enough intensity to move them to action. The average citizen has a dour attitude toward planners who say that if we do thus and so it will not be 40 million dead—it will be 20 million dead. Somehow the impression is left that the planner said that there will be *only* 20 million dead. To him is often attributed the idea that this will be a tolerable or even, astonishingly enough, a desirable state!

The rate of economic recuperation, like the number of lives saved, is also of extreme importance. Very few Americans can get interested in spending money or energy on preparations which, even if they worked, would result in preindustrial living standards for the survivors of a war. As will be explained later, our analysis indicates that if a country is moderately well prepared to use the assets which survive there is unlikely to be a critical level of damage to production. A properly prepared country is not "killed" by the destruction of even a major fraction of its wealth; it is more likely to be set back a given number of years in its economic growth. While recuperation times may range all the way from one to a hundred years, even the latter is far different from the "end of history."

Perhaps the most important item on the table of distinguishable states is not the numbers of dead or the number of years it takes for economic recuperation; rather, it is the question at the bottom: "Will the survivors envy the dead?" It is in some sense true that one may never recuperate from a thermonuclear war. The world may be permanently (i.e., for perhaps 10,000 years) more hostile to human life as a result of such a war. Therefore, if the question, "Can we restore the prewar conditions of life?" is asked, the answer must be "No!" But there are other relevant questions to be asked. For example: "How much more hostile will the environment be? Will it be so hostile that we or our descendants would prefer being dead than alive?" Perhaps even more pertinent is this question, "How happy or normal a life can the survivors and their descendants hope to have?" *Despite a widespread belief to the contrary, objective studies indicate that even though the amount of human tragedy would be greatly increased in the postwar world, the increase would not preclude normal and happy lives for the majority of survivors and their descendants.*

My colleagues and I came to this conclusion reluctantly; not because we did not *want* to believe it, but because it is so *hard* to believe. Thermonuclear bombs are so destructive, and destructive in so many ways, that it is difficult to imagine that there would be anything left after their large-scale use. One of my tasks with The RAND Corporation was to serve as project leader for a study of the possibilities for alleviating the consequences of a thermonuclear war. That study was made as quantitatively and objectively as we could make it with the resources, information, and intellectual tools available to us. *We concluded that for at least the next decade or so, any picture of total world annihilation appears to be wrong, irrespective of the military course of events.*[8] Equally important, the picture of total disaster is likely to be wrong even for the two antagonists. Barring an extraordinary course for the war, or that most of the technical uncertainties turn out to lie at the disastrous end of the spectrum, one and maybe both of the antagonists should be able to restore a reasonable semblance of prewar conditions quite rapidly. Typical estimates run between one and ten years for a reasonably successful and well-prepared attacker and somewhat longer for the defender, depending mainly on the tactics of the attacker and the preparations of the defender. In the RAND study we tried to avoid using optimistic assumptions. With the exceptions to be noted, we used what were in our judgment the best values available, or we used slightly pessimistic ones. We believe that the situation is likely to be better than we indicate, rather than worse, though the latter possibility cannot be ruled out.

Exactly what is it that one must believe if he is to be convinced that it is worth while to buy Counterforce as Insurance? Listed below are eight phases of a thermonuclear war. If our decision makers are to justify the expense (and possible risk of strategic destabiliza-

◇◇◇

TABLE 4

A COMPLETE DESCRIPTION OF A THERMONUCLEAR WAR

Includes the Analysis of:

1. Various time-phased programs for deterrence and defense and their possible impact on us, our allies, and others.
2. Wartime performance with different preattack and attack conditions.
3. Acute fallout problems.
4. Survival and patch-up.
5. Maintenance of economic momentum.
6. Long-term recuperation.
7. Postwar medical problems.
8. Genetic problems.

◇◇◇

[8] *Report on a Study of Non-Military Defense,* The RAND Corporation, Report R-322-RC, July 1, 1958.

tion) that would be incurred in trying to acquire a capability for alleviating the consequences of a war, they must believe they can successfully negotiate each and every one of these phases, or that there is a reasonable chance that they can negotiate each of these phases.

I repeat: To survive a war it is necessary to negotiate *all eight* stages. If there is a catastrophic failure in any one of them, there will be little value in being able to cope with the other seven. Differences among exponents of the different strategic views can often be traced to the different estimates they make on the difficulty of negotiating one or more of these eight stages. While all of them present difficulties, most civilian military experts seem to consider the *last six* the critical ones. Nevertheless, most discussions among "classical" military experts concentrate on the *first two*. To get a sober and balanced view of the problem, one must examine all *eight*.

As an example of the necessity to be concerned about the last six phases, it might be appropriate to quote from testimony before the 1959 Johnson subcommittee on military preparedness during the hearings on the Berlin crisis (italics mine).

MR. WEISL: General White, I hate to keep you here so long, but there are some matters that *we feel ought to be in the record to make it complete.*

On March 9 of this year Dr. Libby, a Commissioner of the United States Atomic Energy Commission, in a public speech stated as follows:

"Now the fallout we fear in the case of a nuclear attack on this country, or in any other country for that matter, is the local fallout, and this arises solely from bombs which hit the surface."

Then I go on to what I consider the important quote:

"But in any case, the area covered can amount to several thousand square miles at such an intensity that it would be hazardous to life to stay out in the open for more than an hour, and the density would be high enough *so that farmland in this area would be ruined for something like 40 years* for anything except the culture of feed for beef cattle, or possibly swine, because of the strontium-90 that would be taken into any other kind of farm product."

I don't know whether it is fair to ask you whether you agree with that or not, but at least that is the statement of a responsible member of the Atomic Energy Commission.

GENERAL WHITE: I think there are other responsible scientists, though, who do not agree. I think Dr. Edward Teller is one such. While I agree that fallout is a terrific hazard and one that we don't know as much about as I hope we are going to know, and it is certainly a consideration in atomic war, I don't think that every horror story should be accepted 100 per cent.

MR. WEISL: I do agree that every horror story should not be accepted, but coming from a responsible member of the AEC, whose duty is to look into these problems, one must take account of it and not look upon it, at least I wouldn't look upon it, as solely a horror story.

SENATOR SYMINGTON: If the counsel will yield, Dr. Teller has opposed those who believe that strontium-90 and cesium-137 will be too damaging from the standpoint of current testing. If there is anything he has said from the standpoint of strontium-90 in answer to Dr. Libby, on the premise of an all-out war, with nuclear surface blasts, I wish you would put it in the record at this point.

GENERAL WHITE: I think the only thing I can say is I am sure there is disagreement among scientists as to the exact effects. I can't go beyond that.[9]

It is clear that if "farmland in this area would be ruined for something like 40 years," recuperation will be difficult. In that case we had better abandon Counterforce as Insurance and retreat to the Finite Deterrence position. However, we are going to consider the strontium-90 problem quantitatively below and will come up with some different results. The only point to be made now is that those waging a modern war are going to be as much concerned with bone cancer, leukemia, and genetic malformations as they are with the range of a B-52 or the accuracy of an Atlas missile. Senior military advisors in particular will increasingly be forced to deal with what would once have been called "nonmilitary" problems. They will need to be armed with documented studies rather than opinions.

Once one accepts the idea that deterrence is not absolutely reliable and that it would be possible to survive a war, then he may be willing to buy insurance—to spend money on preparations to decrease the number of fatalities and injuries, limit damage, facilitiate recuperation, and to get the best military result possible—at least "to prevail" [10] in some meaningful sense if you cannot win.

[9] United States Senate, Committee on Armed Services, Hearings before the Preparedness Investigating Committee, 86th Congr., 1st Sess., March 1959 (Part I), pp. 132–133.

[10] The word "prevail" is much used in official statements. It is a carefully chosen word that shows that the user is trying to do the best he can even though he is aware that many deny the old-fashioned distinctions between victory and defeat. Because its use is ambiguous, the reader does not know whether the author is serious about his goal or is just making a meaningless concession to old-fashioned thinking; it probably does more harm than good to set it up as a goal. It would be better to use the old-fashioned concept of victory, as denoting the one who writes the peace treaty, while at the same time making explicit that victory can be costly.

Insurance Against a Change in Policy. One of the things which I will try to make clear in Lectures II and III is that *the military problem really is complicated and that it is impossible for fallible human beings to predict ahead of time exactly what capabilities they will wish or need.* This does not mean, of course, that one has to buy everything. Resources may not be as limited as some of the more budget-minded people think, but they are still quite limited. However, it does mean that whenever it is *cheap* to do so (and sometimes when it is moderately expensive), we should be willing to hedge against changes in our desires. The fact that it is expensive to buy and maintain a complete spectrum of military capabilities in being does not mean that we should not have what might be called "mobilization bases" for a complete spectrum of adequate military capabilities. The government, relying on current doctrine, current military capabilities, its estimates of the capabilities and intentions of potential enemies, or some aspects of the political situation, might be satisfied with current allocations for national defense. But it should still be willing to hedge against the possibility that circumstances may so change that the reluctance to spend money will also change, either increasing or decreasing. This hedging can be accomplished by spending a relatively small amount on advance planning and physical preparations. We will then be in a position where we can make the most rapid and effective use of larger funds if they become available, or we will be able to get the most value out of a smaller military budget if it seems desirable to cut back on expenditures.

There are many different kinds of programs that come under the heading "Hedging Against a Change in Policy." It is obvious that there is need for very broad research and development programs. While research is not cheap, it is far from true that research is so expensive that it can be afforded only on clearly needful items. The opposite is true. The penalty for not having researched on an item that turns out to be useful is so great that we must have an extremely broad program to be certain that all the things that could conceivably be useful will in fact be investigated. Development is somewhat more expensive than research. As a result, we cannot afford to have quite as broad a menu. But even here we should *develop* many more items than we actually *procure*. We may also procure some systems in part, even if we do not feel they are absolutely needful. Requirements can change.

For example, many people today feel that in the ballistic missile age *air defense* is obsolete. As I will try to explain later, this is by no means true. But even if it were true that air defense should be termed obsolete because it might be unable to give protection against Soviet missiles, we might still be willing to have a "base" for air defense because we may be able to discover an answer to the missile threat, or we may later decide we want air defense against countries like China—or ultimately even smaller countries. We may find it easy to protect against small bomber forces, which could be very lethal if they had a free ride—very much more lethal, indeed, than any small missile forces these same countries might procure. (Of course, such an air defense system might look quite different from our current one.)

Similarly, while it might be our policy at a given moment to fight limited wars with atomic weapons, we may still be glad to have a large reserve force armed with conventional high-explosive equipment. After all, it is relatively cheap to keep up such reserves, and we recognize that we might change our minds—as we did in Korea. The existence of such a force could enable us to fight a war which otherwise we would have to lose by default, simply because we were unwilling to use nuclear weapons when the occasion actually arose.

There is a special type of mobilization base which I will call a "Preattack Mobilization Base." This can be extremely important. It is a capability for being able to improve rapidly our ability to fight or to threaten to fight either a limited or a general war. It includes preparations for putting in *adequate civil defense programs*. It also includes the procurement of very long *lead time* items for our strategic air defense and air offense, so that by just spending money rapidly we could bring all of these capabilities up to an adequate level. There is a very broad spectrum of preparations possible here. One kind of preparation would be useful only if a situation occurred in which substantial tactical warning (hours) was available; another set of preparations would be most useful in situations in which we had strategic warning—days, weeks, or even months. And still another set of preparations could be made to improve our ability to compensate for a possible deterioration in the international situation or an increase in our standards for an acceptable level of defense. I will defer to Lecture II discussion of the role that a Preattack Mobilization Base might play in deterring and correcting provocations or providing extra insurance against a failure of deterrence. I will only make here the obvious point that what might be called the Finite Deterrence function of the strategic force is too important to depend on warning. There should always be an adequate capability *in-being* to deter a surprise attack.

There are large resources available for defense if it becomes necessary to use them. Many economists have estimated that the United States could allocate between 40 and 50 per cent of its gross national product to military purposes for some years without subjecting individual citizens to any appreciable physical hardships. (Postattack living standards would be adequate by almost any reasonable standard. The situation would be much like World War II where we spent, at peak, about 43 per cent of our GNP on military products, and we could still buy phonograph records even if we could not buy phonographs.) In fact, if we make allowances for current unutilized resources, the country should be somewhat better off than in World War II. Such spending would undoubtedly leave a very unpleasant post-crisis legacy of debt, economic dislocation, some inflation, and so on. But if it ever came to a serious question of choosing between such spending and a high risk of national defeat, I think there is no question that the United States would choose to spend between $200 and $300 billion annually on national security—rather than face the alternative. We are actually spending today about one-fifth of this potential. Clearly there is an enormous amount of fat which could be converted into muscle if we felt that circumstances warranted this step. The problem is, Could we move fast enough? Whether we could would depend not only on how critical the military situation was, but also on our stop-gap military preparations, on our ability to recognize that circumstances have changed, on our resolve, and on the preparations already made for such an expansion. It would be most important that the actual physical plant and equipment of the Department of Defense (including installations) be such that it could be used as an existing base for a higher capability.

4. Credible First Strike Capability

The next position on Table 1, that there are circumstances in which a nation may wish to have a Credible First Strike Capability, may seem to many Americans like a possibility for the Soviets—but not for us. One sees many statements to the effect that "We will never strike first." In the context in which the remark is usually made (a "dastardly" surprise attack out of the blue against an unprepared enemy), this position is undoubtedly correct. Such a capability would not be worth much to the U.S. However, we have many treaties and other obligations. There is the obligation to come to the aid of NATO nations if they are attacked. It is generally supposed that this aid includes the use of our SAC against the Soviet heartland, even if the Soviets attack Europe *but not the United States*. From a technical point of view this means that in this instance *we* would strike *first!* The agonizing decision to start an all-out thermonuclear war would be ours. Surely there is a serious question whether we would live up to our treaty obligations under such circumstances.

That this doubt is plausible can be seen in the response of Christian Herter to a question by Senator Morse on the occasion of the hearings on his nomination: "I cannot conceive of any President involving us in an all-out nuclear war unless the facts showed clearly we are in danger of all-out devastation ourselves, *or that actual moves have been made toward devastating ourselves.*" [11]

A thermonuclear balance of terror is equivalent to the signing of a nonaggression treaty which states that neither the Soviets nor the Americans will initiate an all-out attack, no matter how provoking the other side may become. Sometimes people do not understand the full implications of this figurative nonaggression treaty. Let me illustrate what it can mean if we accept absolutely the notion that there is no provocation that would cause us to strike the Soviets other than an immediately impending or an actual Soviet attack on the United States. Imagine that the Soviets have taken a very drastic action against our allies in Europe. Let the action be as extreme or shocking as the reader's imagination permits. Suppose, for example, that the Soviets have dropped bombs on London, Berlin, Rome, Paris, and Bonn *but have made no detectable preparations for attacking the United States, and our retaliatory*

[11] *Hearings on the Nomination of Christian A. Herter to be Secretary of State, Committee on Foreign Relations*, U.S. Senate, 86th Congress, 1st Session, pp. 9–10 (italics mine). Whether he means it or not, Khrushchev speaks a different language. On January 14, 1960, in a speech to the Supreme Soviet, he said: "I am emphasizing once more that we already possess so many nuclear weapons, both atomic and hydrogen, and the necessary rockets for sending these weapons to the territory of a potential aggressor, that should any madman launch an attack on our state *or on other Socialist states* we would be able literally to wipe the country or countries which attack us off the face of the earth" (italics mine). *New York Times*, January 15, 1960.

force looks good enough to deter them from such an attack. As far as we can tell they have done this horrible deed simply to demonstrate their strength and resolve. Suppose also that there is a device which restrains the President of the United States from acting for about twenty-four hours. It is probably true that if the President were not restrained he would order an attack on the S.U. (even if he had previously bought either the Minimum Deterrence or Finite Deterrence positions that no sane decision maker initiates a thermonuclear war against an enemy who can retaliate). However, we have assumed the existence of a 24-hour device which forces him to stop and think and make his decision in cold blood. The President would presumably call together his advisors during this time. Most of the advisors would probably urge strongly that the U.S. fulfill its obligations by striking the Soviet Union. Now let us further suppose that the President is also told by his advisors that even though we will kill almost every Russian *civilian*, we will not be able to destroy all of the Soviet strategic forces, and that these surviving Soviet forces will (by radiation or strontium-90 or something else) kill every American in their retaliatory blow—all 180 million of us.

Is it not difficult to believe that under these hypothetical circumstances any President of the United States would initiate a thermonuclear war by all-out retaliation against the Soviets with the Strategic Air Command? Few would contend that there is any plausible public policy which would justify ending life for everyone. It should be clear that our retaliation would not restore Europe; we could only succeed in further destroying it either as a by-product of our actions or because the surviving Soviet forces would subsequently destroy Europe as well as the United States. I am not saying that the United States would stand idly by. We would clearly declare war on the Soviets. We would make all kinds of *limited* military moves. We would go into a crash mobilization on at least the hundred-billion-dollars-a-year level. But there is one thing that we almost certainly would not do: We would not launch an all-out attack on Soviet cities.

There were two important caveats in the situation described: 180 million Americans would be killed, and the President would have twenty-four hours to think about his response. Let us consider these in turn. If 180 million dead is too high a price to pay for punishing the Soviets for their aggression, what price would we be willing to pay? This is a hard and unpleasant question. I have discussed this question with many Americans, and after about fifteen minutes of discussion their estimates of an acceptable price generally fall between 10 and 60 million, clustering toward the upper number. (Their first reaction, incidentally, is usually that the U.S. would *never* be deterred from living up to its obligations by fear of a Soviet counterblow—an attitude that invariably disappears after some minutes of reflection.) The way one seems to arrive at the upper limit of 60 million is rather interesting. He takes one-third of a country's population, in other words somewhat less than half. No American that I have spoken to who was at all serious about the matter believed that any U.S. action, limited or unlimited, would be justified—no matter what our commitments were—if more than half of our population would be killed in retaliation.

The 24-hour delay is a more subtle device. It is the equivalent of asking, "Can the Soviets force the President to act in cold blood and full knowledge, rather than in the immediate anger of the moment?" This depends not only on the time he has to learn and ponder the effects that would flow from his actions (and I will describe many circumstances in which this time for reflection would occur), but also on how deeply and seriously the President and his advisors have thought about the problem in advance. This latter, in turn, would depend on whether there had been any tense situations or crises which forced the President and the people to face the concept that war is something which can happen, rather than something that is reliably deterred by some declaratory policy that never need be acted upon. (The effects of the war are usually considered irrelevant to one's declaratory policy, since it is assumed that the declarations will deter the war.)

Let me give an example of a crisis that the Soviets could precipitate that would, by forcing both the Europeans and the Americans to face the possibility of a war seriously, give the effect of a 24-hour waiting period. Assume that both the United States and the Soviet Union could reliably annihilate each other in a retaliatory blow so that there was no special advantage in one side hitting the other first. Assume also that the Europeans had bought their own independent nuclear deterrents because they assess such a balance of terror as extremely dangerous to themselves. As De Gaulle explained in a press conference in November 1959,

Who can say that if in the future, the political background having changed completely—that is something that has already happened on earth—the two powers having the nuclear monopoly will not agree to divide the world?

Who can say that if the occasion arises the two, while each deciding not to launch its missiles at the main enemy so that it should itself be spared, will not crush the others? It is possible to imagine that on some awful day western Europe should be wiped out from Moscow and Central Europe from Washington. And who can even say that the two rivals, after I know not what political and social upheaval, will not unite? [12]

However, because they are so close to the Soviet Union, the independent European nuclear deterrent is so vulnerable to a Soviet strike it cannot retaliate effectively. Also assume (because of economy and relative technological backwardness) it is not large enough to destroy the Soviet Union if it goes first. The European deterrent, in summary, can only inflict about as much damage on the Soviet Union as the Soviets suffered in World War II. Therefore, the Soviets can threaten the Europeans with a disarming attack if they go first and with an annihilating retaliation if the Europeans go first, accepting whatever damage the Europeans do on their first strike. They are willing to run the risk of a European first strike because they feel that under these conditions the risk is very small, smaller perhaps than the risk of an accidental war caused by the proliferation of nuclear systems. The Soviets then deliver the following ultimatum: unless the Europeans disarm themselves in 30 days (they have no other demands), the Soviets will proceed to disarm them by force. They could make this demand after some incident, say, after a nuclear missile had been fired accidentally (or by intentional Soviet sabotage) at Soviet territory.

The Soviets might couple their disarming ultimatum with another one that would make specific their immediate goals. They could announce that from then on, Europe, Asia, and Africa would be considered as being in the Soviet sphere of interest; further, they would be willing to respect the Western Hemisphere, Australia, and maybe the British Isles and Japan as being in the American sphere of interest; and they would say they were suggesting this method of organizing humanity in order to head-off an uncontrolled arms race which had already resulted in an incident that could have touched off a cataclysm. The Soviets would claim to be willing to accept responsibility for their area and they would hold the United States accountable for its area.

While the above will strike most people as being closer to paranoia

[12] *New York Times,* November 11, 1959.

than to analysis, it is still worth while to observe that the basic assumption of a firm belief on both sides of a reliable balance of terror is not unreasonable. Given this belief, it is most unlikely that even a Soviet ultimatum as provoking as the above would result in an attack by the United States. Given the time available, the U.S. would feel compelled to ponder the results of an attack before ordering one. We might even feel it was possible to negotiate the Soviet demands. The Europeans would also be unlikely to start hostilities. They would be more likely to do the opposite and take off alert whatever forces they have on alert, to reduce the possibility of accident or sabotage. Having another European missile shot at the Soviets would now clearly bring intolerable consequences.

The Soviet ultimatum in this instance duplicates most of the pressures of the original hypothetical 24-hour delay situation. While some British and American readers may consider such a Soviet ultimatum even more improbable than the hypothetical situation just outlined, I suspect that a number of continental Europeans find it all too plausible. It is most important that we be able to convince our continental allies that the U.S. posture is such that the Soviets really would find it too dangerous to give such an ultimatum, and that if they did the U.S. would be able to take some corrective action that would not result in most of the Northern Hemisphere being wiped out or in a situation such as De Gaulle described in his press conference. I will discuss some of the possibilities in Lecture II.

It should now be clear what I mean by a Credible First Strike Capability. Credibility does not involve the question "Do we or the Soviets have the capability to hurt the other side on a first strike?" It is well known that this capability exists and in all likelihood will continue to exist. Credibility depends on being willing to accept the other side's retaliatory blow. It depends on the harm *he* can do, not on the harm *we* can do. It depends as much on *air defense* and *civil defense* as on *air offense*. It depends on *will* as well as *capability*. It depends on the *provocation* and on the *state of our mind* when the provocation occurs. One should also note that being able to use a Credible First Strike Capability to influence Soviet or European behavior depends not only on our will, but also on Soviet and European estimates of our will. Serious problems may be created for us if either of them does not believe in our willingness to attack under certain kinds of provocation.

Let us consider some European estimates first. I have discussed with many Europeans the question of how many casualties an

American decision maker or planner would be willing to envisage and still be willing to see this country live up to its obligations. Their estimates, perhaps not surprisingly, range much lower than the estimates of Americans, that is, roughly 2 to 20 million (clustering toward the lower numbers). In fact, one distinguished European expert thought that the U.S. would be deterred from retaliating with SAC against a major Soviet aggression in Europe by a Soviet threat to destroy five or ten empty U.S. cities.[13]

Will the Soviets find the threat of U.S. retaliation credible? I have not asked any Soviet citizens, so I lack the advantage of any introspection by Russians. But we do know that their formal writings strongly emphasize that decision makers should be able to control their emotions. The Soviets do not believe in cutting off their noses to spite their faces; they write and seem to believe that one should not be provoked into self-destructive behavior. They probably would assume that we do likewise. One would not think that the Soviets could believe that the U.S. would willingly commit suicide. In fact, I would conjecture that they would feel fairly certain about this matter. They could readily underestimate our *resolve*. We might easily be irrationally determined to resist the Soviets. We have no tradition in the United States of controlling our emotions. We have tended to emphasize the opposite notion (e.g., "Give me liberty or give me death"). A Soviet underestimation of U.S. resolve could create the worst of all situations—one in which we had not made preparations for the failure of deterrence because we knew we had enough resolve, but the Soviets did not believe it so they went ahead and provoked us and we were forced to initiate a war in retaliation, a war in which we were not prepared to do anything more than kill Russians.[14] But it seems likely that unless we institute remedial measures, the Soviets may estimate that we will be deterred, and they will be right in their estimate. It should be realized that a very low additional probability of war might not deter the Soviets. It is not as if there were no probability at all of war and their action had

[13] After observing, in passing, that the case for more civil defense was "perhaps best put eighteen months ago in a study by The RAND Corporation," the London *Times* of January 4, 1960 editorialized, "No amount of money or concrete could guarantee to prevent the deaths of some millions of city-dwellers from blast and heat, and it is just as difficult to imagine an American President willing to risk deaths of five million Americans as of fifty million."

[14] Nathan Leites points out to me that a convinced Communist might be perfectly willing to believe that the cold-hearted capitalist ruling class would be willing to lose 60 million or so of the "lower" classes; but even this ideological estimator would probably feel safe from an attack if a Soviet retaliation could kill many more than 60 million Americans.

created this probability. It would be much more reasonable to say that just the existence of the U.S.–S.U. rivalry means that somehow there is always a probability of war of, say, one in fifty every year, and that if the Soviet action increased this by, in any one year, 50 per cent—from the assumed .02 to .03—that this might not be, for many reasons, as deterring as raising the probability from zero to .01. As the engineer would put it, the increased probability of war must dominate "the noise level" to be deterring. This is particularly true if the Soviets believe that their action would either decrease the long-run probability of war or increase markedly their chance of coming out of such a war very much better than if they had not improved their position. In addition, if the Soviets were not to risk all by a single attempt but tested our resolve more gradually by instigating a series of crises, then without running excessive risks they could probably find out experimentally a great deal about our reactions to extreme provocations. No matter what our *declared policy* might be, our *actual policy* could be probed. Most important of all, it is difficult to believe, in the absence of adequate measure for air defense and civil defense, that the Europeans will have faith in our declared policy when it is strained. The Soviets may be able to make their gains more easily by working on the will and resolve of the Europeans than by working on ours. We must convince the Europeans as well as the Russians of our resolve if we are to prevent appeasement or an undue degree of accommodation.

Here again is a summary of the situation:

❖❖

TABLE 3
TRAGIC BUT DISTINGUISHABLE POSTWAR STATES

Dead	Economic Recuperation
2,000,000	1 year
5,000,000	2 years
10,000,000	5 years
20,000,000	10 years
40,000,000	20 years
80,000,000	50 years
160,000,000	100 years

Will the survivors envy the dead?

❖❖

The first three lines in this table indicate circumstances under which *some* Europeans still believe in U.S. "retaliation." The next two lines show circumstances in which *most* Americans seem to believe in it, and the last two lines indicate states in which *neither* Europeans nor Americans (nor presumably the Soviets) would believe that the use of our Strategic Air Command against the Soviet Union is credible—no matter what the Soviets did in Europe—providing they gave U.S. decision makers time to ponder seriously on the consequences of a war.

Unclassified published estimates of the casualties that the United States would suffer in a nuclear war generally run around 50 to 80 million. If these estimates are relevant (which is doubtful since they generally assume a Soviet surprise attack on an unalert United States), we are already deterred from living up to our alliance obligations. If these casualty estimates are not relevant, then we ought to make relevant estimates for now and the future.

The critical point is whether the Soviets and the Europeans believe that we can keep our casualties to a level we would find acceptable, whatever that level may be. In such an eventuality the Soviets would be deterred from such provocative acts as a ground attack on Europe, Hitler-type blackmail threats, or evacuation of their cities and presentation to us of an ultimatum. But if they do not believe that we can keep casualties to a level we would find acceptable, the Soviets may feel safe in undertaking these extremely provocative adventures; or at least the Europeans may believe that the Soviets will feel safe, and this in itself creates an extremely dangerous negotiating situation—one in which the possibility of extreme pressure and blackmail will always be in the background, if not the foreground.

The situation is actually worse than the mere estimate of the casualties or economic damage is likely to indicate. The most crucial and difficult question is the one asked at the bottom of the table: "Will the survivors envy the dead?" Unless the President believes that the postwar world will be worth living in, he will in all likelihood be deterred from living up to our alliance obligations. We must give some attention to the conditions of postwar life, to the full impact of a thermonuclear war as indicated in Table 4 on page 22.

As has already been explained, one does not have to be trying to achieve a Credible First Strike Capability to be interested in trying to cope with the eight phases of a thermonuclear war. Even if one believes in mutual annihilation, he may still be willing to endorse Counterforce as Insurance Capability (the insurance against unreliability discussed in the previous section). This is because a reasonable person generally knows that his beliefs can be wrong. Many will agree, therefore, that some portion of the defense budget should be allocated to Counterforce as Insurance and to other measures designed to alleviate the consequences of a war. Because paper calculations can be misleading, it is rational to have even an inconsistent program which hedges against this possibility.

There is, however, a difference between Counterforce as Insurance and Credible First Strike Capabilities. In the case of the latter we do not say that there is a *modest* probability that the mutual annihilation theory is wrong; instead, we require that there be a *very high* probability that it is wrong. In short, *the time has come when we must believe that our programs are very likely to be successful under wartime and postwar conditions.*

When this has been said, it is still important to know (abstractly, we hope) that a war in which the U.S. made the first strike would result in more favorable conditions for us than would the wars that are generally considered. And even here we are more interested in *deterrence* than in *striking first!* We are more deeply interested in what the Soviets will conclude when they ask themselves, "If we try this very provoking act, will the United States strike us?" than in speculating on what could happen to us if we should actually strike them. It is quite possible that the Soviets may conclude when contemplating action that their risks are too high (even though the fact may be that we have already concluded that we would not actually dare to initiate the war). It is for such reasons that even a façade may be invaluable. Everyone knows that there is an enormous difference between a probability and a certainty.

5. "Splendid" First Strike and no Limited War Capability

It is difficult for most people to believe that any nation would initiate a thermonuclear war against an opponent capable of retaliation no matter what capabilities it had and no matter how much it was provoked; nevertheless, there are many military planners who oppose having limited war capabilities to handle modest provocations. They say this is a diversion of our resources from more important and essential central war capabilities. They seem to feel that our strategic force can be so effective in Soviet eyes that they would not dare to provoke us in even a minor way. They also believe that if the Soviets did provoke us we should then hit them at "a time and place of our choosing," thereby punishing the Soviets for their provocation. This is, roughly speaking, the massive retaliation theory as enunciated by former Secretary of State John Foster Dulles. While a Credible First Strike Capability to correct or avenge a limited but major aggression also involves massive retaliation, the distinction is that it is massive retaliation over *major* issues, not minor ones. It should also be clear that if the terror in the "balance of terror" intensifies, the line between major and minor issues will shift so that the level of provocation we will accept without triggering SAC will increase.

Anyone who studies even superficially the likely effects of thermonuclear war will inevitably reach certain conclusions. Chief among these is the idea that *even if one could launch a very successful first strike, the net damage, if only from the backlash (i.e., the fallout on the U.S. and the world from the bombs dropped on Russia, not to speak of the Russian people who would be killed), would make it unreasonable to make such a strike on a minor issue.* Is it not true that if we were to launch such a war it would not be over the minor issue bothering us but really because we had decided to engage in a form of preventive war? In the real world we would have to worry about far more than just the backlash from our blow; we would have to worry about Soviet retaliatory action. For such *practical* reasons alone, not to speak of vitally important moral and political ones, the notion of having a "Splendid" First Strike Capability seems fanciful.

6. Dreams

If a "Splendid" First Strike Capability seems in the light of facts and reason to be fanciful, it is no less strange than many of the ideas which make the rounds in Washington or in European capitals. In such places one finds consideration given to very implausible notions. One of these is a conflict in which a thermonuclear blow is followed by a three-year war of production accompanied by the kind of mobilization we had in World War II. Another is the notion that the enemy can go ahead and strike us first, but that our defenses would keep us essentially untouched, and that we in turn can strike back and then survey the situation. There is the fervid belief in the possibility of a "leakproof" active defense system. There is the concept of a long-drawn-out conflict, a "broken backed war," waged with conventional weapons because both sides have simultaneously used up all their nuclear weapons. There is the claim that in a thermonuclear war it is important to keep the sea lanes open. And there is the quaint idea that the main purpose of civil defense is to support a thermonuclear war effort with men and materials. Or the equally quaint notion that after a massive interchange of thermonuclear bombs the major objective of the U.S. Army forces in the United States will not be civilian recuperation but to move to a (destroyed) port of embarkation for movement overseas. While all of these views are most implausible, they can be found in various types of official and semiofficial statements.

Where do such ideas come from? They generally result, it can be assumed, from doctrinal lags or from position papers which primarily reflect a very narrow departmental interest or which are the result of log-rolling compromises between several partisan departments of the government. We are fortunate that on the whole these views are no longer taken seriously even by many of the decision makers who sign the papers. Unfortunately, this does not prevent the papers themselves from influencing public opinion and policy to an important extent.

It should be noted that those who are convinced of the efficacy of Minimum or Finite Deterrence tend to believe that the Counterforce as Insurance, the Credible First Strike Capability, and the "Splendid" First Strike Capability views are as fanciful as the dream capabilities mentioned above. If anything, they find them more dangerously fanciful because so many people take them seriously. In this book only the following strategic positions will be considered seriously: Finite Deterrence, Counterforce as Insurance, Preattack Mobilization Base, and Credible First Strike Capability—all with varying degrees of Arms Control and Limited War Capability. The burden of my discussion will be on the nature, feasibility, and problems associated with each of these strategies, with the purpose of suggesting which one should be the basis of national policy. Our national policy at this writing seems to be drifting (mostly as a result of decisions evaded or decided for relatively minor technical reasons) toward accepting a strategy between Finite Deterrence and Counterforce as Insurance. *It is one of my main arguments that at least for the immediate future we should be somewhere between the Preattack Mobilization Base and the Credible First Strike Capability.* This posture would have, at least, enough capability to launch a first strike in the kind of tense situation that would result from an outrageous Soviet provocation, so as to induce uncertainty in the enemy as to whether it would not be safer to attack us directly rather than provoke us. The posture should have enough of a retaliatory capability to make this direct attack unattractive. It should have enough of a Preattack Mobilization Base to enable us to increase our first strike and retaliatory capabilities rapidly enough so that, if international relations deteriorate seriously, we will be able to acquire sufficient power in time to control or influence events. There should be enough Counterforce as Insurance so that if a war occurs anyway—perhaps as a result of accident or miscalculation—the nation will continue and unnecessary death and destruction will not occur. And lastly, the posture should include enough Arms Control and Limited War Capability to deter and correct "minor" conflicts and to make the day-to-day course of international relations livable until more permanent and stable arrangements are set up.

CHAPTER II

WILL THE SURVIVORS ENVY
THE DEAD?

How Much Tragedy is "Acceptable"?

BEFORE describing postwar problems, let us consider what we mean by an acceptable level of risk. We could start by asking, "How much tragedy can we live with and still not have 'the survivors envy the dead'?", but we will start with a more moderate question: "How dangerous or hostile a world would we be willing to live in and still call it a reasonable facsimile of a Russian or American standard of living?"

Nobody in either country would worry about a situation in which one thousand workers were engaged in some hazardous occupation which inflicted on each worker one chance in a hundred thousand per year of a fatal accident. Over a full year there would be approximately 99 chances in 100 that none of the workers would be hurt (see Table 5). Over a fifty-year period there would be better than an even chance that no worker would have been hurt. However, this attitude may change if the entire world population is subjected, as a result of some governmental action, to the same level of risk.

❖❖

TABLE 5
ACCEPTABILITY OF RISKS

Peace

$$1 \text{ thousand workers} \times \frac{1}{100,000} = 0.01/\text{year}$$

$$0.01 \times 50 \text{ years} = 0.5 \text{ workers}$$

$$3 \text{ billion people} \times \frac{1}{100,000} = 30,000/\text{year}$$

$$30,000 \times 50 \text{ years} = 1,500,000 \text{ people}$$

Postwar

$$180 \text{ million Americans} \times \frac{\overline{100,000}}{1} = 1,800/\text{year}$$

$$1,800 \times 50 \text{ years} = 90,000 \text{ Americans}$$

❖❖

Because the world's population is so large (about three billion), one chance in a hundred thousand of a fatal accident per year means that on the average, 30,000 extra people per year would be killed. Over fifty years, 1,500,000 would die prematurely. While these are large numbers, something like this *might* result if many governments engaged in vigorous programs of weapons testing. Many people feel that any peacetime government action that could result in such a large number of casualties is intolerable.

We are concerned here, however, with the consequences of a war. One might well ask, "If a few bombs in the distant Pacific or Soviet Arctic will cause so much damage, would not a lot of bombs close-in be totally catastrophic?" The answer depends on how one defines "totally catastrophic"; a catastrophe can be pretty catastrophic without being total. Unfortunately, in order to make some necessary distinctions I will now have to treat some aspects of human tragedy in an objective and quantitative fashion even though some readers will find such treatment objectionable. I will tend to ignore, or at least underemphasize, what many people might consider the most important result of a war—the over-all suffering induced by 10,000 years of postwar environment. Instead, let us ask two questions: Can society *bear* the economic burdens caused by the increased sickness, malformations, and deaths? What view should a reasonable (nonhypochondriac) individual hold toward his own future?

The reader can easily see that from the viewpoint of these two questions, decision makers might define a postwar world as "tolerable" if death rates increased by about one per cent for tens of thousands of years, even though this might mean that at long length the war would cause the premature death of more people than are now alive. No doubt most decision makers under extreme compulsion would be willing to countenance the idea that the immediate survivors and later generations be subjected to levels of risk that industrial workers undergo in peacetime. Therefore, if as a result of a thermonuclear war long-lived radioisotopes are created which cause the premature death of some thousands of Americans each year (or hundreds of thousands of deaths over fifty years), simple arithmetic shows that such deaths would be of small significance *compared to the war itself*. Few would call it a "total catastrophe" if *all* survivors of a thermonuclear war lost a few years of life expectancy and even ten or twenty million of the survivors lost an average of ten or fifteen years of life expectancy. To repeat: I think that any individual who survived the war should be willing to accept, almost with equanimity, somewhat larger risks than those to which we subject our industrial workers in peacetime. We should not magnify our view of the costs of the war inordinately because such postwar risks are added to the wartime casualties.

At this point I must make an admission. *The illustrative table is "faked."* A risk of one part in a hundred thousand is actually *far too small* to illustrate the industrial risks we accept in peacetime. We like to think that when we subject people to risk we do it at so low a level there is no discernible damage. But this is not even true of risks taken by all our population, not to speak of limited industrial risks. We design our roads and set up safety regulations to make driving reasonably safe, but rather than accept speed limits of twenty miles an hour we prefer to let automobiles kill forty thousand people a year (or about 25 per 100,000) and injure close to a million (or about 600 per 100,000). This degree of risk is in fact characteristic of a great deal of activity in modern societies.

Some of the risks of living in a modern society are assumed willingly and knowingly by those who bear them; even more are assumed willingly, but not knowingly; and probably most are just assumed. However, many people have a much more favorable attitude toward risks that arise out of useful or pleasurable civilian activities than those that arise from preparations for war—for example, as a result of testing nuclear weapons. These people feel even more

✦✧✦

TABLE 4

A COMPLETE DESCRIPTION OF A THERMONUCLEAR WAR

Includes an Analysis of:

1. Various time-phased programs for deterrence and defense and their possible impact on us, our allies, and others.
2. Wartime performance with different preattack and attack conditions.
3. Acute fallout problems.
4. Survival and patch-up.
5. Maintenance of economic momentum.
6. Long-term recuperation.
7. Postwar medical problems.
8. Genetic problems.

✦✧✦

antagonistic toward risks that could potentially arise from fighting a war. I would like at this point to evaluate these risks objectively, without worrying how they arose, and later we will consider how they might affect calculations of deterrence and defense. More generally, I would like to describe some of the possible forms a postwar world might take in order to evaluate whether it is worth while to survive a war and how decision makers might view their country's prospects. We will be examining points 4 to 8 of Table 4, which is repeated above for reference.

Genetics and Thermonuclear War

Many people who contemplate thermonuclear war have found number 8 on the table, the genetic hazard, particularly frightening. Partly for this reason and partly because it has been so widely publicized, we shall start with this problem. Distinguished geneticists and biologists have made statements which, when quoted out of context (and occasionally even when quoted in context), seem to imply that the human germ plasm simply could not survive a thermonuclear war. Even if one does not adopt this extreme position, the long-lasting and somewhat incalculable nature of the damage has seemed so frightening that even the experts tend to avoid calculating the effects of a nuclear war. By contenting themselves with discussions of the fallout from tests, they have sometimes given the impression that the damage from a war is so great that it does not have to be calculated.

I would now like to give a serious illustration of the kind of risk that is sometimes considered acceptable by discussing current public health standards with regard to the genetic damage caused by the peacetime use of radiation; this discussion will have the bonus value of providing some orientation about this important subject. How much damage would be done if everybody received a radiation dose to his reproductive organs as large as that considered acceptable by the National Academy of Sciences? According to the NAS, every effort should be made to limit the average dose to the reproductive organs to less than 10r (roentgens) during the first thirty years of life, and to no more than another 10r in each subsequent ten years. The reason for this limit is not so much the damage to the individual, but rather the possible genetic damage that will be passed on to his descendants. What would be the genetic effects if the entire world population received doses approaching NAS

limits? Would effects be large or small? Using the best available
information, we get the results shown in Table 6.

◆◇◆

TABLE 6

ESTIMATED GENETIC CONSEQUENCES IF WORLD-WIDE
DOSES APPROACHED NAS 10r LIMITS

Type of Damage	Total Increase [a]		Per cent Increase [a]		Normal Rate (per cent)
	First Generation	Later Generation [b]	First Generation	Later Generation [b]	
Major Defects	1,000,000	10,000,000	0.04	0.4	4 [c]
Minor Defects	10,000,000	200,000,000	0.4	6	100 [d]
Early Mortality [e]	2,500,000	40,000,000	0.08	1.3	25
Decreased Fertility	5,000,000	100,000,000	0.17	3.3	–

[a] World population assumed constant at 3 billion.
[b] Also gives total damage over all generations due to a dose to one generation.
[c] Includes nongenetic defects present at birth.
[d] Everybody has minor defects.
[e] Includes miscarriages.

◆◇◆

The estimated amount of human tragedy and accompanying
misery is uncomfortably high. It is believed that if everyone in the
world were subjected to a 10r dose, approximately one million children, who would not otherwise be defective, would be born seriously defective in the next generation. If this dose should be repeated generation after generation (the world population remaining stable), a new and higher level of defective genes would be
established. When this new level of stability is achieved, every generation might see the birth of about ten million seriously defective
children as a result of this NAS limit exposure. These are very large
numbers, even for a generation.

We can obtain the corresponding numbers for the United States alone (assuming average population to be 200,000,000) by dividing the totals by 15. This comes to roughly 65,000 defective American children in the first generation and 650,000 in every generation when new levels of stability are reached. This would be a large toll; moreover, we are talking about such serious defects as imbecility, crippling, blindness, deafness, and various debilitating or deforming diseases and defects. If not correctable by medical science, these congenital defects are viewed by most parents as human tragedy in its most extreme form—a live defective child. However, some may be surprised and shocked to learn that this toll has not only been judged to be acceptable hypothetically; it seems likely to be accepted by the technologically advanced peoples. The average person in the United States probably *now* receives about one half of the NAS dose to his reproductive organs from X-rays alone. The readers of this book very likely use more medical services than the average American, and as a result receive at least twice the average dose. The resulting damage is just part of the price we have to pay to live in a civilization with nuclear power plants, X-rays, fluoroscopes, tracer elements, weapons tests, and so on.

Many geneticists have raised serious questions about the acceptability of the damage just described. They argue not only that the predicted damage is very high, but also that there is a good deal of uncertainty in the calculations. Still, it has been decided by the geneticists on the NAS committees, and others, that the expected gains from using this level of radiation for medical and other purposes are greater than the losses. Even so, nobody is thinking of lowering the standards by raising the limit. The reason why we are willing to accept such losses is that they are small when expressed as percentages even though they are high numerically.

Referring again to Table 6, we note that the most important genetic effect of radiation—live but seriously defective children—starts from 0.04 per cent for the first generation and gradually increases to 0.4 per cent for later generations if the radiation continues. While four chances in a thousand is a high price to pay for the use of radiation, it is not obviously excessive, especially when one considers that it is only a 10 per cent increase in the natural rate of 4 per cent.

But four chances in a thousand is four hundred times larger than the hypothetical one-in-a-hundred-thousand risk that we originally discussed. Even in peacetime we are willing to subject large populations to significant risks, accepting the resulting damage. War is a terrible thing; but so is peace. The difference seems in some respects to be a quantitative one of degree and standards.

I once mentioned in an unclassified lecture that I could easily imagine a war in which the average survivor received about 250 roentgens. Now 250 roentgens is 25 times greater than the 10 roentgens we have talked about. According to Table 6, 10 roentgens produces about .04 per cent defectives. According to the widely accepted theory of a linear relationship between dose and damage, 250 roentgens would produce 25 times as much damage as 10 roentgens. This would mean that about 1 per cent of the children who could have been healthy would be defective; in short, the number of children born seriously defective would increase, because of war, to about 25 per cent above the current rate. This would be a large penalty to pay for a war. More horrible still, we might have to continue to pay a similar though smaller price for 20 or 30 or 40 generations. But even this is a long way from annihilation. It might well turn out, for example, that U.S. decision makers would be willing, among other things, to accept the high risk of an additional 1 per cent of our children being born deformed *if that meant not giving up Europe to Soviet Russia.* Or it might be that under certain circumstances the Russians would be willing to accept even higher risks than this, if by doing so they could eliminate the United States.

At this point in the lecture a lady in the audience got up and said in a very accusing voice, "I don't want to live in your world in which 1 per cent of the children are born defective." My answer was rather brutal, I fear. "It is not *my* world," I observed, and I then pointed out that if she did not want to live in a world in which 1 per cent of the children were born defective she had a real problem, since 4 per cent of the children are born defective *now*. This story illustrates that peace also has its tragedies, and that we tend in our day-to-day life to ignore the existence of this continuing risk. Unless their own family or close friends or relatives have been affected, most people just ignore these kinds of risks in the environment in which we live and raise families.

I can easily imagine that if we lived in a world in which no children had ever been born defective and we were told that as a result of some new contingencies 4 per cent of the children would be born seriously defective we would consider such a world to be intolerable. We might not believe that people would be willing to bear and raise children if the risk were about 1 in 25 that these children would have a serious congenital defect. However, we live in that world now. We not only bear this relatively high rate of tragedy; we come close to ignoring it. While some women are greatly concerned about such possibilities during their pregnancy, it is only in such critical periods or when they are touched personally that most people think about this continuing burden of life. To add a further 1 per cent to the burden would be a terrible thing to do, but this additional burden is clearly comparable to the kinds of risks to which we have become accustomed in the peacetime world. Most people will be able to live with such increased risks.[1]

A magnified incidence of major defects, while dramatic, is not the only genetic cost of exposure. Table 6 indicates that there will probably also be about 10,000,000 new minor defects in the first generation, rising to an equilibrium in which people have 200,000,000 minor defects that they would not have had if their ancestors had not been exposed. These minor defects might affect the health,

[1] In testifying before a subcommittee of the Joint Committee on Atomic Energy on June 26, 1959, I made some remarks in which the words "peace also has its tragedies" appeared and a little later I said, "In other words, war is horrible. There is no question about it. But so is peace. And it is proper, with the kind of calculations we are making today, to compare the horror of war and the horror of peace and see how much worse it is. This is an emotion-laden issue, partly because it gets mixed up with the question of nuclear testing where many people have overdone such comparisons or said, rather violently, that they are totally irrelevant."

The comment was quoted or misquoted in several places to the effect that, "scientist testifies that peace is horrible." It is partly because of the danger of being quoted out of context that many technical people and government officials are unwilling to discuss these problems soberly. Almost invariably when one tries to put the tragedy into context or proportion, one is accused of either grossly underestimating or of being incredibly callous.

I should like to add another example of either a misunderstanding or a misquote. *On a number of occasions I have remarked that it is not necessarily true that both nations will be destroyed in a war; there are many circumstances in which only one nation will get destroyed and some in which neither will be.* Therefore, depending on the circumstances and the alternatives which a nation has, it is quite possible that decision makers could rationally and sanely choose to go to war. (I will expand on this a bit later.) The immediate reaction many had to this remark was that I was recommending preventive war. That is, they did not attack my estimates but simply some of the conclusions that they thought I would draw from these estimates.

I do not believe it will help us to solve the problems that are coming up in the next ten years to discuss the problems of war and peace on an emotional rather than factual basis. It is not that the problems are not inherently emotional. They are. It is perfectly proper for people to feel strongly about them. But while emotion is a good spur to action, it is only rarely a good guide to *appropriate* action. In the complicated and dangerous world in which we are going to live, it will only increase the chance of tragedy if we refuse to make and discuss objectively whatever quantitative estimates can be made.

happiness, life expectancy, and vigor of the individual, but they generally do not show up in a dramatic way. It is very hard to estimate the over-all impact of such defects. In particular, some geneticists tend to be misleading in their estimates of this impact because they do not think or talk like economists. For example, there is a theorem in genetics which intimates that almost any defective mutation is just as bad as any other mutation because almost every defective mutation eventually causes a death.

Sometimes a geneticist says that insofar as two mutations do not cause exactly the same damage, the one that results in a minor defect may cause more damage. The reasoning goes as follows. A major defect either kills the bearer or at least prevents him from having children, thus causing the genetic death of the line. The minor defect is carried along generation after generation, affecting the health of each of its bearers adversely, until finally it tips the scale against an individual, causing him to die and terminating that genetic line. So while both the minor and the major mutation killed an individual, the minor one also affected the health of many other individuals in the process. One can therefore argue that the minor mutation caused more total damage. While this theorem (due to J. B. S. Haldane in 1931) is a very important insight it can be misleading and in practice seems to affect a great deal of thinking among geneticists in a misleading way. It is misleading because, among other things, it ignores the fact that one normally discounts the future in assessing the current impact of future harm.

Let me give an example of one reason (there are others) why the theorem is misleading if we are to use the words "harm," "damage," and so on, properly. If asked to choose among four situations —one in which 100 per cent of the people were killed immediately, another in which 10 per cent of each generation died prematurely for ten generations, another in which one per cent of each generation died prematurely for a hundred generations, or finally, one in which a tenth of a per cent of each generation died prematurely for the next thousand generations, there is no question which situation most people would prefer. Yet the total number of individuals killed is exactly the same.

In other words, if you can spread the genetic damage over tens of thousands of years you have done something very useful. If one is asking, "How does this damage affect society and its members?" one cannot just add arithmetically the total damage over tens of thousands of years. From some moral points of view the simple arithmetic sum may be the right way to think, but I have doubts even about that. It is true that "a human being is a human being," but it is also true that human beings live in a society. Thus the well-being of the human race as a whole is a value which most people are interested in preserving. The things affecting the human race as a whole are also important, possibly more important than the things that jeopardize a limited number of particular individuals. Even though it seems to many to be grossly immoral to talk about preferences at all in this unpleasant subject, from both the practical and moral point of view decision makers do have preferences. From the viewpoint of how we as individuals view our personal expectations of happiness or our society's ability to function, the simple arithmetic sum is also almost irrelevant. It is probably also worth observing that it would be almost impossible to have a sober objective public discussion of the problem I have just discussed. It is impossible to imagine a public figure stating, "the damage due to fallout is not as serious as is sometimes implied, since most of the burden is borne by our descendants and not by our own generation." While I believe that this statement is a defendable one, it is not one I would care to defend in the give and take of a public debate.

In any case, I am not going to discuss the question: "Is it just as bad to kill a man 10,000 years from now as to kill one today?" It is not that I am disinterested in that question. It is that it is almost irrelevant to the major point at issue: *the deterrence of war*. That kind of question typically will not affect in any serious way most calculations of deterrence.

It is impossible to estimate the absolute effect of the minor defects on society and the average individual. However, we can almost be certain that the relative impact of the new minor-defect genes will be much less than the absolute impact of either the existing minor-defect genes or the relative impact of the new, serious-defect genes. The reason for this is that the major defects are likely to manifest themselves in such a way as to terminate or reduce the number of bearers of that particular line, while a minor defect does not have such a drastic impact on the bearer and, unlike a major defect, may stay in the genetic pool for many, many generations. So the existing pool of minor-defect genes has been built up over many times more generations than, for example, the pool of major-defect genes. Therefore, the war-caused increases in minor defects should be a much smaller fraction of the normal pool of minor defects than are the war-caused increases in major defects of the current pool of major defects. If we make the plausible assumption that the burden to society caused by minor defects is comparable to the burden caused by major defects, then the additional burden due to minor defects caused by the war is clearly much less than the increase due to major defects.

In addition to the minor defects, there should be approximately two and a half million first generation early deaths (a number composed mostly of miscarriages, but including some deaths in infancy or early childhood), and there should be forty million in subsequent generations after stability has been reached.

Probably of limited significance to us are the so-called embryonic deaths. These are conceptions which would have been successful if it had not been for radiation that damaged the germ cell and thus made the potential conception result in a failure. There will probably be five million of these in the first generation, and one hundred million in future generations. I do not think of this last number as too important, except for the small fraction that involves detectable miscarriages or stillbirths. On the whole, the human race is so fecund that a small reduction in fecundity should not be a serious matter even to individuals. It is almost completely misleading to include the "early deaths" or embryonic deaths in the same total with the major and minor defects, but this is sometimes done by scientists who have overemphasized the abstraction "genetic death" and thus lost sight of the difference in terms of human tragedy of a serious defect or an embryonic death.

A final remark on the genetic problem. Only survivors can have children. It would be difficult to have a war in which the average *survivor* got much more than 1,000 roentgens before the age of thirty. (Giving this amount of radiation rapidly will kill a person.) Unless the enemy has deliberately adopted self-defeating tactics (for example, deliberately degraded his wartime capability by using "cobalt" bombs in places and at times he should be using militarily more efficient bombs), the long-term radiation should also be much less than this, particularly if even modest precautions were taken. One thousand roentgens might double the existing burden of genetic defects. Though the total amount of human tragedy that this might

50

cause over the next twenty-five generations staggers the imagination, it is still very far from annihilation. In fact, there are many circumstances in which the issue of "War or Peace?" would not be decided by such long-run costs.

I would like now to give the assumptions underlying the discussion of genetic effects just concluded. At present about 4 per cent of all infants are either born with, or soon develop, a serious abnormality. It is believed that about half these abnormalities are of genetic origin. About 13 per cent of all pregnancies result in an early death (including miscarriages in the definition of early death); of these, 8 per cent are presumed to be of genetic origin. We assume that a dose of 50r to the reproductive organs of both parents would result in doubling the natural rate of *all* mutations.

❖❖

TABLE 7
GENETIC ASSUMPTIONS

Normal congenital abnormality rate	4%
of genetic origin	2%
Normal early deaths (including late miscarriages)	13%
of genetic origin	8%
Dose to double normal mutation rate	50r
Rate for expression of genetic defects	
first generation	10%
later generations	4%
First generation expression rate for 100r dose (factor)	0.2
First generation expression rate for 1,000r dose (factor)	2

❖❖

This assumption is inconsistent with some data from experiments with animals, because some mutations are more likely to be induced than others. But so little is known about the quantitative relationship between dose and human mutation rates that it is reasonable to use a single rate for all mutations, though the average rate could easily be wrong by a factor of 2 or 3 in either direction.

A doubling of the mutation rate for one generation does not mean doubling the total number of mutated genes, for a large pool of defective genes has been created over many generations. Doubling the natural mutation rate just doubles the rate at which this pool is being increased. We assume that about 10 per cent of the new defective genes would manifest themselves in the first-generation progeny of the irradiated parents but would so handicap the bearer that they would not be passed on to later generations. Our calculations also assume that only recessive genes can influence later generations, and that these appear in each generation as follows: 4 per cent of the transmitted genes manifest themselves in each generation as serious defectives that do not breed, and 96 per cent show up as minor defects which do not affect fertility but may affect the happiness and vigor of the carrier.

We also assume a linear relationship between size of dose and number of genetic defects created. This means that if both parents were to receive an exposure of 100r, the number of defects of genetic origin manifesting themselves in the next generation would be increased by 20 per cent, while a 1,000r dose would increase the same number by 200 per cent. From these assumptions it is possible to calculate the first three lines in Table 6. The fourth line is obtained directly from data on the reduction of fertility of radiated mice, which might or might not be applicable to man.[2]

It is clear that there is much uncertainty in using the above assumptions for making calculations. There are equally large uncertainties in calculating other effects of radiation. In fact, one of the things that has alarmed some physicians, perhaps excessively, is how new research has shown that past "allowable" medical use of X-rays was unsafe, at least by current peacetime standards. This, in turn, has cast doubt on the reliability of standards for other risks. For example, many obstetricians once X-rayed pregnant women as a routine precautionary measure. It is now thought that this might give both the unborn child and the mother an exposure of between 1 and 5 roentgens, depending on the quality of the equipment, how well the equipment has been maintained, and the care with which the X-ray is made. This amounts to an appreciable fraction of the allowable thirty-year NAS dose. The routine X-ray, therefore, has been almost eliminated in the last few years.

But this particular practice may have been more dangerous than

[2] For a more detailed discussion of such calculations we refer the reader to Carl Crow's testimony, Hearings before the Special Subcommittee on Radiation of the Joint Committee on Atomic Energy, Congress of the United States, 85th Congress, 1st Session, on the Nature of Radioactive Fallout and Its Effects on Man, June 4, 5, 6, and 7, 1957, Part 2, especially pp. 1009–1028.

the above figures indicate. For example, one study indicates that an X-ray pelvimetry might double a child's chance of getting leukemia before the age of ten, raising it from 1 in 1,000 to 1 in 500, probably because the rapidly multiplying cells of a fetus may be more sensitive to radiation than are the cells of an adult.[3] Such studies, widely publicized, induce in most doctors a deep respect for the potency of radiation and our lack of knowledge about the many ways in which radiation can harm us. Indeed it has induced a feeling close to panic in some physicians, and part of this feeling has been communicated to the general public. While it must be conceded that there are great uncertainties, it should be pointed out that man has been subject to natural radiation for millions of years, and whatever the effects these new peacetime and potential wartime exposures will be, they are not different in kind from the old—just more intense.

What risk of damage are we willing to tolerate for industrial and laboratory workers? In the light of common notions of "acceptable," the amount we are willing to accept in this respect in order to keep our society operating is almost astounding. Before the current controversy about tests and radiation, the nominal dose permitted for industrial workers was 0.3 roentgens per week (in 1931 it was 1r/week or 52r/year). Note that 0.3r per week is 15r a year, or 450r over a thirty-year working life. This is a large dose indeed. Children conceived after one parent acquired such a dose *might* have about 50 per cent greater than normal chance of being genetically defective. This 450r exposure *might* also increase by a factor of 5 or 10 the worker's chances of having such diseases as leukemia and bone cancer. Even if he escapes these diseases, this large dose *might* still cut his life expectancy by a few years. Partly for these reasons, but chiefly as a by-product of the recurring controversy over bomb tests, an additional limitation has been placed on the allowable industrial dose, to no more than 50r in any ten-year period. We will refer to this rate as the permissible dose (PD).

We have argued that this PD, or even a somewhat higher one, is "acceptable" in a postwar world, because if one is forced to undergo risks comparable to those normally undergone in peacetime

[3] A. Stewart, J. Webb and D. Newitt, "A Survey of Childhood Malignancies," *British Medical Journal*, Vol. 1. (June 28, 1958), p. 1495, line 58; reprinted in Vol. 2 of *Fallout from Nuclear Tests*, Hearings before Joint Committee on Atomic Energy, May 1959. Also see article by Jack Schubert, "Fetal Irradiation and Fallout," *Bulletin of the Atomic Scientists*, Vol. XV (June 1959), pp. 253–256.

by industrial workers, this rate (almost by definition) is not cataclysmic. It is not that we are callous to the human tragedy involved. It is simply that if one asks two questions: What are the social and economic consequences of the high postwar radiation risks? and What are the consequences in terms of the average person's standard of living as he sees it? the answers should not change much from the prewar ones, provided we can hold the risks roughly to industrial levels. It is true that the total genetic damage resulting from the war, if totaled over the many generations in which it might manifest itself, would be staggering. It is, in fact, quite possible that the number of casualties represented by this simple *arithmetic* sum will, in some sense, be equal to or even much larger than direct wartime casualties. We observe, however, that it is just because the genetic effects are spread over thousands of years that they become bearable to any particular generation.

It is not obvious, just because we can bear a certain level of defects today, that we could afford to add an equal amount and thus double society's burden; in fact, I am sure we could find some societies with large medical burdens whose character would be sharply changed if we doubled this medical burden. Yet it seemed to those of us who did the RAND civil defense study that societies like those of the United States and the Soviet Union (always abstracting from the humanitarian aspects) are not really strained very much by their current burden of defects. Doubling the burden, we thought, might cause some small decrease in net productivity because of the decreased efficiency of some members of the society, and it might increase somewhat the expenditures on medical and custodial care. But the extra costs would not be large enough to change appreciably the expectations of persons not directly affected.

It is also appropriate to observe that the science of genetics is only about one hundred years old. Along with the other sciences, it is progressing rapidly. It is quite possible and even likely that future generations will develop genetic or medical techniques to eliminate or alleviate this particular legacy of war.

Two Possible Attacks

In order to be as specific and quantitative as possible in discussing fallout effects, we are going to consider two attacks, as shown in Table 8.

TABLE 8
TWO POSSIBLE ATTACKS ON U.S.

	Early Attack	Late Attack
Target points	150	400
Number of bombs	500	2,000
Total *fission* yield (MT)	1,500	20,000

The labeling of "early" and "late" is arbitrary. We could just as well have called the attacks "small" and "large." The labeling that is adopted is useful because it draws attention to the fact that the threat could get much worse with time. Measures which might be valuable for the next few years may prove to be ridiculously inadequate somewhat later.

It is not important to justify the size of the indicated attacks or to try to relate them to our own or enemy capabilities; they were arbitrarily chosen to illustrate what *might* happen in a war. They are not a prediction. In particular, as will be discussed in Lecture II, an actual war is likely to be quite different. These contingencies are fundamentally so uncertain that it is hopeless to try to predict in any detail what is likely to happen. Any plans that depend on detailed predictions are probably unreliable, but this does not mean that quantitative estimates are without value. (It only means that their usefulness is restricted to testing plans and postures under a large variety of circumstances and to making communication more precise. Only in the most general and tentative way should one try to make predictions as to what will actually occur.)

However, it is important to be quantitative. It does no good to use expressions such as *intolerable, catastrophic, total destruction, annihilating retaliation,* and the like. These expressions might be reasonable if it were really true that in a modern war the total target system is "overkilled" five or ten times. It would then be unimportant to calculate the exact degree of overkill. But such expectations do not seem to be realistic, and it is important to get some understanding of what the levels of damage might really be.

The large attack in Table 8 is not really an upper-limit estimate of the enemy capability, but simply one of the cases that should be considered. It probably does not take full account of the possibility that if we establish a civil defense system that is effective against customary attacks, the enemy may develop new weapons systems to meet this challenge. We should evaluate our system in terms of the worst that he may conceivably be able to do. This includes looking not only at larger weapons delivered by conventional means, but also at ingenious and specially designed weapons systems (such as suicide ships or submarines carrying super-large bombs to explode off our coasts, causing tidal waves or extreme fallout). We need information on how our system looks under all conditions of attack, even though in the end we may be willing to gamble on the enemy not choosing to do the worst or not being able to do so. If we design our system to "look" at least moderately effective against these other attacks, the enemy is less likely to spend large sums of money to do this worst, since he may believe it to be relatively ineffective. We should, if we were doing a more complete study, look at both larger and smaller attacks than we will in this book, and also explore unconventional attacks. (I should note that, in the mid-sixties when we are likely to be dependent on Polaris and Minuteman systems, any attack we launch with these systems will be much closer to the "early" attack than to the "late" attack.)

Whenever in the discussion that follows I examine world-wide effects, I will assume that the U.S. and the U.S.S.R. together drop the same amount of fission products on the rest of the Northern Hemisphere as is dropped on the U.S. This is actually an unreasonable assumption since it is quite likely that one side will drop much more than the other, but it is a standard assumption to make, and I will follow the custom. I have used an oversimplified but for my purposes adequate model of fallout distribution which assumes that 80 per cent of the material comes down directly as "close-in" fallout, that 10 per cent goes into the stratosphere to be uniformly distributed over the earth, and that 10 per cent goes into the troposphere to be uniformly distributed north of the equator. These assumptions probably overestimate the level of contamination in the U.S., and they may correspondingly underestimate the Northern Hemisphere and world-wide contamination. The latter underestimate may be large if there are many high-yield air-burst weapons. Furthermore, we have made no allowance for the possible use of atomic or thermonuclear weapons in air defense.

The Radioactive Postwar Environment

Let us start by asking how hostile the postwar environment would be. We will start by examining the situation one hundred years after the war is over. This is just the kind of question a scientist is likely to ask himself, particularly the day or week before he appears at a Congressional hearing. After making some simple back-of-the-envelope calculations the scientist might come up with something like Table 9.

❖❖❖

TABLE 9

RADIOACTIVE ENVIRONMENT 100 YEARS LATER

(As measured by ratio to NAS or Industrial Standards)

Standard	Early Attack		Late Attack	
	NAS	IND.	NAS	IND.
U.S. Maximum	11.0	0.75	48.0	3.0
U.S. Average	0.6	0.04	7.0	0.45
Northern Hemisphere Minimum	0.004	0.003	0.06	0.004
World Minimum	0.001	0.0001	0.01	0.001

❖❖❖

The first column compares the radiation levels with the standards set by the NAS (10r in the first thirty years or 1/150r/week). Since those standards were determined by genetic and not somatic considerations, we are estimating whether or not genetic damage is still being done. It is—and seemingly at a disturbingly high rate. Even in the small attack, this external gamma radiation (almost all due to the long-lived isotope cesium-137) has hot spots about eleven times as radioactive as the NAS suggests is safe. The average over the country is three-fifths of the NAS standard. Therefore, it is almost certain that those parts of the country in the neighborhood (a few hundred miles) of targets will be over the NAS standard. It is this kind of calculation that causes geneticists to have such deep concern. Many of these geneticists thought that the NAS standards were too high, but even one hundred years after a war most of the important areas of the country may have even higher rates of radiation than these. Many naïve people accept a calculation of this kind as showing that the country would be uninhabitable for a century. But would such an attack really mean that we must abandon the contaminated areas of the country for a century? Not at all. The calculation is misleading. First, this back-of-the-envelope calculation used what might be called the "billiard table approximation," which assumes not only that all fission products come down on an infinitely smooth plane, but also that they stay there undisturbed for a hundred years. This is clearly unrealistic. At the least, it ignores the effects of weathering and terrain, which in most parts of the country are likely to improve long-run conditions by as much as tenfold. This calculation also ignores the remedial activities of man, and this is even more important. If we are suitably prepared before the attack, we will be able to decontaminate the more valuable areas. We might put enough effort into the decontamination to clean up a significant portion of the country by factors varying between 2 and 100 in the first two postwar years. Since decontamination would become a more or less continuing activity, where it is feasible we can expect this cleaning-up process to continue even after the passage of two years.

When we put these corrections into the calculation, even the heavy attack does not seem so frightening at the 100-year point. This impression is reinforced when we remind ourselves that the NAS standard was set for the whole population on the basis of genetic considerations. We could tolerate ten or twenty times this dose for a small percentage of the population for many years. This actually means that no part of the country would be inaccessible and, with reasonable risks, no part of the country considered valuable would be uninhabitable.

But this does not mean that every part of the country would be habitable. If, for example, the Air Force followed the suggestions that some people have made—that the Strategic Air Command be moved away from cities and into the Rocky Mountains or the Great American Desert—then some wars might easily result in the creation of large areas that one would not wish to live in, even by industrial standards. It is very unlikely that areas such as the Rocky Mountains would ever be decontaminated. Some people might be willing to visit and perhaps hunt or fish for a few weeks (the game would be edible) but, unless they had a very good reason to stay, it would be unwise to live there and even more unwise to raise a family there.

From our point of view a much more important result of the long-lived radiation is not the genetic effect, but the fact that such radiation seems to induce a sort of artificial aging, to reduce the average life expectancy of the exposed individuals. Table 10 gives the aging assumptions that we used in our study. The concept of artificial aging, while useful, is an approximation and probably overestimates the effect of the radiation on older people. It is believed, for example, that the young probably suffer effectively more life-shortening than do the old from diseases such as leukemia. For this reason some scientists prefer to use another approximation that also fits the known data—that radiation causes, on the average, a fixed percentage loss of the exposed individual's remaining life expectancy (i.e., a forty-year-old adult would be only half as sensitive to radiation as a ten-year-old child).

As Table 10 shows, we assume that on the average every roentgen would shorten life expectancy at birth by three and one-half days. While this number is only one-half to one-tenth as large as some of the numbers mentioned at the 1957 Congressional Hearings on fallout, it is actually large for the circumstances we are considering. Current data and theory suggest a figure closer to one or two days

❖❖❖

TABLE 10

LIFE-SHORTENING

(by small chronic doses)

1 roentgen	3.5	days
100 roentgens	1	year
1,000 roentgens	10	years

❖❖❖

per roentgen for small chronic doses continued throughout the life of the exposed individual. (However, if the dose is more concentrated, as it would be in the immediate postattack exposure situation as opposed to the long-term postwar environment, the loss in life expectancy at birth might be about three times greater or about five to ten days per roentgen.)

If we assume a three and one-half day decrease in life expectancy per roentgen, then 100r would mean the loss of a year and 1,000r the loss of ten years. Ten years happens to be the amount that has been added to an American *adult's* life expectancy since 1900. (Actually, twenty years have been added to the individual's life expectancy, but one-half of the increase is due to a reduction in infant and child mortality and is not pertinent to our problem.) Since it is difficult to have exposures by fallout that would give a person 1,000r without killing him, ten years is about the greatest decrease in life expectancy that could be expected in survivors as a result of long-term chronic exposure.

While it seems possible to devise programs that would keep the total exposure of most of the population to war-induced fallout within currently permissible industrial levels—50r for those less than thirty, 100r for those between thirty and forty, and 150r for those over forty—large groups of people would receive higher doses. These would include persons who have inadequate protection, those engaged in anticontamination activities, and those who must work in highly exposed areas. This condition can be tolerated because an average life-shortening of from five to ten years for, say, a small per cent of the population is not, compared to probable casualties, a catastrophic additional burden. In fact, when we discuss later a "cheap" program, I will argue that programs which could result in greater life-shortening may still be valuable.

Let us now see what the radiation levels might be during the initial recuperation period, which I will assume to start three months after the war is over. A comparison of the postwar rate of radiation with the NAS and industrial standards is given in Table 11.

The *straightforward* factor by which we exceed the NAS standards is now really horrifying. Even the small attack gives, *worldwide,* a dose rate about three times heavier than the permissible level. However, the straightforward calculation is making an additional mistake. It ignores not only decontamination, weathering, and terrain, but also the fact that at three months the radiation emission rate would drop rapidly. If *only* this last factor is put in so that instead of calculating the dose rate we calculate the accumulated dose over thirty years, we get the numbers in the parentheses. These are still rather impressive, however.

We have already stated that the standard that is appropriate for the postwar world is the permissible industrial dose. In addition, we would not accept the situation passively. We certainly would undertake decontamination activities, and would arrange our lives for a time to minimize exposure. Calculations indicate that these measures could reduce the exposure level to about 1 per cent of that indicated by the straightforward calculation.

A reduction in the neighborhood of 100 might be comprised of a factor for decontamination ranging from 1 to 100, a factor of about 3 to 5 for weathering, terrain, and deviation from theoretical decay rate (which is known to overestimate greatly the long-term exposure),

◆◇

TABLE 11
RADIOACTIVE ENVIRONMENT THREE MONTHS LATER

Standard	Early Attack		Late Attack	
	NAS	100 × IND.	NAS	100 × IND.
U.S. Maximum	26,000	17	110,000	75
	(660)	(0.4)	(2,900)	(2)
U.S. Average	1,200	0.8	17,000	11
	(31)		(430)	(0.3)
Northern				
Hemisphere	10	0.007	130	0.1
Minimum	(0.25)		(3.3)	
World	3	0.002	52	0.03
Minimum	(0.08)		(1)	

◆◇

and a factor of 2 to 30 to be obtained by limiting exposure to the unshielded environment. (The rest of the time we would have to live in protected areas. This would not mean that we would have to give up our homes and factories, although we might have to give up some of their aesthetic appearance and convenience. For example, sandbags might be placed around some houses for the first year or two.)

If we assume that we have made at least modest preparations before the war, the over-all factor of 100 is probably conservative for the long-term exposure due to the small attack—at least for any urban area or for any area where the land is of sufficient value to justify decontamination efforts. We do not know whether such a factor would be conservative for those who have to spend appreciable time in large, open spaces such as farms and forests. Not only is shielding (as in, for example, the cab of a tractor) more difficult but experiments in Nevada indicate that it may be more difficult to decontaminate open land than was previously thought, but these data remain to be verified. In any case, considerably more research is needed on the methods and techniques of decontamination.

If these same factors can be applied to the heavy attack, the postwar environment resulting from such an attack would be bearable. Even the hot spots would be accessible for short periods of time, and we could live in them if we wished to accept a somewhat greater dose than our standards suggest, or be more aggressive in our anti-contamination. Unfortunately, the assumption that we would be able to get a factor of 100 seems optimistic for the late attack unless very elaborate preattack preparations, costing in the tens of billions, have been made. The environment in the first few weeks after the attack is just too hostile to allow for much improvising or rationed exposure. However, presumably there is *now* time to put in an elaborate program before enemy capabilities get so large that we are threatened by the late attack.

What we have shown is that *if* we can get through the first three months of the war and postwar period, and *if* we can do the necessary decontamination and provide the necessary protection for most of the working and living hours, we can probably live with the lingering effects of radioactivity. The two *ifs* can scarcely be ignored, however.

We should accept even this qualified conclusion tentatively. We have not undertaken a complete treatment of the lingering effects of radioactivity. In the 100-year table, we were looking at one of the long-lived isotopes, cesium-137, and its effects as an external gamma emitter. In the 3-month table we were looking jointly at all the fission-process products as external gamma emitters. But the fission process produces about 200 separate isotopes. A more detailed treatment of this problem would require the study of every one of these that could cause trouble, either in the short- or the long-run. Then would come the development of measures to prevent this trouble. It is very important that we do this, because isotopes that are unimportant products of past nuclear tests may become of major importance after a war, once the more dominating ones have been treated. Some of these isotopes can get into the human body or into the animals or vegetables we eat or use in a very subtle fashion. They might cause all kinds of unsuspected difficulties. In addition, some of them may have ecological effects that would sharply influence our preparations or expectations. We will examine two of these isotopes in the next section.

On Strontium-90 and Carbon-14

In addition to cesium-137, we have studied two other radioactive isotopes—strontium-90 and carbon-14—in some detail. We studied these last two, partly because they are the ones most often involved in public discussions of world-wide fallout problems, and partly because each illustrates the sensitive nature of our results. However, other isotopes may also turn out to be important.

Strontium-90 emits beta rays that are easily stopped by a few inches of air. It probably will not cause trouble by external radiation unless a person actually gets it on his skin or comes into close contact with it by walking barefoot, picking cotton, and so forth. The major danger from this element lies in the fact that it is chemically very similar to calcium; once it is ingested a certain percentage of it will get into the bones. It is known that in large amounts Sr-90 can cause bone cancer. In smaller amounts it can cause bone lesions and interfere with bone growth, particularly in the young. It is possible that even in very small amounts it increases the probability of cancer contraction, although this is not known for certain (there may be a threshold concentration beneath which it is harmless). It is also suspected that it may cause leukemia, but this is not certain either. Because of their short range the beta particles do not reach the reproductive organs; Sr-90 therefore has no important genetic effects.

The Sr-90 problem has probably created more apprehension than any other problem generated by the nuclear tests. It has been estimated that every time a megaton of fission products is created as the result of a test in the Pacific Ocean or the Soviet Arctic, the resulting Sr-90 may give a thousand living people leukemia or bone cancer. While this figure is probably too high, it is widely accepted, and it is probably the origin of the rather common belief that no country could afford to launch a massive attack on another country in the same hemisphere because the backlash of the radioactive products would make the attacking nation uninhabitable even if the defending nation never got to retaliate.

This belief in what may be called completely "automatic retaliation" is almost certainly wrong. Even if one accepts the given figure of 1,000 world-wide deaths per megaton of fission products, automatic deterrence does not thereby become a certainty. A large attack by the Soviet Union or the U.S. of even 20,000 megatons of fission would then mean about 20,000,000 world-wide deaths in addition to local fatalities. Only about one or two million of the deaths would occur in the Soviet Union. Even the effect of that number of deaths is mitigated by the fact that they would be spread over the following fifty years or so. This would mean an average annual toll of 30,000 deaths. About 1,500,000 people die each year in the Soviet Union, so the above would increase the death rate by about 2 per cent. The backlash from a smaller and more plausible war would be, as deterrence calculations go, much less important than almost any other risk of war.

The Sr-90 problem in peace and in war is summarized in Table 12.

◆◆

TABLE 12

THE STRONTIUM-90 PROBLEM

	Strontium Units [a]	Corresponding Wartime Kt/sq. mi.[b]
Current level in new bone	3	~.0006
Future predicted level in new bone	10	~.002
Population M.P.C.[c]	67	~.013
Industrial M.P.C.	2,000	~.4
Recognizable cancer level	>10,000	• >2.
Serious cancer level	<100,000	<20.

[a] A strontium unit is a measure of Sr-90 contamination, defined as 1 microcurie of Sr-90 per Kg of calcium.

[b] The peacetime contamination would be half as much. I am assuming that as a result of fractionation about half of the Sr-90 is removed from local fallout and goes into world-wide fallout. I am also assuming that 10 millicuries of Sr-90 per square mile will result in the contamination of new bone by 1 strontium unit.

[c] M.P.C. = Maximum Permissible Concentration.

◆◆

Currently, large areas in the United States have an Sr-90 concentration that corresponds to a wartime contamination of .0006 kiloton of fission products per square mile. This is a new development. Strontium-90 is not an element that occurs naturally; all of it has been manufactured by man by fissioning uranium. Children raised in these contaminated areas are supposed to be in a sort of rough equilibrium with their environment. New bones being formed in children have about 3 strontium units. Even this low concentration of Sr-90 may be causing harm. About 10,000 people a year die of bone cancer or leukemia in the United States. E. B. Lewis has estimated that the background radiation of about 0.1r a year may cause about 10 per cent of these cases.[4] Three strontium units probably give the bones and neighboring tissues an average dose of a little less than 0.005r per year. Since .005r is about 5 per cent of the background dose, one could argue that after equilibrium is reached a contamination of 3 strontium units could increase the number of deaths from bone cancer and leukemia in the United States by 5 per cent of 10 per cent, or ½ per cent. This would be about 50 people a year. Even this small number of people being injured has raised serious apprehensions about the tests, partly on moral grounds and partly on public health grounds. Furthermore it is believed that, even if nuclear testing is discontinued, sometime in the mid-sixties when almost all of the Sr-90 in the stratosphere will have come down, the contamination in new bone will rise by a factor of 3, to about 10 strontium units.

The International Committee on Radiation Protection has suggested a maximum permissible adult body burden of Sr-90 of 67 strontium units, or about twenty times what we are finding in children today. Even more than in the case of the NAS 10r standard many experts believe that this limit is too liberal. However, the relatively restricted adult population, represented by industrial workers in hazardous occupations, is allowed thirty times more, or 2,000 strontium units. (No one has yet seen a bone cancer which was *known* to be caused by radiation at a burden of less than the equivalent of 20,000 to 30,000 strontium units. But bone lesions have been seen at lower levels.) A serious cancer-causing level, one at which the average individual rather than the more susceptible (or unlucky) would have an appreciable chance of getting bone cancer, should probably be more than 10,000 and somewhat less than 100,-000 strontium units (s.u.).

If we agree that a wartime local contamination of 0.0002 kiloton (KT) per square mile means that there will be 1 s.u. in the bodies of individuals living in that environment; if we accept that a linear

[4] E. B. Lewis, "Leukemia and Ionizing Radiation," *Science*, Vol. 125 (May 17, 1957), p. 965.

relationship holds between the contamination on the ground and the level in human bones; and if we believe that we would not eat foods which would produce more than the allowable 67 strontium units in new bone, what do we have? Then .013 KT per square mile or a mere 13 megatons (MT) of fission products spread uniformly over the 1,000,000 square miles in which we grow food in this country would make the food unfit for human consumption. And 13 MT of fission products could be produced by one large bomb! If we take account of the inefficiencies of distributing fission products by exploding bombs and also take account of the fact that weathering and decay alleviate the problem, we might increase the requirements for contamination by a factor of 50 to 100. Then we can estimate that *an attack with about 1,000 MT of fission products could suspend agriculture in the United States for 50 years or so.* However, if we are willing to envisage relaxing the peacetime standards to the point that the incidence of cancer begins to change average life expectancy by a significant amount, then we have a problem when there is between 2 and 20 kilotons of fission products per square mile. It would be very difficult to contaminate large areas to this level, for now between 2,000 and 20,000 megatons of fission products would be required to contaminate an area of about a million square miles—without the factor of 75 used in the previous calculation. The late attack shown in our tables would barely do something like this if it were concentrated in such an area, and the simplest decontamination measure or alleviation by natural processes would make the land usable—always assuming we are willing to drop our standards.

How much would we have to drop our standards in a realistic attack situation? I suggest that something like the following rather dangerous-looking standards might be both adequate and acceptable in some postwar worlds. The common contaminated foods which would be the major source of Sr-90 might be classified into five grades—A, B, C, D, and E. Food in each of these five grades, if eaten with no other alleviatory measures (such as supplementary calcium in the diet), might result in the levels of contamination in *new* bone that are shown in Table 13.

The A food would be restricted to children and to pregnant women. The B food would be a high-priced food available to everybody. The C food would be a low-priced food also available to everybody. Finally, the D food would be restricted to people over age forty or fifty. Even though this food would be unacceptable for children, it probably would be acceptable for those past middle age, partly because their bones are already formed so that they do not pick up anywhere near as much strontium as the young, and partly because at these low levels of contamination it generally takes some decades for cancer to develop. Most of these people would die of other causes before they got cancer. Finally, there would be an E food restricted to the feeding of animals whose resulting use (meat, draft animals, leather, wool, and so on) would not cause an increase in the human burden of Sr-90.

❖❖❖

TABLE 13

INTERIM STANDARDS FOR SR-90

Grade	Strontium Units	Use
A	0–200	Most susceptible
B	200–2,000	General (high priced)
C	2,000–5,000	General (low priced)
D	5,000–25,000	Over 45
E	25,000– ?	Animals

❖❖❖

The reason for the suggested difference in price of the B and C foods comes from assuming some sort of a free market mechanism; we wish to encourage the production of the B food and to discourage that of the C food. Price differences would keep the demand and supply in equilibrium. We do not want to *discourage* B food, we want all there is of it to be consumed. If there were no free market, some sort of rationing of B food would be required, but this could introduce all kinds of serious administrative, political, and ethical difficulties and would not encourage expanded production of B food unless some subsidy were granted—implying further complications. A reasonable rationing procedure might restrict the B food to those between the ages 15–30 and the C food to those between the ages 30–45; those over 45 eating the D food.

One official who expressed skepticism about the different grades of food asked me what I thought the difference in cost would be between the B and C foods. I said, "About five cents a quart." "More likely fifty dollars," he replied. If he is right, and unless very extensive preparations have been made or unless we can make arrangements to grow food in other countries, this would mean an allocation of resources to the production of pure food which, if undertaken on a large scale, would condemn us to a slow rate of general recuperation. This is, of course, the reason he is probably wrong. The slow rate of recuperation itself would probably mean a reduction in standards of living, including medical care that would result in more damage than the interim Sr-90 standards.

Some may argue, and perhaps correctly, that to assume that a contamination of 0.0002-kiloton per square mile will result in one strontium unit in the human body is optimistic by a factor of 2 or 3, and that, in particular, the current experimental evidence could be misleading not only because of uncertainties in measurement but because we are not yet in equilibrium with the immediate environment. However, it could also be pessimistic in the long run because there is some evidence that the Sr-90 becomes less available as time passes. In any case, we are actually being conservative because we have not taken account of the fact that it takes a while for appreciable amounts of Sr-90 to enter the body, so there is time to use the known ameliorative measures, not to speak of the ones we still hope to discover. That is, the above standards for strontium-90 consumption would be interim standards because there are things we can do to diminish the problem markedly. Some possibilities are given in Table 14.

❖❖

TABLE 14
SR-90 PALLIATIVES

1. Decontamination of food
2. Decontamination of land
3. Food selection (calcium pills)
4. New patterns of agriculture
5. Medical treatment

❖❖

For example, methods are currently being developed for removing strontium-90 from milk and replacing it with uncontaminated calcium. Similar methods are being developed for the decontamination of land. Some of these methods—for example, the removal of the top portion of the soil—require application soon after the attack. Other methods that are not as effective (such as deep plowing, which mixes the Sr-90 more uniformly) can be applied anytime.

There are also major possibilities in the realm of food selection. They go all the way from feeding special calcium pills to people or cows so as to dilute the strontium-90 in the diet, to the kind of rationing and selection that we have already discussed in connection with A, B, C, D, and E foods. Probably most important of all are new patterns for agriculture. For example, where the strontium-90 falls on sandy soil (which it readily penetrates) one would grow shallow-root crops. Where the strontium-90 falls on clay-type soils, one would concentrate on deep-root crops. In addition, it would be possible to vary the areas in which food is grown. As a sort of extreme, we could imagine growing meat in this country and dairy products in Argentina; we would then sell the Argentineans meat and buy dairy items from them. Such a drastic change would cause an increase in the price of food, but probably not an exorbitant one. Lastly, of course, there is the possibility of medical treatment. The major effect of strontium-90 is cancer of the bone and possibly leukemia. Both of these diseases may be susceptible in the next generation or so to medical treatment. For all the above reasons, it is probably wrong to think of strontium-90 as a one- or two-hundred-year problem that can be mitigated only by the actions of wind, weather, and natural decay.

The notion that it would be acceptable to drop safety standards is not widely accepted in the government. Responsible officials have sometimes talked as if we really would abandon the "moderately" contaminated agricultural areas for fifty years or longer. This does not seem to me to be a realistic view of the situation, even if we do not make allowances for measures of alleviation. After all, the survivors really have no choice, since all alternatives—such as large-scale emigration—would be impractical. And as mentioned, putting inordinate efforts into eliminating or "over alleviating" the problem might mean diverting so many resources into relatively less productive uses with the result that recuperation would be delayed. If this happened it would result in even larger reductions in life expectancy and economic costs than would the adoption of the suggested interim standards and the alleviation measures.

The real question that arises in the prewar period concerns the impact that even a sober estimate of the postwar environment (not to speak of the current apocalyptic views) may have on programs, policy making, and the willingness of governments to take risks. There are likely to be some pronounced asymmetries here between us and the Soviets; it would be well to alleviate these asymmetries insofar as greater knowledge and better preparations can do so.

It is most important to take a realistic view of postwar standards *before* the war occurs. Only if this is done can reasonable estimates be made of the effects of a war and the nature and performance of various preparations. Only in this way can a guide be given for analyzing the effects of the standards and searching for methods for alleviating the effects. It is probably appropriate to point out that while the AEC has a large program (about $20,000,000 per annum) to investigate the peacetime effects of fallout and the corresponding standards, they are spending almost nothing on the wartime situations and standards. While almost everything that they do for the peacetime situation is useful for the wartime situation, there are special problems associated with only the latter that have not been receiving adequate attention. No other government agency is putting in the necessary effort either.

I would now like to discuss what some think of as the most important and menacing aspect of calculations of the sort that I have just gone through.

The relationship of .0002 KT per square mile causing a strontium unit or so in children is due to an accident of chemistry. Sr-90 is very similar chemically to calcium. Therefore, when people tried initially to predict how much Sr-90 would get into the human body, they assumed that it would be the same percentage of the body's calcium as it is of the environment's calcium. The ratio in children's bodies is actually less than the ratio in the soil by a factor between 10 and 20. Every step in the sequence of events that brings Sr-90 into the body—from the soil to the grass, to the cow, to the milk, to the human intestines, to the bone—seems to lower this Sr-90 to calcium ratio. In addition, a fractionation phenomenon that occurs at the time of the bomb burst seems to deplete the Sr-90 in local fallout by a factor of 2 or so.

Before we had acquired empirical evidence, we might have conjectured it was just as likely that this same chain might favor Sr-90 as not.[5] Therefore, in any a priori calculation, since Sr-90 could have had a slightly different chemistry and been favored by a factor of

---

[5] In fact, in the similar problem of cesium-137 (Cs-137) contamination, Cs-137 bears the same relation to potassium as Sr-90 to calcium, only this time the chain seems to favor Cs-137 over potassium by a factor of five or so. Fortunately, the Cs-137 problem is an order of magnitude less serious than the Sr-90 problem, so the reverse discrimination is not a total disaster though it does have serious effects.

20 or so rather than the other way around, we probably should have been conservative and assumed a factor of 20 against us rather than for us. (It would be particularly important to be this conservative if we were making calculations concerning the performance of a Credible First Strike system rather than a Counterforce as Insurance system.) This would mean that the predicted problem would be 400 times more serious than the actual problem. If we had gone ahead with the tests and the pessimistic calculation had turned out to be correct, then the exposed children would have about 1,200 strontium units in their bodies rather than just 3. This, in turn, would probably have put the government into a somewhat difficult position, since if the so-called "no threshold" theories of bone cancer and leukemia are correct, the incidence of these diseases might easily have doubled. While this would not present us with a catastrophic public health problem, it certainly would present us with very serious, to *understate* it, moral and public relations problems. Even more important from the viewpoint of the present discussion, it would be impossible, in the absence of the most elaborate preparations to survive even the early war. Very few people will be able to "rise to the occasion" if they have a few hundred thousand strontium units in them. They are going to get bone cancer and die.

I have laid this stress on the sensitivity of our results to such a minor matter as the chemistry of Sr-90 as compared to the chemistry of calcium because this sensitivity illustrates the situation as we face it today. *It is the thesis of this lecture that if proper preparations have been made, it would be possible for us or the Soviets to cope with all the effects of a thermonuclear war, in the sense of saving most people and restoring something close to the prewar standard of living in a relatively short time. But there is no reason to believe this will be true unless both nations investigate the problem more thoroughly than has been done so far, and then take the necessary preparations.* In particular, the possible role of any of the many isotopes that could be dangerous must be studied. Preparations must be made to alleviate any problems uncovered. If this is not done we may be in for unpleasant surprises.

It is particularly important to set up in time of peace whatever war and postwar standards we think we may have to adopt. In addition to determining these standards, we should formally publish them in some durable and official form that will be available for postattack distribution. It would not be necessary to distribute broadside all the handbooks beforehand. It is important, however, to print them ahead of time so that they will be immediately available and people will trust the information in them. In any crisis, many people will be cynical about the integrity of the government, arguing that the government says these standards are acceptable because it "must" say so, that conditions are such that it has no choice. The knowledge that the standards were set up in peacetime after due care and debate should be reassuring.

The only other isotope that I would like to discuss specifically is carbon-14. Almost all the neutrons emitted from a bomb either get into the air and are absorbed by nitrogen to create C-14, or they reach the ground and are absorbed by the earth. This means that C-14, while not a true fission product, is nevertheless about the most abundant radioisotope produced. While some fraction of it may come down as insoluble calcium carbonate and not cause any serious trouble for many years, if ever, the balance oxidizes to become CO_2 and enters the atmosphere. Part of it eventually enters the biosphere.

❖❖❖

TABLE 15
CARBON-14 PROBLEM

	Approximate r/yr
Current background radiation	0.1– 0.2
Normal C-14 dose	0.0015
Possible increase due to tests	0.0008
Small war might add	0.01–0.1
Large war might add	.1– 5.0

❖❖❖

Currently, we received approximately 0.0015r/yr from C-14. As a result of past tests the amount of C-14 in the atmosphere has probably increased by about 75 per cent, but most of this is in the stratosphere and currently out of harm's way. Some of this stratospheric material will eventually find its way into the troposphere and then into the food we eat. It is quite possible that this process could result in additional radiation to the whole body, including the reproductive glands of about .0008r/yr. While .0008r seems like a very small amount, if one multiplies it by 8,100 years, which is the average lifetime of C-14, one gets about .7r, which is an appreciable dose if one is trying to calculate the damage a genetic line will receive over the next 10,000 years. (Such a dose could, for example, cause about 1,000,000 serious defects.) A war in the early 1960's might cause an increase in the amount of C-14 of at most 100 times that produced by the tests, but probably it would be somewhat less. This could mean an additional .1r/yr, or about a 67 per cent increase over the current background radiation. This condition would be undesirable, but tolerable. It changes none of our considerations. A war in the more distant future could cause an increase over past tests by a factor of 1,000, but it also would probably be *much* less. A factor of a 1,000 might result in an additional 1r/yr, which is "small" compared to industrial levels but still ten times the prewar background radiation. While this situation would be serious, it clearly would not prevent postwar reconstruction.

Unfortunately, as already mentioned, C-14 has an average life of about 10,000 years. A dose of 1r/yr or so for 10,000 years would mean in effect that the average background radiation for the population had been increased by close to a factor of 5 or 10. This would mean more than a 50 per cent increase in the pool of defective genes.[6]

While we could live with this problem, it would still be an immense toll to pay for the next five or ten thousand years. Fortunately, the above estimate in the long-term problem appears to be exaggerated. It may take a very long time for the C-14 to diffuse down to the troposphere. Of that which does diffuse down, then in much less than a generation, about one-half the C-14 would probably be dissolved in the top layers of the ocean, and the effective amount in the biosphere would therefore be reduced by a factor of 2. In some five or ten generations, it would be further dissolved in the depths of the ocean and reduced by an additional factor of 10 or 20. Therefore, the long-term problem is thereby reduced by more than 20 and the short-term problem by an unknown but large factor. While the total amount of human misery caused after several hundreds of years by C-14 would still be very large, it would be comparable to the damage caused by normal background radiation and less than the NAS standard. In addition, a more careful predic-

---

[6] This assumes 50r is the doubling rate. Given the uncertainties, the problem could conceivably be five times better or worse.

tion of the amount of C-14 actually created in either the early or late wars would probably produce a lower figure than our estimate suggests.

I pointed out in discussing Sr-90 that we have been favored by an accident of chemistry. In some sense we have been fortunate here as well. If C-14 had an average life of only 10 or 20 years [7] instead of being spread out over 10,000 years, the entire dose would be received by the first generation. This hypothetical first-generation dose would be about 100 times larger than the actual one. In a very large war this could be lethal, incurably lethal from the practical point of view. Once again, we see that our results are sensitive to a specific empirical constant, in this case the decay rate of C-14. As a physicist would put it, "There are no conservation laws which state that we can survive this kind of war. Any such belief must rest on empirical knowledge and calculations and not on being able to 'rise to the occasion.'" I repeat, *one cannot rely on surviving unless one has made preparations or has verified that the effects can be controlled without preparation.* Much more work must obviously be done before we are in a position to make even modest assertions about the long-term results of large attacks. However, our prognostications concerning the small attack are much less sensitive to specific assumptions; we believe that they are relatively reliable.

Recuperation and Reconstruction

If we assume that people could survive the long-term effects of radiation, what would the standard of living in their postwar world be like? Would the survivors live as Americans are accustomed to living—with automobiles, television, ranch houses, freezers, and so on? No one can say, but I believe there is every likelihood that even if we make almost no preparations for recuperation except to buy radiation meters, write and distribute manuals, train some cadres for decontamination and the like, and make some other minimal plans,[8] the country would recover rather rapidly and effectively from the small attack. This strong statement is contrary to the beliefs of many laymen, professional economists, and war planners.

On what is this statement based? Let us look at the urban United

[7] David Inglis has pointed out to me that the shell model (a simple theoretical picture of the nucleus) seems to predict such a short lifetime. It is only because we have some experimental measurements that we know we can deal with this problem.

[8] See Appendix IV.

States. An air defense study generally considers the 53 industrially important Standard Metropolitan Areas (Table 16) to determine how well they can be defended.

❖❖

TABLE 16

53 STANDARD METROPOLITAN AREAS

	1950 Population (millions)
1. New York–Northeastern New Jersey	12.9
2. Chicago	5.5
3. Los Angeles	4.4
.	.
.	.
.	.
51. Trenton	0.23
52. Erie	0.22
53. New Britain–Bristol	0.16

❖❖

A metropolitan area is larger than a single city, of course. It includes all the contiguous urbanized areas and the county or counties in which they are located. Each one of these areas contains at least 40,000 manufacturing workers (1952 definition). Jointly they contain about one-third of the population of the United States, about one-half of the "wealth," somewhat more than half of the general manufacturing capacity, and almost three-fourths of our capacity to manufacture war goods. In active defense studies, these are the areas of the country that are usually considered to need protection.

If those who conduct the active defense study are incautious and exaggerate the performance of our defense equipment and underestimate the potential of the enemy, it is possible to pretend to protect all but four or five of these areas against a determined attack. A more cautious study will claim to lose about half, and a pessimistic study might anticipate losing two-thirds, or even more, where "losing" means that the enemy has succeeded in placing at least one bomb "on target." In our study we assumed, however, that every one of these areas was totally destroyed—every stick and stone. Generally, such a result could come only from the use of

very large bombs or more than one bomb. For example, it is estimated that one 20-MT and five 10-MT bombs, *accurately placed*,
would be required to destroy the New York metropolitan area. The
total destruction of the 53 SMA is probably greater than that which
would be caused by the early attack. If allowance is made for aiming errors and misallocations, it would probably take many hundreds of bombs delivered to the target area by airplanes to do this
amount of damage, and it might take even more ICBM's—the exact
numbers depending on the warhead yield, reliability, attrition, and
accuracy of the delivery system, and the degree of assurance that
the enemy planner desires.

Of course, no reasonable enemy would use hundreds of ICBM's to
destroy the last 20 to 30 per cent of our 53 largest SMA city areas,
but it is still true—at least for the early time era when ICBM's are
relatively unreliable, may have low accuracy, and may have relatively small warheads—that it could take an extraordinary effort on
the part of the enemy to do an amount of damage to the country
equivalent to the total destruction of the 53 standard metropolitan
areas—an effort that might well be beyond his capacity—particularly if we had a strong SAC to divert and degrade his attack.

If we assume that the destruction has been as specified, we then
might ask, "What's left?" The first reaction of many people is that
there is practically nothing left. The United States is an urban
country. These areas—New York, Philadelphia, Chicago, Detroit,
Los Angeles—*are* the United States of America, they believe. Destroy them and you have nothing left. Not quite so. Simple subtrac-
tion demonstrates that the statement is too strong.

If these cities contain about one-third of the population, than almost two-thirds is outside. If they contain half the wealth, another
half must be outside. If they contain slightly more than half of our
manufacturing capacity, then slightly less than half remains outside.
They do contain an inordinate amount of our war goods manufacturing capacity, true, but we would not be trying to produce jet engines in the postwar world—we would be trying to survive and reconstruct. What is outside the large metropolises—construction,
mining, agriculture, consumer goods, and the like—is what we
would need to do this.

Actually, a country like the United States can about double its
GNP every fifteen or twenty years. A country like Russia, which
works harder and saves a higher percentage for capital investment,

can double its GNP every ten to fifteen years. From this point of view, the above destruction does not seem to be a total economic catastrophe. It may simply set the nation's productive capacity back a decade or two plus destroying many "luxuries."

This statement strikes most people as being very naïve. After all, they point out, a young boy may double his size in ten years but if you cut him in half he does not make up for the loss; his growth simply stops. Most people looking at the highly integrated character of a modern economy argue that a nation is like a body— destroy the heart or some other vital organ, and the body dies even if 99 per cent of it is undamaged; a few cells may linger on for a while, but they will die very soon. What makes those who hold this view most apprehensive is that wherever they look they see vital organs in our economy.

The organism analogy may have some validity in predicting the ability or inability to continue complicated operations in an uninterrupted fashion after some important or vital components have been damaged. The analogy seems to be completely wrong as far as long-term recuperation is concerned. The most important difference is that the economy is even more flexible than a salamander (which can grow new parts when old ones are destroyed) in that large sections of it can operate independently (with some degradation, of course). In addition, no matter how much destruction is done, if there are survivors, they will put *something* together. The creating (or recreating) of a society is an art rather than a science; even though empirical and analytic "laws" have been worked out, we do not really know how it is done, but almost everybody (Ph.D. or savage) can do it.

The next most important difference between a society and an organism lies in the fact that if a critical part of the economy is destroyed, so that the economy grinds to a complete stop, one can still use the remaining parts in the reconstruction effort, while one cannot use the undestroyed portions of a dead organism to build a new living organism.

A more useful and orienting model to use in studying the recuperative powers of a nation like the United States or the Soviet Union is to divide each nation into two countries, an "A" country consisting of 50 to 100 of the largest cities, and a "B" country made up of the remaining rural areas, towns, and small cities. The relationship between the A and B countries of the Soviet Union and the United

States is very similar to the relationship between a mother country and a vigorous, wealthy and diversified colony. It turns out that most of the activity in the A country is spent in running the A country and only a small percentage of its activities are contributed to the B country. (A very rough estimate indicates that the A country exports less than 10 per cent of its "GNP" to the B country.) The most important things the A country supplies are probably managerial and technical services.

It further turns out that as far as we can see, while the A country cannot survive without a B country, the B country cannot only survive without the A country; it also seems to have the resources and skills it needs to rebuild the A country in about ten years. That is, the B country, like any dependent colony, would have a number of troubles if its mother country were destroyed; in particular there would be a critical need to upgrade managers and technicians to make up for the lost services. This would temporarily make for some degradation in efficiency. But for the B countries we are considering these troubles are likely to be less serious than those that would have been faced by India if she had not only cut loose her ties with England but had refused to trade with England any more. I think that all would concede that though India would go through an even more drastic readjustment than she did, that she could have survived and carried through that readjustment. In fact, the problem the B country faces in rebuilding the A country is probably less difficult than the one met by the Soviet Union in constructing the Soviet Union of 1955 from its 1945 base. This last remark is particularly relevant to the often-expressed fear that we will lose our most experienced and trained people. We tend to exaggerate, particularly if we have a "vested interest," the impact of losing valuable people, equipment, or resources.

I will point out in the third lecture that before World War I many people thought a large war would have to be short, simply because they assumed that the interdependence of nations made it impossible for modern nations to exist for very long without the foreign trade that would be curtailed by a long war. Today we know better. We know that there is a good deal of resiliency and flexibility in a modern economy, and we know that in general the more advanced we are the more flexible we are. It is probably not only true that B country could get along without A country and rebuild it, but if the situation were partially reversed and A country happened to be undamaged, it could probably recuperate a damaged B country even faster than B could rebuild A. If B country should be too seriously damaged, A country could probably maintain a reasonable standard of living by trading its products with whatever portions of the world survived—just the way the British now do. Therefore, while it is theoretically interesting to consider the case where A country survives and B country does not, considering tactics the enemy might reasonably use, only the other case would occur. We will therefore restrict ourselves to an examination of the capability of B country after A country has been totally destroyed; at the same time we will also look at a case in which the most valuable resource of A country —the people in it—have been evacuated to the B country.

It is clear that the sciences of economics, sociology, and politics are not sufficiently far advanced today to enable us to chart the rate at which a country recuperates from the precise hypothetical initial state we have assumed, not to speak of the highly uncertain state that would actually occur. Rebuilding society will involve more uncalculated components than calculated ones. However, people do have intuitions and preconceptions, and it is well to check these notions against certain orienting calculations that can be made.

Let us start by considering the gross nature of the recuperation problem. (Hopefully, the following remarks will be orienting. However, if they are taken too literally, they can be misleading. Even though they explain intuitively some important aspects of the recuperation problem, many economists are likely to think that they are more disorienting than orienting.)

Today (1960) there is roughly two trillion dollars' worth (see table 17) of real tangible wealth in the United States. At current rates of investment it would take less than a generation to create this wealth. The postwar restoration may be even faster, not only because so much survives all but the most destructive wars, but also because we are likely to work harder and consume less. Of course the loss in wealth will also cause a decrease in productivity, but this can be overestimated. From the viewpoint of productivity, much of the destroyed wealth will be a luxury. For example, if half of our residential space is destroyed, then, even if everyone survives, these survivors will be better housed than the average (very productive) Soviet citizen. (In 1970 when we might have a large underground shelter system that could be used postwar for temporary housing, we could probably lose three-fourths of our residential space and still be reasonably well-housed in terms of the economic efficiency of the inhabitants.)

◆◆

TABLE 17

THE WEALTH OF THE UNITED STATES °

(*billions of dollars*)

Structures:		960
Residential	455	
Private (non-residential)	235	
Government (civilian)	200	
Institutional	30	
Government (military)	20	
Equipment:		485
Producer durables (non-farm)	205	
Consumer durables	200	
Military equipment	60	
Producer durables (farm)	20	
Inventories:		175
Business (non-farm)	115	
Farm	30	
Government (CCC and strategic)	30	
Land, forests, and subsoil		375
TOTAL		1,995

° An extension of estimates as of the end of 1958 compiled by the National Bureau of Economic Research. Does not include consumer non-durables (45), monetary metals (25), or foreign assets (30).

◆◆

Similarly, we could lose many of our nonresidential structures (the dispensable elements of business, administration, commerce, and government) and still be able to operate our industry and government efficiently. In fact, if we ask what part of the two trillion dollars of assets would both be in danger of being destroyed and would be critically needed in the immediate postwar period, we would find it to be made up largely of some important fraction of the $250 billion in producers' durables and manufacturing structures, and of the $115 billion in business inventories. It would be only a fraction because not all of it would really be in danger of being destroyed or made unusable, and because we could dispense with or greatly cut back many industries for the first two or three years of the reconstruction period. We should not have to manufacture automobiles, most military products, elaborately processed food, nonwork clothes, and so on. (Some industries, of course, would be more important postwar than prewar—the construction industry, building supplies, machine tools, metal works, spare parts, and medical supplies.)

Let us now ask ourselves what the B country of the United States contains in the way of valuable material resources, particularly those industrial resources that do tend to be concentrated in the A country and would probably be among the most important bottlenecks in the effort to rebuild and recuperate the economy.

Table 18 indicates the capacity of different industries of the United States and the proportion that is available outside the 53 metropolitan areas. Superficial examination indicates that B country contains more than one-fourth of our capacity in almost all industries. Actually, this one-fourth capacity means more than this because industries frequently run below capacity in peacetime. In a reconstruction period we would undoubtedly run most of them at more than their theoretical capacity (by multiple shifts and intensive use of equipment).

On the other hand, this table is a gross representation and does not take into account specific bottlenecks that might occur if we do not make advance preparations, such as the stockpiling of certain items. However, experience has shown that entrepreneurs and engineers are very capable at "making do" when necessary. (For examples, we refer to the German and Russian economies during World War II.)

Table 18 indicates capacity. Table 19 is another way of looking at the problem. It gives the value of capital goods used in industry and an estimate of the minimum that should survive an attack that destroyed the equivalent of 53 metropolitan areas. It gives us an idea of the amount of rebuilding that would be necessary. If one looks first at that part of manufacturing which would be necessary for recuperation but would be in short supply, one can estimate that less than $100 billion worth of producers' capital goods might be urgently needed for the first stage of reconstruction, even if every consumer suvived the war.[9]

[9] This figure was arrived at by guessing that an approximate mix would involve something equivalent to one-half of the food manufacturing, all of the tobacco, one-half of the textile, one-third of transportation, all of the electrical machines, all of the chemical, and so on.

Very roughly, then, we seem to be faced with the problem of guaranteeing that we will have, say, two or three years after the war ends a manufacturing industry that at current prices would be worth something like $100 billion. I believe that if we can do this, protect a few special items, and use the things that will automatically survive, such as people, land, transportation facilities, rural areas with

❖❖

TABLE 18

ESTIMATED PRODUCTION CAPACITY SURVIVING
DESTRUCTION OF 53 SMA

	1954 Output Capacity (billions of 1956 dollars)	Per Cent Outside 53 Standard Metropolitan Areas
Instruments and related products	4	20
Transportation equipment	73	23
Electrical machinery	32	23
Primary metal industries	36	23
Miscellaneous manufacturing	7	27
Fabricated metal products	35	28
Rubber products	6	29
Printing and publishing	12	29
Apparel and related products	20	30
Machinery, except electrical	50	34
Petroleum and coal products	18	36
Chemicals and chemical products	25	42
Furniture and fixtures	6	51
Pulp and paper products	14	54
Stone, clay, and glass products	8	56
Food and kindred products	68	57
Leather and leather products	6	58
Construction	91	60
Textile mill products	20	69
Tobacco manufacturing	4	70
Lumber and wood products	9	86
Mining	20	89
Agriculture	92	94.6

❖❖

their power stations, utilities, nonmanufacturing industries, and so on, *there is every expectation that we will have an economy able to restore most of the prewar gross national product relatively rapidly.* Since our GNP is now about $500 billion, it is clear that it would be

TABLE 19

ESTIMATED UNITED STATES CAPITAL SURVIVING
DESTRUCTION OF 53 SMA

(dollar amounts in billions of 1956 dollars)

	1954 Total Stock of Capital Goods	Per Cent Outside 53 Standard Metropolitan Areas	1954 Capital Goods Outside 53 SMA's
Instruments and related products	2.2	20	0.4
Transportation equipment	24.3	23	5.7
Electrical machinery	10.9	23	2.6
Primary metal industries	30.5	28	8.4
Miscellaneous manufacturing	1.4	27	0.4
Fabricated metal products	12.8	28	3.6
Rubber products	5.5	29	1.6
Printing and publishing	4.0	29	1.1
Apparel and related products	0.9	30	0.3
Machinery, except electrical	21.8	34	7.4
Petroleum and coal products	16.7	36	6.0
Chemicals and chemical products	14.1	42	5.8
Furniture and fixtures	2.0	51	1.0
Pulp and paper products	10.7	54	5.8
Stone, clay, and glass products	6.3	56	3.5
Food and kindred products	11.6	57	6.6
Leather and leather products	0.6	58	0.35
Construction	–	60	–
Textile mill products	5.5	69	3.8
Tobacco manufacturing	0.4	70	0.3
Lumber and wood products	3.2	86	2.8
Mining	–	89	–
Agriculture	28.8	95	27.2
Electric public utilities	30.0	54	16.2

feasible for us, if we really wanted to do it, to stockpile the basic $100 billion industrial base in the relatively inexpensive form of critical parts (or even the more expensive form of complete standby plants). However, our calculations indicate that even without special stockpiles, dispersal, or protection, the restoration of our prewar GNP should take place in a relatively short time—*if we can hold the damage to the equivalent of something like 53 metropolitan areas destroyed.* These calculations, the results of which I am going to describe, have in them at least the seven optimistic elements given in the table below, but we still believe that the calculations are more likely to be pessimistic than optimistic.

❖❖

TABLE 20
SEVEN OPTIMISTIC ASSUMPTIONS

1. Favorable political environment
2. Immediate survival and patch-up
3. Maintenance of economic momentum
4. Specific bottlenecks alleviated
5. "Bourgeois" virtues survive
6. Workable postwar standards adopted
7. Neglected effects unimportant

❖❖

Let us go over these optimistic assumptions. First, and most important, we have assumed that we are in charge of our own destinies—that we will be permitted to reconstruct. This may imply that we have not lost the war, though it does not necessarily mean that we have won. It means only that no one is seriously interfering with the reconstruction effort. This war, like many others, may end in negotiation with only a partial victory for one side or the other.

Secondly, we have assumed that society has started to function again—that, where necessary, the debris has been cleared up, minimum communications restored, the most urgent repairs made, credits and markets re-established, a basic transportation system provided, minimum utilities either set up or restored, the basic necessities of life made available, and so on. After the small attack, the physical basis for all of the above will probably exist even if we have made no preparations, but some forethought would certainly facilitate recovery. It may not be feasible to use many of the resources that survive unless certain simple preparations have been made in advance of hostilities. In the large attack the physical basis is almost certain to shrink substantially unless very extensive preparations have been made or the enemy has been "careful" about the targets attacked.

Preparations for survival and patch-up should include provisions for continuity of government, improvised postattack radiation shelter at work and home, food supplies for those communities where food will be in short supply, manuals and instructions to aid adjustment to the new conditions of life, trained cadres, and radiation meters. Let us discuss the last two in more detail.

Most of the skills that would be needed in initial patch-up and repair are very similar to normal peacetime jobs. Such skills as those acquired in operating bulldozers and street-cleaning equipment, in construction, in transportation, and in engineering of various types will all be valuable. There are probably about five million people in the United States with especially useful skills or experience of this kind. One thing which might be valuable would be the creation of a permanent semi-military reserve of between 100,000 and 250,000 cadres. While it would probably cost about 50 to 100 million dollars a year to support such a reserve (about $500 per man per year to cover costs of about two or three weeks of training, including his equipment and supplies), we would only budget less than $50 million for the initial one or two years, because it takes time to build such an organization. If these "trained" cadres could be dependably expanded in the event of impending attack, or afterward, by about a factor of, say, 10, by mobilizing volunteers with the proper skills (who may have signed up in advance and who had at least received training manuals and assignments), we should have more than enough manpower to accomplish the clean-up and repair that would be needed. The same cadres would be most useful in improvising preattack protection in any of the typical tense situations that will be described later.

Probably the most important special equipment that would be needed—and the least improvisable—would be radiation meters of various kinds. These are not only useful during and immediately after the attack; they are necessary for many basic and important postwar activities. Meters could play an essential role in maintaining the morale and the risk-taking capacity of the cadres who would be exposed to radiation. It is easy to see why this is so.

The radiation from fallout has curious and frightening effects. Most people already know, or will know in a postattack world, that if you get a fatal dose of radiation the sequence of events is about like this: first you become nauseated, then sick; you seem to recover; then in two or three weeks you really get sick and die.

Now just imagine yourself in the postwar situation. Everybody will have been subjected to extremes of anxiety, unfamiliar environment, strange foods, minimum toilet facilities, inadequate shelters, and the like. Under these conditions some high percentage of the population is going to become nauseated, and nausea is very catching. If one man vomits, everybody vomits. It would not be surprising if almost everybody vomits. Almost everyone is likely to think he has received too much radiation. Morale may be so affected that many survivors may refuse to participate in constructive activities, but would content themselves with sitting down and waiting to die—some may even become violent and destructive.

However, the situation would be quite different if radiation meters were distributed. Assume now that a man gets sick from a cause other than radiation. Not believing this, his morale begins to drop. You look at his meter and say, "You have received only ten roentgens, why are you vomiting? Pull yourself together and get to work."

This view is in accord with experience in peacetime disasters that have been complicated by epidemics. People often require some kind of talisman before they will expose themselves—a shot, a pill, a gauze bandage around the nostrils and mouth or, in this case, a meter. They need, of course, other equipment in addition to meters, but a meter may well be the most essential. *In the RAND civil defense study we suggested the immediate purchase of about $100,-000,000 worth of radiation meters, so that this nonimprovisable but vitally necessary piece of equipment will be available.*

In addition to sheer survival, it is very important that economic activities be started rapidly, even though society can live for a time on inventory and stocks. For example, depending on the number of survivors and the time of year of the attack, there should be between two and four years' food supply in the country; this means that there is no need for getting agriculture started full-swing immediately, but it would be important to get it started within a year or two. While the other essentials such as fuel, power, transportation, and communications all seem to survive in sufficient supply to get things started, some inventories would be in much more critical supply; unless we started to produce them soon, parts of the economic system might falter or even grind to a stop. Under these circumstances it probably would be difficult to get things started very expeditiously unless we had some outside aid or prewar stocks to draw upon. In some cases, trying to start the economic machine again after an appreciable stoppage could mean an enormous depression of living standards, possibly down to the point where social stability would be endangered. The maintenance of economic momentum mainly concerns the areas which have not been seriously devastated by the attack. When one thinks about war, one normally concentrates his attention on the area of destruction, but the problem of recuperation will most probably involve, at least in the early attack, the areas to which we have referred in the past as the "B country" plus cities which have not been badly hit. Preparations must be made now to facilitate effective use of these untouched resources. There are two points of special importance. One is to see that the economy does not stop, that resources for survival and recuperation are produced. This requires the establishment of markets, and the furnishing of labor forces, credits, and management. In addition to the use of direct allocations and priorities, financial measures may be crucial here. Some of these are dicussed in Appendix II of Part II. Almost as important to the encouragement of useful activities is the discouragement of wasteful or unimportant ones. Thus, in addition to preplanning trigger orders for the crash manufacture of such products as medical supplies, reinforcing steel, concrete, work clothes, spare parts, and the like, we may wish to curtail the manufacturing of noncritical goods whose continued manufacture would use up important resources. We may even wish to plan curtailment of the use of private transportation to preserve vehicles and save gasoline, to institute blackouts to conserve coal at the power stations, and in general to discourage consumption of all potentially scarce resources. It will be important to have studied such matters ahead of time, to have made advance preparations, and to have taken appropriate measures.

The fourth element of optimism in Table 20 was that there be no specific crippling bottleneck problems. The RAND civil defense study analyzed broad sectors of capital. We did not go into such details as, "Are there sufficient 2-inch screws or ½ horsepower electric motors?" Laymen, and some experts, may be disturbed by this, remembering the bottlenecks of World War II, but history is against them. In fact, World War II is an example of our ability when we have a year or two to conquer any serious shortages. In the long run it should be the over-all resources available and not any specific resource constraints which determine the gross output, and we are worrying here of the long run—five, ten, and fifteen years after the war.

If further study should show that there are important specific bottlenecks, we ought to stockpile the scarce items or protect the capability for making them. To assume that bottlenecks are not important does not change the feasibility of recuperation, only the cost of preparation. Our detailed recommendations allocate about $5,000,000 to the search for these bottlenecks, but for the small attack we do not really believe they exist, unless the enemy deliberately attempts an attack against our recuperation potential.

This last caveat is probably very important. The enemy can try three kinds of attacks, aiming at military targets, population, or recuperation potential. In the RAND study we considered only the first two and mixtures of these; we did not study attacks directed specifically against recuperative capacity. For example, in none of the attacks that we looked at did we consider petroleum refinery capacity to be a problem, since about one-third of our refinery capacity is outside major metropolitan areas and would automatically survive attacks directed at military establishments or at the general population. Yet if we had assumed that the enemy had added several dozen aiming points to his target list, he could probably eliminate almost all our refining capacity. If we are anxious to get rid of this problem, it would be possible for us to alleviate our worries for about $100 million. For this sum we could stockpile portable refineries of a type already designed by the Navy that would have about 10 per cent of our prewar capacity.[10] To get more than this basic minimum, we would have to spend more money. This stockpiled refinery capacity would have to be supplemented by some protected oil stocks. This, too, could be relatively simple. There has recently been a tendency in the oil industry to store certain petroleum products underground, either in abandoned mines and caves or in special excavations in rock. This is being done not because of the protection that is afforded by underground storage, but because this type of storage is economical. We suspect that some mild encouragement or inducements from the federal government might spread this practice rapidly.

The government could encourage other kinds of protection. For

[10] The plant is described in *International Oilman*, September 1957.

example, there are at least three large warehouses that have been built in abandoned limestone mines just because it is cheaper than aboveground construction. With the proper encouragement this might become a widespread practice and prove to be a very useful way to decrease the vulnerability of much of our inventory. A sample survey conducted for the RAND study indicated that while most mines cannot be used, there might be as much as 700,000,000 square feet of suitable underground mine space available. With inexpensive inducements, it would probably be possible to get about 50–100,-000,000 additional square feet developed annually—about where we would want it and as we would want it. It might be quite inexpensive to move some kinds of industrial operations underground into such space, if the proper kind of space were ordered from mining companies sufficiently far in advance.

The fifth optimistic element in our calculation was the assumption that people would be willing to work at reconstructing the country and would have a productivity at this task about equal to that of their prewar work. To many this seems like a rather bold assumption. They ask, "Would not the shock of the catastrophe so derange people that every man's hand would be against every other man's?"

This seems entirely wrong. Man never lives in a Hobbesian state of nature. There is always a society of some type. However, this fear is proper if it is stated more cautiously. There would be the possibilities of demagoguery, or sectionalism, or banditry. Some people would not be willing to work hard for the rewards available to them. Possibly the good "bourgeois" virtues so essential to a modern business society would disappear, and many people would become unambitious, irresponsible, dishonest, or lazy. The destitute survivors might war with the less destitute ones.

I do not believe that any of these events would necessarily occur, especially *if we have made preparations* to preserve our society and to alleviate the strains that would inevitably occur. Nations have taken equivalent shocks even without special preparations and have survived with their prewar virtues intact. In past years these shocks were spread over many years; the one we are considering would take place in only a few days. But for individual psychological effects (as opposed to organizational and political effects) this is good, not bad. While many normal personalities would disintegrate under hardships spread over a period of many years, the habits of a lifetime cannot be changed for most people in a few days. If you have to take it at all, then from the viewpoint of character stability it is better to take this kind of shock in a short time rather than in a long one.

It is my belief that if the government has made at least moderate prewar preparations, so that most people whose lives have been saved will give some credit to the government's foresight, then people will probably rally round, especially if the government has the organization, equipment, and manuals that it needs for recuperation and survival activities, and (most important of all) if the over-all plan for recuperation looks sensible and practical. It would not surprise me if the overwhelming majority of the survivors devoted themselves with a somewhat fanatic intensity to the task of rebuilding what was destroyed. Of course, if there is a fantastic disparity between the government's preparations and the problems to be solved, then none of this would hold. Quite the contrary. There would probably be a complete rejection of the prewar government, and possibly the prewar ideals and institutions as well.

One of our most important assumptions was that it would be possible to adopt "workable" postwar health and safety standards —workable in many senses: that people would be willing to accept them from both the political and individual point of view; that they would not be so high as to result in any large economic costs or so low that the medical problems get inordinate. The previous discussion of genetic defects and strontium-90 (pages 64 to 70) illustrates the problem. The important thing is to set up the standards prewar so that they can be thoroughly investigated and *realistic* factors of safety adopted. Doing this may be very difficult because it may make the people setting up the standards look somewhat callous, but unless we do this we will not be able to anticipate contingencies, guide research and planning, or even have available the proper information on which to estimate U.S. or S.U. deterrence calculations.

Finally, we have assumed that the economic and social cost of dealing with "other" postwar problems will not be catastrophic. We have discussed at some length, but probably much too lightly, some of these postwar problems—for example, the effects of the lingering radioactivity on heredity and life-shortening and reduction of vigor. There are others. The war may have important and totally unsuspected ecological consequences. For example, radiation kills a much higher percentage of birds than insects. Even the weather may be affected for some years. We do not believe that the small attack will have any disastrous surprises of this type, but the large attack might. The latter would affect the weather for at least a short period; it might sear a very large area of the country by thermal radiation; and either attack could cause cataclysmic tidal waves, floods, and fires. But perhaps what is most important of all, we did not look at the interaction among the effects we did study.

In spite of the many uncertainties of our study we do have a great deal of confidence in some partial conclusions—such as, that a nation like the United States or the Soviet Union could handle each of the problems of radioactivity, physical destruction, or likely levels of casualties, if they occurred by themselves. That is, we believe if either nation were to be dusted with radioactivity in a wartime manner, and if nothing else happened, this radioactivity could, with minor preparations for a small attack and elaborate preparations for a large one, be handled. With the proper alleviatory measures the resulting environment could be made acceptable (by somewhat relaxed postwar standards, of course).

We also believe that if the destruction of the 50 or so major metropolitan areas in either country were all that happened so that the ensuing reconstruction program was not complicated by social disorganization, loss of personnel, radioactivity, and so forth, neither the Soviet Union nor the United States would have any critical difficulty in rebuilding the equivalent of the destroyed metropolitan areas in the time we have estimated, or even less. Even if 100 metropolitan areas are destroyed, there would be more wealth in this country than there is in all of Russia today and more skills than were available to that country in the forties. The United States is a very wealthy and well-educated country. Even in the early missile era (the next five or ten years), *if we have a reasonable air defense,* it is difficult to imagine an enemy attack that could set us back economically to pre-World War I standards just by destroying physical assets. It is even hard to imagine our being set back to pre-World War II standards, if there is a "reasonable" course of military events and if we prepare ahead of time for what may come.

Finally, we believe that if either nation suffered large casualties, even of the order of a quarter or a half of the population, the survivors would not just lie down and die. Nor would they necessarily suffer a disastrous social disorganization. Life would go on and the necessary readjustments would be made.

But if all these things happened together and all the other effects were added at the same time, one cannot help but have some doubts. Some of these interactions are researchable and should be studied even though we did not do so. However, I believe, though admittedly on the basis of inadequate evidence and subject to the caveats I have already pointed out, that none of the problems encountered in the small attack would prove to be annihilating or even seriously crippling. No such judgment can be passed about the heavy attack without more research effort. Even then doubts may remain, depending on the quality of the preparations and the amount of research that has gone into the problem.

What are our pessimistic assumptions? There are really only two. First, we have assumed that people and equipment will work about as well as they did prewar. Many will be surprised that we consider this view conservative, but we believe that experience has shown people tend to do better in disasters and wartime situations than they expect. They "make do." For example, we have assumed that if a particular machine or factory is destroyed the total output is reduced by a corresponding amount. Often this is not true. People work longer hours, they work harder, and they use make-shift arrangements to make up for destroyed machines and factories.

Secondly, there is much marginal and underutilized plant capability and equipment in the B country which is uneconomic to use to full capacity on competitive grounds or which remains unused owing to a deficiency in over-all demand. We have not accounted for the full use of this existing underutilized capital, or the ease with which the amount of it available could probably be increased by suitable government policies aimed at preserving "obsolete" plant and equipment on a stand-by basis. We believe experience in such situations has shown that both laymen and professionals tend to exceed their own and the experts' expectations, referring to the result as a "miracle of production" or a "miracle of ingenuity." This kind of "miracle" seems very common and is almost to be expected.

We made two kinds of calculations in trying to chart the course of recuperation. The first assumed that people dedicated themselves to the job of recuperation by working hard and investing a relatively high proportion of the resources into recuperation. However, after things have been started again, say after the first six to twelve months, living standards should be quite acceptable, and probably higher than from 1930 to 1940. The other calculation assumed less dedication to the reconstruction effort and more to immediate consumption. In this case it is believed that the recuperation effort should take about five years longer. The results of the first calculation, indicating how recuperation should go with the investment-oriented policy, are given in Figure 1; our consumption and GNP go back to normal in about ten years.

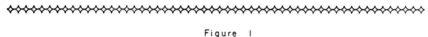

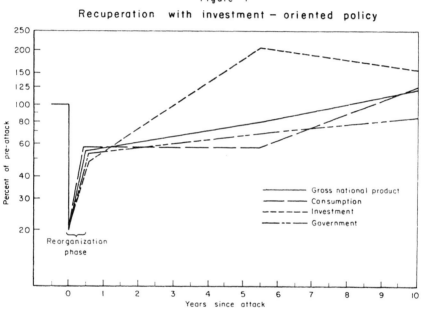

Figure 1

Recuperation with investment – oriented policy

There is one assumption shown in Figure 1 that probably should have been listed with the other optimistic assumptions in Table 20. We have assumed that people would get along with less government services than they did before the war. That is, large welfare programs would be cut back, except for relief for the destitute, and immediate postwar military expenditures would be at a maintenance level.

In Figure 2 we see that once recuperation is complete, all factors, even housing, are brought back to prewar standards. Our calculation may be a little misleading here. These houses would be rebuilt in only a restricted economic sense, that is, to their equivalent value in prewar prices. The consumer may not like this. For example, we might replace a roomy but very old house worth $10,-

❖❖❖

Figure 2

Recuperation of consumption

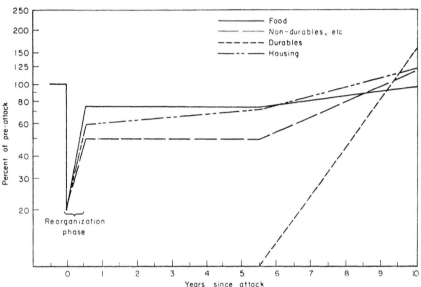

000 before the war with a new trailer, also worth $10,000 before the war. The tenant may not be happy about the change. However, I think it is fair to say that we would rebuild the cities that had been destroyed (complete with slums, and some extra ones) in less than ten years.

How much confidence did our researchers have in these recuperation calculations? In the sense of having taken account of *all* factors, not too much. While in the study we looked at more aspects of the problem than are discussed here, we have already suggested that our study was not complete enough to be a full treatment of this complicated problem. Yet we believe that it shows rather convincingly that if thermonuclear war damage is limited to something like the A metropolitan areas or the equivalent and the levels of radioactivity are about as indicated, then all the usual reasons for being skeptical of our ability to recuperate are probably wrong. We may not be able to recuperate even with preparations, but we cannot today put our finger on why this should be so and I, for one, believe that with sufficient study we will be able to make a very convincing case for recuperation, if we survive the war, and, more important, that with sufficient preparation we actually will be able to survive and recuperate if deterrence fails.

CHAPTER III

NEITHER OBLIVION NOR SURRENDER

Need for More than Finite Deterrence

THE major point of the last chapter is: *If our nation can survive the actual attack and has made some minimum preparations, then in all probability, "the survivors will not envy the dead"; there will be more than a mere technical or academic difference between victory, stalemate, or defeat. Under these circumstances, in addition to having a deterrent capability, we might want an ability actually to fight and survive a war.*

I would like to defer to Lecture II the major discussion of what a "reasonable" course of military events might be and the military measures that will be necessary if we are to be able to limit damage to the extent we have just discussed. However, at this point it does seem appropriate to digress into the active defense picture and some of the objectives in which the public and experts in and out of the Department of Defense should be interested.

I agree with our current national policy that the primary objective of our military forces is to deter war. However, I feel that there is a second but still very important objective: to protect life and property if a war breaks out. This important objective, which we have referred to as Counterforce as Insurance, is currently being neglected—in some cases advertently, but mostly because it is thought to be impossible. This impression of the impossibility of alleviating a war's effects often (illogically) leads to a conviction that war is also impossible.

In addition to the obvious dangers, there is another subtle but by no means minor disadvantage to a pure deterrence posture: the threat of mutual suicide is a very uninspiring concept, no matter how logical it may seem. If it happened to involve explicitly the annihilation of all humanity it would also be totally immoral; one doubts if it could long remain an important part of United States policy. This last possibility is taken seriously today in England, where sober statesmen and retired military officers argue that no nation has the right of all-out retaliation if such retaliation would involve the end of civilization. Therefore, they advocate that after a moderate and *restrained* retaliation, the retaliating nation should admit its defeat and surrender before too much damage is done. Some have pushed the idea even further, almost suggesting a degree of accommodation approaching surrender in the hope of settling differences without a war.

The uninspiring nature of the mutual suicide concept may eventually affect the morale and efficiency of our military forces. Many military and civilian officials who have been excessively preoccupied with the notion of pure deterrence have remarked to me, in effect, that they do not really care how the war comes out; some have even added they do not really care once deterrence has failed if our buttons are actually pushed. This position is not very far from the one of not worrying if the buttons are not connected so long as they appear as if they are. And if one looks soberly at many of the quick-reaction schemes that are proposed, he notices that they are so prone to accident or false alarm that we could only live with them if the buttons were *not* connected. It is then argued that this does not matter because the enemy surely will not rely on their not being connected. I do not believe it is necessary to say how dangerous such an attitude can be. Such sloppiness may pervade all aspects of any operation that is based on trying to keep, to a continuous and instantaneous high level of efficiency or capability, equipment and organizations that will only be used in a very remote contingency; yet if that contingency occurs, we really do not care *how* it operates.

In addition to its effect in improving morale and efficiency, there are objective reasons for believing that a war can actually occur. I said previously that even adequate deterrent forces could fail because of irrationality, miscalculation, accident, or excessive pressures on the potential attacker. These and other plausible circumstances in which deterrence can be strained or can fail will be discussed in more detail in the next lecture. Even at this point it should be clear that being able to fight a war and being able to face up to the threat of a war are important. It might be fatal to the free world, for example, if the Soviet Union felt it could *rely* on its deterrent force to keep us from threatening them no matter what they did short of a direct attack on the United States. I have already pointed out the enormous (though usually unrecognized) difference in a situation in which action by the U.S. might cause us to incur, say, 50 to 100 million casualties, and one in which they would be in the 2 to 20 million range. In the first case, the Soviets could have a high confidence in their hope that we would be deterred *no matter how provocative they were.* They might feel no necessity to restrict themselves to the so-called "ambiguous challenges." In the second case, they know from their own World War II experience that a country the size of the United States can take casualties in the 2–20 million range, and beyond, and still recuperate. They would therefore be forced to consider limiting their provocations, because their ability to deter the United States would be less than total. Our study of nonmilitary defense indicated that there are many circumstances in which feasible combinations of military and nonmilitary measures might make the difference between our facing casualties in the 2–20 million range rather than in the 50–100 million range. This could mark the difference between a world in which the Russians might feel they had an almost completely free hand, and one in which they should feel they had to act with some circumspection.

I would not be willing to predict, if our current inability seriously to threaten war continues, that the Soviets will immediately exploit this by going on a Hitler-type rampage. But if everybody recognizes the situation, it is not necessary for them to be so aggressive to make major gains. The accommodations by the threatened nations would be close to automatic. I also believe that no "moderately prudent man" would ignore the possibility of even Hitler-type threats. I have found among too many people the utmost resistance to taking seriously the idea of "gambling" or "reckless" Russians. I do not believe such resistance to be based on sound intuition that such Russians will not be in power at any time in the next ten years. Under the new conditions of the Soviet counter-deterrent, the past may be a poor guide to the future. Most people resist thinking about the idea of aggressive Soviets in a condition of no U.S. Credible First Strike Capability because the possibility is too horrible to face. Meanwhile, as we shall discuss, a free world posture develops that is ever more vulnerable to such aggressive behavior, and therefore in effect invites it.

There is another possibility that should at least make military planners willing to study and evaluate seriously the civil and air defense of people and property. If (or should I say when) the Russians acquire an effective combination of civil and air defense that we cannot match, they will have an almost incredible advantage at some bargaining tables. Therefore, even though one does not,

98

in the strictly military sense, fight shelters with shelters or air defense with air defense, I feel that at a minimum we ought to have what I have called a Preattack Mobilization Base—to be prepared to go into a crash program either to match any corresponding Russian defenses or to counteract a Russian program of provocation. In addition, both our present and our future weapons systems should be examined to see how effective they would be against a Russia with an existing or plausibly modified civil defense system—one that has had a chance to exploit a few hours of warning, for example. (Such warning is quite possible for the attacker or aggressor even in the ICBM era.) We should be prepared to hedge against a possibility of this kind.

The Soviets already seem to be doing this. *We know the U.S.S.R. takes active air defense seriously.* In addition, particularly during the last few years, there has been a marked increase in civil defense activity in the Soviet Union. A program of mass education in civil defense has been undertaken; indeed, the Soviets claim that every adult in Russia had at least twenty-two hours of instruction in 1958. In addition, some experts believe that urban population shelters are being built, usually in the form of reinforced basements in newly constructed masonry buildings. However, nothing is known, at least in the unclassified literature, about the quality and number of shelters.

Even more important (though as far as we know, they have done nothing until these last few years to exploit it), the Soviets can get a rural fallout program almost for nothing. Most current peasant housing has earth walls 2 to 3 feet thick and small windows. In addition, most Russian villages have large "refrigeration" cellars, which could easily be adapted to provide quite adequate fallout protection. However, even though current Russian manuals have begun to emphasize rural and fallout protection, we just do not know to what extent the Russians have tried to exploit their assets sensibly.

I should point out that the levels of damage and the postwar problems that we have just discussed might be an overestimate of what a retaliatory blow could or would actually do. While few aggressor nations would willingly face either a small probability of total annihilation or a certainty of a high level of damage, an aggressor might be willing to face a small probability of a high level of damage. For such reasons the balance of terror is far from automatic or easy, and even a reliable Finite Deterrence posture is hard to achieve. Even if a nation possesses very impressive deterrent capabilities, war or the serious threat of war will still be sufficiently likely so that even an imprudent government would not ignore the possibility.

Need for Air Defense

Many people believe that in the ballistic missile age there is no need for active air defense. Whether this is true or not will depend on many things, the most important being the ability of the Soviets to destroy the country with ICBM's. In the near future ICBM's are likely to be relatively expensive and limited to small warheads as compared to those the manned bomber can carry. During this period, except for warning considerations, even an unprotected B country probably can survive a free ride by ICBM's *if it has an adequate passive defense system.* In addition it will be some time before Soviet missiles can do as much destruction as Soviet bombers, simply because the Soviets have so many bombers. In the long run, the question of active air defense will revolve partially about the relative efficiency of bombers and missiles. The missile has two great advantages over the bomber:

1. It is more reliable because it is less vulnerable to active defense.
2. It is faster.

The first advantage exists only if the opponent has a very expensive air defense system. Otherwise the bomber is more likely to get to place its bomb load accurately on the target. The fact that the missile is faster is only an overwhelming advantage for some, but not all, tactical situations (e.g., in the long [2–30 days] war for many missions some of the urgency of time disappears). The bomber has some advantages over missiles: it is recallable, can carry many bombs, can carry a man to make last minute decisions (particularly important for mop-up and hunter-killer tactics), is operated in peacetime in a manner similar to its wartime mission, and, most important of all, both we and the Soviets have lots of them. For all of these and other reasons it will be important to be able to defend against bombers in the early and mid-sixties and may be important in the late sixties and early seventies. It should be noted that defense against attack was hard even before the ballistic missile age. In the past those who have looked at the problem of defending

100

the ten or twenty largest cities against a determined enemy attack found that a sober analysis almost always shows this to be an almost hopeless task. The general feeling of hopelessness held by even the advocates of air defense, is indicated in the following quotation: [1]

We believe that the defense of North America is so vital, not only to the people of the United States and Canada but to the whole Free World, that we must build the best air defense that seems possible, because it *might work*—not fail to build it because it might not.

As I mentioned in Chapter I in discussing why some people are willing to advocate Counterforce as Insurance even though they do not believe it is likely to work, the above quotation may represent a correct and sophisticated point of view. But, correct or not, a military organization that is worried about its morale would be extremely loath to raise the question "might work" unless it felt that this view would improve morale; that is, unless it felt that the "might work" position represented a more optimistic point of view than that held by the audience. The budget people will realize this and wonder if it makes sense to support the program. In this particular case analysis seems to indicate that the "might work" hope is pretty weak if "work" is interpreted as preventing a determined enemy from dropping at least twenty or thirty bombs on our largest cities. However, it is our conjecture that (with the caveats to be made in Lectures II and III) feasible combinations of active defense, active offense, and nonmilitary defense can, with at least medium confidence if not with high confidence, protect a nation in the sense that without these measures the nation may be almost totally destroyed. With them, it can recover from a war to an equivalent of its former position in about ten years or less. This can be done because it is much easier to defend B country than A country.

If one agrees that one should prepare to alleviate the consequences of war, he can talk about objectives of air defense beyond protecting our retaliatory capability. In fact, from the air defense point of view the most interesting result of the RAND civil defense study was that nonmilitary defense measures can make these other objectives both feasible and worthwhile. We would therefore suggest that so far as NORAD thinks its function is to protect civilians

[1] Reported on page 102 of *Air Force Magazine* for August 1958 as a motto of the North American Air Defense Command (NORAD); italics mine.

and their property, it could change its briefing to include some such remark as the following:

> With feasible levels of Air Defense, we will have a country after a war. Without an adequate Air Defense, we may not.

In accord with this quotation we can think of at least four things that air defense can do to help make the nonmilitary defense system work.

❖❖❖

TABLE 21
FEASIBLE AIR DEFENSE CONTRIBUTIONS TO NONMILITARY DEFENSE

A. Prevent a free ride
B. Provide usable warning
C. Stop small strikes
D. Help in reorganization and recuperation

❖❖❖

It might turn out, of course, that if air defense is reoriented to maximize its contribution to the objectives in Table 21 it may take a different form than it has in the past.

A. *Prevent a "Free Ride"*

The first and most important consideration is to keep the enemy from getting a free ride in any attack against population or industry.

Usually, when one calculates the effectiveness of air defense measures, it is assumed that the enemy has high-performance bombers with a small number of bombs to the bomber, and that he will use saturation and deceptive tactics. One then calculates the number of bombers that the air defense shoots down and figures any additional costs, difficulties, or inconveniences to which the enemy is subjected by his attempts to prevent being shot down. Because these additional costs, difficulties, or inconveniences often seem relatively small, many people have pinpointed the "inadequacy" of air defense. However, this method of looking at the problem does not give air defense credit for its major contribution: forcing the enemy to use a high-performance bomber, to put only a small number of bombs in his bomber, and to confine himself to saturation and deceptive tactics. By doing this, air defense may succeed in defending the B country, even if it goes down fighting in trying to

102

defend the 53 SMA of A country. It may also do a worthwhile job of defending A country by holding the damage to moderate or partial levels. From the viewpoint of recuperation, saving 10 or 20 per cent of A country would be very valuable.

Let us try to imagine what the situation would be if we had no air defense at all, and the enemy knew this and prepared to take advantage of his golden opportunity. Under those circumstances he would not need penetration aids and could use the resulting savings in weight to load many bombs on each of his long-range bombers and a smaller but impressive number on his medium bombers. Even more menacingly, the enemy might then buy cheaper or slower bombers with longer ranges and capabilities for even heavier bomb loads. However, even if in this example he restricted himself to his current bomber force, he could probably still just about totally destroy the urban part of the United States—and I mean totally, right down to small towns and cities of five to ten thousand population.

It is much more important to prevent that free ride than it is to subject the bombers to some high level of attrition. Even though the enemy might successfully attack and destroy the majority of our largest cities by using the saturation and deceptive tactics we have mentioned, the air defense may still have done its major job by forcing the enemy to concentrate his attack on these largest cities. The mere existence of the air defense system prevented these same bombers from doing even greater destruction.

Let us now consider the warning question.

B. Provide Usable Warning

The second function in Table 21 is surveillance. We want to be able to have some warning of the first strike of the enemy's manned bombers, and possibly even of his ICBM's.

For the general population the warning situation, even in our early ICBM era, may be much better than most people imagine. If we have been moderately intelligent about the number, hardness, and dispersal of our SAC bomber and missile bases, the enemy should not have enough ICBM's to destroy completely all his strictly military objectives. If he is prudent, he will not wish to send very many of his valuable ICBM's against cities, at least in the early 1960's when his inventory will be measured in the hundreds rather than in the thousands. Presumably, he does not care to start a war with the idea of self-destruction; if he is starting the war, his strategy should provide him with the highest possible hope of attaining a meaningful victory. His priority efforts should be devoted to destroying things that could hurt him.

Many of us believe that a future war is going to be fought out of stock and inventories. Thus the things that can hurt the enemy will not be the producing cities but the strategic forces—the bombers, missiles, submarines, and carriers. Even if all of these strategic targets were soft and easily destroyed, the enemy might wish to send many missiles per target, realizing that his missiles are not completely reliable. For example, if he is willing to assume (and rely on) his ICBM's having a reliability of one-half, and if he sends four missiles to a target, there is one chance in sixteen that all four will misfire and the target will survive. This one chance in sixteen means that if we have sixty-four bases, on the average four of them will survive untouched. If the enemy is unlucky, eight or ten will survive for retaliatory purposes. The surviving four squadrons of B-52's, four wings of B-47's, or four squadrons of Atlases could do a great deal of retaliatory damage, probably much more than the enemy would want. Therefore, if he thought his reliability was around one-half, he would probably consider four missiles per strategic target a questionable minimum; if he has the extra missiles available, he may choose to send more per target.

It is, of course, very possible that the Soviets would have confidence in the ability of their active and passive defenses to limit damage done by our small retaliatory attack (from surviving bases) to an "acceptable" level. They might not be deterred from starting a war in which they could hope to destroy all but five or ten of our bases. However, even if they have enough confidence in their defenses and their ability to accept damage to be willing to go to war, they are unlikely to have so much confidence in their untested capabilities that they would be willing frivolously to divert missiles to Grand Rapids or Des Moines. So as far as the larger cities are concerned—New York, Washington, Chicago, Philadelphia—we can be less sure. They might be willing to divert a small percentage of their missile force to destroy these cities that have probably been on their target list for so long. But it may not be militarily rational for them to do even this.

These remarks about the priority targets for enemy missiles also hold for their submarine force, and for the relatively small number of long-range bombers the Soviets are supposed to have. They do not apply to their medium bombers, because they have so many of them. However, such bombers cannot fly far enough for the most devious and deceptive limited-warning attacks. At worst, the medium bombers are likely to be at the DEW (Distant Early Warning) Line when the first ICBM's begin to explode, and therefore two to four hours away from the target. They will more likely be in the interior of Russia and therefore six to twelve hours away from the target when the first ICBM's explode in this country. The reason that the medium bombers may still be in the interior of Russia is that they are of relatively short range; in order to reach deep targets in the United States, even on one-way missions, they will need to refuel in the air or to stage through northern Russian bases. Unless the Russians have been showing activity at these bases in peacetime, they may be loath to manifest such activity just before an attack for fear we might have them under some kind of surveillance and take alarm.

Medium bombers are a "mop-up" force. In the hands of the Soviets they would probably be out to get the municipal airfields and other secondary targets. Some could be after the cities, either to guarantee that in the long run the Russians come out on top, or just because it takes a long time for war planners to change target lists. But even if they are directed to cities, we have already pointed out that they are likely to come at least two to four hours after the first bombs have exploded, and maybe six to twelve hours later. There could be even more warning. Most or all of the Russian medium bombers will be going on one-way missions. It might be that rather than "throw them away" on essentially nonmilitary targets, they may prefer to hold them back. (We shall discuss some of the reasons they might do this in the next lecture.)

We are not saying that we should rely on the enemy's avoiding cities in *the very first waves*. What we are saying is that there are overwhelming reasons why he should not bother to attack cities ranking 50th to 200th in size, very good reasons not to attack those ranking 10th to 50th, and even moderately good reasons not to attack those ranking 1st to 10th. If he waits, it is not wishful thinking for us to prepare to exploit the resulting warning period if there is one, and to design our early warning lines to make this warning more probable.

One way to exploit warning is by evacuation. While evacuation has been one of the official policies of the Office of Civil and Defense Mobilization, it has been without reality—at least partly because our people do not believe it worthwhile. In the RAND study we concluded it is worthwhile and that adequate preparations for it should be made as soon as possible. While a few cities such as New York may take days to evacuate, most American cities could be evacuated in a few hours if the proper preparations have been made. As important as being able to evacuate is the capability to improvise fallout shelters, either for the evacuees or for those who have stayed put.

There are ways other than deliberate enemy use of a limited warning attack in which we might get two to twenty hours of warning before a wave of enemy bombers could enter the continental United States. The enemy might use a mass attack over the North Pole and give us DEW Line warning. A much more reasonable possibility is the outbreak of an accidental or unpremeditated war in which ICBM's land while the bombers of both sides are mainly on the ground and their submarines are in home ports. We are also interested in deterring or correcting extreme Soviet provocations (for example, attacks on Europe) by the use of SAC as a threat. This implies a United States first strike with consequent warning to us. That is, our having a Credible First Strike Capability may depend on our being able to carry out an evacuation in the crisis period. The feasibility and dangers of such a tactic are considered in Lecture II. Most important of all, we have already pointed out that if they think it through, the side which starts the war will see that there are good reasons for not attacking cities in the first wave even if it is not costly to do so. The attacker could threaten to destroy these cities to try to intimidate the country being attacked either into regulating its tactics or into negotiating.

The possibility of having hours of warning makes evacuation and improvisation useful; it also implies that there are plausible circumstances under which there will be both unambiguous warning and time to get "augmentation" forces [2] and nonalert forces ready be-

---

[2] Augmentation forces are forces which are not normally kept ready but which can be made so in a matter of hours or, in some cases, days. They would include most of the military reserves, the civil defense cadres we have already discussed, and military forces which do not normally have a strategic mission but which can improvise one. For example, the Tactical Air Command stationed in the continental United States or the fighter aircraft on carriers that are in port can both be used in air defense.

fore the mass plane attack comes. Again it is not wishful thinking to acquire active and passive capabilities that can exploit this unambiguous warning if it happens to be available.

In addition to warning that the first strike is coming, we want warning of later strikes. This requirement is not generally recognized. If you believe as I do *that a war is likely to continue a few days after the first strike and then terminate (probably by negotiation)*, there are two very important reasons for getting continuing warning. First, there is the continuing need to alert air defense and enable people and air offense to take protective steps. Secondly, there is the need to police any agreements made with the enemy. If we have no postwar surveillance, the enemy may be tempted to break any agreements he makes. Unfortunately, it is not clear whether our current radar systems—both the early warning and the contiguous cover—will have much capability after the first strike, partly because of sheer physical destruction and partly because there have been to date insufficient preparations for guaranteeing even a degraded continuing usability.

C. Stop Small Strikes

The third objective of air defense is really the classic one of attrition, but with special emphasis against relatively small strikes that might occur in the middle and later phases of the war. We are as interested in this capability as in getting an appreciable attrition of early mass attacks. As we have pointed out, even a small strike can do a great deal of damage if it has a free ride and involves many small bombs per bomber. This is especially true if the enemy has done some reconnaissance to learn what is still undamaged, and can allocate his offense efficiently against the undamaged component. It is especially important, therefore, to be able to defend against not only small strikes but even single-plane reconnaissance missions so that the enemy will be forced to direct his offensive blindly. This may mean that we must also try to knock down any reconnaissance satellites he may have.

The high attrition of small and uncoordinated strikes may be a very feasible technical objective. Many of the ills that air defense is supposed to suffer from could occur only in the first strike or two. It is only in these strikes that there is the possibility of the enemy's launching thousands of ground "decoys" together with hundreds of bombers, all coordinated and with "jamming." [3] Such strikes would presumably not be within the enemy's capability after the first day of the war. (There is, as of now, some belief that such strikes would not be within Soviet capability even on the first day of the war.)

D. Help in Reorganization and Recuperation

Lastly, the air defense can help the total war effort, particularly in reorganization and recuperation. The most important part of this function is undoubtedly the reorganization and recuperation of that part of the strategic forces which survives the enemy's first strike and either has not gone off on a mission, or has returned, or possibly is at sea (submarines and aircraft carriers).

It is part and parcel of this concept of *fighting* and *alleviating* a war that we must preserve enough offensive force either to destroy the enemy's offensive forces or to force him to negotiate. Unless specific provisions are made in advance, it is unlikely that many of our bombers, missiles, or facilities will survive the first day of the war. (Some of the proposals for placing complete reliance on alert or airborne systems are presumably based on an operation in which no provisions are made for other than a single retaliatory strike.) However, if we had adequate programs for hardening, dispersal, recovery facilities, command and control, and so on, it might be possible to preserve an even larger strike potential for the second and later days of the war than the forces that take off on alert status. Other sources of strength could be some bombers returning from the first strike and the many bombers in the pipelines, air training commands, depot storage, or even in the air. We must be able to locate these bombers, to count them, to direct them to land on airfields that are not radioactive, to find out what maintenance or repair they need, to locate possible crews, bombs, and tankers for them, and finally, to decide the tactics to be used and to communicate these with the directions needed to launch a reasonably coordinated strike. This calls for the survival of at least a minimum communications, monitoring, data-processing, and computing capa-

[3] Decoys are relatively cheap flying objects which can be made to simulate bombers to radars. By using them one may saturate the enemy's capability or direct his attention away from the real bombers. Jamming means the emission of electronic radiation in such a way as to confuse or saturate the enemy's radar and his data-processing systems.

bility, and for advance preparations to continue operations in a degraded environment. If properly designed, the air defense facilities would be able to supplement the surviving SAC system in a valuable way.

The government needs similar facilities to gather information and process data about the state of the country. Here again, the centralized facilities of NORAD and SAGE are likely to be invaluable if they survive. The newspapers report that the Department of Defense has considered (and reconsidered) placing future headquarters for NORAD and SAGE deep underground. If this were done properly, they should have an equivalent strength per square inch capable of withstanding thousands of pounds of blast pressure. In fact if really well designed, they might be able to accept direct hits of large surface burst bombs. It is important to design in as much invulnerability as possible because one desires the central air defense headquarters to survive even manned bomber attacks. (A possible hardening policy for military and civilian installations is discussed in Appendix III.)

Surviving the War

Let us assume that we develop a sufficient air defense system to prevent the enemy from getting a free ride with his bombers, and also that we have enough offensive strength to be able to terminate the war on some sort of reasonable basis. Then the really serious problem, serious in the sense of actually jeopardizing our ability to survive in a postwar world, will probably turn out to be—not the sheer destruction of wealth, the medical effects of the radioactivity, or the genetic effects—but *the short-run acute radiation effects*. Anyone who gets too high a dose of radiation in the first month or two of the war will simply die, not show a moderate life-shortening.

Table 22 summarizes the mortality expectations resulting from acute radiation exposure. From an exposure of between 200 and 300 roentgens we would expect 5 per cent of the people to die; between 350 and 600, about 50 per cent; and almost everybody at some dose between 600 and 1,000. (The upper figures assume some simple medical care.) The reason we can take the larger doses indicated in Table 10, page 59, over a long period of time is that the body tends to heal the effects of radiation—perhaps 90 per cent of the somatic damage can be repaired over a long period of time. But in a month (as far as lethality is concerned) we probably get very little healing, as indicated by the column labeled "Semiacute." (However, the column may be pessimistic by a factor of 1.5.)

TABLE 22

MORBIDITY OF ACUTE TOTAL BODY RADIATION

	Instantaneous	Semiacute (1 month)
Some die	200–300r	~300r
50% die	350–600r	~600r
All die	600–900r	~900r

There are two possibilities for handling the short-term effects: one is shielding, and the other is the possibility that drugs can be developed which, if taken in advance, will increase our ability to accept large radiation doses. This second possibility is being investigated with some success. One of the recommendations of the RAND study is that this research be pushed vigorously. However, we have (pessimistically) based all our calculations on the first—shielding.

When we build fallout protection, we build into the shelter factors of attenuation of 1,000 or even 10,000 because such attenuation factors are so inexpensive to get—three or four feet of earth will do it. But if we look at the light attack (Table 23), we see that rather small protection factors, say 5, 10, and 20, will in most areas save one's life even though in many places these low factors mean that many would get uncomfortably high doses, higher even than the industrial standards mentioned previously. (These calculations were based on the assumption that adequate radiation shelter would be available to almost everybody, so that the dose most people would get would be determined almost solely by their postwar activities.) However, there is probably a lot of leeway in our radiation standards. While every effort should be made to keep below them, it would not be the ultimate tragedy if doses exceeded them. Therefore, I would value a "cheap" civil defense program (see Appendix IV), one which enables people to take advantage of the natural shelter available in most parts of the United States and which could easily give protection factors of 5, 10, or even 20. We

110

do not know how much of such protection is available, but we recommend that about $150 million be spent on identifying, counting, labeling, and improving the best radiation protection in every neighborhood so that people will know where to go and so that planners and decision makers will know how much of this protection exists and where it is.

❖❖

TABLE 23

FRACTION OF COUNTRY COVERED BY VARIOUS
DOSES IN ONE EARLY ATTACK

48-hour Dose in r	Fraction of U.S.	Minimum Protection Factor Needed
0– 300	0.30	1– 2
300– 750	0.30	2– 5
750– 1,500	0.25	5–10
1,500– 3,000	0.10	10–20
3,000– 6,000	0.04	20–40
6,000–10,000	0.01	40–65

❖❖

An important prerequisite to being able to use this makeshift space is to have a radiation meter available, so that one will know what his exposure is and what is safe and not safe to do. For example, can one expose himself for a short time to improve the protective capabilities of the refuge (such as washing down the roof or piling on sandbags), or to go out to get food and water? One will wonder if he should stay put, crowd into the safer portions of the refuge, or find a safer place. We have already mentioned that wide availability of meters is also most important for postwar patch-up and recuperation. *Unless one knows what the radiation levels are, he is likely to be absolutely paralyzed when it comes to debris clearing, repair, clean-up, decontamination, and the like.*

I mentioned earlier that we have recommended that the government spend around $100 million for the purchase of various kinds of meters. This may seem to be a large sum of money, but actually it is just barely adequate. We had originally recommended spending about twice this sum, but we believe that the institution of the cheap program should stimulate private individuals and organizations to buy substantial numbers of meters on their own.

It is my personal belief that just buying the meters and making preparations to utilize existing protection would be a fairly significant civil defense program. It is also an important part of any larger program, so it seems to be a convenient way to get started.

◆◆

TABLE 24

FRACTION OF COUNTRY COVERED BY VARIOUS
DOSES IN ONE LATE ATTACK

48-hour Dose in r	Fraction of U.S.	Minimum Protection Factor Needed
over 6,000	0.50	over 40
3,000–6,000	0.30	20–40
1,500–3,000	0.10	10–20
750–1,500	0.05	5–10
0– 750	0.05	1– 5

◆◆

If one looks at the larger attack (Table 24), he will readily see that using existing protection is not enough. Unless people find protection factors of more than 20, they are going to be killed by radiation in the first days or hours of the war. And even if they find protection factors of 100, they will probably be killed eventually because they will not be able to go out to decontaminate and get supplies. For this latter threat, adequate, specially-built fallout protection and elaborate preparations to cope with the postwar radiation environment are needed. However, if programs are started in the near future, there is probably plenty of time both to build the shelters and to make the other preparations.

How many civilian casualties can we expect? If we adopt the pure Finite Deterrence position and do not "fix-up" our civil defense and our air offense and air defense, in most cases we can expect as many casualties as the enemy cares to inflict. If, however, we make the necessary changes so that the enemy does not have a free ride on his first strikes and also meets a formidable opposition on his later strikes, there are limits to how many people he can kill. Within these limits, the civilian casualties resulting from an attack on the United States would be a function of the attacker's strategy and tactics as well as our own civil defense measures. For example, if it is assumed that the enemy's strategy would consist of an initial strike mainly at SAC, the particular tactics used would depend on the strength and posture of SAC and on our air defense capabilities. The more SAC is protected by hardening and dispersal, the more it acts as a "Counterforce" by drawing the enemy's attack away from cities.

The effects of various defense measures are shown in Table 25. While the table is approximate, I believe the numbers are accurate enough to be orienting. These calculations may not allow for the range

❖❖

TABLE 25

EARLY ATTACK AGAINST SAC AND FIRST
50 URBAN AREAS

Civil Defense Measure	Casualties (in millions)
None	90
Minimum Fallout	30–70 [a]
Minimum Fallout plus 70% Strategic Evacuation	5–25

LATE ATTACK AGAINST SAC AND 157 URBAN AREAS [b]

Civil Defense Measure	Casualties (in millions)
None	160
A Complete Program	
Protected SAC	8–25 [c]
Unprotected SAC	40–55
70% Strategic Evacuation	
Protected SAC	3– 5
Unprotected SAC	12–20
Minimum Fallout	
Protected SAC	60–85
Unprotected SAC	over 85

[a] Where ranges are given, the particular value in the range will depend on the tactics of the attacker and the physical assumptions made.

[b] In the unprotected SAC cases, attacks extend to targets beyond this list to cities in the 25,000 to 50,000 population category.

[c] In this case the lower figure is for an attack on SAC only in the first 45 minutes; the upper figure assumes that the enemy gives up a slight military advantage and attacks a few population targets with the opening military salvo.

❖❖

of options available to attacker and defender; the problem needs more study. For example, even with a hard SAC, an attacker could increase the casualties beyond the ranges indicated if he chose to give up small military advantages. However, if we have been foresighted, he probably could not increase them by a very large amount without giving up a great deal in military effectiveness.

With a complete civil defense program, adequate warning, and a relatively limited Soviet strike (limited because of the unpremeditated character of the war or because the Soviet strike was blunted by the U.S. attack), U.S. casualties would probably be in the 3 to 10 million range. Once again: *a strong defense program could conceivably strengthen our ability to deter extremely provocative actions on the part of Soviet policy makers who do not want war but are willing to engage in provocative or testing actions short of war.* Those policy makers would have to concede to themselves the possibility of a deliberate U.S. decision to fight on provocation.

A Point of View

While many pay lip service to the weaknesses of pure deterrence strategies, few take these weaknesses seriously—often not because they do not recognize that they exist, but because they feel it impossible to do anything realistic and useful other than deter. The "rosy" results of the RAND study were surprising, even to ourselves. Let me summarize why the RAND study discussed in *A Report on a Study of Non-Military Defense* (R-322-RC, July 1, 1958) brought in results so different from those that are often accepted. First, even though we could not go too deeply into particular questions, we still tried to perform careful and objective studies rather than trust "first impression" calculations. Second, instead of asking "What happened?" we asked "What can we do about it?" For example, in evaluating the problem created by fallout, rather than use the peacetime standards in the handbooks, we made realistic assumptions on the internal and external doses that people could receive and still get along by "acceptable" postwar standards. We looked into the possibilities for significant levels of cheap protection (one of our programs for the whole nation is only $500 million) for the immediate future. We were also willing to look at the very expensive measures needed to meet attacks of the late 1960's and early 1970's. We explored unconventional and sometimes extreme (though we feel practical) solutions. (Some of the programs we explored envisaged people living hundreds of feet underground for as long as three months, having three years' stocks of food supplies, putting 20 per cent or more of our industry underground, and so forth.)

Last, and most important, we allowed for the fact that we do not have to be passive; we can do and will do things to ameliorate such problems as the long-term effects of radiation—for example, decontamination and behavior that minimizes both internal and external exposure.

In the case of the recuperation problem, the biggest contribution we made was in taking a long view. Instead of asking, "How terrible is the war?" we asked, "How does the country look five or ten years after the war as a function of how the war starts, of the preparations we have made, and of the course of military events?"

We did not cry "uncle" because we could not produce war goods in the first year of the war. In fact, we chose to ignore the problem. We believe that everyone who is interested in properly protecting people and property during a war would do well to do the same. The "War Value Added in Manufacturing" criterion that has been used in almost all defense studies is misleading and should be dropped. (This does not imply that we will not need military forces in the immediate postwar world. It means that, with preparations, our surviving military forces should be sufficient to handle third powers—if we have been successful in handling our opponent.)

People often feel they make a case for nonmilitary defense by saying it is part of our deterrent posture—by which they mean deterring an attack against the United States. Except for increasing our ability to withstand the postattack blackmail tactics discussed later, this deterrent is so small [4] compared to the role the strictly military deterrence plays that it seems proper to ignore it.[5]

Many civil defense enthusiasts feel that they are making a disas-

[4] For example, it would not surprise me if a careful study showed that the net military resources in our cities as represented by the communication centers, municipal airfields, valuable off-duty personnel, and the makeshift possibilities for an improvised second- and third-strike capability could, with preparation, be made to add up to the equivalent of a number of wings of B-52's. In order to simplify the discussion we are ignoring this contribution except when it is central to a point we are trying to make.

[5] As we have already discussed, and will add to in Lecture II when we discuss the different kinds of deterrence, nonmilitary defense may have an important role in deterring the Russians from extremely provocative behavior, but this is different from deterring an attack on the United States.

trous admission if they concede that our nonmilitary preparations may not have a crucial effect on the military course of events. But it is not the purpose of people and property to fight a war; it is the purpose of the military to protect people and their property. Far from being a weakness to concede this, it shows you to be hard-headed, and it isolates you from antiquarians who do not yet realize the implications of the existence of megaton bombs and believe that a World War III initiated by an all-out exchange of thermo-nuclear bombs would be followed by an industrial mobilization.

Taking the long view—that is, asking the question, How will the country look five or ten years after the war?—is important. Few people differentiate between having 10 million dead, 50 million dead, or 100 million dead. It all seems too horrible. However, it does not take much imagination to see that there is a difference between having a country which five or ten years later has a population of 150 million (or more) and a GNP of over 300 billion dollars and is strong and prosperous, and one which has only a few million scattered survivors grubbing out a miserable existence. The former is not only the richest nation in the world, it is also one of the largest in population. It is not a bare remnant. One need not live with this problem very long to accept these long-term differences as significant. It is absolutely essential to take such a long view if one is to think constructively on defense, deterrence, and national survival.

LECTURE II

THE FORMULATION AND TESTING OF
OBJECTIVES AND PLANS

CHAPTER IV

CONFLICTING OBJECTIVES

An Essential of Good Planning

ABOUT six or seven years ago there was a "technological breakthrough" at The RAND Corporation in the art of doing Systems Analysis and Military Studies. This technological breakthrough was of so simple and common-sense a nature that some readers will be annoyed at me for even inferentially claiming a patent for RAND, and others will be annoyed that I used the grandiose word "breakthrough." Both annoyances are probably justified, but it was nevertheless a very important event for RAND.

The nature of the breakthrough was simple. In the early days at RAND most studies involved an attempt to find the "optimum" system, given some reasonably definite set of circumstances, objectives, and criteria. The emphasis was on comparing thousands, sometimes tens of thousands, of different systems under idealized conditions; then the "best" one would be picked. We actually tried to select such things as the optimal turbine inlet temperature of a turbojet engine by a detailed campaign analysis. If the analysts were a little sophisticated, they also did a sensitivity analysis to study the results of varying the assumptions slightly. However, with or without a sensitivity analysis, the attention was still directed toward finding the single "optimum" system out of the millions of possible systems where the comparisons were all made within a rather narrow and definite context. Naturally, the high-speed computer often played a central role in all this.

Sometimes our researchers took a curious pride in the prowess of their high-speed computers. They would make such remarks as, "More than a million campaign calculations went into this analysis." Or, "This is the first analysis done by man in which 10,000,000 multiplications were made." Or even a more extreme boast, "These results came out of a complicated calculation performed by the most modern of high-speed computers using the most advanced mathematical techniques available. Do you want to argue with an electronic machine backed up by all the resources of modern science?" The only possible answer to that question is, "Yes."

The new viewpoint is different. We now tend to compare a rather small number of different systems under widely varying circumstances and objectives. No simple criteria of performance are used. The major attention is focused on the uncertainties. A system is preferred when it performs reasonably well under probable circumstances in terms of the high-priority objectives, and yet hedges against less probable or even improbable situations, and does more than just pay lip service to medium- and low-priority objectives.

It is obviously better to do something such as we have just described than to pick out a single major objective and a most probable situation. It is proper to do this in a more fundamental sense than many people realize. One cannot, for example, just eliminate the problem by weighting the objectives by importance numbers and the circumstances by probabilities and then reduce the problem, in a mathematical sense, to the use of a single super objective and a single super circumstance. Yet if one did this he would run into less trouble than if he tried the more classical method of a single pure objective and a single pure circumstance.

The reason a simple weighting does not work is that anyone doing such studies is working for a committee—fundamentally a committee formed of the people of the United States or of the free world, but more directly a committee formed by the policy advisors and decision makers. In general, there is no way for a committee to arrive at a consensus on weighting numbers or probabilities. Because this point is important, I would like to illustrate it by two examples, which may impress some as being academic but which really are not. (I will go into more detail, in the next lecture, on some ways in which the committee structure of the decision process affects our studies.)

❖❖

TABLE 26

GROUP CHOICES [a]

Chooser	Preference
Tom	A to B, B to C, A to C
Dick	B to C, C to A, B to A
Harry	C to A, A to B, C to B
All	A to B, B to C, C to A

[a] This "paradox of voting" seems to have been first pointed out by E. J. Nanson. The reference is given by Kenneth J. Arrow in *Social Choice and Individual Values*, Wiley, New York, 1951, p. 3.

❖❖

Consider a committee formed of three people, Tom, Dick, and Harry, as shown in Table 26. Tom has the set of preference relations A to B and B to C. Because Tom is a rational person, I do not have to ask him which he prefers between A and C. If he prefers A to B, and B to C, then he prefers A to C. Similarly, Dick prefers B to C, and C to A, and therefore B to A. Lastly, Harry prefers C to A, A to B, and therefore C to B. Now if we ask this committee to vote for their preferences between A and B, we note that they give two votes, Tom's and Harry's for A over B. Similarly, if we ask them to choose between B and C, B will win out over C by two to one. We might then conjecture that since the committee is composed of reasonable people it should not be necessary to ask which they prefer between A and C. We ought to be able to deduce that they prefer A to C, since they prefer A to B and B to C. However, being experimentally minded, we might just go ahead and ask the committee which they prefer between A and C and find, to our amusement or horror, that two to one, they prefer C to A. This is most disturbing. If one is a rigid type, it may be extraordinarily distressing. It turns out that it is perfectly proper to be disturbed because, even after analysis, there seems to be no way in principle (and very often in practice) to make this committee act reasonably—unless we accept a rule of autocracy and delegate the decision making to one of them, to a dictator. Even this may not solve our difficulty. Some dictators, though they have the external appearance of being integrated, are really committees. In any case, there is no subtle voting method for a committee that is even mildly democratic that seems to avoid the difficulty.

It should be noted that in our example instead of having them use the word "prefer" we could have substituted "more probable" or "more important" and still have had the same situation. In general, the concepts denoted by the words "preference," "probability," or "importance" have a different connotation for a group than they do for an individual—so different that it is sometimes misleading to use the same words in the two situations. In the case of the individual they have to be transitive or we would judge the individual to be illogical or unbalanced; in the case of the committee there is no necessity for these concepts to have any transitive connotations.

Let me give another example of committee behavior that is both instructive and amusing.[1] Assume that the members of our com-

---

[1] This example is based on one given in *The Foundations of Statistics*, Leonard J. Savage, Wiley, New York, 1954, p. 207.

mittee go into a butcher shop. They want to pick out some meat for a picnic so they ask the butcher what he has available. He tells them he has turkey and ham. They consult for a few minutes and decide to get turkey. The butcher then notices that he also has chicken available. The committee goes into a new huddle and then decides that if he has chicken available, they no longer want turkey, they want ham. That is the way committees often act, and it may be a perfectly reasonable way to act. The reason the committee changed its mind was that one member of the committee really liked chicken and "sort of" preferred ham to turkey. Once chicken was available and he could not have it, he forced his colleagues to concede to him on the ham.

These two examples should illustrate that even conceptually it may be nonsense to talk of the *most important* objective, the *most probable* circumstance, or the *optimum* strategy, when "important," "probable" or "optimum" refer to a committee's utility function or estimate. If we are working for a committee we have to design satisfactory systems (including military systems) in the same way that legislators satisfy people as part of a political process. We have to have something in the chosen system for everyone who is "reasonable," and even something for some of the unreasonable people too. This is the sense of what we mean when we refer to a contingency design or contingency analysis. We cannot be fanatic and focus all of our attention on a numerically complicated but theoretically straightforward optimization calculation or the deduction of some best system from a few simple assumptions or postulates. In peacetime planning we must do the exact opposite of what the textbook recommends we do in war. During a war people cannot only force themselves to agree on objectives and circumstances, but the agreement itself is easier because both the objectives and the circumstances are relatively simple and certain. This is just not so in peacetime. How does this work out in practice?

Table 27 illustrates the problem. A, B, and C are either different circumstances or objectives; systems I, II, and III are designed to grapple with A, B, or C, respectively. The table gives a hypothetical scoring for how each of these systems might work in three different circumstances or objectives with a score of 100 for "best." While each of the three systems does admirably at the job for which it was designed, they all perform miserably at off-design points. If the problem were to choose between the given alternatives—that is, systems I, II, or III—both the analyst and the military planner would have a hopeless task as far as analysis goes—they could act as advocates, but not as objective students of the problem.

❖❖

TABLE 27
CONTINGENCY PLANNING

Objective or Circumstance	System					
	I	II	III	IV	V	VI
A	100	50	20	90	85	75
B	30	100	40	80	95	80
C	10	30	100	85	75	95

❖❖

Fortunately the situation is not so bad. It is usually possible to redesign systems I, II, and III into systems IV, V, and VI, which have appreciable off-design capabilities, without spectacular loss in performance in the highest priority position. Because the most extreme supporters of systems IV, V, and VI will still differ among themselves as to whether A, B, or C is most important, the argument may still be bitter. Futhermore, because the redesigned systems do not differ as spectacularly as the original ones did, the argument will probably be decided even more arbitrarily than would the original argument. This will make the losers even more bitter. That is, if the decision makers choose I over II, the supporter of II can console himself with the thought that this time the decision maker was misled into feeling A was more important than B and maybe next time the argument will come out differently. But if the decision makers choose IV over V, the difference between the two systems is so slight the supporter of V is forced to conclude that those in charge do not like him (i.e., the choice is less between systems than between "roles and missions"). However, any who are not severely partisan will not care much which system is chosen, so long as it is one of the collection of IV, V, and VI and not one of the collection of I, II, and III. It is not really the job of the analyst to advise directly on the choice problem. His major job is one of design—design to make the choice problem less agonizing. So long as he is an objective analyst, he does not really care as much which system is chosen as that the chosen system be one of the right set.

It is clear that we should prefer IV to I even if we do not happen to care much about B or C, because we understand that we are human and may be wrong. Even a fanatic about A will pretend to prefer system IV to system I because he does not want to look like a fanatic. Only a fanatic's fanatic is not willing to yield a *little* on his most cherished objective or worry in order to be able to give a *lot* to other people's cherished objectives or worries. Now what does all this mean in the context of this book?

In what follows I am going to ask the reader to go along with the notions I have just expressed. When I suggest designs for systems, and when I discuss their performance, I would like the reader to concede, at least for the sake of discussion, that *so long as every legitimate risk is taken into account, and every legitimate circumstance considered (being quite generous about how we define the word legitimate), then even though my emphasis may be different from his our quarrel is not serious. I am not asking the reader to agree with me precisely on the relative importance of all the things that I will compare, but only to understand and agree that my views and those of others should be considered seriously along with any purely "idiosyncratic" views he may have.* The reader as well as the planner should be willing to "give a little" on his most cherished objectives in order that others can gain a bit on the things they consider important.

It is important to realize that over-all planners must design from the beginning for the complete range of plausible objectives. In olden times, when the problems were simpler and events moved more slowly and the corrective effects of experience played a bigger role, it was possible to get good designs by a process of political compromise. Various individuals and groups advocated specific and often parochial systems, but as a result of the political give and take in the bureaucracy a design evolved which did embody concessions to the multiple objectives and estimates of everybody who had influence. This is no longer a feasible process. Technology and events move so fast that most trial and error processes become too catastrophe-prone to be satisfactory. It is therefore the responsibility of every designer to take seriously not only the problems and desires of his immediate superior, but also the problems and desires of all who have a right to influence the final decision. This is true of more than just intraservice rivalries. It is true in a larger political sense. For example, one must reconcile proposed solutions of military problems with those who desire arms control, relaxation of tension, and lower national budgets, *just as the exponents for these views should understand and appreciate the narrow military problems.*

There is another way in which we can have too narrow a focus. We can refuse to entertain or consider seriously ideas which seem to be "crack-pot" or unrealistic, but which are really just unfamiliar. In more casual days one could dismiss a bizarre-sounding notion with a snort or comment about being impractical or implausible. Things moved slowly, and no real harm was done if a new idea took several years to prove itself. Indeed, allowing a notion to stay around for several years before giving it serious intellectual attention meant that most of the "half-baked" ones got scuttled and never had to be considered seriously at all. The consequent saving on the use of both time and "gray matter" must have been enormous.

Today the situation is different. The world really is unstable. We have a revolution in military technology about once every five years. This means that the military planner who refuses to accept rapidly the unconventional implications of eagerly accepted unconventional gadgets is often one or two revolutions *behind* current technology. He has to be one or two revolutions *ahead* if he is to do successful planning. The only way for him to do this is to put time, energy, and thought into exploring unfamiliar and often, to the individual concerned, unpleasant or distasteful ideas.

Nothing in the above suggests that one should accept a new idea just because it is unfamiliar or glamorous. Historically, the conservative and "practical man" has been correct more often, particularly when one takes timing into account, than the radical or "dreamer." The problem is partly that the phenomena of modern war are such that the approach of the radical (theorist) is more appropriate than it ever has been, while the approach of the conservatives and practitioners has lost in effectiveness in such areas. There is a great dearth of people with experience in fighting thermonuclear wars; there is even a dearth of experience of how to conduct international relations in a world in which force is so much more available, and yet so much less usable. For some of the questions that arise, notions acquired as a result of experience in World War II or in the peacetime tasks of operations and adminstration can be worse than irrelevant; they can be *dangerously disaster prone.*

Peacetime Objectives of a Strategic Force

As the picture of horror of a modern thermonuclear war grows, we tend to consider weapons less and less usable, and we emphasize more and more their role in deterring an enemy, rather than their objective capability to punish or defend. That is, *we emphasize the impact of our capabilities on the enemy's mind rather than on his body.* This introduces many subtleties and some wishful thinking into discussions of modern war. En route, the word "deterrence" gets sadly misused. If one wishes to discuss deterrence precisely, then one should first specify all the alternatives available to the enemy, and then the various threats and promises we can make to influence his choice among these alternatives. Even for those occasions when one wishes to speak loosely and generally about deterrence, it is still important to distinguish clearly among different kinds of deterrent situations. I will emphasize in what follows three kinds of provocations, labeling them Type I, Type II, and Type III, respectively.

The Three Kinds of Deterrence

Type I Deterrence is the deterrence of a direct attack. It is widely believed that if the United States were directly attacked, its response would be automatic and unthinking. The British call this "passive deterrence" on the plausible, but possibly incorrect, assumption that it requires no act of will to respond to a violation. *Type II Deterrence* is defined as using strategic threats to deter an enemy from engaging in very provocative acts, other than a direct attack on the United States itself. The British call this "active deterrence" because it clearly takes an act of will to initiate. *Type III Deterrence* might be called "tit-for-tat," graduated, or controlled deterrence. It refers to acts that are deterred because the potential aggressor is afraid that the defender or others will then take limited actions, military or nonmilitary, that will make the aggression unprofitable.

One can visualize a hypothetical set of rules or a code as governing the permissible acts of nations and think of Type III Deterrence as covering provocations "within the rules" and therefore giving no cause to go outside the rules in reprisal. A failure of Type I or Type II Deterrence involves a "breaking of the code" and thus justifies and perhaps *demands* the most extreme reprisals. However, being within or without the rules will depend on more than just precedent, custom, and declaratory policy. The military and political situation will affect the interpretation. Such nuances are included in the definition.

❖❖❖

TABLE 28
PEACETIME OBJECTIVES OF A STRATEGIC FORCE

A. Deter Direct Attack
  1. Second Strike Capability
  2. Attacker's Defense
  3. Need for Quality
B. Deter Provocation
  1. Necessary and Feasible
  2. First Strike Capability
  3. Compatible with Arms Control
C. Not Look or Be Too Dangerous
  1. To Us
  2. To Allies
  3. To Neutrals
  4. To Enemy
D. Not Look or Be Too Expensive

❖❖❖

Our attention should be focused first on the peacetime objectives of a strategic force. Table 28 lists those of major interest. At the top of the list we have put the objective of deterring a direct attack. Most experts today argue that we must make this deterrence work, that we simply cannot face the possibility of a failure. Never have the stakes on success or failure of prevention been so high. Although I will attack the extreme view that deterrence is everything and that alleviation is hopeless, clearly Type I Deterrence must be our first priority.

In spite of (or possibly because of) the many words that are lavished on Type I Deterrence, most discussions of the conditions needed for such deterrence tend to be unrealistic. They rely more on assumption and wishful thinking than analysis. Typically, discussions of the capability of the United States to deter a direct attack compare the preattack inventory of our forces with the preattack inventory of the Soviet forces (i.e., the number of planes, missiles, army divisions, and submarines of the two countries are directly compared). This is a World War I and World War II approach. It can look very impressive in the columns of the Sunday newspaper or speeches of a leading statesman, but it can be very misleading.

The really essential numbers are *estimates of the damage the retaliatory forces can inflict after they have been hit and hit hard.* The most important calculation that is relevant in evaluating Type I Deterrence is the one we have previously mentioned; it is a Russian calculation in which the Russians hypothesize striking at a *time and with tactics of their choosing.* We strike back with a *damaged* and perhaps *uncoordinated* force, which must conduct its operations in the *postattack environment.* The Soviets may use *blackmail* threats to intimidate our response. The Russian defense is completely *alerted.* If the strike has been preceded by a tense period, their active defense forces would have been *augmented* and their cities would have been at least partially *evacuated.* (As explained later, this step does not necessarily give us strategic warning that is as useful as people sometimes think it should be.) Every one of the italicized words in this paragraph may be of vast significance, and yet most published analyses of Type I Deterrence ignore these possibilities.

The first step of this calculation—the analysis of the effects of the Russian strike on the U.S. ability to retaliate—depends critically upon the exact nature of the enemy's attack and on our corresponding capabilities. The question of warning and reaction is generally uppermost. Many analyses of the effect of the enemy's first strike neglect the most important part of the problem *by assuming that the defender's bombers and missiles were launched and sent on their way to the target.* But as we will point out in our third lecture when we discuss World Wars III, IV, and V, *this assumption may be the heart of the problem.* The weapons may be destroyed on the ground or not get the order to go ahead. The enemy may not only use tactics that limit our warning so that he can catch us on the ground, but he may also do other things to degrade our retaliatory blow, such as interfering with command and control arrangements. Thus it is important in evaluating enemy capabilities to look not only at the tactics and responses that past history and standard assumptions lead us to expect, but also at any other tactics that a clever enemy might use. We should not always assume what Albert

Wohlstetter has called "U.S. preferred attacks" in estimating the performance of our system. We should also look at "S.U. preferred attacks"—a sensible Soviet planner may prefer them.

The enemy, by choosing the timing of an attack, has several factors in his favor. First, he can choose a time when he is prepared and we are not. This does not mean that he necessarily plans years ahead of time to strike at some definite date in the future. It only means that as the cycle of military advantage passes to and fro, the aggressor is much more likely to be willing to make the decision to attack when he is ahead or losing an advantage than when he is behind or when he is still gaining. In addition the attacker can select a time of day calculated to force our manned bomber force to retaliate in the daytime, when his day fighters and his air defense systems will be much more effective, or he can choose the season of the attack so that his postwar agricultural problems and fallout protection problems will be less difficult.

The second part of the calculation—consequences of the lack of coordination of the surviving U.S. forces—depends greatly on our tactics and the flexibility of our plans. Much of our force may not get the order to go ahead. In addition, because we cannot predict which part of the force functions properly, there will be target misallocations. If, for example, our offensive force is assigned a large target system so that it is spread thinly, and if because of a large or successful Russian attack the Russians have succeeded in destroying much of our force, many important Russian targets would go unattacked. If, on the other hand, to avoid this we double or triple the assignment to important targets, we might over-destroy many targets, especially if the Soviets had not struck us successfully. For this and other reasons, it would be wise to evaluate the damage and then retarget the surviving forces. Whether this can be done depends critically on the timing of the attack, the nature of the targeting process, our postattack capability for evaluation, command, and control, and the things the enemy has done to prevent us from exercising command and control.

Our attack may also be degraded because of problems of grouping, timing, and refueling; in some instances our manned bombers might be forced to infiltrate in small groups into Soviet air territory and lose the advantage of saturation of the Soviet defenses. Whether or not this would be disastrous depends a great deal on the quality of the Russian air defense system, especially on whether it has any

129

holes we can exploit, and the kind and number of penetration aids we use. If the enemy has an anti-ICBM system, similar problems can arise with regard to missiles. The problem of penetrating active defenses in a retaliatory blow is complicated and classified, so I will not discuss it further here except to say that it may be much harder than the same problem in a first strike.

Another point that is of great importance and is often overlooked is that modern nuclear weapons are so powerful that even if they do not destroy their target, they may change the environment or damage critical equipment so as to cause important parts of the retaliating weapon system to be temporarily inoperable. The various effects of nuclear weapons include blast, heat, thermal and electromagnetic radiation, ground shock, debris, dust, and ionizing radiation—any of which may affect people, equipment, propagation of electromagnetic signals, and so on. One might say that the problem of operating in a postattack environment after training in the peacetime environment is similar to training at the equator and then moving a major but *unpredictably incomplete* part (that is, a damaged system) to the arctic and expecting this incomplete system to work efficiently the first time it is tried. This is particularly implausible if, as is often true, the intact system is barely operable at the equator (that is, in peacetime).

In addition to attacking the system, the enemy may attempt to attack our resolve. Imagine, for example, that we had a pure Polaris system invulnerable to an all-out simultaneous enemy attack (invulnerable by assumption and not by analysis), and the enemy started to destroy our submarines one at a time at sea. Suppose an American President were told that if we started an all-out war in retaliation the limitations on the Polaris system would make it unsuitable as a counterforce weapon and our active and passive defenses are so weak the Soviets could and probably would destroy every American. Now if the President has a chance to think about the problem, he simply cannot initiate this kind of war even with such provocation. Against even stronger strategic postures there will still be opportunities for using postattack coercion. In some cases it will cost the Soviets nothing to use tactics combined with threats which, if they work, will greatly alleviate their military problems; if they do not work, the situation will be almost unchanged anyway. I will discuss later some of the timing, control, communication, and persuasion problems involved in making different kinds of postattack coercion feasible.

One of the most important and yet the most neglected elements of the retaliatory calculation is the effect of the Soviet civil defense measures. The Soviets are seldom credited even in calculations by experts with even the most simple and primitive civil defense preparations or capabilities. Analysts sometimes go so far as to assume that peacetime civilian activities will continue on a business-as-usual basis, hours after Soviet missiles or planes have been dispatched, worrying, for example, about conventional day-night variations in population tens of hours after the war has started.

I have seen many calculations that assumed that Russian bombers take off and some ten hours or so later drop their bombs; our bombers then take off and drop their bombs, some ten or twenty hours after the Soviets have dropped their bombs. While each Russian may be given credit for having sought the best protection in his immediate neighborhood, it is somehow assumed that he is still pursuing his normal routine and is at his post office address or place of work or in transit between (probably waiting for his newspaper to tell him the results of the attack). He has never, in these calculations, evacuated to improvised or prepared fallout protection outside the immediate target area, nor is he even on his way to such protection. I have even seen calculations which did not give the Russians credit for enough sense to take "duck and cover" precautions a dozen or more hours after the war had started. *Not giving the Soviets credit for rather obvious measures is a continuing weakness of U.S. and of Western calculations generally.* This is not only ridiculous, it is also symptomatic of a certain lack of realism and of the prevalent tendency toward underestimating the enemy, especially since Soviet civil defense manuals (see Lecture III, pages 440 to 442) indicate that the Soviets are making reasonable preparations for protecting themselves. The Soviets claim to have given every adult in the Soviet Union between 20 and 40 hours of instruction in civil defense, followed by a compulsory examination. Perhaps most important of all, their program seems to include preparations for evacuation to improvised fallout protection. How effective would such an evacuation be?

About 50 million Russians live in the 135 largest Soviet cities. If, say, 80 per cent of these 50 million were evacuated to their B country and the remainder were left to operate the cities, all essential functions could be maintained while exposing only about 10 million citizens. Also, having evacuated most of the urban population, they could evacuate those remaining with comparative ease. So long as our ICBM force is small, the Soviets would not even have to execute the evacuation before they launched an attack, since they would have time to do so before our retaliatory force reached the majority of their cities.

Under these circumstances, if the Russians should strike first and be reasonably successful, our retaliation attack would not kill more than 5 or 10 million Russians and probably considerably fewer —unless things went inexplicably badly for them. Thus they might lose only a fraction as many people as they lost in World War II.

The Soviets also know that they can take an enormous amount of economic damage and be set back only a few years in their development. Not only did they do something like this after World War II, but what is even more impressive, they fought a war *after* the Germans had destroyed most of their existing military power and occupied an area that contained about 40 per cent of the prewar Soviet population—the most industrialized 40 per cent. According to Soviet estimates, by the time the war ended they had lost about one-third of their wealth—almost the proportion we would lose if we lost all of the A country. The Soviets rebuilt the destroyed wealth in about six years. Moreover, since 1931 they have had a vigorous program to disperse their industry, a program that seems to have been stepped up since World War II. It is quite likely that their B country (small cities, towns, farms) is at least as capable of restoring society as ours is.

In a particularly tense situation the Soviets could deliberately evacuate their A country in order to put pressure on us. Such an evacuation would make it credible that they might go to war unless we backed down. While this would give us a sort of warning, we might not act on it. We might refuse resolutely to be "bluffed." Unless we were willing to accept a Soviet retaliatory blow, the only practicable counteraction that we would have would be to back down or to put our Strategic Air Command on alert and hope that this action would be enough to deter them. The other possibility— to assume that they did not mean what they seemed to mean—might be too risky. If we wished to be in a good bargaining position we would probably have to evacuate our own cities. (We have made almost no realistic preparations for such a step.)

Evacuation-type maneuvers are risky because they may touch off an attack by the other side. But so far as the Soviets are concerned the probability of such an attack by us is small, particularly because we have made negligible preparations to ward off, survive, and recover from even a "small" Soviet retaliatory strike. No matter how menacing they look, it will be irrational to attack and thus insure a Soviet retaliation unless we have made preparations to counter this retaliation. If our Credible First Strike Capability is weak, they might accept the risk. They would then be in a relatively good position to go to war if we did not attack or back down. As I shall try to illustrate later, the Soviets could risk this tactic in any circumstances in which Khrushchev finds the risks of not going to war comparable to those of going to war.

All of the above leads us quite naturally into the next topic on Table 28, "*How high a quality deterrent does a country need? What kind of strains should the deterrent be able to resist?*" After all, even if the Soviets could survive a retaliatory blow, it is most unlikely that they would be willing to repeat their World War I or II experiences. Both of these were extraordinarily unpleasant times for both the government and the people.

In the first lecture, I pointed out that it was quite conceivable that the Soviet deterrent force could be so good and our offense plus civil and air defense so bad that we might be deterred from attacking the Soviet heartland even to avenge a Soviet attack on Europe; it is even conceivable that the Soviets might have such confidence in their Type I Deterrence that they might be willing to subject it in cold blood to this kind of strain. Under some circumstances the balance of terror might not be symmetrical. For one thing the Soviets, being more dispersed and less industrialized than we, are intrinsically less vulnerable. (For example, our ten largest metropolitan areas contain about 50 million people. The ten largest Soviet metropolitan areas probably have less than half as much.) Not only are the Soviets intrinsically less vulnerable, they are doing things to reduce their vulnerability. They seem to have or are acquiring a civil defense program that is of somewhat higher quality than the one recommended later (Appendix IV) for the United States. In addition, it is often stated that they have spent from two to three times as much as we have on air defense. Last and most important, there is some question about how fast the Soviets are advancing in offensive technology and capability and if we are reacting rapidly enough to these possible changes (i.e., the alleged missile gap) so that our SAC may both be more vulnerable to this attack and less effective on the offense in the counterforce missions. For all these reasons there may well be circumstances other than a U.S. attack on the Soviet heartland in which the Soviet Union might be willing to attack the United States and accept our retaliatory blow, while the converse may not be true. What these circumstances are depends on their alternatives, that is, upon a comparison of the risks they run by attacking as opposed to the risks incurred by pursuing some other alternative.

It is important to state the Soviet calculation in this form and to use the term "risk" rather than the logically equivalent term "gain" (a risk is a negative gain). Phrasing the question in terms of choosing between unpleasant alternatives makes it plain that a force sufficient to deter in times of peace might not be sufficient to deter under certain conditions of stress or crisis when not attacking might also look dangerous—that Type I Deterrence could fail if a situation arises in which the other side feels there is a reasonable probability that the damage it suffers will be less than losses incurred by not fighting. One could expect the calculation to be made conservatively (in the sense that governments will tend to choose an inert strategy over a dramatic change). In fact, in most circumstances the U.S.S.R. might well be deterred from starting a war just by the threat of losing Leningrad and Moscow, as these cities appear to play a more central role in the Soviet Union than even Washington and New York do in the United States. While an intelligence briefing on Soviet intentions might start out with the remark that the Russians seek world domination, Khrushchev probably does not want it in the immediate future even at such a relatively low price. He may want it and want it very much, but not enough (we hope) to start a war in cold blood—at least not unless we have been incredibly careless.

If Khrushchev is as cautious as I have indicated he may be, then if he starts a thermonuclear war, he will probably start it because he is under some great pressure—because a situation actually has arisen in which the risks of not going to war loom larger in his eyes than the risks associated with going to war. Let me give an example of such a possibility, which seems quite realistic to me. In 1956 the Hungarians had a revolution which the Soviets suppressed very harshly. There was a lot of pressure on the United States to intervene. We did not. In fact, there are reports that we did exactly the opposite, by broadcasting to the Poles and East Germans not to "rock the boat," since no American aid was on the way. But let us assume that we had intervened. The Russians would then have been faced with three fairly serious choices.

1. *They might have done nothing.* This would almost automatically have meant a Polish and East German revolt. (They almost revolted, anyway, without any hopes of American aid.) Such a revolt would have been a serious event in itself, and it would also have caused serious repercussions inside Russia. We do not know how serious these repercussions would have been, but we know that Russians worry about internal political stability. While many Soviet experts think that the Soviet regime would be stable enough to ride out such a revolt, these same experts usually do not believe the Soviet government has such confidence in its internal stability. The Soviet government might have considered such a satellite revolt as having intolerably serious consequences.

2. *They might have fought a limited action.* But that would have brought its own risks. The satellites were still likely to revolt. In addition, if we fought a limited action and stuck with conventional high-explosive weapons we would have lost just by the weight of numbers, and the Soviets could then have asked, "Why did we intervene in a self-defeating way? Perhaps we were planning to widen the area of the conflict?" If we had gone to atomic weapons at a high enough level to give the Soviets a serious fight (as our preparations and announcements suggested we might try to do), it would have been even harder for many on both sides to believe that the war could stay limited. How could we have used nuclear weapons successfully without either going to the self-defeating level of destroying Hungary, or taking the risky and provocative course of attacking Soviet logistic and military support areas? Nuclear weapons could only have been successful and yet very limited if our use frightened the Soviets with the idea that we were prepared to go further if they resisted effectively (i.e., we are presenting the Soviets with the alternative of a resistance on our terms or a possibility that the violence will escalate into World War III). Under these circumstances, it should not surprise us if the Soviet decision makers viewed the prospect of a limited conventional or atomic war close to their heartland as intolerably dangerous. If the Soviets were to reply in kind they might easily have believed that they still ran great risks of a satellite revolt and that in addition the Americans were capable

of expanding the scope of the war with a surprise attack at their strategic forces. Such considerations might have led them to their third alternative.

3. The third possibility might have appeared safer to the Soviets. Rather than wait for the satellites to revolt or for the limited war to erupt into a general war at a time chosen by the Americans, *they might have decided to hit us right away.* They could argue that this would guarantee them the all-important first strike, *at least if they hurried.*

This last is a very important remark. Most governments when asked to choose between war and peace are likely to choose peace, because it looks safer. These same governments if asked to choose between getting the first or the second strike will very likely choose the first strike. They will do so for the same reason they chose peace in the first choice; it is safer. All theories of Finite Deterrence and automatic mutual annihilation to the contrary, most governments would much prefer getting in the first strike once they feel war is inevitable, or even very probable. However, there is a fortunate stabilizing effect. As I will discuss in Lecture III when I discuss World Wars I and II, most governments are extremely loath to go to war at a time not of their choosing and in a crisis are deperately anxious to believe that war is not inevitable. Nevertheless, the element of instability remains. As soon as either side thinks that war is probable it is under pressure to pre-empt. I will point out later that the instability is increased by the "reciprocal fear of surprise attack," in which each side feels a pressure to strike mainly because it feels the other side has exactly the same pressure.

I am not saying that U.S. intervention in Hungary would have inevitably resulted in a Soviet attack on the U.S. From the end of 1956 on, our ability to deter Soviet attacks on the United States probably reached a peak, which should not decay appreciably unless the Soviets obtain a significant number of ICBM's before we have made counter-preparations. I am just saying intervention would have been dangerous both because the strain on the Soviets would have been greater than some Western experts realized and because the Soviets are not quite as vulnerable to retaliatory strikes following a crisis situation as we like to think.

It is possible that a situation as potentially dangerous as the Hungarian revolt could arise again. We could get deeply, if involuntarily, involved. If any events of this sort ever happen, our Type I

Deterrent must be so good that even if the Soviets evacuate their cities they will feel that a strike by them would be more risky than accepting whatever alternative seems to be in store. As I will discuss later, it may be much more difficult to achieve this capability in the 1960–75 period than many suppose.

Some readers may find the Hungarian scenario unconvincing. They may find it hard to believe that we would ever, willingly or unwillingly, intervene in such a crisis, or they may not believe that even in such circumstances the Soviets would be under great pressure to attack us. I do not at this point have too much of a quarrel with the first group, since I am trying to suggest that if we have a weak Type I Deterrent there are many provocative or strong actions which we would or should fear to take because they might strain our Type I Deterrence to the failure point. However, I will try to point out later that situations can exist in which we may want to, or even have to, take such actions, and we will then desperately want a high enough quality Type I Deterrent to make taking such action safe. I challenge the second group (those who believe that intervention in a satellite revolution or similar crisis could not strain our Type I Deterrence) to make up their own scenarios. It is not really very hard if one puts one's imagination to work. I would suggest as possible examples to be considered a U.S.–Chinese war in which Siberia and Japan had been sanctuaries but were about to be violated. Or, there could be a large Middle East war, in which first Turkey and then Russia got involved. A drawn-out revolt in East Germany, in which the West Germans felt obligated to aid their countrymen, might take place. A second Polish revolution which also stimulated a revolt in East Germany could occur. Yugoslavia could get embroiled in a conflict with the East—or with the West. Even the relatively docile Czechs or Bulgarians could cause trouble.

History has a habit of being richer and more ingenious than the limited imaginations of most scholars or laymen. Few, if any, would have predicted, for example, the course of events in either the Polish or the Hungarian uprisings. Rather the opposite: many wrote that such things could not occur. Even fewer would have predicted, in 1930, the kinds of challenges the Germans actually gave the British and French in 1938 and 1939 (or the reaction of the British and French)—challenges which did eventually induce the relatively pacifistic British and French to declare war.

The point is that we should not evaluate our Type I Deterrence

137

by its ability to deter a complacent and cautious enemy. Even a frown might do that. Our attitude should be the same as an engineer's when he puts up a structure designed to last twenty years or so. He does not ask, "Will it stand up on a pleasant June day?" He asks how it performs under stress, under hurricane, earthquake, snow load, fire, flood, thieves, fools, and vandals. Even if he is an optimist and does not wish to consider the "worst case," he still asks, "Viewing the next twenty years optimistically, what is the worst load this building will have to survive and what is the minimum factor of safety that I can design into the building and still feel safe?" Deterrence is at least as important as a building, and we should have the same attitude toward our deterrent systems. We may not be able to predict the loads it will have to carry, but we can be certain there will be loads of unexpected or implausible severity.

Type II Deterrence (Deterrence of Extreme Provocations)

The first question that comes up when Type II Deterrence is discussed is, "Does the U.S. really wish to have a Credible First Strike Capability? Is it really true that we may get into trouble unless we have this capability to initiate a thermonuclear war?" I tried to make clear in Lecture I that there are many occasions in which the enemy can do things which no limited reaction on our part can possibly alleviate satisfactorily. Let me give another illustration. Consider the possibility that limited war capabilities may be able to handle our problem. The question then immediately comes up: "How do you limit the limited war?" If, for example, we are trying to defend Burma by using some sort of limited capabilities, either conventional high-explosive or small atomic weapons, and the enemy starts using multimegaton bombs on us, either in retaliation for our use of small atomic weapons, or simply because he does not care to lose the war. He might end up by destroying Burma totally. There could be some Americans who would then believe we had defended Burma successfully on the grounds that we did not really care whether Burma was with us or not—"She meant no real addition to our strength." These Americans only care if the Communist bloc has acquired Burma as a going concern, because unlike us, the Communist bloc has been able to exploit countries such as Burma to add military strength and mischief-making capability to their arsenal.

Now, there are at least two groups of people who will disagree with this notion that we can claim a success in the limited war even if Burma is accidentally or deliberately destroyed. First, of course, the Burmese. Secondly, Burma's neighbors. For example, India. The question that would arise in the governments of these neighbors would not be, "Should we invite the Americans to defend us?" The answer to that question has already been settled. The only question that could arise would be, "What arrangements can we make ahead of time in order to prevent an American defense?" It may, of course, turn out in practice that limited wars are self-limiting. Finite Deterrence advocates often argue that this would be so because there is what might be called a "residual fear of war" left even in a seemingly reliable balance-of-terror situation and that this residual fear of war would deter the other side from starting a process that could lead to escalation. This argument is often made by people who wish to escalate a little themselves, but somehow feel that the other side would not be willing to go one step further. I agree that a residual fear of war will probably exist; all I am denying is that it is of the right type or exactly the right amount to solve our problems. It may turn out that we may want to manipulate this fear of war—to have less or more. It seems quite clear to me that in the world of the future we must pay attention to this problem or find ourselves facing a series of Munichs, "Rotterdams," [2] and "Hachas" [2] not so much because the other side is so nasty (though on many occasions it has been), but simply because we are so vulnerable to this tactic that we are almost inviting it, and when one asks for something like this one oftens gets what he asks for. In any case, a crisis can come unwilled by either side, and if we have no effective threats to make, if a continuation and exacerbation of the crisis looks safe, then the other side may not feel under any pressure to compromise his position.

A quite different calculation is relevant to U.S. Type II Deterrence, than to U.S. Type I Deterrence, although it is still a Soviet calculation (but this time a Soviet calculation of an American calculation). The Soviet planner asks himself, "If I make this very provocative move, will the Americans strike us?" Whether the Soviets then proceed with the contemplated provocation will be

[2] These events are discussed on pages 528 and 403. The Germans destroyed Rotterdam as an example to other cities not to resist and they forced Hacha, the President of Czechoslovakia, to surrender without resistance in March 1939 by threatening to destroy Czechoslovakia before the allies could rescue it.

influenced by their estimate of the American calculation as to what happens if the tables are reversed. That is, what happens if the Americans strike and damage the Russian strategic air force, and the Russians strike back, uncoordinated, in the teeth of an alerted U.S. air defense and possibly against an evacuated U.S. population? If this possibility is to be credible to the Soviets, it must be because they recognize that their own Type I Deterrence can fail. If Khrushchev is a convinced adherent of the balance-of-terror theory and does not believe that his Type I Deterrence can fail, then he may just go ahead with whatever provocative but profitable action he may contemplate.

It is important to realize that the operation of Type II Deterrence will involve the possibility that the United States will obtain the first strategic strike or make some temporizing move, such as evacuation. Many people talk about the importance of having adequate civil and air defense to back our foreign policy. However, calculations made in evaluating the performance of a proposed civil and air defense program invariably assume a Russian surprise attack and, to make the problem even harder, a surprise attack directed mostly against civilians. This is unnecessarily pessimistic. The calculation in which one looks at a U.S. first strike in retaliation for a Russian provocation is probably more relevant in trying to evaluate the role that the offense and defense play in effecting some important aspects of foreign policy.

Under this assumption, if we have even a moderate nonmilitary defense program, its performance is likely to look impressive to the Russians, and probably to most Europeans. For example, the crucial problem of obtaining adequate warning will have been greatly lessened, at least in the eyes of the Soviets. They are also likely to think that we have more freedom than we will have. The Soviets may believe that we are not worried by the possibility that they will get strategic or premature tactical warning. This could be true in spite of the fact that in actual practice such an attack would probably involve a considerable risk that the Soviets would get some warning. Any planning would have to be tempered by the sobering realization that a disclosure or mistake could bring a pre-emptive Russian attack.

The possibility of augmenting our active and passive defense is very important. That is, rather than striking the Russians if they do something very provocative, we might prefer to evacuate our city population to fallout protection, "beef up" our air defense and air offense, and then tell the Russians that we had put ourselves into a much stronger position to initiate hostilities. After we had put ourselves in a position in which the Russian retaliatory strike would inflict much less than a total catastrophe, the Russians would have just three broad classes of alternatives:

1. To initiate some kind of strike.

2. To prolong the crisis, even though it would then be very credible that we would strike if they continued to provoke us.

3. To back down or compromise the crisis satisfactorily.

Hopefully the Soviets would end up preferring the third alternative, because our Type I Deterrence would make the first choice sufficiently unattractive and our Type II Deterrence would do the same for the second.

It is important to note that we do not have to have super alert or trigger-happy forces for Type II Deterrence. There is no need to promise to destroy the enemy within fifteen minutes. It is perfectly all right to promise to destroy him somewhat later. This means that the forces needed for Type II Deterrence may still be quite compatible with many important and desirable arms control measures intended to reduce the danger of a surprise attack or the possibility of an accidental war. In fact, the first thing one would do, if one was sufficiently provoked, would be to denounce the arms control agreement. I will try to make the point in Lecture III that even medium-term defense policies must be compatible with arms control agreements if these policies are to be satisfactory. I am now making the point that having quite competent Credible First Strike Capabilities for use in Type II Deterrence, particularly capabilities which will exploit the augmentation capabilities we have just mentioned, is quite compatible with various agreements to lessen the danger of accidental war or surprise attack.

It is also important to note that it is possible for two opponents simultaneously to possess reasonably satisfactory levels of both Type I and Type II Deterrence. Let us define this situation as Multistable Deterrence (to distinguish it from the Stable Deterrent situation—which term implies symmetrical Type I Deterrence and no Type II Deterrence). A sample Multistable Deterrent situation could be the following:

1. That an attacking nation, if it directed most of its surprise attack at the enemy's civilians and recuperative ability, could destroy the defender totally, but in doing so it would either have given re-

liable warning to the defender's retaliatory capability or damaged it so little that with the remaining force the defender could either destroy or grievously hurt the attacker.

2. That if the attacking nation concentrated its attack on the enemy's retaliatory force, it automatically gives, say, 75 per cent of the enemy civilians enough warning to get to shelter, and that even the other 25 per cent (if there are elaborate shelters available) have some chance. This is a reasonable assumption since it is tactically difficult, given probable constraints imposed by warning, salvo capability, and deployment considerations, to attack all of even these most vulnerable civilians at the same moment that the defender's retaliatory force is attacked.

3. That even when the attacker concentrates on destroying the defender's strategic forces, the attacker cannot be completely successful. The defender's retaliation, when completely directed against the attacker's recuperative capabilities, could kill about 10 per cent of the attacker's civilians and destroy about one-third of his wealth. (For future systems, say a decade or so hence, this probably assumes that the attacker has: (1) succeeded in getting in an annihilating first strike, (2) built an adequate shelter system for people and capital, (3) evacuated his cities, or (4) has successfully used what I have called postattack coercion to limit the retaliatory blow. In addition to suffering the immediate damage, the attacker should be able to handle all the postwar effects with about the efficiency suggested in Lecture I.

4. That the capabilities described above are symmetrical.

Under these circumstances it is clear that neither nation would be likely to initiate an attack against the other in cold blood. Losing 10 per cent of one's population and one-third of one's wealth is a very frightening prospect, even if one can console oneself with the thought that the enemy has been eliminated. And if one gives full credit to the inevitable uncertainty in the calculations regarding performance during the war and recuperation afterward, it is an even more ferocious thing to contemplate. The threat of such a catastrophe would clearly deter in most circumstances. However, it is not an absolute deterrence. In fact, the assumed losses happen to be rather close to the amount the Russians actually suffered in World War II. It is true that they did not make a deliberate and conscious choice between the two alternatives of acquiescing or accepting the kind of damage they suffered. Still, it is quite probable that they would have preferred accepting that damage (hoping to conquer the Germans) to not accepting it—that is, accepting immediate defeat instead. Given the nature of the Nazi regime, it also seems quite reasonable that the choice would have been correct. A similar situation in the sense of choosing between awful alternatives could arise. This means that while neither of the two nations described in the assumptions would be likely to start a war in cold blood, it would still be risky to be extremely provocative or to let an unwilled crisis develop too far. After all, it is just possible that the provoked nation would then decide that it preferred eliminating the source of the provocation, and accepting the damage inflicted by the retaliatory blow, to living with the consequences of the provocation. It also means that even though it lost the war, the defending nation would have gotten a great deal of benefit out of its Counterforce as Insurance capabilities.

I will try to indicate in the next section that if deterrence fails and a war breaks out there is a reasonable possibility that the damage level might not be as great as we have assumed. If the attacker is sensible he will avoid the defender's cities, civilians, and recuperative capability in order to maximize his postattack blackmail threats. The defender, if enough of his force has survived, will presumably try to use it to get a bargaining advantage.

The symmetrical state described in the assumptions is not a prediction that the military situation will be as described, though I think that something like that condition could be achieved if both sides put enough resources and intelligence into prewar preparations. It has been described only to illustrate that it is theoretically possible for two opponents simultaneously to have reasonably satisfactory levels of Type I and Type II Deterrence. If I had to predict what was going to happen, I would probably conjecture that we will procure a "Finite or Minimum Deterrence" offense force and a completely inadequate active and passive defense, while the Russians will presumably pursue something between Counterforce as Insurance and Credible First Strike, so that the actual situation may become very asymmetrical, indeed.

The symmetrical deterrent situation that we have just described can be thought of as a deterrent situation which has a three-way stability. It is stable against first strike because the retaliation, while not annihilating, is certainly cataclysmic enough to deter in most circumstances (particularly since if the calculations go astray the retaliation may turn out to be annihilating). It is stable against extreme provocation. Both sides have a Credible First Strike Capability—good enough so that the calculated consequences of use are comparable to recorded (and recovered from) events. This means that each side can conceivably be provoked into an attack. It also has some moderate stability against small provocations because both sides will realize that small provocations can lead to large ones and because an increase in tension could lead to an acceleration of the arms race; in particular, any Preattack Mobilization Bases might be activated. (The arms race has a strategic significance here because it is not true that both sides can overkill the target so that an increase in the size or quality of active or passive, offensive or defensive forces will affect the outcome of a war and the reliability of the deterrent.) Lastly, it should be stable against accidents. The accidental war is the one war in which both sides are most likely to get destroyed, partly because the first strike uses only the alert part of the force and partly because the war plans are likely to be inappropriate. This means that both sides should be careful. In addition, the deterrence against extreme and even moderate provocation means that the kind of tense situation in which the two sides are most likely to be accident prone is less likely to come up than a situation in which extreme provocations are not deterred. In addition to having a three-way stability, the above posture has a considerable capability to alleviate the consequences, if stability fails and war or provocation occur.

The situation has two major instabilities, however. One, it encourages an arms race, since improvements in numbers and quality are of significance. Secondly, in most postures that do not involve automatic mutual annihilation there will be an advantage in striking first. (There is no logical necessity that this be true. One could imagine a situation in which the attacker used up more resources than he destroyed, but I think of such a situation as being technologically improbable unless one or both sides have deliberately accepted weak postures or tactical restraints.) We will consider the significance of both instabilities later in this chapter.

Not Look or Be Too Dangerous

I would like to start this section on "not looking or being too dangerous" with some comments on the strategic theory of three con-

144

ceptualized devices, which I will call the Doomsday Machine, the Doomsday-in-a-Hurry Machine, and the Homicide Pact Machine. Discussing these idealized (almost caricaturized) devices will both focus attention on the most spectacular and ominous possibilities and *clarify a good deal of current strategic thinking*. A Doomsday weapons system might be imaginatively (and entirely hypothetically) described as follows: Assume that for, say, $10 billion we could build a device whose only function is to destroy all human life.[3] The device is protected from enemy action (perhaps by being put thousands of feet underground) and then connected to a computer which is in turn connected, by a reliable communication system, to hundreds of sensory devices all over the United States. The computer would then be programmed so that if, say, five nuclear bombs exploded over the United States, the device would be triggered and the earth destroyed. Barring such things as coding errors (an important technical consideration) the above machine would seem to be the "ideal" Type I Deterrent. If Khrushchev should order an attack, both Khrushchev and the Soviet population would be automatically and efficiently annihilated. (The emphasis is deliberate. This deterrent is more efficient since in most practical cases deterrents destroy populations—not decision makers.)

Even though it is the ultimate in Type I Deterrence, the Doomsday Machine is an unsatisfactory basis for a weapon system. It is most improbable that either the Soviet or U.S. governments would ever authorize procuring such a machine. The project is expensive enough so it would be subject to a searching budgetary and operational scrutiny—a scrutiny which would raise questions it could never survive.

Before considering these questions, let us discuss how one might adapt the Doomsday Machine to Type II and Type III Deterrent purposes. For reasons that will become clear, I would like to call this model the Doomsday-in-a-Hurry Machine. The computer would be given all the facilities it would need to be "well informed" about world affairs. We could then unilaterally legislate into existence a

---

[3] While I would not care to guess the exact form that a reasonably efficient Doomsday Machine would take, I would be willing to conjecture that if the project were started today and sufficiently well supported one could have such a machine by 1970. I would also guess that the cost would be between 10 and 100 billion dollars. Even then it might not be possible to destroy groups of especially well-prepared people. The mechanism used would most likely not involve the breaking up of the earth, but the creation of really large amounts of radioactivity or the causing of major climatic changes or, less likely, the extreme use of thermal effects.

Soviet (or Chinese) Criminal Code. This would list in great detail all the acts which the Soviets were not allowed to commit. The Soviets would then be informed that if the computer detects them in any violations it will blow up the world. The logicians (and some so-called practical men) might then believe that we had solved all of our deterrence problems. After all, we will now have drawn a line across which the Soviets would not dare to cross. We could relax forever our interest in defense and turn our attention to other matters.

Unfortunately, the world is not that simple. First, the Soviets would rush to build their own machine. There would be a rather hectic race to publish first. This race to publish first involves more than prestige. There almost has to be an incompatibility between the two sets of rules, since paragraph one of each probably states that the opponent shall not build a Doomsday Machine! To many people, to build a Doomsday Machine would be the most provoking thing short of an attack that the opponent could do. In fact, because it may destroy so many people, some find it more provoking than an attack. It should also be noted that even if we succeed in publishing first, and even if the Soviets believe our machine will work as advertised and are deterred from publishing, trouble is still almost certain. It will simply turn out in practice that it is impossible to draw a useful and unambiguous line for most Type III situations—it may even be difficult to draw an unambiguous line for all possible Type I and Type II situations. The first time there is a difference in interpretation, the world will be blown up.

Let us examine the use of both imaginary Doomsday Machines as deterrents in more detail. Table 29 lists some desirable characteristics of a deterrent.

❖❖

TABLE 29

DESIRABLE CHARACTERISTICS OF A DETERRENT

1. Frightening	4. Cheap
2. Inexorable	5. Nonaccident prone
3. Persuasive	6. Controllable

❖❖

As far as the first five characteristics are concerned, both of the Doomsday Machines are likely to be better than any current or proposed competitor for deterrence. They are as *frightening* as any-

146

thing that can be devised. They are more *inexorable* since they can be made almost invulnerable to direct physical destruction (electromagnetic waves which would set them off go faster than shock waves which might destroy the device); the operation is in principle so simple and reliable that one can really believe it will work (as opposed to some complex weapon system which requires the split-second coordination and almost perfect operation of many complex parts in a strange postattack environment); and the automaticity eliminates the human element, including any possibility of a loss of resolve as a result of either humanitarian consideration or threats by the enemy.

The machines are certainly *persuasive*. Even an idiot should be able to understand their capabilities. Most likely such machines would be *cheap* compared to present weapons expenditures.

Finally, they are probably relatively *foolproof*, in the sense that the probability of an accidental or unauthorized triggering should be low—that is, while the possibility of an unauthorized or accidental use of such a machine will, in spite of all precautions, be too high to be acceptable, it will still be lower than the probability of such an action in complicated and dispersed systems as Polaris, Minuteman, airborne alert, and so on. The Doomsday weapon system is so simple that one can see clearly most of the places where trouble can occur, and one can take all possible precautions.

The difficulties lie in item 6 of Table 29. The Doomsday Machine is not sufficiently *controllable*. Even though it maximizes the probability that deterrence will work (including minimizing the probability of accidents or miscalculations), it is totally unsatisfactory. One must still examine the consequences of a failure. In this case a failure kills too many people and kills them too automatically. There is no chance of human intervention, control, and final decision. And even if we give up the computer and make the Doomsday Machine reliably controllable by the decision makers, it is still not controllable enough. Neither NATO nor the United States, and possibly not even the Soviet Union, would be willing to spend billions of dollars to give a few individuals this particular kind of life and death power over the entire world.

If one were presenting a military briefing advocating some special weapons systems as a deterrent and examined only the first five qualities on the list, the Doomsday Machine might seem better than any alternative system. Nevertheless, the Doomsday Machine is unacceptable. This could imply that either some of the weapons systems currently being proposed are also unacceptable, or that the way we talk about these weapons systems is wrong—very likely both. Most decision makers, if forced to choose between accommodation to the point of surrender, a large risk of surprise attack, and buying a Doomsday Machine, would choose one of the first two as against the last one.

I have been surprised at the unanimity with which the notion of the unacceptability of a Doomsday Machine is greeted. I used to be wary of discussing the concept for fear that some colonel would get out a General Operating Requirement or Development Planning Objective for the device, but it seems that I need not have worried. Except by some scientists and engineers who have overemphasized the single objective of maximizing the effectiveness of deterrence, the device is universally rejected. It just does not look professional to senior military officers, and it looks even worse to senior civilians. The fact that more than a few scientists and engineers do seem attracted to the idea is disquieting, but as long as the development project is expensive, even these dedicated experts are unlikely to get one under way.

To the extent that the Department of Defense and the Executive Office are interested in getting support for budgets and proposals, they should make it very clear that they are not advocating Doomsday Machines in any form. The closer a weapons system is to a Doomsday Machine, the less satisfactory it becomes. The military people may have hurt their case by appearing (often inadvertently) to be oblivious to the Doomsday aspect of some of the public discussions of the military problem. They have also looked parochial to many observers, for some of the time they seem to advocate the most narrow and shortsighted views rather than show a concern with the over-all security of the United States or the Free World. For example, some of the talk about using "quality" weapons for occasions when they are clearly inappropriate automatically gives an appearance of callousness to such larger issues as the importance of preserving the implicit agreement not to use nuclear weapons or the legitimate fear of escalation. (Both of these problems are discussed later.)

Attempts to use the threat of all-out nuclear war to deter minor provocations are even more disturbing, looking much like the Doomsday-in-a-Hurry Machine. I would agree with these objections. Any attempts to get security cheaply by the use of even sanitized versions of the Doomsday-in-a-Hurry Machine are likely to cause more harm than good, to create more insecurity than security. To the extent that the appearance of a narrow professional approach images reality, the parochialism itself is dangerous and should arouse hostile reaction. To the extent that the appearance is illusory, our military leaders are unnecessarily hurting their case. If military leaders (including senior civilians) expect to exert the influence on these issues that they should, they must make it clear that they are speaking from a viewpoint of over-all national and human interests first; and they must examine their programs from time to time from this same position. In my opinion, they do this more often than they are given credit for, but less often than they should.

The unacceptability of the Doomsday Machine raises awkward, unpleasant, and complicated questions that must be considered by both policy maker and technician. If it is not acceptable to risk the lives of the three billion inhabitants of the earth in order to protect ourselves from surprise attack, then *how many people would we be willing to risk?* I believe that both the United States and NATO would reluctantly be willing to envisage the *possibility* of one or two hundred million people (i.e., about five times more than World War II deaths) dying from the immediate effects, even if one does not include deferred long-term effects due to radiation, if an all-out thermonuclear war results from a failure of Type I Deterrence. With somewhat more controversy, similar numbers would apply to Type II Deterrence. (For example, some experts would concede the statement for an all-out Soviet nuclear attack on Europe, but not if the Soviets restricted themselves to the use of conventional weapons.) We are willing to live with the possibility partly because we think of it as a remote possibility. We do not expect either kind of deterrence to fail, and we do not expect the results to be that cataclysmic if deterrence does fail. However, even those who expect deterrence to work might hesitate at introducing a new weapon system that increased the reliability of deterrence, but at the cost of increasing the possible casualties by a factor of 10, that is, there would then be one or two billion hostages at risk if their expectations fail. Neither the 180 million Americans nor even the half billion people in the NATO alliance should or would be willing to design and procure a security system in which a malfunction or failure would cause the death of one or two billion people. If the choice were made explicit, the United States or NATO would seriously consider "lower quality" systems; i.e., systems which were less deterring, but whose consequences were less catastrophic if deterrence failed. They would even consider such possibilities as a dangerous degree of partial or complete unilateral disarmament, if there were no other acceptable postures. The West might be willing to procure a military system which, if used in a totally irrational and unrealistic way, could cause such damage, but only if all of the normal or practically conceivable abnormal ways of operating the system would not do anything like the hypothesized damage. On the other hand, we would not let the Soviets cynically blackmail us into accommodation by a threat on their part to build a Doomsday Machine, even though we would not consciously build a strategic system which inevitably forced the Soviets to build a Doomsday Machine in self-defense.

Aside from the obvious moral and political reasons, and the repugnance policy makers and practical men have for a device which is aimed at their own population, the main reason the Soviet Union and the United States would not build a Doomsday Machine is that they are both *status quo* powers, the U.S. because it has so much, and the Soviet Union partly because it also has much and partly because it expects to get so much more without running any excessive risks. Even if we consider that neither the Soviets nor the Americans, nor other technically competent and wealthy but "satisfied" powers (such as England), would deliberately build a Doomsday weapon system, at least three important problems arise:

1. Would a nation build one inadvertently?
2. If not now, will it change its mind in the future?
3. Would a determined *non*-status quo nation build one?

I do not believe that any nation will build a Doomsday Machine inadvertently, partly because it is hard to build one, but mostly because current discussion is succeeding in focusing attention on this problem, and decision makers are becoming conscious of its implications. As far as a technically advanced *status quo* country changing its mind is concerned, I could easily imagine a crisis occurring in which a nation might desperately wish it had procured such a machine. Fortunately, it seems to be even less likely that a nation would procure a standby capability that could be connected up at the last moment than that it would procure a continuous capability in being; and the lead time for designing and constructing such a machine would be so long that the crisis would be settled before the

150

project could get under way. In the long run (one to three decades), the third question, "Would a determined non-status quo nation build one?", may turn out to be the most important.

Many scientists believe that with the passage of time Doomsday Machines will inevitably become both clearly feasible and much cheaper than I have suggested, so that the developmental gamble will be much less risky than it is today. In addition, a number of powers which, unlike the United States and the Soviet Union, may not be so cautious in outlook, will be getting both richer and technically more competent and may yet retain their non-status quo outlook. For example, a nation may be wealthy and technically competent enough to have an advanced military technology and yet desperate or ambitious enough to gamble all.[4] Or some of the underdeveloped nations may become rich in the sense of gross national product, but have such a low per capita income or other social anomaly that they retain attitudes more appropriate to a desperate claimant on the world's resources than a responsible "bourgeois" member of international society. The outstanding possibility in the next decade or two is China. Such a third nation might well decide that an investment in a very high-quality Type I Deterrent would pay dividends. It is unlikely that the leaders of this nation would plan on threatening the world with annihilation or extreme damage if they are not given their way, though even this is not impossible. If they can do the damage gradually they can both make the threat clear and demonstrate their resolve, without actually committing suicide. As an example of this possibility, suppose that the blackmailing nation started a process which it could reverse, but which could not be reversed or negated by others, in which the temperature of the earth was artificially dropped five degrees a year. If they also had a Doomsday Machine to protect themselves from attack (one which might depend on the same mechanism), one could easily imagine that they could demonstrate enough resolve to bring most of the other major nations to terms. A much more likely possibility for the possessor of a Doomsday Machine would be to exploit the sanctuary afforded by his "excellent" Type I Deterrent

[4] Germany in the decade 1934–1944 came close to being such a nation. As far as Hitler personally was concerned, he probably would have been delighted to procure a Doomsday Machine. However, during most of the period between 1934–1944 Hitler was restrained by "responsible" elements, and many of his gambles were actually hedged. On many occasions in which he seemed to be too reckless, military groups prepared what amounted to a standby *coup d'état* should he go too far or get into serious trouble.

to be as aggressive as he pleased against his neighbors and to threaten any who interfered with all kinds of punishment—for example, some form of controlled nuclear retaliation, in which he destroyed two or three of the major cities of his interfering opponent. Even if it were feasible to retaliate in kind without setting off the Doomsday Machine, the social and political impact of accepting such losses would raise much more serious internal and external problems in the United States than in China. It seems most likely, for example, that having to accept and explain the rationale of an exchange of two or three major U.S. cities for an equal number of Chinese cities would result in political suicide for the party in power in the U.S., plus some alliance instabilities, but only in some serious inconvenience to the Chinese government. It should therefore presumably be a major objective of arms control to prevent such hypothetical, but not unimaginable, problems from occurring. (Here is one clear case of joint Soviet–U.S. interest.)

There is another form of deterrence which, while not a Doomsday Machine, is still an "ultimate" of a sort. This could be called the Homicide Pact Machine, an attempt to make a failure of Type I Deterrence mean automatic mutual homicide. The adherents to this somewhat more practical device hope to divide the work of deterrence in a natural way: We destroy the enemy and the enemy destroys us, neither of us cheating by buying any effective Counterforce as Insurance for our respective societies. The Homicide Pact Machine is clearly more satisfactory to both humanitarians and neutrals than the Doomsday Machine and both should make the distinction.

As far as patriots and nationalists are concerned, I believe that the Homicide Pact system has many of the same drawbacks as the Doomsday Machine, though not in so extreme a form. The major advantage of the Homicide Pact is that one is not in the bizarre situation of being killed with his own equipment; while intellectuals may not so distinguish, the policy makers and practical men prefer being killed by the other side. It is just because this view no longer strikes some people as bizarre that it is so dangerous.

The Homicide Pact used to be, albeit only semiconsciously, NATO policy and recently has become extremely close to being consciously adopted as official U.S. policy. It is not known to what extent the Soviets are planning to live up to "their part of the bargain" and move in the same direction. While Khrushchev's speech of 14 January 1960 indicated that Soviet decision makers have begun to accept some of the concepts of deterrence which have so persuasively swept the West since the mid-fifties, there is no indication that this acceptance will lead to a relaxation of current Soviet attempts at a capability to fight and survive wars as well as deter them. The opposite may be true. As the quotation from his speech on the bottom of page 28 indicates, he may intend to increase Soviet Credible First Strike Capabilities. The main specifics of the speech were not that the Soviets were disarming, but rather that by cutting back on conventional capabilities they would gain in their capability to fight modern thermonuclear wars. Whether this is the somewhat misleading "more bang for the buck" program we followed or a serious attempt to be prepared for any eventuality, only time or Khrushchev can tell.

Just not building Doomsday Machines or near approximations does not resolve all the problems of not being too dangerous. The day-to-day operations of the Department of Defense should also be safe. This gets to be quite a problem with modern weapons. The introduction of such weapons systems as the atomic Nike-Hercules, air defense fighters with kiloton weapons, the ground alert of SAC planes complete with megaton bombs, the ground alert of armed and dispersed IRBM's and ICBM's; and finally the existence of alert mobile systems such as Polaris, train mobile Minuteman, and Air Force SAC bombers has given a new intensity to the peacetime safety problem.

Here is one place where, surprisingly perhaps, one may be able to distinguish between kiloton and megaton. Suppose an air defense fighter carrying a low-kiloton weapon crashed in a lightly inhabited area, and due to some coincidental malfunctions and mistakes the plane crash led to a small nuclear yield. A serious public relations problem would be created, I expect, but the incident would not necessarily have a catastrophic effect on future operations of air defense fighters (provided the accident had been in a lightly populated area, which is why we prefer to operate our air defense fighters away from heavily populated areas in peacetime). If the same thing occurred to a SAC bomber carrying a multimegaton weapon, the situation would be catastrophic. It would not be surprising if, as a result of the accident, SAC were forced to go off alert status. To the extent that our security depends on SAC being kept on alert, such an accident might dangerously increase our vulnerability. Therefore, both for normal considerations of public safety and because of the possible catastrophic effects on our Type I Deterrence, it is crucially important that the operation of the force contain safeguards against the occurrence of an unauthorized explosion, safeguards which reduce the probability of this event to as close to zero as is humanly possible. This must be done even though it results in serious compromises and inefficiencies in the operation of the force. I use the words "unauthorized behavior" rather than "accident" because we must guard against many types of events—psychopathic or irrational individuals, mechanical or human failure, sabotage, irresponsible behavior, and so on. *Some proposals (for example, unmanned space bombardment platforms or decentralized decision making on the issue of war or peace) do not take sufficient account of the necessity to prevent unauthorized behavior of either men or equipment.*

It is not that any of these possibilities has a very high probability of occurring. The point is that the results would be terribly serious if they did occur.

There is another type of accident that would not be quite as cataclysmic but would still be serious. This is an accident in which the high-explosive part of a nuclear weapon is detonated, but the nuclear part is not (because it is normally kept safe). This episode might cause trouble because of the primary effect of the explosion, and because of such secondary effects as the scattering of radioactive material or poisonous plutonium. Even very light levels of contamination might cause alarm among the uninformed residents of the area. Therefore, in addition to making adequate physical preparations for handling such residual effects, it is important that we have a good "public relations policy" that includes setting up, *in advance* of an incident, reasonable standards on what is a "dangerous" or "safe" level of contamination. Then we will know what to say —as well as what to do. It might even be judicious to encourage a moderate amount of public discussion of this problem now, to indicate that it is one of the perils of the age in which we live and that it has to be accepted as such.

A problem on which there is much discussion but which seems almost irrelevant to me is the "conventional" damage that our weapons will do to ourselves during the war. For example, there has been some worry about the damage the Nike or Atlas boosters will

154

do when they fall back to earth. While it seems clear that one should attempt to minimize the amounts of "friendly" metal dropping on the heads or property of American citizens and allies, it is hard for me to believe that we should accept any compromise in efficiency to do this. After all, the comparison of the damage likely to be done by an enemy's multimegaton bombs as opposed to the return of boosters somewhere in the United States makes the latter trivial.

To some extent the same holds true for the use of atomic weapons in air defense. It is perfectly possible that a 20 KT bomb, exploded at ten, twenty, or thirty thousand feet, may cause moderate damage to people and property below that would be totally unacceptable by *peacetime* standards. However, these peacetime viewpoints should not confuse us into handicapping our prewar preparations for the inevitable wartime use of these weapons.

In addition to not looking too dangerous to ourselves, *we must not look too dangerous to our allies.* This problem has many similarities with the problem of not looking too dangerous to ourselves, with one important addition—our allies must believe that being allied to us actually increases their security. *Very few of our allies feel that they could survive a general war*—even one fought without the use of Doomsday Machines. Therefore, to the extent that we try to use the threat of a general war to deter the minor provocations that are almost bound to occur anyway, then no matter how credible we try to make this threat, our allies will eventually find the protection unreliable or disadvantageous to them. If credible, the threat is too dangerous to be lived with. If incredible, the lack of credibility itself will make the defense seem unreliable. *Therefore, in the long run the West will need "safe-looking" limited war forces to handle minor and moderate provocations.* It will most likely be necessary for the U.S. to make a major contribution to such forces and to take the lead in their creation, even though there are cases where the introduction of credible and competent-looking limited war forces will make some of our allies apprehensive—at least in the short run. They will worry because such forces make the possibility of small wars seem more real, but this seems to be another case where one cannot eat his cake and have it.

In addition to the limited war forces, we still need Type II Deterrence to force the enemy to limit his provocations *and to limit lim-*

ited wars. There is here a rather important interaction between limited war forces and Type II Deterrence. Because we are reserving the use of Type II Deterrence for rather improbable events, the thought does not frighten us and our allies so much. At the same time, its use is more credible because the provocations that require its use will be extreme. However, we must envisage the possibility of a failure of Type II Deterrence or the Soviets may be tempted to create a crisis which is far too weak to touch off a U.S. attack but intense enough to raise the fear of war or intense crisis as a real possibility. If the West is to have the resolve, in a time of need, to stand firm, the United States needs to have capabilities and war plans designed to give a reasonably credible and *explainable* possibility that our allies will be able psychologically to endure the strain of a prolonged crisis and physically to survive the war which might result from a failure of Type II Deterrence. Otherwise the Soviets may be able to develop and use tactics that could strain the alliance to the breaking point.

As will be discussed later, a satisfactory alliance posture might involve such things as the careful placement of strategic forces away from bonus civilian targets, a cheap civil defense both to make this placement feasible and to make destruction of civilians at least moderately difficult, the announced use of withholding and post-attack coercion tactics to encourage the enemy not to hit nonmilitary targets, and possibly some independent nuclear deterrents.

We must not look too dangerous to neutrals. While this is probably less important for us than not looking too dangerous to friends and allies, it is still too important to be ignored. Here again, we must not look excessively destructive. It may be all right to promise the Soviets that if they attack us we will destroy every Soviet citizen in retaliation (though personally I think this far too destructive a proposal), but we should not threaten nonbelligerents with near annihilation because of our quarrel with the Russians. Many of the world's inhabitants—perhaps two-thirds of them—do not feel it is their quarrel but feel it is their world. The more destructive we look, the less they like us and our program. To the extent that some in our midst talk and threaten potential world annihilation as a U.S. defense measure, we focus undeserved attention on ourselves as being dangerous and even irresponsible—appearing to be willing to risk uncounted hundreds of millions or billions of bystanders as pawns to our selfish ambitions and desires. Neutrals and bystanders will inevitably suffer heavily in any thermonuclear war. But there is a difference between damage and annihilation.

We must not look too dangerous to the enemy. This does not mean that we cannot do anything that threatens him. After all, our mere possession of a Type I Deterrence capability implies that we can harm him if we desire. But it does mean, to the extent that is consistent with our other objectives, we should not make him feel any more insecure than is necessary. We do not want to make him so unhappy and distraught that he will be tempted to end his anxieties by the use of drastic alternatives. We do not wish him to conclude, "better a fearful end than endless fear." We must not appear to be excessively aggressive, irresponsible, trigger-happy, or accident prone, today or in the future.

Still, we cannot afford to make the enemy feel too safe. As already mentioned, our Type I Deterrent depends upon having the ability to hurt the enemy. Even if he is reasonably certain we would not rationally use it, the mere existence of this power must give the enemy some qualms. He cannot be certain we might not use it accidentally, irresponsibly, or in desperation. Some experts on Communism have argued that Soviet leaders may have a special compulsion to destroy anything that could conceivably harm them; that they compulsively feel that the mere existence of a hostile enemy is intolerable. In any case, the thought of a catastrophe or holocaust unleashed by accidental (i.e., nonhistorical) causes might be very unsettling to any Marxists who had a passionate belief in a deterministic theory of history. Instead of saying "It is inevitable that we will take over the world in fifty years," this Marxist would have to add, "Always assuming some capitalist fool doesn't press a button." In addition, the existence of the United States as the leader of an independent bloc makes it difficult to control the arms race and therefore reliably to prevent the coming into being of other nations or power blocs with weapons with which they might do all kinds of mischief. *Therefore, the mere existence of a retaliatory force and nothing else may look provoking to a Marxist.* However, the situation is worse than this.

Since we wish to be able to limit Soviet behavior to deter them from acts which cannot be met by limited means, we must have a Credible First Strike Capability. To the extent that we have such a first strike capability over and above our Type I Deterrent, the enemy is under additional pressure to initiate a preventive or pre-emptive war. In normal circumstances this extra pressure must be very small. It should be quite clear that we are not going to initiate a war deliberately, one in which we may lose fifty or a hundred cities and create a radioactive environment, just because there is a belief among some of the planners that the country could survive and rebuild after the holocaust. The only time in which the Credible First Strike Capability would be destabilizing would be when we were being cruelly provoked or in a desperate crisis—a circumstance in which, destabilizing as it would be, we would feel we would need an ability to rescue ourselves from a more dire eventuality either by increasing our bargaining power or by actual use of the Credible First Strike Capability. We may also need some Type II Deterrence to protect our Type I Deterrence. I have yet to see a posture de-scribed in which the Soviets could not degrade seriously the capa-bility of our Type I Deterrent in peacetime by acts of violence which would not be deterred if we only had a Type I Deterrent. Therefore, we cannot afford to eliminate completely our ability to go to war if provoked in some extreme fashion. *But we should be careful in our use of threats and not be excessively or unnecessarily provocative.* We should not add strains in any greater intensity than seems neces-sary for the purpose we are trying to fulfill. In particular, we should not put any unintentional strains on the enemy.

The easiest way in which one can put unintentional strains on the enemy is to have a force which looks "trigger-happy." *The one cir-cumstance under which almost-all Soviet experts agree the Russians might strike is the one in which they feel they are anticipating a strike by us.* It will be difficult for them to read our intentions. They will doubtless err on the side of caution. But it is not clear which side will *look* cautious, particularly if there is a crisis which creates apprehension. It will add a real element of stability if our posture is such that we do not look as if we have to be "trigger-happy" in order to survive. This is an important reason for not relying solely on quick reaction as a protection and for not having forces so vulnerable that we could lose most of them from a Russian first strike. Under some circumstances our vulnerability to a Russian first strike would *both tempt the Russians* to initiate a war and at the same time *compel them,* because they might feel that we would be tempted to pre-empt for our own protection. If we are sufficiently vulnerable they

158

might find it impossible to believe that we were willing, in this crisis, to rely on their good will, morality, caution, or sense of responsibility as a protection.

The problem here is that we do not want the enemy to think that in a tense situation he must strike first or at least very early, reflecting that if he does not, we will (not because we want to, but because we have to if we are to have any capability). The enemy must feel that we do not have to be "trigger-happy." He must sense that we know there is a good possibility that even if he should strike first we have a capability to hurt him enough so that even though he may win the war he will be sorry he started it. Let us turn this around. If *we* feel confident that *he* will not be tempted by our vulnerability to solve his problems by quick action, we can afford to hold back. The enemy will know this and be reassured that *he* has no need to be "trigger-happy." If both sides are vulnerable to a first strike, then we have a very unstable situation in which even a minor crisis or accident may touch off the "reciprocal fear of surprise attack" which in turn may touch off a war.

Equally important to not appearing "trigger-happy" is *not to appear prone to either accidents or miscalculations.* Who wants to live in the 1960's and 1970's in the same world with a *hostile* strategic force that might *inadvertently* start a war? Most people are not even willing to live with a *friendly* strategic force *that may not be reliably controlled.* The worst way for a country to start a war is to do it accidentally, without any preparations. That might initiate an all-out "slugging match" in which only the most alert portion of the forces gets off in the early phase. Both sides are thus likely to be "clobbered," both because the initial blow was not large enough to be decisive and because the war plans are likely to be inappropriate. To repeat: On all these questions of accident, miscalculation, unauthorized behavior, trigger-happy postures, and excessive destructiveness, we must satisfy ourselves and our allies, the neutrals, and, strangely important, our potential enemies. Since it is almost inevitable that the future will see more discussion of these questions, it will be important for us not only to have made satisfactory preparations, but also to have prepared a satisfactory story. Unless everybody concerned, both laymen and experts, develops a satisfactory image of U.S. strategic forces as contributing more to security than insecurity, it is most improbable that the required budgets, alliances, and intellectual efforts will have the necessary support. To the extent that people worry about our strategic forces as themselves exacerbating or creating security problems, or confuse symptoms with the disease, we may anticipate a growing rejection of military preparedness as an essential element in the solution to our security problem and a turning to other approaches not as a complement and supplement but as an alternative. In particular, we are likely to suffer from the same movement toward "responsible" budgets, pacifism, and unilateral and universal disarmament that swept through England in the 1920's and 1930's. The effect then was that England prematurely disarmed herself to such an extent that she first almost lost her voice in world affairs, and later her independence in a war that was caused as much by English weakness as by anything else.

I believe that, in the long run, a purely military approach to the security problem can lead to disaster for civilization, and by long run I mean decades, not centuries. But this does not mean that while trying other approaches, we can cut back on the energy, thought, and appropriations needed by military approaches. I believe that even with large-scale use of "nonmilitary" approaches we will have to do better in the military field than we have in the past if we are to preclude the possibility of disaster. However, unless a much better case is made for constructive reforms and the corresponding budgets in coming years, I strongly suspect the necessary efforts are not going to be made.

The Department of Defense

Our Department of Defense should not be or look too expensive. Basically this means that it should be worth its cost. But it should also look efficient. It should not look full of fat that could be squeezed if necessary to pay for new weapons systems. It is very difficult for the Department of Defense to do this, partly because it does have some fat, but mainly because even the most efficient department of defense cannot (under modern conditions) be or look "efficient" as the term is normally used in business practice. It is easy to see why this is so. Let me suggest to any Congressmen, members of the Budget Bureau, and others who tend to be overcritical of minor inefficiencies in the Department of Defense that they imagine themselves in the following position: They are made responsible for the operation of all aspects of a business and must make all the decisions; but they are to make them in a curious environment. They are told in only the most approximate and casual way what things cost and when they will be available, often by people who are actually trying to mislead them; in any case, nobody really knows. They are not told what items "sell." They are not told what items are causing extreme dissatisfaction among customers. They have to deduce these things by reading records of what similar stores sold ten or twenty years ago and by making some general and purely theoretical calculations on what current customers are like. No specific observations on real customers or their buying habits are allowed. The business is a highly fashionable one in which the desires and tastes of the customers are known to change rapidly, though the management has only the most indirect clues and paper studies as to what these changes are. Nevertheless, they have to order merchandise years in advance to meet the fickle whims of their customers.

Finally, this business makes most of its money on a sale day which occurs once every decade or two at a time unknown to the management. The management does have a signal on the morning of the sale that *this is the day*. This helpful signal consists of leading competitors coming into the store, breaking up all the equipment, shooting most of the help and generally causing as much damage as they can.

In the circumstances under which this business is operated, it is quite likely that there will be some minor inefficiencies and maybe even some major ones in the preparations and operations. In particular, there may be some inconsistent and overlapping facilities as safety factors.

I think it should be clear that the above is a quite reasonable description of how the Department of Defense must operate. While they could know their costs a great deal better than they do, and while they could do a lot more work in trying to estimate the efficiency of the things they buy, their problems will remain pretty close to those of the foggy businessman just discussed.

In these circumstances, huge mistakes must necessarily be made; the only question is the size and frequency of the mistakes, and what can be done to keep them as small and infrequent as possible. But fat there will be.

It is, of course, extremely aggravating to members of Congress and others to see more money allocated to defense when they are morally certain there is a lot of fat in the existing defense budget. They feel that if the new money is not allocated the three service chiefs will find the resources they need by cutting the fat; if they cannot, then it serves them right not to get the money.

There are several things wrong with this view. The first, of course, is that it is more than the Department of Defense that is "served right"; the country also has a stake in this problem. The second is that it is quite clear that there is going to have to be a lot of fat in the Department of Defense, some of which is not really fat but only seems to be.

And, of course, lead time is so important that we should be willing to spend money on several competing, duplicating, and overlapping projects, because it may take a multipronged approach to eliminate the uncertainties that must be cleared up before a decision can be made. We do not wish to lose time while eliminating these uncertainties. Almost equally important, we may be willing to spend appreciable sums of money carrying along several projects just to buy the time we need to be able to study the situation before we can responsibly decide what to do. Nobody in the Department of Defense, including its senior members, can possibly have the kind of trained and tested intuition that is expected of a normal executive. There is no one with experience in the conduct of thermonuclear war. That means we must depend on *hypothetical experience*, i.e., paper studies. These take time to do. It may be desirable not only to keep open several alternatives until the studies are done, but even to push the more likely looking alternatives vigorously, so that we will not lose excessive amounts of lead time. I feel sure that Lecture III will show how difficult it would be for even a "superman" to keep up with just the major implications of our rapidly changing military technology.

Wartime Objectives

We have just considered the major military objectives of a strategic force in peacetime. I am now going to ask the reader for an unpleasant feat of imagination, one which very few Westerners seem willing to achieve—to try to project himself into a future wartime situation and to ponder the questions seriously. *Why and*

162

how might a thermonuclear war be initiated? Is it really true that only an insane man would initiate a thermonuclear war, or are there circumstances in which the leaders of a country might rationally decide that thermonuclear war is the least undesirable of the available alternatives? What are some of the different ways in which a war might be fought and terminated?

In answering the above questions, one should not shroud the possibilities or consequences of a war with an air of hypotheticalness, unreality, or improbability with which most people associate the risk of war. We are assuming that the unthinkable has actually occurred and are asking: Why?, When?, and How? with the emphasis on the last two questions rather than the first.

The wartime objectives overlap to some extent with the peacetime objectives and are, of course, an expression of these peacetime objectives, but they are different enough to make them worthy of separate discussion. It may be difficult for some readers, particularly any who are used to thinking of a future war as automatic mutual annihilation (or as a sort of orgiastic spasm of destruction) to take seriously a discussion of "rational" wartime objectives and of the strategy and tactics necessary to achieve these objectives. They may find it particularly hard to accept the classical notion of "strategy" as an attempt to force one's will on the enemy.

Some war planners find it as hard to think through the course of a war as most of the lay readers of this book will. In previous times it was not essential for the war plans staff to think through the many steps of the war *before* the event, for campaigns moved slowly enough so that they could improvise as problems arose. Today, this is no longer possible. One of the reasons why modern war is likely to be excessively destructive is that, with events moving so fast, unless preattack preparations for evaluation, negotiation, and operational flexibility have been made there is no way for knowledge of the actual military course of events to improve the conduct of operations. It has always been possible for two nations to fight to the death, but (normally) one side or the other sees that things have gone too far and calls a halt. Today these possibilities must be thought about in advance. *To some extent we must try to think a war right through to its termination.* This does not mean that we can predict the details of what will happen, but only that it is valuable to think through many possible wars to their termination points.

Doing this will enable us to prepare for contingencies in advance and to develop correct approaches and doctrines.

Table 30 outlines the wartime objectives.

TABLE 30
WARTIME OBJECTIVES

    A. Of attacker
        1. Limit damage
            a. Counterforce
            b. Postattack coercion
            c. Objective capability
        2. Win war
        3. Win peace
    B. Of defender
        1. Punish enemy
            a. Priority affected by damage accepted
            b. Population and recuperation targets
        2. Stalemate war
            a. Conflicts with "punish" enemy
            b. Requires staying power
            c. Feasibility varies
        3. Limit damage

Somewhat misleadingly, I used to label the wartime objectives as "non-psychological objectives," to distinguish them sharply from the peacetime objectives with their heavy emphasis on the psychology of deterrence. Yet I hasten to emphasize that even in war we may be, or at least should be, coercing and seducing the enemy, which automatically means we are working on his mind as well as his body. However, given the current overemphasis on psychological tactics, I think it is a valuable corrective to emphasize the need for an objective capability. We want an objective capability for the simple reason that equipment that is bought may be used and, contrary to the automatic mutual homicide view (Minimum Deterrence), one cares how efficiently the equipment is used.

In most situations there will be a clear distinction between the attacker and defender, though this will not always be so. It is also possible that the distinction may become blurred, as far as objectives go, as the war progresses. The first half of Table 30 lists the main objectives of the attacker. The first and most important of the attacker's objectives is *to limit damage to himself*. A modern thermonuclear war is a frightening thing, and even a nation that is confident of its strength must be worried about the uncertainties. In all likelihood, the highest priority objective of the attacker will be to survive in some acceptable fashion. He might even be willing to choose damage-limiting tactics at the cost of seriously compromising his chances of victory. But fortunately for him, most of the things which he can do in order to limit damage are most likely to increase his chances of victory. The first thing he must do is to counter the force of the enemy.[5] This is likely to mean an extreme emphasis on tactics designed to destroy the defender's strategic force on the ground.

It would not surprise me to find that actual Soviet war plans are completely inappropriate. War plans usually are so, because they are drawn up in peace rather than in war. There once was a saying among staff planners that the purpose of war plans is not to guide the initial tactical operations but to give people a chance to exercise their skills in peacetime and to jog their memories on their responsibilities. Thus the first thing one does when a war starts is to throw away the war plans and write something sensible. But there is no longer time to do that. If the war plans are not sensible, the war will not be sensible.

Now I do not know what the Soviets consider "sensible." But I am certain that if they ever deliberately planned to initiate a war, they would think much more clearly than they do in peacetime— when war is for most people (even professional war planners, I suppose) a sort of hypothetical and abstract notion. In particular, they would undoubtedly notice that, in wartime, American cities are not particularly dangerous to them. It is true, as we have mentioned, that these cities do contain resources and capacities vastly useful to military operations. Still, if we have a properly designed strategic force, very few of them will be essential. On the other hand, it is clear that our strategic force can hurt Russia. If the Soviets are limited in the size of their initial blow (perhaps because they do not have a large force or because of constraints on what they can deploy or put into one *salvo* due to warning or timing considerations), it is likely that the bulk of their blow will be directed toward

[5] As always, I am using the word counterforce in the most general sense to include active and passive defense as things which counter the force of the other side as well as the possibility of destroying the enemy forces on the ground.

destroying, crippling, or degrading the operation of our retaliatory forces. In the main, of course, this implies interfering with control and communications or trying to destroy weapon carriers on the ground, at sea, in port, or even in the air. This portrait of their first-priority target system tends to agree with most published Russian discussions of their military doctrine, though there are some contradictions (see Khrushchev's speech of January 14, 1960).[6]

SAC bases therefore have urgency for the Russians. But there are targets other than SAC bases that the Soviets might wish to hit early in the war—for example, headquarters installations, communications, and possibly certain important cities, such as Washington or New York—in order to maximize confusion and delay reaction, thus giving them more time to complete their work of destruction. It is possible, however, that they would choose the opposite technique of deliberately avoiding certain of our top echelon headquarters communications and completely or almost completely avoiding cities in order to maximize their postattack blackmail possibilities.

Let us consider why and how the attacker would use postattack blackmail tactics. The attacker, whose highest priority objective is to limit damage to his country—that is, to evade the punishment which the defender is trying to inflict—must worry about three kinds of forces:

1. Reflex
2. Ready
3. Unready

Reflex forces are those that are available for instant retaliation. As we shall see later, there are several reasons for wanting some degree of flexibility in the operation of even these forces, but it may be difficult to achieve much. The reflex forces are typified by bombers, ICBM's and IRBM's on ground alert, air-borne bombers that have bombs and adequate fuel, Polaris submarines at battle stations, and the alert planes aboard aircraft carriers within range of targets. Because of the shortness of time available before these forces are committed, about the most flexibility that can be expected might be about two or three fixed-alternative attack plans.

The *Ready forces* are forces that are combat-ready or almost combat-ready but still take hours to become committed. They are typi-

---

[6] *New York Times*, January 15, 1960, p. 2.

fied by combat-ready bombers without their bombs or crews, standby ICBM's and IRBM's, Polaris submarines at sea but not at station, combat-ready bombers in the air but without either bombs or adequate fuel, and so on. Because it takes time to commit these forces, there may be a great deal of flexibility possible in their committal.

The *Unready forces* include the rest of the strategic weapons, and may include such things as bombers not in SAC (in Air Training Command, at depots, in pipelines, and at proving grounds), and even improvised bombers. We are likely to have many more bombs than bomb carriers available and it might be possible, if we have prepared in advance, to modify rapidly jet and propeller transports and cargo carriers to carry bombs on one way (but not necessarily suicide) missions. (Soviet civil transport seems designed with this thought in mind.) As we shall see later, such forces may play an important role on the second and later days of the war. And the second or later days of the war could be important.

Ready and Unready forces are likely to be somewhat larger than alert forces. That is, for every plane on ground or air alert, there are presumably two or more planes not on alert. There may also be several hundred bombers in the air. Unless there is an air-borne alert, these will not be combat-ready. They must land and get crews, fuel, and bombs. In addition, there are likely to be many missiles not fired in the first few minutes of war, because they do not receive the fire order, malfunction, or are in a standby or backup condition, or because being mobile they are not in a position to fire. It is therefore my belief that, even with relatively inexpensive measures, the non-Reflex forces can be made to be as important in deterring an attack as the Reflex forces, and they can be *much more important in terminating a war.* Unfortunately, we have been so preoccupied with alert and fast reaction as *the* means of protection that most military experts seem to think of these non-Reflex forces only as being necessary but unusable components of an alert force. Most "progressive" experts on war seem to be willing to have these nonalert forces, for all practical purposes, "thrown away." They probably find their destruction acceptable, in spite of the fact that these same forces compose the bulk of our inventory, because they are so used to thinking of the war as a momentary spasm rather than as a continuing activity that may terminate in less than total destruction.

The attacker will, of course, try to destroy all three kinds of forces in his first attack. But if we have prepared sensibly, he may have trouble destroying his first-priority target—the Reflex forces. He may not have the capability to mortally wound the other forces in the first wave or two. This is particularly likely to be true if the alert character of the Reflex forces has compelled the attacker to use a limited-warning attack. If we prepare moderately, it may be very difficult for the attacker to destroy completely the Ready and Unready forces on the ground, even in several wave attacks.

The attacker, at essentially no risk to himself, can hedge against the possibility of failure. He can adopt the following tactic, which, if it works, may save him a great deal of damage; if it does not work, it will cost him very little in relation to his possible gains. This tactic is to avoid the cities deliberately and to concentrate his first waves on our offensive forces and air defense. If he succeeds in destroying enough of our air defense, so that the remaining active and passive defenses give almost no protection, our cities will be helpless before the fury of even a "small attack." For, as we pointed out in the first lecture, just a few wings of heavy bombers carrying multiple bombs in a ferrying operation could destroy even a good civil defense system if they "got a free ride." The enemy could then make some ferocious threats that might well cause us to be discriminating in our later counterattacks. He could say, for example, "I have deliberately avoided your cities. I have treated them as open cities, and I wish you to treat my cities in the same way. In the confusion of the first attack you inadvertently or advertently may have tried to attack my cities. However, it is most unlikely that the handful of attacking planes got through, since I have such an adequate air defense. If they did, I will be more angry at my air defense commander than at you. However, from now on for every city of mine you destroy I will destroy five of yours." If he has been reasonably effective in his first strike, this is a credible threat. If he makes it dramatic enough, it might influence our action. For example, he could be specific and say, "If you destroy Moscow, I will destroy New York, Washington, Los Angeles, Philadelphia, and Chicago. If you destroy Leningrad, I will destroy Detroit, Pittsburgh, San Francisco, New Orleans, and Miami." He could finish his list with a remark to the general effect that "you know better than I do what kind of a country you want to have after this war is over. Pick which American cities you wish to have destroyed." This would be in any event a very credible threat, but particularly so if our air defenses had been destroyed. However, to the extent that our air defenses can survive his attack, and are capable of attriting his later missions, there may be significant limits to the damage he can do. In this respect, I would like to point out again that there is an enormous difference between a threat of total annihilation and a threat of extreme damage. The first cannot be bargained with; the second can be. A nation such as the United States might be willing to fight to the last man, but there are *almost no circumstances that are likely to occur* in which it should be willing to fight to the last woman and child.

If one gives any credence to the missile gap, the possibility of a blackmail threat is particularly serious in the immediate future. In the years 1960 and 1961 most of our bases will be soft. From the viewpoint of maximizing the amount of damage done by blast, it is advantageous to the enemy to use air-burst weapons. If all of the attacker's weapons are air burst, there will be no local fallout to kill civilians hundreds of miles away from the targets. The locations of SAC bases are such that if the enemy does air-burst megaton weapons over these bases, and if none of the weapons goes astray, he will kill less than 5,000,000 Americans by direct effects such as blast and thermal radiation. In fact, casualties could be in the neighborhood of 2,000,000. To most American officials who have been facing the possibility of 50 to 100 million deaths, the above would seem like a rather small number, very much closer to the peacetime state of zero damage than to the usually-visualized wartime state of total annihilation.

It is interesting to note that in the early 1950's when a colleague (Bernard Brodie) pondered on separating the strategic military and civilian targets, calculations which predicted a couple of million deaths were considered to demonstrate the infeasibility of such a separation. Two million deaths is about three times as many deaths as were suffered by the North and the South together in the bloodiest war of our history, the American Civil War. It is more than five times as many deaths as we suffered in either of the two World Wars. It was difficult for people to distinguish in the early 1950's between 2 million deaths and 100 million deaths. Today, after a decade of pondering these problems, we can make such distinctions perhaps all too clearly. Most of the decision makers and planners who have been facing the prospects of a thermonuclear war would find it difficult to distinguish between zero and two million deaths and very easy to distinguish between two million and a hundred million deaths. This means that in such a carefully designed and

169

executed attack most responsible Americans would think of the United States as being essentially untouched. In a sense, the awful decision of all-out war, limited war, or peace would then be on *their* shoulders. The decision might be made under circumstances in which we could scarcely hurt the enemy and in which he could annihilate us. No public policy can possibly justify anything that means a high probability of total suicide in exchange for inflicting "moderate" damage on the attacker. And if the attacker succeeds in destroying the defender's air defenses while holding back a small percentage of his force, he is in a position to guarantee annihilation. If we are to have any large number of survivors *and* be able to recover, either the damage an enemy can do must be limited or we will have to accede to his threats or make effective counterthreats. The damage he can do might be limited by such factors as his own voluntary actions, involuntary internal constraints (for example, having only a limited number of the right kind of bombs stockpiled, or the action of our military forces and threats). If the Soviet Union were to initiate an attack with a volley of ICBM's, *then unless we have made adequate active and passive preparations, it is very possible that this first ICBM volley may take out the bulk of our air defense, almost all our nonalert offense, and a portion of our alert offense.* On their side they would doubtless have many hundreds of medium- and long-range bombers in their reserve, in addition to whatever ICBM's that aborted in take-off. Under these circumstances there is at least a possibility, if not a certainty, that blackmail tactics would affect both the tactics and choice of targets of that part of the force still under Command and Control. Any responsible officials who were not just reacting in a blind and uncontrollable anger would certainly consider temporizing, at least to the extent of being careful in the use of these surviving and controllable offense forces. In fact, if the first attack were sufficiently successful in destroying our offensive and defensive forces, we might well be tempted to negotiate.

Remember, we are not talking about a heroic individual sacrificing himself for his regiment, or a regiment sacrificing itself for the division, or the division for the army, or the army for the nation, or even the nation for the world. I believe that countries other than ours, if they had the chance to vote, would also favor our temporizing. It is the nation that is at risk, and the nation does not destroy itself in cold blood. Neither does it frivolously or uselessly generate problems for the entire world and for unborn generations. It seems to be difficult for many Americans to understand the point that if the President's anger abates long enough for him to consider the situation, he will realize that there is no way to undo the damage that is done and that *revenge may appear to make less sense than trying to make the best of a bad situation.*

The ability of the defender to counter postattack blackmail will depend on many things. It will depend on his obtuseness (his inability to recognize that he would only hurt himself), the population and wealth that has survived the initial attack, the decision makers' physical, legal, and moral ability to Command and Control, and to evaluate damage, his inflexibility of character, how well the offense and defense survive the enemy's first strike, the counter-threats that can be made against the enemy, and on the quality of the preparation the defender has made to limit the damage the enemy can do on subsequent strikes.

The views that I have just expressed go contrary to the notion of "bonus" damage that is prevalent in some military and other expert circles. The idea common there is that "anything that hurts the defender must help the attacker." From the viewpoint of putting the defender in a position where he can readily be coerced, this clearly is not true. The notion of "bonus" damage is wrong in another sense. It is basically an immoral idea. It became reputable and could be justified in World War I and World War II, only because of military necessity. In those wars civilian morale played an essential role in furnishing men and materials to the fighting fronts. This is no longer true, and therefore civilians and their property are no longer military targets. The idea of bonus nonmilitary damage is now not only immoral, it is senseless. It is hard to conceive of a Premier of Russia or a President of the United States who would prefer to go to war—other things being equal—with a plan that would exterminate the enemy's civilian population, rather than one which would simply force the enemy to acquiesce on certain points. Even if military advantages were not to be had by deliberately limiting attack to counterforce targets, I suspect that most governments would still prefer to observe such limits. Almost nobody wants to go down in history as the first man to kill 100,000,000 people.

There are many who will disagree with the above analysis. Even those who agree with the logic behind it may wish to point out that the example of World War I and World War II is just too firmly entrenched in men's minds. Planners have become used to thinking it

171

is important to afflict civilian casualties and property damage on the enemy to wear down his will to resist. Lengthy attrition campaigns and attacks directed at morale played such an important part in forcing the Germans and Japanese to consider the possibility of surrender that it is difficult for those who have the example of these two wars firmly before them to believe that the attacker would understand the force of the arguments I have given, even if they are correct. It is believed that the decision makers will prefer to follow the road pointed out by custom and experience. Khrushchev's speech of January 14, 1960 indicated that he thinks along these now old-fashioned lines rather than the ones that I have indicated. (Of course, this is scant evidence. After all, he would scarcely be willing to picture himself as a potential blackmailer and aggressor.) However, some Soviet experts have argued that it might be particularly difficult for the Communists to adopt a plan that deliberately avoided cities because the Communists tend to equate victory in a war with an overturn of the opposing government by civil war. They tend to think that the destruction of existing social and governmental restraints will create civil war or at least civil strife. Blackmail of the type just outlined would look inappropriate since it scarcely touches the existing government.

All of this may be true, but I find it most doubtful that the Soviets would give up the advantages of the pure counterforce attack unless, of course, the Soviets went to war under conditions which gave them little chance to rethink their philosophy. After all, the Soviets, more than any other group in the world, are used to thinking of rational and profitable connections between force and coercion, between power and policy. It should not be too difficult for some bright young colonel or civilian to convince his superiors that the use of postattack blackmail tactics is the best way to maximize the impact of his force. This is not a prediction of what would happen, but simply the statement of a possibility that must be seriously entertained and prepared for.

There are many interactions between passive defense and the possibility of postattack blackmail—interactions which can go in the direction of increasing or decreasing the possibility and effectiveness of the tactic. Let us consider first some ways in which the passive defense of civilians increases the possibility of postattack blackmail.

To take an extreme case, *imagine that we put all our missile bases in the hearts of cities and made no preparations to evacuate the population* so that the only way the enemy could destroy our retaliatory force would be to destroy our cities and people at the same time. If we did a good enough job of placing SAC within our civil society I think it is quite clear that we would have minimized the possibility of postattack blackmail. We would also have shown our peaceful intentions. Some seemingly sober military planners have found this concept so attractive that they are actually advocating a similar policy, though usually not quite so bizarre and open. They merely content themselves with advocating the placement of hard or mobile SAC bases in the populated areas of the country, leaving civilians unprotected. It is these planners I was thinking of when I was discussing those who found the concept of the Homicide Pact Machine a desirable one.

While I agree with some elements of the above analysis, I find myself forced to disagree with the desirability of the resulting posture for many reasons, some of which have already been explained, and others which I will explain. However, it should be clear that a policy of separating the offense system from civilian society by the use of modest civil defense measures good enough to prevent population and civilian property from being bonus targets but not good enough to prevent the enemy from destroying these nonmilitary targets if he desires, will have a tendency to increase the feasibility and performance of postattack coercion tactics. Such a policy does this not only because of the physical preparations but also because of the psychological by-products. Planners are forced to think of a war as something to experience, survive, and rebuild from afterward, rather than as an "end of history." This is the proper psychological preparation for a potential victim of postattack blackmail. *But if the civil and active defenses are so good that it is impossible for the attacker, particularly on his later, reduced strikes, to threaten civilians with total annihilation or even extremely large amounts of destruction, then the civil and air defenses will tend to degrade the effectiveness of postattack blackmail. Such defenses will at least put the defender in a good negotiating position.*

The proper kind of nonmilitary defense, combined with the proper military measures, may be important in making the defender less vulnerable to blackmail tactics. Even though civilians are not military targets they are hostages, and protecting them can negate some important enemy tactics. In this new and rather subtle sense, nonmilitary defense can contribute to Type I Deterrence, even if civilians and their property no longer contribute to the war effort.

Even without any detailed investigation of the possibilities it seems probable to me that the winning side can with some confidence use the threat to annihilate civilians to prevent the losing side from continuing long, hopeless retaliatory measures. For example, if the losing side has Polaris-type submarines, and if these turn out to be as invulnerable as claimed, they could by firing their missile stocks gradually over a period of weeks or months, delay or impede the recuperation activities of the victor. However, if the victor has left a sufficient portion of the losing country intact, he can threaten to destroy the rest and expect with some confidence that his threat (perhaps combined with some concessions) will neutralize the threat of these Polaris submarines.

Whether, given current attitudes on the part of decision makers, the attacker can expect blackmail techniques to work in a matter of minutes rather than hours or days is doubtful. But all these possibilities should be investigated. Unfortunately the investigation of the feasibility of various blackmail tactics is not only a difficult technical problem but it seems to be contrary to public policy as set forth in recent legislation forbidding the use of federal funds for the study of "surrender." Nevertheless, such research is important. Research on the costs and risks of the various offers that can be made and on the mechanisms available or desirable for communication, negotiating, and persuading could be especially important. Such studies may give us valuable clues to possible Soviet strategies and calculations. These studies should be symmetrical and include possible United States attempts to use postattack blackmail on Russia since these tactics could be of interest to us also.

The above remarks can be generalized into the parallel concepts of Controlled Reprisal and Controlled (or Limited) General War. The notion of Controlled Reprisal (which includes the much-discussed Controlled Nuclear Retaliation as a limiting case) envisages each side engaging in a series of tit-for-tat attacks (nuclear or nonnuclear), whose object is not the destruction of the other side's military power but the destruction of his resolve. Each side attempts by threats and actual punishment to force the other side to compromise or back down.

The Controlled War, on the other hand, visualizes reciprocal attacks on each other's military power with the object of attriting the opponent's retaliatory capability down to the point where it begins to be a doubtful Type I Deterrent. The Controlled War tries to extend deterrence to the intrawar period by using the threat of Reprisal or escalation to induce the other side to avoid nonmilitary bonus or collateral damage, perhaps even at the cost of handicapping military operations. If the intrawar deterrence does not break down completely, the war will end by negotiation (perhaps preceded by a period of Controlled Reprisal). The stakes in this negotiation will be the surviving people and resources; the cards will include the surviving offense, active defense, passive defense, Command and Control, and such imponderables as resolve, deception, and morale. If the intrawar deterrence does break down, then the failure of the restraints may result in much less destruction, since the controlled phase of the war may see a massive attrition or degradation of the forces available to one side or the other. If (or as) the balance of terror becomes more stable we can expect to see more study and discussion of the theory and practice of Controlled Reprisal and Controlled War.

The next item on Table 30 refers to the need of the attacker to believe he has an objective capability; he must have some confidence in his plans and paper calculations. This is difficult to attain. If the attacker is planning to rely on some complicated mix of air offense, air defense, and civil defense, in order to limit damage, he will be depending on what can only charitably be called untested capabilities. This means that the attacker, no matter how good his plans look on paper, will be anxious to buy whatever insurance he can to hedge against disaster—and in particular to limit damage. This should increase his willingness to use intrawar deterrence plus generous peace offers to induce the defender either to cease fighting or at least to fight "carefully."

If the first objective of the attacker is to limit damage, his second objective is to win the war—either to destroy the other side or force him to sue for peace. In peacetime, this objective puts more emphasis on offense and less on civil and air defense than would the objective of limiting damage. While the wartime operation of the force is quite similar in these two objectives (both emphasize the counterforce mission and the use of postattack blackmail), there may be some tactical differences. For example, if we are trying to limit damage to ourselves, we might be more interested in directing our attack to Russian staging bases than to their home bases, from which the combat-ready bombers have already flown. If we are trying to win the war, we might be more interested in destroying the grounded part of the Russian force as rapidly as possible so they would be more inclined to surrender or negotiate—rather than try to prevent Soviet planes that had managed to take off from reaching targets in the United States. That is, *winning the war* puts more emphasis on improving our bargaining position than *limiting damage* does.

It should be clear by now that under many circumstances winning a war would involve some kind of bargaining with the enemy. I will defer discussion of the details of this bargaining. I would only like to point out that any bargains the attacker might enter into could complicate his postwar problems—the third of our points, the "Win the Peace" objective.

This last objective of the attacker, *to make sure that the postwar situation is such as to further his long-range objectives,* is an important one, but one on which the critical issues have been little discussed. Many times, in discussing this objective, people will ruminate as follows: "The enemy is going to try to destroy our cities so he will have no postwar competition problems to worry about, a problem which might worry him even if he won the war." Or, "The enemy will try to preserve our cities because he wishes to use them to *increase his standard of living.*" However, given the enormous uncertainty associated with the future and the acutely uncomfortable dangers of the present, it is hard to imagine an attacker with so much confidence in the success of his plans that he would give up substantial immediate gain in order—by preserving or destroying our cities—to improve his position in the distant future.

But to spare the defender's cities may well be strategically advantageous. We have already pointed out that if the defender has been reasonably successful in his defensive disposition it will be very difficult for the attacker to destroy the defender's force completely on the first blow, although it may be clear to both the attacker and defender that the defender has been damaged so grievously by this first blow that he has no hope of winning the war. Under these circumstances, even though the attacker could physically destroy the defender's military forces, it would make sense for the attacker to offer some kind of bargain, since the attacker would then be limiting the retaliatory damage *he* would suffer. It would also make sense for the defender to listen to those terms. We discussed one aspect of this situation in connection with the postattack blackmail problem.

If the defender can win reasonable terms for himself—particularly if he can retain the ability to keep at least a modest deterrence force so he can make the attacker observe his promises—the attacker may then indeed have a very serious problem of postwar competition to worry about. He may face a problem similar to that Germany faced in 1871, or that the French faced in 1918. From the time Germany took Alsace-Lorraine from the French in 1871, the French had as their highest priority foreign policy objective to revenge their defeat and regain this territory. Likewise, it did not take the Germans long after their defeat in 1918 to devote themselves to negating the Versailles Treaty. On the other hand, if the attacker is not willing to offer decent terms, then even though he will win the war, he is likely to lose many more cities than if he had been willing to offer terms.

I would argue that it makes sense to offer generous terms. The war itself will make such a dramatic impression on all that there will be an enormous pressure to outlaw such levels of violence. Whether or not this pressure would be successful in setting up an explicit system, it is quite likely to be very effective in deterring those who would plot revenge, or at least those who would support them. If an effective system is set up, this system will certainly be acceptable to the victor; it may even be dictated by him in spite of the bargaining strength retained by the loser.

There are several circumstances in which it would especially make a great deal of political and military sense for the attacker to offer extremely good terms. The first is if a war started because of a failure of Type II Deterrence. Assume, for example, that the Russians were threatening a massive attack on Europe and refused to back down even though we went through the temporizing measures of evacuating our cities, alerting our SAC, and augmenting our air defense.

The Soviets think that we will still be deterred from attacking them because they can destroy 50 partially empty cities in their retaliatory blow. We, on the contrary, do not intend to let the Soviets get away with their aggression. If necessary, we are willing to lose these 50 cities, but we are in no sense anxious to lose them.

Under these circumstances we might initiate thermonuclear hostilities and restrict ourselves to the most sanitary and controlled counterforce operations.

We might hit missile bases in Siberia, Soviet bomber bases away from cities, identified submarines at sea, and in general, any target that does not involve the destruction of important nonmilitary assets, particularly civilians, as a "bonus." If the Soviets happen to have a bomber base in Moscow, or a Polaris base in Leningrad, we would avoid these particular targets, even though this might result in our suffering more damage in the long run. We would then point out to the Soviets that since we struck them first (successfully), there was no possible way that they could win the war. Our only war aim, we would say, was that they remove their threat against Europe. And we would ask, "Do you really want to choose this particular time to start a city exchange?" If we had achieved enough of an advantage, we could use the five-city-for-one-city threat on them (including European cities under the protective umbrella).

Even if our first strike had been only moderately successful, it should be successful enough under these hypothetical circumstances, so that the Russians have no reasonable choice, since if they continue the war they will be beaten. The only rational thing for them to do at this point would be to sign a truce. However, human beings being what they are, it is implausible that they would be this rational. But even if they struck back so that hostilities continued for a short time, they might be willing to limit their counterblow to pure counterforce targets. They might do this since it would be clear to them that should the war end in a stalemate, the stalemate would be much less costly to both sides if each is careful how it uses its strategic forces. Care on their part is made probable by our own care and the limited objectives we will have proclaimed. *Even if events go astray and the war degenerates into a city-busting phase after ten or twenty hours, the attacker has gone a great distance in achieving his "limited damage" objective* because after ten or twenty hours of war much of the defender's forces should have been used up or made inoperable.

Insofar as our European allies have any say in the matter, this is the only kind of thermonuclear war it would pay them to fight. In most wars, because of their proximity, it would be much easier for the Soviets to destroy Europe than the United States. It may even be reasonable in some cases for us to encourage the Europeans to declare an armed or unarmed neutrality, depending on our tactics and strategy and their capabilities. Because of security, vulnerability, and warning considerations, European based forces are not as valuable military assets to the United States as is often believed. For this reason a declaration of neutrality or partial abstention might in some circumstances be almost costless to the United States. There is also a possible bonus in this action. To the extent that the Europeans can decrease the vulnerability of their forces, they represent a force which, after the U.S. and Soviets have attacked each other's military forces, may be able to exert pressure on both sides to be reasonable in their negotiations.

The second circumstance in which it might be both useful and feasible to try to terminate the war by a stalemate or cease-fire is when the attacker's first strike has not done much damage. This could happen if the war started by accident or miscalculation—a war which nobody wanted. It could also happen if the first strike were small, because the attacker started the war with very little notice, or possibly because he tried a sneak attack and failed. We will point out in the next section in the discussion on flexible war plans that this is one time when the defender should be careful how he uses his force. It is probably also the right time for the attacker to start negotiations.

❖❖

TABLE 31
WARTIME OBJECTIVES OF DEFENDER

I. Punish Enemy
   1. Priority affected by outcome of first strike
   2. Countervalue targets
II. Stalemate War
   1. Conflicts dramatically with "punish enemy"
   2. Requires staying power
   3. Feasibility varies according to how war started
III. Limit Damage

❖❖

The last set of objectives we must discuss is the defender's objectives. The counterpart of the peacetime objective of Type I Deterrence (and the attacker's wartime objective of limiting the damage) is the defender's objective of punishing the enemy. It is my belief that if we adopt a rational war plan we may not make this last objective as overriding as it has been, or at least not as overriding as public discussion indicates it has been. In particular, the intensity with which we pursue this objective should be made quite sensitive to the outcome of the attacker's strike.

In strict rationality, once the war has started, deterrence has failed. The sensible thing to try for is a military victory. If this seems infeasible, we should try to bring about a stalemate of some sort by negotiating an end to the war—all the while trying to alleviate the damage. Given the enormous advantages of striking first, it is probably realistic to assign a modest ambition to the defender, so in Table 31 we refer to stalemating the war rather than winning the war. Unfortunately, going to war is much safer for the attacker, if he has reason to believe that we will use our surviving forces rationally. Therefore, it is necessary to appear to have the "Punish Attacker" objective, otherwise our deterrent objective would not be credible. As a nation, we have always talked as if the only way to make the deterrence objective *credible* is to have it as our sole war plan. And, indeed, if there is only a small force left after the attacker has made his strike, the military potentialities of the surviving force would be relatively limited. Under these circumstances, unless the surviving force is devoted to the objective of punishing the enemy, the enemy will get away almost scot-free. To the extent that the enemy is willing to believe that this could happen, the deterrent effect of our forces is decreased. Therefore, there is a very dramatic conflict in wartime, between the Punish Enemy and Stalemate War objectives. The first argues a concentration on population and recuperation targets; the second argues a concentration on the enemy's strategic forces with a deliberate avoidance of nonmilitary targets in the hope of using them as hostages.

If a quite large force survives the attacker's strike, we can afford to shift the priorities and put the Stalemate War and Limit Damage first, probably without losing much in the quality of our deterrent, since we would then have plenty of force available to punish the enemy later if this becomes necessary. Our Type I Deterrence would not be weakened even if the enemy knows our plans.

In peacetime, the procurement and deployment policies for the Punish Attacker and Stalemate War objectives seem to emphasize offense, and to that extent they overlap, but even in peacetime the overlap is not complete. For example, the Punish Attacker objective

180

might involve certain unconventional forces, such as one-way cargo carriers containing extremely large weapons. These could be menacing to people and to recuperation. They might not have much military use against the enemy's offensive forces. Such weapons could contribute to the Stalemate War objective only if they could be made so invulnerable that the defender could safely hold them back for days to use as a threat in bargaining.

To the extent that the defender wishes only to deter a war and not to try for a stalemate or to limit damage, he can sometimes use measures which work on the psychology of the enemy, but which may not give much objective capability and, at best, may be relatively unreliable. For example, if we put our forces on alert one-quarter of the time, but keep very secret which quarter it is, we might be able to save much of the cost of the alert, and yet those enemies who tend to focus attention on the worst that can happen might be almost as deterred as if we were alert 100 per cent of the time. Of course, a more optimistic or gambling enemy might have a different reaction. One serious trouble with such low confidence forces is that they will most likely not be able to play a role in stalemating the war or limiting damage. They also have an equally serious psychological trouble.

An emphasis on façades tends to encourage wishful thinking. It is dangerous to use measures that work on the psychology of the enemy, because they work on our psychology also. I mentioned in Lecture I that it is difficult for some people to distinguish between four things. These are: an objective capability to hurt the enemy, a high probability that the enemy will be damaged, a small probability of the same thing, and finally a posture in which there are conceivable circumstances in which a very cautious enemy might worry about being hurt. An official emphasis on façades tends to increase enormously the number of people who cannot make the distinctions. However, to the extent that we cannot afford measures which give us an objective capability, we may wish to utilize low-confidence forces either as a substitute or a supplement.

In peacetime, the third objective—to Limit Damage—conflicts somewhat with the other objectives. First, and foremost, it requires a greater objective capability. Unless the equipment actually works, it will not stop enemy attacks or limit the effectiveness of the attacks that get through. Secondly, it gives greater emphasis to active and passive defense.

In wartime, the Stalemate War and Limit Damage objectives seem to overlap to a considerable extent. For example, both involve attacking the enemy's offense and trying to terminate the war. The Punish Attacker objective conflicts quite sharply, since it seems to involve attacking the enemy's population and industry. But the Stalemate War and Limit Damage objectives do not overlap completely. One way to describe the Limit Damage objective is to say that we are trying to conduct the war so as to make the position of the country as favorable as possible five or ten years after the war. In many circumstances this could lead to a quite different course of action than if we were trying to force the enemy to negotiate a reasonable settlement without worrying how much damage is done (either to the country itself or to its relative position in the world).

We have already discussed briefly one case in which the Limit Damage objective should be placed uppermost by both defender and attacker in a war started by accident. For example, one of the enemy's or one of our ICBM's might be fired accidentally, precipitating an exchange of ICBM's. *This would be a war no one wanted and one which it would be well to terminate as quickly as possible.* It would be almost but not quite completely senseless to expend much effort deliberately to punish the enemy rather than to try to blunt his attack, destroy his military forces, and defend ourselves from damage. Even if it did not take urgently needed resources, it could still be disastrous to arouse his ire by destroying cities.

Even though this would be a war that should be terminable very rapidly by negotiation, our capabilities for and interest in negotiating would depend upon how badly we had been hurt and on how badly we could still be hurt, just as in the preplanned blackmail situation. Whether ending the war by negotiation would be feasible would depend upon the mechanics of the situation, such as our and his capabilities for communicating, persuading, making, and enforcing decisions. This is one area in which, as soon as the problem gets acute (and hopefully even before), we could expect both sides to be willing to make both unilateral and bilateral arrangements, not only to reduce the probability of an accident, but also to reduce the possibility of terrible consequences if an accident should occur.

The accidental war is another case in which even modest civil defense programs might perform reasonably well. Because the war would not be premeditated, it would be unlikely to start with a large, full-scale coordinated attack, so both the active and passive defense should work much better than the standard calculations would imply. Because the war would be unpremeditated (and therefore unwanted), it should be easier to settle by negotiation than a war which was started intentionally as a result of a crisis or provocation. Of course, it is not at all clear that once such a war had started the winning side would be willing to stop, short of a complete victory. He might argue, "Sure I stand to lose another twenty or thirty cities if I continue this fight, but I have already lost twenty, and it is worth taking these additional losses in order to guarantee that this 'problem' is not repeated in the future." It is therefore very important to enlarge so far as possible the disparity between the damage the enemy has already suffered, and the damage that he will suffer if he continues the war. This means having an appreciable offensive system survive the first day of the war in addition to deliberately avoiding destruction of too many of his cities on this first day of the war. It is also crucial to have enough active and passive defense to protect the surviving strategic forces necessary for bargaining purposes and to preserve enough of our civilian society from his first and later strikes to make it worth while, from our point of view, to settle.

In such a war, even if there were no intention at all of punishing the other side, and even if he successfully induced us to restrict our attack to pure military targets, the enemy would still suffer a great deal of "bonus" damage. But the defender may still want to punish the attacker even more, as a secondary objective, because he may feel that the prospect of bonus damage is not enough to make the enemy extremely careful about accidentally starting a war. *It is important that all possessors of nuclear capability be fearful of starting an accidental war, so fearful that they will be willing to accept large peacetime operating costs and substantial degradations of capability in order to decrease the possibility of accidents and to increase the likelihood of error-free behavior.* However, I would tend to feel that the expected bonus damage plus the risks of more extensive destruction are so high that it is presumably not necessary to threaten any additional punishment. Such punishment has the extreme disadvantage of complicating negotiations.

The whole problem of *flexibility in war plans for use in the retaliation mission* is a relatively unexplored one. While much work has gone into studying targets and target systems, changing conditions and technology have tended to make most of the work obsolete long before it is completed. I would like to discuss the value of having flexible war plans in the context of a specific proposal. (I am not advocating this proposal; I am only using it to illuminate the questions that come up.) The guiding principle followed in designing the proposal was fully to implement the Stalemate War and Limit Damage objectives (not only to ourselves, but to allies and neutrals and even to some extent the enemy) without weakening our Type I Deterrence excessively.

Table 32 indicates the basic proposal. The first column describes the postattack capability of the force. The second column assumes that these capabilities correspond to a certain level of damage. The numbers in this second column are arbitrary. They are just supposed to illustrate one set of possibilities.

❖❖❖

TABLE 32
FLEXIBLE WAR PLANS FOR DEFENDER

Capability of Surviving Force	Assumed Level of Damage	Action
Negligible Counterforce Moderate Countervalue	80–100%	All-out countervalue
Some Counterforce High Countervalue	40–80%	All-out counterforce Some withholding
High Counterforce High Countervalue	10–40%	Careful counterforce Much withholding
More than 90% of original capability	0–10%	Temporizing Measure or very discriminating counterforce

❖❖❖

The table suggests that if the enemy is lucky enough to destroy 80 per cent or more of our strategic force, we should devote the remaining force to malevolent (i.e. countervalue) objectives—to punish the enemy in that way which is hurtful to him. We might plan to do this even though he maximizes his blackmail threat, which would now be a very credible threat. In a way, I am saying that under these circumstances we would risk annihilation rather than attempt to alleviate the war. This notion may seem to contradict some other views that I have expressed. I stated earlier, for example, that no nation such as the United States should or would deliberately choose to commit suicide; yet it is clear that if we lost 80 per cent or more of our force and attempt to use the rest malevolently in the face of an overwhelming enemy superiority, he may, in his anger, literally destroy the United States. The reason I think this contingency plan is reasonable is partly that *every effort should be made to insure that the enemy could not possibly destroy 80 per cent or more of our force on his first strike.* If we are successful in this attempt, then the 80 per cent destruction case cannot occur and we do not care if the corresponding plan is reasonable or not. However, as I will try to illustrate in the next lecture, it is very difficult in this uncertain world of rapid technological change to guarantee that we will have a posture in which this will be true. It is just possible that the enemy, in spite of our best thought and preparation, may (either because he is clever, or because he or we have made a miscalculation) develop a technique which *he believes* will destroy more than 80 per cent of our strategic force on the first blow. We wish to assure him that *even if he thinks he can be this successful, he is still in serious trouble.* To the extent that he could *rely* on our using our small remaining force "sensibly," this might not be true.

Sometimes people argue that it is all right to assure the enemy before the war that if he attacks we will be irrationally malevolent, at the same time knowing that in the event itself it would be silly to carry out the threat—particularly at a moment when the enemy is so far ahead. I believe this is substantially true. But I do not believe that the idea of using our small remaining SAC against his society, rather than against his strategic force, is credible *unless we really intend to do it.* If we are only *pretending* that we would do it, the credibility and therefore the deterrent value of our force is almost certain to be lessened by the automatic and inevitable leaks. While we can probably keep the details of our war plans secret, it is most unlikely that we can keep the philosophy behind them secret. If there were some politically acceptable accident-proof way to make this kind of retaliation completely automatic, it would be sensible to put it into immediate effect.[7]

The second set of war plans is implemented when he succeeds in

[7] It should be noted that this kind of retaliation may be acceptable in another way. Even though the defender is trying to be malevolent, his force is small. Therefore his retaliation is "relatively humanitarian," that is, it does not involve the annihilation of continents; it is no Doomsday Machine.

destroying between 40 and 80 per cent of our force. At this point we have a large enough force remaining to do considerable damage. I would suggest that this force mostly be devoted to destroying his force—that is, to a counterforce mission. Subject to pursuing the mission aggressively, we should leave his cities alone, particularly if he has obviously tried to avoid ours. However, we should withhold enough forces to be able to threaten his cities.

This situation raises some big targeting uncertainties. For example, if he has planned the war weeks or months in advance, it is quite unlikely that we will find many enemy Polaris-type submarines at home ports and bombers at home bases, or any especially vulnerable concentrations of unfired missiles (e.g., missiles in such places as Kamchatka). On the other hand, if he had only a few hours or possibly even a few days of preparation, this might not be true. All of the above might then be very valuable military targets. Similarly, in some cases we may want to hit staging bases, and in other cases home bases. It is not necessary to discuss such an operation in detail here, but I think the essential ideas should be quite clear.

What if the enemy only succeeds in destroying 10 to 40 per cent of our force? This makes for a rather peculiar war. Most likely he did not initiate the war with the expectation of seeing the majority of our strategic force survive. The war may have started by accident. Perhaps it was by miscalculation. Or he ran into bad luck. In each of these cases it should be possible to terminate a war quite rapidly, if we and he can exercise enough self-control to prevent the war from degenerating into an "all-out slugging match." Even if we are so provoked at the attack that we wish to destroy the enemy, this is probably not the time to try it. Though the initiative he had did not prove devastating in the first few hours, it may be enough to give him the advantage. We should still devote our surviving forces, now quite large, to the counterforce mission, but we should be extremely careful how we carry out this mission, refraining from attacking any enemy "Polaris" bases in the harbors of important cities, or "SAC" bases near very large cities, and so on. The aim should be to institute negotiations toward a cessation of hostilities while at the same time trying to destroy the enemy's offense and defense, both as a hedge against the failure of negotiations and to improve our bargaining position by blunting the later waves of the attacking force. Both need to be done quite carefully. By being careful, unfortunately, we take the risk that if the negotiations do not work we will suffer more damage than if we had not been careful. On the other hand, we are probably maximizing the probability of sharply decreasing the damage.

What if the attacker succeeds, in his first strike, in getting less than 10 per cent of our force? If the previous 10–40 per cent war was peculiar, this one is even stranger! In all likelihood, this is an accidental war or a sneak attack gone awry, or the Chinese or some other third power trying to touch off a United States–Soviet conflict. Whatever it is, it is not the result of a deliberate and successful surprise attack by the enemy. In the case of 0–10 per cent destruction we should temporize—perhaps by doing nothing more than putting his military establishment on a state of alert. If this seems too innocuous, or if he wishes to hedge against the possibility that an all-out war might break out, we can possibly destroy some especially threatening portions of his force (e.g., ICBM's close to U. S. territory, as on Kamchatka,[8] or especially important strategic home bases). While either of these two "limited" reactions might strike most readers as being unrealistic, they are not as unrealistic as initiating a city exchange at a time when we are totally unprepared for war and there is a reasonable possibility that the enemy did not intend to start one. I repeat, there is clearly something incredibly wrong in the attacker's initiating a war and doing it so badly. Under these circumstances the defender should only attack the other's force when it can be done in the most sanitary way possible. And he should send him an explanation of what he is doing. Even if the attacker does not immediately concede that he initiated the blow and is willing to make amends, the proper thing to do may still be to break off diplomatic relations, to appoint an investigating committee to look into what happened, or to do something else on this level. While these reactions may strike the reader as inappropriate, none of them is as inappropriate as the initiation of a mutual holocaust.

All the above assumes that there is some kind of information-gathering network and data-processing centers that can receive and

[8] Any bases the Soviets put on Kamchatka will be only three or four thousand miles away from their probable targets—hardened U.S. ICBM bases. Because they are so close they will be able to carry a much heavier bomb and be more accurate than ICBM's stationed in the interior of the Soviet Union. This means that these ICBM's are much more dangerous to our retaliatory force. In addition, because they are so close to Alaska we should have both the information and the capability we need to be able to destroy them.

evaluate information, make decisions, and transmit orders—all in a matter of minutes or even seconds. It seems to be feasible to build systems that will do this even under enemy attack. Such systems will rely heavily on certain kinds of fixed installations, particularly headquarters buildings. The systems have to gather the information automatically. And the evaluation, decision, and transmission of orders will probably also be done by automatic machines using pre-set instructions. There will, of course, be data displays and human interference (overrides) available at various points to countermand the automatic machinery. (Nobody is yet willing to trust the decision of war or peace to a computer.) But every delay that is introduced increases the risk of destruction—these will have to be kept to the minimum necessary to prevent accidents or irresponsible behavior.

There are some very knotty questions that come up here about executive responsibility and civil-military relations. The most important constraint is the requirement that the President or his authorized representative have final control as to whether war is on or not, whom he intends to attack, and how he intends to conduct military operations. Because any single headquarters may be vulnerable to a direct or subtle attack, it is very likely that the President will need the equivalent of many "assistant presidents" sitting in protected places (such as underground air defense, SAC, or civil defense headquarters) with adequate communications, information, and data-processing equipment.[9] These "assistant presidents" will each have the responsibility, in some order or priority, to:

(1) recognize that there is a state of war on;
(2) assess the damage;
(3) make the decision about what to do;
(4) communicate these decisions to the proper places;
(5) regulate and monitor the ensuing activities.

These are all very critical functions now, and they are likely to become more critical in the future.

The first question that comes up is whether the individuals who sit in the protected headquarters and have this responsibility should be military or civilian. Some who have thought about this subject believe that if "assistant presidents for war or peace" are appointed

---

[9] For a discussion of some of the technical possibilities for deep underground buildings, see RAND Report R-341, *Protective Construction*, March 1959.

they should be civilians. They argue that the principle of civilian control must be upheld in this most crucial of all decisions. However, I think that in actual practice the deciding thing should be the quality of the man rather than whether he is wearing mufti or not. I find it difficult to envisage recruiting first-rate civilians for such a job—one in which they live or spend many hours a week in a military installation and have no stimulating civilian occupation. Even time-sharing arrangements are probably too onerous a duty for senior civilians to assume in peacetime. In addition, time-sharing of the one-day-a-week variety would inordinately multiply the number of assistant presidents required. No such difficulties arise, or at least not in such severe form, with military decision makers.

It may be important to give these decision makers rather rigorous training courses on the various circumstances that can arise and what the corresponding decisions should be. Such training courses would be of great value to military decision makers. Even aside from the palatability of special courses, the background and training that one would want these assistant presidents to have is a natural for a senior military commander (while quite foreign to the tastes and capabilities of most of the civilians who would be available).

Whether they are in uniform or not, it is important to have these decision makers responsive to Presidential control. This, in turn, may mean some organizational and administrative problems, but with some thought we ought to be able to work out an adequate system. Here, as elsewhere, everything depends on knowing what we want, and initiating the proper measures before the situation becomes critical. Since the lead time for the installations and communications is likely to be five or six years, we must face up to these problems now if we are to be prepared for the mid-sixties when the question of Command and Control gets more critical. Unfortunately, as far as public discussion goes, the whole problem of Command and Control in both wartime and the transition to war is often neglected, and it is quite possible that some serious defects will develop in our posture.

CHAPTER V

STRESSES AND STRAINS

Planning for a Complicated World

IN addition to trying to satisfy multiple and in some cases conflicting objectives, *sensible military planning should try to take account of the fact that wars can arise in many different ways.* Let us, therefore, ask ourselves, What are the various types of situations in which we might expect war or the threat of war to occur? How do these different situations change our concepts or our preparations? It is important to answer these questions if we are to design military and nonmilitary systems which are sufficiently flexible to meet the complexities of the real world and which do not suffer from fatal omissions, weaknesses, or premature obsolescence.

◆◆◆

TABLE 33
EIGHT BASIC SITUATIONS

I. Five Classes of Wars
    A. Normal Alert Status
        1. A Soviet attack "out of the blue"
        2. An "accidental" accident
    B. Tension Alert Status
        1. The Soviets solve a problem
        2. A "non-accidental" accident
        3. The Americans solve a problem
II. Change of Policy
        1. Technological breakthrough
        2. Deterioration of international relations
        3. Arms control

◆◆◆

It is most unlikely that we will be able to make equally satisfactory preparations for all the situations in Table 33. If it turns out that a certain system is especially useful in one of these situations, but not in the others, we should not reject the system as inadequate, but instead ask if its cost and performance justify procuring it for the specialized use. If there then are deficiencies in the preparations for the other situations those deficiencies must either be countered by other means or tolerated. In the United States there is an overconcentration on the first war (a premeditated S.U. attack out of the blue), and in NATO there seems to be an overconcentration on the third war on the list (a premeditated S.U. attack after an alerting period of tension). The suggestion in Table 33 that in addition to being prepared with a capability in being we should make preparations for a change in policy as brought about, for example, by a technological breakthrough, a deterioration in the international situation, or arms control measures is almost uniformly ignored. In principle, even those studies that examine hedging against a change in policy should include analyzing the performance of the hedged system under each of the previously mentioned wars both before and after the change in policy has been made. It is most unlikely that any actual studies will be that thorough, but even modest study and preparations can make an important difference in our ability to react. We do need more than just study; we need physical preparations if our posture is to be prepared to accept changes easily and efficiently.

In our research and development (R&D) programs we should push "state of the art" work in all kinds of interesting fields so that we will be in a position to create and exploit breakthroughs and meet totally unexpected challenges. Until a project gets to be moderately expensive (usually at the weapon system stage), the limiting factor should be—at least under current conditions—the scarcity of good people and ideas rather than money. I will have more to say on this important topic in Lecture III. In Lecture II, I will consider the Preattack Mobilization Base for use if and when the international situation deteriorates, and I will also consider some of the problems of arms control.

Let us start now with some details of the nontense situation.

A Soviet Attack "Out of the Blue"

It is hard for most people, including the author, to believe that any nation would violate the balance of terror and start a war unless it was under great pressure to do so.

A modern thermonuclear war is, after all, a completely hypothetical operation. There will always be chilling uncertainties—some of them completely unexpected. No matter how much care has gone into making plans and no matter how much peacetime training and careful evaluation is done, it is hard to believe that any sober plan-

191

ners will assign this unprecedented and complicated operation a probability greater than, say, .9 of achieving even a partial success. This means that there would be .1 chance of a disastrous failure. The issues are so great that one chance in ten of the attack going awry and failing, perhaps totally, seems to be too big a chance for most decision makers to take. This is, of course, one of the main arguments of the adherents to Minimum Deterrence. It is most unlikely, therefore, says this calculation, that any nation will go to war. I tend to agree with the judgment if one adds "for positive gains." As I have said several times, a nation is most likely to go to war when it believes that it is less risky not to go to war. However, it is always possible for an enemy to decide to go to war in a crisis and then deliberately act in a conciliatory fashion to persuade the opponent to relax his alert status. It might therefore be necessary to be prepared to maintain some type of super-alert long after the crisis seems to have relaxed—but not for an indefinite period. (Presumably there are limits to how long the enemy can wait, either because the temporary settlement that he accepted is resulting in a rapid deterioration of his position or simply because it is difficult for most human beings, including decision makers, to hold such a resolve for a long period.) From the analytic point of view, the problem is to be able to spend a great deal of money in a postcrisis period in a very small amount of time to keep a super-alert posture, as opposed to the normal problem of being willing to spend a small amount of money in a large amount of time. However, being able and willing to do this does not dispose of the problem. Even the situation without any tension (everybody seeming to be relaxed and happy, or at least at a normal temperature) may have its dangers.

I used to feel strongly that the "normal" situation was relatively safe. Thus I ventured to make at that time the following analogy. Assume that we put all of SAC's three thousand bombers and tankers into Times Square, turn off the radars, and announce in the newspapers that we had done so. Would the Soviets attack? I suggested that they would not, at least not in the first week, or even in the first month. Somehow, no reasonable country starts a fight with an opponent who owns almost two thousand H-bomb-carrying planes just because he seems to have dropped his guard momentarily. However, there is an important caveat. It would be dangerous to leave those planes sitting there and have our radars turned off indefinitely. We do not want a potential enemy's high command contemplating for months or years a possible opportunity to eliminate most of his supposed troubles at one blow.

Let us consider a hypothetical but not completely manufactured example that has some similarities with the Times Square example. During the early months of 1958 there was much discussion in newspapers and magazines that we might be doing something very much like putting our bombers into Times Square by failing to react quickly and adequately to a developing Russian missile threat. I would like to make some comments on the situation, not to prolong that controversy (though it might be desirable to do so), but only to discuss the issues involved and to point out that it is necessary to react vigorously to "hypothetical" changes in the threat if we are not to run excessive risks. In discussing this problem, I will assume that in 1957 the Strategic Air Command was normally stationed on about twenty-five bases.[1]

The Russians announced in August 1957 that they had tested an intercontinental ballistic missile, and in October 1957 they launched their first Sputnik. At the same time there were many stories in United States news journals and magazines to the effect that the Russians had had a very vigorous ballistic missile program for many years and had developed reliable intermediate and short-range missiles. This indicated to many people that the Russians might possess a rather advanced missile technology and that it might only be a few years, if the Russians went into a crash program, before they might have quite a large number of reliable ICBM's in their operational force. In fact, even people who were trying to look calm agreed that the Russians would probably have an operational missile capability in a few years.

While very few numerical estimates were given by those who were trying to reassure, some mentioned two, three, or four years. Those who were advocating crash programs for the United States tended to make somewhat shorter estimates. Finally, in early 1959

---

[1] General Power suggested (in a speech before the New York Economic Club, January 19, 1960, reported in the *New York Times*, January 20, 1960, p. 14) that we had fifty SAC home bases within the continental United States. I got the number of twenty-five by dividing this number by two to account for the fact that there has been a publicly announced expansion of the number of bases. The number 25 is also consistent with General Washbourne's testimony ("Study of Airpower," *Hearings* before the Subcommittee on the Air Force of the Committee on Armed Services, U.S. Senate, 84th Congr., 2nd Sess., 1956, Vol. I, p. 393) of two medium or one heavy bomber wing per base. The reader can make any adjustments in the argument he desires to for a different number of bases.

Khrushchev boasted that the Soviet Union had intercontinental rockets in serial production.

I do not wish to make any comment on the possible accuracy of the above estimates. I just wish to consider a hypothetical situation. What would happen if these estimates were reasonably accurate and the Russians had appreciable numbers of operational ICBM's, say, three years after their announcement of a successful test of a prototype (that is, August 1960), and if, in addition, we took our own defense problems very calmly and did not react by initiating long

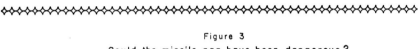

Figure 3
Could the missile gap have been dangerous?
SAC assumed on 25 soft bases

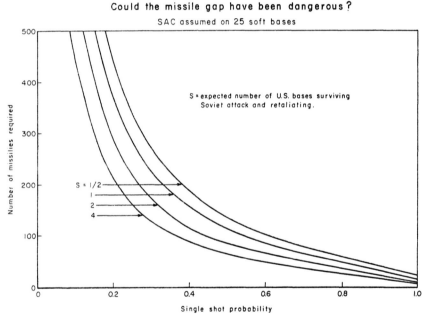

Single shot probability

lead-time programs within a matter of months to meet "hypothetical" changes in Russian posture? If these changes turned out not to be hypothetical, what kind of risk would we run?

Figure 3 illustrates the number of missiles that the Russians would need in order to destroy the postulated 25 SAC bases. It indicates that we might be accepting quite substantial risks. For example, assume that the Russians have achieved a technological capability halfway between perfection and worthlessness; that is, they have a

194

probability of ½ of destroying any soft SAC bases they shoot at. Then if they have, say, 125 missiles, even if these missiles could not be fired in a closely coordinated fashion (that is, even if their firing time is spread out over an hour or so), it would still be possible for the Russians to push 125 buttons and expect to have almost an even chance of destroying *all* the planes that were on the ground at SAC home bases, about one chance in three that *one* such base would survive, and a small probability that *two or more* would survive. It would presumably be no problem at all, if the Soviets were unlucky, for their air defense to handle attacks launched by planes from one or two of our bases. If they wished to accept the risk involved in facing an attack from, say, three or four bases, they would only need about 75 missiles, each with a single-shot probability of ½; if they had 150 missiles, the single-shot probability could be as low as ⅓ and still be satisfactory to a Soviet planner willing to accept an attack from three or four surviving bases.

The above discussion illustrates earlier remarks that missile attacks are more calculable than almost any other kind of attack. Indeed, missile attacks of this kind are so calculable that many people believe that the results of such an attack can be predicted just by applying well-known principles of engineering and physics. They look so calculable that even a cautious Soviet planner might believe that he could rely on the correctness of his estimates; thus *he might find it the path of caution to attack while the opportunity to rid himself of his dangerous opponent was still available.* If, for example, the Russians have been able to fire enough missiles in their test programs to get a fairly accurate estimate of reliability and accuracy, they might easily be persuaded that they have most of the information they need. If the stories about their intermediate-range and short-range missiles are correct, they can learn a good deal from these previous missile programs, and they might feel that they would not need to test as many ICBM's as we might feel that we had to. They might feel that they could predict the results of such an attack with almost complete assurance.

Actually, even with tested missiles, results of attacks are not really mathematically predictable. The probability of extreme variations in performance, the upper and lower limits, cannot be calculated accurately. But laymen or narrow professionals persist in regarding the matter as a simple problem in engineering and physics. Therefore, unless sophisticated objections are raised, even an inarticulate

Russian general could probably force the following conclusions on a group of hostile, skeptical, and busy civilians, whether they wanted to believe them or not: that in this hypothetical case (where the Russians had 125 missiles, each with a single-shot probability of ½), if they were to push these 125 buttons and also launch a supplementary coordinated attack with IRBM's and tactical bombers on U.S. and allied overseas bases, there would be a reasonable chance that the Soviet Union would get away scot-free; that there would be a good chance that they would suffer very little damage; and that there would be no chance at all that they would suffer as much damage as they suffered in World War II.

Let us consider some of the caveats that this Russian general would have to face if somebody brought them up, and try to judge how serious Khrushchev or the Presidium would find them.

♦♦♦

TABLE 34

FOUR TYPICAL CAVEATS

1. Unreliable basic data
2. Field degradation
3. Intelligence leak
4. Unreliable discipline

♦♦♦

The first caveat is that they must have accurate data with which to calculate the attack. They must know the location and hardness of each SAC base and the existence of holes in any open or clandestine warning networks. Given the newness of the threat and U.S. security practices currently in vogue about the position and use of our SAC bases and the ease with which information could be obtained about last minute changes, this could look feasible. Probably the only requirement is to try to get the information.

They need accurate data about themselves—the yield, accuracy, and reliability of their ICBM's, for example. While it is surprisingly hard to get reliable estimates of these quantities, only very sophisticated people will know this. If the Soviets have some extra margin of performance for insurance—that is, if they have a much better technological capability than they need—they do not require extremely accurate estimates of this capability. On the other hand, if their equipment is just marginally satisfactory, then even though

196

they have an adequate capability they are unlikely to know this.

In talking about the performance of equipment, one usually differentiates between the intrinsic capability of the equipment and what actually happens in the field; that is, the question of field degradation. Let us go back to our Russian general's persuasion problem. It is perfectly possible, for example, for this general to take the members of the Presidium out to the range and show them, say, 5 or 10 ICBM's lined up, and ask them to select one missile and then make a cross on a world map. The range personnel could proceed to fire that ICBM and hit near enough to the cross to make the general's point. Or even more convincingly, they might fire all 5 or 10 ICBM's at once—all of them falling in the target area.

This would be an impressive demonstration, but a question arises. The demonstration shows what can be done with factory maintenance and operation by the most skilled personnel available. What happens when the missiles are operated in the field by regular military personnel? While in the past century or two the Russians have established a tradition of initial incompetency in a war, they have, since World War II, emphasized reliability of equipment, sometimes at the cost of other performance. One would assume that if they could obtain accuracy and yield at all, they could obtain it reliably. Nevertheless, the worry might remain, How far from range performance will we be?

Khrushchev might or might not feel that with 125 missiles the Soviets should be able to attain near theoretical range performance. They might operate these 125 missiles from one or two secret bases—this would simplify both security and control problems. In any case the Russians should be able to get close to factory maintenance performance with a much larger number of dispersed missiles. As we all know, they do have an enormous number of engineering graduates, a high percentage of whom undoubtedly go into the armed services. This means that the average technical ability of the people they have available to fire and operate missiles is probably relatively high. Nevertheless, the nagging worry might remain, How much off range performance will we be?

The third caveat is that there be no intelligence leak. Given the small number of missiles involved and the tight security in the Russian empire, this might be a reasonably safe assumption. But whether the Russians would be willing to rely on our lack of intelligence is very hard to say. The Russians might think it possible for us to have

197

a very senior spy or, even more worrisome, for them to have a defector—possibly in the Presidium itself.

The fourth caveat concerns firing discipline, that is, that nobody fires either prematurely or too late. If we work on our original assumption that the U.S. posture remains unchanged since 1957, when alerts were measured in hours or so, this is not a rigid requirement. However, if we give ourselves credit for a 15-minute alert, this would mean that the Russian missiles are so reliable that when they want to press the buttons the majority of the missiles are actually ready to be fired. If the Russian missiles have a "hold" capability—that is, if they can be ready some minutes or hours early and then maintain this ready position—this may not be a difficult requirement, although it could decrease the effective reliability.[2] A small reduction in reliability would simply mean that the Russians would need a few more ICBM's. A large reduction would most likely put them out of business.

There is an interesting interaction between firing discipline and measures designed to reduce the possibility of intelligence leaks. If the Soviets trained with very realistic exercises so that even the people involved in the exercises could not distinguish until the last minute the exercise from the real thing, such exercises could be used to disguise preparations for attack. But there would be a tendency for somebody to fire prematurely, perhaps causing an accidental war. If, on the contrary, the Soviets tried to prevent this breach of firing discipline by the use of severe threats and indoctrination so that nobody would fire prematurely, they would run the opposite risk that people might refuse to believe the order when it came, unless they were alerted ahead of time.

One could imagine the following dialogue between Khrushchev and his inarticulate general.

G: So you can see that if you press these three hundred buttons there is a good chance of us getting away scot-free, a small chance of us suffering moderate damage and no chance at all of us suffering as much damage as we suffered in World War II.

K: The Americans are on a fifteen-minute alert. If they have any spies or even if we have a defector we will be destroyed!

G: Don't worry. I have arranged to have a training count-down operation at noon every Saturday. All you have to do is pick up the telephone

---

[2] We are defining a missile's reliability here as including the probability that it takes off within a few minutes of the assigned firing time. Given that the Soviet missiles have a "hold" capability, this may not be a much smaller number than if we define reliability as the probability that the missile takes off within a few hours of the assigned firing time.

and give the order. You will be the only one who knows when the attack is going to take place.

K: I don't believe it. What if some Ukrainian who is still mad at me presses one of the buttons ahead of time just to get me in trouble!

G: Don't worry. I know that some Ukrainians are still harboring un-justified grievances against you. There are no Ukrainians in this force. In addition to being specially selected for reliability every officer is married and has children and we have told these officers that if they fire early not only will they be shot but their families will be severely punished. We can do this extraordinary measure without hurting morale, because every officer realizes that this issue is of overriding importance.

K: I still don't like it. I can imagine what will happen. I will pick up the phone and say 'fire!' The officer will reply, 'What did you say?' I will repeat, 'Fire!' He will say, 'There seems to be a bad connection. I keep hearing the word "fire." ' I will say, 'If you don't fire I will have you boiled in oil.' He will say, 'I *heard you* that time. *Don't* fire! Thank you very much!'

Khrushchev in this hypothetical example is of course quite correct. *There must be preliminary alerting and verifying orders if all the people are to believe the orders and press the buttons at the right time.*

It should be noted that *so long as our strategic bases are soft, missile attacks present the Russians with possibilities for the use of a postattack blackmail strategy almost as extreme as the one mentioned previously.* If the Russians concentrate their attack solely against strategic bases and air-burst their weapons (which is the most efficient way to use a weapon against a soft target), there will be no local fallout effects. Then, unless one of the weapons goes astray and hits a major city, deaths would be limited to a few million Americans as the result of blast and thermal effects. The Soviets could then point out (unless we had appreciable surviving levels of air offense, air defense, and civil defense) that they could totally destroy our country (while we could only hurt them), and did we really want to pick this moment to initiate the use of nuclear weapons against open cities?

Even with the hypothesized assumptions, it would take a moderately reckless Soviet decision maker to press the 125 ICBM buttons, but such things have happened. It would be even more reckless for the United States to rely on extreme Soviet caution and responsibility as a defense. In any case, our Type I Deterrence can be strained, and in some moderately plausible situations even a cautious Soviet government might prefer pressing buttons if the odds were for it. *The*

mere recognition by U.S. and European decision makers of the pos-
sibility of such an attack could dominate or distort all international
relations.

Actually, the situation differs from this hypothetical one, because
we have taken many measures to alleviate this problem. But the
measures we have adopted may or may not give us an adequate
factor of safety. In any case, it is necessary to react rapidly to changes
in the enemy's posture.

The need for quick reaction to even "hypothetical" changes in the
enemy's posture is likely to be with us for the indefinite future, in
spite of the popularity of the theory that once we get over our current difficulties we will have achieved at least a stable Finite Deterrent.

Dropping now the hypothetical assumption that we did not react
at all, I should make the point that while the measures we took in
1957, 1958, and 1959 helped alleviate the problem, they may not be
enough. I have already discussed the most important measures—
the ground-alert capability of getting our forces off the ground with
fifteen minutes of warning. There may, however, be no method of
getting reliable warning of an ICBM attack in most or all of the
1960–1961 time period, except from Russian sloppiness in the timing
of their salvo. This does put constraints on them on both firing time
and reliability. While such constraints may keep them from attacking, this is still a very unreliable measure of security. We have no
way of knowing that the Russians could not shoot the required number of missiles within two or three minutes. At the least, they might
get one out of two missiles off in the required time.

The dispersal we have undertaken is a most important measure. In
our calculations we arbitrarily assumed that we have dispersed by a
factor of 2; that would about double the Russian missile requirements.

Airborne alert would probably be a very effective measure, but
it has been announced that because of the expense and operational
complications we have not instituted one at this writing.

The publicly discussed defensive measures—such as *BMEWS*
(Ballistic Missile Early Warning Systems), Polaris firing submarines,
and hardened ICBM bases—will just barely be coming into service
in the year following August 1960 and are likely not to be entirely
operational. However, even if the early systems are unreliable for a
time, so that they are not objectively available until much later, they

should at least introduce sobering uncertainties into any Russian calculations.

What I am saying is that our protection may have depended (and possibly will depend) on extreme responsibility and caution on the part of Soviet decision makers or on Soviet inability or unwillingness to carry through the kind of crash program for ICBM's which they have previously carried through for their TU-4, Bear, Bison, and Badger bomber programs (or which we have carried through in the Thor and Atlas programs).

All the crash programs that I have just mentioned involved getting into fairly large-scale production programs while the prototypes were still being tested. The produced articles were then retrofitted with any changes that the operational suitability test program showed were necessary. This is not an uncommon practice. In fact, it is almost standard in the development of a modern weapon system.

Our government has assured us that the Russians have not carried through a successful crash program resulting in their having numbers of operational ICBM's. However, an examination of Congressional testimony and other public sources raises a sobering thought. Some feel there is more than a mild indication that we got the information late—so late that one doubts that we could have reacted in time even if the Russians had carried through such a program. Secondly, many of the measures seem to have been put in as a reluctant response to Congressional and public pressure, rather than as a routine response to staff recommendations. Another and much more important consideration is the reliability of the information on which the government's feeling of safety is based. It is not true, as is often stated in Congress, that one can take no chances with national security. Today's world is full of risks. Still, it is not sufficient merely to say that one is taking a calculated risk. (The term "calculated risk," as nearly as I can see, is always used in the sense that there is a risk of which we are aware but have not been able to calculate.) *One would like to actually calculate this "calculated risk"—to get some numerical orientation on what the risks are.* Are we taking one chance out of a hundred that the Russians have a disguised program we do not know about? Is it one in ten, or one in three, or what?

What I am trying to say is that the most frightening thing about this possible Deterrent Gap (or as I will refer to it from now on, Operational Gap) is not that it probably exists, but that we *do not seem to worry enough about the possibility.* At least from 1957 to

201

1959 we did not. A handful of critics, many of whom were obviously trying to make political capital out of the situation and were therefore suspect, raised some fuss, but these critics mostly emphasized the gaps in research and development, or in procurement. With a few exceptions, no one stressed the nature of the possible Operational Gap. We should always remember that this kind of Operational Gap is very dangerous. It may be much more tempting to a Russian planner than one which could look equally good on paper but which involved many relatively imponderable risks, such as their ability to make long, circuitous, over-water flights undetected, or sneak through holes in our radar cover, or clandestinely smuggle suitcase-bombs into this country, and so on.

We have already discussed how evaluation of the effectiveness of an ICBM attack seems to involve mostly problems in physics and engineering, utilizing what to the Russians could be well-known and documented constants. If they have run enough tests, they may persuade themselves that they can estimate accurately both the upper and lower limits of performance, even though we think that they cannot. Furthermore, this possibly extreme weakness in our deterrence capability would not last for a momentary point in time; rather, if it existed at all, it would be likely to last anywhere from a number of months to a few years.

It would be imprudent for us to take, say, even one chance in ten that the Soviets would sit for a somewhat lengthy period with a few hundred buttons or so at a time when we might be, for all practical purposes, defenseless. As far as we know, it would have been well within Russian resources, if they made the decision in 1957–58, to enter into such a crash ICBM program. With a little luck, they could have achieved the necessary technological capabilities. Still our government has assured us that they have intelligence information that the Soviets did not enter into a crash program along those lines.

What are the availability and extent of Russian resources for such a crash program? After an initial spurt of production, the Russians seem to have cut back, around 1957, on the procurement of heavy bombers and, in 1958, they dumped surplus aluminum on the international market. They also seem to have made reductions in other parts of their armed services. Many people have conjectured that they may have originally intended to produce a very large number of long-range bombers and then changed their minds. The lack of a

202

large heavy bomber program may be a case where Soviet "intentions" were misleading to both us and the Soviets. There could be at least four plausible reasons why they changed their minds.

1. Perhaps the performance characteristics of both the Bear and the Bison were disappointing. (General White, Chief of Staff of USAF, indicated that he believed this to be the reason.[3])

2. It may be that they planned to introduce superior follow-up bombers. (There has been no public disclosure of such a program. However, the last few May Day programs of the Russians de-emphasized military products; this indicates that if they had such new bombers they would not necessarily have displayed them to the West.)

3. Perhaps they decided to switch their resources into ICBM production. (The transfer of this quantity of resources would mean a very large crash program.)

4. They might be disarming, or at least not expanding their strategic forces.

While it is easy to be an alarmist and point only to the crash program in ICBM's as the most probable thing, disarmament is also a possibility. There was a great debate in Russia during 1954–1956 about whether they could get along with only a Minimum Deterrent force and not bother to buy an expensive "Win-the-War" capability. As often happens, even though the win-the-war advocates seem to have won the political battle, a good deal of the opposition program was adopted. In 1957 the Russians raised minimum wage rates for many workers, increased some pensions, and in other ways introduced expensive welfare measures. They also greatly increased their rate of investment in agriculture, and instituted or increased foreign aid activities. In addition, due to the changed political situation, they were not able to draw as much from the satellite countries as they had been in the habit of doing. Rather the opposite. It is probable that a number of the satellites came to represent a net economic drain. We do not know if all this required a cutback in armaments, but it is a plausible hypothesis that they did at least absorb the major part of the resources saved by the cutback in bomber production that we mentioned. This pressure on their budgets could also be the reason why they may not have gone into a crash ICBM program—

[3] *Hearings* before the Preparedness Investigating Subcommittee of the Committee on Armed Services, U.S. Senate, 86th Congr., 1st. Sess., March 1959, p. 127.

if that was the case. *It should be clear that* things could have gone the other way and a situation might have arisen in which they accelerated rather than decelerated their program.

Some experts have argued that even if the missile gap existed it would not be important. Sometimes they belong to the Minimum Deterrent school (in which many facts fail to influence them), and sometimes they have the theory that even if our U.S.-based forces were an unreliable Type I Deterrent the overseas forces of the West would make up for any deficiencies. The last idea is not a comforting theory. Sober examination indicates that given estimated Russian tactical capabilities, the overseas weapons systems as currently deployed should not really complicate their wartime problem of reducing our retaliatory force to an acceptable level. They should have an excess of IRBM's and medium and light bombers to handle all overseas points, presumably including our carriers. Any small number of planes that inadvertently survived their offense would have to penetrate a prepared and expectant air defense system. Overseas problems are also probably simplified for the Russians, because the warning networks seem to have gaps and weaknesses which the attacking Soviet bomb carriers can exploit. (A recent incident in which unidentified planes bombed some point on the German coast indicates there are gaps in the warning networks.)

There are many things that we might do to ameliorate or to insure against the possibility that the Russians produce more and better ICBM's than we are expecting them to. But nothing at this late date (1960) except *certain* knowledge that the Soviets do *not* have the capability would make our strategic posture completely satisfactory. This is not the place to discuss these things in detail. *For any who are deeply disturbed over the possibilities we have just discussed there are a number of measures to be examined. Among these are: increased ground alert; some interim "psychological" anti-ICBM capability; a crash hardening program for both planes and missiles; an emergency dispersal program—possibly including the deployment of simple H-bomb-carrying missiles on ships at sea; a full airborne alert or perhaps just keeping a somewhat larger portion of our planes aloft than is currently the practice (possibly on a random basis); an increase in the Atlas, Titan, and Polaris programs; credible plans to increase and to use the unready forces which might survive a first attack; and a "quick fix" of any holes in our air defense. Additionally, we need an ability to improvise at least moderately effective civil defense measures so that we will not be so vulnerable to either the preattack or postattack blackmail tactic.* Some of the measures suggested are now in programs in a tentative way and some might not be available until 1963 or 1964. But if the Russians have produced a large number of missiles in 1959 and 1960, we will want at least some of these measures in 1963 and 1964—that is, if we get through 1961 and 1962!

An "Accidental" Accident

Let us now turn to the second of our eight basic situations. *There may be an appreciable possibility of an accidental or otherwise unpremeditated war even when the situation is not tense.* Almost all military planners believe that unless forces are much more alert and dispersed in the future than they have been in the past they will be extremely vulnerable to surprise attacks. As a result, there are all kinds of proposals to use extremely *quick reaction* or *extreme dispersal* with *correspondingly dispersed control* as a protection. But many who have studied the situation think that some proposals calling for forces of this kind can make us dangerously prone to accidents. For example, many studies indicate that *unless a strategic force occasionally reacts in some appropriate way to false alarms, it runs a risk of not reacting at all when the real thing comes along.* Some of the proposals advocated for quick-reacting or dispersed control systems could not survive many false alarms without some appreciable risk of setting off an accidental war. Even the current relatively reliable "fail-safe" or "positive control" systems may become dangerous if the Soviets adopt similar measures and either of the two sides is so careless in his operating practices that "a self-fulfilling prophecy" is set into motion. For example, consider some of the problems of our current "fail safe" (or "positive control") system. This system was described by Frank H. Bartholomew (President of the United Press at the time), in a dispatch that was distributed by the news agency on April 7, 1958:

. . . you were airborne in six minutes; you have been flying for eight minutes. Enemy missiles that must have passed you in flight would be due to strike North America in one minute. Other United States bombers are in the air all over the world with reprisal bombs.

But this is one thing you alone do not know: Since your take-off, the foreign objects picked up on the radar scopes turned out to be a shower of meteorites.

Other aircraft in your sortie have been turned back by radio. But in spite of the trigger-quick efficiency of the command that dispatched you, and of the giant aircraft under your hand, there has been a failure: You did not receive a turn-back signal.

You have been dispatched with a complete invasion plan—routes across the enemy border to your target, alternate routes to an alternate target, routes across enemy country. You have more than one bomb. You have fuel for 6,000 miles.

Do you proceed to your target, does your bombardier press the button and does the first nuclear bomb go 'down the chimney' to start World War III? All this because one of the Strategic Air Command's vast fleet failed to receive a turn-back order?

Not so. You are saved, you and many others by a a powerfully simple plan called "Fail Safe." It is proof against error, human or mechanical.

Fail Safe, a term borrowed from the engineers, simply instructs you to proceed toward your target for a fixed number of nautical miles and then turn back if for any reason you do not at that point and at that moment receive coded orders to continue.

This actually has happened many times. The great counter-offensive striking force of the Strategic Air Command has been sped on its way by alerts created by meteoric flights registering on the DEW line radar-scopes, by interference from high-frequency transmitters or by the appearance of foreign objects, flying in seeming formation, that simply never have been explained.

"The compression of time in the Atomic Age is such that SAC must be in constantly alert status and ready for instantaneous counterattack," says Gen. Thomas S. Power, its commander.

Time does not permit holding bombing aircraft on the ground while alarms are investigated. The investigations take place while the bombers are on their way toward the target.

The Air Force planners believe that if World War III occurs, the first phase of nuclear bombing will all be over in the first four hours.

You are at the controls of the B-52 again, your radio is functioning, you have reached the Fail Safe line. This time, instead of an order to return or no orders at all, a voice in your earphones orders you to continue to target. . . .[4]

The U.P. dispatch created quite a furor. On April 18, Reuters in London made available the text of a statement by Foreign Minister Andrei A. Gromyko at a news conference, as issued in English by Tass, the Soviet news agency. In it, Gromyko said:

. . . American generals plead that thus far United States aircraft re-turned to their bases from half-way as soon as it became clear that the alarm was false. But what will happen if these generals whose nerves, as shown by the facts, frequently play them false, do not realize in time

[4] *New York Times*, April 19, 1958, p. 4.

that the meteor they see is not a guided missile, and American aircraft proceed with their mission and approach the Soviet Union's frontier? . . .

All this shows that mankind has on several occasions been on the brink of another war which could have flared up instantly through irresponsible or provocative actions on the part of the United States military command, and the peoples have not even suspected what danger overshadowed the world. . . .

The world is finding itself in a position where atomic war can result from a slightest mistake on the part of an American technician, from carelessness, miscalculation or faulty conclusion on the part of some American officer. . . .

Taking into account the grave threat which these flights spell for the peace of the world, the Soviet Government submits the question of stopping them to the Security Council of the United Nations. . . .[5]

On the same day the State Department issued the following reply to Gromyko's charges:

It is categorically denied that the United States Air Force is conducting provocative flights over the polar regions or in the vicinity of the U.S.S.R. Mr. Gromyko's charges appear to be an attempt to raise fears of mankind in the nuclear age.

What we do is public knowledge. What happens behind the Iron Curtain menacing to the free world is carefully hidden by the Soviets. We will be glad to discuss this question in the United Nations as we are always willing to discuss there any charge made against us. . . .

The Strategic Air Command is the mainstay of the free world's deterrent position. . . . It can only accomplish its mission of deterrence in the future if it is well known that it is so trained, so equipped and so situated that it cannot be surprised and destroyed on the ground by an enemy.

Therefore, it has in the past and will continue in the future to maintain its high state of efficiency through constant practice. All these training exercises, however, are designed to maintain the force within areas which by no stretch of the imagination could be considered provocative to the U.S.S.R. So far, the S.A.C. force has never been launched except in carefully planned and controlled exercises and practices.

Should there be a real alert based on a warning of a possible attack, the force would be launched under a procedure which makes certain that no S.A.C. airplane can pass beyond proper bounds far from the Soviet Union, or its satellites, without additional unequivocal orders which can come only from the President of the United States. The procedures are in no sense provocative, and could not possibly be the accidental cause of war.[6]

[5] *Ibid.*, p. 2.
[6] *Ibid.*, p. 2.

The matter gave rise to a Security Council debate on April 21, during the course of which the Soviet delegate, Arkady A. Sobolev, declared:

American generals refer to the fact that up to the present time the American planes have taken off on their flights and returned to their bases as soon as it became clear that it was a case of false alarm. But what would happen if American military personnel observing their radar screens are not able in time to determine a flying meteor is not a guided missile and that a flight of geese is not a flight of bombers? Then the American planes will continue their flight and will approach the borders of the Soviet Union.

But in such a case the need to insure the security of the Soviet people would require the U.S.S.R. to take immediate retaliatory measures to eliminate the oncoming threat. The Soviet Government would like to hope that matters will not go so far.

In order to get a clearer idea of the extremely dangerous character of acts of the United States dangerous to peace, it is enough to ask the question what would happen if the military Air Force of the Soviet Union began to act in the same way as the American Air Force is now acting? After all, Soviet radar screens also show from time to time blips which are caused by the flight of meteors, or electronic interference. If in such cases Soviet aircraft also flew out carrying atom and hydrogen bombs in the direction of the United States and its bases in other states, what situation would arise?

The air fleets of both sides having observed each other, having discerned each other somewhere over the Arctic wastes or in some other place, apparently would draw the conclusion natural under those circumstances, that a real enemy attack was taking place. Then the world would inevitably be plunged into the hurricane of atomic war.[7]

While it is clear that the Soviets were deliberately being alarmist and trying to make some propaganda out of an unfortunate news story, it can also be inferred from these quotations that, irrespective of how safe current American preparations are (and I should probably add that I do believe current preparations are safe), the problem may get worse in the future, unless *both* sides are careful, and unless there is some understanding on *both* sides of each other's operations.

Therefore in some sense the Russians have a legitimate right to ask certain kinds of questions about our operations, and we should be willing to answer these questions. Insofar as our system depends on things which cannot be explained to the Russians and which they may worry about, the system has a serious inadequacy. It is to our

[7] *New York Times*, April 22, 1958, p. 10.

208

interest to convince the Russians that they do not have to be trigger-happy. (They ought to do the same with us.) To the extent that they raise serious issues, they should be treated seriously, and we should even give careful consideration to their relatively clumsy propaganda campaigns. Unfortunately, the Soviets do not seem to be as interested in this problem as they ought to be. The U.S. Technical Experts at the 1958 Geneva Conference on Safeguards against Surprise Attack tried to discuss with the Soviet delegates measures that would reduce the risk of misunderstandings that might lead to an "accidental" war, but the Soviet delegates stressed the "larger issues" and refused to look at "narrow technical problems." (However, our own position may have been excessively narrow.)

Fortunately, if proper preparations have been made, it is not necessary to take off on a false alarm just because the other side has done so. On the other hand, unless both sides make preparations for some kind of "hold" ability—for example, by refueling the airborne planes or bringing reserve planes to an alert status—it could be dangerous to call back the bombers unless it were certain that the triggering signal was a false alarm. Even with preparations, there may be some degradation if the timing is interrupted. Once this force has turned back or tried some temporizing measure, schedules are deranged. Some bombers will lack fuel to turn back again! A large number of those planes that land may for some time be unavailable for a coordinated strike for various reasons connected with maintenance, crew fatigue, timing, and so on.

Unless we are properly prepared, fear of accidental war may lead to crippling restraints. Most people, when asked to choose between (1) a force which is invulnerable but achieves this invulnerability by having (every year) one chance in a hundred of starting a war accidentally, or (2) a force which is non-accident prone, but as a result is so handicapped that it is vulnerable to clever attacks, will choose the second. They do not believe anyone would be so insane as to launch a deliberate attack, but the thought of accidental war is all too real. (A psychologist friend tells me that if one asks a ten year old what he expects to be he will often answer, "An engineer, unless some fool accidentally presses a button, in which case I'll be nothing.") Therefore, unless nonaccident-prone reactions are designed into the system, this could mean that the buttons will not be fully connected. If a surprise attack actually occurs, an appreciable portion of the offense may be destroyed on the ground. While this would not disturb the façade school, the possibility does disturb those who believe that as much of the offensive force as possible should play a role in punishing the enemy or in limiting damage.

I should like to point out that Table 33 does not contain an entry corresponding to a U.S. premeditated attack in a normal (non-tense) situation. Sometimes people postulate wars in which the United States got off a first strike and caught the Soviet air force on the ground, unalerted. This seems to me to be the one case worth ignoring.

While I am perfectly prepared to believe that the United States SAC might strike Russia if the Russians ever provoke us by some extreme action, I do believe that it is so unlikely for a situation to arise in which we would strike the Russians "out of the blue" that calculations for this eventuality are not worth bothering with. Perhaps it is a mistake to be too reassuring to the Russians on this point. If they completely discount the possibility of a United States surprise attack, they may be able to save large sums of money on their day-to-day operations, diverting these funds into increasing the size of their striking force. For example, instead of five crews on a 24-hour day, 7 days per week, for each alert missile they would need only one or two crews if they could depend on warning; they would not need so many hardened and dispersed facilities; and so forth. In spite of this last point, calculations on the United States capability to strike an unalerted Soviet air force make little sense to me—nor will they to most Americans. After all the mere existence of the United States SAC probably puts enough pressure on the Russians to be reasonably alert, dispersed, and hardened no matter what our intentions might be.

Defense in a Crisis

The next three basic situations occur when things are tense, when there is a crisis in which each side's "minimum" objectives are incompatible; that is, the Soviet Union and the United States each claim to be determined to force the other to do or not do something. I do not want to be specific about what the crisis is—it might be similar to such situations as Korea, Suez, Hungary, the Berlin Blockade, or a Russian ultimatum to the British, but in a somewhat more severe form than those which actually happened. The Munich crisis, the German ultimatum of 1939 to the Poles, or the situation which developed out of the Sarajevo incident of World War I might be more typical of what I mean. One new type of situation could occur if there were a limited war raging and one side had gotten an advantage and the other, not willing to concede victory, was threatening to use some tactics or equipment that violated the limitations.

As I have mentioned many times in this book, most people, even experts, somehow do not believe in premeditated thermonuclear war. They find it "unthinkable" that a sane decision maker would ever deliberately authorize war, no matter what the compulsion. This is, of course, their privilege. However, even these disbelievers have to concede that a tense situation might arise. "Have to concede" may be too strong. By my definition of the word *tense,* no such situation has occurred in the years from World War II to this writing. Normally when there is a mild crisis, people will say: "Neither side wants war; therefore the Soviet Union must back down." (This is not even good logic.) I am here defining *tense* as implying a situation in which each side will be saying that if the other side does not back down it will be attacked.

Sometimes people think that in such tense situations the military problem is alleviated because we have a sort of "warning." As we shall see, however, it may be worsened. In any case, each side is trying to force the other to back down, and each at least pretends that nothing can make them give way and that they will consider war seriously if the other side does not back down. Whether they are truly serious will be hard to tell; nobody pays that much attention today to notes, even notes phrased as quasi-ultimatums. *Real ultimatums of the "You must back down by 12:00 noon!" type are vastly too dangerous to give because if they are unequivocal they are quite likely to touch off a pre-emptive strike at 11:00 A.M.* Yet each side may wish to increase the apprehension of the other side in a marked degree without pushing it to the point of a pre-emptive strike.

This inability to convince the other side that one may prefer going to war to backing down raises an interesting theoretical and practical question: *How can a nation be convincing in its threats if the ordinary diplomatic techniques are either unconvincing or too dangerous?* [8] We have already indicated the answer. The most impressive

---

[8] I have asked this question of many people in and out of government, American and European, and rather amazingly almost none of the experts or officials can come up with any suggestions. Laymen and wives do much better. In particular, one's wife will usually say something to the effect, "Let's get the children out of town and then go talk to him," reflecting the fact that it is difficult to give a credible ultimatum as long as a country has 50-100 million of its most valuable citizens exposed to the enemy's retaliatory strike. The most significant thing about the above poll is that today all-out war is so unthinkable that many officials not only do not know how to threaten credi-

demonstration that a nation can make to convince its opponent to back down is to do something that is both dangerous and at the same time shifts the balance of power appreciably in favor of the side making the move. Because it is dangerous, it demonstrates resolve; because it shifts the balance of power, it makes it credible that the resolve will be translated into an attack if the other side is not reasonable.

What kinds of moves are likely to be effective? The most obvious is putting one's forces on an alert status. This would probably take the form of a "stand-down" operation on both sides. All ordinary flying, training, routine preventive maintenance, leaves, and so on are cancelled. All equipment is brought to a state of maximum readiness. As many crews as possible are kept at the base on an alert status. Forces are deployed. Security is enhanced. Going on alert is a sensible thing to do because it maximizes the number of the aircraft and missiles available. It means that if the enemy becomes so provoking that he provokes an attack, this attack will be large. It also means that you are alert and in a position to exploit any warning received. Yet, as we will see, it may also mean that if you are serious about exploiting warning you may turn out to be trigger-happy.

Just going on alert may not be very convincing to the opponent. The unreality with which nations regard war is not based on a belief that the attacker cannot launch a very powerful blow, but rather that he is not willing to accept the retaliatory strike. Therefore, merely increasing the power to strike is not necessarily persuasive. *Unless the increase in striking power gives one an annihilating capability, the ability to accept retaliation must also be increased.*

Parochial or uninformed people sometimes measure our offensive power—our power to regulate enemy behavior—just in terms of the number, quality, and operational capability of the offensive vehicles we own. Actually, our ability to regulate enemy behavior depends as much, if not more, on our active and passive defensive capability as on our offensive capability. Unless an enemy is incredibly careless, we cannot hope to destroy anywhere near 100 per cent of his force on the ground. Unless we can alleviate or accept the retaliatory blow

bly, but have suppressed the knowledge that they do not know. This is sometimes known as psychological denial and is a typical reaction of an individual who is faced by a situation he believes to be intolerable, but which does not call for immediate action. It seems far better to forget about it rather than engage in useless and disturbing worries.

launched by his surviving "SAC," we may be effectively deterred from trying to regulate his behavior.

The most impressive move comes after the alert. One possibility would be to evacuate the urban population to existing or improvised fallout protection. This is quite likely to be convincing. Any power that can evacuate a high percentage of its urban population to protection is in a much better position to bargain than one which cannot do this. There is an enormous difference in the bargaining ability of a country which can, for example, put its people in a place of safety in 24 to 48 hours, and one which cannot. If it is hard for the reader to visualize this, let him just imagine a situation where the Soviets had done exactly that and we had not. Then let him ask himself how he thinks we would come out at a subsequent bargaining table. As I will describe in Lecture III, the Soviets seem to be preparing a program of civil defense which will enable them to complete such an evacuation. They have not only had extensive training programs, but they seem to have the physical capability, in terms of roads and truck transportation, to evacuate almost all their cities in about eight hours or so. And in the kind of crisis we are considering they can and probably will do this even if the act seems to give us some sort of warning. It is most unlikely (given our current and future lack of a Credible First Strike Capability) that in our fear of the effects of a Soviet retaliatory strike, we would react to such a Soviet evacuation by attacking them. Many, especially those who find the concept of a deliberate war inconceivable, will discount the evacuation as a war-of-nerves move intended to frighten us. We might be so resolute that we would not even order a formal evacuation of our own cities. Unless the Soviets deliberately publicized their evacuation (as a war-of-nerves move or an effort to make it seem so), Western governments might conceal that dramatic information to avoid frightening their own people. As I will try to bring out in Chapter VIII when I discuss the Munich crisis, completely extemporary preparations to meet the threat of attack can have a disastrous effect on national morale. This means that unless adequate preparations have been made in peacetime (preparations in which the government and people have confidence), it would be disastrous for a government that wanted to stand firm to extemporize measures to reduce the vulnerability of its population. This would be true even though both the bargaining situation and the military and civilian preparations of the enemy seem to make it mandatory. About all an unprepared government can do is to say over and over, "The other side doesn't really want war." Then they can hope they are right. However, this same government can scarcely expect to make up by sheer determination what it lacks in preparations. How can it persuade its opponent of its own willingness to go to war if the situation demands it? *An unprepared government will have a poor chance of forcing a prepared government to back down.* And *our* government could not put its people in places of safety on even a week's notice.

Long before the day of crisis, and peace-loving as most of us are, we must understand that unless we have confidence in our ability to initiate and terminate a war under some "reasonable" conditions, the Russians can with safety do almost anything they want in the way of preparations to launch an attack. And if at a time of crisis both sides may seem superficially to be making the same kinds of moves, they may still differ enormously in quality—assuming that we have not used the intervening years to improve our posture. In fact, as long as we do not have *many* IRBM's or ICBM's that can *survive a Soviet attack*, it is not really necessary for them to give us even ambiguous warning by evacuating their cities before the attack. Evacuation moves, in addition to reducing one's vulnerability, have some of the character of burning one's bridges. Unless the crisis appears to be over, it is now quite difficult to imagine a democratic nation meekly backing down and asking its people to return to the cities. Even a totalitarian nation might have trouble manipulating its population under these circumstances. There is a possibility, of course, that rather than make people bolder, the evacuation may so frighten everybody that enormous pressure will be brought to bear to preserve the peace at any cost. The last minute (and obviously unplanned) preparations in London and Paris during the Munich Conference of 1938 seem to have had this effect. I know of no way to predict how things would go, but I would conjecture that if the evacuation plans are at all competent, they will have a reassuring effect, or at least tend to make people resolute. In fact, they may go too far in this direction. It is important to make it clear to the enemy that if he backs down you will not strike him. He must believe that you will then go at least partially back to a normal posture.

However, a stand-down operation and evacuation are not the only impressive things that can be done. One side or the other can indulge in massive "jamming" and "spoofing" tactics. Spoofing means to pretend to attack by making feinting moves that could actually mask

214

an attack. This is dangerous because it may touch off an attack by the nation that is being spoofed. However, if the nation being spoofed is loath to attack, all it can do is take interim measures. If the spoofing continues, the defenders may find it too costly or wearing to take the most advantageous interim measures. Thus their defensive capability is degraded if the spoof turns out to be the real thing. Jamming (to emit electronic radiations that will cause interference and make radar protection ineffective) can be considered a form of spoofing, since the nation being jammed does not know if an attack is under way or not.

Such tactics really begin to show that one is serious about not backing down. They are also very effective in shifting the balance of power by sharply increasing the other side's vulnerability to surprise attacks. If the warning system has not been built to deal with peacetime spoofing and jamming tactics, and if the enemy institutes these, the capability to tell the difference between small "training" missions and actual attacks is reduced or even eliminated. By making the possibility of a successful surprise attack much greater, the enemy succeeds in looking much more threatening. He *is* more threatening. It is quite possible that spoofing and jamming will take the place of the classical ultimatum or quasi-ultimatum.

What can be done about these tactics? If, for example, the Russians used aerial jammers against our early warning lines—either the over-water or over-land portions—there is very little we could do, even if we wished; at present it is difficult to defend these lines actively. This could change in the future; the F-108 (now cancelled) is supposed to have been designed for this capability. Or we could outfit B-58's as long-range supersonic air defense fighters. We might even develop long-range ground-to-air missiles for this purpose. However, it might be both cheaper and more satisfactory for the Russians to use ship-borne jammers. They might even get very aggressive and station a half-dozen ships 50 to 100 miles off our shores to jam our contiguous radar cover. Then even our hard missile bases might suddenly become vulnerable to a surprise attack by Soviet bombers, since the jamming would put the radars out of commission. They could get still nastier and deploy, in addition, missile-launching or small airplane-launching submarines and ships.

It is hard to predict what we would do by way of reply under any of these circumstances. If the Soviets used civilian ships to do this jamming, we would almost undoubtedly board them and throw the

215

equipment overboard. If they used naval vessels, the problem is much harder. We know that a naval vessel is unlikely to let itself be boarded. Any attempt to do this may be considered virtually an act of war; in any case, it will be resisted. Perhaps we would start sinking their military ships. But this is a symmetrical world, and we have many military and civilian vehicles close to their borders. If we start sinking ships they may do so also. It is hard to tell where this kind of exchange will end. Equally important, it might alienate neutrals, allies, or even our own citizens. After all, the Soviets' actions are perfectly "legal"—or have been so regarded to this day. They can pretty well do as they please on the high seas. What we will do will presumably depend critically on the specific circumstances that initiated and prolonged the crisis. Inaction, dangerous as it is, is by no means an impossible reaction.

If none of the above measures worked and the Soviets still preferred to make us back down instead of backing down themselves or attacking, they could try limited attacks against critical and exposed elements. The most innocuous way would be to start attacking Polaris submarines, airplanes, or isolated vessels. It would be very difficult for us deliberately to start a war because of some relatively minor engagement that we might not even hear about directly. The risk of touching off a war by a properly executed attack on some kinds of ground installations is also slight. If the Soviets really wished to be frightening, they could destroy some crucial component of our warning systems in the Far North. We have been building a Ballistic Missile Early Warning System (BMEWS). Some people propose that we place our main reliance for the defense of our strategic forces on a combination of quick reaction and warning to be obtained from BMEWS. If these notions are accepted, and if the Soviets could seriously degrade or eliminate the warning by physical destruction, they could pose some serious challenges to us. In order of increasing provocativeness, they could jam or sabotage communications, dynamite installations by means of "unidentified" raiders (probably Soviet "juvenile delinquent" Eskimos), bomb them with high explosives, or, finally, bomb them with nuclear weapons. The physical result would be the same. The only difference that the more violent means would make would be on our morale; because the means are more provoking they are more effective in showing that the Soviets are serious.

Perhaps the most important sanctions to keep the Soviets from indulging in extreme tactics are the chances that they might touch off an accidental (or as I call it, have a "nonaccidental" accidental) war or the chance that they might provoke a deliberate United States attack. If they are serious enough about the crisis or if they are inclined to gamble, they may be tempted to push their luck. They are likely to act provokingly enough to raise the chance of a deliberate U.S. attack or accident *in their estimation* sufficiently high to scare us—but not high enough to run a serious risk. They will, of course, realize that even if our push buttons previously were disconnected they are now wired. The prospect of our wiring these buttons might in itself have a deterring effect on the Soviets before the crisis, because it increases the chances of an accident. Connecting the buttons, if they are normally left disconnected, is a fearsome thing to do. In addition, the psychological bloc against believing in war will be removed. Whether the attitude of the Soviets toward touching off an accidental or deliberate war will coincide with ours is very hard to say. One can but hope that they will favor caution rather than recklessness and that in their calculations caution will indicate compromising the crisis rather than striking or putting extreme pressure on us.

If we have a Credible First Strike Capability, a capacity for deliberately initiating a war, then even if the Soviets doubt that we would have the resolve to use our SAC they must have some doubts about their doubts. *Such a "capability" on our part should discourage them from even thinking about using extremely provocative tactics.* It should also encourage them to consider backing down. But as we have already discussed, the existence of such a capability puts pressure on the Soviets to strike us before we strike them, since they now run the risk of provoking us into an attack or putting ourselves in a position to attack. It works the other way also. If the Russians have a Credible First Strike Capability—even one depending on evacuation to make it credible—then they are in a much stronger position to bargain with us and, failing adequate bargaining, to strike. If we have bought a Finite Deterrent and nonaccident-prone force, then we have no sanctions to use against them. Accident proneness seems like a bad tool to use in this situation; hence the emphasis on having a Credible First Strike Capability.

Table 35 summarizes the United States preattack bargaining problem if we are to be able to use our strategic forces to make the Russians back down in these situations. The table is symmetrical. If we substitute "United States" for "Soviet Union" and vice versa, we indicate the Russian problem we have just discussed.

❖❖❖

TABLE 35

U.S. MUST CONVINCE S.U. THAT:

1. U.S. prefers U.S. strike to U.S. acquiescence.
2. U.S. prefers S.U. acquiescence to U.S. strike.
3. U.S. is unlikely to pre-empt or to be accident-prone.

❖❖❖

We have pointed out that the first proposition is the most difficult to make convincing. It means we must persuade the Russians that we and maybe our allies are willing to accept all the costs and risks of a war (that were discussed in the first lecture) rather than back down. At least they must be persuaded that there is sufficient *probability* that we will accept a *possibility* of incurring these costs—that they prefer the alternative of accepting a compromise of the crisis which is satisfactory to the U.S. to prolonging the crisis. I use the words, "possibility of incurring these costs" because it should be clear to the Russians that if we do strike them, we will maximize our potential for postattack blackmail. This tactic has a reasonable chance of making the Russians careful in the planning and execution of their retaliatory strike. It should be relatively easy to convince the Russians that we have enough confidence in the success of our "Controlled War" to raise appreciably the probability that we will not back down.

While the Russians are mulling over the "probabilities" and "possibilities," we must keep them continuously convinced of points 2 and 3. Otherwise they may decide to pre-empt. More precisely, we must convince them that our retaliatory blow will be so unpleasant that rather than striking us and touching off a retaliatory blow they will prefer to believe that points 2 and 3 are true to believing that we will strike them, even though we have made the probability of a U.S. strike high enough so that they prefer compromising the crisis satisfactorily to continuing to provoke us. Our Type II Deterrent makes them want to believe point 1 and our Type I Deterrent makes them want to believe points 2 and 3.

The Complete Hedger

There are many kinds of changes in policy for which we might wish to prepare, but I would like to start with what I have called the Preattack Mobilization Base. It has become fashionable among the

218

more sober military experts to regard mobilization capabilities as examples of wishful thinking. While this was a step in the right direction, it has probably gone too far. I agree that all-out wars are likely to be short (probably between a day and a month). Therefore, they will be fought with forces in-being, perhaps supplemented by equipment in the pipe lines and by trained reserves. Thus it would be a mistake to accept much smaller capabilities in-being to improve the postattack mobilization capability. However, when we ask ourselves what it is that deters the Russians from a series of Koreas and Indochinas, we come to an important conclusion. It is probably less the fear of a direct U.S. attack than the probability that in response to such crises the U.S. and its allies will greatly increase both their military strength and their resolve. I have referred to the deterrence of moderately provocative behavior by such threats as a Type III Deterrence capability. This differentiates it from the previously described Type I and Type II Deterrence threats.

It is clear that Type III Deterrence cannot be expected to work 100 per cent of the time. The enemy will do moderately provocative things occasionally, if not frequently and we will either have to acquiesce or react against them. There are, of course, many things which give us Type III Deterrence as well as alleviatory capabilities if deterrence fails. These extend all the way from diplomatic protests, through Limited War, to Controlled Nuclear Retaliation. There is *a special type of capability* we can have that may regulate the degree and frequency of the provocation more effectively than will the all-out Type II Deterrence military threats we mentioned previously or any limited military reaction. It may do this more effectively because it is more credible. It is the explicit capability for increasing our strength very rapidly whenever the other side provokes us. For example, in June 1950 the United States was engaged in a great debate on whether our defense budget should be 14, 15, or 16 billion dollars. Along came Korea and Congress authorized 60 billion dollars, an increase by a factor of 4.

No matter what successes the Communist cause had in Korea, that authorization represents an enormous military defeat for the Soviets, since after the authorization, the Soviets came at length to face a very impressive military power. If they had not invaded Korea their opponent would likely have had scarcely a housekeeping establishment in the early mid-fifties. What result this would have had is hard to say, but it could have been disastrous. It was almost three

219

years before that authorization was fully translated into increased expenditures and corresponding military power. It is very valuable to be able to increase our defense expenditures, but this ability becomes many times more valuable if authorizations can be translated into military strength in a year or so. If the Russians know that deterioration in international relations will push us into a crash defense program, they may be much less willing to let international relations deteriorate. The problem is, would we have time to put in a useful program? After all, the basic military posture (including installations) must be of the proper sort if it is to be possible to expand it within a year or so to the point where it is prepared to fight a war in addition to being able to deter one. Our current posture (1960) is probably far from optimal for doing this.

If preparations like these were at least moderately expensive and very explicit, the Russians might find it credible that the United States would initiate and carry through such a program if they should be provocative even, say, on the scale of Korea or less. The Russians would then be presented with the following three alternatives:

1. They could strike the United States before the buildup got very far. This might look very unattractive, especially since the buildup would almost certainly be accompanied by an increased alert and other measures to reduce the vulnerability of SAC.
2. They probably would find it difficult to match the U.S. program, but to the extent that they did it would mean that their aggression had at length cost them tens of billions of dollars annually.
3. They could accept a position of inferiority. Such an acceptance would be serious, since the United States would now come to have a "fight the war" capability as well as a "deter the war" capability. In addition, we would be very angry—at least for a while. This would not only mean that they could not afford to challenge us again but that even a relatively slight and unintended incident could result in a blow-up.

In each case the costs and risks of their provocation would have been increased, and it is likely that the Soviets would take these extra costs and risks into account before attempting any provocation. If they were not deterred, we could launch the crash program. Then we would be in a position to correct the results of their past provocation or at least to deter them in the future from exploiting these results.

It might be particularly valuable to have credible and explicit plans to institute crash programs for civil defense [9] and limited-war capabilities. It seems to be particularly feasible to maintain inexpensive and effective mobilization bases in these two fields, and the institution of a crash program would make it very credible to the Russians, our allies, and neutrals that we would go to war at an appropriate level if we were provoked again. To give an idea of the kind of thing that is possible I need only point out that the construction industry is one of the most readily deployable industries we have and that its theoretical capacity is about $100 billion annually. This means that if inexpensive but time-consuming preliminaries—such as those involved in research, development, planning, analysis, design, programming, and legal hurdles—have been eliminated, we might expect to get permanent installations within a year and improvised ones in much less time (possibly a few hours or days). Because of our increased capability, it would not be necessary for us to back down again, and the initiation of an expensive program of the proper kind would, in itself, indicate a resolve not to be blackmailed again.

It is important to understand that we have this asset: the ability to spend large sums of money rapidly. Let us, for example, assume a new Berlin crisis in two or three years. Assume also that the United States has done nothing to improve its Type II Deterrence capability, and very little to improve its limited-war capability, but it does have a first-rate Type I Deterrence (one that could punish the Soviets if they attacked us, but one that could not protect the United States). Under these circumstances it would be most improbable that we would initiate either a thermonuclear or limited war if the Russians gradually put the squeeze on Berlin. Nevertheless, State Department negotiators would try in all likelihood to get the Soviets to back down by threatening that we would do something very violent—that we would use our military forces. But our negotiators would be afraid to spell out our threat, for nothing that they could present would be both credible and effective.

Even today the Russians have told us that any talk of our maintaining our position in Berlin by force is "bluff." If we send soldiers, they say they will kill them; if we send tanks, they will burn them; if we send bombers, they will destroy our cities. The Soviets are saying that at any level of violence we care to use they can either meet

---

[9] For a discussion of the possibilities, see Kahn, et al., *Some Specific Suggestions* . . . , RM-2206-RC.

221

that level on the spot or promise such a severe punishment that we will be deterred. The Russians also point out that Berlin is a chess game, not a poker game, and that everybody can see what our capabilities are.

If the Soviets are right—that our only alternatives are violence or defeat, where defeat would be an acceptance of some new and unsatisfactory status of Berlin—they could probably succeed in talking us into adopting a face-saving method of losing Berlin rather than one that would make it clear to all that we had suffered a serious defeat.

This is not to say that the face-saving device would be effective enough to prevent us from suffering the repercussions of this defeat, but only that we would be able to kid ourselves. The capacity of Western governments to indulge in wishful thinking in the military and foreign policy fields whenever it is possible to do so is almost unlimited.

In actual fact we do have some very strong cards to play, but if we do not know what these cards are we may be tricked out of playing them. If we refuse to accept a face-saving defeat and the Russians persisted in rubbing our noses in the dirt, then it would be clear to all in NATO that unless we did something spectacular to recover the situation, these nations could no longer rely on us for any kind of protection; under such circumstances the United States might order an attack, but it is much more likely that it would authorize enormous defense budgets, probably at least at the $100 billion a year level. These funds would be used not only to improve our current posture but also to buy large limited-war forces and such things as civil defense and the corresponding military forces that would give us a credible capability for initiating a war at some appropriate level of violence if a humiliating crisis should be repeated. There would also be enormous pressure on the NATO nations under these circumstances to combine into an even tighter alliance and to mobilize their resources for their defense. This would mean that as in Korea, even if we lost Berlin in the military sense, the Russians would have lost this particular campaign. While Berlin is important ethically and politically, its loss would not compare to the greatly increased power and resolve on the side of the West.

This is one of the major threats we can bring to bear on the Russians. If we are not aware that we have this threat, if we believe that doubling the budget would really mean immediate bankruptcy or other financial catastrophe, then the Russians can present us with alternatives that may in the end result in their winning the diplomatic, political, and foreign policy victory. It is important that we understand our own strengths as well as our possible weaknesses.

Reaching 1975

In the fifteen years since World War II, international relations have been mainly concerned with postwar reconstruction and settlements, the liquidation of some Western influence in colonial areas, and the cold war. Much of the complication and ferment of the first two matters have been generated as much by the rivalry between the Communist and NATO blocs as by the problems themselves. This rivalry is likely to continue to dominate every aspect of international relations. In spite of some speculation, it seems most unlikely (though not impossible) that any third force will come into being that could challenge or endanger either of the two blocs on its own (as opposed to exploiting the rivalry between them). While there have been and will continue to be uncommitted and independent nations that blur any simple picture of a world divided into two disjoint camps, the most basic ingredient of international relations for the next decade or so is likely to be the cold war—a war which is as likely to be exacerbated by the existence of third powers as to be mitigated by their throwing their might on the side of peace. The third powers are all too likely, particularly in an unregulated world, to have the strength, desire, and opportunity to do the former—but not the latter.

Intense rivalries like those in the present cold war have in the past been settled as a rule by a hot war or a series of hot wars which end in a reasonably clear-cut victory or defeat. Less often, the wars prove to be merely exhausting. The passage of time and the enervating effects of the losses finally convince the contenders that it is not worth while to press the conflict to the limit. Both sides then settle for some sort of a stalemate, sometimes even forgetting what the original issue was or at least forgetting the reason for their passion. Even less often, but often enough to be noted, the rise of a third power will create a greater danger, one which causes the contenders to submerge their differences and join forces in the interests of joint survival. However, almost never do conflicts as bitter and longlasting as those of our current cold war get settled amicably simply because it may be the sensible thing to do.

This latter possibility seems somewhat more likely today. War at this writing looks more dangerous to decision makers than it ever has to most such leaders in the past. In addition, an unrestricted and uncontrolled arms race itself looks like such a dangerous thing that it may play the same role in bringing together the United States and the Soviet Union that the growth of German power after 1900 did in bringing those long-time enemies, Britain and France, together after centuries of rivalry.

Both sides today have common interests, not only in regulating their mutual conflicts, but also the degree and manner in which third parties join in the conflict or in the arms race. No matter how intense the rivalry, the sixties and seventies are likely to see each side collaborating with the opposed power for certain common objectives, possibly without any real slackening of the basic rivalry.

While the main theme of these lectures is that we cannot afford to ignore the military problem generated by the cold war, there is a co-equal theme. I would like to have devoted more space to it than is possible here. This theme is that the purely military solutions to our security problem are likely to be grossly inadequate in the long run, and may prove to be so in the short run. If we are to reach the year 2,000, or even 1975, without a cataclysm of some sort (in particular, if we are to obtain the time to work out the rivalry peacefully), we will almost undoubtedly require extensive arms control measures in addition to unilateral security measures. I am going to use the words "Arms Control" rather than "Disarmament" because they indicate explicitly that the problems are more general than some pacifists or budget-minded people think. One may accept the existence of both the rivalry and the weapons and still be interested in nonmilitary measures to increase the security of both nations. The Soviets have recently indicated that they are not interested in arms control but only in what they call "disarmament," but in practice they seem to use this position only as a bargaining device when we propose some specific arms control measure they do not like. There have been several occasions when they are willing to discuss the problems of arms control as a related and equally important but still distinct problem from that of total disarmament or the settling of U.S. and Soviet conflicts by negotiation or other nonviolent means.

It is often said that reaching an arms control agreement must wait the settlement of international political problems. It is certainly true that such a settlement would greatly facilitate the achievement of arms control (including even a limited disarmament). It is probably equally true that it would be very dangerous to wait for such a settlement before trying to alleviate some of the most dangerous aspects of the arms race and the general military competition. Competition will complicate the process of arriving at an agreement, for each side is likely to try to use the mutual threat to make unilateral gains, but this does not make limited collaboration impossible. It simply makes it *harder* to reach. This is one of the major differences, for example, between total disarmament and arms control. It should not be necessary to progress very far toward settling our basic disagreement before agreeing to whatever arms control measures seem likely to have mutual advantages; yet it would be inconceivable to engage in voluntary disarmament or to agree to any world government without such a settlement. One can express the problem abstractly and rather crudely as follows:

Imagine there were two countries which were competing with each other. Both would prefer having their way without fighting, but neither is willing to surrender without a fight. Both feel so strongly about this that if necessary they are willing to lose some millions of their citizens rather than surrender or accommodate too far. But neither feels so strongly about its objectives as to be willing to accept a large risk of total annihilation, or something approaching that. Neither is willing to risk a major fraction of humanity (one-fourth or one-half) while protecting itself or furthering its objectives, but each is willing to risk some hundreds of millions of lives for both of these ends. Both nations are very anxious to prevent war from breaking out unintentionally. If they think about the problem they will probably be quite anxious to alleviate the effects of an unintended war if one happens to occur, since such a war is particularly likely to result in mutual devastation and it seems possible to have control measures to both prevent and, failing prevention, limit the consequences of an unintended war without presenting either side with important military advantages.

I do not say that the above is an accurate picture of the world. Many will deny that it describes the Soviet Union (which is often pictured as being willing to risk all for world domination) *or* the United States (which is sometimes pictured as being indifferent to such issues). Others will deny the existence of either the competition or the mutuality of interests. The question I wish to raise is this: assuming that the above is to some extent a reasonable description, could one design within those constraints a security system in which neither side gives up very much but in which both sides gain symmetrically in security?[10] I am not denying that so far as the real world is concerned, under almost any reasonable definition of Soviet or U.S. goals, both would gain more if they compromised the ideological conflict than if they fought it out. I am only trying to make the abstract but important conceptual point that even if they cannot or will not compromise the long-run ideological battle, they might still wish to be in the arms control business, if only to obtain the time they need to let their more dastardly plans (if any) mature. And, of course, the arms control area itself becomes a battlefield of the cold war with each side trying to achieve quick propaganda victories and ultimate advantage in a possible hot war.

Various Ways in Which War Can Start

The major objective of arms control should be to reduce the risk of damage by war without jeopardizing unduly other aspects of national security. From the viewpoint of arms control there are three major things that can be done to diminish the risks entailed in the perennial possibility of war:

(1) Arms control can reduce the probability of events, both international (tensions and crises) and technical (accidents, false alarms and misunderstandings), that could give rise to war.

(2) Arms control could reduce the probability that a war-causing type of event would actually cause a war.

(3) Lastly, arms control can reduce the damage done if a war actually occurs. It can do this not only by abolishing the use of cer-

---

[10] This last symmetry is not essential to the arguments. Imagine that one is asked to choose between two situations:

    a. He and his enemy will inevitably be engaged in a mortal struggle. The probabilities are .8 that this mortal struggle will result in mutual annihilation, .1 in victory for oneself, and .1 in victory for one's opponent.

    b. He and his enemy will still inevitably be engaged in a mortal struggle, but now it will be conducted by rules. As a result the probabilities now are .1 of mutual annihilation, .3 of victory for oneself, and .6 of victory for one's opponent.

While the rules have had the asymmetrical effect of making one's opponent twice as likely to be the victor as oneself, they have still increased by 3 one's own security. For this reason most people would prefer *b* to *a*. (Though it is unlikely, unless they are analytically minded, that they would recognize the superiority of situation *b*. It is also unlikely that situation *b* could be negotiated if the asymmetry were this transparent. It could only be negotiated if the asymmetry were obscured by uncertainties.) Even more people (in the West at least) might prefer an alternative set of rules which yields .8 chances of a viable stalemate, no chance of a clearcut victory for oneself, and .2 chance of a victory by the opponent, even though the opponent's chance for a clear-cut victory were thus doubled and one's own chance went to zero.

tain weapons and controlling the use of others, but by facilitating
ahead of time the machinery by which wars are ended *before* they
become overly destructive.

It will be well at this point to list systematically ways in which a
war could arise. This will remind us of some of the specifics that
have to be considered. Table 36 covers basically the same area cov-

◆◇

TABLE 36

THE ARMS CONTROLLER'S VIEW OF WAR

1. Accident
   a. False pre-emption
   b. Unauthorized behavior
   c. True mechanical or human error
2. Miscalculation
   a. Escalation
   b. Rationality of irrationality
   c. Overconfidence
3. Calculation
   a. Reciprocal fear of surprise attack
   b. Type II deterrence situation
   c. Other crisis (internal or external)
   d. Preventive war
   e. World domination
4. Catalytic
   a. Ambitious third nation
   b. Desperate third nation

◆◇

ered by the five classes of wars in Table 33, but this time the viewpoint is that of the arms controller rather than the strategist. While
the two viewpoints should be much closer than they have been in
the past since both are trying to enhance security, it is almost inevitable in this world of parochial interests and bureaucratic specialization that they should differ. Table 36 tries to take account of the
differences. The strategist is mainly trying to improve his nation's
military position and international influence; the arms controller
is trying to reduce the risks of war. However, the best members of
both occupations may find their outlooks quite close, and in some
ways, perhaps, identical.

The foregoing list is neither exhaustive nor disjoint. It is not exhaustive because our weapons systems are so new and their impact

on each other and on international relations are so unknown that it would not be surprising if a war could start in some unforeseen manner. They are not disjoint because the causes of a war can occur in series or overlap in subtle ways. The four major topics are listed in the author's personal order of decreasing probability of actually being a cause of war in the next decade or so.

The first item on Table 36, *false pre-emption,* is the most publicized possibility and one difficult to consider objectively. I have pointed out that in a properly designed system it is most unlikely that this could be caused by a simple false alarm, but such an attack could be triggered by a series of false alarms if a chain of self-fulfilling prophesies should be set into motion (see page 205). The prevention of this last possibility may be one of the most important objectives of arms control. It is also conceivable that a pathological individual will deliberately try to start a war. The Soviets have made much of the possibility that a deranged American pilot on airborne alert would take it in his head to attack the Soviet Union. However, there are many safeguards against this behavior. Also it is most unlikely that an attack by a lone plane would touch off a war. Another possibility is given by Peter Bryant.[11] He discusses how a determined SAC general, who, unknown to his superiors, is incurably ill and whose judgment and sense of discipline are affected by this knowledge, decides to end the Soviet problem. Bryant is most interesting when he discusses the clever way the general negates the elaborate system set up to prevent unauthorized behavior. And last there is the possibility of a genuine accident—a switch failing, some ICBM's being launched through some mechanical or human error, some stockpile weapons accidentally exploded—any of which might, in spite of the safeguards, set off a self-fulfilling prophesy. These possibilities (*unauthorized behavior* and *true mechanical or human error*) can be influenced by collaboration with potential enemies in the sense that the degree of alertness or decentralized control that is required for one's force may be dependent on the overall strategic environment. Basically, however, the problem of unauthorized behavior or true mechanical or human error must be handled by unilateral action. Accident proneness may increase somewhat simply as a by-product of the number of alert weapons. However, the really dangerous intensification is likely to come from the proliferation of independent capabilities, each with its own standards of training, reliability of personnel, and safety practices.

[11] In *Red Alert,* Ace Books Inc., New York, 1958.

Nearly as worrisome as the war by accident is the war by miscalculation. The most likely way that this would occur is by *escalation*—the unpremeditated increase or spread of a limited operation. I have already discussed how the threat of escalation is today an important deterrent to limited actions and said that the introduction of reliable measures to limit escalation will inevitably increase the probability of the use of limited levels of violence. Yet it seems to me that it is still important to control or limit the possibility of escalation even if doing so decreases deterrence. The example of the Doomsday and the Doomsday-in-a-Hurry Machines was supposed to illustrate convincingly that it is not enough to maximize the probability that deterrence will work, but that one must also consider the consequences if deterrence fails. Another likely possibility for a war by miscalculation comes from the misuse of a strategy of *rationality of irrationality* or committal. This possibility will be discussed at some length in the next chapter in the section on bargaining. It involves such things as one side making an irrevocable committal for action in the belief that taking a firm stand will induce the other side to back down. But suppose they do not? Arms control can lessen the likelihood of war from these two types of miscalculation by setting up machinery for less risky methods of alleviating, avoiding, and settling conflicts. Also encouragement can be given both sides to be skillful and responsible in the use of the more dangerous weapons on the occasions when they resort to them.

The final possibility of a war by miscalculation mentioned in Table 36 occurs when one side has greater faith in some war plan than is justified by the objective facts. Given current beliefs in the West, it is almost impossible to imagine this happening to a Western government unless the decision makers have their judgment clouded by desperation or madness. The situation is less certain in the Communist bloc. The Chinese clearly underestimate the effects of nuclear war. Hopefully, it will be some time before they have the power to use nuclear weapons, and time may bring them greater wisdom. The Soviet estimates, as gleaned from their public statements, seem plausible, though whether this comes as a result of more or less sophistication than is prevalent in the West is hard to tell. They talk in a manner quite close to the discussion of Lecture I, where the possibility of great destruction and suffering is emphasized together with the likelihood of both survival and recovery. The Soviets do not seem to be trigger-happy or reckless, one judges at this writing, so that it does not seem to be necessary to put much effort into attempts to educate them on the danger of being over-confident about the use of modern weapons. The Soviets may under-estimate the need for collaboration in controlling the technological development and dissemination of new weapons and thus be un-willing to make the necessary compromises entailed in getting feas-ible programs accepted by both sides. If they go to war, however, it is as likely to be as a result of calculation as of miscalculation. This thought brings us to our next topic.

It is difficult for us in the West, with our abhorrence of the use of force and the widely prevalent view of automatic mutual homicide as the only result of a modern war, to believe that a situation could occur in which a perfectly sane but calculating, decisive, or ruthless decision maker could rationally decide that he is better off going to war than not going to war. In particular, we do not believe that any such calculation could make full allowance for uncertainties and still be correct. Yet sober studies indicate that this widely prevalent belief may be wrong.

Table 36 lists five calculated war situations. While all of them have been discussed, arms control adds some new aspects. The most obvi-ous is that a reduction in the absolute level of the balance of terror may reach the point at which an aggressor no longer fears annihila-tion or even unprecedented destruction if his plans go awry, but only defeat. It will then no longer be true that, "Even if the proba-bility of success were 90%, war would still be preposterous." Nine out of ten chances are pretty good odds and the war would now only be immoral, not unthinkable.

Disarmament can also create pressures toward preventive war. If a disarmament agreement breaks down and if one side obtains a significant lead either because of previous evasion or greater ability to rearm, then it might feel compelled to perform a great public service by arranging to stop the arms race before a dangerous bal-ance of terror was restored. It could do this most reliably by stopping the cause of the arms race—its opponent. Most writers ignore this situation and focus all their attention on conditions at the moment the agreement was openly abrogated rather than on conditions some months or years after an uncontrolled arms race has started again.

The arms controller should not advocate anything to decrease the possibility of the accidental and miscalculation wars that so weakens us militarily that he has, inadvertently, excessively in-creased the possibility of war by calculation. Almost inevitably, he is going to make the deterrence of war harder by reducing the risks of war. He is even going to make the deterrence of limited threats or violence less feasible by reducing the probability that war will occur as the result of provocation or limited violence. He is going to try to balance these effects, by making the peaceful alternatives to war more attractive, but there are limits on what he can accomplish. While I have indicated my belief that the probability of war by calculation is low, this stems from the thought that this is the one place where deterrence is most likely to work (and—perhaps optimistically—that we are going to be competent about deterrence). If we weaken our deterrent prematurely—possibly because so many naïve people interested in disarmament or agreements at any cost (not to speak of many professional war planners) refuse to take the possibility of war by calculation seriously, then of course this possibility may move to the top of the list. There are, and in spite of anything we do there will remain, great pressures to go to war. These pressures are unlikely to be restrained except by the fear of punishment.

The last possibility shown in Table 36, that a third country may try to touch off a war between the major powers, has been named "catalytic war" by Amrom Katz. If both powers have slow-reacting and flexible systems or can stop a war before both are destroyed, then starting a catalytic war would both be very difficult and very risky. It would be so risky that it is implausible that any third power would try to start one for the objective that is usually considered— to advance its position in the international hierarchy by inducing the two top nations to destroy each other. However, there is another type of catalytic war which may be more plausible—where a desperate third nation has a problem which can be solved if it touches off the right kind of catalytic war. Imagine, for example, a war between India and China, which the Indians were losing. The hard-pressed Indians might feel that the United States was morally obligated to come to their aid and that any way of obtaining this aid was as good as any other. Or imagine a situation in which the Chinese felt hard pressed by the United States—possibly over Formosa. The Chinese might tell the Soviets, "We are going to strike the imperialists at 5 A.M. tomorrow and you might as well come along and help us do a thorough job, for they will undoubtedly strike you even if you don't."

It is clear that many of the ominous possibilities just discussed might be alleviated by proper arms control measures.

Some readers may find it difficult to take seriously the possibility of any collaboration with the enemy. In particular, they may not take arms control as seriously as the other topics in the table of basic situations of Table 33. This is a very shortsighted point of view. Not only are the current dangers great but, as I try to make clear in Lecture III, the future promises to be even more dangerous. A contemplation of 1970 or 1975 without arms control should change the ideas of many people on what is practical, feasible, or desirable. If one is seriously trying to design an over-all military establishment to meet the problems we will face over the next decade or two, he should be as interested in designing a capability for accepting various types of control measures as a capability for accepting attack and striking back. The designer must ask himself more than "Are the envisaged equipment and operating practices consistent with necessary and feasible arms control measures?" He should design in such consistency—where consistency implies ability to operate with the measures in peacetime and being able to cope satisfactorily with feasible violations. He should also be constructive, asking what types of measures we could negotiate with the Soviets or institute on a unilateral basis that would improve the short- and long-run stability of the system.

It is psychologically very difficult for responsible military planners to take arms control seriously and constructively. To some extent this is because the point of view is new and unfamiliar. Partly it is because the thought of collaboration with the enemy seems vaguely disloyal and potentially dangerous. Then there is the point that military planners tend to confuse arms control measures with some form of premature disarmament, or at least with a general neglect of the armed services. *Premature disarmament is a real danger.* But the danger is increased if the technological race causes, correctly or incorrectly, a widespread fear that the weapons themselves are more dangerous than the enemy or the quarrel. People interested in defense must not only take a responsible interest in controlling the arms race; they must show this interest. There must be good faith between them and all who are conscious of the dangers of an unrestricted arms race and the burning need for stable, long-term arrangements. By being constructive on this problem, rather than blindly opposing all measures, they are more likely to increase their influence against undesirable programs and to promote constructive measures. In the short run, such measures are unlikely to involve a major degree of disarmament.

In fact, successful and responsible *short-run* control measures are more likely to require large military establishments on both sides than the opposite. While this will strike many as paradoxical, there are many reasons why this is true. A trivial one is that a small residue of a large force can still be very destructive. For example, if each side has only one hundred missiles and each missile has a .9 probability of destroying its opponent's missile, the 10 missiles that would survive an attacker's strike might not deter an attack. If each side has 1,000 missiles, the thought of 10 per cent (or 100) of his opponent's missiles might well deter an attack. Even more important than the small residue argument is the fact that a "balance of terror" between two large military establishments tends to be much more stable against crises, accidents, cheating, minor changes in technology or posture, or miscalculations—for example, of the effect of the arms control measures or performance of equipment—than a balance of terror stabilized with small establishments. In particular, if we are not to be excessively vulnerable and if we are to have the necessary confidence to be willing to live with the new dangers that arms control agreements can bring, the military establishment should be large enough to be able to include mixed forces with overlapping functions.

It is extremely bad (both tactically and analytically) for those interested in "first steps" to ignore these problems. Experts and decision makers are now very sophisticated and perhaps *overly* aware that careless agreements are dangerous. Our ability to negotiate useful agreements will be related to the confidence responsible people have in the continuing effectiveness of the military establishment. I would like to emphasize that this is only partly a question of abating the fears of the "militarists" as a political and bureaucratic pressure group; the problems raised by having an inadequate military establishment are genuine. To the extent that there are important measures that can be and should be instituted, it may be irresponsible to jeopardize them by asking for the unobtainable— that is, those who ask for some form of universal disarmament or nothing are probably asking for nothing.

Table 37 indicates major areas in which one might consider explicit and implicit arrangements for arms control. The first area is control of the development and introduction of new weapons. This is a very attractive thought. It is quite clear that many of our problems are a result of technological progress. Future progress promises to accentuate most of these problems. Unfortunately, it is very difficult to prevent governments, private parties, or clandestine groups from financing rather large projects in research and development.

So long as activities are confined to office-type buildings, laboratories, and reasonably small factories, it is practically impossible to
monitor them reliably by international regulating agencies—though
clandestine intelligence agencies may do very well if they can get
proper access. In the next lecture, when we consider how the Germans systematically violated some of the provisions of the Versailles
Treaty, we will have an example of how easy it might be to hide such
activities, even in a parliamentary democracy, from official groups
—though many unofficial groups knew about the violations. It is
far easier to hide them in a totalitarian state.

TABLE 37

AREAS FOR ARMS CONTROL

    I. Peacetime
       A. Development
       B. Number and Kind
       C. Deployment
       D. Operational Practices
   II. Wartime
       A. Number and Kind
       B. Operational Limitations

One major problem in trying to control research and preliminary
development is that it is difficult to draw a line between warlike and
peaceable activities; as a result, violations tend to be ambiguous.
Even if both parties start with the best will in the world, the impact
of science and technology is so broad that they will tend to find
themselves gradually shifting over into the impermissible field. In
addition, unless the violation is very flagrant, it will be difficult for
political and psychological reasons for either side to charge the other
with a violation, unless it wants to make trouble, in which case it is
likely to describe even innocuous activities as a violation. *An accu-
sation of cheating is as likely to result from a hostile attitude by the
accuser as by an act of the accused.* Since this will be widely recognized, it may be difficult to muster public opinion in a democracy
to take any counteractions. The problem of mobilizing allies or neutrals would be even more difficult.

The situation becomes quite different with some of the later stages
of some kinds of weapons development—the testing of nuclear devices or ICBM's, for example. These are large and spectacular proj-

ects. If they were banned at the present time they would be easily distinguished from legitimate peaceful activities. Detected activities are probably going to be unambiguously classifiable into the allowable or the forbidden. However, as we shall see in the next lecture, this may not be true in the future. I will discuss there the very real possibility that there will be large-scale use of nuclear explosives in peacetime applications. It should also be clear that satellite and space research is going to be an attractive and ever-increasing peacetime activity. But there are still good possibilities for control, because in both cases there is likely to be a limited number of allowable events (nuclear explosions for scientific purposes or the launching of space probes). Both sides could be required to register all such events in advance and to disclose all details of the equipment being tested or used. If such a rule could be enforced—and it is easier to enforce rules in which only a small number of events are being monitored, and in which violations are clear-cut, than when the activities are continuous or when the violations can be obscured—in that case the rate of technological development of forbidden devices could be made more controllable. Because this is an area where we can readily separate suspicious from ordinary civilian activities, it is reasonable to examine ways of restricting the activities—possibly even at the cost of limiting some valuable future peacetime developments. *In particular, it may be practical to restrict development and ownership of "advanced" weapon systems to a small number of nations.* I am personally of the belief that to do only this would go an appreciable distance toward meeting some of our most pressing future problems. The suggestion of the British Labour Party for a non-nuclear club with the initiative taken by England is of special interest, and it is unfortunate that it does not seem to have been taken more seriously.

The second area of importance in control agreements is the number and kinds of weapons that will be permitted. In some ways this problem is easier to cope with than the previous one. Under most arrangements, we would not be worried about minor violations on the number and kinds of weapons, since we would probably be considering only a reduction in our force or the prevention of an increase. We would not be considering a total ban. Therefore, minor variations in the enemy's strength would not be serious. This is quite different from the development picture where one side is worried about the other side getting a technological lead, and where a single experiment may be sufficient to establish such a lead. There is also an interaction between control of development and some types of control in the number and kind of weapons. If one has the latter control also, violations of the former may not be as serious, since the violator is handicapped in translating his clandestine knowledge into forces in-being.

Presumably the only way to enforce controls on numbers and kinds would be to require a complete listing of the allowable weapons by location, and a continuous inspection to verify that such listing was correct. We presumably could do almost nothing about stocks that were hidden before the inspection system was set up. For most modern weapons (except bombs) this might not be too serious. Complicated weapons have some tendency to deteriorate, and they require quite a bit of equipment, installation, and organization to support. (But will this be true in the future? Minuteman, for example, is supposed to be almost maintenance-free.) For most weapons there will be an appreciable lead time from cache to force in-being; if the agreements have allowed for preparations designed to allow the nonviolating nation to catch up with the violating nation if the violating nation starts to uncache its hidden stocks, then the existence of clandestine stores may be tolerable. The simplest way to achieve this might be to allow the parties to the agreement to keep officially inspected caches. If these are large, invulnerable to feasible surprise attack, and maintained satisfactorily, their existence would go some distance in alleviating the quite reasonable fears of those who would worry about being defenseless against an enemy who cheated.

But preparations must be made. Just because violations of certain kinds of bans can be detected does not mean that we could enter into such an agreement and then tailor our defense establishment around the existence of the ban. We must always ask, "What would happen if it is violated?" Would we then be in a position to take corrective action or to stand pat, or would we be completely defenseless (either at the time of the violation or later)?

For nuclear weapons, the problem of the clandestine cache is overriding. While nuclear weapons do have some maintenance problems, they are relatively storable and would be simple to hide in large numbers. It is also relatively simple to put most designs back in working order. We can therefore assume that a total ban on nuclear weapons would not be enforceable, since preparations to counter the effect of a violation imply the existence of counter nuclear weapons to use either as a deterrent or for waging war.

236

It would be rather easy in the case of a democratic society to enforce a ban on large-scale manufacture of new and complicated weapons. This would be especially true where the nation allowed free movement of inspectors and access to people and places. In the case of a totalitarian society, it is doubtful that such a ban could be enforced, unless clandestine intelligence came to the rescue. This would especially be true if the totalitarian government allowed only very limited inspection at fixed times and places and if in addition could discipline its own citizens. The official system could then only hope to control *the rate at which these weapons entered service.*

The next area to consider is *the deployment of weapons.* If aerial or ground observation is allowed, an absolute ban should be relatively easy to police. If an appreciable number of weapons are present it should be a relatively easy matter to find at least one of these weapons and, if a single weapon is found in the banned area, a violation has occurred. If the ban is not absolute, but on some quantity, it may be difficult to distinguish whether there are n or $n + m$ weapons in the area. However, it is not essential to have an absolute ban if the Arms Control Commission is informed of the location and status of every weapon in the area, and if this information can be frequently and readily checked. In that case it would still be true, most of the time, that a single discovery of an unauthorized weapon meant a deliberate violation.

Control of the deployment of weapons is most likely to be useful in specialized circumstances, as a supplement or addition to existing defense arrangements. The deployment of weapons could be limited in order to reduce the possibility of a surprise attack, false alarms, accidental war, creation of tense situations, and so forth.

Control over the deployment of weapons is often advocated as a method of reducing international tension. This objective usually emphasizes removing the more open manifestations of the arms race—for example, the suggestion for an atomic-free area where the two power blocs directly impinge on each other. It strikes me that while such proposals may be useful if only because people really prize them, their value lies mainly in this rather than in any objective effects. The "reach" of modern weapons is such that withdrawals of from 50 to 100 miles, or even many hundreds of miles, can be meaningless from a tactical or strategic point of view. This meaninglessness is likely to be realized soon after the agreement is put into effect. This is one of the difficulties with putting much effort into such "psychological" gains. This statement about the insignificance of moderate withdrawals is also likely to be true of the alleviation of frontier incidents, which are much more likely to be related to conventional forces than nuclear forces. (Of course, I do not imply that it may not be of great value to prevent the diffusion of nuclear weapons into the control of many different sovereignties.)

Probably a much more reasonable form of deployment control is one that removes or alleviates a real military threat or problem. For example, if we are worried whether a certain country will be responsible in their use of modern weapons, one way to handle the surmised danger would be to ban the weapons from that area by agreement. Or if we are worried about early warning lines being spoofed, it may be reasonable to ban planes or submarines from crossing the warning line. One could not depend on the other side's permanently observing the no-spoofing rule, and it would be necessary to maintain stand-by capabilities, but during the existence of the controls both operating and safeguarding problems would be reduced.

Very closely related to the control of deployment would be *limits on operational practices*. These, too, can be relatively easily monitored if frequent inspection procedures are allowed, because the detection of a single aberration would mean a violation. However, the inspection requirements would become much more rigorous than those needed for controlling deployment. In fact, limitations on operational practices generally presuppose deployment control or at least information on deployment as a first step.

Some of the most useful arms control measures on operation and deployment are those designed to reduce the probability of accidental war, fatal human errors, or miscalculations. This could be done by not having forces on super-alert, by restricting operations on both sides to reduce the rate at which false alarms might be generated, by the banning of any peacetime practices that could be used to mask a surprise attack, and so on.

One measure that could be of great importance would be to institute direct peacetime communication channels between the two strategic forces. This would enable them, in case anything untoward happened that seemed to threaten the security of one side or the other, to communicate their fears and assurances, and possibly even their proposals and counterproposals. In its most advanced form this would lead to the precrisis adoption of orderly procedures to handle unexpected incidents. Nobody wants to live in a world in which an all-out war could be touched off accidentally. Therefore, in addition to operating to reduce the chances of accident, we should be able to agree on additional, even if unconventional, measures to ameliorate the effects of an accident.

There are dangers in such proposals. For example, the enemy could launch a sneak attack with several hundred ICBM's in such a way that he did not think we could pick up any of them at all. The enemy could then take out insurance against our picking up one or two of them by calling us up and announcing that two ICBM's had been fired by mistake, but that "everything is all right—they do not have armed warheads." The enemy might well gain a crucial five or ten minutes by doing this; on the other hand, he is also likely to lose a crucial five or ten minutes if we refuse to believe him. In any case, proposals for establishing such prewar communication channels and procedures will have to be examined for the possibility that they might be exploited. This would have a significant impact on both physical and legal arrangements for Command and Control.

We might even wish to establish in time of peace channels for postattack communication to carry through bargaining and negotiating. We have already discussed the value of this. It is a controversial proposal, because it does make Type I Deterrence weaker by making it more credible that postattack blackmail will work. On the other hand, it makes it much more likely that any war which does occur will not be irrationally or excessively destructive. I would conjecture that if we took the possibility of war seriously we would find that the latter effect would dwarf the former.

It should be repeated that having Type II Deterrence can be consistent with precrisis limitations on deployment and operations. Type II Deterrence does not require ultra-fast reaction. Rather the opposite. Here the wish normally is to threaten the enemy and to give time for the threat to sink in. Denouncing the arms control agreement or announcing that one is changing one's posture to be more threatening might be very effective ways of exerting pressure.

It is also possible, strangely enough, to have arms control agreements operate in *wartime*. Such agreements are actually traditional, particularly in wars among moderately civilized people. Almost unrestricted war as a norm is a relatively new thing in the affairs of civilized nations. One has to go back to barbarous times or to wars over religious matters to find wars equal in fury to World War I and World War II. For example, I am told (but have not been able to verify) that in the Tourag society, which has learned to cope with the problem of living in the Sahara Desert where there are only a small number of oases, an enemy can commit all types of atrocities, such as torturing and murdering one's son, violating one's wife, selling one's daughter into slavery, and yet the injured party will not poison the wells of his attacker. He has simply learned that nothing that anybody does justifies poisoning wells. The Tourags had to learn this, otherwise they would not have lived very long. (If the story is not true it ought to be.) Similarly, it is conceivable that civilized nations will ban the most destructive practices, *particularly those that have little to do with winning wars.* I realize, of course, that the whole theory of the balance of terror lies in making war more and more destructive, but it is hard for me to believe that this is a *permanent* state of affairs. We will either eliminate the balance of terror by eliminating the need for it, or if the need cannot be eliminated, we will find more reasonable forms of using violence (i.e., the use of Limited War, Controlled Reprisal, or Controlled War). It is almost likely that future limitations on the use of violence will be either explicitly negotiated or voluntarily self-imposed. The threat of the most destructive types of action will then be reserved to enforce these limitations. While it is often stated that no country will accept defeat without using every weapon it has in its arsenal, if a nation is losing it may not be in a position to increase the level of violence advantageously. I would like to point out again that no civilized nation really is willing to fight even a semicivilized opponent to the last woman and child rather than sue for peace.

It is rather unlikely that we will have explicit agreements with the Russians on acceptable military operations in the near future. Perhaps, however, we will be able to arrive at implicit agreements, tacit understandings, or shared expectations. If these "agreements" are not established *before* the event, they can be made *during* the event. The Korean war was an example in which both sides kept the war under close control without ever having a conference about ways and means.[12] The future will see more of this. Even in a so-called all-out war some limitations are likely to be observed.

There is one wartime control measure that already exists; a ban on the use of atomic weapons in minor conflicts. Official statements to the contrary, *it would be almost unthinkable for the United States or the Soviet Union to use atomic weapons against a small country that did not possess atomic weapons.* Only a few government officials do not realize this. Of course, we might use atomic weapons

---

[12] We did not bomb across the Yalu River or blockade Chinese ports, while the Communists did not use their submarines or bombers against our troops or logistics. Mining was either very discreet or nonexistent, and, most important of all, such sanctuary areas as Siberia and Japan were religiously observed.

in reprisal for a large attack by the Russians or Chinese, even if this attack were restricted to conventional weapons. However, even in this case we are likely to be deterred from using atomic weapons. Thus it is quite possible that there could be a large, mostly conventional war in which the use of nuclear weapons would be limited at most to air defense and naval actions.

It might be a very good move for us to recognize the existing situation, by offering to accept (with the modification to be noted) a long-standing Soviet proposal to ban the *use* of nuclear weapons in war or to just make the unilateral announcement that after a certain date we would not be the *first* to use atomic weapons, (except possibly in air defense and naval warfare). The date should be set far enough ahead to give us time to fix the various gaps and omissions in our posture so that we will no longer have to depend on atomic weapons. Such a move could be made in conjunction with some revision of the NATO alliance. We could suggest to the Europeans that the defense of Europe by means of conventional weapons, and possibly even the defense of the Middle East, is mainly their job, though we would help. (I will discuss in the next lecture the possibility of this assignment of responsibility.) After all, such areas are much more valuable to the Europeans than to us. We could take responsibility for South and Southeast Asia, the Japan-Formosa-Korea area, and other places, either alone or in combination with allies. We could also take the responsibility for guaranteeing that the Russians did not use atomic weapons. *We would need to have the capability to enforce that ban; a credible capability to initiate thermonuclear war would be required.* (Many would deplore this, of course.) The Europeans could also have a modest "independent" nuclear deterrent to increase the credibility of U.S. response, but by being explicit as to the actuating mechanism (the use of nuclear weapons by the Soviets), there would be no encouragement of the kind of wishful thinking that leads to neglect of conventional capabilities. Under these circumstances, use of atomic weapons by the Soviets would be such a provocative and significant event—it would not take very much retaliatory capability to be credible—decision makers might easily prefer a thermonuclear war to living in a world where the Soviets used such weapons at times and places of their choosing and without much other restraint.

My suggestion seems attractive in many ways. It tends to put the Soviets under pressure to match *Europe* in conventional weapons and to match *us* in nuclear weapons. This should be a real strain on them if both we and the Europeans go about our military affairs diligently. It should be emphasized that this suggestion is not a disarmament suggestion. Rather the opposite. Unless both we and the Europeans are willing to increase our forces—we, in the Central War (offense and defense), and the Europeans in the Limited War areas —the reassignment of responsibilities would cause a dangerous weakening of our capability to defend Europe.

One could make a more thoroughgoing set of suggestions. As part of an arms control agreement, the U.S. and the Soviet Union not only agree that they would not use any nuclear weapons first —again with the possible exceptions of use in air defense or naval warfare (my personal views favor neither exception, but others seem to find them very desirable)—but they could further announce that they would consider the first use of a nuclear weapon by any third power, with the possible exception of the peaceful testing of bombs, to be an act of war. The proposal could be made more acceptable internationally if it were made part of a general Hague Convention-type of pact with regard to nuclear weapons, but the teeth would come from U.S. and S.U. adherence. The major impact of the agreement would be in improving Soviet bargaining power versus China and U.S. bargaining power versus its own allies and the bargaining power of both nations versus third parties. If either party did not want its bargaining power increased, the treaty would be ineffective. The pact should discourage third powers from expensive programs to obtain "useless" nuclear weapons. (It is for this reason, to make the weapons useless, that I oppose even the limited and otherwise reasonable use of nuclear weapons in air defense or naval warfare.) One could tie the Treaty to an additional proposal. The U.S. could give up operating on its overseas nuclear bases (since they are mainly useful for a first strike by the U.S., they would be kept on a standby basis to be reactivated only if the Soviets precipitate a crisis that causes the U.S. to abrogate the agreement), in return for which we would expect the Soviets to open up their society to inspectors and to provide opportunities for clandestine surveillance.

I do not wish at this point to discuss the merits and demerits of the above proposal. (I will describe later the importance of the "open" society.) The "Hague Convention" seems so close to some past Soviet proposals, one suspects that its effects may well be asymmetrical. Still, I think a hardheaded look would disclose that neither side would get extremely large gains at the other's expense, while both sides may get some very large gains in terms of a more stable world. It should also be clear that this proposal is another example of how increased armament can be combined with measures that alleviate some of the most important and dramatic problems. *It assumes that the U.S. first obtains a Credible First Strike Capability and the West obtains large conventional forces.*

One objection that is sometimes made to the "Hague Convention" is that such collaboration with the Soviets weakens the resolution of the West and discourages the captive nations. This seems to me to be very shortsighted. We have accepted coexistence and it may be worthwhile to accept small competitive losses now, not only to increase stability, but to head off the more cataclysmic losses that could ensue later if, as seems quite likely, an increasingly dangerous arms race makes the weapons seem more dangerous than the Soviets.

Another wartime limitation that has some attractive features (as suggested by both Colonel Leghorn and Admiral Buzzard some years ago) is to use atomic weapons freely (in the military sense, but with due regard for friendly civilians and property) when defending against even conventional attacks, but only over our own territory; we would threaten to use limited or unlimited "strategic" nuclear retaliation if the other side should use atomic weapons over our territory. I think this, too, could be made very credible. It might eliminate some of the problems of keeping large conventional establishments in many areas of the world. Once again, a credible Type II Deterrent or belief that Controlled Nuclear Retaliation can be made to work is required to make this notion feasible. But ambiguity must be avoided. For example, is Taiwan our territory or not? We would get into a nasty crisis if the Soviets made the same rule and the "atomic rights" status of some disputed territory came to be itself disputed. Probably the announcement of the rule would have to be accompanied by the publication of a map that would clearly mark off the restricted area. To be included in such an area might be very valuable to a country. It could be made an inducement for them to join alliances, and so forth. We would have to make it clear that we were in no sense writing off the excluded areas; instead, we were reserving some freedom of action as to our reaction to aggression against such neutrals. Most likely we would have to have some capability to fight limited, nonnuclear wars in these gray areas. While we would reserve the right to use nuclear weapons, their use could not be made automatic.

Some of the problems of arms control are shown in Table 38.

First, and possibly most important, are the limitations themselves.

If, for example, we successfully ban the testing of nuclear weapons, we cannot then develop with assurance certain types of new weapons. Contrary to much popular opinion, this is of major military significance. Occasionally one hears remarks to the effect that since we now have weapons large enough to destroy the world, why should we bother to improve them? This is really a variant, and a very misleading one, of the over-kill theory. When we look at actual military operations, it is easy to see that improved weapons could increase the utility of our force by an order of magnitude. It is therefore going to be important to keep up with the technological development of the other side.[13]

◆◆

TABLE 38

SOME PROBLEMS OF ARMS CONTROL

   I. The Limitations Themselves
  II. Decreasing Uncertainty   •
 III. Cheating
  IV. Asymmetrical Effects of Reduction of Tension

◆◆

Banning or controlling the further testing and development of nuclear weapons will have side effects. It will reinforce the moral and political sanctions against using nuclear weapons in limited warfare. To the extent one feels it desirable to be able to use nuclear weapons, this is another potent argument against banning tests. If one wanted to discourage the use of nuclear weapons in limited wars, this particular side effect would be regarded as beneficial rather than harmful.

[13] It might be worth while to give one illustration. It turns out that the effectiveness of a missile in either destroying a protected military base or in laying waste an area (as in city bombing) goes as the ⅔ power of the yield of its warhead for any target that is not over-killed by launching a single missile at it. If the yield and accuracy are such that the target is over-killed, increasing the yield will not give an increase in efficiency. In plain English this would mean that, other things being equal, an improved ICBM carrying three times the yield of an unimproved ICBM will do the same amount of damage as two of the unimproved ICBM's. If testing is permitted it is probably not very hard to develop weapons which will give about three times the yield in about the same weight (in a decade or so of testing we went from 20 KT to 20 MT, or a factor of 1,000). If one makes the assumption that clandestine testing could mean improvements by some factors of 3, then every factor of 3 that was obtained would be the equivalent, at the minimum, of doubling the size of the force. This is a minimum because it does not take account of the fact that improvements in the KT/lb rating of bombs do more than just increase the efficiency of the old ways of doing things—they enable one to do new kinds of things (e.g., Polaris and Minuteman depended on achieving this kind of improvement).

244

The mutual benefits to both sides from a reliable freeze or slowing down in the development or testing of nuclear weapons seem to be much larger than any asymmetrical losses or gains. Such an agreement could be negotiable. I would conjecture that a successful freeze in phases of nuclear technology would tend on the whole to hurt the Soviets more than the United States. At the worst it would not hurt us very much.[14] This conjecture on the "safeness" of arms control agreements, while plausible, needs more analysis than has been given it. It is subject to many caveats, the most important of which is the problem of cheating. The main problem seems to be that the Soviets are willing to accept an enforceable ban (one that they could not evade clandestinely), if one could be devised that would not give the United States any opportunities to gather military intelligence. Our decision makers seem to be willing to accept a test ban that would prevent the Soviets from conducting clandestine experiments, even if it did not give us any opportunities to gather intelligence. Unfortunately, every proposal to date either gives us bonus intelligence about the Soviets or seems to give them real opportunities for cheating. We refuse to trust the Soviets and the Soviets want to preserve an iron curtain. *Even modestly reliable arms control measures may be infeasible if any large or technologically advanced segment of the world is left outside the controlled area.*

Similar remarks can be made about *restrictions on operational practices.* Insofar as a particular practice is important to our defense, restrictions on its use have the obvious effect of denying us the benefits from it. For example, many valuable safety measures on operational practices might be inconsistent with alert status and quick reaction. To the extent that we wish to depend on alert and reaction for protection, we may not wish to limit ourselves. Probably the most serious problem of this sort arises in connection with those arms control measures that require each side to give to the other detailed information on deployment and operation. On the surface, such measures help the United States more than the Russians because they are more successful than we at hiding information. But we are unlikely to strike first. If the Soviets do, then any extra information they got in this way would be very helpful to their plans. Even if the arms

---

[14] This remark will be debated by those who wish to develop special weapons for limited war, active defense, or mobile missiles. Only the last strikes me as being of major importance, and even here the disadvantages to the U.S. are exaggerated because insufficient account is taken of the effect of the same constraints on the Soviet offense and defense program. Of course if the Soviets cheat and we do not, the last remark does not hold and the asymmetry can be dangerous.

control measures, on the average, increase the punishment that the aggressor must accept, in most cases they will reduce his uncertainty. Many students of the Soviet government have conjectured that this could have a destabilizing effect. The reduction in uncertainty may more than recompense them for any moderate loss in the effectiveness of their attack. It should be clear that uncertainty in the outcome could be more deterring than the prospective losses. Suppose the Russians had to choose between two tactics. One would give them the certainty of losing, say, 10 per cent of their population, but no more and no less. A second tactic would be one in which they had a 90 per cent chance of getting away scot-free and a 10 per cent chance that things would turn out so disastrously that they would lose 100 per cent of their population. Most experts would guess that the Russians would prefer the first tactic. While losing 10 per cent of the population is a terrible disaster, it is (as we pointed out before) not an unlimited disaster, nor is it entirely unprecedented in history. The Russians would be more than 90 per cent certain that they could survive such a disaster. In this respect, nations may be very different from criminals, for whom the certainty of some punishment seems to be more deterring than a small likelihood of a very large punishment.

One of the most important problems of arms control, and one which has received the most attention, is *the problem of detecting cheating.* The problem will exist even if the original signers to the agreement are sincere. People and governments change. The evasion problem may be more severe than most people think. The would-be evader has an almost incredible advantage vis-à-vis the overt and official system. It is very difficult to negotiate these agreements. While we do not have much experience, one can confidently predict that once negotiated, they will tend to become very rigid. In fact, it may be impossible from the practical point of view to change them even though new technical information comes up and provisions have been made for taking account of such changes. This rigidity will occur even if neither side wants to cheat but just entertains suspicions of the other. Revision will be even more difficult if only one party intends to cheat. As a result of this rigidity in the original agreement, the would-be cheater has quite an advantage. He can use all his ingenuity and expertise to devise methods for evading a fixed control system. Any method that works may serve his purpose, and *he may have years to work out the method,* having almost complete flexibility in choosing his means. The would-be controllers, on the other hand, are attempting to set limits on the ingenuity and cleverness of man for years in advance. They are trying to protect against all possible ways of cheating. The methods they can use are rigidly limited to those the contracting parties can agree on. In addition, because of the inadequacy of our research programs, those who set up the plan will generally have only weeks or months to study their problem and to work out methods, while the evader not only knows everything the enforcer knew when the agreement was set up, he also has the benefits of later research and development. He has the lifetime of the agreement to work out his countermeasures.

The problem of detecting a violation is very similar to the standard problem of law enforcement. Society sets up many different systems and mechanisms to prevent crime, but none of them is depended on to work perfectly. In addition to use of preventive methods such as guards, auditors, safes, locks, and other devices, we have a police force which tries to detect criminals by using both covert and overt methods. The monitoring of an arms control agreement is likely to be a similar problem, so that covert methods of detecting violations are likely to play an important role.

By contrast with the official inspection system (which is restricted to methods that have been agreed upon after lengthy negotiations), the covert inspectors can use any method that they can devise within the rules of the game; that is, if they are doing something forbidden, they must not get caught or at least the system must be able to continue operation after any penalties that are levied for getting caught are paid. Thus, the situation is almost the reverse of the official inspection system. As far as the official inspection system is concerned, the violator has a great deal of freedom. Any method of evasion that he can dream up is as good as any other method. But once he begins evading he has to work with one fixed method or vary his violations between a few methods. The covert inspectors can now use any method that they can think of to pick up the violators. It is not quite symmetrical. The violator knows all the details of the system he is evading, while the covert inspector may have only a fragmentary idea or no idea at all of what to seek.

In most cases the searchers will have some idea of what they are looking for, and any method that they can devise to find it is as good as any other method as long as it works. I mentioned earlier that when most people who have studied this field are asked, "Which would you rather be, a hider or a finder?" they generally answer, "A hider." Some of them would change their minds if they were told that they had to hide a fixed operation of some magnitude and that there was an active group of finders using a spectrum of methods, including clandestine intelligence activities, to pick them up. The agreement should allow for the possibility of clandestine intelligence. While the main purpose of the official system is to prevent open violation, it has a secondary but very important objective—that is, to increase the capability of the unofficial snoopers and to force the violators into using tactics which make it easier for the unofficial snoopers to detect them. Unless there is the possibility of such unofficial activities, then there will be very few agreements possible which would have even a medium confidence of detecting violators.

I would like now to take up, very briefly, two of the most important and least discussed aspects of arms control:

1. How does one deter, punish, and correct arms control violations?

2. How does one operate the controls in a strained situation? For example, two of the nations being controlled are at war with each other and worried about the use of the control system to give military intelligence to the enemy.

Let us consider the problem of deterrence, punishment, and correction. We have mentioned several times that the correction part of this must involve having a posture which is not absolutely dependent upon there being a zero rate of violation, but that preparations must be made so that if the violation is detected it will be possible to react quite rapidly. This is one of the major reasons why I do not believe that we can afford to reduce our armament too much. The ability to correct violations means that the military effect of the violations must be small in percentage terms of the current strategic balance. It should also be clear that a credible ability to correct violations may go a great distance to remove temptations from a potential violator. On the other side, one wishes also to punish the violator. Many people have conjectured that just the public reaction from world opinion on being caught red-handed would deter the violator. Fred Iklé [15] has called this the "cover themselves with shame" hypothesis. The term comes from the January 14, 1960 speech of Khrushchev's in which he stated,

[15] The next two pages owe a great deal to an unpublished paper by Fred Iklé on the evasion of arms control agreements and the use of deterrence and punishment in controlling such evasion.

248

If some side violates the agreement it assumed, the instigators of this violation will cover themselves with shame, they will be condemned by the peoples of the whole world.

Khrushchev has also had a different attitude. For example, speaking in Hungary on December 2, 1959, he said,[16]

. . . international reactionary circles still seek to have the so-called Hungarian question discussed in the United Nations. Let them have it as a souvenir, if this consoles them.

It is hard to believe that public opinion is either a very sure or effective punishment. It is likely that it could only deter if there is no great pressure to violate. I believe that most of the people who hold the public opinion hypothesis are basically members of the Minimum Deterrence school who really think of armaments as being psychological, and therefore argue to themselves, either consciously or unconsciously, that the net psychological effect of a violation is likely to be negative and therefore why would a nation take the chance; and in any case, "Who cares?" If one takes the question of objective capabilities seriously as I have done in this book, one has a quite different estimate of the possible motives and pressures. It should also be clear that rarely, if ever, will a violation be as flagrant and shameful as the Hungarian intervention. Even if it is picked up by the official inspection system there is likely to be at least some ambiguity involved. An ambiguity which the violator will exploit. If the evidence has been picked up by clandestine intelligence or by an unfriendly monitoring power, then of course the violator will accuse the accusor of fabricating the evidence for some nefarious purpose. Or the violator who is caught can always blame the other side for having violated first. He had become aware of the violation by clandestine intelligence, but rather than denounce the arms control agreement he simply took some measures in self-defense. Finally, and not at all improbably, the violator can argue the absolute historical necessity for doing whatever he did. While this strikes people always as a very weak defense before the event, it is amazing how strong it looks after the event. For example, practically nobody would have predicted that the U.S. government would ever say it had a right to fly over the territory of a sovereign nation with which it was at peace. But when we were caught doing exactly that we did assert the right as being absolutely necessary in an age of push-button warfare in which one could easily and quietly

---

[16] *New York Times*, December 3, 1959.

procure enough missiles to wipe out an unwary and unknowing opponent. The argument, of course, is quite strong.

Another punishment would be to resume the arms race which would entail both sides being subjected to all of the risks and costs which had been ameliorated by the broken agreement. This second kind of punishment one can take more seriously. At least the author of this book would, though it is not at all clear whether the Soviets would. As far as the risks are concerned, resuming the arms race is presumably only a punishment if one takes seriously the technological race and the problems that the arms control agreement tried to ameliorate. It is difficult to judge how important this would be in Soviet eyes.

The third and the most important punishment, particularly if it is made credible and sure, is the effect of a subsequent deterioration of international relations; particularly between the two major powers. This would not only show up in an increased hostility, general distrust, and unwillingness to negotiate future agreements, but in an accelerated technological and material arms race; it would then cost both sides money as well as risk if one side were caught in a violation. The money threat could be particularly credible if the U.S. government had made a public previolation commitment to double or triple its budget, making it quite clear to a Soviet decision maker that a detected violation would cost them 10's, if not 50's, of billions of rubles a year in counterprograms. I am suggesting that one of the major values of a Preattack Mobilization Base may well be in an arms control situation. The arms control agreement may ban certain capabilities which frighten or irritate the other side. We may still want a Preattack Mobilization Base for these capabilties so that if the agreement is broken, these capabilities will rapidly come into being.

The last possibility and one very much to be considered for deterring and punishing smaller powers is the use of military and economic sanctions. It is difficult for me to believe that we can have a stable world under arms control agreement unless we are willing to use violence to enforce these agreements. It is also quite likely to be true that we may have to use or threaten violence to gain universal acceptance in the first place. This is, of course, the exact opposite of the pacifist position.

Let us now consider the second question. What happens if the arms control agreements are put under stress and strain because of a war, civil strife, or other crisis arising? If the success of arms control depends on the creation of a world in which all violence and conflict have been banished, it is most unlikely that a successful arms control system will be developed. Stresses and strains will arise even in the best-run worlds. It will probably turn out that it will be impossible to devise a system that can work if either the U.S. or the Soviet Union defy it. Let us therefore assume that both of these countries are anxious to keep the system working. Even given this optimistic assumption, one wonders if a system can be designed which will work even if some third or fourth power decides to defy the system or to denounce the agreement, possibly announcing that the agreement has been denounced temporarily for some overwhelming reason (real or simulated, deliberate or unpremeditated), and promising that as soon as conditions have returned to normal they will be glad to return to the fold. In the meantime they would say they have no intention of violating the agreement, but they find it necessary in view of the special condition to throw out the inspectors and their equipment (temporarily, of course).

It seems to me that as much as possible the necessary inspection and monitoring of the arms control agreement should be carried out even against the will of the violator, but unnecessary or marginal frills dropped. This may be especially feasible to the extent that these activities can be done from the air or space. If this is not possible, then it seems to me that the time has come to apply the economic or military sanctions I have mentioned previously. One simply cannot allow any and every nation to decide at times of its own choosing whether or not it will agree to accept regulation. It may not be possible to force regulation on the U.S. and the S.U.; it ought to be possible to go a great distance in doing so on other nations, once there has been a reasonably widespread (but not necessarily unanimous) consensus on principles and methods.

It should be clear that even with the suggested measures it is most unlikely that any inspection or monitoring scheme can be advertised responsibly as "100 per cent reliable," many public remarks to the contrary notwithstanding. It is far easier to design a low-quality system than a medium-quality one. Even modest high quality—say a 50 per cent chance of detecting a determined violator —may be beyond us. Even though I hold this view, I think it may still be worthwhile under some conditions to enter agreements which involve some moderate risks. Agreements seldom last indefinitely.

Furthermore, as I will try to show in the next lecture, there are a great many risks in not having an agreement. One must seek a balance. While I do not pretend to have reached one, it is almost inconceivable that we should not be able to arrive at agreements with the Soviets that are less risky than an unrestricted arms race, or even a race with the current implicit agreements. While there are reasonable and relevant calculations and studies that can illuminate the problems, we will have to end up taking the usual uncalculated "calculated risk" on one side or the other. The next lecture will try to make it clear that the risks of doing *nothing* are also fearful. If events are not controlled, it may just turn out that there are going to be too many risks and tensions combined with too much technological progress: too many missiles, too many buttons, too many people with potential decision-making power, and too many countries with nuclear weapons and missiles.

It is important that we take some control of our destiny, not just go along with events. But it is also important that we do it intelligently and cautiously. If things go poorly some may say that they would prefer a Russian-dominated world to a war. Even that unpleasant choice is unlikely to be the one that is presented. In a multiweaponed world, the actual problems and choices are likely to involve accident, miscalculation, blackmail, or the irresponsible use of weapons, and it would be folly not to consider these problems on their own merits because of an over-concentration on some extreme solution.

Some of these specific dangers can be the subject of negotiations. They probably can be controlled successfully, but only if we put more imagination and work into it than we have in the past. We may already have missed some chances. There may have been some golden opportunities from 1953 to 1955, though this is controversial. The Russians seemed to be willing to accept a test ban and also seemed willing to accept U.S. inspectors at fixed points in Russia. It is generally agreed that at that time we were far ahead of them in thermonuclear capability. From both the narrow (military) and the broader (public policy) points of view, this seemed to many Americans to be exactly the right moment to stabilize the situation. If the Soviets really were willing to accept a ban at that time it was probably because they were just beginning to emerge from the "three year war" doctrine and did not understand the full significance of our technological lead. However, we did not really try to exploit the opportunity. Rather, we assumed that such Soviet proposals as a desire to have inspection posts at railroad terminals and posts for the purpose of detecting classical World War I- and World War II-type mobilizations were evidence of insincerity rather than a possible doctrinal lag.

I had some small contact at that time with a number of people who were against accepting Russian offers. One was even against negotiating with them. I would like to go over a few of their objections.

One worry for the technical people was the possibility that a test ban would be likely to wreck the Livermore and Los Alamos Laboratories. This worry may be legitimate (even the current moratorium could be doing some harm). There has always been in peacetime a slight onus on working on nuclear weapons, and we would expect prejudice on this to increase sharply if a test ban were agreed to and no special measures were taken to prevent undesirable side effects. Judicious salary raises of 25 to 50 per cent for personnel would be helpful here. (Too much would look as though you were trying to buy people.) Other fringe benefits, pleasant working conditions, and lavish research budgets might help. These could be combined with a deliberate public indoctrination campaign to remove the onus. This campaign could, for example, include a Presidential announcement at the time he accepts the ban that he is doing so only because he has faith that patriotic and public-spirited scientists will continue doing the paper and pencil work necessary to maintain standby test capabilities and theoretical development. The President could supplement this announcement by occasional visits to the laboratories. There is, of course, the serious problem that in a relaxed world most U.S. Presidents are going to want to look like peacemongers, not warmongers. This brings us to the major asymmetry between the United States and the Soviet Union—the effect a reduction in tension was thought likely to have on our respective defense postures.

When faced with possible bans on tests, the nontechnical people were sometimes preoccupied by certain fears motivated by lack of confidence in the future action of the government or people of the United States. They wondered if we would have the courage to accuse the Russians of violations on the basis of evidence that was good but slightly ambiguous, particularly if relations between the two countries were superficially satisfactory and it should seem undesirable to disturb them. (That this worry was legitimate is shown by the fact that we allowed the Chinese and North Koreans to violate *unambiguously* the Panmunjom truce terms in a flagrant fashion and waited some years before we denounced the agreement.)

Another worry in this same class was that the slightest relaxation in tension would be likely to cause a reduction in our military budgets that would prove dangerous. That this worry was legitimate is shown by the number of people, some of them in high places, who have expressed publicly and privately fears that we could not continue indefinitely to spend something like 10 per cent of our gross national product on national defense. I have discussed this problem with many who are familiar with both economics and the military problem; they discount this fear. It is difficult to find a respectable economist who is willing to endorse the notion, but the idea that our current defense burden is unbearable is nevertheless prevalent. As a result, the pressure to reduce military budgets is so strong that it is quite likely that any Soviet–U.S. agreements would touch off such action.

The major purpose of a disarmament agreement should not be to relieve the so-called "crushing" burden of defense. (There is a belief though that this is the major Soviet motivation.) As far as I can see, the best that could be accomplished in the immediate future via practical and responsible agreements is to prevent the budget from getting enormously larger, or equally important, to insure that the current "burden" gives us satisfactory security. If the conclusion of a successful agreement were the signal to go into another Louis B. Johnson era (when our defense budget was less than fifteen billion a year and scarcely enough for housekeeping), then I suspect we are facing a very grim future. It is unlikely even though they are under greater objective pressure that the Russians would also reduce their budget so drastically. In addition, due to the problems of scale, a symmetrical reduction of the budget may destabilize the objective "balance of terror." This destabilization while objectively symmetrical, may be more dangerous for us than for them.

Nonmilitary defense and disarmament appear to be somewhat complementary. Most nonmilitary defense expenditures seem to be consistent with all current negotiations and suggestions in the disarmament field. An adequate combination of military and nonmilitary measures should provide an objective and credible capability for calling attention to the enemy's violations and lead to either punishment or negotiations. Military measures alone may not do the trick because they are so vulnerable to blackmail tactics. Just a modest but realistic Credible First Strike or even Counterforce as Insurance Capability might be adequate in the context of a slowed-down arms race.

A rather important and valuable effect of such a realistic defense program, particularly in a disarmament situation, is psychological. If one country designs its military establishment to *terminate* war rather than *deter* war (by punishing the enemy with a retaliatory strike), it is much less likely to indulge in wishful thinking. Even today, without any disarmament schemes, Western military organizations and their governments have psychological and motivational difficulties in maintaining a high operating state of readiness and adequate combat capabilities. This is partly due to the fact that many feel that such weapon systems will never be used and that even if used they would be so destructive that it makes no difference if they operate well or badly. If this attitude is combined with the moral onus on military preparations and planning that a disarmament agreement might bring, we could almost confidently predict an undue and possibly dangerous degradation of Western military capabilities. If we are emotionally committed to the belief that deterrence or the disarmament or control agreement is foolproof, there is only a short space between being satisfied with a system that is objectively capable of destroying the enemy in a retaliatory blow and a system that can only hurt the enemy. Small spaces also separate a system that *might* hurt the enemy from one for which there are circumstances in which it is conceivable that the enemy *will* be hurt. To repeat a previous remark, *"The capacity of Western governments and peoples to indulge in wishful thinking about military problems is almost unlimited."* An official goal that calls for an objective capability to terminate a war in a fashion other than envisaged in the Homicide Pact concept might have a most salutary effect in restraining fanciful notions.

CHAPTER VI

ADDITIONAL REMARKS ON THE MILITARY PROBLEMS

WHAT are the requirements that our military forces must satisfy if we take seriously the objectives and circumstances discussed in the last chapter? To start with a narrow view of the problem, we will first consider *the protection of the SAC alert forces.* (Many people think that this is all that is necessary to meet our strategic problems. They also tend to think of it as simple and easy. Actually even this relatively straightforward objective is complicated.)

❖❖❖

TABLE 39

TO PROTECT STRATEGIC ALERT FORCES

1. Mixture of *warning and reaction,* shelter, concealment, dispersal, and active defense
2. Protected "go ahead" order
3. Reliable safety measures
4. Some command and control
5. Protection against peacetime attacks
6. Capability to limit peacetime attacks

❖❖❖

Table 39 lists the minimum ingredients needed to protect an alert force. First, we have to provide some mixture of warning and reaction, shelter, concealment, and dispersal. Warning, as a defense, implies that we will be able to react and exploit the warning, which is why I have coupled the two concepts together. Thus we must get into a place of safety, otherwise reduce our vulnerability, or launch an attack between the time the warning is received, evaluated, and acted upon and the time the enemy's bombs arrive at the target. Sole reliance on warning and quick reactions may be an unreliable security measure, however. This is partly because dependence on some kinds of quick reaction so increases the chance for an unpremeditated war that the quick reaction schemes tend to be a façade; the buttons are not really connected. Additionally, quick reaction seems particularly susceptible to degradation by clever tactics on the part of the enemy that have been overlooked or underestimated. Among these tactics are clandestine delivery of weapons, spoofing, jamming, or circumvention of the warning network (for example, by infiltration or masquerade), or even the possibility of physical destruction of a crucial element of the warning system by sabotage or peacetime attack. This hardly means that warning and the possibility of quick reaction should not be an important component of a retaliatory system, but only that sole reliance on these measures is unsatisfactory.

In evaluating the efficiency of warning and reaction it is convenient to define two kinds of mistakes. The first is to react to a false alarm and thus be subject to some needless cost or risk—for example it is possible to react to a false alarm in such a way as to dangerously increase the probability of war. The second kind of mistake, is *not to react* adequately when a real attack is taking place.

It can be shown that with most systems the two kinds of mistakes are closely related. If we refuse to react at all to false alarms we increase markedly the probability of being caught on the ground if an attack actually occurs. On the other hand, if we wish to take no chance at all of being caught unprepared, and react whenever there is ambiguous evidence that an attack may be taking place (no matter how ambiguous the evidence is), we will have to react to so many false alarms that the system would be too "costly" to operate in peacetime. (I am using the term *cost* to cover such things as lowered morale, increased chance for war by mistake or accident, interference with civilians, and so on, as well as direct dollar costs.) It is necessary to balance the probability of being caught on the ground against the cost of reacting to a false alarm. The exact point at which the balance should be achieved depends rather sharply on the rate at which false alarms occur and the "cost" of the reaction. These costs in turn depend on how we react to the alarm. These costs are not negligible. If the cost of some possible action were very low, we would do it normally. We would not wait for an alarm to initiate the action.

Table 40 indicates some possible reactions to varying degrees of warning. The most innocuous would be *to increase the alert status of the strategic force.* If we normally keep one-third of the bomber force on ground alert, we could take account of the alarm to increase this proportion. It is also possible to increase the number of ICBM's by postponing effective routine maintenance and replacement and keeping those ICBM's that are on alert farther along the countdown. The costs of these reactions are measured mainly by the effects on crews, training, maintenance, morale, and the increased possibility of an accident.

The second measure would be *to decrease the vulnerability of the force by methods supplementing the alert.* For example, decision makers and other normally vulnerable personnel could go to their battle stations, planes could be dispersed to other than their home bases, and friendly air traffic which might be used to conceal a sneak attack could be curtailed. If we have had only a ground alert we

◇◇

TABLE 40
REACTIONS TO WARNING

I. Increase Alert
II. Decrease Vulnerability
III. Initiate "Positive Control"
IV. Local Counterforce
V. Institute Negotiations
VI. Limited Counterforce
VII. Controlled War
VIII. Unlimited Retaliation

◇◇

could even temporarily institute an airborne alert and at the same time bring additional planes and crews to a state of ground alert. This last measure would have a double value, since it would discourage the enemy from deliberate spoofing in addition to decreasing our vulnerability; whenever he spoofs we would put one-third of the force in the air and bring perhaps another third of the force to ground-alert status. We would have twice the force available for striking at a time he had deliberately aggravated us.

The third possibility is *to initiate a "positive control" or "fail-safe" reaction.* For the bombers this could mean sending them off toward their target but giving them orders to return to their base if they do not get a confirming go-ahead signal at the proper spot. We have already mentioned that unless this is done carefully it could involve an appreciable possibility of touching off a war by accident either because one of our bombers makes a mistake or because the enemy reacts and a self-confirming chain of action and counteraction that leads to war is set off. It also has the sharp disadvantage that, unless plans are made to institute some form of continuous airborne alert, the calling back of the planes may result in a reduction of capability. This means either a weak point in the system or a proneness to war by miscalculation.

A complete "positive control" reaction is not possible for the ICBM. It cannot "fail-safe." Even if one had a destruct-mechanism, whereby ICBM's that were shot off by mistake could be destroyed in the air, it would not be satisfactory to react to a false alarm. First, it would be too expensive. Second, and even more important, we could not be sure that the destruct-mechanism would be 100 per cent reliable. Therefore, it is quite unlikely that any order could or should be given to fire ICBM's on any but the most certain type of evidence. However, a partial "positive control" system can be used with ICBM's; the order could be given to start the count-down and then to stop and hold at a convenient spot. This, too, increases somewhat the chance of an accident, but with the proper safeguards only to a negligible degree. The major effect is the removal of all the safeties in the system since it now takes only a simple "go ahead" order to launch this attack.

In later time periods, when we have many protected and dispersed ICBM's, it may be possible to fire ICBM's on the basis of radar or other tactical warning, since under these circumstances the enemy must fire large numbers of missiles and thus possibly be forced to give certain evidence of his intentions. This is unlikely to be true in the immediate future. For this and other reasons the early ICBM's cannot now rely solely on quick reaction for their protection. This does not mean that we do not wish to have a capability to react rapidly. There are several reasons for this. First, the enemy cannot be sure that we will be unwilling to shoot on the basis of ambiguous evidence. He does not know what would appear to us to be ambiguous. This increases his uncertainty and complicates his planning. Secondly, if the enemy spreads his attack over many minutes (and it may be that he is forced to do so, either because of incompetency or technological and geographical difficulties), those of our ICBM's that are not hit by the very first bombs can be launched before the second wave. It is quite probable for the early time period when only the Soviet Union and we have ICBM's that the landing or explosion of just a small number of foreign ICBM's anywhere in the United States might well cause us to launch our ICBM's in retaliation. In the later time period, as I explained under "Flexible War Plans," we will have to be more cautious. It might even be prudent to be more cautious than this in the early time period.

A fourth possible reaction would be a local counterforce operation. For example, if Soviet or even unidentified planes were found flying within the continental United States, particularly near an important installation such as a control headquarters (one which was protected from ICBM or IRBM attack by adequate shelters or warning) one might possibly shoot the menacing plane down first and ask questions afterward. The trouble, of course, is that one may be shooting down one's own planes. Such an incident is not only deplorable in itself, but it is likely to cause such bad public and interdepartmental relations that the future alert status of the warning and reaction system will suffer. Sometimes, however, the warning signal may be of such a magnitude that mistakes can be tolerated, at least in comparison with the warning signal. For example, if a nuclear bomb exploded in the United States, that incident could be used to actuate an order allowing local defenses to shoot at any unidentified planes in forbidden areas. If it turns out that the nuclear weapon was not a premature firing by the enemy, but one of our own or one of his that was accidentally exploded, people will be so angry at the nuclear accident that they are unlikely to become more angry if a few friendly planes get shot down. On the other hand, one should not use such a signal to launch our own ICBM's. The mere knowledge that a nuclear weapon has exploded is not reliable evidence of a sneak attack by the Soviets.

Sometimes it is suggested that one could use a local counterforce operation against "legal" but threatening maneuvers by the enemy, such as planes or ships that spoof early warning lines from international waters, Soviet submarines in the Gulf of Mexico, submarines shadowing our Polaris submarines or aircraft carriers, and so on. I suspect that within wide limits we will have to live with such practices if the Soviets start them, contenting ourselves with "retaliation in kind." However, such practices can certainly be subject to negotiations and forbidden by agreement. To some extent they are forbidden by current implicit agreements, that is, by precedent and custom.

The next item in Table 40 is not normally considered when one is discussing various standard operating procedures. It is to warn the enemy, probably very discreetly, that you have received certain information that is making you very nervous; in fact you believe that he is planning an attack, that you are thoroughly alerted, that as a result the attack is almost certain to be a failure, and it would be much better for all concerned if he would call off his attack. This warning could be coupled with an ultimatum or semiultimatum that whether or not the other side is actually planning an attack it would be better for all concerned that he do or not do certain things; for example, remove medium bombers and Polaris-type submarines from advanced positions. It might be necessary to do similar things oneself, in order to assure that one was not planning on exploiting the situation for a surprise or pre-emptive attack. It should be clear that at this point both sides will be trigger-happy and possibly even accident prone. After all, the feeling of safety due to the mutual belief in the preposterousness of war has been shattered, and both sides now must seriously consider that the other side is nervous, or desperate, or optimistic enough to do something "decisive" to end once and for all its anxieties and desperations.

The sixth reaction would be a *limited counterforce*. This could occur when we might be almost, but not quite, certain that the enemy was attacking. Suppose a small number of ICBM's were fired at us, but the number was so small that we felt fairly certain they came as the result of an accident on the other side rather than from a breakdown in firing discipline. However, because we are not certain, we feel we could not take the chance of doing *nothing*. We might then be willing to fire a number of ICBM's or IRBM's at his "first strike" forces (i.e., radio guidance installations, ICBM's in Kamchatka, etc.), while making other moves to reassure the Soviets that the strike is defensive and will stay limited.

The seventh reaction is *the initiation of a controlled but all-out counterforce mission*. While the limited counterforce reaction may or may not initiate a Central War, the all-out counterforce unquestionably does. However, the enemy may be induced to control his reaction by the suitable use of intrawar deterrence plus reasonable peace offers.

The eighth reaction is *an all-out retaliation against his cities*. This in turn means that he will shoot at our cities. In spite of the many trigger-happy quick-reaction proposals that are often made, this is the final decision and should only be taken with the most positive evidence. For example, one would not really wish to institute such a reaction if the other side had started the war accidentally. It should also probably only come at a point when the enemy has done so much damage that prospects seem fairly hopeless. If we have not made satisfactory preparations to survive the war, it means an attempt to bring about a mutual homicide situation, since it is almost certain that it will bring about our own homicide.

In analyzing the usefulness of any warning and reaction proposal, we should differentiate between the *physical* reaction time—that is, the time it takes the system to implement the order to institute any particular reactions—and the *effective* reaction time, which includes the time for receiving information, evaluating it, and making the decision to react in an appropriate way. The more innocuous the reaction and the better the information gathering and evaluation, the more automatic and fast we can afford to make the reaction. The reason I suggest considering at least the eight different reactions in Table 40 is that having such a large number of reactions available gives us the flexibility we need to react to different kinds of situations with varying degrees of ambiguity in the signals. Contemplating these alternatives, it is clear that the decision processes and the allowable false alarm rates are quite different for each of the reactions. Because of the shortness of time that is available, each of the reactions must be studied ahead of time and standard operation procedures worked out as far as possible. We may end up wanting more flexibility than I am suggesting: it is most doubtful that we can safely do with less. It is particularly dangerous to try to dispense with the more innocuous reactions. In the next lecture I will give several instances where a planned defensive reaction turned out to be unreliable because its consequences were so vast the government preferred to take the hypothetical risks incurred by temporizing, rather than the certain risks to be incurred by instituting the planned reaction.

Shelter tends to be a good deal more stable than quick reaction alone as a defense, because it is much less accident prone and the number of ways in which it can fail seem relatively low. Unfortunately these few ways can be important. The most worrisome is that if the enemy's attack proves "larger" than the shelters were built for, the shelters may be negated. The attack can become too large if the enemy has some combination of bigger warheads, higher accuracy, or more numbers than were planned for. The attacker may also be able to negate the defender's shelters by exploiting special effects or techniques. For example, he can emphasize ground shock by using weapons that penetrate the earth and explode underground. Unless the equipment is properly shock-protected, it is perfectly possible for the shelter to survive, but for the contents to be useless. This is a particularly worrisome form of attack because no matter how well the equipment is shock-mounted and tested, it is not likely that we will be able to work out realistic "shakedown" tests. There may be other special attacks or effects that the attacker can exploit to damage the operation of the equipment in the shelter or the system as a whole, such as destruction or disruption of control, communications, guidance, and so forth.

One way to prevent the attacker from mounting too large an attack is to disperse shelters to many distinct target points. This forces downward the number of missiles the enemy can shoot at each point. If hard shelters are built, it is not necessary to separate points by as great a distance in order to get the effect of dispersal. This cuts costs by simplifying maintenance, operations, and logistics. However, we have already pointed out that the side that prepares to shoot first can often more cheaply put a large number of missiles in its first salvo than the defender can disperse his missiles to a comparable number of points. Whether the salvo is enough larger depends on such factors as the relationship of the attacker's yield, circular probable error (CEP), reliability, and coordination—as compared to the vulnerability of the defender's shelters, the amount and reliability of warning, and the effective alertness of his force. No one can today make precise estimates of the interaction of these parameters for the time periods of interest.

Shelters work out a great deal better if they are combined with other measures. If the attacker is trying to swamp the defender by sheer numbers and the defender can react quickly, the attacker must deliver his missiles within an extremely short time. This makes the warning problem simpler for the defender and cuts down the effective reliability of the attacker's missiles. Quick reaction can also be helpful against a joint missile and bomber attack. If the defender has the capability to accept the first wave missile attack and still launch his missiles or fly away his planes before the attacker's planes arrive, it greatly simplifies the kind of shelters that have to be built. (Shelter against large, accurately aimed bombs delivered by planes presents a much more difficult problem than shelter against the higher CEP and lesser bomb yields of at least the early missiles.)

Concealment can also be a helpful addition to a shelter. It is not necessary for a protected weapon to be well hidden. If the enemy can only guess location within a few miles (or even just a few thousand feet in the case of very hard shelters), the shelters may well be close to invulnerable. The West may have given up too easily the possibility of hiding the location of its shelters; there are techniques available by which even a democracy should be able to make the enemy slightly uncertain as to the exact location of missile silos.

The most exciting kind of protection that is currently being considered is *concealment by continuous mobility or reasonably frequent changes of position*. Now either nobody knows where you are, or it takes extremely up-to-date intelligence for the enemy to be able to follow your movements. It is also possible to combine a limited mobility (perhaps better called portability) and dispersal in cases where the bases are relatively inexpensive and the weapons system is rather expensive. It may then be practical to build a great many more bases than needed. They can be occupied at random or in a concealed manner, the missiles moving relatively frequently from one base to another. The same tactics are currently used, to some extent, for the protection of British and American medium bombers. In the future they may be even more valuable for planes that do not need runways (vertical take-off or zero-length-launched tactical planes that might be able to use very primitive fields).

A variation of this can occur when both missiles and bases are inexpensive but maintenance or operation are expensive. In this case a relatively small number of crews could secretly be moved around to make the missiles operational.

Effective concealment, either by mobility or by the use of large-scale security measures, could be one of the most reliable methods of protecting a force. For this reason mobility has recently attracted much attention. In particular, three kinds of mobility—Polaris submarines, train-mobile Minuteman, and airborne alert B-52's—are being proposed as the final answer to the vulnerability problem. Desirable as mobility is likely to be, for a portion of the force, it has problems which make it unlikely that it will prove to be the sole answer. While these problems vary from system to system, there are certain typical ones which seem to affect all or most of the systems being considered. Some of these problems are listed in Table 41. The first, the method of achieving mobility, may put severe constraints on the system. To take the most obvious, oceanic systems are restricted to the oceans, train-borne systems to tracks, and airborne systems are hard to keep in the air. The size and weight of the vehicle are severely restricted by the requirement of mobility, and the possible arrangements for command, control, communication, guidance, and maintenance are all affected. As a result the systems tend to be relatively expensive, which means many fewer missiles per dollar. For example, if an invulnerable system happened to be five times more expensive than a vulnerable one, then, per dollar spent, we would get only one-fifth as many invulnerable missiles than if we had bought the vulnerable system. Unless the enemy can destroy 80 per cent of the vulnerable system, the more expensive invulnerable system would have been a bad buy. In addition, we

◆◇◆

TABLE 41
PROBLEMS OF MOBILE SYSTEMS

1. The Method of Achieving Mobility
2. Reliable Command and Control
3. High Operating Costs
4. Low Performance
5. Area Attacks
6. Security Leaks
7. Peacetime Attacks

◆◇◆

should give the vulnerable system credit for forcing the enemy to use up some of his offensive force in destroying this portion of our force. It should be clear that mobility is expensive, and that the costs are often underestimated. To quote a column by Hanson Baldwin:

> Navy witnesses also testified that it cost three to four times as much to operate a nuclear submarine as it did to operate a conventional Diesel-engined electric battery "boat."
> Moreover, the cost of overhauling the Nautilus, first of our nuclear-powered submarines, and the time required to give her a thorough going-over have surprised the experts. The Nautilus has been in the dockyard for more than a year and her overhaul has cost about $11,000,000 so far.
> One estimate is that this cost-time factor is about four times that of a conventional powered submarine; others think it is much higher. Some Navy experts estimate that it will cost the Navy more in the near future to overhaul our fleet of nuclear submarines than the present overhaul bill for the entire Navy.
> There are, of course, caveats to these somewhat alarming statistics. . . . the first nuclear core provided about 60,000 miles of cruising; the third . . . is expected to provide about 130,000 miles. . . . With greater experience overhaul cost will be reduced.[1]

If, in addition to being of high cost, the warhead yield is relatively low and the guidance system inaccurate, then the mobile system may not have much counterforce capability, since relatively simple

[1] *New York Times*, May 6, 1960, p. 9.

shelters can now protect the target. In fact, if the system has small enough warheads or a large enough CEP, it may not only be unsuitable for the counterforce mission, it may be weak for the retaliatory mission as well. Such measures as evacuation and improvised shelters are very effective against "small" warhead systems. For these reasons some kinds of mobility entail buying a "lower performance" system. The value of mobility as compared to other protective measures must be judged by how seriously the mission is compromised by the "lower performance" or by what the extra money put into mobility could otherwise buy in the way of protecting more conventional systems. I would conjecture that sole dependence on mobile systems will prove to be a mistake, but that such measures will play an increasing role in the future.

To mention another possible weakness of concealment by mobility, it is sometimes possible to gain intelligence even about moving forces. For example, if mobile forces were put on either the land or waterways of Europe (an area which contains some of the largest Communist parties in the world, the Russians could probably build up a last-minute reporting network that could keep track of most of the force. It would take real effort to prevent this. It is also possible in some circumstances to have peacetime surveillance on aircraft carriers by submarines, seemingly neutral vessels, or airborne radars, or even by the same kind of reporting systems suggested by the mobile land systems. Under some circumstances similar systems might keep track of Polaris submarines or airborne alert planes.

If headquarters knows where these forces are—and it may be important for them to know—the security of the mobile bases then depends completely on the security of this information. The American experience in breaking the Japanese code shows one way in which such security can be lost.

Lastly, protection by pure concealment, either mobile or otherwise, can sometimes be negated by area attacks, unless there is specific protection against such attacks. Mobile systems are likely to be very soft—vulnerable to just a few psi (pounds per square inch) overpressure or to relatively mild ground or water shock. It is possible, of course, that ships, barges, and Polaris submarines might be made relatively invulnerable, but even they might have their contents degraded by subtle effects such as ground shock and radioactivity.

If the enemy wishes to use an area attack against a mobile or concealed system, the effectiveness of his attack will be sensitive to the lethal radius of the weapons he can deliver. The lethal radius in turn is dependent on the size of the warhead in the attacking missile and the vulnerability of the system being attacked. A convenient parameter that can be used to define the vulnerability of a system is the "psi resistance"; that is, the number of pounds per square inch of pressure that the system can withstand and still remain operable. We will consider three warhead sizes: 1, 10, and 100 megatons, because these are round numbers, and six levels of psi resistance: ½, 2, 10, 25, 100, and 500.

While the range of warhead sizes from 1 to 100 megatons is a reasonably large one, it may not cover the entire region of interest. It is possible, for example, that Russian bombers could carry air-to-ground missiles with less than 1-megaton warheads. In any case, published reports have indicated that the American Minuteman and Polaris systems may at least initially carry warheads smaller than this. On the other hand, while the idea of a 100-megaton weapon may strike most readers as extreme, it is not at all unreasonable to make plans against the possibility that such bombs may be developed and carried in the 1965–75 time period. In fact, 100 megatons may not exhaust the upper range of the possibilities or, at least, speculations. There have been several published references to the possibility of 1,000 megaton or begaton bombs (sometimes more accurately, if pedantically, referred to as gigaton bombs). If we were vulnerable to attack by much smaller bombs, it might be reasonable to suppose that the enemy would not bother to develop very large bombs. However, once we have acquired a mobile system of the sort we are discussing here, we have challenged him. If he can meet this challenge by building 100-megaton bombs and the corresponding delivery system, he is very likely to do it. Enemies are like that: always spoiling and making obsolete a perfectly good idea. There are restrictions on the maximum size of bomb that can be delivered practically, but very few technical people would bet that these limits will be much below 100 megatons in the 1965–75 time period.

The six pressures we are considering may not give a sufficiently large range. The lowest of these, ½ psi, exceeds the force of a hurricane wind by a factor of 2 or 3. While the pressure would only last for a very short time—a fraction of a second—it is clear that lower pressures may well be able to damage many systems. On the other hand, while 500 psi is five times the announced hardness proposed for the Titan missile system, it is by no means an ultimate level. The pressures 2, 25, and 100 psi would correspond respectively to the

267

likely vulnerability (to moderate damage) of a completely unhardened system, the early hard Atlas, and the early Titan respectively. Table 42 indicates what could be done in various kinds of area at-

◆◇◆

TABLE 42

EFFECTIVENESS OF AIMED AND AREA ATTACKS

psi Resistance of Target	Lethal Radius (miles)			Lethal Area (sq. miles)		
	1 MT	10 MT	100 MT	1 MT	10 MT	100 MT
½	9	20	42	260	1,200	5,600
2	5	11	25	90	400	2,000
10	1.9	4	8	10	50	200
25	1.2	2.5	5.4	4	20	90
100	.6	1.4	3	1.3	6	30
500	.4	.8	1.7	.4	2	9

◆◇◆

tacks. It should be clear from Table 42 that if the system were vulnerable to a few psi, even the entire area of the United States (3,000,000 square miles) would not be enough to hide it. On the other hand even 10 psi protection gives a sizeable reduction in vulnerability, though, if the enemy can locate any single 10 psi missile base within some ten square miles or any large group (5 to 10) of 10 psi missiles within some hundred square miles, he can probably afford to attack these points by a barrage. For a very hard system (100–500 psi) the enemy needs a very accurate location or a very large yield to be able to destroy it.

The last item on Table 41 is Peacetime Attacks. One must differentiate here a number of cases. There is clearly a great difference between a system which is based on international waters and one which is based on sovereign territory. There is also a great difference between a mobile system which is a component of an over-all posture that includes a Credible First Strike Capability and one which is restricted to Finite Deterrence. In the first case the mobile system helps protect the Credible First Strike from a surprise attack and the Credible First Strike protects the mobile system. In the second case the mobile system is protected by Type III Deterrence if it is protected at all. I will consider all of these matters in a somewhat more general context when I discuss points 5 and 6 of Table 39. (Table 39 is on page 256; discussion is on pages 271–273.)

The second important requirement for the protection of the SAC alert force is to have a *reliable "go ahead" order,* reliable not only in the sense that it can be made and communicated despite all the enemy does to prevent it, but reliable also in the sense that the problems of accident, miscalculation, and unauthorized behavior are kept to the point where excessive worries about these problems or the actual occurrence of accidents will not cause us to handicap the operation of the force. This may get particularly difficult with forces that are widely dispersed, extremely alert, and depend on quick reaction for their protection. There are many safety possibilities here. One would be to have some kind of mechanical (or psychological) lock or safety that could only be released by *central* authorities; such locks and safeties could include an extreme indoctrination of crews and officers on the absolute necessity of not firing without an official, verified order. While such devices may be essential if the strategic force is to be allowed to have hundreds of missiles on a high degree of alert, they may create a special kind of vulnerability if the thing that releases the safety is itself vulnerable, either physically or in method of operation. For this and other reasons, we also need protected headquarters and control centers—preferably mobile or very deep underground.

We have already stressed why centralized decision making and communication is essential. Everybody, even those who find deliberate war implausible, are likely to be very worried about the possibility of starting a war by accident or miscalculation. Because there will be so many people with authority over weapons systems, it will be necessary to make it clear to everyone that he cannot act on his own, no matter how many fireballs or mushrooms he "thinks" he sees. Unless an official, verified order is received, no one will be authorized to push any buttons, irrespective of any evidence he may think he has that the war is on. Unless this is done, we could almost guarantee that a war would occur by accident.

This in turn means that there is a potential weak spot in the system if the enemy can destroy certain headquarters or interrupt or delay communications so as to keep the alert forces from reacting quickly. This gives him two possible advantages. First, it gives him more time to destroy these forces. Second, and probably most important, it enables him to use the postattack blackmail tactics we have already discussed to disarm or degrade the forces whose reaction had been delayed.

Of course, in order to use blackmail, the enemy must have someone with whom to negotiate, so he must be willing to let at least one senior headquarters survive, though he can cut off or degrade its communications. It is a nice point as to whether or not he would prefer to negotiate with the military or the civilians. The military are likely to be of tougher fiber than the civilians, but they are also likely to be quicker to recognize the nature of the problem and the dimensions of the disaster if the enemy happens to have been lucky on the first strike. I would conjecture that there would be many circumstances in which an attacker would prefer to negotiate with the tougher, but better informed group.

If it is also important to regulate and monitor subsequent activities, then the headquarters will probably have to be deep underground rather than mobile. (The communications, data processing, display, and manning in a mobile headquarters are likely to be insufficient to enable much more command and control than just the "go ahead" order.) For example, insofar as our retaliatory force might be composed of manned bombers, we surely would not want our defenses to fire on our manned bombers as they pass out of the United States. The flight plan and identification data needed to prevent this from happening probably need to be kept in some centralized headquarters. Another monitoring and control function occurs when we have to adjust target assignments either to make up for the damage that he has done to us or to negate or adjust to some last minute moves of the enemy, such as evacuation. We will then need some sort of centralized data gathering, processing, and assessment facilities. If the enemy can destroy the buildings that house these facilities he will significantly degrade our capability.

In laying down the requirements for these buildings it is important for us to realize that if they have not been put very deep underground the enemy may be able to design special missiles with the specific objective of destroying them. These might be more accurate and carry much larger yields than the backbone of his force. That is, when these buildings are put underground he is challenged to destroy them and, as with the mobile system, we should not be surprised if he reacts to that challenge, or at least tries to, by the use of special equipment or tactics. We may therefore want some active anti-ICBM defense for these buildings. Active defense of a hard point target should be easier than of a dispersed city, and we may wish to exploit this difference. In addition to decreasing the vulnerability of our Command and Control, we may try to gain more reliability by the use of intrawar deterrence. We could have a specially strong back-up system for the simple purpose of a go-ahead order to attack cities. If by Herculean efforts the enemy destroys our control he activates the back-up system and guarantees an all-out attack on his cities. While this tactic could be used in any Controlled War, it is probably most likely to work in the Counterforce as Insurance posture.

We will also need some active air defense, though perhaps less than we have today if we are only trying to protect the SAC alert forces from a small surprise attack and give up trying to protect other facilities or civilians. For example, if we had no active air defense force, the enemy might be able to attack a SAC complex with a single bomber carrying a large number of bombs. In some circumstances this could cause a great deal of trouble. Once we have some active air defense protecting the places the enemy might be most eager to attack with these bombers, he is likely to be unable to drop more than one or two of his bombs before the bombers are shot down. By having some active defense, we force him to increase the size of any attacking force. We thereby increase the probability that we will get warning. Because of the short reaction time required between warning and firing, local defense missiles may play a special role here.

By proper use of active defense we can also force the enemy to separate in point of time his missile and bomber waves. He may, under some circumstances we have discussed, be able to sneak a small number of bombers through or around our early warning lines. He would find it much harder to sneak even a small number of bombers through the much higher quality contiguous radar cover in the continental United States. However, he might take the risk of keeping these bombers hovering outside this cover and then use them as an immediate follow-up to a missile attack. This tactic could be made to look even more unattractive to them than it already is if we had only a moderate level of active defense, one which could protect against this small attack even if it could be swamped by a large bomber force. (The enemy presumably would not be willing to try to sneak a large bomber force through our early warning lines.) Thus the follow-up attack would be delayed by some hours. These extra hours would be very useful to us.

Lastly, as I already pointed out, we might need some active defense and some Type II Deterrence to protect those components of our SAC alert forces and supporting system that are vulnerable to enemy interference or attacks in peacetime. Either we need this or we have to build systems that cannot be seriously degraded by minor (in scale) enemy actions during peacetime. Unless this is done, the enemy might be tempted to attack the system in peacetime, especially critical elements, or carry on activities which seriously degrade the over-all operation of the system. If he does any of these cleverly, it is not all clear that he cannot do them safely and cheaply. In fact, if we have no credible capacity for protecting our system or initiating a war, the opposite is true: it is quite clear that in peacetime he can do small-scale but significant things that will make life intolerable for an unprepared system.

This last possibility gets particularly important if we go to a pure Finite Deterrence position—say a SAC completely composed of Polaris and Minuteman so designed as to be effective against Soviet cities, but not against SUSAC, and in addition we have no effective civil or active defense for our people or property. We have now guaranteed the enemy that we will not go to war no matter how much he provokes us short of an an all-out attack, and unless we are willing to try our luck with things like controlled nuclear retaliation, we may be in for serious trouble. It is now conceivable, if he wants to be aggressive, that our opponent will hunt down our Polaris submarines in peacetime, interfere with Command and Control, destroy early warning networks, and so on. Under these circumstances, we must charge the Finite Deterrence system with the cost of active defense measures and replacements for the peacetime attrition. We will have some of these costs even if the Soviets or others do not behave this way since we must make advance preparations to meet this contingency. This may increase the system costs of the Finite Deterrent posture markedly.

Active and passive defense may provide a valuable strengthening to our Type II Deterrence, by acting similarly to the NATO trip-wire or plate glass concept [2] in a new role. If our active and passive defenses are good enough so that the forces or resources he must put into attacking or degrading our Type I Deterrent in peacetime are large, such an attack or act is much more eventful and provocative than if it can be done on a very small scale. This, in turn, makes it more credible that he is risking touching off our Type II or Type III Deterrent, and so he may be restrained from such tactics even (or

[2] Under this concept, one of the major purposes of the relatively small forces in Europe was to prevent the Soviets from making large gains by relatively small (and therefore innocuous or safe looking) probing actions. The same concept can be applied in the future to the actual peacetime defense of our strategic forces.

especially) in a tense situation. If we do not have such a plate glass or trip wire, then we must persuade the enemy that we have the resolve to initiate effective and punishing reprisals to any acts of his that seriously degrade our capability, even though on an absolute level the act may look rather trivial, and even though the other side may raise the level of provocation gradually.

In addition to protecting our alert forces, we may wish to protect all the forces that could hurt the enemy. There are two reasons for doing this. First, even if all we are interested in is Finite Deterrence, the enemy may still be deterred by the threat of the damage we can do in second and later attacks of some future war. If we are interested in more than just Finite Deterrence, for example Counterforce as Insurance or Credible First Strike Capability, then these second-day forces are not only useful in Limiting Damage by his later operations, but they can also be used to conclude wars on terms other than outright surrender. In general, we must do the same things for these "second-day" forces that we do for the alert forces, only more —and then some additional things. Table 43 lists some of the essentials.

❖❖

TABLE 43

TO PROTECT ALL DETERRENT FORCES

1. More shelter, concealment, dispersal and control
2. Late-strike facilities and use of improvised forces
3. Warning and defense against second and later strikes
4. Protection against postattack blackmail

❖❖

First, we need more and perhaps better shelters to protect those missiles and planes which either cannot react rapidly or which we wish to hold back. We may want to protect vehicles that are not combat-ready, because we may be able to evacuate them to safer spots or even leave them where they are for use in later strikes of the war. And, of course, if we hope to utilize the nonalert deterrent forces, we must have facilities for these later strikes. For the manned bomber, this may be just some communication facilities and radiological protection of a large number of alternative bases in the hope that a small number survive.[3]

_____

[3] Radiological protection here refers to sufficient ability to decontaminate or protect from the effects of fallout so that the alternative base is not a bonus target.

It may strike some as wishful thinking to expect to have any forces on the second day of the war, when it is so difficult to have forces survive the first hour or so. Actually, the second problem is somewhat easier than the first. Imagine, for example, that we had 1,000 hardened ICBM sites and that the enemy fired many thousands of missiles at these 1,000 sites. It would not be at all surprising if he took out, say, three-quarters of the sites, leaving only 250 surviving intact. This is a pretty grim prospect for losses on the first day of the war. However, if we can prevent the enemy from reconnaissance or free-ride tactics, it will be practically impossible for him to destroy these 250 survivors because he will not know which of the original ICBM's were destroyed and which were not. If he wishes to try to destroy the small remaining force, he would have to fire at the total target system of 1,000 points; this takes four times as many missiles as firing at 250 points and is quite likely to be far beyond his capacity. This means that, subject to preventing the enemy finding them by reconnaissance, these 250 survivors are essentially invulnerable, and we can take our time about firing them. It also means that these same missiles would have been useful even if they had not been alert or combat-ready. Even reloads may be useful.

A similar situation exists in regard to manned bombers. In order to hold down costs, manned bombers operate in peacetime on a relatively small number of home bases, and the enemy presumably knows where they are. Once the war has started, if we have made preparations, we can protect our force but complicate our operations by dispersing these bombers to hundreds of bases, or we can choose the riskier but simpler tactics of dispersing to only a few bases—but to which ones the enemy presumably will not know. Even if he can afford to attack this whole base system in the first few minutes or hours of the war, if we have some sort of evaluatory and monitoring system we can keep the bombers airborne and disperse them to only those bases which survive the first attack. Since he is unlikely to know which bases survive, these bombers are effectively hidden and, like the missiles, are almost invulnerable to second and later strikes.

These late-strike facilities must be protected against free-ride tactics. We therefore need warning and defense against second and later strikes, but most particularly the second. It is quite likely that bombers carrying many bombs (perhaps in short-range air-to-ground missiles) will be much more effective in such mopping-up operations than ICBM's. This would be particularly true if the bomber has some

Hunter-Killer capability (ability to examine an area for targets and then destroy these newly found targets). In particular, if the enemy can destroy the air defense system on the first strike of missiles, he can then use the hundreds of medium- and long-range bombers that he has had in reserve and literally clean up the country and remove from us any capability for firing or launching anything that was not committed in the first few hours of the war. He cannot do this unless he gets a free ride, but unless we have an air defense system that can survive the first wave of ICBM's, he will get this free ride.

If we are to use deterrent forces in the second, third, or later days of the war, we need some protection against blackmail—against all-out threats of total or partial annihilation that might force us to disarm ourselves or to limit our tactics. This last requirement presumably requires that we be able to protect both the population and recuperation ability, which survive the first attack, from later attacks and threats.

Actually, the protection of people and property is an ancient function of the Department of Defense which goes back to the Indian wars, but which has lately received diminished emphasis. Some people think of it as an end in itself and not merely an adjunct to the protection of our strategic forces. (I am of that group.) Since I further believe that in the pre-1965 period, possibly extending into the late '60's or early '70's, it will indeed be possible (if proper preparations have been made) to still have a country after most wars, we should make those preparations. While it is clear that we cannot restore pre-World War II standards of protection, we *can* buy Counterforce as Insurance Capabilities which will make exactly the kinds of distinction illustrated in Table 3 in Chapter I (page 20), and we may even buy some Credible First Strike Capabilities.

◇◇

TABLE 44
TO PROTECT THE UNITED STATES

1. Counterforce as Insurance or Credible First Strike
2. Preattack Mobilization Base
3. Arms Control

◇◇

The first item on Table 44 means having at least an inexpensive civil defense capability in the early '60's, plus a good enough air defense to prevent free rides by bombers. If the threat gets worse, we must either change the cheap civil defense program to an expensive capability or give up our capability for fighting any but the most carefully conducted wars. This presumably weakens our Type II Deterrence and increases markedly our vulnerability to postattack coercion. In addition to continuing defensive capabilities, we need a continuing offensive capability to be able to destroy and harry the enemy's forces so that they cannot operate at leisure (and hopefully cannot operate at all after the first few hours of the war), and to threaten his civilians and property with additional damage so that we can bargain with him. We need at least the kinds of flexible war plans we have already discussed and an adequate command and control and material basis to implement them.

Because it is expensive (and possibly destabilizing) to buy the items on the scale one would like, we need a Preattack Mobilization Base so that, if the international situation ever deteriorates to the point where we feel we must spend very large sums of money, we will be in a position to spend money rapidly and efficiently. Finally, we need Arms Control in addition to military preparations if we are to survive the arms race.

Military Requirements for a War-Fighting Capability

Once one rejects the notion of a war necessarily being a momentary spasm of destruction involving only a "go ahead" order to an invulnerable alert force, then he realizes that preparing for war and deterrence is somewhat more complicated than is usually envisaged by those who have *overadjusted* to the impact of thermonuclear bombs. What are some of the specific capabilities that our military forces will need to be able to fight and terminate wars in addition to deterring them? (It is important to realize that acquiring many of these things will also improve our Type I Deterrence.) Some valuable capabilities are listed in Table 45.

I have mentioned the first and most important capability several times. In order to be able to do anything you have to survive—you must exist. If any important element of the offense or defense is destroyed or used up, it cannot continue to protect, threaten, or attack. We have described the problem of protecting the offensive forces. Let us now consider active defense. I have already pointed out that even if we do not have any anti-ICBM capability we may still want defense against bombers. Even here, in the part of the system that is clearly assigned to a war-fighting rather than a war-deterring mission, it is not all clear that sufficient thought has gone into the problem of "being." As a result, it would not be surprising if large portions were not there. For example, *some basic parts of our defense are located on SAC bases.* They are, therefore, quite vulnerable to attacks that are not directed against *them,* but only against

◇◇

TABLE 45
"LONG" WAR CAPABILITIES

1. Survive!
2. Staying Power
3. System Damage Control
4. Off-Design Operation
5. Postwar Capabilities

◇◇

SAC bases. It should be quite clear that if there are any soft installations or equipment on SAC bases that are so vulnerable that a "small" bomb exploded within a few miles would either destroy them or so damage them that they would be out of the war, we can confidently expect these objects to disappear in the first wave. Now it is possible for people to believe that non-SAC installations will not be objects of enemy attacks (though I do not subscribe to that belief). However, whether you believe this or not is academic so far as installations or equipment on SAC bases are concerned. No one can believe that SAC would not be an object of enemy attack. This means that in any war that is started by a respectable volley of ICBM's, portions of our defense establishment that are soft and on SAC bases will disappear before they can fire a shot.

We have not yet discussed the vulnerability of the local and area defenses that are not on SAC bases. Let us consider the local defenses first. In the past they have often been considered to be defending a definite target point. As a result, some people were not worried if these local defenses were destroyed along with the target they were defending. Here, however, I am tentatively assigning to the local defenses a somewhat larger role; I do not want them to be a bonus target. First of all, it is possible that a city will only be partially destroyed. Thus I want to prevent the enemy from using his bombers as a "mopping up" followup to his ICBM's. Second, the enemy himself often does not realize when a city is destroyed. If the local defenses survive they can attrite his later attacks and even his reconnaissance missions. Third, and most important, such local defenses as the old Nike-Ajax have some capability for protecting suburban areas as well as urban centers, and the newer Nike-Hercules will cover much larger areas. Therefore, if the Nike batteries survive the first strike, they may be an important element of our continuing capability.

From the viewpoint of direct damage by blast, the local defenses are in a somewhat better position than the area defense installations because they are more dispersed. However, they are not necessarily so dispersed that vulnerability to blast is not a serious problem. In any case, both the long-range and short-range Nikes are dependent on timely identification information and supervised fire coordination if their performance is not to be degraded. Therefore, if command and control arrangements such as SAGE or Missile Master are vulnerable, the performance of the weapons system may suffer.

Probably most important of all, unless they have been specially protected, outdoor installations such as Nike are extremely vulnerable to close-in fallout. It is likely that in a widespread attack this effect alone will disrupt operations at any installation that has not been protected, whether it is attacked or not.

The military establishment must do more than just survive; it must have *staying power*. It must have enough endurance capability to fight a "long" war (a war lasting between two and thirty days). While there are no explicit requirements that we be able to fight only a one day or a one hour or a fifteen-minute war, in practice it is difficult to buy a screwdriver for any of the newer systems unless one can justify its use in facilitating the operation of the alert force. It is most likely, as a result, that only the alert force will be operable. It is most unlikely that any of this equipment will work in some post-attack situations unless there have been expensive preparations made ahead of time for such an eventuality. One obvious thing that may be lacking is a reload or repeat capability. Missiles for air defense will serve as an example. Most military planners argue that an installation has enough missiles if it will just run out of them during the first strike. Even on this basis we are not sure that sufficient missiles have been allotted, because these same planners may not have allowed enough for the use of both area and local decoys and a possible degradation in kill probability with jamming and deceptive tactics.[4] In any case, there may not have been sufficient allowance made for having extra missiles for the second and later days of the war. If it were cheaper to do so, these extra missiles could be kept on a standby basis in which they could be made ready in a few hours.

As with air defense, we need air offense (both missile and bomber) on the second and later days of the war, not only to increase our deterrence, but to threaten and harass the enemy's surviving air offense, to draw his attacks away from our cities (this may mean the relocation of at least two or three SAC bases and the careful location of future missile bases), and most important of all, as crucial cards in the negotiations that terminate the war. This last role may eventually be an important one for those of our Polaris-carrying submarines which may have missiles but which are out of position to attack immediately or for various other reasons have trouble firing in the first hours of the war. Our command and control arrangements must be able to survive enemy attack sufficiently well to carry through the above.

We presumably need preparations for the use of alternate SAC bases or "recuperation" fields, so that planes which are in the air or which happen to be evacuated or return from strike will also have a place to go. Once such preparations have been made, we will have much greater interest in a multiple strike capability. This latter may call for an increase in our tanker requirements, so that the utmost value can be gotten from the bombers we have already bought.

Alternate fields could have a valuable bonus effect in further attracting Soviet attack resources away from cities, and should be chosen with this possibility in mind. We should probably also make preparations to use planes not assigned to SAC—that is, bombers in ATC, AMC, depots, factories, pipelines, and the like, and even readily adapted nonbombers for one-way missions. In all probability, we are going to have many more bombs than carriers.

No matter how much care has gone into reducing the vulnerability of the system, it will be damaged. Preparations must be made to control the extent and consequences of the damage. In addition to redundancy, this probably means that we need a capability to repair damage and to restore, possibly with some degradation, interrupted operations. The value of patching-up is particularly clear in the communications field.

While it is perfectly true that what a military establishment needs most in a communication system is *survival* in the proper sense of the word, it is also true that it is useful to have an additional capability for restoration, and the prewar designs and preparations should consider this possibility.

Some restoration capability might be provided by mobile equipment; for example, to replace radars or microwave towers that have been destroyed. A great deal of mobile equipment has been developed for use by organizations such as the Army, the Marine Corps, the Corps of Engineers, and the civilian telephone companies. I am told that the use of such equipment has been of only modest value in typical civilian disasters because it is generally faster to use emergency repairs than to substitute mobile elements. It is very possible, though, that such equipment would be relatively more effective in alleviating the effects of widespread damage and multiple breaks. Prepositioned standby equipment could possibly play an important role. It is also possible that some of our mobile early warning equipment—either ship or air—can be redeployed to plug gaps in the contiguous radar. These units might be supplemented by standby mobile radars, perhaps using equipment similar to that developed for the Army and Marine Corps.

One of the most important tasks of damage control is anticontamination. Except in the worst areas, this is probably quite simple if one has the manuals, meters, water, brooms, specialized equipment, and SOP's, and has adapted construction to prevent contamination or to make decontamination easy. For those installations which are not prepared, it may be quite difficult to improvise. Except in the case of airfields, decontamination will probably not require heavy equipment, such as bulldozers and mechanical sweepers. The value of anticontamination will be particularly great in the prevention of sickness and nausea, which brings consequent degradation of the capabilities of the afflicted. Since nausea is psychologically very catching, healthy persons may be affected.

Last, but by no means least important, is the whole question of spares and equipment to replace and repair damaged parts. In addition to using the regularly assigned forces, there are today plans for using nonregular forces such as Tactical Air Command, Navy and Reserve fighters, and so on. Such plans may not only increase our capability on the first day of any war in which there is warning, but they may also be one of the main sources of area air defense on the later days of the war.

In addition to the military forces, there are the civilian radars, air traffic control centers, a possibly expanded ground observer corps (now cancelled), and so forth, which may all be capable of contributing to "long" war capabilities if plans have been made. At a minimum, we should consider hardening potentially useful government facilities and even some that are privately owned—at least where it is very cheap to do this—as a hedge against a future desire to use them.

A good military system must have an "off-design" capability. An enormous amount of damage will occur as a result of the strike. Things will happen that are not expected to happen. The system should not be designed against a single preferred attack or be able to operate only when all of its parts are working perfectly. While computers with fixed programs will undoubtedly play an important role, the system must give scope to the capability of men to improvise and rise to the occasion. For example, wherever we use centralized techniques actually to regulate defense activities, unless they are "invulnerable" they should be used as an override to improve capability. Still there should be back-up capabilities in case the centralized setup becomes degraded or impaired. It should not be a system that is only as strong as its weakest link, unless that weakest link is very strong.

Lastly, there is a problem to which very little attention has been given—the question of postwar capabilities. As I have already twice pointed out, if a war occurs one is inevitably going to have an end of the war, and this end is likely to occur in a very few days. If one believes that the war may end by negotiation, then both sides may have appreciable capabilities left. It might be well if we investigate to see if there are inexpensive things that we can do that would improve our postwar capabilities. It is clear that there will be no time to build new defense systems, or even make any additions during or immediately after the war. Most important of all, our ability to supply certain kinds of specialized spare parts for even a small military system may be sadly degraded; prewar stocking policy should take account of this problem.

More on Deterrence

Because the subject is so important, I would like to summarize, review, and amplify some of the remarks I have made about deterrence.

Let me start by reviewing the three kinds of deterrence I have discussed. *Type I Deterrence refers to the deterrence of an attack by the fear of a retaliatory blow by a damaged SAC or a pre-emptive strike by a SAC which has gotten tactical warning.* Type II Deterrence refers to the deterrence of provocative actions by fear of a premeditated first strike by the nation being provoked. Type III Deterrence refers to the deterrence of provocative actions by a counteraction which is expected to be so effective that the net effect of the "aggressor's" action is to cause him to lose in position.[5]

The concepts of Controlled Reprisal and Controlled War really fall between Type II and Type III Deterrence. However, I have somewhat arbitrarily included the Controlled War in Type II Deterrence and the Controlled Reprisal in Type III Deterrence and I will continue this practice. This implies that Controlled Reprisal is "within the rules." This is certainly true for lower levels such as frontier incidents, blockades, spoofing and jamming, and probably very limited counter force operations. It is, to say the least, controversial whether such Controlled Reprisals as envisaged in graduated deterrence or controlled nuclear retaliation would today be considered within the rules. However, the twentieth century may yet see one or two limited city exchanges occur without actuating the Type

[5] It might be appropriate to make some remarks on nomenclature at this point. Probably because I was trained as a physicist and mathematician, I find it both satisfying and illuminating to distinguish the three kinds of deterrence by I, II, and III. Many people have been distressed with the nonsuggestive nature of the ordinal numbers and have tried to come up with something more descriptive. John Grant, Denis Healy, and some other British authors have used the terminology "Passive Deterrence" for Type I and "Active Deterrence" for Type II. The thought here is that Type I Deterrence does not really take an act of will, while Type II does, hence the labels passive and active. The word passive, however, is not really accurate and in addition has the unfortunate connotation of being easy. First strike and second strike deterrence or primary and secondary deterrence have similar troubles. Harold Lamport has suggested Reflex for Type I, Conscious for Type II, and Tit-for-Tat for Type III. Again the connotation problem bothers me, and I have more or less decided to stay with the brilliant invention of counting until some other terminology has gotten so widely used that it would be foolish to resist further.

II Deterrent. This is particularly likely if the balance of terror gets more stable and the Soviets less so.

In discussing Type I Deterrence I have usually assumed that only adequately protected forces count. This simple view must be modified in two ways. The first exception concerns the fact that, even if the aggressor is reasonably certain that he can destroy the other man's first strike forces, he would still probably prefer attacking a country which did not have such forces over one which did. That is, his certainty is not 100 per cent. If anything goes wrong with his plans, particularly if the other side happens to get tactical warning or there is an intelligence leak, his opponent's first strike forces may turn out to be lethal. This means that vulnerable first strike forces play an ambiguous role in deterrence. To the extent that the enemy feels threatened by them and feels that he can destroy them by his own attack, they actually invite attack. To the extent that he is so uncertain about his plans that he prefers to "let sleeping dogs be" they can act as a Type I Deterrent, even if they are vulnerable.

The second exception about only strike second forces being valuable in Type I Deterrence concerns the Type I Deterrence capability of a third power that cannot afford more than a modest budget for its strategic force. For example, if soft IRBM's are placed in Europe, it would probably be relatively easy for the Soviets to destroy them with their own IRBM's or with tactical aircraft using air-burst weapons with only kiloton yields. Since the Soviets are likely to have more than enough IRBM's and planes to do this job *reliably*, having soft IRBM's in Europe does not increase by any large amount our ability to deter a simultaneous surprise attack on the United States and NATO forces. This may still be true even if we harden these IRBM's, as this might mean only that the Russians would have to go to megaton ground-burst weapons to destroy them. Because of the short range, this probably would not change very much the cost of the weapons system to the Soviet Union.

However, from the viewpoint of a third country, creating a situation in which the enemy would be forced to go from a kiloton air burst to a megaton ground burst may increase its Type I Deterrence enormously. The fallout from such an attack would kill millions of people in neighboring countries, not to speak of the fatalities in the attacked country. The attack would automatically involve much more eventful decisions and risks and even undesirable internal reactions than would a local attack with KT weapons. These possibilities should tend to deter a Soviet attack. Yet, if deterrence failed, there would be a great deal more damage to the country being attacked.

It may be hard for most readers to visualize a situation in which the Soviet decision makers would feel that an attack on a small power with air-burst kiloton weapons was "safe" or "acceptable," but that one which involved ground-burst megaton weapons was not. Actually, there may be many cases where the Soviets would incur only a very slight risk of involving us or the NATO alliance in an all-out war if they were to limit their attack to conventional or low kiloton air-burst weapons. If this is correct, they might choose this tactic even if it meant that they had to spare certain hard installations and run the risk that the attacked country, at its option, could use those unattacked weapons to destroy or damage some major Soviet cities. It is unlikely, and under most circumstances *reliably* unlikely, that this option would be exercised. The Soviets could point out, very credibly and persuasively, that even though the defender could do a great deal of damage to the Soviets (as measured by peacetime standards), the Soviets would take a most terrible revenge for what could by comparison be only a minor setback to them. If the Soviets were to use ground-burst megaton weapons, they would greatly increase the risk of involving other countries. The precedent would be most menacing, the violence itself would be more provocative, and, finally, the use of megaton bombs would cause a great deal of damage to neighboring countries and thus automatically cause the damage and possibly the conflict to become general.

The above discussion on third power deterrence can be turned around. Imagine, for example, that by sometime in the late '60's or early '70's the Chinese had acquired about fifty ICBM's and that they had put these ICBM's in hard bases in the fifty largest cities of China. If we then got into a war with China over some local issue such as Korea or Formosa the Chinese could, at great risk to themselves, put us in an awkward dilemma. If, as is often recommended, we chose to use atomic weapons locally, the Chinese could probably match us *locally*. It could easily turn out that they would win the issue either by actually beating us or by threatening enough local damage to force the country being fought over to surrender. If we try to limit their use of nuclear weapons by threatening retaliation against them or by actually destroying their home bases, they could retaliate by taking out one or two major American cities, perhaps after warning them to evacuate. If we tried to prevent such nuclear blackmail by destroying the hard Chinese missiles, we would have to destroy the surrounding cities and kill several hundred million Chinese.

Such action would be likely to touch off a Soviet strike against us unless we had a much better Type I Deterrent than we are likely to have. It is most improbable that we would launch such an attack until after the Chinese had provoked us in some extreme way; it is even doubtful that we would be willing to make such an attack if they destroyed only one or two American cities in a somewhat legitimate-looking retaliation for some act of ours. About the most that we would be likely to do would be to take out a small number of Chinese cities in return. Such an exchange would clearly cause much greater internal problems for us than for them.

To summarize, the Chinese could obtain some of the performance of a Doomsday or Homicide Pact Machine very inexpensively by putting their ICBM's in their own cities and then exploiting either their Soviet allies' fears of alienating them (or loss of prestige), or even by exploiting our own humanitarian instincts.

I would like now to make some general remarks on the nature of deterrence and bargaining. It is clear that so far as day-to-day activities are concerned, what regulates a country's behavior are non-military calculations in the Type III Deterrence area. Among other things, for example, a potential provocateur may be deterred by any of the effects shown in Table 46.

❖❖

TABLE 46
NONMILITARY DETERRENTS

1. Internal Reactions or Costs
2. Losing Friends or Antagonizing Neutrals
3. Creating or Strengthening Coalitions of Enemies
4. Lowering the Reaction Threshold of Potential Opponents
5. Diplomatic or Economic Retaliation
6. An Increase in the Potential Opponent's Military Forces
7. "Not Going to Heaven"

❖❖

We have discussed only the second from the last on this list, but all of them can be important. It is easy to exaggerate their importance and to think of them as all that count, simply because in about 99 per cent of the conscious peacetime calculations that are made by each side they *are* the things that count. If the above deterrents are to work reliably, there must always be in the background the knowledge that if they did not, other kinds of deterrents or corrections would come in. It could be disastrous to have a conspicuous gap in the spectrum of deterrents and capabilities. For example, when President Eisenhower remarked at a press conference that it was unthinkable that he would call out federal troops to enforce federal law in the Southern states, some Southerners immediately did something to make it thinkable. Something similar may happen if he convinces the Soviets that he means what he says when he says that "war is preposterous." I suspect that many in the West are guilty of the worst kind of wishful thinking when, in discussing deterrence, they identify the unpleasant with the impossible. It is particularly hard to understand why this is so when almost all who write on this subject were adults during the later part of the Hitler era and presumably were educated in some of the ways in which all these types of deterrence can be strained. (If it were not for the fact that my colleagues and I have lived through this era, most of us would need to have much more knowledge of history than in fact we possess before we could find illustrations to make credible the kind of threats that Hitler made and the reactions of his opponents.) It is interesting to point out that in 1930 and even later practically nobody would have conjectured that the British and the French and others would be subjected to the challenges that they came to face. Even less could they have foreseen the inadequate reactions of the challenged nations. Even if some scholar or statesman had fully appreciated these possibilities, he could not have made them dramatic or plausible enough to have induced these countries to make specific preparations. However, with the record of the 1930's plainly before us, we should all be able to realize that it is possible for all these kinds of deterrence to be strained.

Now the capabilities for such blackmail are much larger. When Hitler gave his ultimatums, he really could not threaten immediate and total annihilation, but Khrushchev can and does so threaten. It was quite possible that the British and French could have rescued Czechoslovakia (later, as a matter of fact, they did—with the help of the Russians, of course), but if all we have is a Type I Deterrent force, it is clear that neither rescue nor preventive action is possible.

Because the Soviets today, and in the future the Chinese or any aggressive nation, can make such convincing threats, and because the possibility of rescue is much more remote (in most people's eyes the rescue would look more dangerous than the original act of aggression), it is absolutely essential that we do not allow a position to develop that tempts such action. I am not saying that we need always make immediate threats of "massive retaliation" or pre-emptive action. Rather, the opposite. I believe that the threat should be held in reserve, but at the same time preparations ought to be made to make it more credible that it will be used in extreme provocation. For "moderate" provocation we should not even discuss the possibility. Even for "extreme" provocation, it is only after the nonmilitary deterrents have been exhausted that we should think of military deterrents to restrain a potential aggressor's behavior. These military deterrents are listed in Table 47.

❖❖❖

TABLE 47
MILITARY DETERRENTS

1. Some temporizing military measures—alert, mobilization, etc.
2. Direct military support for the threatened area
3. A small Controlled Reprisal
4. A small Controlled War
5. A large Controlled Reprisal
6. A large Controlled War
7. A Spasm War
8. A Countervalue War

❖❖❖

If we wish to have our strategic air force contribute to the deterrence of provocation, it must be credible that we are willing to take one or more of the above actions. Usually the most convincing way to look willing is to be willing.

We have already discussed the first item on the list. It envisages sharply increasing our capability for safely striking an opponent. In many cases the easiest and cheapest way to increase this capability for striking him involves use of a vulnerable go-first force. I have mentioned before that if we are to put such forces on alert, we are putting pressure on the enemy which he may be tempted to relieve by pre-empting. It may therefore be essential to increase simultaneously our capability for retaliating after being struck in order to preserve our Type I Deterrence.

Let me give an example of a system that uses alert to deter provocation—although I hasten to add that I am not recommending this particular system. We could station a large number of ICBM's or large IRBM's in centralized areas in Europe, North Africa, or Turkey, and in the Far East. These could be operated, concentrated, and unalert, so that it would not be costly to maintain them. Because the missiles would be large and very close to Russia, they could carry enormous warheads, be very accurate, and have a short flight time. This would make them ideal counterforce weapons, particularly against very alert systems or hard-point targets or soft mobile systems. They might even have some effectiveness against hard hidden bases as area weapons that depend on such low confidence phenomena as ground shock, thermal radiation, and radioactivity to degrade the operation of the hidden system. If a crisis occurred, these missiles would be put on alert so that they could all be fired in a single salvo. They would be maintained in this status until the Russians chose to back down. The Russians would then be faced with the normal triplet of choices. They could strike, they could back down, or they could try any of a number of temporizing measures. Because the first choice would now be relatively attractive to them, since it might be quite credible that we were going to strike, our retaliatory capability must also be increased or at least assured, perhaps by the use of temporary measures that are considered too expensive for noncrisis use.

The second item on the military deterrent list is direct military support for the threatened area. Insofar as this really works, it is probably a better policy than any of the remaining reactions since it involves the least risk of Central War. However, having sufficient capability to be effective will be very expensive unless we can get our allies or neutrals to share a larger portion of the burden. For many reasons, we cannot get away "on-the-cheap" by using our so-called "quality" weapons.

The third possibility is a *limited reprisal*. This is really a classic reaction to provocation, but one which has partially gone out of favor in recent years. It would not surprise me at all, however, if such actions came back in some specialized form, perhaps against purely military installations. These could be naval forces, airplanes close to the enemy border, or even fixed installations such as the early warning lines. It is hard to believe, though, that any nation will have enough faith in its own Type I Deterrence, the rationality of the enemy, and the stability or reasonableness of its own population to initiate punishments of a much greater order of magnitude (such as destruction of large cities) so this option is deferred to a later point in the table (and many would leave it out). Insofar as such an option is available, it seems to be more likely to be used by a country like China in the manner described earlier than a country like the United States or even the Soviet Union. Limited reprisals need not involve actual destruction or even illegal activities; they need only involve the kind of spoofing and jamming I discussed when I tried to illustrate how an opponent could put pressure on us (or the other way around) in a tense situation. Jamming or spoofing can negate a warning system as effectively as physical destruction.

Next in the scale is a military reprisal at a high enough level to weaken the opponent's military capability significantly as in a limited counterforce operation. This could be designed to take out things that were especially threatening—missile bases in Kamchatka, reconnaissance satellites, identified Polaris submarines, and so on. Next, one could have the unlimited or almost unlimited counterforce attacks combined with postattack coercion (i.e., the Controlled War). Then there is the uncontrolled (Spasm) War, and, finally, an attempt to annihilate the enemy.

While many readers will think of the eight options of Table 47 as being too many and too sophisticated to be of practical import, I am willing to make again the statement that *a serious planner may wish to study even more options; it is most unlikely that he can get away with less.* The known existence of a sequence of options of gradually increasing risk and severity removes from the other side the temptation to raise the ante, because he believes that we would prefer appeasing to going all out with the Spasm or Countervalue Wars.

Because it is closely connected with the idea of deterrence and the notion of a series of threats as just discussed, I would like to make some comments about bargaining. Many of these will simply repeat or summarize remarks I have already made, but it seems worthwhile to do this.

The simplest form bargaining could take would be to make an offer or threat on a take-it or leave-it basis. This simplest form is often urged. For example, people sometimes argue that since we can clearly do great destruction to the Soviet Union, all we have to do in order to regulate her behavior is to tell the Soviets that unless they do so and so—or, more often, unless they refrain from doing so and so—

we will punish them so severely they will be sorry they did "it." We then lay down the rules and regulations by which this punishment is to be imposed, commit ourselves irrevocably to carrying it out, and our problem is solved.

Unfortunately, this attempt to look like a force of nature that cannot be influenced or reasoned with, but can only be taken account of when calculations are being made, ignores the fact that the enemy also can threaten us, and he will simply refuse to believe that we will ignore his threats. If we believe the enemy is listening to our threats, then somehow we have to believe that he thinks we are listening to his threats. Even if we think we are sincere in our irrevocable commitments, the probability of a total response to a moderate provocation is still going to be close to zero, since the enemy can make such a response costly. When the time comes to act it just will not be worth it. The closest one can come to making this stand credible is to program it in a computer, to take a high moral position (saying, in effect, I would like to compromise but my integrity will not let me) or to look slightly mad, intemperate or emotional. This technique was used by Hitler. It may also have been the technique used by Khrushchev in recent years).[6] Let us discuss all these possibilities systematically.

✦✦✦

TABLE 48
BARGAINING ABILITY

   I. Your Threat
      1. Your available offensive forces
      2. His available defenses
      3. His assets at risk
  II. His Threat
 III. Your Resolve versus His Resolve
  IV. Communication and Persuasion Techniques Available
   V. Capability for Self-control and Committal

✦✦✦

Table 48 indicates what is involved in bargaining between two opponents, in both peace and war. The first thing is obviously your

---

[6] For example, on the occasions of Macmillan's visit to Moscow during May 1959, Khrushchev's speeches during the Foreign Ministers' Conference of June 1959 and at the World Affairs Center at Los Angeles in 1959, Gronchi's visit to Moscow during February 1960, and the Summit Conference in Paris in May 1960.

threat—what you have "to sell." The only special comment we should make is on item 3, his assets at risk. To the extent that he can put the most important of these into places of safety, particularly his *people,* he can naturally improve his bargaining position. Insofar as the same item applies to wartime situations, we have already mentioned that one may deliberately refrain from destroying some of the opponent's assets in order to use them as hostages.

We have a similar situation with his threat, which of course is measured by his available offense force and our available defenses and our assets at risk. It is the object of the military operations of the Controlled War to reduce the enemy's threat and to increase our own. Taking account of the two threats, we now have to match our *resolve* against his. While announcements and pledges play an important role, they may still have only a limited effect. Resolve is best shown by action. The bigger the risk the more resolve it demonstrates. The use of Controlled Reprisal is a direct matching of our resolve against his.

The use of resolve is closely connected to what are sometimes called *rationality of irrationality* or committal strategies. In any bargaining situation it can make sense to commit one's self irrevocably to do something in a certain eventuality and at the same time it may not make sense to carry out the committal if the eventuality occurs. A very graphic example is given by Bertrand Russell.[7]

"This sport is called 'Chicken!' It is played by choosing a long straight road with a white line down the middle and starting two very fast cars towards each other from opposite ends. Each car is expected to keep the wheels of one side on the white line. As they approach each other mutual destruction becomes more and more imminent. If one of them swerves from the white line before the other, the other, as he passes, shouts 'Chicken!', and the one who has swerved becomes an object of contempt."

If one wishes to win this game his best (rational) strategy is to put on a blindfold and commit himself irrevocably to going ahead. If the blindfold is visible and the committal convincing (this can be done by noticeably raising or, better, by removing the steering wheel), the other side must back down. However, if the other side still refuses to back down after the irrevocable committal has been made, it would be irrational to carry out the rationally made committal. Since both sides might use this strategy, the game may end in a disaster.

[7] Bertrand Russell, *Common Sense and Nuclear Warfare,* Simon and Schuster, New York, 1959, p. 30.

According to Bertrand Russell, the above game is played by degenerates in America and nations everywhere. Russell is too hard on the diplomats. The above is a caricature of power politics, even if it has enough realism in it to make it an educational analogy. In addition, insofar as the game is played, it is not played for some frivolous reason. Life, liberty, and security may depend on playing a variation of the game of "Chicken." Russell himself explains why the game is played. "Practical politicians may admit all this, but they argue that there is no alternative. If one side is unwilling to risk global war, while the other side is willing to risk it, the side which is willing to run the risk will be victorious in all negotiations and will ultimately reduce the other side to complete impotence. 'Perhaps'—so the practical politician will argue—'it might be ideally wise for the sane party to yield to the insane party in view of the dreadful nature of the alternative, but, whether wise or not, no proud nation will long acquiesce in such an ignominious role. We are, therefore, faced, quite inevitably, with the choice between brinkmanship and surrender.' " [8]

Short of an objective arbiter or judge to decide disputes (possibly with power to enforce his decisions), one must be willing to play the "game" in some form or another or surrender. The above is a most powerful reason for creating an objective arbiter or judge. However, the diplomatic game is not normally as ferocious as Russell's analogy would suggest. The following example is more typical. Let the reader imagine a situation in which a used-car dealer has a car to sell. Assume also that this dealer is being foreclosed so that if he does not get rid of his merchandise by, say, 12 midnight the sheriff will get it and it will be worthless to him. Imagine, at the same time, a purchaser wanders in at 11:30, quite clearly the last possible purchaser of the day. Assume the purchaser is willing to pay $100 for this same car. There is now a bargaining region from 0 to 100 dollars for the price of the car. Where it will fall will depend on the respective skill of the bargainers. One cannot even apply the "ethical" idea of splitting the difference since neither bargainer will admit ahead of time what his final price is. That is, the used-car dealer will not admit he is facing bankruptcy and the purchaser will not agree that he will go to $100.

If now the purchaser tries to play this game the way "Chicken" is played he can go to the dealer with the following verifiable state-

[8] *Ibid.*, pp. 30–31.

ment: "I have put up a bond with a trustee which states that if I pay you more than $5 for the car I am forced to give some $10,000 to some charity I don't particularly like, so it is impossible for me to pay you more than $5." The dealer must in fact sell the car for five dollars or get nothing for it. On the other hand, if the dealer tells the would-be purchaser that he has put up a bond making it impossible to sell the car for less than $95, then the purchaser must pay $95 or go elsewhere and pay $100. So, the man who commits first does in fact get the bargain. The analogy with the Doomsday Machine and game of "Chicken" should be clear. It should also be clear that if both sides commit, there will be no bargain. Most important of all, if one side has the attitude that it will not bargain at all because it does not want to take any risks of ending up with "no sale," this side is going to do very badly in a whole series of circumstances, not only in the current bargain, but on all later bargains. Barring an outside adjudicator, one must be willing to bargain even if the state of no-bargain is dangerous or even disastrous. But if the bargaining is carried on with skill, and if both sides are cautious, then the bargaining will take on the aspects of a normal commercial transaction in which both sides gain, the exact division depending on their relative skill, but neither is driven to the wall. A war caused by Rationality of Irrationality should be distinguished from one caused by two sides having incompatible objectives which they are determined to achieve no matter what the risks. In this case war must result. The Rationality of Irrationality war corresponds to a situation in which neither side really believes the issue is big enough to go to war but both sides are willing to use some partial or total committal strategy to force the other side to back down; as a result they may end up in a war that they would not have gone into if either side had realized ahead of time that the other side would not back down even under pressure.

Such bargaining is a battle in which one uses communication and persuasion techniques in addition to military devices and threats. In peacetime there is a persuasion asymmetry in favor of the Soviets. They do not have the same restraints on the kind of speeches and notes that they write that we have. I have already noted that Khrushchev can afford to lose his temper to the point where he can pretend or actually be irrational. The Soviets can also use semi-official media in a way that is difficult for us. For example, during the Suez crisis they sent a note to the British that was quite threatening, but nowhere near as threatening as a Russian broadcast said it was.

A broadcast itself might be as persuasive as a note in raising apprehension and yet be much less risky in terms of arousing counteractions.

In wartime persuasion techniques might be even more important than in peace. I pointed out in Chapter I that if the Russians could restrain the President for twenty-four hours it would take a relatively modest retaliatory capability on their part to keep us from honoring our obligations to our allies even if the Russians attacked Europe. The figure twenty-four hours is picked to allow them to communicate to us the exact significance of what the retaliatory blow would be, to allow the notion of thermonuclear war as a real event rather than a hypothetical possibility to sink in, and finally to persuade us that we have better alternatives available than suicide or something close to suicide. Insofar as they can improve their persuasion techniques, either by using prewar tension periods to educate us or by being able to make very dramatic postwar threats, they need less time. *I cannot stress too much that this is one place where there are great differences among their being able to threaten us with a high assurance of total damage, a great probability of total damage, and a possibility of large but not total damage.* Any asymmetry in our threats vis-à-vis each other may also be of great importance—if, for example, they can threaten to destroy fifty American cities and their population, while we can only threaten to destroy fifty empty Soviet cities because they have evacuated them during the crisis. An even more extreme advantage would accrue to the Soviet Union in any conflict with a third nation that only had a small independent nuclear deterrent and no allies or other support.

Finally, there is the capability for self-control and committal. The more one can control his force, and the more freedom he therefore possesses, the worse off he may be in the bargaining situation. The person who can first give the appearance of having committed himself irrevocably has a much higher chance of coming out on top in a bargaining situation than the one who can always keep control of his behavior. However, some of the committal strategies that can be used most effectively to increase one's capabilities of getting a bargain are also dangerous. There is the risk of a mutual devastation. The unilateral commitment we mentioned at the start of this section is an example of how effective a committal strategy could be if the other side was sure to believe the committal and how dangerous if they did not and went ahead anyway with their provocation. It is possible that from the bargaining point of view the asymmetries in being able to commit may be in our favor both prewar and postwar because of the relative difficulty a democratic government has in backing down, but nobody has investigated or written on the problem systematically. This strategy is also open to a totalitarian society, for the leader can always say (and perhaps correctly), "*If* I do not succeed in obtaining a diplomatic success, I will be overthrown. Therefore, I will not back down." He can get a double income from this plea by adding, "The man who replaces me will be much worse than I am. Therefore, in your own interest, you should compromise this issue."

A Summary of Lectures I and II

Let me now make some suggestions regarding the kinds of studies we need if we are to understand our national security problems.

TABLE 49

IMPLICATIONS FOR STUDY AND ANALYSIS

1. Contingency Planning
   a. With many objectives
   b. Under many situations
2. Complex Justification
   a. Complete description of a war
   b. Doomsday machines unacceptable
   c. Homicide pact machines undesirable
   d. Arms control important
   e. Low, medium, and high confidence
3. Re-examining such subjects as—
   a. Being able to fight as well as to deter war
   b. Long war (2–30 day) capabilities
   c. Flexible war plans
   d. Reliable command and control
   e. Preattack and postattack coercion
   f. Controlled war
   g. Improvised protection (U.S. and S.U.)
   h. Tense situation
   i. Protection against second-order threats
   j. Suitable language, doctrine, and concepts for military planners

These suggestions comprise a partial summary of Lectures I and II. They are listed in Table 49.

Let us go over the topics in Table 49. *Contingency Planning.* The evaluation of our over-all military posture and the corresponding weapon systems, tactics, strategies, and policies must by its very nature be quite complex. (The word "complex" should be taken as having a connotation of many separate aspects, each of which, separately, might be simple.) One must consider all the objectives in Tables 28 and 29, which we have called Peacetime Objectives and Wartime Objectives, respectively, and the Eight Basic Situations in Table 33. It is quite possible that after study we will find we have to be even more complex than I am suggesting. I seriously doubt that we will be able to be less complex and still do a satisfactory job of planning or analysis for our over-all posture. The simple-minded optimization using only the "best" assumption and "best" criterion is dangerous. In addition to requiring sophisticated analysis, a competent over-all design and evaluation cannot be done quickly nor can its results be summarized readily. *Complex Justification.* In olden days the justification for military forces was very simple. If the enemy attacked, you resisted him and your military forces acted as a physical barrier between the enemy and the homeland. In addition, there might have been many controversies about offense and defense, but with a few exceptions basically the same equipment could be used for both jobs. This meant that these controversies did not greatly effect the training or equipment of the military service.

None of this is true today. When we defend a country by deterrence, we are employing an extremely subtle notion. Or, if we defend the B country by forcing the enemy to use up all his forces in attacking A country, this too is a subtle notion. In addition to such subtleties, the very idea of war has become incredibly complicated, as indicated by my Table 4, Complete Description of a War. Particularly if one is trying to "sell" some weapons system on the grounds that it contributes to a Counterforce as Insurance or Credible First Strike Capability, one has a difficult job on one's hands. One must convince his audience that the problems associated with all eight stages of the Complete Description of a War can be handled or that some technological innovation may come along. Justification may not only depend on the actual battle performance of the system, but on such things as the chemistry of strontium-90, the lifetime of cesium-137, and the recuperative powers of the B country. This means that, if one is trying to justify the procurement of a certain weapons system or the initiation of certain research and development, it may be impossible to justify these actions simply in their own terms. It may be necessary to justify the system as part of a larger picture or as a speculative venture that might pay off. It is especially difficult to justify Preattack Mobilization Bases that depend on a change in doctrine, objectives, or technology for activation. And if the audience does not understand the larger picture or is hostile to speculation, it will be impossible to make the justification.

More and more, military people will have to be at home in discussing the wider implications and connotations of both weapon systems and thermonuclear war. This is even important on the public relations level, not to speak of the decision level. If officers of the Army, Navy, and Air Force are going to be in contact with Congress or the public on the many questions related to military matters, and if they are going to work with other government agencies, they must have as complete a picture as possible of the characteristics of thermonuclear war, from weapon systems and strategies to radiation effects, civil defense, and economic recuperation. In a phrase, they should understand Thermonuclear War.

In addition to making clear that their weapons systems are useful—that is that they can do something—the military must also make clear that the weapon systems are not overly powerful, that they will not do certain other things which many may consider well within their power. They must not be Doomsday Machines, or Homicide Pact Machines. They must not even look like they could be a Doomsday Machine if misused, much less when used as authorized.

I cannot stress how important it is that it be made clear that we are not developing and planning the use of Doomsday Machines—or even systems which, if they should be used (whether they are good deterrents or not), will destroy the defender and a large portion of the world along with the aggressor. One might note that until the Congressional hearings of 1959 on thermonuclear war there was no official documented statement that the weapons systems that the U.S. was buying were not Doomsday Machines. In fact, about the only unofficial but documented statement was the RAND Corporation Report of July 1958.[9] On the other hand, there were many semiofficial and unofficial statements or assertions that the U.S. had already built a Doomsday Machine, so there was no reason for most lay-

[9] *Report on a Study of Non-Military Defense*, R-322-RC.

men and some experts to believe differently (and many still do not).

Closely related to not building Doomsday Machines is designing weapons systems that are compatible with arms control. If one seriously pictures the world over the next fifty years, and perhaps just the next ten years with arms control and without arms control, he is almost compelled to conclude we will and should be actively and earnestly seeking *arms control* agreements. It is important to note that arms control does not necessarily mean disarmament; in fact, if you look at the *short-run* problems that people worry about most, the dispersion of nuclear weapons and the danger of accidental war, neither necessarily involves disarmament, but just control. In the *long run*, the arms control must involve reliable controls on the availability and use of violence. Many people, including the author, believe that this cannot be done without the sacrifice of some sovereignty, but it also seems possible that we may be able to devise a satisfactory system that involves a minimal loss of sovereignty. We should start studying such systems now and also even start looking into important long lead-time items (such as an international police force).

Let us now discuss the very important roles that *low, medium, and high confidence measures* can play, and some of the difficulties that war planners and others have in making clear the distinctions between them and the necessity for making such distinctions.

There is no precise distinction between these three classes of measures. Still, in order to orient the discussion, let us say that a *low confidence measure* is one to which most people assign less than one chance in four of working. A *medium confidence measure* would have an estimated reliability of between one in four and three out of four, and a *high confidence measure* would have more than a three in four chance of working. This means that "low" may sometimes be very far from a forlorn last hope or a desperate measure; it also implies that "high" may be very far from what we would really like. For example, a 75 per cent chance to deter war in the next ten years (about one chance in forty per year of war) would not be very satisfactory to many people. Nevertheless, I think the above divisions are quite reasonable. In the dangerous world in which we are going to live, both now and in the foreseeable future, we simply cannot achieve the degree of security we would like to have. Some of the problems which will come up are so important that we may be willing to spend many billions of dollars a year on medium or even low confidence measures, simply because we cannot get high confidence measures.

Yet in other cases even feasible "high confidence" measures may fall far short of what we would desire. It should, of course, be clear to the reader that what I mean by *probability* is a subjective judgment by most of the people concerned.

Let me try to give an example of the distinction between low and medium confidence. Assume for example that we want to build a warning or air defense system that will take five years to create, that it could easily be negated if the enemy worked out a clever tactic, and that the tactic was of such a character that within one year of the enemy's decision to use the tactic he would be able to do so. One would have to call the system a low confidence measure. We would have to call it that even if we thought it was quite unlikely that the enemy would develop the tactic immediately because it was against his doctrine or we did not think he was smart enough; over time his doctrine might change and his knowledge increase. On the other hand, let us assume that a certain countermeasure does exist and that it is just as simple to recognize this countermeasure as it was to recognize the opposing tactic. Still, there is one important distinction: the enemy must decide on a vigorous program to implement the countermeasure five years before the date that he can have the capability; moreover, the countermeasure is expensive in absolute terms— though a very good buy in terms of system performance. The enemy now has both a lead-time and a resource problem. Under these circumstances, there are many cases where we should be willing to put in a certain system which itself had a five year lead time and argue that the useful life of that system should be about five years. Somehow it is difficult for the other side to react fast with expensive and vigorous programs because of hypothetical possibilities that might result from even known development programs on our own part. It does not help his inertia problem much that these hypothetical possibilities are actually almost certain. At least, this tends to be true of our ability to react to him; there is a great deal of evidence that it is even more true of his ability to react to us.

A typical example of both types of situations would be the development of a warning line such as the DEW Line that has ends around which the enemy can go with his long-range planes but not his medium-range planes (unless he has bought a lot of tankers). The first decision would be tactical, and it would be low confidence to assume that he would not make it. The second decision would involve an expensive procurement and training program. Or consider the use by the enemy of ground-launch decoys to saturate our air defenses. This program makes a great deal of sense in the bomber era. For a rather small percentage of the cost of this strategic air force he can buy thousands of cheap flying objects which our radars cannot distinguish from bombers. On his first strike he can saturate our defenses with these thousands of objects. However, there are many reasons why he may not wish to spend some billions of dollars on such a capability in the early 1950's. During this period the Soviets seemed to believe in lengthy wars—three years or so—and decoys are not a good buy under those circumstances because they can only be used once. Secondly, using decoys is a very subtle tactic. Thirdly, while as a percentage of the strategic budget the decoys look cheap, they will still cost many billions of dollars.

There is no public evidence that the Soviets have ever had a ground-launched decoy program, and we have cancelled our own. Therefore, as far as is known, nobody has ever had an existing operational capability of ground-launched decoys. It is nevertheless true that air defense studies in the U.S. have been plagued by the possibility of such tactics by the enemy, and many valuable measures have not been put into effect because they could be negated in such a way. I would argue that even if we had put these measures in, it is most unlikely that the Soviets would have reacted early enough to our capability to negate it, at least not until it had some years of useful life. There are circumstances in which such "counterable" measures should be considered as quite reasonable measures and about as likely to work as one could expect—rather than as desperate last-ditch attempts by wishful thinkers.

It is difficult for most government planners and decision makers (and even more difficult for the Executive Office, Congressmen and laymen) to distinguish properly between low, medium, and high confidence measures. In the past I have found that many military planners distinguish only between "low" and "high." This meant that in many cases where they analyzed an important problem and found that a certain measure could not *really* be called high confidence, they automatically relegated the measure to the category of low confidence. This somehow meant that it was not worth buying. On the other hand, many people react to the cliché that one cannot have 100 per cent surety with the advocacy of any program that has more than a zero probability of working—in particular, they tend to ignore the important distinction between low and medium confidence.

It may be of some value at this point to list some of the special subjects that I have dwelt on that seem generally ignored in most discussions of thermonuclear war to the time of this writing. Since in a democracy like ours public opinion has a vast influence, even on professional students of war, one can assume that there could be a certain neglect of these particular subjects among many in the Pentagon and the Executive Office. Here are some of the ideas I have in mind when saying this:

Being Able To Fight as Well as Deter War. In the current enthusiasm for the notion of deterrence, the value of objective capabilities has been neglected. Very few people would be willing to sign their name to a statement to the effect that the invention of nuclear bombs in the middle of the twentieth century successfully abolished all-out wars. Many of these people are acting as if they believed this to be true, however. They show only the slightest interest in *reliable* Finite Deterrence or Counterforce as Insurance, much less in any Credible First Strike Capability or a serious Preattack Mobilization Base.

Long War (2–30 Day) Capabilities. Almost no matter how well one does on the first day of the war, if he has no capability on the second day—and the enemy does have some capability on that day —he is going to lose the war. In order to limit damage and terminate a war, we need surviving forces which have the weapons, delivery systems, command and control, supplies, and bases they need to operate. In addition, there may well be time to bring into action many military assets that are not part of the alert force. Complete preparation should be made to utilize these assets.

Flexible War Plans. We must not encase the President or the Commander of SAC in concrete. We need to have available a series of options during the very first minutes of the war in order to be able to react safely and surely to varying kinds of warnings and varying kinds of provocations. We need the ability to evaluate the posture of both ourselves and the enemy after the initial strike in order to bargain and use our remaining forces effectively. In addition, it is almost certain that the course of the war will reveal surprises. We must have the ability to react to those surprises.

Command and Control. In addition to all of the requirements for command and control that are required to handle the first three topics discussed, we should become much more conscious of the central role that command and control is likely to play in the future

301

as a possible Achilles heel of otherwise invulnerable systems. The problem seems to be particularly acute with mobile systems. It is difficult, for example, to provide protected and reliable communication with submarines deep under water. Fixed systems also seem to have troubles. One problem is that we do not want to start a war *accidentally*. Another is that we do not want the enemy to exploit the resulting requirement for officially verified "go ahead" orders to degrade the performance of the system.

Preattack and Postattack Coercion. The main objective of our military forces is to protect ourselves and to influence others. This is sometimes forgotten. In particular, we do not really want to destroy the enemy; we want to coerce him. Before the war, we attempt to *prevent* the enemy from attacking us by having an effective Type I Deterrence. We attempt to *regulate* his behavior by having effective Type II and Type III Deterrence. After a war has started, under most circumstances we ought to be interested in Limiting Damage and Stalemating or Winning the War. Whether we pursue these objectives by destroying the enemy's forces, attacking his resolve, or negotiating, is a tactical and strategic question, but under conditions of modern warfare attacks on resolve (the use of postattack coercion) and negotiation are much to be preferred to attacks on people and property. Similarly, we must be prepared for the enemy to use such attacks on us.

Controlled War. If we add together the capabilities just discussed (a–e on Table 49) and also add a discriminating use of force, post-attack blackmail, and intrawar deterrence and bargaining, then we are in the Controlled War area, an area we should never have left.

Improvised Protection (U.S. and S.U.). The many proposals for twenty, thirty, and fifty billion dollar civil defense programs have tended to confuse some important issues. While such programs are necessary for adequate protection, inexpensive programs costing a billion dollars or less might be very useful in many situations in the early 1960's. We should examine such possibilities both for ourselves and for the Soviets. If we do so we may decide to increase markedly our own capabilities for Counterforce as Insurance and Credible First Strike. We may also question more deeply thereby the adequacy of many suggestions for a Finite Deterrent force, if we test them against improvised Soviet civil defense programs, *including the evacuation-type maneuvers*. The Soviets can feel quite safe in carrying out such maneuvers if we have bought only a Finite Deterrent force.

Tense Situations. We must get out of the habit of thinking of our National Security System in the day-to-day context of normal relations. We must ask how the system performs under strain—for example, in a Munich or Hungarian crisis situation. We will then find that all kinds of capabilities, such as evacuation, augmentation, super-alert, and so forth, make sense. We will also understand that there is a difference between a high quality and a low quality deterrence capability. We will also investigate more carefully the kinds of things we or the enemy can do in a peacetime crisis to degrade and damage his opponent's weapons systems.

Protection against Second-order Threats. It is quite clear that in the late '60's and early '70's it will be very difficult to protect this country adequately against attacks by the Soviet Union. Even if one believes that it will be impossible to do so, he might be willing to buy *active defense against lesser threats.* For example:

1. Missile or airplane attacks by China. (The technology of China should be at least as far behind Soviet technology as NATO is behind ours—or about five years. The size of the attack should be much smaller. Both of these considerations make defense much easier.)

2. Missile or airplane attacks by even smaller countries than China.

3. Missiles fired accidentally at the United States.

4. The smaller and less coordinated attacks that might occur in the second day of the war or after a U.S. first strike. (Such a capability would help in reducing the effects of postattack coercion.)

5. Airplanes dispersing super-lethal bacteriological or chemical weapons. (Some writers believe that the future will see some very cheap and lethal forms of warfare developed along these lines. The subject is discussed in Lecture III.)

6. A mobilization base for a system that would be effective in an arms control situation or if there were a breakthrough in the art of defense.

At least points 1, 2, 3, and 6 are of sufficient importance to justify now a few billion dollars a year. Even if we do not start from scratch, but have done the R&D, the lead time to a reliably operating and deployed system is likely to be five to ten years. We must decide now if we want such capabilities, and if so, what kind of equipment will do the job best. One trouble is, it is difficult to take such threats seriously until they have actually matured, even though most people are agreed that they will mature. Another trouble is that planners may use reasons 1 to 6 above to justify continuing a defense system which was provided for other reasons, rather than design a new system or modify the old system in the way one would if he took the new objectives seriously.

Suitable Language, Doctrine, and Concepts for Military Planners. This is of really crucial importance if we are to meet our military problems satisfactorily. As will be discussed in Lecture III, the technological, political, and military situation changes so rapidly that we must make a conscious and vigorous effort to keep our conceptual, doctrinal and linguistic framework up to the needs of the moment. As soon as one uses a word or short phrase to characterize an idea it becomes oversimplified and misleading. That is true. Yet it may be better to have such oversimplifications and accompanying misconceptions, perhaps, than to have to go through a lengthy and almost unintelligible explanation every time one wishes to bring up a concept. We must have this shorthand way of posing and considering subtle and complicated military problems. Otherwise, discussion, research, communication, and formulation of problems are all hampered or degraded to the point of ineffectiveness.

I have discussed in this section many important shorthand concepts such as contingency planning; low, medium and high confidence; the eight phases of a war; arms control; Doomsday Machines; fighting versus deterring wars; flexible war plans; improvised protection; preattack and postattack coercion; and so forth.

Table 50 lists some other important ideas that are often imperfectly understood, but which one must have at his fingertips if he is to understand and discuss the deterrence and the waging of thermonuclear war. *The first four are, of course, the basic alternative strategies we are comparing.* Let me review them very briefly.

The *Finite Deterrence* strategy takes the position that the only strategic objective is to annihilate or punish the enemy reliably, and that there is no other job that we should or can expect our strategic forces to do. *The Counterforce as Insurance* strategy is an attempt to pick up the pieces if deterrence fails—to achieve the best possible postwar situation without making too many promises in advance about how well we can expect this salvage operation to work. The *Preattack Mobilization Base* tries to buy and design enough flexibility into our posture to make it possible to change our capabilities on notice as short as a week, month, or year as the case may be.

◆◆◆

TABLE 50
OTHER IMPORTANT CONCEPTS

(1) Finite Deterrence
(2) Counterforce as Insurance
(3) Preattack Mobilization Base
(4) Credible First Strike Capability
(5) Three Kinds of Deterrence
(6) Postattack Environment
(7) A and B Country
(8) Declaratory Policy
(9) Action Policy
(10) Rationality of Irrationality
(11) Calculated Win
(12) Spasm Theory of War
(13) Precedent and Custom

◆◆◆

Lastly, the *Credible First Strike Capability* implies that it is desirable to be able to threaten the enemy with some dire punishment to prevent him from engaging in extreme provocations and to limit limited wars. It argues that if we lack a Credible First Strike Capability, then in all logic we presumably need something else with which to deter or punish the enemy for extreme provocations. The main possibility here can be summarized as Controlled Reprisal. If used on a violent level and the enemy has a Credible First Strike Capability, this strategy is very dangerous. (This is true even if he mistakenly thinks he has such a capability.) In order to discuss and distinguish the above strategic views we have to delineate at least three kinds of deterrence and the corresponding notions of provocations and problems "within the rules" (Type III Deterrence) and "outside the rules" (Types I and II Deterrence). I have tried to do this with some thoroughness.

It is very important that the next concept, *the Postattack Environment*, be clearly understood. We are so accustomed to operating our forces *in peacetime* that it is difficult to imagine the difficulties of operating *after the enemy bombs have dropped.*

I have been connected with a number of projects in which important problems, that would be created by the postattack environment and would hinder the operation of our forces, came up for discussion. In every case there was the utmost resistance to the idea that these difficulties should be taken seriously. That money should be spent or operational changes made to alleviate these "hypothetical" problems were unpalatable ideas. It is only if this is conceptually understood to be a major problem that we will find people willing to listen open-mindedly to the statement of problems and the postulation of solutions. It is not a matter of just the obvious physical damage the bombs will do; it is also the subtle weapons effects. (Some of these are discussed in Lecture III.)

The concept of the A and B countries stresses the notion that nations can endure a lot of damage and recuperate but that they do not enjoy the process. On the one hand, it is suggested, no country is willing lightly to lose 50 to 100 cities. On the other hand, this amount of damage (particularly if the cities have been partially or totally evacuated) is far from total destruction. It is quite conceivable that decision makers may be willing to accept some risk of such destruction rather than accept an even more unpalatable alternative. There is no implication that countries are anxious to go through the experience. It is only urged that planners explicitly recognize that the risks a nation runs under some kinds of attacks are substantially less than is generally supposed. There is obviously a difference between *damage* and *annihilation*. It is high time that the distinction was drummed into many key minds in our society.

The next two items to be summarized emphasize another kind of distinction—that there may be a difference between the declaratory policy of what we *say* we will do and the action policy of what in fact we *will* do. The declaratory policy may claim that our action policy is something which it may not be. No matter how much we may fool ourselves or attempt to fool others, the enemy—and even allies—will be aware of this possible difference. They will make plans accordingly. The main reason for having a difference in declaratory and action policies is that there is the desirability of keeping our response ambiguous in certain circumstances and the possibility of bluffing, especially in the use of Rationality of Irrationality or committal strategies. Such strategies are actually quite familiar in one's daily life, but not clearly understood in international relations. If we refuse to use such strategies, we will be giving up an important set of options that may cause us very serious handicaps; on the other hand, we must resist the temptation to get off cheaply by overusing or otherwise abusing Rationality of Irrationality strategies.

Calculated Win. It is very important to understand the concept of the calculated win—that the other side may make a calculation which indicates to him that he can *win* the war, and that the calculation may be correct. The word "win" is being used in the classical sense of being better off after the war than one was before the war. Here, "better off" may be in the restricted sense that one is in a crisis and the best way out of it seems to be to try to destroy the other side or to make him back down through the use of force. The reason why it is important to emphasize the notion of "calculated win" is that the common jargon has it just the other way—that a war could only start by miscalculation. The possibility that a war would start by a calculation which is in fact a correct calculation is scarcely mentioned.

When I say that a war may start by calculation, I do not wish to imply that the enemy decision makers will believe that the calculation is 100 per cent reliable. They will worry that it may turn out to be a miscalculation. The point still remains that the other side may soberly and carefully make the best estimate it can. They may check and recheck it and decide that as far as they can see they can actually win the war. Of course, there will still be uncertainty; because of this uncertainty the side that makes this calculation may be unwilling to start a war. It would still be a terrifying decision. The carefully checked calculation may still turn out to be a miscalculation. There will also be moral, political, and social restraints. The concept of the "calculated win" only means what it says—that as far as the decision makers can calculate and estimate the problem, they expect a win. If the plans are actually implemented and they do achieve a win, one can say that *the nation has achieved a calculated win.* The war did not start by miscalculation.

Many people are deeply disturbed by the notion that there can be such a thing as a calculated win. The idea that this possibility should influence our behavior because *it may influence the enemy's behavior,* is also rejected without further consideration. And, as I pointed out in the first chapter, all the language normally used is against the notion. Consider, for example, the statement often heard, that we and the Soviet Union must live together or die together. Compare this with the much more frightening statement, "We must live together or *one of us* will die." While neither statement is accurate, the latter is more nearly accurate than the former. (An accurate statement, of course, is likely to be rather dull. It would run somewhat as follows: "We must either live together or one of us is quite likely to get destroyed, or at least get set back enormously, and the other will be hurt—to exactly what degree is very hard to predict.")

Spasm Theory of War. Almost completely opposed to the notion of a calculated win (with its connotation of war as a controlled operation) is the idea of the spasm—that one simply launches out suddenly, almost blindly doing the greatest possible destruction to the enemy without asking specifically, How does any particular part of this destruction aid one to achieve his final goal? In its purest form, this way of looking at a war considers only the alert force. It is very acceptable to many Minimum or Finite Deterrence advocates with their view of war as automatic mutual annihilation or a near equivalent. Surprisingly, experts sometimes have even the attacker acting this way. (For example, Khrushchev in his speech of January 14, 1960 [quoted on page 28], indicated that he would retaliate against attacks on any satellite socialist nation with an attack against both civilian and military targets in the U.S.)

Precedent and Custom. The reader will sense by now (and it will emerge more clearly after Lecture III) that it is going to be very difficult to live in a world of the future unless there are implicit agreements on behavior between us and the other nations. It will be important to get explicit arms control agreements. Still, many important aspects of international security will be regulated by precedent, custom, and other implicit agreements. In particular, shared and unshared expectations, previous behavior, and "fairness" or "legality" all play a crucial role in negotiations.[10] All of us will find it to our self-interest to preserve many of these precedents and customs. This means that even if there should be a momentary advantage occurring to one side or the other by breaking one of these unwritten laws, the decision makers concerned might think long and carefully before acting, pondering on the possible long-run consequences of the new precedent. The most important examples which come to mind are the distinction between nuclear and non-nuclear weapons, the use of violence in peacetime, peacetime spoofing and jamming, and general observance of the law and custom of nations.

[10] For a fascinating and illuminating discussion of bargaining in all its ramifications see Thomas C. Schelling, *The Strategy of Conflict,* Harvard University Press, Cambridge, 1960.

LECTURE III

WORLD WAR I THROUGH WORLD WAR VIII

CHAPTER VII

THE ROLE OF ANALYSIS

I AM going to discuss eight wars, some real and some hypothetical. Each war is supposed to be one technological revolution ahead of its predecessor; that is, *the wars have been chosen sufficiently far apart to illustrate how strategy and tactics change as technology has changed in the past and may change in the future.* Because the wars are supposed to occur *"in real time,"* they can also be used to illustrate certain real or hypothetical historical themes. The dates of the eight wars and their main themes are listed in Table 51.

The first two wars, World Wars I and II, are history. The main

❖❖

TABLE 51
THE EIGHT WORLD WARS

I.	(1914–1918)	An Accident-Prone World
		Unexpected Operational Gaps
II.	(1939–1945)	The Failure of Type II and III Deterrence
		The Technological Seesaw
		Unexpected Operational Gaps
III.	(1951– ?)	A Peacetime Revolution in the Art of War
		Unexpected Operational Gaps
		Re-emergence of Russia as an Eurasian Power
IV.	(1956– ?)	The Problem of the Postattack Environment
		The Waning of U.S. Type II Deterrence
V.	(1961)	S.U.–U.S. Parity
		Emergence of the S.U. as a World Power
		No Type II Deterrence Programmed
		Potential Failure of Type I Deterrence
VI.	(1965)	Prematureness of Minimum Deterrence
		Possibility of S.U. Strategic Superiority
VII.	(1969)	Possibility of Reliable Finite Deterrence
		Emergence of "Third" Powers?
		Arms Control or "?"
		World is ⅓ Rich, ⅓ Aspiring, and ⅓ Desperate
VIII.	(1973)	Thirteen Years of Progress (or 50,000 Buttons)

❖❖

value to us in examining them here is to improve our understanding of the kinds of things that can actually happen in war and peace. It oftens occurs when one presents the results of an analysis—as has been done in this book—that the psychological, political, or bureaucratic possibilities of certain hypothetical actions on the part of some government must be evaluated. Often the analyst will think that these possibilities must be taken seriously, but some critics will challenge him, arguing that it is not reasonable to suppose that actual decision makers or others could or would do such things. It becomes appropriate, therefore, to observe that historically such things have been done. History will not slavishly repeat; yet it may paraphrase itself. Faced with the record, the critic can no longer say that particular events "cannot" happen. He can only say that they are "unlikely" to happen—a much weaker statement. Therefore, one thing that we should try to get out of World Wars I and II is some orientation about what kinds of actions, situations, and capabilities are possible or plausible in the future.

Both wars illustrate how poorly even the experts can estimate the impact of new and untried military technologies. Both wars illustrate the prevalence of unexpected (but in retrospect obvious) operational gaps. World War I also illustrates how a seemingly unstable international security system can be made to work for years, but how eventually the law of odds will catch up with it. World War II illustrates even more dramatically how Type I and Type III Deterrence can fail as a result of almost incredible blindness and apathy on the part of seemingly responsible decision makers with more than enough information and motivation to take action.

In a sense, what we have called here World War III is also "history." Although no Soviet–U.S. war was fought in 1951 the capabilities on both sides are reasonably well known. We can conjecture with somewhat more confidence how such a war *might have been fought* than we can about our conjectural World War V, for example, which may lie in the future. In both cases there are enormous uncertainties. These stem not only from the normal capriciousness of war but from the fact that World War III would have been the first war to see a complete technological revolution in the art of war in peacetime. Unlike almost every other war in history, a war in 1951 would not have started off with a mere modification of the technology and tactics of the last previous war. Partly because of the newness of the equipment and partly because people are always blind to the obvious but unfamiliar, World War III would have also illustrated some startling operational gaps.

Like World War III, fictitious World War IV is also semihistory. But partly because it is closer to us (so that we do not understand it as well), and partly because some of the details are still classified, we cannot be as precise in our conjectures. This war, too, would show unexpected operational gaps. We will not discuss these for either this war or any of the future wars, since the discussion would almost by definition involve classified information.

The most important technological development of World War IV is the fact that it would have been a thermonuclear war rather than an atomic war. The difference between megaton and kiloton is very large, in some ways larger than the difference between kiloton and ton. Megaton weapons are comparable to gross forces of nature, such as earthquakes and hurricanes. The effects of the use of such weapons are not only extremely widespread; they are also occasionally very subtle and hard to predict. As a result, for the first time in the history of war we have what might be called *the problem of the postattack environment.* Partly because of one of these environmental effects—fallout—and partly because we had not thought about or prepared for nonmilitary defense including recuperation, it is most unlikely that the U.S. really possessed in 1956 and later years much objective Type II Deterrence. Nevertheless, relative to the past (and maybe the future), 1956 represents a peak. The West has shown that communism can be contained, most colonial questions settled reasonably amicably, incredibly (by 1951 standards and expectations) vigorous economies developed, a surprising ability to cooperate has been demonstrated, and enough military and political skill is at hand to hold the line on the communist rim between Turkey and Korea.

There are chinks though. The Soviets have solved the problem of succession. They have also displayed amazing economic vigour and technical skill, plus a new and unexpected diplomatic and political flexibility. They have shown in East Germany, Hungary, and Poland that they can put down internal disturbances without fear of Western intervention (a bitter and discouraging pill for those in the Satellites who thought of the Soviet Empire as a house of cards that would collapse at the first wind from the West). Most menacing of all, the Soviets have begun, tentatively but successfully, to act as a world power with a right to influence events in any corner of the globe.

313

World Wars V (1961), VI (1965), and VII (1969) are the possible wars for which we ought to be preparing, for they might be thrust on us. As far as World War V is concerned, our preparations can only affect operational decisions. It might be possible to speed up some development and procurement programs, but it would be hard to affect even by crash programs very much of the 1961 posture. World War VI on the other hand, will be affected by the procurement decisions and, in a much more modest fashion, by some of the development decisions we are making today. World War VII represents a possible development war. We are today instituting the long lead-time programs which will to a great extent determine our capabilities for national survival in 1969. These may turn out to be inadequate or marginal. 1961 should see the full emergence of the Soviet Union as a World power whose "presence" will be felt everywhere; under current programs 1965 may see a significant Soviet strategic superiority; and 1969 could bring a flowering of the post World War II military technology to the point where it will begin to be available to all.

Finally, there is a conceivable World War VIII, which we have relegated to the year 1973. In principle we should be studying this "war" today, but it will appear in our discussion that it is much too difficult to do this in any explicit and detailed fashion. The main purpose of our discussing it is to make some conjectures about the long-run future, so that we can have some notion about where we are trying to end up and what we are trying to avoid.

I mentioned that *the wars postulated here for educational purposes are spaced roughly one technological revolution apart.* One of the most interesting things in Table 51 is the estimated time it takes for a technological revolution to be superseded by a new one. There was practically a hiatus in technical development between Wars I and II, compared to the rate of development during the wars themselves. But things have been quite different since 1945. Figure 4 indicates how "official" Research and Development expenditures have increased in the last two decades. The reason for the quotes around the word official is that it turns out there is about twice as much spent for R&D as is usually officially allocated to R&D. The difference is buried in procurement budgets and military pay and allowances. However, the official curves do indicate the trend. Observe that R&D expenditures by the Department of Defense are now about four times what they were during the peak of World War II. One effect of this increased expenditure is that there is more technological progress in peacetime than there used to be in war, but with one important difference. During wartime we use the weapons we are developing, learning by experience their limitations and capabilities. This learning is purely hypothetical, of course, for imaginary World Wars III through VIII; as a result, it is possible for doctrine and reality to become almost unrelated to each other.

◆◆

Figure 4

Annual expenditures on research and development
(billions of dollars)

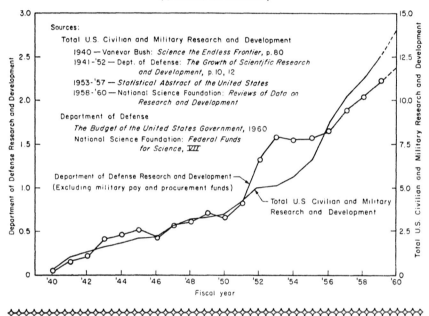

◆◆

I have allowed five years between Wars II, III, IV, and V and then only four years between Wars V, VI, VII, and VIII. In recent years it has taken about five years to have a revolution in the art or technology of war. However, we are getting more skillful at managing R&D programs and are also spending more money; we have reason to believe, unless we deliberately slow it down, that this process is going to be speeded up in the future. Thus, the four-year allowance for future revolutions.

Some Remarks on Lead Time

Before turning to World War I, I will make a few remarks on the subject of lead time, to show why it is important to look now at World Wars VII and VIII. I will then make some additional remarks on the role of analysis in defense problems, trying to illustrate some of the problems with which planners and decision makers have to cope in dealing with the kind of technological race that is discussed in the eight World Wars.

Since I have said that there has come to be a revolution in the art of war every four or five years, it may strike the reader as unreasonable to try to look ahead ten or fifteen years to the early and middle 1970's. Unfortunately, as far as programming or planning is concerned, the fact that a revolution occurs every four or five years does not mean we start from scratch every four or five years. The lead time for really *new* weapons systems, from the point when the "go ahead" on research and development is given to the attainment of appreciable numbers in inventory, is closer to ten or fifteen years, and the system itself should have a useful life of five or ten years more. That is, a system on which R&D is started today will have its useful life in the environment of two to four technological revolutions later. Since it is impossible for fallible humans (and maybe even infallible ones) to project two to four technological revolutions ahead, much of our preparation must be made in a partial fog.

Because of these long "lead" times we must work on a number of systems simultaneously. Typically there will be, first, a system that is being phased out of inventory, another more modern system composes the bulk of the inventory, a much more modern system is being phased into the inventory, and another system that will make all the other systems obsolete will be in operational suitability testing or some intermediate development phase. This last system will be thought of by most laymen and some experts as *the* strategic system, the one which solves the strategic problem once and for all. Finally, there will be a futuristic follow-on system under development, one advertised to the skeptics as the final answer to all the problems, a system so good that the budget people argue it is a shame to buy the one in operational suitability testing. However, some of the "experts" will have looked at this system and noticed that it has some possible defects. Luckily there will be another system not quite on the drawing boards that really is the final answer to all our problems.

The only reason we do not get technological revolutions every three years is not because of technological or economic infeasibility,

though these are problems, but because of the intellectual impracticability of juggling even more balls at the same time.

A typical schedule for a future weapons system is shown in Figure 5.

I have tried to picture on the figure a reasonable projected history of a current system that is just coming under study. While the
schedule illustrated is a normal development program, or even a
bit slow for today, four or five years ago we would (properly) have
called it an accelerated or crash program (or a "pipe dream" drawn
up by the "sales department"). If the R&D were being done calmly
and systematically, not only would every line in this figure be in

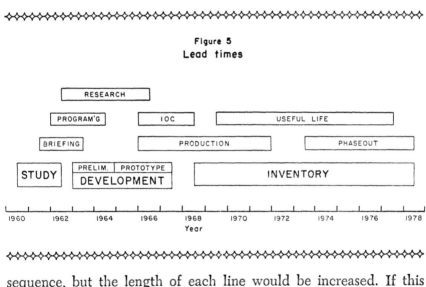

Figure 5
Lead times

sequence, but the length of each line would be increased. If this
were done, in an attempt to eliminate risk and waste, the lead time
would be approximately doubled. This would be an intolerable
hardship unless the enemy were courteous enough to follow the
same policy.

Let us start with the first box. It is my observation that almost
every study conducted by research organizations such as RAND,
SRI, ORO, and so on that has made a significant impact on understanding and reoriented people has taken at least two years to complete, and generally longer. If one waited until the final report was
written before starting a briefing he would lose one or two years;
thus preliminary briefings begin after you have been in the study
for about a year—and sometimes less. The study continues while

the briefings are going on. In a sense you start your briefings before you know what the whole story is about. Furthermore, you try early to get small sums allocated to study or research crucial questions, that is, you try to get the preliminary recommendations into "programs" without full coordination with all the relevant staff. If you had to wait until every person who might legitimately "coordinate" was persuaded before you could get the research part of the programming started, it would mean an excessive loss of time. It is very important to get the cheap programming decisions made early —the $2,000 for a consultant to study or comment on some technical question, the $20,000 for a preliminary feasibility study, the $50,000 for a preliminary design contract, or the $100,000 to $200,-000 for initial R&D. It is important to get these things started early, sometimes because they represent relatively long lead-time items, and sometimes because the information is needed before one can complete the study. Only when this research is completed can one obtain the information that is needed to formulate specific recommendations and make the kind of case that could persuade all the echelons of decision makers and thereby get the rest of the programming under way.

Fortunately, the Department of Defense always has a number of old programs phasing out, with the money being allocated to new ones, and in spite of all the criticism, it does have a sophisticated attitude toward R&D. This means that, unlike other government agencies, there is a lot of money available in DOD for speculative and even marginal projects. Unfortunately, though, if the study is really important, it is usually so because it is coming up with unpleasant ideas or it conflicts with the accepted views. (In general, people have difficulty understanding these kinds of ideas, not because they are difficult, but because they do not want to understand them. If they are forced to face up to the problems, they tend to transfer their dislike of the problem to the person that is forcing them to regard seriously what they would prefer to ignore.) Even though DOD encourages a very broad program of research, it is still possible to tap this available money only if you have the confidence of the people who control it. Almost automatically, an earth-shaking study is trying to sell unpopular notions, and this is one way to lose friends rather rapidly. So the analyst is in the peculiar position of, on the one hand, trying to keep on good enough terms with those who have easy access to money so they will have sufficient confidence in his judgment to initiate these necessary preparatory contracts, and, on the other hand, he must be willing to antagonize many of these same people by advancing startling, unpopular, or even unpleasant notions, sometimes even before he has them fully documented. In fact, in most cases the study cannot be documented before some money is allocated to get preliminary answers to the most important questions.

The initial development phase is often started before the briefings have been completed. If things are being done sensibly and the work is oriented toward answering technical and operational questions and advancing the state of the art, and not toward final prototypes, this is not too risky. So long as we are not trying for a weapons system or factory prototype we are not talking large sums of money—typically $1 to $50 million, not $50 to $500 million. If things go wrong, it is reasonably economical to cancel the program, since no commitments have been made for really large expenditures. (If individual or organizational prestige or vested interests are involved in the programs, cancellation will be politically difficult.) It does not take very long in the development cycle, on the other hand, before it becomes necessary to make fairly expensive decisions or to begin deferring the procurement date. For example, if you wish to have an initial operating capability in about 1968, you have to make some decisions on real estate, installation design,[1] and pro-

[1] The over-all installation period is one area in which our country is unnecessarily handicapping itself. With the exception of a handful of top-priority programs it seems to take about four to five years from the time senior decision makers agree to go ahead with a project until one can walk into a new building ready for occupancy. And it generally takes another six months to a year after the BOD (Beneficial Occupancy Date) before the building is functioning as an operating installation. If that kind of time had been taken in World War II, we would not have built a single usable building in that war. Even allowing for the fact that much World War II building was of temporary or substandard construction, our present time lag is still excessive. It does not have to be like this. Ordinary businesses which do not have the same pressure for speed that the military do in their life and death race with an aggressive enemy, manage to beat this time by factors of 2 and 3, just to save a few months' interest on the idle capital.

The installation "lead" time to which we have just referred concerns normal installations. The problems get much more severe for installations of particular importance—the hard or protected installations. Here again, the United States has been unnecessarily handicapped because of refusal to put enough effort into the theoretical and practical problems that come up. The traditional problem which innovators have had with military organizations—an excessive conservatism on the part of the military—no longer prevails. The military today are more than eager to be progressive and pick up any useful ideas, and this is also true of their supporting organizations. However, there are some fields which for one reason or other are "unromantic" and which have never really stirred up much interest. This has been particularly true of protective construction. As a result, there has been much less technological progress here

duction tooling around 1965 or 1966. Figure 5 allots about 4½ years to the development phase. This is a relatively short time for most weapons systems.

We show on the figure that we begin production for inventory about eighteen months before we have finished operational suitability testing. There actually have been at least two publicized cases —the B-52 program and the Thor missile—in which the Air Force ordered production before the first prototype model had been produced. But even the relatively slow program I have illustrated in the figure, one in which the production decisions come relatively late, involves many technological risks. I should point out that the Russians quite likely took such risks in their TU-4 aircraft program, and probably also in their Bear and Bison aircraft programs. There is some belief that they did not do this in their ICBM program, or if they did, they ran into trouble; in which case it was a gamble they lost. Some people have conjectured that the Soviet ICBM program is completely dominated by the Ordnance Department, which is traditionally very conservative. As Vannevar Bush once said, in commenting on the relatively slow development of artillery between the wars, "There is something about the word ordnance that produces stodginess in its adherents. Again this is not a matter of this country alone; it seems to be a general affliction." [2] If the ordnance hypotheses are true it would not be at all surprising that the Soviets did not launch into a large-scale production program until after all the testing had been completed. This is the traditional approach in the peacetime ordnance field as opposed to the much riskier practices common to the aeronautical field. It is the latter field that we illustrate in Figure 5. In 1967, the new weapon system starts to enter the inventory in reasonably large amounts. Just because it has entered the inventory does not mean that the technological race has stopped. For example, our B-52 airplane was being procured in the G model in 1959–60 with the H model in production. The changes from the A to the G models were large enough almost to justify a new numerical designation. The G models were not only larger and faster, but they will carry two Hound Dog air-to-surface missiles with five hundred miles range in addition to the regular

---

than in other military fields. Because of this lack of research, the uncertainties are so large that programming is slowed down and the installations themselves are inefficiently designed. Appendix III discusses some of these installation problems in more detail.

[2] *Modern Arms and Free Men*, Simon and Schuster, New York, 1949, p. 25; quoted by permission of the publishers.

bomb—a change that enabled each B-52 to fire two missiles at targets without penetrating any defense around these targets. If the Soviets are given credit for a competent local defense, this change alone could make an order of magnitude of difference in performance.

It should be clear that not all programs go through the stages that I have mentioned. Some of the most important and successful skip the first three or four years because they are not the result of systematic studies and programming. Rather, they are the happy outcome of a marriage of convenience, often hastily arranged, of devices that just happen to be available. The Hound Dog missile just mentioned belongs in this category.[3]

MONGREL MAKES GOOD

Air Force missilemen made a convincing display last week of a new missile that they have put together out of the parts and pieces of old projects. The mongrelized missile is aptly named Hound Dog. It has real bite. As the U.S.'s first effective plane-launched, jet-propelled air-to-ground missile, Hound Dog adds range and firepower to 1960's most potent operational weapon, the intercontinental B-52's of the Strategic Air Command.

To prove it, an eight-jet B-52G lifted off from Florida's Eglin Air Force Base last week with a 43-ft. Hound Dog slung under each wing. Air Force Captain Jay L. McDonald, 36, piloted the bomber over Cincinnati, Lake Superior, Hudson Bay and to the North Pole; then he wheeled it back all the way to Florida and unleashed one of the Hound Dogs. Still fully operative after the rigors of a combat-type, 10,800-mile, 22-hour plane flight, the missile streaked off on a northern course at close to Mach 2 speed. Then it turned around as directed, headed south, made "dog leg" evasive turns of well over 90°, and landed on target more than 500 miles down the Atlantic firing range.

Hound Dog was developed in record time of 30 months. Back in August of 1957, SAC put in a hurry call for an air-launched missile. The order: get it ready by 1960. To meet the deadline, Air Force Research and Development people made a missile out of existing systems. They:

Dusted off the old X-10 frame that North American Aviation had begun working on way back in 1946 for its air-breathing Navaho missile, since scrapped.

Salvaged an inertial guidance system that North American had been working on since 1950 for a fighter plane (the system has yet to go into a fighter but its kissing-cousin now guides Polaris subs).

Picked up a Pratt & Whitney J-52 jet engine that had been under

---

[*] The quotation that follows appeared in *Time*, April 25, 1960, p. 18.

low-priority development for planes for two years, used it to power Hound Dog, which is like a pilotless bomber.

The mixed ancestry produced bright offspring. The Hound Dog, now operational, weighs less than 10,000 lbs., has a thrust of 7,500 lbs. The engines may even be used as secondary power sources to give an extra 15,000 lbs. of thrust to the B-52 on takeoff. The Hound Dogs do not interfere with the B-52's normal H-bomb load; each missile simply adds a one-megaton hydrogen punch and an extra reach that combine to make a single B-52 the mightiest weapon ever seen.

The successfully improvised Hound Dog replaced the much more systematic Rascal missile program, before the Rascal missile reached the procurement stage. This is typical. The Hound Dog type of shotgun marriage is often more important than the systematic program illustrated in figure five. For example, our two most recent systems, the ICBM and the Polaris, are also examples of hasty marriages. To paraphrase an article in *Time* magazine on the development of the ICBM:

The ICBM program suffered from a lack of support because the guidance problems were so severe that the rest of the program was not pushed. The *unexpected* development of the H-bomb suddenly made even very inaccurate ICBM's useful. We were unfortunately in no position to benefit immediately from this development. We would have been in an even worse position but, luckily, an *entirely different program*—the rocket booster for the Navajo cruise (nonballistic)-type missile—had been pushed so far that we could use it as a basis for the ICBM engine.

As a final irony, the accuracy of the missile itself exceeded the expectations, so that it would have been a useful military device, at least against large cities, even if the H-bomb development had not come along. The Polaris program would have also been unpredictable (by reasonable war planners or arms controllers) in the early fifties. It depended on some breakthroughs in the development of lightweight thermonuclear bombs, the discovery of higher specific impulse solid fuels, improvements in missile technology and guidance, the newly launched nuclear power submarine, and the new Ship Inertial Navigation Systems (SINS). Most or all of these developments were unexpected successes in terms of performance, reliability, and date at which they were attained.

Because such marriages of convenience have been so important in the past, it is widely believed by many experienced people that a large part of our state-of-the-art development programs should be undertaken without worrying in great detail or specificity how the particular device will fit into the over-all military picture. It is only after the development has been carried through and we can survey all the other technological developments that we can get a moderately reliable idea of what particular combinations are going to be valuable. *Unless we undertake a great deal of risky development, for its own sake, we will not be able to arrange so many marriages of convenience.* It is not the purpose of the kind of study I have been describing to set up rigid programs into which all research and development must be fitted. Insofar as they are trying to guide Research and Development rather than procurement and operation, their main purpose is to look over all the programs that are going on to see that there are no important gaps and to find new uses and tactics for the products of the going projects, rather than to emphasize the avoidance of "duplication and waste" in R&D or the cancellation of projects which do not fit into the current official views and policies.

I mentioned earlier that we can expect lead time for the 1960's to be less than in the 1945–1960 time period. This should be true even though the systems that are currently being developed are more complicated than the early postwar systems. Almost all the postwar systems slipped back about five years or so, not from the earliest promises (which literally did come out of the "sales department"), but from schedules that were estimated *after* the various companies had gotten some distance into the projects. There are many reasons for this. Some involve administrative difficulties such as erratic financing, design changes, delayed decisions, over-frequent bureaucratic reviews, and so on, but in my opinion one of the single most important reasons was that in most cases the projects were beyond the skill of the contractor.

During the war development was relatively easy because it involved either improvements of existing models or innovation of specialized components—as in the radar field where the direction and requirements were furnished by technical people who understood their problems very well. In the late 1940's and early 1950's many of the most complicated weapons systems were in the hands of the aircraft companies, who then knew a great deal about aeronautics and air frames, but little else. Of all the classifications of engineering, the aeronautical engineer is among the most technically competent: in addition, he has always placed a premium on imagination and willingness to be daring. However, even the best aeronautical engineers were not physicists, electronics experts, propulsion specialists, and mathematicians. When they were given a series of problems in which success and failure depended on advances in the fields of propulsion, guidance, computing, and the like, they did not do at all well.[4]

I am not making these remarks about the aircraft companies because they were the worst offenders, rather the opposite; they were among the best of the industrial contractors. I should also make the point that the above discussion of the shortcomings of aircraft companies no longer holds. Major companies now have not only a spectrum of skills on their staffs, but they also have divisions and subdivisions which are comparable to university or government laboratories in the background and competency of their personnel; they have come to be better in most practical applications than academic or semiacademic institutions. In addition, they have become much more skillful in their letting of subcontracts for the development of the more specialized parts of weapons systems.

There are many other reasons why Americans do R&D better today than we used to, but the one I have just mentioned—that the technical managers of the program are more experienced—is one of the most important.

Different Kinds of Gaps

There is a connection between lead time and what has come to be called "gaps" between our position and that of the Russians. There are three types of gaps for us to consider.

1. *The R&D gap:* The other man knows more about some piece of hardware weapons systems or weapons effects than you do. This is a serious gap, but unless it involves immediate exploitation of a new weapons effect or other phenomena against existing equipment and posture, it is not suicidal, or at least not for that year. It may

---

[4] To give a typical example of the kind of misunderstanding many aircraft companies had about how to go about their work, they tried to hire technical staff in the fields of mathematics and physics through newspaper classified advertisements. It turns out that you can put an ad in the newspaper for an aeronautical engineer at, say, the $15,000-a-year level and people will in fact apply who are worth $15,000 a year. The same procedure would not work for physicists or mathematicians at the $7,500 a year level. People in these professions just do not read the classified ads. There is really no snobbery involved; it is just not their habit. They are hired through universities, personal acquaintances, meetings of their professional societies, and through ads in their professional journals. I mention this single incident just to illustrate one way in which the traditional aircraft companies misunderstood an important aspect of their problem.

be a dim prognosis for the future, of course, and it is almost always bad for public relations and prestige.

2. *The procurement gap:* The enemy has bought more of some weapons systems than you have. Whether this kind of gap is serious or not depends on what you are trying to do. But it is also almost always bad for public relations.

3. *The operational gap:* He can present you with a problem that you cannot solve satisfactorily. An operational gap could arise out of an R&D or procurement gap but normally it arises out of a failure to react properly to a change in the situation. This failure to react is often the result of an intellectual or doctrinal lag in understanding and facing up to the results of changes in technology. It is the operational gap that kills you. It is also the most subtle and hardest to recognize and guard against.

These three kinds of gaps can exist independent of each other. It is perfectly possible for the enemy to have a much larger force than you do and for you still not to suffer from an operational gap. This is the popular view as embodied in the Minimum and Finite Deterrence theory, which holds that so long as you have enough armed force to destroy his cities it is irrelevant to you how much armed force he has. While there is a germ of truth in this theory, as it is ordinarily applied, it can be very misleading. On the other hand, both sides could have exactly the same equipment, but if both sides were vulnerable to a first strike, the situation would be symmetrical but unstable and very unsatisfactory. We will both have inadequate Type I Deterrence. Or contrariwise (and more likely), in the late sixties if we both buy Homicide Pact Machines we would both have operational gaps as far as Counterforce as Insurance or Credible First Strike are concerned.

In the body of this lecture I am going to try to show as we go through the eight wars that it has been historically true and will continue to be true that seemingly obvious and important gaps can and do arise and are either totally unnoticed or noticed and disbelieved. Such gaps do not show up in the prewar critiques as sharply and clearly as the R&D and procurement gaps that are detectable even by a novice and that make such embarrassing headlines for the government. These unnoticed operational gaps may determine the course of events and are most likely to cause catastrophic failures of the system, but until one is faced with a disastrous failure, it is most difficult to take them seriously. In general, the only way to find operational gaps is by intense observation of the whole system, reflection on unconventional possibilities, and paper and pencil studies. This means that any gaps that are found will look hypothetical and unreal. It will be difficult for rigid thinkers, the budget-minded, the "by assumption"-type of analyst, the loyal member of an operating organization, or the partisan advocate to take such worries seriously. It is particularly easy to be apathetic about operational gaps if one has accepted the notion that the purpose of the military forces is purely psychological and designed to impress the enemy rather than to have an objective capability. Modern weapons are so destructive that even a flimsy façade of an objective capability looks impressive to most laymen and some experts. I will try to show that the façade business can be a very dangerous one.

The Role of Paper and Pencil

I have mentioned before that there is a dearth of people with relevant practical experience in the conduct of thermonuclear wars. Rather surprisingly, one can make almost as strong a statement about the conduct of international relations in a world in which the contending powers have modern weapons systems. One reason for this latter lack is because our understanding and doctrine tend to lag behind the existing technology. Thus both sides may be running unnecessary risks and neglecting strengths of which they are not aware. The misunderstandings on the two sides can be very different, moreover, so there is an additional complexity introduced. The only way to alleviate the situation is by appeal to analytical thinking. It will do no good to inveigh against theorists. In this field everybody is a theorist. Table 52 outlines the basic problems of theoretical analysis.

◆◆◆

TABLE 52

ON THE ANALYTIC APPROACH TO DEFENSE PROBLEMS

I. What are the questions?
II. How do we get the answers?
III. Do we believe the answers?
IV. Do we care?

◆◆◆

It is probably clear to most people that asking the right questions is far more important than having a good technique or methodology for getting answers, although the latter two are also important. Let me give some examples (from memory) in the field of ordinary operations research. We will then go on to the subject of war planning.

I recently had occasion to read about a group of operations researchers who were studying methods of using bags more efficiently in a supermarket. They found that the checkers at the cash registers tended to use a larger paper bag than was necessary when they packed orders. In order to counteract this "bias" the analysts suggested putting the large bags in a somewhat inconvenient position so that the checker would prefer to use the smaller bags that were closer and more convenient. This did not seem to work, so they finally went to the extreme of taking the large bags away. This meant that quite often the checker had to use two medium-sized bags rather than one large one. The article concludes with the rather naïve and somewhat wistful remark that the whole experiment was discontinued because all along the customers wanted the large bags to use for their garbage; and they had started going across the street to another market that prized science less and customers more. It is important to note that *the analysts would never have found out their mistake if they had not been able—a little late—to observe the behavior of customers.* They could not depend on theory to bring them back to reality.

An interesting example of very successful operations research occurred in World War II. In setting the timing on fuses for air-dropped depth bombs for use against submarines, the following question was asked: What is the average depth at which submarines travel? It turned out that on the average submarines seemed to travel at depths of about fifty feet, so the fuses were set for fifty feet. In practice, however, air-dropped depth bombs were very ineffective against submarines. In investigating this, the researcher noticed that airplanes only dropped bombs against submarines that they had seen and they only saw submarines that were on the surface; therefore, the submarine was on the surface when the depth bomb was dropped, or at the worst, it had just started to dive and had not gotten very deep. Since the radius of damage of a depth bomb was only about ten feet, a bomb fused to explode at fifty feet tended to explode harmlessly beneath the submarine. It was calculated that the optimum depth to set the fuse should be about ten feet. This could not be done for technical reasons, but the fuses were set at the minimum depth possible, which turned out to be thirty feet. A spectacular improvement in capability was achieved.

Another example of *asking the right question* is given by analysts who were asked to study the problem of expediting the delivery of truck loads of merchandise to a chain of markets. The stores had found that because of traffic and other delays they could not predict when the trucks would get to the store, making it necessary for them to keep an unloading crew waiting until the truck actually arrived or to keep truck driver and the truck waiting until the unloading crew came on duty. The analysts were asked to improve the chain's ability to predict the arrival time and thus schedule trucks and crews better. The problem as posed turned out to be rather unfruitful, but the researchers suggested that a much better way to do things would be to use trailer-truck combinations and deliver the goods at night, leaving the loaded trailer at the store one night and picking it up again the next evening. It turned out that it was thereby possible to cut transportation costs (because there was less traffic congestion at night) and to make deliveries completely predictable.

A last (and apocryphal) example: It seems that one of our most distinguished operations researchers who was in Korea during the early days of the war noticed that soldiers, after finishing up their meals, had to queue up in very long lines to wash their mess kits. The mess kit washing was done in two steps. There was a first GI can in which the soldiers washed the mess kit and a second one in which they rinsed it. The washing took a few minutes, the rinsing a matter of seconds, but there were the same number of rinse cans as wash cans. This operations researcher suggested that if every other rinse can were made into a wash can there would be three wash cans for every rinse can. The 50 per cent increase in wash cans would permit a 50 per cent increase in the speed of washing, while the decrease in the number of rinse cans would not create a bottleneck because so little time was spent in this operation.

Because the operations researcher was a very good friend of the general's, his suggestion was carried out. However, a few months later the new method was dropped—as soon as the general was transferred, as a matter of fact. When the sergeant in charge was asked why the new method had not been kept, he said, "Oh, yeah, I remember that nut. He had a crazy idea that the Army wanted to get people through lines 'fast.' We *like* lines in the Army—they strengthen the guys' legs. Everybody got so soft after we eliminated the lines that instead of just going back to the old way, we set up only one wash can for every *three* rinse cans. Not only did the bacteria count go way down, but what's more important, the lines got so long the men got their legs in damn good shape. We're a real fighting *army* now."

Again, it is all-important to ask the right questions. When we discuss World War II, particularly when we discuss the German breakthrough at Ardennes Forest, the vulnerability of the Maginot Line, the fall of Singapore, and the Japanese attack on Pearl Harbor, we will see that it is sometimes very hard to formulate the right questions.

I do not want to spend very much time on the second item in Table 52, How do we get the answers? Even if the right questions have been asked, working out the correct answers is by no means a routine endeavor to be entrusted to excessively narrow-minded technicians and professionals. We will content ourselves with an example from World War II on how far off an answer can be.

Goering once boasted that no British planes would reach Berlin. He said, "If that event ever occurs, you may call me Meyer." I have been told this boast was based on some calculations the German antiaircraft people had made on the efficiency of their weapons. They first figured that the theoretical kill probability would be .25 per round fired; that is, on the average they would shoot down one plane every time they fired four rounds. These theoretical calculations were then checked by some experiments at the proving grounds which verified this .25 figure. This gave them a great deal of confidence in the over-all result and led to Goering's boast.

In the war, the kill probability turned out to be .0002 rather than .25—or about a thousandth as large as the predicted number. Even if the decision makers had discounted the claims by a factor of five or ten, they would have been incredibly misled. This is an example of how badly off a prediction can be, even though a great deal of technical work, computation, and experiment may go into documenting it.

❖❖

TABLE 53

THE GERMAN AIR DEFENSE ANALYSIS

  I. Selected Crews
 II. Single Plane Targets
III. Selected Fuses
 IV. Experiments at 10,000 feet
  V. Scale

❖❖

Table 53 shows why the calculations and validating experiments were so wrong. The German antiaircraft battery was a rather complicated affair requiring the split-second coordination of six people. One man found the height of the plane, another man found its speed, a third man estimated the range, a fourth set the fuse, and so on. Of course, as soon as there are two planes in the sky simultaneously one man will find the height of one plane while the second man is finding the speed of the other. Mistakes of this kind multiply fantastically when there are many planes in the sky and when the pressure of combat intensifies. Since the Germans ran the experiments with select crews (they might well have been described as athletes with Ph.D's in Physics) and used these select crews against single-plane targets, they naturally did not have many crew errors.

Another part of the experiment that was misleading was the use of specially selected timing fuses. The most critical element in shooting down a plane is getting the shell to burst at exactly the right altitude. If it bursts a few feet too high or a few feet too low, the target will go unscathed. By using a higher quality timing fuse than could in fact be mass produced they got misleadingly good results.

The most important mistake they made, however, was in flying the target at only 10,000 feet; at this altitude World War II antiaircraft was extraordinarily effective. For this reason, attacking planes flew at 20,000 feet or even higher. At such altitudes antiaircraft efficiency diminished dramatically. If you were to ask why they did the experiments at 10,000 feet, I would have to say I do not know. (The reason is probably the same as ours if we do our calculations and experiments these days at 10,000 to 30,000 feet—perhaps because that is a convenient altitude and one at which our weapons work well.)

The final problem that the Germans ran into was scale. Once they found out how far off their original plans were they had to increase greatly the number of antiaircraft batteries. This in turn led to a further degradation in the quality of both crews and equipment.

The next question asked in Table 52 is, Do we believe the answers? This question is, of course, highly relevant. Even conventional scientific and engineering analyses are much more uncertain than most laymen realize. In this subject, which is more of an art than a science, it is quite clear that most of our studies and conclusions must be taken tentatively.

For example, I hope that the first lecture is an example of a reasonably good study. The finding that if a nation such as the United States or Russia makes very moderate preparations it can survive a "small" war was made quite plausible, I think. It is not really unreasonable on the basis of our study to conjecture that if either of these nations made elaborate preparations they could survive and rebuild after an extremely "large" war. However, I think it must also have been clear to the reader as he went through the material that, even if one accepts the idea of quality and reliability in our work, there remain many uncertainties. It would be difficult for a policy maker to rely on our study if it came to a decision of war or peace. (He may have to if he does not have any better analyses, but where he can he will usually act "conservatively," where "conservatively" can mean inertly—which is not in all cases the conservative thing to do.)

Analytic treatments of war during the last five or ten years have a real possibility of being more reliable than the same kind of attempt made in preceding decades. The reason for this is partly because we have new tools and techniques available, but mainly because in a nuclear war many of the problems that arise really are problems in physics and engineering. For example, the destructive effect of H-bombs can be predicted with sufficient reliability for most purposes. The effects of fallout are likewise susceptible to reasonable prediction. Most important of all, in many analyses, individual components or systems often end up with a score of either 0 or 100. It is usually possible to predict 0 or 100 relatively reliably, even though one could not predict some in-between number. If, for example, one is calculating the probability of penetrating a defense barrier and if there are very large holes in the barrier that the enemy can easily exploit, it may be quite simple to show that with some enemy tactics the barrier has zero effect. In other circumstances, if the equipment is working as it should work and the enemy uses a tactic for which the equipment was appropriately designed, it may be quite easy to show that if the barrier works at all it should provide about 100 per cent effectiveness. As I have said, it is of course difficult to estimate the level when the number is between 0 and 100 per cent, but this most difficult problem is often not the most important. Often all we need really to know is whether the system works or falls flat on its face. In any case it should be clear that, good or bad, for many questions paper analyses are all we have.

As we change the bulk of our strategic force from planes to missiles, the war gets even more calculable than it was before. The use of planes involves many imponderables, such as the skill and performance of the crews under stress, the evaluation of the possibility of casual detection when trying a sneak attack, the effectiveness of complicated active defense systems, the competing countermeasures, and so on. The missile, however, is particularly a product of the engineering sciences. Its major parameters involve such things as circular probable error, yield, reliability, vulnerability of the targets, accuracy with which location of target is known, and so forth. The effects of these variables can be described quite accurately by mathematical formulae and much of the basic information is likely to be available to both sides, so that to an heretofore unprecedented extent campaigns really are problems in applied mathematics. However, as I tried to point out in Lecture II, there still are chilling uncertainties.

The point that I wish to stress here is not, What are the questions? though we will spend a good deal of time on this theme, and not, How do we get the answers? or even, Do we believe the answers? but, Do we care? Even if we conclude that we have asked the right questions, that we have been competent about getting an answer, and that we believe our answers, we still may not care.

There are many reasons why decision makers do not care. Four of them are shown in Table 54.

✧✧

TABLE 54

WHY DON'T WE CARE?

I. Doctrine
II. Politics
III. Point of View
IV. Irresponsibility

✧✧

The first is doctrine. The answer does not accord with the official ideology. Let me give a slightly farfetched but, I think, rather revealing analogy. Imagine that you live in a community where people have been brought up to detest the color *gray*. They detest it to the extent that some proportion of them literally retch when they see the color. Assume now that you had been given the job of designing some kind of prefabricated housing for this community and you came up with the marvelous idea that aluminum fits the bill exactly.

This material is light, ductile, corrosion proof, inexpensive, strong, fabricates easily, and so on. You then get up before an audience in this community and extol the virtues of this wonderful material. However, you soon notice that most of the people in the audience leave with expressions less than rapturous on their faces; the few who remain are scarcely able to hide their disgust. When you inquire as to why they are not entranced by your proposal, they keep making some irrelevant comment that the material is "gray." You explain that color does not affect the structural strength of the other admirable qualities of the material. You point out logically and carefully that the proposed material is better than any alternatives, but the argument has no effect. If you are a typical operations analyst it may be months before you accept the fact that these people are just not going to accept a gray material. At this point you decide to paint it red and thus make it acceptable. After all, paint is cheap. They may still reject the material. (They say, "It is *still* gray—underneath!")

This example may strike you as being farfetched, but some of the offense *vs.* defense arguments have some of the same quality about them. This is even true when one tries to disguise a defensive position by saying you are "defending an offensive force." The answer is, "It is still gray (defensive) underneath."

As most readers will know, Western military schools try to train their students in the so-called offensive spirit. The idea is that there is a natural division of labor between you and the enemy. On the whole you should concentrate on what you can do to hurt the enemy and not worry about what he can do to hurt you. He will take care of that. Actually there are very good reasons for trying to inculcate an offensive bias in the military. Here are some rather interesting quotations from Gordon Waterfield's book, *What Happened to France,* on the effect that the Maginot Line had on some French soldiers:

"'Fine concrete,' he kept on muttering as we strode through the woods along the Rhine bank; 'they'll never get through this! Magnificent concrete!'

"I asked if the Germans had such good concrete on the other side of the Rhine, a few hundred yards away.

"'Oh no,' said the colonel, rather coldly, 'nothing like so good.'

"'Is there any reason,' I asked, 'why you should not attack to prevent them making their defenses stronger?'"

"The colonel smiled reprovingly at me as if I had made a blasphemous remark, but he was too broadminded to take offense at it. He made no reply. The truth was that nobody wanted to attack; their job was to go on making concrete until the Germans took the initiative. On both sides of the Rhine they were building hard, often in full view of each other, but the Germans did not fire on the French, nor the French on the Germans. Every evening a few salvoes were exchanged to relieve the infinite boredom. I spent a night at a well-defended outpost on the banks of the Rhine, and in the morning I walked along the trenches to the look-out post on the water's edge. Across the river a young German was standing in the sun, naked to the waist, washing himself. It annoyed me that it should be possible for him to go on washing calmly there with two machine-guns on the opposite bank. I asked the French sentry why he did not fire. He seemed surprised at my bloodthirstiness. " '*Ils ne sont pas méchants*,' he said; 'and if we fire they will fire back.' "

At a later visit to another fort Waterfield comments:

"We left the hot sun and went down into the Maginot Line. It was like going down into a coal mine. A lift took us into the bowels of the earth, and we walked for a mile along a tunnel, meeting occasional soldiers on bicycles or an electric train bringing up ammunition along a small line. The troops ate, slept and worked underground, seldom going out into the open air. . . .

"As I drank Pernod in the officers' mess, also underground, I said: 'It certainly seems impregnable.'

" 'It's impregnable all right,' they said.

"All the same there was one form of attack they were nervous about, and that was an attack by parachutists. A single courageous man could put the guns out of acting by throwing incendiary grenades at the gun turrets; the heat fuses the metal dome, thus sealing the gun in its chamber. The officers told me that the Germans had put the Liége fort guns out of action in this way, and that they were keeping a sharp look-out to prevent similar attacks. . . . If anyone had suggested to the French military staff some months before that a few resolute Germans, dropped from the sky or infiltrating through under cover of night, could put the guns of the Maginot Line out of action, he would have been ridiculed or arrested as a defeatist." [5]

These quotations illustrate one of the major troubles with fortifications. It may or may not be hard for the enemy troops to get into the forts, but it is almost always hard to get friendly troops out of them and into the field. Actually, the defensive attitude affects more than just fortifications. It is obvious that excessive caution may afflict any individual on a battlefield and that it makes sense to indoctrinate fighting men against this very human trait. It is even

[5] Gordon Waterfield, *What Happened to France*, London, John Murray, 1940, pp. 14–16, 18–19; quoted by permission of the publishers.

more important to indoctrinate leaders than followers against excessive caution. Many commanders do indeed have a bias to act too cautiously. It is, for example, very natural for a responsible and fallible human being during a battle to overemphasize the troubles he has and underestimate the difficulties his enemy has. After all, he knows what has happened to him; he can only conjecture what has happened to the enemy.

A few years ago I read a newspaper story about how Generals Montgomery and Eisenhower criticized General Meade for not having vigorously pursued General Lee after the Battle of Gettysburg. Meade's excuse at the time was that his men were tired and disorganized. This was perfectly true, but Lee's men seemed to have been even more tired and more disorganized, and many military experts think that Meade might have come pretty close to winning the war then and there; that in comparison to Lee's men, his men were in fine shape. I do not want to belabor this point, except to say that while I am personally sympathetic to the notion that offensive strategies are to be preferred to equally good-looking defensive strategies, it does not seem to be technically feasible to do this in an objective analysis. In what follows we will not give ourselves any such extra bonus; there may even be a tendency to do the opposite. As a critic of the military scene, I will have a tendency to emphasize the things that are overlooked. Because the official agencies have in the immediate past almost all had an offensive bias, it was most likely to be the defensive side of things that got overlooked. (This remark may no longer be true for the future. In fact, as we shall see when we discuss World Wars V and VI, the pendulum may have swung too far in the other direction.)

Being occasionally afflicted with doctrinaire blinders is not a monopoly of the military. Until the notion of a missile gap made the possibility of a thermonuclear Pearl Harbor crystal clear, most military experts in and out of government—foreign and domestic—refused to consider the possibility seriously. Since the early 50's all retaliation has been considered "annihilating" and that was the end of it. Or consider the example of many of those who are opposed to military preparations on moral or political grounds. These "nonmilitarists" usually also deny that there can be a military problem in the technical sense. That is, they also assume (generally without a shred of evidence either way) that the "militarists" are overspending, even granting that the military-minded are honestly but objectively concerned with the military aspects of national security. And most im-

portant of all are those who are so preoccupied with fiscal responsibility that this seems to them to be the only legitimate concern.
These persons correctly observe that one can never really satisfy a
cautious general; he will always notice that he can fulfill his responsibilities better if he has more resources. He is always willing to ask
for more. Therefore (in their eyes) the mere fact that a general is
asking for more money may not really give any information on the
relative state of our national defenses; even if they were good he
would not be satisfied. This same individual, who is always talking
about the parochialism of the generals, does not notice that the
comptroller-type also has *his* foibles. He is always anxious to reduce
expenses. Even if budgets have been cut to the danger-point, this
person will notice that *we are still spending money* and will argue
that the Department of Defense cannot possibly be 100 per cent
efficient; that it must be possible to make savings, it must be possible
to buy more defense with less money. Finally, there are the "practical men" who simply cannot make themselves believe in the existence of a problem they have not personally experienced. Paper calculations and theoretical studies do not impress these individuals.
There have been too many calamity-howlers in the past few years
to take any particular one seriously—no matter how good his case
may be.

The second reason for not caring is that we may feel that the
recommendations that result are incompatible with the political
process. Decision making, either in a democracy or in a totalitarian
society, is a political process, and sometimes reasonable-looking recommendations cannot get through the decision-making machinery.
It is useless to urge things that are politically impractical—useless,
at least, in the short run. It may still be sensible to urge "impossible"
programs as part of an educative process that ripens in a crisis.

There are many ways in which the political process influences
what people care about. Table 55 illustrates one way in which the
political nature of our system, particularly our reliance on committees (formal and informal), influences decision making. (The reader
will recognize this table as a repeat of the one that appeared on page
120 on committees. I have substituted the words planner, operator
and staff, for Tom, Dick, and Harry, and for preferences A, B, and C,
I have substituted an adequate system, a minimum system, and a
zero system.)

Let us assume that some problem has come up in which the *plan-*

ner has suggested making a considerable change from the customary way of proceeding in order to get an adequate system. However, he also has a minimum recommendation that could be followed; while it has some faults, it does go some distance in meeting the problem. The planner will then have the following set of preferences: adequate to minimum, minimum to zero, and therefore, by logic, adequate to zero.

❖❖❖

TABLE 55
GOVERNMENT COMMITTEE

Chooser	Preferences		
Planner—	Adequate to Minimum	Minimum to 0	Adequate to 0
Operator—	Minimum to 0	0 to Adequate	Minimum to Adequate
Staff—	0 to Adequate	Adequate to Minimum	0 to Minimum
Committee—	Adequate to Minimum	Minimum to 0	0 to Adequate

❖❖❖

The *operator* is in a slightly different position. He is influenced by the worries of the planner and feels he must do something. He prefers minimum to zero. But because there are many planners coming into his office every day with ideas, he tends to be cautious about going off half-cocked. If his choice was between doing everything or nothing, he would prefer doing nothing. This means that he prefers zero to adequate. Therefore, by logic, he prefers minimum to adequate.

The *staff* are in a still different position. As with the operator, if the choice is between everything and nothing, they prefer doing nothing. However, if the choice is between doing something that is adequate or minimum, they prefer doing an adequate job, at least adequate in the peacetime bureaucratic context. For example, they would find it difficult to defend building an installation with an insufficient number of toilets or other amenities, even if the operator was willing to skip some of these amenities and accept the consequences in lower morale, reduced re-enlistment rate, and so on, if by doing so he can then afford an important new installation. The staff do not feel that they can live with the minimum facilities. The boys are entitled to the proper number of toilets, PX's, and so on, they feel, and as far as the staff are concerned, they are not going to fill out endless forms explaining why they do not have them. They prefer having no building at all to a substandard building. (This desire for the adequate does not, of course, extend to performance in an unreal and hypothetical war that most of the staff does not really think can occur. But that is a separate question.) Since the staff prefer zero to adequate and adequate to minimum, they prefer zero to minimum.

Let us now see what is likely to happen when we take a vote, assuming for the sake of the example that the planner, operator, and staff each have equal influence. If the choice is phrased as being between the alternatives adequate and zero, the zero will be chosen 2 to 1. So, having political savvy, the planner suggests choosing between minimum and zero. Minimum wins 2 to 1. However, once a decision has been made to do *something*, a different group is called together to propose exactly what should be done. This group, even if it has the same representation as the original group, will have to choose between the alternatives of an adequate job or a minimum job. The zero choice no longer interests them. They will then choose adequate 2 to 1. Their tendency to choose adequate, or even an extreme form of adequate, is increased by the belief of some members of the committee that it improves one's bargaining position to pad programs.

This might be all right except that the nation has many echelons of decision making, and this last choice means that the alternatives presented to the next level of decision makers is between zero and adequate; we know what they will do—they choose the zero system. This could terminate the program. Usually it does not, but after some time a new committee is chosen to decide if anything at all is to be done, and the whole process starts over again. While the example may strike some readers as artificial, it is, in my experience, by no means so. In fact, I have just given a capsule history of too many important projects.

When we refer to political considerations we also use the word in the customary sense—that is, many decisions are influenced by the character of the relationship between the Services and the Executive, the Executive and Congress, the Services and Congress, and the relation of all three to what could be lumped together as the "outside world." One of the most important ways in which these relations influence studies and their acceptance is that it is always easier to "sell" something that can be presented as carrying out an existing program or as being in support of an existing program, or (a last resort) as a necessary modification of such a program. Barring a crisis or an exceptionally "glamorous" idea, it is usually risky to phrase the recommendation as an expansion of an existing program and disastrous to let it look like the initiation of a new program. Let me give some examples of how this might work out in practice, with particular relevance to the Air Force, with which I am most familiar.

The first and most obvious is the notion (common from 1950 to 1958) that the Air Force is entitled to a fixed number of wings, no more and no less. This can be misleading in two separate ways. If the enemy threat is fixed, then when we replace old equipment with new equipment that is more expensive but more efficient, we can presumably do the same job, not only with less equipment but at less cost. That is, in the business world when one modernizes, one generally saves money. Historically, it is exactly the opposite in the military field; modernization almost always increases current costs. This is to be expected since the enemy's force is not fixed. He is also modernizing and may be increasing his forces, and we must make corresponding increases and changes to meet the threat. In particular, both of us are growing richer and so can afford to put more resources into "nonproductive" military systems. If one does so, the other must too. In this country, the most palatable way to increase or change our force to meet new threats is to cloak the new program under the guise of modernization without putting too much stress on the fact that in addition to modernizing we are also increasing the force size. Let me give a hypothetical example.

Assume that we have, say, 100 units of old equipment, and the enemy's threat has increased so that we have to double our capability if we are to hold our own. It may be that there are two ways to meet the threat. One is to replace the 100 units of old with 100 units of brand new equipment that is twice as effective but twice as costly. The other way to meet the enemy's threat is to keep the 100 units of old equipment and add 50 units of new equipment; this also doubles one's effectiveness and might be much cheaper than the first procedure since we are only buying 50 new units. Unfortunately this second alternative, unless there happens to be a crisis atmosphere, will be almost impossible to sell because it looks like what it is: an increase in the size of the force to meet a *hypothetical* increase in enemy capability, an increase which skeptical people will not be willing to believe it is necessary to meet. (They either do not believe that the enemy has increased his force, assume we cannot afford to match him, or conclude that the increase is meaningless *à la* Finite Deterrence.) Therefore, the first alternative, while actually more expensive than the second, can be more easily defended. It is defended on the plausible and often correct grounds that irrespective of what the enemy has done in the way of increasing or decreasing his budget we must modernize our force. Let us therefore go ahead and do it.

It is also possible actually to increase the force by putting more things in the Air Force wings (or to decrease the force by taking things out). Something like this actually seems to have occurred since the end of the World War II. We used to have one wing of 12 heavy bombers on a base. Today we have 45 heavy bombers in a wing, composed of three squadrons of 15 planes each with one squadron per base. Actually each of the new squadrons represents many more dollars, planes, and men than did the old wing.[6]

Let me give a hypothetical example of a necessary modification in operation that could disguise an increase. Consider "alert" as a protection. The important thing is to have a satisfactory number of planes on ground or air alert. There are two ways to increase the number of planes on alert. One is to leave the total size of the force fixed but increase the percentage of planes on alert. This obviously increases costs. The other is to have a smaller percentage on alert but to increase the size of the force until one has the same number of planes alert. This also increases costs. Even if it turned out to be true—and I am not saying that it is—that the second way was the least expensive way of getting additional planes on alert and had the additional bonus value of having more planes available during tense periods, it would probably be rejected in favor of the

---

[6] (One of the most amusing and brazen examples of disguising procurement occurred in the early days of the Republic. It seemed that Congress was unwilling to retire old naval ships and replace them with new ones, so the Navy disguised its replacement program as a repair and maintenance program. They took old ships, tied them up at the docks and let them deteriorate. They then put in annual requests for money for repair, operation, and maintenance. The money was saved, and as soon as it amounted to enough a new ship was bought and given the same name as the old ship. In some cases, to add verisimilitude, large sections of the old ship were salvaged and used in the construction of the new ship. In other cases not even this was done.)

first method. The second looks as if it is an expansion of the force and the first one does not. Insofar as pure expansion (buying more planes) is concerned, it will be disguised. For example, one can shift training and maintenance away from the wing's organization, requiring the Air Training Command and maybe the Air Material Command to buy more planes.

Similar problems exist in the Army and Navy. For example, if one had the choice of increasing the number of divisions or ships or of increasing the amount of equipment per division or ship, both ways might end up with roughly the same effective force—but the second way is much more palatable. Or one can replace an obsolete ship with a much more expensive and capable modern ship.

The concept of a "fixed budget" approach deserves some discussion. In this approach it is assumed that one has a fixed sum of money to allocate and asks, What is the preferred method of allocating this money among the various components of the system under study? Perfect freedom (fungibility) in allocating dollars is assumed, and the final allocation is chosen either to maximize the over-all performance of the system or to match a range of contingencies. If one wishes to get the most value for the money, this approach is appropriate. Unfortunately, the approximation of fungible dollars is not a good one. For example, it is easier in peacetime to get money for procurement of equipment than of people. For some reason the civilian decision makers—both legislative and executive—do not seem to object to spending large sums of money for the best equipment possible, but they often object to spending money for the best people, probably because the second option is much more subject to bureaucratic judgment and hence to bureaucratic abuse. Therefore, it can be easier to sell a program that involves obtaining good equipment than one that involves obtaining good people.

The military construction budget is another example of especially "expensive" dollars. It is separately presented to Congress and involves much more political byplay and examination than the other parts of the defense budget. This occurs, among other reasons, because most Congressmen feel quite competent on details of construction and the politics of base location, while they feel very dubious about their competence in fields of electronics, radar, high-speed aeronautics, and so on. This makes the military department much

341

more cautious when asking for money for construction of new facilities—overly cautious, in my opinion. Finally, and most important, the fixed budget approach ignores both inter- and intra-service rivalries. Nevertheless, with all its faults, the fixed budget approach, with its assumption of fungible dollars, is, in a real sense, the only workable approach. While recommendations may have to be modified to take account of the non-fungibility of dollars, it is well to have the idealistic study first to provide a guide to use in judging the compromises.

In a more slowly moving world, the political constraints would not be very serious. When they want to be, bureaucrats are very skillful in dealing with them and can generally do so without making disastrous compromises that affect either the costs or performance of the system, though it may do horrendous things to the logic and language of the justifying arguments. However, the use of misleading and unclear language may be disastrous in a rapidly changing situation where it is necessary to discuss the issues in a reasonably relevant and accurate manner. For example, it would be difficult to debate the merits of aircraft carriers *vs.* battleships if one were not willing to concede that one wanted to or was building new ships. It may just be that we cannot afford the luxury in the future of pampering, to the same extent as in the past, irrational attitudes and positions. The deliberate fostering of a lack of clarity on what we are trying to do could be disastrous.

There is one important caveat about fixed budget studies. The scope of the study in which the monetary trades are worked out is usually so narrow that the trades that are analyzed are not directly applicable to the decision maker's problem. For example, imagine that one were studying how to improve the operation of an authorized B-52 force of, say, 14 wings. When using the fixed budget approach, one might then find out that by reducing the number of wings to 12 and spending more money on reliable Command and Control the over-all performance of the system would be improved. In presenting the results of such a study it would be very important not to make the mistake of saying that the study indicated that the force should be reduced to 12 wings. All that the study really indicated would be that better Command and Control is so desirable that even if the Air Force finds it necessary to reduce the number of B-52's to get the funds for this additional Command and Control, it is still worth doing. In actual practice it is quite likely that the

Air Force or the Executive Office will prefer to get the funds by cutting another program rather than the authorized number of wings. I have found in practice that very few analysts or their clients really understand this point. It is that the fixed budget study does not usually attack the problem of *where* to get the money but only shows some restricted "trades" that may or may not be directly applicable to policy.

A rather amusing case of using language to confuse occurred in the early days of the postwar atomic energy program. A certain reactor was being built that could be used for many different purposes, and as each annual budget came around the name of the reactor was changed in order to emphasize the particular purpose which was most romantic that year.

While this is an almost harmless example of playing politics, it is easy to imagine cases where playing such games could cause serious trouble. We live in a democracy. One of the characteristic weaknesses of democracy is an inability to carry out complicated long-term programs in a steadfast and competent way. In Appendix II, I have some suggestions for improving long-term policy planning on the Executive side. We are going to need corresponding improvements on the Legislative and public opinion sides. One way to do this is to make a serious attempt to lift the level of discussion. I believe it can be done, but only if there is on one hand some self-restraint on the part of those who are trying to facilitate a program by the adept use of language and, on the other hand, much more savage criticism and punishment for those who are caught confusing or oversimplifying issues when it is inappropriate. The cure will not and cannot be complete. There is a serious and only partially reconcilable conflict between the "politician" and the "educator." There are many occasions when the first is trying to diffuse issues to get a more flexible system in the sense of contingency analysis and so that diverse groups will find it possible to support him, as discussed on pages 122 to 124 of Lecture II. On these same occasions the second may be trying to make the issue sharper so that people will understand intellectually what the choices are. It is clear that both things have to be done; often the only question is emphasis, timing, and place. With care it is not difficult or unethical for responsible people to practice this form of double-think without doing any harm.

Another reason why we "may not care" is that our point of view may be different from that of the person doing the analysis. Often this means that we believe that the analyst has asked the wrong question, but we cannot officially or openly admit this objection, so all we do is ignore his argument. A spectacular example of this has been the government's position on stockpiling strategic war materials and war reserve machine tools. It was the official theory of the government that war would be initiated by an exchange of thermonuclear bombs and that we should then be prepared to fight a war of attrition lasting three years or so. In preparation for this war we stockpiled $11 billion worth of war reserve tools and strategic war materials. Almost all of this was done since Korea. Many people think of this program as a disguised subsidy, to lead and zinc producers, for example. On the whole this is not true, since most of the stockpile was bought from foreign sources and was bought during a period of scarcities and inflation. *It was in no sense initiated as a subsidy.*

I suppose I should point out that this long-war concept, which presumably would involve sending millions of soldiers to Europe, was shared by the Russians, who seem to have built hundreds of submarines to stop these soldiers and an air offense and defense designed to fight World War II in Europe and Asia. Actually, these long-war ideas might have made sense in the very early 50's, but at the height of the program, in the mid-50's, they had already become obsolete. This is not to say that we may not have to fight a rather large conventional European war, much like World War II, but only that we will not fight such a war immediately after a World War III fought with thermonuclear bombs. If we happen to get into a large conventional war, then at least some of the Russian preparations for a long war make complete sense. Ours probably make less—at least if one believes in fungible dollars. While these stockpiles could certainly be valuable in case of a long conventional war, there are other ways of spending the money, which, most analysts are agreed, would be a great deal more valuable if we are worrying about a large conventional war.

If some analyst had come up with a study which showed that under the going concept of an exchange of thermonuclear bombs followed by a long conventional war we did not have enough 2-inch screws or ½ horsepower motors, or something of that kind, nobody would have taken him seriously. Most decision makers were really quite clear in the middle 1950's that this concept either did not make sense or was a much lower priority objective than many other objectives that were not being satisfied. While they did not have the courage or influence to cut back the going program, they were certainly not willing to increase it, no matter what weaknesses were found in it.

To some extent the same situation seems to be true of air defense. One way not to make a reputation as an analyst in the last five or ten years would have been to find a hole in our air defense system. As I pointed out in Lecture I, people mostly think of it as being full of holes. For that reason it was often very difficult to get people excited over any *particular* hole. I once had occasion to make a series of recommendations in the air defense field. While the recommendations themselves were simple and could have been explained in fifteen minutes or so, I found that in order to make the recommendations sound convincing, it was necessary to precede them with a two-hour briefing which attempted to show that there is a reasonable and *practical* mission for active air defense of people and property, one which air defense could perform if this particular hole were fixed. Only after that was done were we able to get more than just a *pro forma* agreement—more than the kind of agreement which says, "You certainly are right but nobody here is going to do anything about it."

Probably the most important way in which a "don't care" attitude arises is when the "don't carer" does not care because he exalts a single overriding objective or circumstance over all the competition so that other objectives or circumstances seem unreal or unimportant. Sometimes this occurs because the people involved are too strongly partisan to a single service, sometimes because they are simply fanatics, and sometimes because they have some good or bad reason for believing that their pet project is so neglected and underfinanced that getting funds or support for it is of such overriding importance that it is proper, temporarily at least, to sacrifice all else for this objective.

The same kind of partisanship occurs outside the services in the normal political arena. I have tried to emphasize that we will probably have to concentrate on five major issues if we are to solve our security problems for the next ten to fifteen years. These by now familiar problems are listed in Table 56.

345

Typically, those individuals both in and out of government, who are deeply concerned about the way things are drifting, wish to concentrate on only one of those problems—usually, numbers I (in the form of Finite Deterrent postures), III (in the form of limited war capabilities) and V (in the form of proposals for universal disarmament and world states), and as a result refuse to be interested in any of the other problems or even more complex approaches to their favorite problems. I do not believe it is possible to devise a

❖❖❖

TABLE 56
THE PROBLEM OF SECURITY

I. *High-quality Type I Deterrent Forces.*

II. *Ability to fight and survive wars*—perhaps with special emphasis on controlled, accidental, and Type II Deterrence wars.

III. Increase in our *ability to handle limited provocations,* threats, and ordinary disagreements, by both military and nonmilitary means.

IV. *Short-term nonmilitary arrangements* and arms control agreements to increase the current stability of the international system and to prevent undesirable long-term developments.

V. *Long-term programs* to encourage permanent and stable solutions to the Security problem.

❖❖❖

satisfactory security system without using mutually supporting and integrated measures in all five areas, and it is most important that those who are most deeply concerned should also take a broad viewpoint.

I believe that events are moving so fast that it will be impossible for us to devise satisfactory over-all and interacting systems by the normal process of political give-and-take. The people who are formulating narrow programs for specific situations must, themselves, take a responsible interest in all five of the problems and contribute to the joint designs. Naturally, we will still have the normal process of political give-and-take in order to decide upon the proper emphasis, but we should not depend completely on the political process to design balanced alternative programs.

People May Not Care Simply Because They Do Not Care

There are occasionally individuals in responsible jobs who are phlegmatic to the point of irresponsibility. They are not going to be concerned—no matter how convincing the argument for being concerned—if being concerned implies exertion or bureaucratic risk-taking. Unless or until there is a clear and present crisis which cannot be banished by any degree of wishful thinking or distortion of the facts, they refuse to take any unaccustomed problems seriously. One argument that sometimes works with such individuals is to point out that bureaucratically or politically speaking, apathy may eventually prove even more risky than action. The following (paraphrased) quotations are typical of the bureaucrat or decision maker who simply cannot imagine that his safe, snug world can really be dangerous. (The quotations are not exclusive. The determined do-nothing advocate will go through each in turn.)

1. The problem is *hypothetical*. You cannot *prove* it exists. There is no need to get *hysterical*.
2. The problem is there, but there are many other problems. In your *parochialism* and *naïveté*, you have gotten hysterical. We have known about the problem for some time and we are not excited. Why are you?
3. The problem is there. It is insoluble. (Or, it is too late to do anything.) For God's sake don't rock the (political or public relations) boat.

The key words in the above are *hypothetical, parochial, naïve,* and *hysterical.* That is, any specialist who raises a problem in his specialty is accused of being hypothetical and parochial, of not taking a practical over-all view. This is often true, but in the overwhelming majority of cases his detractor has not taken an over-all view either and is being equally parochial in not being able to visualize the possibilities.

To the sober (but irresponsible) bureaucrat, any problem that cannot be proved to exist by objective scientific verification or by legal rules of evidence is "hypothetical." In fact, the attitude is sometimes worse than this. I can remember an occasion when I was discussing with one of these critics what seemed to me like a problem approaching potentially crisis proportions. He insisted that I was comparing hypothetical Soviet programs with hard American programs. I pointed out with some asperity that the Soviets up to that time had refused to allow our staff access to their records; naturally we would have some trouble proving that these programs existed and would actually meet the hypothetical dates. On the other hand, our staff did have access to U.S. data, so it was easy to show that our counter programs were not as firm as advertised. They were very likely to have some disastrous slippages. These slippages were so likely that the announced dates really should not even be dignified by the adjective "hypothetical." Of course, similar slippages might develop in the Soviet program, but since the slippages were avoidable if appropriate advance action should be taken, it was *possible* that the Soviet programs would not slip. Given the inadequate support of our counter program, even bearing in mind possible Soviet red tape and inefficiency, it would at best be a medium confidence measure in meeting the new threat. And even a mildly skeptical person might judge it to be only a low confidence measure.

A typical hypothetical possibility is illustrated by the ominous possibilities for Hitler-type blackmail tactics created by the waning of our Type II and Type III Deterrence capability. There is a great deal of worry today that the Russians may make impressive gains utilizing only "ambiguous challenges," without presenting us with any direct challenges. This may be so, but if the thermonuclear stalemate (in the sense of inevitable mutual homicide) actually exists and we do nothing about it, we might be in a much worse position. Once the facts are brought home to all, there would be almost no necessity for the Russians to restrict their behavior to the "ambiguous challenges." Their success to date in using "ambiguous challenges" should be nothing to what they could do if they could afford and desired to be unambiguous.

There is an important psychological difference between the post-sputnik and pre-sputnik eras. Previously, the Russians felt like the underdog and, being a sensible underdog, they refrained from extreme tactics involving either risk-taking or provocations. Today they no longer feel the restraining influence of overwhelming American military superiority because it does not exist. Weaknesses or mistakes in our posture which would not have been important in the fifties (because the Soviets would have been too cautious to exploit them) may be disastrous in the sixties. I think we can expect much firmer, confident, and imaginative behavior, if not audacious and reckless conduct, from Khrushchev and his successors than we had from Stalin. This assumes that some situations arise in the next ten years or so which make such behavior profitable. I am not predicting an inevitable war of nerves or a Pearl Harbor attack. I am only pointing out that we cannot prepare for such eventualities at the last moment. Therefore, we should not only be preparing for such possibilities but we should also be trying to discourage the Soviets from acquiring the habit of thinking in these terms. We should not even look so vulnerable as to encourage Soviet speculations on the gains to be realized by this type of behavior. This is not a day-by-day problem or one to be solved by better public relations. We cannot make the necessary physical preparations overnight. We cannot even easily close doors which should have never been opened. We must take seriously the hypothetical possibility of either direct attack or extreme provocation, with or without sophisticated and subtle tactics, long before the challenge materializes.

It seems to me all too possible that at some future date we will be listening to some indignant bureaucrat saying one or more of the following:

1. We were not attacked. (Or: The alliance was not challenged.) Why were we bothered with such groundless worries?
2. Some more years later (1961?): We were attacked! (Or challenged.) Successfully! How could anyone have believed that such an obvious façade would fool the enemy?

We must also, of course, take seriously the hypothetical danger of war by accident or miscalculation or we will find someone saying:

Who really believed that one could have thousands of weapons on alert and not have a button pressed? How could people have lived so dangerously and not have been worried to death? How could they have slept with the knowledge that the other side had a missile aimed at their city and ready to go? [7]

[7] There is an uncomfortable similarity between Damocles, who had everything but security, and the West today. The major difference is that Damocles could see the sword that threatened him and the thin thread that restrained it, while today both sword and thread seem unreal to all too many.

CHAPTER VIII

THE REAL PAST

World War I—The War Itself

LET us now consider World War I. The last previous "world" war had been the series of wars that followed the French revolution of 1789, which, developing into the Napoleonic wars, were not terminated until 1815. It was not believed by most military experts at the time of World War I that this long war of attrition and relatively unlimited objectives was going to be the model for a future conflict. Most experts argued that the Austro-Prussian war (seven weeks) or the first phase (five weeks) of the Franco-Prussian war would be the model of the future. The feeling was that the objective of war was to improve one's position and that both sides would pursue the objective conservatively, trying to limit the risks that they would take; that as soon as one side had been beaten in a significant battle, it would admit its defeat. It was also assumed that the victor would make some reasonable peace offer, this being one of the main reasons why the loser would be willing to concede defeat. In particular, both the military and political lessons of the American Civil War were ignored—the military lessons because it seemed like an out of the way war in a semicivilized nation; the most important political lesson, that in a democratic age war was likely to be so intense as to prevent rational calculations of risk *vs.* gain, was also ignored because the Civil War, being a *civil* war, did not seem to be a good analogy to an international conflict waged between civilized nations.

In addition, most people were very impressed with the volume and importance of foreign trade, and argued that the economic interdependence of nations was so great that the sheer interruption of normal commerce would cause a collapse after a few weeks or months in much the same way that people argue today that if the A country (big cities) is destroyed, the B country (small cities, rural areas) must also necessarily collapse. Therefore, almost everybody expected the war of 1914 to be short, particularly the Germans, who had the famous Schlieffen Plan that called for them to destroy the French army in about six weeks, then move their army to the Russian front and destroy the Russians in the next few weeks

350

or months. The French also expected the war to be short, only they expected the victory to be on their side. Both sides enormously underestimated the impact of the machine gun, barbed wire, and trenches, and most important of all, the resilience and staying-power of their soldiers and civilians, and the economic and political necessity in a relatively democratic age to paint the enemy as inhuman and of making a total commitment to defeating him—a necessity deriving both from the need to justify past casualties and sacrifices and to preserve morale for future efforts. There had been clues as to the effectiveness of both the new devices and the capacity of the new societies in the American Civil War, clues which had been noticed by at least one writer, a Polish banker Jean de Bloch, who, however, seemed to have had no impact on either preparations or calculations, even though he was reasonably widely read.

As a matter of fact, the Germans did come very close to meeting their schedule, but once they failed to meet it the war degenerated into a battle of position in which much of the training and doctrine that the military had received proved to be irrelevant. In particular, the mystique of the offensive and "the will to conquer" proved to be tragically misleading. Military leaders on both sides were quite upset by the development of "the war of position" and did everything they could to eliminate it. But mostly they thought they could solve their problems by the use of the traditional tactics and tools —that is, they thought of more and better frontal attacks, more and better artillery barrages, strike, counter-strike, and quick decision —those were the traditional weapons. Their minds did not turn to the development of new techniques and equipment to meet the problem. The philosophy of the mid-twentieth century that seeks a solution to problems in technology and invention did not fully develop until World War II. (I will later make some comments to the effect that it has probably been overdeveloped.)

However, on both sides there were a few individuals who saw that one way to break the stalemate might be by an appeal to technology. On the Allied side the most outstanding innovation was the *tank*. Many readers are familiar with the fact that gaining acceptance for the tank was an uphill fight almost all the way. There was apathy, skepticism, and opposition. The project would almost undoubtedly have been cancelled if it had not gotten support in the Admiralty under Churchill. The navy saved the day for the army (a typical example of the value of inter-service competition). Perhaps not surprisingly, the people who developed the tank had better ideas of how to use it than the operators, at least for the first year or so. The developers urged that the initial impact and surprise should be maximized—that the tanks should not be used at all until an inventory had been built up, all operational problems had been worked out, and there were sufficient reserves of both tanks and infantry to exploit any breakthrough. In this way, they argued, the initial use of the tanks could be exploited to the maximum—possibly even leading to a strategic decision right then and there. They also urged that there be no preparatory artillery barrages before the tanks were put into battle, because the bombardments would chew up the ground and make it hard for the primitive tanks to move around. It would also alert the enemy and give him the opportunity to build up reserves. (The purpose of the bombardments, of course, was to eliminate the barbed wire and the machine gun nests, and kill or stun the soldiers in the opposing trenches. Since the tank did not need such preparations, it was presumably a mistake to accept the disadvantages associated with them.)

The first use of tanks in September 1916 completely ignored the tactical and strategical ideas of the innovators and was carried out as a sort of field trial. It was a complete success as a field test of the ability of the new weapon to go through barbed wire in the face of machine gun fire, but this lesson was learned at the cost of both alerting the Germans and losing valuable time. In fact, it was not until the battle of Cambrai, more than a year later and almost two years after the originators of the tank had worked out detailed tactics, that their ideas were put into practice. The operation was a huge success for both the tanks and the conceptions. It was not until the end of the war that General J. C. Fuller and Captain Liddell Hart had worked out the modern use of tanks—a mechanized substitute for cavalry that would stab through the enemy lines and range through his rear area, destroying his supplies, communications, and leadership, and in other ways creating panic and havoc. They also suggested the use of airplanes to protect the flanks of the probing tank columns. The British made plans in the last year of the war to use tanks and planes in exactly this way. Those plans probably would have been put into operation if the war had continued another six months. Colonel William "Billy" Mitchell of the American Air Force had some similar ideas for the use of airplanes to interdict and to carry paratroopers—ideas that also got very close to the stage of execution. Of course, between the wars the British, French, and Americans promptly forgot all about the new ideas, and, as always, it was the defeated who learned best the lessons of war.

The German *poison gas* story has some interesting analogies with the British tank story. This too had an uphill fight with the authorities. Again, even after the weapon had been developed the command did not wish to take the risk of using the untried weapon on a large scale, though the inventors urged it, until the military had developed some experience on the capabilities and limitations of gas warfare. It was first tried at Ypres on April 22, 1915 and proved a tremendous tactical success. In fact, a five-mile gap was opened in the Allied lines, but the Germans were not prepared to exploit the opportunity. They were not really making an attack, they were just trying an experiment.

The British reaction to the use of poison gas by the Germans was very fast. About the end of March 1915 when rumors persisted that the Germans would use poison gases, the British War Office tried to ascertain both what gases might be used and the best means of protection. Then the German gas attack of April 22 was made. Within a day Sir William Ramsay had guessed from the description of the battle reports that chlorine had been used and came to the War Office with a protective measure, some sample mouth-pads made of flannel or wool soaked in hyposulphite of soda. British women were asked to furnish 1,000,000 at once. Thanks to their help and Red Cross efforts the necessary quantity came in several days. Within a fortnight every man in the British army at the front was supplied with a rudimentary respirator. Fast as the reaction was, it would be too slow in a modern war, one in which the decisive events are likely to be over in the first day if not the first minutes. It might even have been too late in World War I if the Germans had been prepared to exploit their new weapon.

One can only sympathize with the Allied and German high commands for wishing to test the new devices and learn about their capabilities and limitations and unsuspected weaknesses before they gambled large resources that they would work successfully. History is filled with examples of impractical notions or, equally important, notions that proved to be just fine but which were tested prematurely. (The trouble with going whole hog on a new idea in the 1960's is that when you make a mistake it is not a $10 to $100 million mistake but a $1 to $10 billion one, and there are so many more ways to making mistakes than of being right.)

Unfortunately for those who would urge caution, it is clear that the early and presumably decisive phases of the next war will not allow much time for learning. This automatically means that if we want to be decisive we must be willing to run the risk of letting our mistakes be very large ones rather than just minor fiascoes. This problem becomes even more acute if we are trying to run a technological race.

Table 57 below lists some of the technological innovations of World War I. Some of them (machine gun, trench warfare, and infiltration tactics) had seen use before, but even these had a special impact in World War I.

❖❖❖

TABLE 57
SOME WORLD WAR I INNOVATIONS

1. Machine gun	6. Antisubmarine warfare
2. Trench warfare	7. Big Bertha
3. Tank	8. Airplanes
4. Poison gas and smoke	9. Infiltration tactics
5. Submarines	

❖❖❖

The most spectacular military event of World War I, the development of two parallel lines of trenches from the Swiss frontier to the English Channel, while predicted by Bloch, came as a complete surprise. In place of the "war of movement," the "superiority of the offense," and the "decisive battle," the largest armies yet seen peered at each other through screens of metal. It took four full years to find some way out of the resulting impasse. In retrospect—particularly given the examples of such warfare in the American Civil War and the Sino-Japanese War—it is hard to see how military experts could have overlooked the possibility that the widespread availability of machine guns and barbed wire might result in static trench warfare, but the military planners on both sides completely overlooked the possibility.

In addition to the machine gun, trench warfare and gas, I have listed submarines, Big Berthas, and airplanes as some of the World War I innovations. The prewar German submarine was somewhere between a mistake and a success. The submarine turned out (un-expectedly) to be most useful as a weapon of economic attrition. Economic attrition is useful only when a war is long. If the original estimates of both sides for a short war had been correct, it would have been a mistake for the Germans to put a large investment into submarine warfare. As it turned out, the mistake was the other way— in fact, they came close to winning with the inadequate investment they made.

The battle between measure and countermeasure in the anti-submarine warfare of World War I illustrates in a small way what was to become *a* major theme of World War II and *the* major theme of the post World War II period. Nobody at the start of the war was too sure of the role of submarines in naval warfare. The Germans had been the last of the great powers to acquire submarines, and they were even more doubtful than the others of their value. However, at the outset of the war, on September 5, one German submarine (the U-21) sank a British cruiser, and on September 22 the same submarine sank three battle cruisers. The British fleet at that point almost panicked, and the submarine was suddenly recognized as one of the potentially decisive weapons of naval warfare.

As it turned out, the impressive beginning turned out to be misleading. The submarine was only moderately effective against armed, alert naval vessels or properly protected fleet formations. Its real success came as a menace to commerce. At the peak of effectiveness the Germans had only about 110 U-boats, but this handful of vessels managed to sink one out of every four ships that left port.

It is interesting to note that in terms of matching submarine against submarine the British had no research and development or procurement gap; that is, their submarines were qualitatively better than those of the Germans, and it was not until late in the war that the Germans had more submarines. However, almost from the beginning of the war they had an operational gap; the German submarine presented the British with a problem they could not handle.

The passive defenses developed for use against the submarine included booms, nets, minefields, and camouflage. The active defenses included ruses to lure the submarine to expose itself, destruction by gunfire, and the hunting down of the submarine and its subsequent ramming with explosives. *Almost all the devices and tactics used were worked out under the stimulating effect of actual experience after the war started, most of them after the first year of the war.*

Of all the devices, the depth charge was the most successful, and it was not developed until the second year of the war. It was not until 1916 that efficient depth charges were available, and these were so scarce that they could not be used except under the most advantageous circumstances. It was not until 1918 that they were available for routine use against fleeting and ambiguous targets.

The next two items on the list of World War I innovations—the *big cannon* and the *airplane*—could not have been decisive weapons in that war. It would therefore have been a mistake if either side had directed resources from higher priority tasks into producing these devices on a mass basis, at least until the weapons improved somewhat, as they did about 1918.

It is interesting to note that there were other ways to break the deadlock caused by trenches and machine gun than inventions and technology. Ludendorff introduced a new type of infiltration tactic in 1917, which, combined with the classical principle of surprise, proved successful in the 1918 offensive in penetrating the Allied lines. The new tactic came close to winning the war for the Germans; they were just too late in introducing it; by 1918 they lacked the resources to exploit the new tactic against the reinforced Allies.

In comparison with the old tactic of advancing in a straight line, the new tactic called for specially trained, heavily armed, picked troops to probe for weak spots in the enemy's line and to push through these weak spots. This did have the danger that the attacker had exposed flanks which might be pinched off by the defender, but it was assumed, and correctly, that in the confusion of the attack the defender would generally not be able to exploit this weakness of the attacker; that before the defender could organize a counterattack and cut off the penetrating troops, they would have had time to fan out and attack the bypassed troops from the rear. Since the new tactic was not so dependent on a lengthy preliminary artillery barrage it allowed the Germans to use surprise attack tactics. The Germans also developed the counter to this attack, which was to organize a defense in depth, a defense that did not care if it was penetrated.

The new tactic was not invented by the Germans. A French officer, a Captain Laffargue, had found out experimentally the value of the new tactic and had written a remarkably complete pamphlet on the new ideas. His ideas had no effect on the French or English, but a copy fell into the hands of the Germans, and according to Captain G. C. Wynne it was:

". . . the concise expression of a doctrine which exactly corresponded to the course they themselves had been trying to follow by cumbersome and slow degrees. The pamphlet was at once translated into German and issued as an official German training manual, eventually becoming the basis of General Ludendorff's textbook for 'the attack in position warfare.' It was with an elaboration of Captain Laffargue's doctrine of infiltration that the Germans so effectively broke through the British position in March 1918, and the Chemin des Dames position in May; and his ideas have remained the foundation of the German training manual for attack to this day."

The idea of appealing to new tactics, strategies, or objectives *in addition to technology* for solutions to difficult military problems has obvious relevance today, as I tried to point out in the first and second lectures. We seemed to have been so bemused with the spectacular successes of technology that we rarely ask ourselves searching questions about what we are trying to do with these new gadgets and how we should do it.

How World War I Started

The most interesting thing about World War I in addition to its technology and tactics is the prewar situation, the manner in which the war got started. The last really big European war had ended in 1815 with the defeat of Napoleon. The last moderately large war in Europe, the Franco-Prussian, had terminated in 1871. The next forty-three years, until 1914, were for the European continent years of almost complete peace, marred only by small wars between relatively unimportant Balkan nations and a relatively innocuous war between the Russians and the Turks in 1877. That is, Europe had had about a century of relative peace and almost half a century of almost complete peace. The thought of war had grown unreal to the governments involved. They got used to making threats to go to war, either directly or by implication, and they even got used to getting their way when they made these threats strong enough. There were a number of crises which made newspaper headlines and scared both governments and people, but after a while even these became unreal and the armies were thought of more as pieces in a game played by diplomats (called "let's find a formula") than as tools to be used. Even though the two sides snarled ferociously at each other, one side was always expected to give way graciously, or ungraciously, before it came to a trial of arms. Both consciously and unconsciously, all the top decision makers were afraid of being involved in a large war. In spite of the optimistic calculations of some of the military, there was a feeling in all the governments that the war would be big and that it was too risky an activity to engage in unless the odds were overwhelmingly in one's favor, and none of the nations felt the odds were sufficiently high in 1914. Therefore, *just because neither side really wanted war, one side or the other would presumably withdraw before things got out of hand.*

As far as I know, just about all modern historians agree on this thesis—that none of the top statesmen or the rulers and very few, if any, of the soldiers wanted a world war in 1914 (though some wanted a war somewhat later, after certain preparations had been made), and only the Serbs and the Austrians wanted even a small war. And yet war came. How did it happen?

The British historian A. J. P. Taylor described the prewar situation in an article in *The Observer*.

July, 1914, has produced more books than any other month in modern history. Yet, to adapt a sentence from Sir Lewis Namier in a different context: there would not be a great deal to say on this subject were it not for the nonsense that has been written about it.

Most of the nonsense has sprung from the very human conviction that great events have great causes. The First World War was certainly a great event. Therefore great causes have had to be found for it . . .

The truth is that the statesmen of Europe behaved in July, 1914, just as they had behaved for the preceding thirty years, neither better nor worse. The techniques and systems which had given Europe a generation of peace now plunged her into war . . .

The statesmen of Europe with one accord accepted the theory of "the deterrent": the more strongly and firmly they threatened, the more likely they were both to preserve the peace of Europe and get their way. . . .

. . . the German rulers were firmly wedded to the theory of the deterrent. A resolve to go to war, loudly proclaimed; and the other side would give way. In Jagow's words: 'The more boldness Austria displays, the more strongly we support her, the more likely Russia is to keep quiet.' Those who condemn the German policy should reflect that Sir Edward Grey did the opposite from the Germans: he failed to make his position clear in advance. And for this he has often been saddled with responsibility for the war. . . .

The amateur strategist, devising actions without inquiring whether they were technically possible, was a recurring theme in July 1914. . . .

It was no doubt the penalty for forty years of peace, years in which armies and campaigns had been weapons of diplomacy, not of war.

The most striking feature of the July crisis was the total lack of contact in every country between the political and military leaders. Military plans were at their most rigid in the railway age; yet no statesman had the slightest idea what the timetables involved. Their sensations, when diplomacy collapsed, were those of a train passenger who sees the express thundering through the station at which he intended to alight.[1]

As Taylor says, World War I was a railroad war. It was a war for which the general staffs of the four great continental powers had spent decades planning meticulous timetables. The war plans were literally cast in concrete in the sense that governments built railroads according to the requirements of the war plan. One could look at a nation's railroads and get a very accurate idea of what its war plans were. All nations except Britain had very large numbers of trained reserves available that were quite different from the kind of manpower we refer to as reserves today; the 1914 conscripts were prepared to be mobilized into fighting armies. As soon as they were called to the colors, most of them could march into battle on an equal footing with the best professional troops available. This ability to increase one's force by a large factor and in a very short period of time gave a disastrous instability to the situation, because it promised to give the nation that mobilized first a crucial advantage.

As General Boisdeffre, the assistant chief of the French General Staff explained to Tsar Nicholas:

The mobilization is the declaration of war. To mobilize is to oblige one's neighbor to do the same. . . . Otherwise, to leave a million men on one's frontier, without doing the same simultaneously, is to deprive oneself of all possibility of moving later; it is placing oneself in a situation of an individual who, with a pistol in his pocket, should let his neighbor put a weapon to his forehead without drawing his own.[2]

While the Tsar answered that that was his understanding also, his general staff in 1912 decided that the belief that "the proclamation of mobilization is equivalent to the declaration of war," had serious disadvantages for the Russians, since it took them so long to mobilize. Therefore, they formally annulled the rule and instructed the Foreign Office, "It will be advantageous to complete concentra-

[1] *The Observer* (London), November 23, 1958.
[2] Sidney B. Fay, *The Origins of the World War*, New York, Macmillan, 1931, Vol. II, p. 480. Copyright 1928 and 1930 by The Macmillan Company and used with their permission.

tion without beginning hostilities, in order not to deprive the enemy irrevocably of the hope that war can still be avoided. Our measures for this must be masked by clever diplomatic negotiations, in order to lull to sleep as much as possible the enemy's fears." [3]

While the above is a perfectly reasonable "military requirement," since it is very valuable to be able to steal a march on the enemy, it is not a reasonable diplomatic requirement. The Foreign Office felt that the enemy was just not going to be fooled by soothing words while the Russians prepared to draw (rather noisily) their pistols. As a matter of fact the Russian Foreign Office was wrong; they did succeed, in the crisis of July 1914, in holding off a German mobilization for about a week while the Russians went through preparatory moves. They did this not by being superlatively clever, but by not knowing themselves what they really intended to do and managing to transmit this confusion to the Germans. The Germans had not prepared any temporizing measures; unlike the other nations they had no plans to mobilize and then hold, but only plans to mobilize and attack. From the precrisis viewpoint of the German General Staff this was not a serious disadvantage, since they felt that it would be a military disaster to hold off and let the Russians complete their mobilization; but in the event itself, the government could not make the decision for war. As long as the situation was ambiguous, it was not willing to make an irrevocable step, and no temporizing measures had been prepared, so the German government did nothing while its enemies stole a march on it. As we know, when war finally came the Germans were not able to meet their schedule, but it is possible that if they had not allowed the Russians to steal this march, they might have met the original timetable and won World War I according to plan. The trouble was that the Russians attacked East Prussia in the second week of the war in such strength that Von Moltke got frightened and detached two army corps from the crucial right wing of the German offensive against the French and sent them East to reinforce the German army in Prussia. It is widely believed that if he had not done this the Germans might have won the battle of the Marne and defeated France, though it is clear that troop fatigue, logistic problems, and possibly some poor tactical decisions played an important role. The final irony occurred when the Germans succeeded in defeating the Russian attack before the two army corps reached the Eastern front.

Fay describes the indecisiveness of the Germans:

[3] *Ibid.*, p. 308.

There was thus the danger that the Russian military authorities would take such wide-reaching preparatory measures that Germany would become alarmed and resort to countermeasures, which in turn would lead to a general European war. The German Foreign Office in fact received, as the Kautsky Documents show, between the morning of July 26 and the evening of July 30 twenty-eight reports of Russian military preparations no less than sixteen of which related to the Russian frontier against Germany; and the German General Staff and Navy Department received many more such reports. But in spite of this, Germany refrained from corresponding preparatory measures until she received on July 31 official news that Russia had taken the final military step of openly announcing by placards throughout the streets of St. Petersburg a general mobilization of the whole Russian army and navy. These secret "preparatory measures," which had been decided on at the Ministerial Council on the afternoon of the 25th, and ordered before dawn of the 26th, enabled Russia, when war came to surprise the world by the rapidity with which she poured her troops into East Prussia and Galicia.[4]

Fay also gives some interesting quotations from Von Moltke on how reluctant he was to react to the Russian mobilization.[5]

Though he had two reliable reports concerning Russian general mobilization, Moltke added: "Before advising His Majesty to mobilize, I wish to await a third confirmation of the news about Russian mobilization."

About 7 A.M., July 31, Moltke received a telephone message from a Staff Officer at Allenstein in East Prussia, stating that the frontier had been completely closed by the Russians and that the red placards ordering mobilization had already been posted up. Moltke replied: "It is necessary that you procure one of these posted orders. I must have certainty as to whether they are really mobilizing against us. Before having that certainty, I am not able to elicit a mobilization order."

Thus, it turned out that the German plan for protecting themselves by quick countermeasures failed. There were many reasons for this failure. We have mentioned the first and most important, the Germans' failure to react quickly. This is, of course, the standard problem in dealing with any situation in which there might be false alarms and in which the reaction to a false alarm is costly. One may be unwilling to react. Countries are usually reluctant to go to war except at a time and manner of their own choosing, and as long as there is any chance of peace they usually feel obligated to discount the signals they are getting; because they do not want to be premature, they accept the risk of giving the enemy precious time until the threat becomes unambiguous.

[4] *Ibid.*, pp. 320–321.
[5] *Ibid.*, p. 513.

A second reason that the timing of the German plan was thrown off was that the Russians turned out to be somewhat better at mobilizing than expected. In addition to mobilizing faster than the experts thought they could, the Russians attacked before being fully prepared. Either out of enlightened self-interest or possibly from loyalty to their alliance they were determined to create a diversion that would help the French, even if it meant attacking prematurely and risking a disaster (which it did). This, too, is a standard problem. Whenever a plan depends on a very precise estimate of either the enemy's capability or his willingness to run risks, it is automatically unreliable.

Like the Germans, the Russians had a rather rigid war plan. All their thinking had been devoted to the problem of how to attack Germany and Austria together, and they had not considered any other kind of large war. In particular, they had made no plans for attacking just Austria-Hungary. The Russian government found, to its surprise and consternation, that it could not even carry out a partial mobilization for the purpose of threatening Austria without threatening the Germans by troop movements on their frontier and at the same time leaving themselves helpless before a German mobilization or attack, because they could not reverse their movements. The rigidities and pressures toward pre-emptive action contained in the Russian and German war plans proved disastrous in the events that followed. In much the same way, careless and rigid plans today by either the Russians or the Americans to use certain kinds of quick reaction as a defense might be disastrous.

Many people realized then that the basic situation was unstable and that a chain of events could erupt into a conflagration, but I think relatively few people took the possibility seriously; that is, few of the decision makers "cared" until events had gone too far. The possibility of war by miscalculation was too hypothetical; the civilians tended to leave such matters to the military and the military tended to take a narrow professional view of the risks. The fact that the hypothetical situation could be predicted made it seem even more impossible that it would happen. People do not deliberately walk off cliffs; they believe that only hidden cliffs are dangerous. Only it did not prove to be really like that.

Having described the qualitative character of the prewar situation, let us now go briefly over the chronological events.

On the 28th of June the Archduke of the Austrian-Hungarian Empire was assassinated. A wave of indignation swept over Europe.

The justifications and enthusiasm exhibited by the Serbian newspapers were very much criticized. However, nobody particularly expected the Austrians to do much about it because Austria was thought to be a decadent or decaying country without either the resources or energy to do anything decisive. But the scoffers had forgotten that only the year before the Austrians, by putting on an unexpected demonstration of decisiveness, had achieved a significant diplomatic victory. Possibly this went to their heads. In any case, the Austrian government finally decided that they had to settle the Serbian situation once and for all, and that the way to do that was to go to war and inflict a total defeat on Serbia. No halfway measures would do.

Even if the rest of Europe had realized Austria's resolve, I do not believe they would have been too worried. This kind of extreme resolution is typical of a weak man or country in the initial phases of a crisis—but who later on is quite willing to back down. In fact it was more than a week before the Austrians really did anything at all, and then all they did was consult with the German Emperor as to his position in the matter. The German Emperor on July 5th gave them the famous "blank check" promising to support them in any action they undertook. This was a purely diplomatic move; he did not expect the Austrians to do anything drastic or dangerous; the main reason for giving them this carte blanche was so that he would not be blamed later for Austrian weakness or indecisiveness.

It still took more than two weeks before the Austrians did anything. On the 23rd they sent an ultimatum to Serbia, an ultimatum which most people thought would be unacceptable. The Serbian government, however, originally seems to have planned to accept the ultimatum but checked with the Russians first. It is believed, but not known for certain, that the Russians told the Serbians to temporize and that if the Austrians proved difficult, the Serbs could depend on Russian support.

The Russians were willing to let Serbia be punished; after all, the Tsar felt a fundamental antipathy to regicides, but they were determined not to let Serbia be destroyed or forced to become an Austrian protectorate. They warned the Austrians of their views on the 24th. On the 25th the Serbians replied to the Austrian ultimatum in an extremely well-drawn document which, while seeming to give in on all of the *legitimate* demands of the Austrians, was in fact, as they knew, not acceptable. The Austrians therefore broke off diplomatic relations. Meanwhile, in the rest of Europe sympathy for the Austrian position evaporated, partly because the lapse of time had cooled the indignation that had been aroused by the assassination of the Archduke, and partly because the seeming conciliatory nature of the Serbian reply had made the Austrians appear unreasonable.

At this point the Russians got worried. They had a Council of War at which the Foreign Minister, Sazonov, asked for the right to order a partial mobilization against Austria in order to be able to threaten that country. While the new Chief of Staff, Ianushkevich, concurred in Sazonov's request, his staff was horrified. They tried, unsuccessfully, to explain to both Sazonov and Ianushkevich, that it would be impossible to mobilize adequately against Austria without allowing troop movements in the Warsaw military district. These troop movements would very likely be taken by the Germans as a mobilization against them, which in turn would touch off a German mobilization and attack. Worse, once the mobilization against Austria was started, it would be impossible to turn it around if the Germans decided to move; this would mean that the Russians would be in the worst possible position for the very war that the partial mobilization quite likely would touch off. Sazonov and Ianuskevich were unconvinced. A compromise was reached in which Sazonov was given the right to call for a partial mobilization against Austria and, in the meantime, the military were to put in measures "preparatory to war."

Meanwhile, the Germans had begun to get worried and started to put pressure on their Austrian allies to moderate their demands. Unfortunately, the degree of pressure that they were willing to exert was very mild because of the previous "blank check." The Germans were in no position to antagonize their only reliable ally by abandoning or even seeming to abandon them.

On the 28th of July the Austrians showed an unexpected determination and declared war on Serbia. This was another purely diplomatic move since it would take until August 15th for the Austrians to finish their mobilization and be in a position to move against the Serbs. The Austrians felt that, tactically, the declaration was a good way to take a firm position. Once they had unequivocally staked their prestige, it would be impossible for their German allies or even their opponents to expect them to back down under any reasonable pressure. In a way, the move was a success, since it had the proper effect on both the British and the Germans, but it was too successful on the Russians. The Germans and British then came up with the so-called "halt in Belgrade" plan, which probably would have satisfied all their "legitimate demands," but the Austrians really wanted to destroy Serbia and nothing short of a German declaration that the Germans would not support them would have dissuaded them from continuing on the course they had started. Such a declaration was very improbable, since at this point, it could easily have wrecked the alliance.

And now some crucial miscalculations were made. The Russians overestimated the Austrian capability to implement their declaration of war; in addition the Russians were not informed of the English and German peacemaking attempts. As a result, they panicked at the Austrian declaration of war. Sazonov wanted to go ahead and order partial mobilization against Austria even though the new chief of staff had finally been persuaded by his aides that such a mobilization would be disastrous, and had withdrawn his support for the plan. At this time, the German ambassador delivered a telegram from his government that was intended to inform the Russians that a partial mobilization against Austria was acceptable but that any mobilization on the German border would be taken as an unfriendly act. Due to a misunderstanding, this was wrongly interpreted as a warning against any kind of mobilization, even one that affected only the Austrian border. At that point Sazonov allowed himself to be persuaded that, since partial mobilization seemed to be as provoking to the Germans as general mobilization, the *safest* choice was general mobilization. Together with the Russian chief of staff they went to see the Tsar and persuaded him to sign the full mobilization papers, partly on the dubious grounds that it was not clear that "mobilization would mean war."

Ludwig Reiners points out that:

When the Czar and his foreign minister made this decision they were acting under the influence of three misconceptions which would not have existed if the European diplomats had done their work somewhat more intelligently. They believed that Austria was on the point of invading Serbia; in reality she would not be ready for two weeks, and there was therefore no need to rush decisions. They believed that Germany would answer partial mobilization with German general mobilization; Bethmann had not made himself clear. And they did not know that Kaiser Wilhelm was acting as peacemaker and had sent his "tangible-pledge" plan to Vienna. . . . Had they been aware of these three facts, they would not have ordered general mobilization.[6]

[6] Ludwig Reiners, *The Lamps Went Out in Europe*, trans. by Richard and Clara Winston, New York, Pantheon, 1955, pp. 136–137.

In commenting on these and other mistakes, Fay points out:

Not only in St. Petersburg, but everywhere in the Foreign Offices of Europe, responsible officials now began to fall under a terrible physical and mental strain of overwork, worry and lack of sleep, whose inevitable psychological consequences are too often overlooked in assessing the blame for the events which followed. But if one is to understand how it was that experienced and trained men occasionally failed to grasp fully the sheaves of telegrams put into their hands at frequent intervals, how their proposals were sometimes confused and misunderstood, how they quickly came to be obsessed with pessimistic fears and suspicions, and how in some cases they finally broke down and wept, one must remember the nerve-racking psychological effects of continued responsibility for the safety of their country and the fate of millions of lives.[7]

By sheer happenstance, before the final orders could be given, the Tsar received a personal telegram from the German Emperor warning him that a Russian mobilization would, in fact, mean war. The Tsar cancelled the order for mobilization. There is an impressive description of the sequence of events in Fay's book.[8] He describes how all the telegraph machines were lined up in the Moscow telegraph office ready to give the orders to mobilize the great Muscovite Empire, when at the last moment the cancellation order came in. The chief of staff is furious at what he considers a dangerous and irresponsible delay. He insists on going back to the Tsar with Sazonov to get the mobilization order reinstated, only this time he will "tear his telephone out and disappear" to prevent another change of mind. They get to see the Tsar and after some heated and emotional discussion he agrees to mobilize, and on the 30th of July the Russian mobilization gets under way.

On the 31st the Germans gave an ultimatum to the Russians, and on August 1st the Germans gave an ultimatum to the French. The French had started their mobilization but, in order to prevent any incidents, had carefully ordered their troops not to get closer than ten miles to the frontier, mostly because such care might make a good impression on their British allies. They were very anxious that, if there was a war, they not look like the aggressors. However, when the Germans asked them what they intended to do if the Germans attacked the Russians, they did not reassure the Germans; they said that they would do what was best for France. This implied that they would support the Russians. If they had tried to assure the Germans

[7] Fay, *Origins of the World War,* Vol. II, pp. 288–289.
[8] *Ibid.,* pp. 455–486.

that they did not intend to go to war, the Germans intended to make another demand: that France give up two of their frontier fortifications as a hostage for their good behavior.

It is not at all clear that it would have done the Germans any good if the French had been willing to stay neutral, for at one point the Kaiser asked Von Moltke, his Minister of War, whether the Germans could mobilize only against the Russians in case the French stayed neutral. Von Moltke is said to have been horrified. Initial deployment in the East had been de-emphasized since 1905, when Schlieffen devised his famous plan. It had not even been discussed or planned for by the general staff since 1911. It would not be possible to rectify the omission by improvisation. He replied to the Kaiser that if the deployment plans were changed, the Kaiser would possess a loose horde of armed men without supplies, rather than an army ready to strike. The Kaiser properly took this as an admission of inefficiency and angrily replied, "Your uncle [the great Von Moltke] would have given me a different answer."

In any case, on August 3rd the Germans declared war on France and delivered an ultimatum to the Belgians concerning free passage. The Belgians refused to allow the German army to march unopposed on their territory, so on the 4th the Germans started an armed invasion of Belgium. Later that day the British declared war on the Germans.

While in retrospect the sequence of events tends to look almost inevitable, they by no means looked so to the British, for example. Churchill discusses the attitude of the British cabinet as follows:

The Cabinet was overwhelmingly pacific. At least three-quarters of its members were determined not to be drawn into a European quarrel, unless Great Britain were herself attacked, which was not likely. Those who were in this mood were inclined to believe first of all that Austria and Serbia would not come to blows; secondly, if they did, Russia would not intervene, thirdly, if Russia intervened, that Germany would not strike; fourthly, they hoped that if Germany struck at Russia, it ought to be possible for France and Germany mutually to neutralize each other without fighting. They did not believe that if Germany attacked France, she would attack her through Belgium or that if she did the Belgians would forcibly resist; and it must be remembered, that during the whole course of this week Belgium not only never asked for assistance from the guaranteeing Powers but pointedly indicated that she wished to be left alone. So here were six or seven positions, all of which would be wrangled over and about none of which any final proof could be offered except the proof of events. It was not until Monday, August 3, that the

367

direct appeal from the King of the Belgians for French and British aid raised an issue which united the overwhelming majority of Ministers and enabled Sir Edward Grey to make his speech on that afternoon to the House of Commons.[9]

I have given a much too superficial account of the sequence of events. However, the more historians examine World War I, the more it seems to be clear that this was a war none of the responsible governments wanted, a war set in motion by relatively trivial circumstances, a motion which, given the state of the world, could not be stopped. It is quite possible that if there had been a really great statesman in a responsible position the war could have been averted. But there was no such statesman, and so the automatic machinery that had been set in motion ground on to its inevitable conclusion.

Because the whole concept of a war by accident or a miscalculation is so important, and because there seem to be many valid analogies between July 1914 and almost any crisis month in the 1960–1975 period, I should like, at the risk of belaboring the obvious, to list some of the analogies:

1. The need to meet or even beat the enemy's mobilization timetable has a number of similarities to many current quick reaction schemes. We have today, even more than in 1914, the possibility of setting into motion a series of self-confirming signals generated by reactions and counteractions taken on almost sheerly technical grounds without much reference to further developments in policy. There is also the opposite problem (which paradoxically can occur simultaneously). The dangerous counteractions may not be adequate countermeasures, because the signals which are setting them off are disguised as peacetime training maneuvers, as moderate measures undertaken to reduce vulnerability, or as bargaining threats to bluff the opponent into acquiescence.

2. The need to have a quick victory or stalemate to prevent a situation in which both sides lost. It is interesting to note that Schlieffen recognized this and suggested that if the initial campaign against the French failed, the Germans should try for a negotiated peace. Unfortunately for the moderates, the consequences of not terminating hostilities were not recognized by the decision makers; the desire for victory and "the honor of the battlefield" was too strong.

[9] The Rt. Hon. Sir Winston Churchill, *The World Crisis* (London, Odhams Press Limited) New York, Charles Scribner's Sons, 1923, p. 211; quoted by permission of the publishers.

3. The rigidity of the war plans. In 1914 this occurred because they were so complicated that the general staffs felt that they could not draw up more than one. This single war plan was then made even more rigid because it depended on such detailed railroad schedules. In 196X there is a fair chance that the war plan will be handled by a high-speed computer—if we have not made a real effort, nothing could be more rigid. While there will doubtless be opportunities for human intervention, events may move so quickly that these opportunities may be formal rather than of real effect. It is also likely that there will be only one plan because some planners find it hard to take seriously the thought of a number of different situations. They want to examine and plan for only the most obvious one, and ignore the others.

4. As in 1914, in 196X the various governments, having seen the world go through so many false alarms and crises, will have become blasé. Most people today, in and out of government, find it difficult to believe that any sane decision maker would deliberately initiate a thermonuclear war, no matter how tense the crisis. Therefore, temptation for both sides to take firm (and incompatible) positions is likely to become irresistible.

5. Even more than in 1914, governments in our day are likely to be ignorant of the technical details of war and the tactical measures that can or cannot (or, more important, must or must not) be taken in various specialized situations. In peacetime the study and preparation of these measures will be relegated to military staffs as being narrow and technical. As a result they may be considered in a narrow and technical way. In 196X the ignorance of major decision makers is likely to be more profound than in 1914, because at that time the ignorance was related mainly to disuse; there was no philosophical and doctrinaire position that war was "unthinkable." The study of the strategy and tactics of the actual fighting as opposed to deterrence was considered an eminently practical and respectable subject. Today, on the contrary, it is almost impossible to get people interested in the tactics and strategy of thermonuclear war. It is now believed that only the prewar moves are of interest, and even these are not too important because deterrence is supposed to be so close to "automatic." Also, war is technically more complex today than in 1914, and the technological situation changes rapidly.

6. The year 196X should have at least as many chances for decision makers to make mistakes due to having been under physical

and emotional strain and pressures for quick reaction. The issues are bigger, crises develop faster, and the time for reaction may be less.

7. Probably the most important similarity between 1914 and 196X is the ease with which small powers and allies may be able to manipulate the major powers for their own ends. Instead of Serbia and Austria, we can think of China and almost any Asiatic power; West Germany and East Germany; France and the Middle East; and so on. On the other hand, the military situation is such that allies are both more firmly tied and less important to the United States and the Soviet Union than they once were to Germany, Russia, France, and England. With the possible exception of the Soviet Union's relations to China (Khrushchev's announced policy to support the Chinese in the Formosa dispute), neither country really has to sign "blank checks" to hold its allies.

There are, of course, major differences between 1914 and today. On the stabilizing side, the most important difference is that the thermonuclear balance of terror is much more effective than the 1914 fear of defeat or revolution. However, for that reason, the balance of terror is also more likely to be strained since blackmail, firm positions, reckless actions, and sheer ignorance of the details all look safer. *It is reasonably likely that the passage of time will see a gradual growth in the willingness of all parties to be both provoking and careless about their actual capabilities.*

The other differences seem to be mostly on the destabilizing side and make the balance more precarious. Today, because both sides are in effect permanently mobilized, it may be possible to strike without giving any internal or external advance signals. In addition, there are now so many ways to destroy a nation or its armed forces that the danger of unconventional attacks or the exploitation of unconventional effects is ever-present. As we pointed out, sometimes these unconventional attacks, while seeming to be bizarre or reckless, are still more calculable than was a 1914 offensive. Even with the most careful mutual and unilateral arrangements, the possibility of accidents or errors by relatively minor officials, setting off a disastrous chain of events, will exist. In addition, measures designed to limit this last possibility will themselves create new vulnerabilities of either a physical or psychological sort. Lastly and most important, the fear of future instability caused by an insufficiently controlled arms race is so great and growing that it may create pressures for preventive war or other destabilizing moves.

Before we leave World War I, I should like to quote a number of passages from Volume I of Winston Churchill's *The World Crisis*. I know of no better textbook on the subject of war, prewar preparations, and peacetime risks.

The first excerpt is about some of the arguments that raged before the British put into effect the policy that for every battleship the Germans built under their declared naval program the British would build 1.6 battleships; and for every increase the Germans made over their declared naval building program the British would increase two for one. In effect, the British government told the German government that by spending a great deal of money it could increase the number of ships at sea but it could not change its position vis-à-vis the British. If it increased its efforts it would actually increase its inferiority. This was the reaction of a people whose power was threatened and who understood the relationship between power, safety, and prosperity. Churchill wrote:

> The dispute in the Cabinet gave rise to a fierce agitation outside. The process of the controversy led to a sharp rise of temperature. The actual points in dispute never came to an issue. Genuine alarm was excited throughout the country by what was for the first time widely recognised as a German menace. In the end a curious and characteristic solution was reached. The Admiralty had demanded six ships; the economists offered four; and we finally compromised on eight.[10]

Let me now quote Churchill on the possibility of a surprise attack. He is discussing the tension during the 1911 Agadir crisis. Lloyd George had just made a speech with the idea of forcing the German government to back down. The Germans did not like it, and some cold correspondence had been exchanged between the German and British governments.

> They sound so very cautious and correct, these deadly words. Soft, quiet voices purring, courteous, grave, exactly-measured phrases in large peaceful rooms. But with less warning cannons had opened fire and nations had been struck down by this same Germany. So now the Admiralty wireless whispers through the ether to the tall masts of ships, and captains pace their decks absorbed in thought. It is nothing. It is less than nothing. It is too foolish, too fantastic to be thought of in the twentieth century. Or is it fire and murder leaping out of the darkness at our throats, torpedoes ripping the bellies of half-awakened ships, a sunrise on a vanished naval supremacy, and an island well guarded hitherto, at last defenceless? No, it is nothing. No one would do such

---

[10] Churchill, *The World Crisis*, p. 33.

things. Civilisation has climbed above such perils. The interdependence of nations in trade and traffic, the sense of public law, the Hague Convention, Liberal principles, the Labour Party, high finance, Christian charity, common sense have rendered such nightmares impossible. Are you quite sure? It would be a pity to be wrong. Such a mistake could only be made once—once for all.[11]

The next excerpt is also about an event that occurred during the same crisis. Churchill at that time was Home Secretary, and as far as he knew had no specific responsibility for defense of the island. He happened to be at a party having a good time when he fell into a conversation with a chief of police.

We talked about the European situation, and I told him that it was serious. He then remarked that by an odd arrangement the Home Office was responsible, through the Metropolitan Police, for guarding the magazines at Chattenden and Lodge Hill in which all the reserves of naval cordite were stored. For many years these magazines had been protected without misadventure by a few constables. I asked what would happen if twenty determined Germans in two or three motor cars arrived well armed upon the scene one night. He said they would be able to do what they liked. I quitted the garden party.

A few minutes later I was telephoning from my room in the Home Office to the Admiralty. Who was in charge? The First Lord was with the Fleet at Cromarty; the First Sea Lord was inspecting. Both were, of course, quickly accessible by wireless or wire. In the meantime an Admiral (he shall be nameless) was in control. I demanded Marines at once to guard these magazines, vital to the Royal Navy. I knew there were plenty of Marines in the dépots at Chatham and Portsmouth. The admiral replied over the telephone that the Admiralty had no responsibility and had no intention of assuming any; and it was clear from his manner that he resented the intrusion of an alarmist civilian Minister. "You refuse then to send the Marines?" After some hesitation he replied, "I refuse." I replaced the receiver and rang up the War Office. Mr. Haldane was there. I told him that I was reinforcing and arming the police that night, and asked for a company of infantry for each magazine in addition. In a few minutes the orders were given: in a few hours the troops had moved. By the next day the cordite reserves of the navy were safe.[12]

The important thing about Churchill's concern about the possibility of a surprise attack on the Navy's magazines was that while the Germans had no such intentions (they were in fact very legalistic and unimaginative and probably would not have dreamed of

[11] *Ibid.*, p. 45.
[12] *Ibid.*, pp. 47–48.

such illegality or ingenuity), *Churchill is not ashamed of his worries but is proud of them; he considers it an example of how a responsible person should act.* He "cares" even if the nameless Admiral does not. Even though the magazines had been unguarded for years, he would not wait until office hours the next day to rectify the situation. The issue is much too big and the cure much too cheap for him to rely on any lack of intention of the enemy, no matter how reasonable others may think it is to rely on such intentions.

Now a bit of literature approaching poetry on how delicate was the basis of Britain's power, safety, and influence. The analogy with the position of the United States during the period 1950–1962 with regard to the small number of SAC bases (including land and sea missiles) and their possible vulnerability to nuclear attack is obvious.

For consider these ships, so vast in themselves, yet so small, so easily lost to sight on the surface of the waters. Sufficient at the moment, we trusted, for their task, but yet only a score or so. They were all we had. On them, as we conceived, floated the might, majesty, dominion and power of the British Empire. All our long history built up century after century, all our great affairs in every part of the globe, all the means of livelihood and safety of our faithful, industrious, active population depended upon them. Open the sea-cocks and let them sink beneath the surface, as another Fleet was one day to do in another British harbour far to the North, and in a few minutes—half an hour at the most—the whole outlook of the world would be changed. The British Empire would dissolve like a dream; each isolated community struggling forward by itself; the central power of union broken; mighty provinces, whole Empires in themselves, drifting helplessly out of control and falling prey to others; and Europe after one sudden convulsion passing into the iron grip and rule of the Teuton and of all that the Teutonic system meant. There would be left far across the Atlantic unarmed, unready, and as yet uninstructed America to maintain, singlehanded, law and freedom among men.

Guard them well, admirals and captains, hardy tars and tall marines; guard them well and guide them true.[13]

A final excerpt from a chapter entitled "The Romance of Design," discusses the decision to jump from a 13.5-inch to a 15-inch gun on the battleships to be laid down that year. The quotation gives a feeling for the gains that can be achieved and risks that must be taken if a nation tries to obtain or keep a technological lead. The decision that the quotation describes had far-reaching effects, not only on the design of every part of the battleship, but on the de-

---

[13] *Ibid.*, pp. 123–124.

cision of the British Navy to switch from coal to oil. This last decision, of course, had a major impact on British foreign policy in the Middle East. Churchill writes:

The Director of Naval Ordnance Rear-Admiral Moore was ready to stake his professional existence upon it. But after all there could not be absolute certainty. We knew the 13.5 inch well. All sorts of new stresses might develop in the 15 inch model. If only we could make a trial gun and test it thoroughly before giving the orders for the whole of the guns of all the five ships, there would be no risk; but then we should lose an entire year, and five great vessels would go into the line of battle carrying an inferior weapon to that which we had it in our power to give them. Several there were of the responsible authorities consulted who thought it would be more prudent to lose the year. For, after all, if the guns had failed, the ships would have been fearfully marred. I hardly remember ever to have had more anxiety about any administrative decision than this.

I went back to Lord Fisher. He was steadfast and even violent. So I hardened my heart and took the plunge. The whole outfit of guns was ordered forthwith. We arranged that one gun should be hurried on four months in front of the others by exceptional efforts so as to be able to test it for range and accuracy and to get out the range tables and other complex devices which depended upon actual firing results. From this moment we were irrevocably committed to the whole armament, and every detail in these vessels, extending to thousands of parts, were redesigned to fit them. Fancy if they failed. What a disaster. What an exposure. No excuse would be accepted. It would all be brought home to me— "rash, inexperienced," "before he had been there a month," "altering all the plans of his predecessors" and producing "this ghastly fiasco," "the mutilation of all the ships of the year." What could I have said? Moreover, although the decision, once taken, was irrevocable, a long period of suspense—fourteen or fifteen months at least—was unavoidable. However, I dissembled my misgivings. I wrote to the First Sea Lord that "Risks have to be run in peace as well as in war, and courage in design now may win a battle later on."

But everything turned out all right. British gunnery science proved exact and true, and British workmanship as sound as a bell and punctual to the day. The first gun was known in the Elswick shops as "the hush and push gun," and was invariably described in all official documents as "the 14-inch experimental." It proved a brilliant success. It hurled a 1,920-pound projectile 35,000 yards; it achieved remarkable accuracy at all ranges without shortening its existence by straining itself in any way. No doubt I was unduly anxious; but when I saw the gun fired for the first time a year later and knew that all was well, I felt as if I had been delivered from a great peril.

In one of those nightmare novels that used to appear from time to time before the war, I read in 1913 of a great battle in which, to the amazement of the defeated British Fleet, the new German vessels opened fire with a terrible, unheard-of 15-inch gun. There was a real satisfaction in feeling that anyhow this boot was on the other leg.[14]

While the kind of technological risk that Churchill took in 1911 was almost unprecedented, it would today be routine. In fact, critics of the U.S. defense posture sometimes criticize our programs for not taking much larger risks.

The small and scattered collection of excerpts I have just given should give an idea of the gems to be found in the book. However, most of them were obviously selected for their emotional impact; they are a little misleading as to the general tone of the book. Most of the book is taken up with sober and very illuminating discussion of problems, many of which seem to be quite similar to problems we face today. For both pleasure and orientation there are few investments that would repay the military planner or critic more than reading these volumes.

World War II—The War Itself

This was the first war in which people began to take seriously the possibility that the outbreak of war would touch off an orgy of immediate—almost instantaneous—mutual annihilation. Both the French and the British air power experts talked often and convincingly of the "knock out blow" in which the side with the superior air force would win the war in a few days or weeks. We know now that the capability for strategic bombing as it existed then had been exaggerated, but it took three or four years of war to show this convincingly. The British had learned during World War I that a small bombing attack could come close to paralyzing a city. They assumed that in some sense a linear relationship must hold between the size of the attack and the disorganization produced; that if the size of the attack was increased by a factor of a hundred or so, the resulting havoc, destruction, and disorganization would also be increased by a hundred or so. Well, it is not like that. To give a homely example, if we put one lion on the streets of New York City, one might find every other mother paralyzed with fright. She just would not allow her children out on the streets. However, even if one increased the number of lions by five or ten and kept them on the streets permanently, people would soon learn that lions do not eat

[14] *Ibid.*, pp. 127–128.

very much and that the average pedestrian's life expectancy would not be greatly decreased if they ignored the danger. After all, five or ten lions might kill about as many people each year as would be killed by automobiles in New York City and injure far fewer people. While presumably pedestrians would take precautions—it is, after all, an extraordinarily unpleasant way to die—they probably would not desert the city. If for some reason they could not hunt these lions down, they would just learn to live with them, bizarre as the situation might seem to us. If one made it fifty lions, however, large numbers might well begin to leave. The lions probably would then be a good deal more dangerous than automobiles (though not as dangerous as heart trouble). While one can and should make distinctions between the impact of 1, 10, and 100 lions, 10 lions will cause less than ten times as much trouble as 1 lion, but 100 may make the city unacceptable for business or residence for a large portion of the inhabitants.

To go back to British expectations, the official government staff estimated on the basis of World War I and the Spanish Civil War that the Germans would achieve about 50 casualties per ton of bombs dropped, one-third of which would be fatal (actual World War II experience was less than a tenth of this) and that for every physical casualty there would be about three psychic ones roaming around the streets and countryside contributing to the chaos and disorganization. These psychic casualties would range from acute hysteria and neuroses to madness. Not all the experts believed the worst of the horror stories, but enough of them did to have an enormous impact of policy. In discussing these expectations, J. W. Wheeler-Bennett makes the point:

> . . . in retrospect of the Second World War, it is difficult for those who have survived the blitzes and V-bombings to understand or to recapture the sense of fear and apprehension which oppressed Britain in these days. Our imagination had been whetted by the works of those uninhibited writers of "next war" fiction, who had assured us that within a week of the outbreak of hostilities London would be rendered uninhabitable by bombings and by gas. The actuality, when it came two years later, was hideous enough, but not so horrific as those nightmares of the unknown which rode us during the September nights of 1938. . . .
> "Black Wednesday," dawned bright and clear over Paris and over London. Men and women woke with an eerie feeling that this was "the last day," and that by to-morrow night Paris and London might be in flaming ruins. In each capital there were some who remembered that, if this were

so, Prague might have disappeared even earlier. In Paris they were fighting for seats on trains, and the roads out of the city were choked with traffic; in London they were digging trenches.[15]

One might have thought that in the face of such a threat the reaction of the British government would be to take every possible measure for its defense, but it was not like that at all. The very enormity of the threat paralyzed action. War, unrestricted war, seemed like an unbelievable nightmare and therefore somehow unreal. *The very terror of war powerfully reinforced all those who wished to reject military solutions or palliatives in favor of much more attractive schemes for world government or universal disarmament or some major step in that direction.* While the "pacifists" were undoubtedly right in recognizing that the character of war had changed, they were not right in ignoring the military and security problems that still remained. Many of them refused to recognize that even if a disease cannot be completely cured by currently available techniques, one may still wish to use palliatives either because extending life is itself a useful thing to do or gain time by the use of interim measures to arrange for better treatments.

In 1934 Churchill warned about the German air program to achieve air parity, and in 1935 Hitler himself told the British embassy that they had in fact achieved it.

It is very possible that Hitler was exaggerating in 1935, but it is clear that by 1936 he had in fact achieved air parity. Once the facts were clearly established the British did not take the German advances in military capability complacently; however, their reaction, while large in absolute terms (they did things like doubling the budgets for certain military items) was small compared to the threat and their mobilization capabilities. In fact it was not until April 1939, after the second invasion of Czechoslovakia, that the British went all out and limited their program only by the resources available and the size of the German threat they were trying to meet. It was by that time far too late.

Sir John Slessor comments on the problem of financing military preparations as follows:

Looking back on it now in the atmosphere of 1953, it is almost impossible to believe the extent to which financial considerations were allowed to exert such an influence in bringing us to the very lip of disaster in the

[15] J. W. Wheeler-Bennett, *Munich: Prologue to Tragedy*, New York, Duell, Sloan, and Pearce, 1948, pp. 158, 167; Copyright 1948 by John W. Wheeler-Bennett.

face of the Nazi menace, in the years immediately preceding Hitler's war. Every undergraduate knows that a sound economic situation is an essential basis of military strength; but that principle was carried to ludicrous extremes under Mr. Chamberlain's Government. I remember one of the Chiefs saying in this connexion that, as far as he could see, a certain Cabinet Minister was primarily concerned to ensure that we had enough money left to pay the indemnity after losing the war; naughty, no doubt, but this is uncommonly like what it seemed to us in those days. There was the extraordinary idea that, disregarding what your potential enemy was doing or what your military advisers said were the absolute minimum requirements of security, you could get by with rationing the fighting Services to a fixed sum, not to be exceeded over a number of years. Even in the full knowledge of facts such as those I have just described, the Government continued to rule early in 1938 that the three fighting Services between them should not be allowed to spend more than about £1600 millions over the five years 1937 to 1941—an average of little over £300 millions a year *for all three Services;* and this eighteen months after the Prime Minister, as Chancellor of the Exchequer, had confirmed that he knew the Germans were spending £1000 millions a year on warlike preparations, a figure which by now, of course, was being greatly exceeded. Add to this the fact that, for a year after this, intelligent and really patriotic men were still opposing compulsory military service, and who can doubt that there is some special Providence that presides over the destinies of drunk men and the British Empire? [16]

The whole history of the 1933–1939 period is a clear example of the failure of Type II and Type III Deterrence. These failures occurred because neither the British nor the French had the resolve to use their superior military power or their superior resources to check German aggression until it was too late. While initially there was sufficient military power available to control German behavior, it was not credible to the German government that they would use it. The longer they put off using their superior power the less credible it became that it would ever be used. Finally their power itself became inferior so that even when its use was seriously threatened, the German government was no longer impressed.

I suppose that it will be hard for future historians to explain this failure convincingly. We now know that the Germans had ambitions completely incompatible with British and French security, and it seems clear in retrospect that the British and French should have known that Hitler was very unlikely to stop at any reasonable point unless confronted with superior power and determination. The

[16] *The Central Blue: The Autobiography of Sir John Slessor, Marshall of the RAF,* New York, Praeger, 1957, pp. 160–161.

failure of the British and French to fight when they were both challenged and still superior represents a failure of Type II Deterrence.
Their failure to convert their superior resources into military power
represents a failure of Type III Deterrence. To quote Churchill again:

It [the Munich Agreement] is the most grievous consequence of what we
have done and of what we have left undone in the last five years—five
years of futile good intention, five years of eager search for the line of least
resistance, five years of uninterrupted retreat of British power, five years of
neglect of air defences. . . . We have been reduced in those five years
from a position of security so overwhelming and so unchallengeable that
we never cared to think about it. We have been reduced from a position
where the very word "war" was considered one which would be used
only by persons qualifying for a lunatic asylum.[17]

We in the United States, of course, have had and may be having,
a rather similar record of too little and too late; so it really is not
for us to throw stones.

To continue our discussion of the war of nerves, one of the big
disappointments of World War II was the impact of strategic bombing. While such bombing proved to be very important, possibly
even decisive, the effort required to make it effective was an order
of magnitude more than most air power enthusiasts had estimated.
The underestimation continued through the war. It was only after
four years of war and the report of the strategic bombing survey
that we were able to evaluate the effectiveness of strategic bombing
soberly.

Rather interestingly, the Germans, who used the threat of strategic bombing, war of nerves, terror tactics, and so on, were not
really prepared for that kind of war. As far as they were concerned,
the bomber was mainly an adjunct of the army. Its major responsibility was tactical support of the infantry and tanks, in which tasks
the German air force proved superbly expert. However, as the
record shows, they were relatively inept at strategic bombing.

This was the first war in which the engineer, the scientist, and the
technologist were as deeply involved as the military. There was no
reluctance on the part of the established military departments of the
democracies to accept the gifts of technology. The opposite was true.
They went out and sought them eagerly, in some cases prematurely.
This was not quite true for the Germans and the Japanese. Hitler
and some of his staff were victims of overconfidence. By the time

---

[17] Winston S. Churchill, *Blood, Sweat, and Tears*, New York, G. P. Putnam's Sons,
1941, p. 60.

the war started, they felt that they had more than enough of a lead to win. Since the war would doubtless be short, all long-range development programs were either stopped or curtailed. German scientists were subjected to the draft, and the contribution that they could have made in the laboratories and proving grounds was ignored. The Japanese military also did not work closely with their scientists. This seems to have been partly from an excess of chauvinism. Most Japanese scientists had been trained in the United States or England and the militarists were suspicious of them. In any case, the relative backwardness of the Axis powers in using the scientific and technical resources available to them undoubtedly played a major role in their defeat. This emphasis in the democracies on technological developments was almost completely absent in the interwar period. A good description of the hiatus is given by Vannevar Bush:

When the First World War ended there were thus in existence nearly all the elements for scientific warfare. The principal devices had been tried out in practice. There were automatic guns, self-propelled vehicles, tanks, aircraft, submarines, radio communication, poison gases. More important, mass production had appeared; complex devices had been made reliable; the petroleum, automobile, chemical, and communication industries had approached maturity; thousands of men had become skilled in techniques. The long process of applying scientific results, all the way from the original academic theory or experiment to the finished device, had become ordered. The world was fully launched on mechanized warfare. For all the technical devices that were later to be used in the second war, except only atomic energy, practically every basic technique had appeared, waiting only construction and development. And this was in 1918. . . .

What did the world do about it? It went to sleep on the subject. In this country, a decisive factor was the general atmosphere of isolation; here and elsewhere in the world there was a feeling—closer to hope than to conviction, but still a powerful feeling—that great wars were over. Fundamentally, lethargy gripped the technique of warfare between the First and Second World Wars. Those who were familiar with modern scientific trends did not think of war, while those who were thinking of war did not understand the trends.

So the Second World War began where the first one ended. There were a few exceptions. A very few new technical weapons were worked on. . . . There were a few small wars, like the one in Spain, which were regarded by some military men as practice in the techniques of modern total war. Development of new machines for commercial purposes, of course, produced astonishing results, which could later be exploited for military purposes. But despite the change in the whole nature of war that was obvious in 1918, there had been almost no serious exploitation of its technical lessons by 1939.[18]

In sharp contrast to the lethargy of the interwar period, the war brought a whole series of separate wars of measure and countermeasure fought in the laboratories and proving grounds in which victory and defeat were as much or more determined by the respective technological "lead times" of the two antagonists as by the traditional men and materials. Table 58 lists some of the battlefields.

◇◇◇

TABLE 58

MEASURE AND COUNTERMEASURE IN:

Navigation	Tanks
Radar	Naval Mines
Strategic Bombing	Undersea Warfare
Land Mines	Amphibious Landings

◇◇◇

I will not have the space here to more than mention some of the complexities of the technological war.

Consider the search problem for submarines transiting the Bay of Biscay on their way to the Atlantic. The early submarines had to spend a major portion of the day on the surface charging their batteries. The British therefore tried intensive search during the day. For a while this worked fine, but then the submarines began to stay underwater during the day and surfaced only at night. The British then put on planes with L-band radar and searchlights to fly at night. These were so effective for a while that some of the submarines began to surface during the day again, so the day patrols had to be kept up to discourage this practice. It was not long before the Germans outfitted their submarines with L-band receivers that enabled them to know when a plane was in the vicinity; they then submerged before the plane could detect them. The British replied by changing their frequency and equipped their search planes with S-band radars. The obvious German countermeasure was to equip their submarines with S-band receivers, but they ran into technical difficulties. In the interim period they cut down on

[18] *Modern Arms and Free Men*, pp. 16, 17.

the use of the Bay of Biscay and ordered the submarines which had to use it to stay submerged as much as possible. Both practices caused serious operational inconvenience.

That war of frequencies in a much more elaborate form is one of the outstanding characteristics of air defense today, only it is now measure and countermeasure in abstract and hypothetical form. Aside from the information that is obtained through intelligence, neither side has any way of knowing at what stage the opponent is.

One of the most interesting examples of measure and counter-measure is the V-1, the Buzz bomb of the Germans. This device was a simple airborne cruise-type missile that would carry a half ton of high explosives about 200 miles. At the time the Germans started to develop this weapon, there would have been no way of shooting it down, but by the time it was brought into service there had been three devices produced; the VT fuse, the M-9 gun director, and the SCR-584 radar, which in combination proved to be more than a match for the V-1. *None of these devices were developed for the specific purpose of destroying V-1's, but were designed against airplanes.* At the start of the V-1 campaign the British tried to use manned aircraft against them, but these proved ineffective. It also turned out to be operationally complicated to use both manned aircraft and antiaircraft in the same London areas. So after the V-1 campaign had been on for about a month the British moved the antiaircraft to the coast and left the local defense of London to fighter aircraft. This proved to be very effective. For example, in a four-week period of the bombing of London the score was as follows:

TABLE 59

ATTRITION OF V-1 BY ACTIVE DEFENSE

Week	Per Cent of Targets Destroyed
1	24
2	46
3	67
4	79

The same combination succeeded in destroying 90 per cent of the V-1's engaged in the V-1 assault against Antwerp. Toward the end of the V-1 campaign the defense succeeded in shooting down more than 95 per cent of the V-1's that came into range. To finish the story it should be mentioned that the Germans had developed the counter to the counter along with the V-1, the V-2. For all practical purposes this was invulnerable. We are today just developing the kind of defense that would have a chance against the V-2. However, it was not at all clear that the cost of the V-2 justified its use— to deliver a one-ton load of explosives once. Unlike the V-1, the V-2 was expensive and complicated. Many military experts believe that even taking into account that it had valuable psychological effects, the V-2 was a "bad buy." The missile just did not do enough destruction to justify its cost as compared to other means, even if it was invulnerable to active defense.

Another example of the use of countermeasures is described by Terence Robertson. It seems that early in the war the German naval vessels, the Scharnhorst, Gneisenau, and Prinz Eugen, were bottled up in the harbor of Brest. The British instituted a number of measures to keep these ships bottled up; among them was a continual radar observation of the channel to look for any sign of these ships escaping. Even though the British were looking for this specific thing the Germans managed to hoodwink the radar. As described by Robertson:

Meanwhile the Luftwaffe's Director of Communications, General Martini, had recently completed successful experiments with a new and strictly secret method of jamming British radar stations along the south coast. From the beginning of February onwards he directed a planned operation of interference. Each day at dawn our radar stations were subjected to a few minutes of jamming which resembled atmospheric interference. The length of the jamming increased daily, until by February 11 our radar operators were thoroughly accustomed to the particular type of interference which they reported normally as caused by atmospheric conditions.

This cleverly executed plan was to be largely responsible for the delays in the British attack.[19]

The example is especially interesting, because it has some analogies with the problem of detecting ballistic missiles and indicates one technique which a clear and determined enemy might use to evade detection of an attack.

Another interesting example of the importance of having actual

[19] *The Channel Dash*, New York, E. P. Dutton, 1958, pp. 57–58.

experience is the United States experience with submarine torpedoes. To quote an official U.S. Navy report:

United States torpedoes were variously described as running too deep, not exploding, exploding too soon, or not packing enough punch when they did explode.

The indictment unfolded point by point during the first 2 years of war. As each defect was exposed, the morale of the submariners who risked their lives to take the war to the enemy suffered, the enemy was given further respite from the full potential of torpedo warfare, and the Bureau of Ordnance was faced with the task of uncovering and correcting the mistakes of peacetime . . . the problem was compounded by the Bureau's reluctance to accept the fleet evaluation of its weapon. This reluctance was born not of any petty attempt to cover past errors, but from misplaced confidence in its own past work. . . . *Security, a necessary concern of the armed forces, became such a fetish that measures designed to protect a device from enemy eyes actually hid its defects from those who made the regulations. Ironically, some of those defects were already known to the foreign powers who later became our allies or enemies. . . .*

A long succession of complaints poured in from submarine commands: The torpedo ran deep, the detonators were faulty, the arming distance was too great, the magnetic exploder was undependable, the anticountermining device was improperly designed, the firing spring was too weak, and, even when the torpedo exploded properly, it lacked the punch submariners desired. The situation would have been bad if discovery of all of the defects at the outset had required a redesign of the weapon; what was worse, however, was the diabolical way in which each defect concealed another. No sooner was one kind ironed out before another was exposed.

. . . The villain at this point turned out to be the long secret Magnetic Exploder Mark 6. Its poor performance was obscured as long as torpedoes ran so far under a target that the exploder could not be expected to perform, but by the early fall of 1942 some of its weaknesses began to become apparent. . . . The Bureau was reluctant to believe that the secret weapon long regarded as one of our greatest assets should turn out to be a liability. After considering and experimenting with several different types of exploders, the Bureau had regarded the Mark 6 as the ultimate in development.[20]

It is worthwhile to ponder the above example. We have here what was believed to be a thoroughly tested weapon system—tested by peacetime techniques. One of the two torpedoes in service, the Mark 10 had been in service for well over a decade. Nevertheless, the actual wartime experience showed that it ran four feet deeper

[20] Buford Rowland and William B. Boyd, *U.S. Navy Bureau of Ordnance in World War II,* Bureau of Ordnance, Department of the Navy, Washington, D.C. (1953), pp. 90, 96, 99, 100; italics mine.

than set; in many cases the torpedoes passed beneath the targets at which they were aimed. The announcement of the serious defect in the torpedo might have been demoralizing, but fortunately for morale only 15 or 16 shots had been fired in anger when this defect was found. The other torpedo—Mark 14—had a much more disastrous history. It started out armed with a Mark 6 magnetic exploder, which turned out not to work. In spite of report after report from the field that the torpedo was defective, the ordnance people claimed that these reports were just excuses by the men in the field to excuse bad markmanship or other inefficiency. It was eight months before they were convinced that the torpedoes ran ten feet deeper than they were supposed to. (Imagine how long it would have taken if there had been no war.) After they were convinced of the deep-running trouble, a new problem turned up—the fuse operated erratically. It was almost two years before the torpedo was finally fixed to operate properly.

Having defective torpedoes was in itself a semidisaster; in addition it had a very serious effect on the morale of the submarine captains. Some of them, unwilling to blame the equipment, had come to doubt their competency. A few, terribly disturbed, actually quit the submarine service. Rather interestingly, the Germans had shared a similar experience and after they had found that torpedo failures so seriously undermined the morale of the U-boat crews they eliminated all their trickier and more subtle devices in favor of devices which might not perform as well in the peacetime proving grounds but which were much more dependable in the wartime environment and whose failure did not have such a disastrous effect on the morale of the U-boat crews.

One of the most important of the new weapons of defense was the mine. The Germans started their land-mine campaign with two basic kinds of mines: the Teller mine, which was antitank, and the S-mine, or Bouncing Betty, which was antipersonnel. At first they kept the mine fields separate, which made it relatively easy for the Allies to combat them, since they could simply run tanks over the areas in which they worried about antipersonnel mines, and used personnel without any heavy equipment to de-mine areas with tank mines. Later, the Germans began not only to mix the two mine fields, making it very difficult for the Allies to neutralize them, but they also began attaching booby traps to the various types of Teller antitank mines.

The measure and countermeasure battle moved into several phases, but in the end the defense came out more or less ahead. Vannevar Bush describes it in his book:

In the contest between land mines and means for removing them, the mine won out. Portable devices for detecting metallic mines were successfully developed; they worked along much the same lines as the defective radio set that whistles when one waves his hand near it, but they were avoided by the plastic mine. Dogs were taught to smell out mines, and they did, but there are too many ways of tricking dogs for this to be of much use. Great rollers, pushed ahead of tanks, capable of withstanding mine explosions, had some success, but not much; an occasional very large mine could wreck them. Snakepieces of hose full of explosive, capable of being pushed ahead or pulled ahead by a small rocket—could be exploded to clear a lane. Tanks equipped with a succession of these devices could and did proceed a way, provided the tank itself was not destroyed, but this was a laborious method indeed for fields of great depth. Very light vehicles, in particular the Weasel, a treaded vehicle of low-unit pressure originally developed for use in snow fields, could proceed over mine fields set for heavy vehicles, but this machine was not armed or armored, and mines set for light pressure could stop it. The Russians apparently merely ignored the fields, moved ahead, and accepted the losses. These could be very large, for example when mines were built to project a can of explosive into the air to explode there and spread fragments over an area. The days when hordes by their mere number could overwhelm fully prepared positions approached their end.[21]

I will not discuss the measures and countermeasures of World War II any further, but it should be clear to the reader that our day is not one of relaxation. The technological battle is being fought even more intensely today, in peacetime, than it was fought at the height of hostilities in World War II. But a brand new thing has been introduced in the battle—no actual battles. We have today no substitute for the sobering effects of actual experience except pallid and hypothetical paper studies and peacetime tests. As a result, both the estimates and the expectations of each side are likely to be widely out of line with reality.

Even in World War II, relatively simple innovations changed the performance of weapons systems by many factors. For example, the introduction of proximity fuses had exactly the same effect as multiplying the amount of artillery by a factor of five or ten, depending on the application; the introduction of simple guided bombs in a bridge-busting campaign in Burma multiplied the effectiveness

[21] *Modern Arms and Free Men*, pp. 29–30.

of the planes by a factor of 100. There must be many such minor but important items in today's preparedness techniques. There will be even more factors available in the future as each side invents new techniques or tactics. It is possible that the introduction of a new gadget could shift the balance of power, particularly if we were so incautious as to rely on a single weapons system for our defense. What this will mean if the equipment that is being bought so lavishly is ever used is hard to say, except that it will certainly increase the uncertainty of many forms of attack and defense. From the viewpoint of Type I Deterrence planners, this may be all to the good. Uncertainty ordinarily exerts a sobering effect on those who would be audacious; it may restrain a potential agressor from attacking, although a lot depends on the personality of the man making the decisions.

German Disarmament [22]

Let us now consider some other aspects of the prewar period. I will start by considering the German defense effort between 1918 and 1933, the pre-Hitler period. The Versailles Treaty imposed some very severe arms limitations on Germany. Because of our current interest in arms control it is of some value to examine how well the limitations worked.

In some ways the problem of arms control in post-World War I Germany was much simpler than we would have today vis-à-vis Russia. Germany was defeated and so her desires did not have to be too carefully considered. The country was democratic in theory and to a large degree in fact. This meant that it was difficult to hide any large enterprises. In addition, there was a reasonably large anti-militaristic and pacifistic movement which meant that there were a lot of disaffected people around who would make disclosures of clandestine operations. The government itself was Social Democratic and therefore officially antimilitaristic. On the other side there was a widespread belief that the Versailles Treaty was harsh and unfair. This belief was encouraged by many liberal and other elements in the democracies. This tended to water down the moti-

---

[22] Much of the material in this section came from "Disarmament and Clandestine Rearmament under the Weimar Republic," by E. J. Gumbel, in *Inspection for Disarmament*, edited by Seymour Melman, Columbia University Press, New York, 1958, pp. 203–219; and *The Politics of the Prussian Army*, by G. A. Craig, Oxford University Press, 1956, pp. 382–426.

vation and the will of those who were trying to police the arms limitation clauses. I would conjecture that the pressures of those who would want to be friendly with the Russians at any cost, plus those who do not want to rock the boat, might play a similar role in any contemporary arms control agreement with the Russians.

According to the Versailles Treaty, the German army was to be reduced to 100,000 men. In order to prevent the training of large numbers of cadres in short intensive courses, enlisted men had to sign up for twelve years and officers for twenty-five years of active duty. The General Staff was abolished. The manufacture of arms and munitions was subject to Allied supervision, and the manufacture of heavy arms, artillery, and tanks was forbidden. The manufacture of light arms was to be carried on in small factories which would not be able to expand easily. The Navy was limited to six battleships of less than 10,000 tons, six light cruisers, six destroyers, and no submarines. The rest of the Navy was to be surrendered to the Allies. There was to be no air force and the Rhineland was to be kept permanently demilitarized.

The above restrictions seemed quite severe to many contemporaries. In order to see that they were carried through, an Inter-Allied Control Commission was established to supervise, monitor and enforce the disarmament provisions. While in some ways conditions for enforcement of the treaty provisions were ideal, the Germans managed to violate almost every one of them either in spirit or in letter. They got around the limitations over numbers of men in the military service by clandestine private armies. Government employees were trained as troops disguised under such innocuous façades as the Boy Scouts, various kinds of local municipal forces, secret police, and secret government auxiliary forces. They organized the "Black Reichswehr," a reserve army of so-called labor troops in 1923. In 1926 when one of the organizers was interrogated on the existence of this illegal formation, he replied that they were organized to collect, sort, and destroy stocks of illegal weapons and other war weapons, the existence of which was a danger to the state. It was true, he added, that they were trained in the workings of the various weapons, but only so that they would know whether those that they collected were usable or not. As to why the organization was kept secret, this was to avoid arousing "unjustified suspicion," which might give the Allies an excuse for conducting espionage.

In addition to violating the provisions on the numbers of soldiers they could have, the Germans manufactured illegal arms. In one instance, when a cache was discovered in a factory, the manager claimed that a disgruntled employee had smuggled the arms in and then notified the Arms Control Commission. There were many hidden caches of ammunition and arms, some hidden very ingeniously. For example, a floating stock of arms was kept in transit on railroad cars or on unused sidings where railroad cars could sit for quite a while.

The Germans manufactured such things as flame throwers on the excuse that they were necessary for insecticide spraying; range finders, on the grounds that they were necessary for meteorological observation; airplanes for export; powder for sporting arms; and so on. In addition, they kept and increased their skill in research and development by doing design work for foreign subsidiaries.

Financing was done in a number of ways. In some cases the German government used neutral banks to lend money to its own industries. The funds themselves came from illegal transfers from government accounts, excessively high prices charged by private industry and then partially rebated back to the government, and private donations.

That most important of organizations, the German General Staff, was never actually disbanded; sections were kept in operation in various government bureaus. Organizations such as the pensions bureaucracy were used to keep records for the purpose of later setting up a draft. The government set up a special demobilization organization whose actual purpose was mobilization. (This one was too flagrant, and the organization was banned by the Allied Control Commission in 1921.)

The army of 100,000 men was organized on the basis appropriate to an army of many millions. Each company got the numbers and the colors of an Imperial regiment. This meant that the four companies of a battalion corresponded to a division. In order to violate the provisions requiring each soldier to serve for twelve years, they used devices such as premature and feigned illnesses to discharge people after they had been trained for a couple of years. These discharged soldiers were either in the reserve or in illegal military organizations. Naturally, all of this activity did not go unobserved; terrorist methods were used to discipline the population and to keep people from large-scale disclosures. There were 400 political assassinations during the period of the Weimar Republic.

In the face of this wide-scale violation, one can ask if the Versailles

Treaty provisions were of any effect at all. I think the answer to this must be that they were at least a partial success. That is, in spite of the tremendous scale of the violations it still took the Germans five years, from January 1933 when Hitler came in to around January 1938, before they had an army capable of standing up against the French and the British. At any time during that five-year period if the British and the French had had the will, they probably could have stopped the German rearmament program. This important illustrative example makes me feel that the treaty provisions were as successful as one had a right to expect.

It is not essential to have an arms control agreement work 100 per cent. We must estimate the feasible rate of violation (an admittedly very difficult problem), and then ask if we could live with that rate of violation before we reject the agreement. I suspect that in many cases agreements can be made with the Soviets which would allow a moderate rate of violation by them without seriously jeopardizing us. The fact that the British and the French did not react to open and flagrant German rearmament is less a charge against the disarmament agreement than a charge against the British and the French themselves. While it is an important defect of "arms control" agreements that the punishment or correction of even outright violation is not done automatically by some bureaucracy but takes an *act of will* by policy level people in the nonviolating governments, it takes a similar act of will if one is to compete without arms control.

I would now like to discuss one of the most important aspects of the interwar period: the enormous and almost uncontrollable impulse toward disarmament that governed many of the democratic but particularly the British government in the interwar period from about 1922 to 1935. It was not long after 1919 when many people became disillusioned with the Treaty of Versailles. Many scholars and seemingly disinterested people said it was an "unfair" treaty. There was an even greater disillusionment with the whole notion of "war," and as a result there developed an enormous impulse to remove this disease or at least its manifestations. As late as 1934, after Hitler had been in power for almost a year and a half, Ramsey MacDonald still continued to urge the French that they disarm themselves by reducing their army by 50 per cent, and their air force by 75 per cent.

In effect, MacDonald and his supporters urged one of the least aggressive nations in Europe to disarm itself to a level equal with their potential attackers, the Germans. They were also dilatory, to say the least, about the rearmament of Great Britain. *Probably as much as any other single group I think that these men of good will can be charged with causing World War II.* I do not mean to imply by this that in some fundamental sense they were not "correct"; they did understand that the waging of war was getting more and more anachronistic and that some dramatic moves had to be made in order to abolish or reduce the role war had in human affairs. It is, however, one thing to fear and detest an evil and a quite different thing to ignore all of the realistic aspects of a problem. Much of the current discussion about arms control strikes me as being very similar to the disastrous and unsophisticated disarmament spirit of the twenties and thirties. For example, there are many reasons for stopping nuclear tests if possible, but until recently the one which is probably *least* important, the biological damage that is being done, was generally emphasized. Other reasons, particularly the controlling of the technological race and the diffusion of technology, far outweigh the biological damage in their impact on humanity. Many idealists, by concentrating on the biological damage, almost made a trap for themselves. It is very easy to prevent biological damage. One simply has to test underground or in outer space, and it is perfectly possible for those who wish to continue the technological race to satisfy those who are worried about biological damage, without in fact answering the major issues. It is very typical for those who would try to attack the symptoms rather than the disease or those who refuse to worry about temporary constructive measures to get trapped into spending their energies on issues that turn out to be irrelevant or even hurtful to the main problem—the organization of a stable, secure, and livable international order.

Hitler came into power in January 1933 and almost immediately Germany began to rearm. Both the actions and the character of the new German government raised the gravest apprehensions among the French and British and their allies, but it was not until October 14, 1933, when Germany withdrew from a disarmament conference and the League of Nations, that these apprehensions came into focus. Hitler's advisors seem to have been greatly worried that this action might trigger off a violent counteraction—for example, a French occupation of the Ruhr. But the British and the

French contented themselves with denouncing the action. The British were less worried about Germany than they were that France would do something drastic. (They needn't have worried; the French were not going to do anything without the support or even leadership of the British.)

In March 1934, Stanley Baldwin, in answer to a statement by Winston Churchill to the effect that Germany was rearming and growing stronger than Great Britain, made his famous statement: "If all our efforts at agreement fail, and if it is not possible to obtain this equality in such matters as I have indicated, then any government of this country—a national government more than any, and this government—will see to it that in air strength and air power this country shall no longer be inferior to any country within striking distance of its shores." In spite of this pledge, by 1935 the Germans had achieved parity or even air superiority over the British and their rate of expansion was much larger than that of the British; thus the disparity grew with the years. On May 22, 1935, Baldwin confessed that this and other predictions had turned out to be wrong:

First of all, with regard to the figure that I gave in November of German aeroplanes, nothing has come to my knowledge since that makes me think that figure is wrong. I believed at that time it was right. *Where I was wrong was in my estimate of the future. There I was completely wrong. We were completely misled on that subject.* . . . But I will say this deliberately, with all the knowledge I have of the situation, that I would not remain for one moment in any Government which took less determined steps than we are taking today.[23]

Unfortunately, the steps they took were less than sufficient. As is always the tendency, the British made modest program increases over what they had done in the past rather than ask themselves what the actual needs were and whether the country could afford these needs. On March 9, the official constitution of the German air force was announced. On March 16, 1935, Hitler decreed conscription in Germany. In April, the League Council, composed of Argentina, Australia, Great Britain, Chile, Czechoslovakia, Denmark, France, Germany, Italy, Mexico, Poland, Portugal, Spain, Turkey, and the U.S.S.R., unanimously voted that treaties should not be broken by unilateral action. They referred this sentiment to the plenary assembly of the League. At the same time, Sweden, Norway, Denmark, and Holland also met and announced their sup-

---

[23] Winston S. Churchill, *The Gathering Storm*, Boston, Houghton Mifflin Company, 1948, p. 123; quoted by permission of the publishers.

port of the League's action. Not one of these nineteen nations was willing to contemplate the use of force; therefore, this world-wide protest simply strengthened Hitler by showing both the Germans and their potential victims that he could safely ignore public opinion and moral outcries. It is simply not true that a potential aggressor who is contemplating doing something inherently unpopular is likely to be restrained from preliminary actions by foreign public opinion—particularly if he can justify his action by pleading historical necessity or some other reasonable-sounding excuse or, even better, make the charge uncertain by making the action ambiguous. It is important to understand that the fear of alienating public opinion is often not very deterring, if one is trying to estimate how a potential evader of an arms control agreement will judge his risks.

In May of 1935 the British, *anxious to allay their anxieties cheaply,* signed a naval agreement with the Germans, an act which probably ranks as the height of idiocy. Even the published memoirs of those who initiated the action fail to disclose any rationale for the agreement that will withstand even momentary scrutiny. While this naval agreement "reduced tension" it also in effect formally condoned Germany's breaking of the naval restrictions of the peace treaty. It aroused the gravest suspicion among Britain's allies that as long as Britain's naval position was protected she did not really care what happened to the others. Most important of all, the treaty did not protect Britain's naval position; it authorized the Germans to build to about 35 per cent of Britain's naval strength. While this was much less than the Germans had in 1914, it was much more than they had in 1935, so the treaty did not restrain the Germans from doing any building. It did the opposite; it authorized them to build to utmost capacity for the next five or six years. Among other things, the Germans agreed in this treaty that they would not use submarines in warfare against merchant shipping. This was an obviously worthless promise, since they had no other worthwhile purpose for their submarines. Worst of all, the treaty succeeded in its purpose; it decreased tension in the very circles which should have become most alarmed. Of course, some diplomats might have hailed the treaty as a "first step," but one has only to look at the subsequent course of events to see how dubious such a principle can be.

In October 1935 Mussolini launched his invasion of Abyssinia. This was the most dramatic challenge yet to the authority of the League of Nations. In commenting on the attitude of the British government, Churchill states, "The Prime Minister had declared that sanctions meant war; secondly, he resolved there must be no war; and thirdly, he decided upon sanctions. It was evidently impossible to reconcile these three conditions." [24] The sanctions were applied, but in an innocuous fashion that irritated but did not handicap Mussolini, but only discredited the idea of using sanctions in the future.

In March 1936 Hitler marched into the Rhineland. In spite of assurances to the contrary, the Germans immediately started to fortify the frontier. Thus in case of war the French might not be able to attack Germany successfully and come to the early aid of their allies, Poland and Czechoslovakia. Once this doubt was raised it became a certainty in British and French planning. It meant that while the British and the French could promise revenge they could not promise protection or even relief of any military pressure on their allies. Rather strangely, the impact of this move was not fully understood in Poland and Czechslovakia. Even more strangely, it took more than a crisis to teach them this elementary lesson; it took a war. But the effect of taking the Rhineland was well understood by the Germans. For example, Winston Churchill in *The Gathering Storm* reports that the German foreign minister, von Neurath,

told the American ambassador in Moscow, Mr. Bullitt, on May 18, 1936, that it was the policy of the German Government to do nothing active in foreign affairs until the Rhineland had been digested. He explained that *until the German defences had been built on the French and Belgian frontiers,* the German Government would do everything to prevent rather than encourage an outbreak by the Nazis in Austria, and that they would pursue a quiet line with regard to Czechoslovakia. "*As soon as our fortifications are constructed,*" he said, "*and the countries in Central Europe realize that France cannot enter German territory, all these countries will begin to feel very differently about their foreign policies, and a new constellation will develop.*" [25]

If any Britishers had succeeded in pointing out to the Czechs and Poles that their position was precarious and that they and their allies should do something about it, these Cassandra's would have been accused of unpatriotic behavior, rocking the boat, and so on. Most people prefer deferring consideration of hard and unpleasant prob-

[24] The contradiction is reminiscent of the common Western attitude on Berlin that: (1) any Soviet aggression there will be forcibly and successfully resisted; (2) nuclear war is unthinkable; (3) conventional war is ridiculous. (The above quotation is from Winston S. Churchill, *The Gathering Storm*, 1948, p. 175; it and other selected quotations that follow in this book are reprinted by permission of and arrangement with Houghton Mifflin Company, the authorized publishers.)

[25] *Ibid.,* pp. 205–206.

lems until they go away by themselves or reach the crisis stage. This would be as unfortunate a strategy today as it was yesterday. The similar problem created by the Soviet counter-deterrent requires the initiation of long lead time items to handle. In any case, this time the allies have led the deterred power (the United States) in recognizing (belatedly) the existence of the problem.

During the occupation, Hitler announced that the operation was purely symbolic; that there would be no fortification. This was completely untrue, but it did not cost anything to make the announcement, and making it helped to increase the uncertainty of the French and the British. The French considered mobilizing and reoccupying the Ruhr, but once again they wanted British support. They even knew that the German army had forced Hitler into agreeing in advance to retreat if the French mobilized. But according to Churchill, Baldwin said to Daladier as he pointed out that a show of force would be safe, "You may be right, but if there is *even one chance in a hundred* that war would follow from your police operation, I have not the right to commit England. . . . England is not in a state to go to war." [26] There was not much of an outcry at the lack of action by England and France. After all, the Rhineland was German, and the seeming justice of the German position looked much more important than any strategic considerations, even to those who opposed the new German state. By 1936 anybody who was making strategic calculations as opposed to applying (nonexistent) universal principles of justice and law ran some danger of being considered a warmonger. In 1936 the British government conceded in answer to a question by Churchill that the Germans were spending around five times as much on war preparations as they were. As a result of this and other worries about the developing defense picture, a delegation of about twenty people from the House of Lords and the House of Commons called on the Prime Minister to review the defense needs of Britain and to make recommendations on rearmament. Baldwin listened carefully to the description of the danger and the call to arms, but he refused to do anything about it. (An analogy with the Gaither report is perhaps appropriate here.)

On the afternoon of November 5, 1937, Hitler called a meeting of his military advisors and described to them the future military policy of the Reich. It was then almost five years since Hitler had taken over the direction of Germany, and at this point Hitler (but not the generals) believed that German armament was superior or

[26] *Ibid.*, p. 197.

equal to any hostile combination in Europe. According to Hitler this was the time to exploit the superiority. Unless Germany increased its resources and capabilities by means of this military superiority, it would soon find its newly won superiority passing to the French and the British. At this meeting he laid down a pattern for future conquest, which started with Austria and went to Czechoslovakia, Poland, and finally Ukrainian Russia. Most of his hearers were upset and disturbed by Hitler's program. It seemed to be far beyond Germany's resources and entirely too reckless and dangerous, but Hitler would brook no opposition.

In England, Chamberlain was now Prime Minister. He was supremely confident of his ability to deal in a reasonable way with people in general and Hitler in particular. He chose this moment to begin an exploration of the basis on which he might build up a general scheme of appeasement.[27] Five days after the secret meeting of November 5, 1937, Lord Halifax arrived in Berlin to explore the possibility of a settlement with the German foreign office. He met with Hitler at Berchtesgarten on November 19. Hitler gave his visitor no hint as to the fateful decisions that had been made on November 5; on the contrary, he was the epitome of reason and moderation. While the British were being lulled, preparations were speeded up. Hitler may have felt that if the British were so anxious to be obliging it would be almost discourteous not to take advantage of them. It was not long before Hitler began to show what could be done by a man who was willing to threaten and take chances. To quote Churchill again:

It was thought that the hour had now come to obtain control of Austrian policy by procuring the entry into the Vienna Cabinet of the leaders of the lately legalized Austrian Nazi Party. On February 12, 1938, eight days after assuming the supreme command, Hitler had summoned the Austrian Chancellor, Herr von Schuschnigg, to Berchtesgarten. He had obeyed, and was accompanied by his Foreign Minister, Guido Schmidt. We now have Schuschnigg's record, in which the following dialogue occurs. Hitler had mentioned the defenses of the Austrian frontier. These were no more than might be required to make a military operation necessary to overcome them, and thus raise major issues of peace and war.

Hitler: I only need to give an order, and overnight all the ridiculous scarecrows on the frontier will vanish. You don't really believe that you

[27] At that time the word "appeasement" had none of the connotations that it has today. It was considered almost as a synonym for a flexible and reasonable attitude toward the unsettled questions that the Versailles Treaty had left. As a result of the events which ensued from Chamberlain's attempt to be reasonable, the very meaning of the word changed. It now carries the connotation of a shameful and cowardly settlement.

could hold me up for half an hour? Who knows—perhaps I shall be suddenly overnight in Vienna: like a spring storm. Then you will really experience something. I would willingly spare the Austrians this; it will cost many victims. *After the troops will follow the S.A. and the Legion!* No one will be able to hinder the vengeance, not even myself. Do you want to turn Austria into another Spain? All this I would like if possible to avoid.

Schuschnigg: I will obtain the necessary information and put a stop to the building of any defence works on the German frontier. Naturally I realise that you can march into Austria, but, Mr. Chancellor, whether we wish it or not, that would lead to the shedding of blood. We are not alone in the world. That probably means war.

Hitler: That is very easy to say at this moment as we sit here in club armchairs, but behind it all there lies a sum of suffering and blood. Will you take the responsibility for that, Herr Schuschnigg? Don't believe that anyone in the world will hinder me in my decisions! Italy? I am quite clear with Mussolini: with Italy I am on the closest possible terms. England? England will not lift a finger for Austria. . . . And France? Well, two years ago when we marched into the Rhineland with a handful of battalions—at that moment I risked a great deal. If France had marched then, we should have been forced to withdraw. . . . But for France it is now too late! [28]

Having suitably weakened the resolve of the Austrians by such previous crises and having blackmailed them into not reinforcing their frontiers, on March 11, 1938, Hitler marched into Austria. The French and the Czechoslovakians did not even threaten to do anything about it. Only the British looked as if they might take some action, but they finally backed down with a formal protest. On the whole, the Chamberlain government looked rather sad during this incident. Only the week before Chamberlain had reassured the House of Commons and the nation that the government was satisfied with the progress of their rearmament program. In a now famous quote, he had said, "The almost terrifying power that Britain is building up has a sobering effect on the opinion of the world."

It was now Czechoslovakia's turn. Almost immediately after Hitler's march into Austria, despite his assurances of "peaceful coexistence," he started to wage a campaign in behalf of the Sudeten Germans. At this point, the campaign concentrated on obtaining minority rights for these Sudeten Germans. There was no talk, or almost no talk, of breaking up the Czech state to "return" the Sudeten Germans to the German homeland. (The reasons for the quotes around the word "return" is because the Sudeten Deutsch

[28] Winston S. Churchill, *The Gathering Storm*, Boston, Houghton Mifflin, 1948, pp. 262–263.

had never been part of Germany, but had been part of the Austria-Hungarian empire. In that sense, the Germans had no claim at all to the territory.) The Czechs seemed to have a formidable position. They had a treaty of mutual assistance with France, signed December 1925, pledging each party to come immediately to the support of the other in the event of unprovoked aggression on the part of Germany. They had concluded a similar treaty with Russia in May 1935, which would apparently bring the Soviets to the aid of Czechoslovakia if the Franco-Czech pact went into operation. In support of these two agreements, France had signed a pact of mutual assistance with Russia in 1935. With French cooperation they had built a miniature Maginot Line providing for a defense in depth behind which the Czech General Staff were confident that their excellently equipped army of forty divisions could hold up any German attack for at least six weeks, by which time it was supposed that France and Russia would be engaging the aggressor on the West and the East, respectively. This plan ignored the extreme defensive-mindedness of the French and the counter-deterrent of the Siegfried Line built in 1936. On March 15, 1938, the French foreign office reaffirmed on behalf of the Blum government the intention of France to stand by her obligation to come instantly and effectively to the support of her ally; these assurances were reiterated by Daladier and Bonnet a month later on behalf of the New French government.

But the Germans began to look around for excuses to attack Czechoslovakia—excuses which would look reasonable and particularized enough so that this phase of the general "march of conquest" could be taken as a singular and atypical event by the other powers. Hitler was always conscious of the rationalizations and wishful thinking in which frightened or apathetic people indulge. Among the various pretexts considered by the Germans was the assassination of the German minister at Prague, which would provide all the provocation needed. (They had considered a similar scheme for Austria. In this case, it was Franz Von Papen and his military attaché, Colonel Von Muff, who would be assassinated.)

They finally decided to work mainly through the Sudeten Nazi party led by Conrad Henlein and an external propaganda campaign to whip up the German people and frighten those who would resist with the determination and recklessness of the German government.

The campaign began immediately to have results.

Early in May, Mr. Chamberlain dropped some hints at a formal luncheon party given by Lady Astor that he felt that the Czechoslovakian state was an abnormal creation and that the state could not continue to exist in its present form; that something would have to be done to regularize the situation. These remarks "leaked" (perhaps intentionally) and created profound depression, despondency, and suspicion in Moscow, Prague, and Paris—but elation in Berlin. Possibly as a result of this, possibly independently, Henlein began putting real pressure on the Czech government. It was even hinted among his followers that the day was at hand. As a result, an atmosphere of great tension was created on both sides of the Czech frontier. This was increased by the use of conspicuous German troop movements. While these movements might be explained by the fact that this was the normal seasonal Spring maneuvers, they might also be explained by the possibility that Hitler was thinking of repeating his Austrian maneuver.

Real or imagined, the crisis reached a peak on May 19. Henlein left Czechoslovakia for Germany after declaring that negotiations were at an end. Czech and British intelligence received reliable reports that an attack was imminent. Although no explicit ultimatum had been given by Hitler, the four powers concerned, Czechoslovakia, Great Britain, France, and Russia, acted with an amazing degree of vigor, resolutions, and coordination.

The Czechs ordered a partial mobilization; the British ambassador in Berlin had four interviews with Ribbentrop, in which he refused to be reassured by the same kind of pacifying statements which had worked so well before the Austrian Anschluss; in London, Lord Halifax assured the German ambassador that a Czech invasion would mean a Franco-German war in which Great Britain would inevitably become involved; French Foreign Minister Bonnet announced that if German troops crossed the Czech frontier France would at once come to the support of her ally. Daladier in the course of an interview with the German ambassador, showed him a mobilization order lying on his desk. The Soviet government announced its determination to stand by its treaty obligations.

To Hitler, this display of solidarity on the part of the Allies was astonishing; he had every reason for believing—and events were eventually to prove him right—that the Allies would not fight. And yet it is clear that by Sunday, May 22, if he had had any intentions of moving on Czechoslovakia *he was now deterred.* From Prague came reports of a calm, united nation, girded and ready for war. From Paris and Moscow the German Embassy reported determination to support Prague. From London came a declaration of nonneutrality which gave unmistakable indication against whom Britain would be nonneutral. Hitler's advisors at this point said that some reassuring moves were absolutely necessary. Though it was gall and wormwood for him to do so, he gave the orders and the following day the Czechs were recipients of assurances that the Germans had no immediate intention to do violence to their country. Hitler was furious at being forced publicly to back down. On May 30, he gave a secret general order fixing four months in the future, October 1, 1938, as the deadline for the invasion of Czechoslovakia. (Events were to show that he had picked the day correctly.) On the other side, the Allied Powers, instead of being elated at their success, were terrified by how close they had come to world war; in France and England, at least, they were determined that never again would they run such risks. To quote Wheeler-Bennett,

The annals of history can rarely have afforded so remarkable an example of successful Powers terrified at their own success as that presented by Britain and France after the May crisis. What had been generally believed to be a threat of aggression had been met, and apparently deterred, by an outstanding display of united action on the part of the European Powers concerned. This might reasonably have been accepted as a cause for satisfaction and for the further cementing of those bonds of cooperation which had already proved salutary, at any rate as a warning. The French Government might have been expected to follow up the long-deferred Soviet proposals for consultation between the French, Russian and Czech General Staffs for the possible implementation of their common treaties, and it would not have been extraordinary if the British Government had encouraged them to do so. In any case, in view of the intensified military preparations which Germany had undertaken, and of which there was ample evidence and information to hand, it would have been only common sense for Britain and France to overhaul their own war machines.

In effect, none of these things happened. Instead, Mr. Chamberlain, appalled at the chasm of war which had seemingly opened suddenly at his feet, became more and more determined that never again should he be placed in such an unhappy position, and, instead of taking practical measures to strengthen the powers at the command of those who were opposed to the potential aggressor, he set about weakening still further the position of the victim of aggression . . .

It was now also that, among responsible people in London there began to be repeated what had so long been an insistent refrain of Nazi propaganda, namely, that Czechoslovakia was a ramshackle-state—an Austria-

Hungary in microcosm—a mere collection of mutually antagonistic races held together by force. This offered an obvious solution to those who, on these grounds, contemplated the placation of Germany, and *The Times* openly urged the Prague Government to grant "self-determination" to the national minorities "even if it should mean their secession from Czechoslovakia."

The British people were still generally ignorant of, and apathetic to, the dangers of the situation in Central Europe, despite the eloquent efforts of Mr. Churchill to enlighten them. Mr. Chamberlain alternately lulled them into a sense of false security by statements in the House of Commons as to the satisfactory progress of British rearmament, or endeavored to infuse them with his own sincere belief that in war there are no winners. This was an argument he was to employ more vehemently with President Benes at a later moment in the drama.[29]

There is no need to recount in detail how Hitler resumed his campaign of alternating manic threats and reasonable appeals. The campaign culminated in the all too well-known events of the Munich crisis. Chamberlain, Daladier, Hitler, and Mussolini met in a room (from which the Czechs and the Russians were both barred) and arrived at a settlement that has gone down in history as the epitome of dishonorable international relationships.

Both Daladier and Chamberlain had some misgivings over what they had done; both more than half expected to be mobbed when they returned to their respective countries. However, the exact opposite occurred. When their planes landed at their respective airports, there were crowds waiting to cheer; the awful specter of war had been lifted. In England, at least, almost all the editorial opinion was laudatory. This was on Friday. Over the weekend, second thoughts occurred to many. On the following Monday, when the respective parliaments met there was a sharp criticism from a minority about the behavior of the respective governments. Rather interestingly, of all those who actually voiced criticisms on Monday, only one said that the French and the British should have fought; the others said that Chamberlain and Daladier should have stayed firm and then Hitler would have backed down.

That Hitler would have backed down is most improbable. While it seems quite clear from the record that the German people did not want war and that the German army did not want war, it also seems equally clear that Hitler was quite willing to fight. Whatever the motives we wish to impute to Chamberlain and Daladier, it

---

[29] John Wheeler-Bennett, *Munich: Prologue to Tragedy*, pp. 62–64.

should at least be realized that *a declaratory policy of deterrence might not have worked. It was necessary to be willing to go to war. The democracies were incapable of this.* To go back to Wheeler-Bennett's book:

> The fundamental and salient weakness of the Opposition was that, in the majority of cases, they evaded the issue of peace and war. Just as, on September 28, no one of them had interrupted Mr. Chamberlain's speech to protest against the acceptance of the Berchtesgaden terms, so now, with one exception—Mr. Duff Cooper—no Member of the House was sufficiently certain of himself to stand up in his place and say that the terms of the Munich Agreement should have been rejected at the price of war, because no Member of the House was sufficiently assured that the people of Britain would have endorsed such a rejection. They said, which was not true, that there would have been no war, because Hitler was bluffing; they said, which was possible, that a different attitude on the part of the Prime Minister would not only have averted war with Germany, but also the mutilation of Czechoslovakia and the humbling of Britain and France; but they would not say that at Munich or at Godesberg Mr. Chamberlain, in face of what certainly was not bluff, should have taken a determined stand, saying: "Very well, we shall fight." Whether Britain should or should not have accepted Hitler's challenge at that moment is another question, but it was clear from the debate that very few of the Prime Minister's critics, had they been responsible for the direction of affairs, would have picked up the gage.
>
> Many Members of Parliament, of all parties, shared the sentiments expressed by Mr. Victor Raikes: "There should be full appreciation of that fact that our leader will go down to history as the greatest European statesman of this or any other time." A heartfelt sense of thankfulness for the avoidance of war was the underlying and predominant feature of the debate, and it is significant that nearly all speakers, opponents as well as supporters, paid tribute to the unremitting efforts of Mr. Chamberlain in this regard.[30]

The most fitting and poignant comment of all was the announcement which the Czech government had read in every church in the land:

> The land of St. Wenceslas has just been invaded by foreign armies and the thousand-year-old frontier has been violated. This sacrifice has been imposed on the nation of St. Wenceslas by our ally, France, and our friend, Britain. The Primate of the Ancient Kingdom of Bohemia is praying to God Almighty that the peace efforts prompting this terrible sacrifice will be crowned with success, and, should they not, he is praying to the Almighty to forgive all those who impose this injustice upon the people of Czechoslovakia.[31]

[30] *Munich: Prologue to Tragedy*, pp. 184–185.
[31] Quoted in *ibid*, p. 196.

By the use of repeated crises and maneuvers Hitler had been able to force the democracies to face the awful thought that war might have to be fought rather than deterred. *Hitler had in effect created the equivalent of the twenty-four-hour waiting period I hypothesized earlier.* At several points the democracies seemed willing to fight—when Hitler relaxed the pressure ever so little and dropped some straws which the drowning democracies desperately grasped. The more often Hitler presented the choice of war or peace as a real choice, the more the democracies were demoralized. At no time did Hitler threaten to initiate war against France and England. He simply threatened to "retaliate" if they attacked him.

The Munich crisis had an incredible sequel in March 1939. In spite of all the protestations of Hitler and the guarantees of Chamberlain and Daladier given just six months before, Hitler occupied the rest of Czechoslovakia. The technique he used is such an obvious prototype for a future aggressor armed with H-bombs that it is of extreme value to all who are concerned with the problem of maintaining a peaceful and secure world to go over the story in some detail. I will quote at length from Daniel Ellsberg.[32]

. . . There was the problem of the plate-glass window. This time the vulnerable point in the alarm system was not so clearly England and France; they were not likely again to hold their ally down and stifle her protests while he operated. There must be no cries of protest, no unruly disturbance to challenge them to fulfill their commitment. As in the Anschluss, a *fait accompli* required that the occupation be fast and quiet; and both of these requirements indicated: *there must be no resistance at all.* An unresisted occupation would not call for large-scale mobilization, which might alert the Allies. As in Austria, the Wehrmacht could bring victory over its single adversary; but the Wehrmacht alone could not guarantee a victory without resistance, without outcries, without delaying actions. Lacking a method of entry that would shut off the burglar alarm and dull the Allies' reflexes, the Wehrmacht could not promise victory at all. For this job, Hitler had his "intellectual weapons"; now, having tested them, in Austria, he trusted them enough to schedule in his military plans a scant few hours for the decisive coercion of the Czechoslovak head of state. This would seem to be cutting it fine; though at this point in our story, we might well be wary of criticizing Hitler's judgment in matters of blackmail. To create the necessary impression in such a

---

[32] Daniel Ellsberg, The Lowell Lectures: "The Art of Coercion: A Study of Threats in Economic Conflict and War," Lowell Institute, Boston, March, 1959. Footnote references have been omitted here; quotations have been drawn from the Nuremberg Documents, the French Yellow Book, and memoirs of Paul Schmidt and Ernst von Weizsacker; Documents on German Foreign Policy. Documents on British Foreign Policy, and the memoirs of Neville Henderson and Robert Coulondre are additional sources for this account.

short time, of course, a personal audience was essential. So, on the afternoon of March 14, the army being ready to move, the Czechs were informed that the presence of President Hacha and the Foreign Minister,
Chvalkovsky, was desired in Berlin.

Hacha took the journey with his daughter as nurse and companion. He
was an old man, older than his years, and in bad health. . . . In his last
hours as a head of state, Hacha received all honours due him. A guard
of honour awaited, to be inspected by him, at the station; and Ribbentrop
was present, with a bouquet of flowers for his daughter. At the Adlon
Hotel, an aide presented to the daughter a box of chocolates, with the
compliments of the Fuehrer. . . . Chvalkovsky held a preliminary conference with Ribbentrop, after which he assured Hacha that nothing
drastic was in the offing. Finally, at one o'clock in the morning, after his
long journey, the old man was called to the Reichschancellery for his
audience. In the courtyard, he and Chvalkovsky were welcomed by a
company of the SS bodyguard, whose band played the regimental march.
Hacha inspected the guard. . . .

Then the Czechs entered the presence of Hitler, who was attended by
Goering, Ribbentrop, Keitel, Weizsacker, and others. On the table in
front of Hitler were documents for signing.

Hitler's interpreter, Paul Schmidt, describes the setting: "The dark
panelling of the room, lighted only by a few bronze lamps, produced a
sinister atmosphere—a suitable framework for the tragic scene of that
night."

Then Hitler spoke. He was sorry, he said, to have had to ask the President to undertake this journey; but he had reached the conclusion that
the trip might prove of great service to his country, "since Germany's attack was only a matter of hours." He launched into a diatribe against the
spirit of Benes that still stalked in Czechoslovakia; he cited provocations
(that day the German press was reporting the same atrocities against
Germans in Czechoslovakia that had been described at the time of Munich: the student beaten, the pregnant woman thrown down and tram-
pled, etc.); e.g., "why had Czechoslovakia not reduced her army to a
reasonable size?" Now "for me the die was cast." He had issued the order
for German troops to march, and to incorporate Czechoslovakia into the
German Reich.

Hacha and Chvalkovsky, Schmidt writes, "sat as though turned to
stone while Hitler spoke. Only their eyes showed that they were alive.
It must have been an extraordinarily heavy blow to learn from Hitler's
mouth that the end of their country had come."

But why had they been brought to hear this? The invasion would begin at 6 A.M. that morning: in five hours. There were, said Hitler, "two
possibilities. The first was that the invasion of the German troops might
develop into a battle. This resistance would then be broken down by force
of arms with all available means. The other was that the entry of the German troops should take place in a peaceable manner, and then it would be
easy for the Fuehrer . . . to give to Czechoslovakia an individual exis-

tence on a generous scale, autonomy and a certain amount of national freedom."

It was simply up to the Czechs; if they did resist, the punishment would be automatic; indeed, it would be out of Hitler's hands.

"If, tomorrow, it came to a fight . . . in two days the Czech army would cease to resist. Some Germans would, of course, also be killed, and this would produce a feeling of hatred which would compel him, from motives of self-preservation, to refuse any longer to grant autonomy. The world would not care a jot about this.

"This invitation was the last good deed he would be able to render to the Czech people. If it came to fighting, then the bloodshed would compel us to hate also. But perhaps Hacha's visit might avert the worst.

"The hours were passing. At 6 o'clock the troops would march in. He felt almost ashamed to say that, for every Czech battalion, a German division would come. The military operation was not a trifling one, but had been planned on a most generous scale."

But how, in any case, asked Hacha, could it be arranged within four hours to hold back the entire Czech nation from offering resistance. The Fuehrer advised him to telephone Prague. "It might be a great decision, but he could see the possibility dawning of a long period of peace between the two nations. Should the decision be otherwise, he could foresee the annihilation of Czechoslovakia."

Hacha asks whether the whole purpose of the invasion is to disarm the Czech army. This might, perhaps, be done in some other way.

Hitler signed the documents, left the room. The Czechs were closeted alone with Goering and Ribbentrop. On this discussion the German minute is tactfully silent; but details emerge, secondhand, from the dispatches of Henderson and Coulondre, and from Schmidt's account. Schmidt's job was to contact Prague, so that the President could send his crucial instructions to a cabinet meeting then in session. But at this moment the telephone line to Prague was out of order. "A nervy Ribbentrop told me to find out 'who's gone and let us down.'" All Schmidt could find was that Prague did not answer. " 'Call the Postmaster-General at once, for me personally,' screamed Ribbentrop, scarlet with rage. I redoubled my efforts, with the knowledge that failure to get through might cost many lives."

And inside the room, Hacha and Chvalkovsky had come at last to life. They turned from the documents and refused to sign. "If we should sign those documents," they said, "we would be forever cursed by our people."

But the Germans pursued them around the table, thrusting the documents before them and pressing pens into their hands, shouting "Sign! If you refuse, half Prague will lie in ruins from aerial bombardment within two hours."

"I have nothing at all against your beautiful city," Goering told Hacha. "However, if you want to do anything at all against the decision of the Fuehrer, especially if you should attempt to get help from the West, then I shall be forced to show the world the 100 per cent effectiveness of my Air Force." A warning example for England and France: there was a rationale, only too credible, for the action Goering threatened. "Sign!" Goering ordered; hundreds of bombers waited only for his signal; the signal would be given at six, if the signatures were refused; the life of Prague was at stake.

Outside Schmidt was dialing; Ribbentrop had told him to "get the Postmaster-General out of his bed," snarling at "ministers who sleep during such a situation while we're hard at work here."

"Suddenly [Schmidt's account continues] there was a commotion; Goering was shouting for Professor Morell, Hitler's personal physician, who had been detailed to stand by. 'Hacha has fainted!' said Goering with great agitation, 'I hope nothing happens to him.' He added thoughtfully: 'It has been a very strenuous day for such an old man.'

"If anything happens to Hacha, I thought, the whole world will say tomorrow that he was murdered at the Chancellery."

And, though Schmidt knew little of this, more was at stake than world public opinion. Hacha was revived by Morell, with injections. He continued to resist, fainted again, and was revived again. But if he had fainted once too often; or if the telephone line to Prague had stayed out three more hours, Hitler might have lost his gamble. With the burglar alarm unsilenced, with resistance starting in Czechoslovakia, even in an unorganized way, the Second World War might have started in March of 1939.

At 3:55 Hacha signed the documents. He called Prague, Schmidt finally having gotten through, and ordered that there should be no resistance. There was a final conference with Hitler, who assured him: "We do not desire nor do we intend de-nationalization. They, on one hand, shall live as Czechs, and we wish to live contentedly as Germans." Germany and Czechoslovakia would get orders which would certainly double her production.

Here and there, the Germans concluded, there might be clashes where Hacha's message had not gotten through, but by and large they could count on an entry without opposition. The agreement that the Czechs signed told the world:

"The conviction was expressed on both sides that all endeavours must be directed to securing tranquility, order and peace in that part of Central Europe.

"The President of the State of Czecho-Slovakia has declared that, in order to serve this aim and final pacification, he confidently lays the fate of the Czech people and country in the hands of the Fuehrer of the German Reich. The Fuehrer has accepted this declaration, and has announced his decision to take the Czech people under the protection of the German Reich, and to accord it the autonomous development of its national life in accordance with its special characteristics. . . ."

Later when the British and French called to file protests, Weizsacker reports, "I called attention to Hacha's signature." It was not the document, of course, but the speed of the occupation, unresisted on Hacha's orders, that stayed the hands of the Allies; until too late. Only two days later, in his speech at Birmingham, Chamberlain made his spectacular about-face in his evaluation of Hitler; but by then, he could only resolve not to be caught *next time*. If segments of the 40 Czech divisions had still been fighting when Chamberlain prepared that speech—and even Hitler had predicted they could hold out that long—what action might the Allies have taken? One thing is sure: Hitler did not care to find out. And, as he read the document that lay before him at 4 in the morning, March 15, with the signatures of Hacha and Chvalkovsky, he knew he would *not* find out.

The Wilhelmsplatz was still dark as the two Czechs left the Chancellery. It was two hours before the invasion.

"Our people will curse us," said Chvalkovsky to the President, "and yet we have saved their existence. We have preserved them from a horrible massacre."

The War Itself

One of the most interesting aspects of World War II was the way expectations were shattered—just as in World War I. First and foremost there was the unexpected German breakthrough at the Ardennes Forest. The Germans originally had a war plan which was close to a repetition of the Schlieffen Plan, but with not quite as strong a right wing. Fortunately for the Germans, their war plans fell into the hands of the British. They had to cancel them and postpone the operation by about six months. In the interim period, Hitler began to think of some new approaches. His thinking was crystallized when von Mannstein, over the official objections of the General Staff, was able to discuss with Hitler a new war plan which envisioned the major thrust going through the Ardennes Forest and which was very much in accord with what Hitler had been working out himself. The French had not extended the Maginot Line past this area because they felt that the Ardennes Forest was impassable. This opinion was shared by many members of the German General Staff. History, of course, has showed the opposite, for by 1940 mechanized equipment had developed to the point where it could negotiate terrain as inhospitable as the Ardennes Forest, and the German breakthrough at the Ardennes was incredibly successful. (This was the same mechanized equipment, or at least the same army, that had disgraced Hitler at the time of the Anschluss by barely being able to negotiate the concrete road between the German border and Vienna.)

It is worth pointing out again that a *single man or a few people with a good idea, who have contact with one senior decision maker, can gain adoption of a plan with which 90 per cent of the other decision makers and advisors may disagree.* It is also worth pointing out that the area of the Lowlands in which this battle was fought is probably the best-known area in military annals. Members of every General Staff in Europe had personally gone over that ground, which has been fought over for hundreds of years. In spite of the fact that the area was very well known and the problems very carefully delineated, a huge misjudgment could still be made; mainly because tanks and wheeled transport were substantially better and improving all the time. The earlier estimates may have been correct *at the time,* but they did not allow for this technological improvement in tanks and transport and therefore had not adjusted to it.

An interesting example of an operational gap occurred with the Maginot Line itself. I have already mentioned (page 334) that it was found possible to destroy the Maginot-Line-type forts by dropping a few paratroopers on the top armed with thermite bombs. Now in the prewar evaluation of the Maginot Line this tactic had not even been considered. Instead the experts concentrated on such things as the field of fire, and the weight of bombs, cannon, artillery, machine gun fire that they could put in a particular area. The design was tested by rushes on the ground by tanks and men. As always, it is the unexpected attack one must worry about.

I would also like to make a few more comments on the psychology of the Maginot Line. In principle, the idea was very sensible. The French had two-thirds of the population of the Germans and only about half as many young men in the draftable age categories. Under these circumstances it made a great deal of sense for them to supplement their manpower with fixed fortifications which they could use to defend the flanks of an offensive force, contain the freedom of maneuver of the enemy, and to be used as a strong spot from which they could sally forth and to which they could retire. To some extent, this was the original conception of the Line. However, the French both adopted a defensive psychology and put all their faith in a single, simple solution to their strategic problem—a war of economic attrition behind the protection of the Maginot Line.

The French had no plan for attacking the Germans at the outbreak of war. They only had a plan for occupying the Maginot Line where they simply intended to sit. This meant that the Germans had a free hand in any military operations they undertook. When the war started the French refused to stir from their fixed positions and allowed the Germans to concentrate their best troops in the

East to destroy Poland undisturbed. This was very different from the actions of the Russians in World War I, who took very large risks in order to divert the Germans from their attack on the French. As important as this lack of military vigor, was the lack of intellectual vigor. The French felt that the Maginot Line solved all their military problems. In order for them to feel comfortable with this notion of *a single panacea* they not only had to refrain deliberately from examining all other ideas but they had to refrain from examining soberly the risks involved in putting all their bets on the single idea they chose. The intellectual analogy with the Finite Deterrence notion of mutual homicide as the simple solution to our own strategic problems is very strong. The analogy may be more than intellectual, there may be a repetition of history. The Finite Deterrent posture we are developing may not only in the end fail to defend our country but, in the interim period, it may fail to meet all the other strategic demands that are placed upon us.

One of the most disastrous surprises of World War II occurred when the "impregnable" fortress of the Far East, Singapore, fell to the Japanese.

Russell Grenfell describes the prevailing prewar attitude toward Singapore (and current attitude toward protection by mobility) as follows:

The proper journalistic role for a new weapon system is to be revolutionary, throwing all the older ones into obsolescence. The correct attribute of a fortress is impregnability. Every fortress that has come into the news in my lifetime—Port Arthur, Tsingtao, the great French defensive system of the Maginot Line—has been popularly described as impregnable before it has been attacked.

Politicians also favor impregnability for fortresses.[33]

One can today add to the list of desirable military attributes by assumption that all strategic forces have an "annihilating" retaliation, that all "limited wars" are successfully limited, that all forms of controlled nuclear retaliation terminate in a simple and mutually satisfactory exchange, and that all decision makers are cautious, responsible, and, most important of all, too sophisticated to believe and act on calculations.

The military attitude toward Singapore was based on a little more than just invulnerability by assumption in that it was believed that the city would hold out for seventy days, at which point aid would

[33] *Main Fleet to Singapore,* New York, Macmillan, 1952, p. 64.

be on the way. Both of these ideas also proved wrong, for as Grenfell continued:

> The assumption that the fleet would have seventy days in which to relieve an uncaptured Singapore was much too optimistic, especially on the above assumption that only the island had to be held. When the matter was put to the test, the Japanese completed the conquest of the whole of Malaya from the far north-west downwards in less than seventy days. Had there been no defending forces beyond Singapore island, as was the original and for many years the ruling policy, the Japanese conquest would have been quicker still. This could have been foreseen. In 1914, the Japanese had captured Tsingtao, a naval base with much better natural defensive positions and much more strongly fortified than Singapore against land attack, in a very leisurely siege of sixty-six days, of which only seven were devoted to the actual assault. Why, then, were seventy days accepted as being within the safety period for Singapore? *Possibly because any period much less than seventy days would have knocked the bottom out of the Government's "main-fleet-to-the-east" plan by leaving insufficient time for the fleet to get there.*[34]

Churchill describes the fall itself as follows:

> On January 16 Wavell telegraphed: "Until quite recently all plans were based on repulsing sea-borne attacks on (Singapore) island and holding land attack in Johore or farther north, and little or nothing was done to construct defences on north side of island to prevent crossing Johore Straits, though arrangements have been made to blow up the causeway. The fortress cannon of heaviest nature have all-round traverse, but their flat trajectory makes them unsuitable for counter-battery work. Could certainly not guarantee to dominate enemy siege batteries with them. . . ."
>
> It was with feelings of painful surprise that I read this message on the morning of the 19th. So there were no permanent fortifications covering the landward side of the naval base and of the city! Moreover, even more astounding, no measures worth speaking of had been taken by any of the commanders since the war began, and more especially since the Japanese had established themselves in Indo-China, to construct field defences. *They had not even mentioned the fact that they did not exist.*
>
> All that I had seen or read of war had led me to the conviction that, having regard to modern fire power, a few weeks will suffice to create strong field defences, and also to limit and canalise the enemy's front of attack by minefields and other obstructions. Moreover, it had never entered into my head that no circle of detached forts of a permanent character protected the rear of the famous fortress. *I cannot understand how it was I did not know this.* But none of the officers on the spot and none of my professional advisers at home seemed to have realised this awful need. At any rate, none of them pointed it out to me—not even those

[34] *Ibid.,* pp. 65, 67; my italics.

who saw my telegrams based upon the false assumption that a regular siege would be required. I had read of Plevna in 1877, where, before the era of machine guns, defences had been improvised by the Turks in the actual teeth of the Russian assault; and I had examined Verdun in 1917, where a field army lying in and among detached forts had a year earlier made so glorious a record. I had put my faith in the enemy being compelled to use artillery on a very large scale in order to pulverize our strong points at Singapore, and in the almost prohibitive difficulties and long delays which would impede such an artillery concentration and the gathering of ammunition along Malayan communications. Now, suddenly, all this vanished away, and I saw before me the hideous spectacle of the almost naked island and of the wearied, if not exhausted, troops retreating upon it.

I do not write this in any way to excuse myself. I ought to have known. My advisers ought to have known and I ought to have been told, and I ought to have asked. The reason I had not asked about this matter, amid the thousands of questions I put, was that the possibility of Singapore having no landward defences no more entered into my mind than that of a battleship being launched without a bottom. I am aware of the various reasons that have been given for this failure: the preoccupation of the troops in training and in building defence works in Northern Malaya; the shortage of civilian labour; prewar financial limitations and centralised War Office control; the fact that the Army's role was to protect the naval base, situated on the north shore of the island, and that it was therefore their duty to fight in front of that shore and not along it. I do not consider these reasons valid. Defences should have been built.[35]

The quote illustrates one of the major problems. *If you do not know about a problem, it is very hard to worry about it. People at the top have no way of getting information about things which their subordinates do not think are important.* The same remark holds even more strongly for the various official and unofficial committees which review our defense preparations, but must receive all their data through official channels.

Probably the most interesting single operation of World War II was the Japanese attack on Pearl Harbor,[36] the considerations which influenced the decision, the competent way in which the planning was done, and finally the manner in which the attack was executed.

The Japanese had the following problem. They were virtually certain that the United States was going to be their enemy (though they were also preparing to fight other enemies such as the Chinese,

[35] This selection from Winston S. Churchill, *Memoirs of the Second World War,* 1959, pp. 536–537, is reprinted by permission of and arrangement with Houghton Mifflin Company, the authorized publishers. Italics mine.

[36] Almost all the material on Pearl Harbor came from an intensive study made by Roberta Wohlstetter.

the Russians, the British, and the Dutch). For years the Japanese Navy had done their planning with the expectation of fighting a fleet action in Japanese waters; that is, the Navy was defensive-minded. Probably up to the year 1940, the United States fleet could have been incredibly careless about its posture and still have been safe from a sneak attack by the Japanese. However, that psychological invulnerability started to disappear toward the end of 1940 when Admiral Yamamoto asked for a high-ranking Japanese aviator, who was not bound by convention, to study the problem of attacking the American fleet while it was in Pearl Harbor.

Admiral Yamamoto was given an Admiral Onishi who soon decided he had a hard problem. The fleet in Pearl Harbor was considered by experts, seemingly including the Japanese, to be close to invulnerable. One U.S. naval expert even delivered the following passage which illustrated the prevailing attitude.

The greatest danger from Japan, a surprise attack on the unguarded Pacific Fleet, lying at anchor in San Pedro Harbor, under peacetime conditions, has already been averted. The Pacific Fleet is at one of the strongest bases in the world—Pearl Harbor—practically on a war footing and under a war regime. There will be no American Port Arthur.[37]

Ambassador Grew heard rumors in January of 1941 about the attack plans, but he rejected the whole notion as fantastic—an opinion he shared, unknowingly, with the Japanese naval General Staff.

There were many reasons for thinking the American fleet impregnable. One of the more important was that the most effective weapon against a battleship or aircraft carrier, the torpedo, was impossible to use in Pearl Harbor; or, rather, it was *supposed* to be impossible. The textbooks stated that a minimum of 75 feet of water was necessary to use torpedoes and that 150 feet was desirable. The water at Pearl Harbor was only about 30 feet deep, except in the channels where it was 40 feet.

Admiral Onishi immediately grasped that the heart of the problem lay in achieving surprise and in developing techniques for exploiting the surprise by launching torpedoes in shallow water, so he instituted a technological program of research and development. Instead of admiring the clear way in which nature had protected the carriers, he succeeded in his program, actually developing torpedoes that could be used in the shallow waters of Pearl Harbor.

[37] W. D. Puleston, *The Armed Forces of the Pacific*, New Haven, Yale University Press, 1941, pp. 116–117.

It is important to realize that much of this activity was done without any specific intention of implementing an attack in the immediate future; Yamamoto simply realized that much of the time our fleet was in Pearl Harbor and it would be prudent to have a capability that *might* be able to destroy that fleet, even though he did not have any specific intention of using it. *It should not surprise us that a nation might do something sensible, even if unexpected.* It is, after all, the job of some individual on the other side to do exactly that. (Once in a while people do the jobs they are supposed to do.)

In April 1941 Onishi completed his general plan and in May Yamamoto had pilots practicing the specialized launching techniques that would be needed. He did not inform either the army or the government of his ideas until much of the training had reached the point that he knew he could settle any arguments about operational infeasibility. By September the originator of the plan, Admiral Onishi, lost heart and tried to persuade Admiral Yamamoto to give it up, but the latter was adamant.

The shallow water torpedo was not the only technological problem the Japanese had to solve for their Pearl Harbor attack. For example, they had decided to concentrate *all* of their large carriers on the attack. (This in itself was an unprecedented decision. Standard naval theory argued that no nation would risk more than two carriers on such a gamble.) There were only two small carriers left to support the assault on the Philippines. This worried the Japanese, because there were a number of B-17's in the Philippines and they felt that these planes were a rather lethal threat. They did not believe they could adequately support operations from the two small carriers. The only alternative was to support operations from a land base, but this too seemed infeasible. The nearest land base, Formosa, was 550 miles away from targets and this was about 150 miles more than the radius of their fighter plane, the Zero.

Here again, the Japanese instituted a program of research, this time to increase the range of the Zero. They succeeded in doing this by decreasing the revolutions per minute of their engines, using a leaner gas mixture, training their pilots in much better flying discipline, and so forth. Even after they had carried out the above research program the Zeros did not quite make it on the average by about 50 miles, but the Japanese simply told the pilots they would have to rise to the occasion.

The Japanese had another serious problem which is worth com-

413

menting on. They had learned in the Chinese war that they could not bomb effectively at night, so they wanted the attacks on both Hawaii and the Philippines to take place simultaneously at dawn. Unfortunately for them, dawn comes up about three and a half hours later in the Philippines than it does in Hawaii. Their answer to this problem was to jam communications from Hawaii to the Philippines in the hope of keeping from MacArthur the knowledge that the war had started. However, they did not expect the jamming to work and, in fact, it did not. Not only was MacArthur informed almost immediately of the attack on Pearl Harbor but the Japanese attack on the Philippines was delayed another six hours because of fog at the home base. So MacArthur had roughly nine hours of warning before the Japanese attacked. Nevertheless, when the Japanese did attack they achieved perfect tactical surprise. All the B-17's were lined up on the ground, a perfect target for the attacking planes. They had taken off and then landed again—a perfect example of how a "fail-safe" procedure could be disastrous.

The last and most interesting detail about the attack was that the Japanese had more and better information about the location and number of our forces than we did. It is very common for critics of studies to say that the Russians cannot possibly know that much about us—after all, we do not have the information ourselves. But the situation is not really symmetrical. *In warfare the motto is often not "know thyself" but "know thy enemy."* On the whole, we are not trying to gather this information about ourselves because we do not worry enough about our vulnerabilities. But the Russians presumably do worry about U. S. vulnerabilities; at least one rather expects that they do. It should not surprise us if they put many people on the task of finding out about these vulnerabilities. *Simply because they put a greater effort into it they may easily know more about us than we do, just as the Japanese did.*

A last point—the operation was very complicated—almost incredibly complicated, as shown in Table 60. It involved about 1,400 land-based planes. There were about 2,000 vehicles with a very large spectrum of speeds that had to be coordinated. Many of the decisions had to be made a long time in advance. For example, there were 33 days between the time of the initial decision to go ahead to the time a bomb was dropped. The fleet was irrevocably committed to the action for a full 24 hours before anything happened.

Now, I am not saying that this operation was a typical operation.

It was not. It was a magnificent and complicated operation, about two orders of magnitude more complicated than those that experts sometimes say cannot be done.

◆◆◆

TABLE 60
TIMING AND COORDINATION PROBLEMS OF JAPANESE ATTACK ON PEARL HARBOR

Aircraft (land-based)	1,478
Aircraft (carrier-based)	537
Surface Craft	169
Submarines	64
Total	2,248

Time From Initial Decision to First Bomb Drop	33 days
Time From First Departure to First Bomb Drop	20 days
Time from Final Decision to First Bomb Drop	24 hours
Aircraft Speeds	150–250 knots
Surface Craft Speeds	10–35 knots
Submarine Speeds	12 knots, average
Greatest Speed Difference between Vehicles	240 knots

◆◆◆

One question is particularly worth asking: What was the Japanese estimate of the probability of success of this complicated operation? They gave themselves a probability of about 50 per cent of achieving surprise at Pearl Harbor and a much lower probability of achieving surprise in the Philippines. They also felt that surprise was essential. In spite of these low estimates, they went ahead with the operation anyway. What, then, was the pressure on the Japanese? Why did they feel it was less risky to go to war than not to? The pressure was not very much. If they did not start a war, they would have to slow down or possibly even temporarily stop the expansion of their Asiatic co-prosperity sphere. This does not seem to us a really great pressure, so let us look at the other side of the picture: What was the carrot that led them on into this mad venture? It turns out that they did not really expect the operation to achieve a decisive victory that would win the war. It was done to achieve an initial position of advantage. In fact, Admiral Yamamoto is alleged to have said that in the first year of the war they would run wild and achieve all kinds of success, but at the end of that year if the Americans were not ready to acquiesce in the Japanese conquest, from that time on the Japanese would start to lose.

This finishes our "lessons from the history of The Real Past." I am not, of course, saying that World War I or World War II will slavishly repeat themselves; nor am I implying that Khrushchev is like Hitler. I do claim that the problems with which the major European powers contended may arise again in some modified form—particularly if we do not make preparations to prevent this from happening. I will now shift my ground and consider The Hypothetical Past of what I will call World Wars III and IV. Since some challenge the idea that "history teaches," it may be that hypothetical history will teach even less. But the effort must be made. An intellectual effort to supplement our calculations and analysis with ersatz experience drawn from the postwar world can be most rewarding. In some ways the unrealized and unexperienced, but historically plausible, problems of World Wars III and IV are more valuable than the experienced problems of World Wars I and II.

CHAPTER IX

THE HYPOTHETICAL PAST

A. WORLD WAR III (1951)

A Peacetime Revolution in the Art of War
The Emergence of Russia as an Asiatic
and European Power
Unexpected Operational Gaps

ALMOST all of the World War II belligerents have by 1951 displayed the extraordinary recuperative power of a modern economy by either restoring or bettering their prewar levels of industrial production in spite of damage levels that in Japan, Germany, and Russia were in the neighborhood of one-fifth to one-third of the wealth of the country. The most startling political change of 1951 is the emergence of Soviet Russia as a great European and Asiatic power—in fact, the most important European and Asiatic power by a large margin. The most obvious manifestation of this is the creation of the Satellite Empire, the communization of China, and various degrees of major war, civil war, or insurrection in Korea, Indochina, Greece, and Iran. A more subtle result of this expansion of Soviet interests is the creation of a bipolar world—a bipolarity which dominates all international relationships and is reminiscent of the struggle between Carthage and Rome or the Catholics and the Protestants during the Reformation. Given the seeming failure of most postwar "bold new approach" proposals, many think that the struggle will end as almost all major struggles have ended—in a war to the death or continuous and exhausting fighting which finally fades out in an implicit truce, but only after a frightful slaughter.

There are uncommitted nations who will be known in a few years (with some exaggeration) as the "uncommitted billion," but on the whole most people know in 1951 whose side they are on. This known and relatively stable line-up simplifies military planning, at least for the all-out war. The United States has shown in the Truman Doctrine for Greece and Turkey, Berlin Airlift, Marshall Plan, formation of NATO, and the "police action" in Korea that we have a keen appreciation of the necessity for holding the line in Asia and Europe and for the importance of international affairs, and of the need to be willing to make comparatively large sacrifices to influence them.

Despite the Soviet A-bomb and the approaching balance of terror, almost no one is thinking about the *concept* of limited war, much less about the utility, complexity, and requirements of such operations. This is true even though a limited war has been raging since June 1950 in Korea. In a sense the government behaves better than it knows how to.

However, when it comes to the real test of resolve—*our willingness to accept casualties in order to improve our total bargaining position*—1951 is to show the country failing. In all probability the immediate slackening of our "victorious" offensive as soon as the Chinese offered to negotiate, and our subsequent unwillingness to use serious military operations to put pressure on the Chinese, not only caused the negotiations to be drawn out, but may have easily resulted in larger over-all casualties, despite lower daily rates. In addition, partly because we did not understand the rationale of wars (which being limited could only end by negotiation and not by total victory), the war left a very bad taste with most Americans. It is believed by some that an important factor in the loss of the 1952 election by the Democrats was their involvement of the country in this very unpopular war. *It is quite clear that if there is another unpopular Limited War followed by the loss of the ensuing national election by the party in power, the ability of the United States to fight Limited Wars will be sadly impaired.* In a way, Korea represents a major test of the ability of the free world to handle the problem of force and policy in a world soon to be armed with thermonuclear bombs. One very proper type of reaction was that large-scale rearmament was undertaken. This was less to influence future Soviet behavior (as in Type III Deterrence) than for more immediate reasons. There was a widespread belief that the Soviets would soon be on the move in Europe.

The year 1951 is an especially good year to examine how the rapidity of the technological revolutions creates difficulties for both the Soviets and us in evaluating the impact and significance of the new developments. This postulated World War III is far enough past World War II to illustrate how spectacularly technology can change in five or six years. Yet enough time has passed so that one can claim to have developed some understanding of its problems. (Also it is enough in the past to be mostly unclassified.) A partial list of the new possibilities (with particular reference to the United States and air warfare) that the military planner (or Arms Controller) of 1945 should have anticipated is given on Table 61.

It should be clear from the table that any attempt to apply concepts and rules of common sense derived from World War II experience run the grave risk of being as outmoded as some American Civil War concepts would have been in World War II. Insofar as we are trying today to plan for the late sixties and early seventies, we are projecting into an environment which is two or three revolutions ahead of where we are today. An examination of the development of military doctrine in the postwar years, in both the official agencies and the *avant garde,* indicates that the possibility of great

◇◇

TABLE 61
TECHNOLOGY, 1951

Third or fourth generation atomic bombs
B-50 and B-36 form backbone of U.S. SAC
Initial production of B-47
First flight of XB-52
Manual air defense system started
Air defense has F-80, F-86, F-89, F-94
Production order for Nike A
Range extension (aerial refueling and overseas bases)
Nuclear-powered airplane under development
Many organizations, in and out of government, to institutionalize innovation in air warfare and to rationalize research, development, procurement, and operation
Russians have TU-4 and MIG-15 and have tested 3 nuclear weapons

◇◇

success in such planning is not high. While doctrine has evolved with meteoric speed as contrasted with the rates before World War II, it has been hopelessly behind events rather than successful in anticipating the future. I will not try to describe this process in any detail, though I would like to describe the technological revolutions, so as to emphasize the difficulties both we and the Soviets have in evaluating the impact and significance of the new developments.

The most pressing questions in 1951 involve the impact of fission bombs. These devices have had a very vigorous development program and we have third- or fourth-generation models available. Are they or are they not decisive? The Soviets do not think so, and they talk smugly of the "permanently operating factors" and the impracticality of blitzkrieg tactics. Many Americans, particularly advocates of air power, tend to think their use would be decisive, but we have not bothered to buy as many bombs as we could or (from the strictly military point of view) should have. Of course, the Soviets have gone into a vigorous development and procurement program for nuclear weapons. But they do not seem to have made any preparations specifically designed to meet the threats that nuclear weapons pose, though they have done a great deal to meet conventional World War II-type threats.

There is still much talk about the scarcity of uranium—a view which is reinforced by most of the technical people. Few people in or out of government think that the atom bomb will soon be plentiful; nobody realizes that practical and convenient thermonuclear bombs will be available before long. But a few people with high clearances know that some work on a rather impractical thermonuclear device is going forward. Though there is some discussion in 1951 about "baby atom bombs," that is, bombs about the same power as the Hiroshima and Nagasaki bombs but much smaller in both weight and size, not even the experts have any idea of the flexibility, efficiency, and economy soon to be available in the atomic weapons arsenal.

Almost all discussions about defense against nuclear weapons assume that the bombs are too precious to be used on anything but important cities or the most extremely lucrative production targets such as Oak Ridge and Hanford. Similarly, NATO planning is done on the basis that nuclear weapons will not be generally available for the European theatre except for very special and very high-priority targets. However, a few economists are already pointing out that since there is a large disparity between the value of uranium and the marginal cost of production, there is every reason to imagine that much more uranium can and will be produced. There is even some reason to suppose that this large increase in production will be roughly at current prices, but very few of the technical or military people who set policy think in these terms.

This overvaluation of bombs as being too precious to use on most military targets affects defense planning in our Zone of the Interior. Because of the threat of Soviet attacks, the Air Defense Command and the associated Army Anti-Aircraft Command is set up in Colorado Springs in 1951, but they think of their highest priority job as defending the large cities and nuclear facilities, and the initial deployment of their forces (radars and fighters) almost ignores warning and defense for SAC in the contingency of a surprise attack directed at SAC and not at the cities.

At this time, SAC is composed mostly of B-36 and B-50 bombers. The latter is an improved version of the B-29 of World War II fame, but it is so changed as to deserve a new model number. The B-36 is a true intercontinental bomber that depends mainly on altitude for its defense. The history of this bomber is a slightly atypical but not extreme example of how difficult it is to prepare for an uncertain future.[1] The B-36 was designed during World War II when people were thinking first of Germany and then of Japan as the enemy. It was designed to carry high explosives. It was designed when its chief enemy was thought to be the propeller-driven interceptor.

None of the analyses which went into it and determined how we should go about trading range, weight, altitude, and speed considered the possibilities that (1) the B-36 might carry atomic bombs; (2) the enemy might be Russian; (3) it would have to fight its way through jet fighters and guided ground-to-air missiles; (4) we would have overseas bases; or (5) refueling techniques would be available. Any one of these changes might have been sufficient either to eliminate its value completely or to increase it enormously. Somehow, it is up to the man who is designing such vehicles to produce equipment which will be able to fight effectively in virtually unpredictable situations or, better, a flexible development and procurement position must be maintained until enough information has come in to enable one to make firm decisions.

I mentioned in discussing lead-time problems that it helps, in trying to anticipate future problems and improving performance generally, to allow fairly frequent and rather drastic model changes, even after full-scale production has been started. Unless there are contract troubles or competitive weapons systems in the offing, these changes tend to be resisted by the manufacturer and his engineers as too costly and difficult, although with a few exceptions they turn out to be rather inexpensive (if one does not count sweat and tears, but only dollars). As an example of such a change, the sixth model of the B-36, the B-36F, is in production in 1951. This is substantially faster and has twice the altitude capability of the early model. (There will be an H model in 1952 and a J model in 1953.) Also in

---

[1] I am indebted to Albert Wohlstetter for suggesting this example. He discusses it in detail in his paper, *Systems Analysis versus Systems Design*, The RAND Corporation, Paper P-1513, October 29, 1958.

1951 all of the B-36A's have been converted into strategic reconnaissance aircraft and are renumbered B-36E.

In spite of the emphasis by Air Force planners on short wars, it was not until 1948 that we seriously started to mold SAC into an ever-ready instrument of war. (The accession of General Curtis LeMay to the command of SAC, and the Berlin Blockade seemed to have played the main roles.) We have not quite finished the process by 1951. Neither have we accepted the implications of the Soviets' testing of an atom bomb. For example, the official point of view (to be reflected soon in the investment of some $11 billion in war reserve tools and raw materials) holds that an all-out war of the mid-1950's will be long—three to five years—even though initiated with atomic weapons. While it is easy to show that most of these planners have not thought about the problem and are just reacting in a World War II fashion, given the official assumptions about the scarcity of bombs, they may well be right about the length of the war. Nobody can show just by physics and engineering that a small number of atomic bombs dropped on Russia would in fact cause them to sue for peace. In fact, one can almost show the opposite: that the Russians accepted much more damage in World War II and continued to fight, so that unless such imponderables as the psychological and disorganizing impact of using even a small number of bombs is very large it is possible that the war will be long.

One thing is almost always completely overlooked in 1951; the possibility that a war could break out under such circumstances that the United States might not get to drop very many bombs. At that time we have only a small number of SAC bases (18 in 1950,[2] which small number included some strategic fighter bases that did not pose a serious threat to the Soviets) and no warning system worthy of the name. (There was not even a Ground Observer Corps, since this organization started on July 14, 1952.)[3] Furthermore,

[2] Testimony of General LeMay before 1956 Subcommittee on the Air Force, Senate Armed Services Committee, "Study of Airpower," 1956, Vol. I, p. 135.

[3] However, the system was alert enough on April 17, 1952, to trigger a false alarm, according to Arnold Brophy (Reprinted by permission of Gilbert Press, Inc., from *The Air Force* by Arnold Brophy; © Copyright 1956 by Arnold Brophy): "Heessen looked up when the yellow lights flashed on and the bell rang. Four vapor trails had been sighted over Nunivak Island, heading SES. They had been seen a full hour and 27 minutes earlier and the report had come through the Air Defense Control Center at Elmendorf to the 25th Air Division at McChord AFB, Tacoma, Wash., to the Western Air Defense Force at Hamilton. The young captain immediately called Captain Joseph Wood, intelligence duty officer. Wood had spent the afternoon studying intelligence material which, because of security, has to be called simply X. It

under normal conditions, SAC operates unalert (at that time) and takes some hours before it can get its planes into the air just to evacuate; it takes even longer before the airplanes can be prepared

---

concerned the Soviet Air Force and it looked very important. X had a possible direct bearing on the mission of the Air Defense Command but nothing definite could be confirmed or denied at that time. Heessen knew nothing about X. But Wood did and he immediately called Colonel (later Brigadier General) Woodbury M. Burgess, ADC's Deputy Chief of Staff, Intelligence. Burgess was concerned with X. All that afternoon and evening until 10:30 P.M., he had worked on X, telling Major General Kenneth P. Bergquist, Deputy Chief of Staff, Operations, about it.

"Captains usually pause before calling their bosses in the middle of the night. Wood had every reason to do so. Who had made this sighting? An Eskimo. How reliable was it? After all, only supposed contrails had been reported, not any aircraft. Wood did not know the answers to these questions but he didn't hesitate. He telephoned Burgess and then notified the Air Defense Command of the Royal Canadian Air Force at St. Hubert.

"Burgess hurried to headquarters. He went over the situation carefully with the two captains and then woke up Bergquist and told him about the Nunivak contrails. The general did not waste any time in getting to the command post. Again, everything was checked and the officers attempted to clarify the Nunivak sighting by contacting Elmendorf through the Western Defense Force. At this point the message came into Colorado Springs: 'Nothing here.'

"And then all the lines to Alaska went dead.

"By now the tempo of activity had been shoved into high gear. Telephone lines were loaded with calls back and forth with the three defense forces. Conferences were held over classified circuits.

"The general officer on duty at the U.S. Air Force Command Post in the Pentagon, Washington, D.C., was informed of the situation.

"At 2:20 A.M. Bergquist called Major General Frederic H. Smith, Jr., Vice-Commander of ADC. 'We have something hot—I think you'd better come over,' Bergquist said, his voice calm but firm. That was enough for Smith, who also had been briefed on X. He made it downtown in record time.

"Smith checked on what the others had done. An estimated time of arrival for the unknown planes had been computed. They would, if they were going at 400 knots, hit the Seattle radar net at 4:30 A.M., Colorado time. It was then 3:00 A.M., an hour and a half to go. Smith weighed possible courses of action. One was to notify Western Air Defense Force to alert its Aircraft Control and Warning sites—the radar stations. A second was to call a full Air Defense Readiness in Western alone. But, reasoned Burgess and Bergquist, the arc of a circle to Chicago is just as practical as the arc to Seattle. And so was the concept of simultaneous attack.

"Smoking cigarettes and talking quietly together, the two men, from a distance, looked as if they were discussing politics, baseball, or their families. It was 3:10 A.M. when Wood walked over to the two senior officers. 'Eastern has just called in and reported five unknowns coming in over Presque Isle.' Presque Isle is in Maine.

"Smith looked up quickly. 'This triggers it. The Air Defense Command goes on full Air Defense Readiness immediately,' he said.

"The time was 3:11 A.M., April 17, 1952. Air Force headquarters in Washington was notified, the Joint Chiefs of Staff alerted. President Truman was awakened."

It is because of the possibilities of such coincidences—a menacing intelligence situation, a careless Eskimo, a telephone line failure, and some B-47's off course at Presque Isle—that we will need centralized and responsible decision making on the issue of war or peace. It is also most likely that this centralized decision-making apparatus will involve the President of the United States or his authorized "human" representatives. Nobody has yet designed an automatic system for deciding to go to war that will withstand experimentation.

to go on a mission. Under these circumstances just a handful of Russian planes carrying a very small number of atom bombs might well be able to wipe out a large segment, approaching 100 per cent, of our strategic military power in a few hours. (I use the term "few hours" deliberately. The Russians need no superb coordination or piloting to do this task. They simply must be able to fly from one point to another point more or less on a Great Circle route.)

In some ways the lack of concern for the ground vulnerability of bombers was surprising. Many people had written or lectured about the importance of our having a secure and invulnerable SAC. Furthermore, it was part of both Douhet and Air Force doctrine that war in the air is decided by the destruction of the enemy air force on the ground. Last, less than a decade had passed since the "bolt out of the blue" at Pearl Harbor. Nevertheless, there is a real doctrinal lag in 1951 (which was just being made up by 1956). Rather interestingly, it is the advent of the ICBM which made the problem crystal clear rather than the fact that the Soviets had acquired a strategic bombing force that persuaded most people to think the vulnerability problem through and learn to distinguish between First and Second Strike forces. As long as the problem had any subtlety at all most people managed to ignore it. One wonders what subtle doctrinal lags exist today.

If the Russians had made a successful surprise attack on our SAC, they would presumably have taken over most of Europe easily. When one senior NATO officer was asked what kind of equipment the Russians would need in order to be able to reach the Pyrenees, he answered, "Shoes." Another referred to NATO as being like Venus de Milo, "All SHAPE and no arms." After occupying Europe they could have launched into an expanded strategic and nuclear program which might have given them a counter deterrent to our recovering and reopening the war.

It is, of course, quite true that even though the Russians in 1951 have the basic equipment they need—(1) the bomb, and (2) a plane which when refueled could reach its target—they probably have neither the tactical knowledge, the operational capability, nor the strategic doctrine which would enable them to launch such an attack out of the blue. In fact, given their strange lack of emphasis on aerial refueling (an absolute must for any Soviet war planner devising an attack on the U.S.), one can argue that the Soviets are basically planning to refight World War II and, for example, have bought hundreds of submarines to stop World War II-type convoys. However, we should always remember the example of the Japanese attack on Pearl Harbor. It was not until about a year before the attack that the Japanese even considered such an operation, and I believe that it is fair to characterize the operation as being completely outside their doctrinal framework for using the bulk of the fleet in home waters and using only small and unimportant units in such desperate raids.

In addition to having doctrinal lags, Stalin and his military advisors seem to have been reasonably cautious. They were willing to fill power vacuums and to press relentlessly (but not too aggressively). They were willing to take small but not large risks. There is even some evidence that they tried to restrain the Yugoslav, Greek, Indochinese, and Chinese Communists from being too provocative.

However, it also seems likely that Stalin's caution did not stem from fear of the atomic bomb as a decisive weapon. What alarmed him about the United States was Detroit—not SAC! He appears to have felt very strongly that no sensible government tangles with a nation with a GNP of $300 billion a year. Luckily we had both assets—the bomb and the GNP—so that any difference between U.S. and Soviet calculations was not crucial.

It should be quite clear from even the above superficial discussion that any arms control system set up in 1951 might have easily been based upon some serious misunderstandings of the implications of the then current technology and even more serious misunderstandings of the future. In particular some kinds of inspection schemes might have resulted in making our vulnerabilities both crystal clear and very tempting to Stalin or some of his military advisors. Even forcing the Soviets to go through the intellectual exercise of thinking these problems through could have been dangerous. Before we could have safely started discussion of "the control of surprise attack" we would have had to fix up the gaps in our posture—that is, had a limited rearmament program.

There is one moderately amusing but frightening vulnerability that we had in the late forties or early fifties. There was a short period when all of our atomic bombs were stored at just one site and then another period when they were at two sites. I do not know about the second site, but I know some details about the first one, and it was similar to the Churchill incident of the naval magazines (page 372)—a handful of Russians could have had their way.

It is improbable that the Russians would have started a war in 1951 no matter how successful calculations indicated they might be. If they had started such a war, however, the fact that they might launch a sneak attack on either the national storage sites or the SAC bases, or both, is not at all improbable. After all, the Russians must understand that one of their major problems is to prevent U.S. atomic bombs from landing on their country. It is not unlikely that some Russians would ask, How can we stop this? They would then notice that there are several ways to stop such an attack.

It does not take much daring or imagination to dream up a raid or sneak attack against a storage site if it is openly vulnerable. Given that the Russians have made the decision to go to war, it may not even take much persuasion to sell the project. It risks little and could gain much. What would take imagination and daring would be, if instead of destroying the bombs, they had tried to steal them for use against us later. This, too, is neither ridiculous nor farfetched. The bombs themselves are probably too heavy, but one might easily be able to steal the uranium. (The technical problems and logistics of the operation did not seem too complicated to me when I checked into the subject.)

One of the most crucial considerations in the 1951 war is the "range extension" methods used by both sides. It is generally believed the Russians do not have refueling techniques. We ourselves have started to acquire two types: air refueling and the use of overseas bases. Since the Russians have at least a small number of atomic bombs, the latter may be very vulnerable, and we do not have much refueling capability in 1951. So, even if the war is started with an initial tense period which allows us to make preparations to forestall a Russian sneak attack against the U.S., it is not at all clear that we can strike heavy enough blows at the Russian heartland to cause them to collapse; still, it is clear that we would get in some rather impressive licks.

For some years, by 1951, people have been talking about the possibility of having nuclear-powered airplanes flying around. A small group thinks of these as being a competitor to or a close follow-up of the B-52. However, early studies by the NEPA division of Fairchild Aircraft and the Oak Ridge National Laboratory indicate that the problem is going to be difficult. Nevertheless, the Air Force and the AEC think that there is enough promise in this early work to give contracts to Convair and Pratt and Whitney for the development of an airframe and an engine, respectively.

As part of the technology (technology of R&D), I have put in Table 61 the establishment of institutions to encourage and rationalize innovation. One of the most important is the Air Research and Development Command. While the organization was actually started as an independent command in the Air Force in June 1950, it did not assume major responsibility for development until more than a year later. Some may think of the establishment of ARDC as a mere organizational detail; it is actually an important innovation in the art of research. Previously, research and development had been a responsibility of the Air Material Command—an agency whose main job was procurement and which therefore tended to neglect the long-range problems of research and development for the more pressing problems connected with its major duties. In addition, the atmosphere of a procurement agency was not suitable to the flexible and relaxed requirements needed to encourage innovation and good technical work. Other important organizations include RAND, Lincoln Laboratories, and many university groups.

The Russians have come to exhibit, by 1951, some impressive technical capabilities. In August 1944 four B-29 aircraft crash-landed in Siberia. In August 1947 the Soviets publicly unveiled the TU-4, a copy of these bombers. It would have been a real feat for the Soviets to copy such a plane in only three years, but since the war did not end until November 1945, it is not at all unlikely that the time from the decision to copy the plane to the first prototype (which of course may have been produced sometime before they unveiled it) was significantly less than three years. In any case, three years or less for the production of the prototype was a significant technical achievement that should have given us a clear warning of things to come.

The achievements in the long-range bomber field were followed by the testing of an atomic bomb in August 1949, less than four years after the end of the war. This successful test was an outstanding surprise to many Americans, even those who at the end of the war had argued that it would take around five years for the Soviets to test their own bomb. (Even then most Americans thought it would take much longer, estimates of ten years and up being common.) The reason why those who predicted five years were surprised was because there is a very human tendency to forget the passage of time and think of five years as being always five years after the moving present rather than as five years from a fixed date. Secondly, even though nobody in 1945 would have claimed an accuracy of 20 per cent in his prediction, once a number like five years is repeated often enough, it gets to be sacred. If the Russians had beat the schedule by only one month some people would have been surprised.

Finally, the Russians exhibit their MIG-15 in Korea in 1951. This plane turns out to be roughly equal in aerodynamic performance to anything the Americans have in the theatre. While the original design for the engine had been bought from the British, the Russians made some very significant improvements on their own, thus showing that they either had mastered the intricacies of jet propulsion or were well on their way toward doing so.

Nevertheless, even Americans who should know better find it difficult in 1951 to take the Soviets seriously as technical rivals. All their successes are thought of as flukes or propaganda build-ups. This is in spite of the fact that they have clearly shown a capability to approach our performance and do it in a shorter lead time. For example, in just a few years former President Truman is going to cast doubt publicly on whether the Soviets really have an atom bomb or not, even though he personally announced in 1949 that they had tested one.

B. WORLD WAR IV (1956)

The Problem of the Postattack Environment
Type II Deterrence Begins To Wane

The most startling change is the development and perfection of thermonuclear bombs. I mentioned earlier that this probably introduces a more radical change in the technology of war than the introduction of the atomic bomb, that the difference between megaton and kiloton is larger than the difference between kiloton and ton.

The effect of the innovation shows up in the nature of the questions one tends to ask. For kiloton bombs, one asks how much is destroyed—but, banning an extreme course of military events, no one doubts that the nation will continue in some form. With multimegaton weapons, the question of the continuation of the nation (to some, of civilization) is raised even in the shortest of wars. From the technical military point of view one of the most important consequences of the use of thermonuclear weapons in a war would be the creation (at least temporarily) of a radical difference between the preattack environment, in which all our operating experience and training takes place, and the postattack environment, with its likelihood of having strange and unexpected phenomena.

◇◇

TABLE 62
TECHNOLOGY, 1956

Third generation thermonuclear bombs;
Flexible, efficient fission bombs;
Three nuclear countries;
Last B-47E produced;
B-52 and KC-135 being phased into SAC;
B-36 being phased out (last B-36J produced in August 1954);
B-52D in production;
B-58, Snark, and XP6M-1 (Martin Seamaster) fly;
Regulus I, Nike-Hercules, and Falcon missiles in service;
Atlas, Titan, and Thor in crash programs;
Many other missile programs in progress;
Century Series of fighters (F-100 to F-104) phased into Air Defense Command;
DEW Line being built;
MB-1 (nuclear warhead for air-to-air rockets) tested;
Production order for Missile Master and Sage;
U-2, Turkish radar, and other intelligence devices;
Atomic-powered plane and rocket under development;
Atomic-powered submarine launched;
Research and development become major business of aircraft industry; procurement is secondary;
Russians have Badgers, Bears, Bisons, IRBM's and their own model H bombs.

◇◇

The various effects of nuclear weapons include blast, thermal and electromagnetic radiation, ground shock, debris, dust, and ionization—any of which may affect people, equipment, propagation of electromagnetic signals, and so on. It would not be surprising if much equipment that had not been permanently or seriously damaged was still rendered temporarily inoperable by some subtle or simple effect that had not been allowed for.

It is quite possible that some of our current systems may have important hidden defects that will only be disclosed by an attack. In the last few years I have worked on several weapons systems in which new weapons effects or new interpretations of old weapons effects were found that had not been thoroughly allowed for and which could have been disastrous. I therefore find it hard to believe that we have uncovered all of the problems from which our systems may suffer. Extreme dependence on such theoretical investigations as a substitute for (unobtainable) experience can be dangerous. For example, imagine that our total posture has ten serious weaknesses in it, but by dint of hard work and much investigation we discover nine out of ten of the weaknesses and correct them. Imagine also that the enemy is trying to find these same weaknesses and succeeds in finding nine of them. Unless the overlap is complete and we have found exactly the same weaknesses, the enemy has discovered a weakness which he can exploit. If the processes involved were purely random there would be a 90 per cent probability that the enemy had found the one weakness we failed to correct. In practice, the situation should not be that bad: the weakness that was hard for us to find is probably just as hard for the enemy to find. But even if the enemy does not find some weakness that he deliberately exploits, it is not at all clear that we will be able to predict the postattack environment in enough detail to be able to take into account adequately all the phenomena that will occur.

This problem of finding and correcting weaknesses is compounded by the rapid rate of technological advance, a rate that seems much faster than our cultural absorption rate. It is difficult to study seriously what one must do to make our own new measures work and to counter those of the enemy until both have been around awhile. By that time it is too late to develop, proof-test, and install the remedial systems and fixes because the technological race has set up still newer problems.

Let me consider some examples—some serious and some hypothetical but all educational—of the kinds of problems that can arise.

Consider the problem of shelter. It is quite likely that the object being protected will be vulnerable to shock and vibration. It is therefore quite possible for the shelter to survive the blast wave but be so shaken that its contents are damaged. In order to decrease this vulnerability to shock, sensitive equipment is usually either shock-mounted, or the shelter itself is isolated from the earth shock waves that are created by the bomb. There is probably no question that such shock-mounting could be made to work if we could carry out enough experiments. But it is not at all certain that all or most of the schemes that may be used will work on the first try. There is some evidence to the contrary. For example, the problem of protecting naval turret electronic equipment that is subject to extreme shock conditions when guns are fired is well understood. It is perfectly possible to shock-mount such equipment adequately. However, our ships do go out and fire off some test shots to test the adequacy and the reliability of any new kinds of shock-mounting. I am told that in many cases adjustments or minor repairs have to be made after such proof-testing before the equipment is in reliable working order. Because of the weapons test ban, our shelters will not be adequately proof-tested. Shock may also be a problem for mobile systems because it can have an extremely large lethal radii against any systems in which it is difficult to provide elaborate shock-mounting.

There is another weapons effect that could cause trouble if it is not predicted and adequately prepared for. That is the blackout of high-frequency communications of the type that occurred when we tested some high-altitude weapons in the Pacific Ocean. News stories mentioned that about 3,000 square miles were blacked out. Any system that depended on high-frequency communication and did not realize and correct for this effect might have run into serious, unexpected, and possibly disabling trouble in the first few minutes of the war.

Let me mention one last example of how we can get into trouble. Suppose we try to predict the effects of radioactivity from a nuclear explosion on the operation of our system. If we used the standard methods we would assume that the fission products spread according to some pattern in time and space derived from theoretical or experimental evidence. It would then be assumed that these fission products decay according to the so-called $t^{1.2}$ law. Assume also that this law has been verified in laboratories as being accurate enough for our purposes. However, no one has actually measured the radioactivity close-in soon after the explosion. One uses the theoretical law plus measurements made some hours later to predict the radioactivity in the first few minutes, using the mathematical rule to extrapolate backwards from the measurements made at the time of entry to estimate what the radioactivity must have been. People had confidence in this technique, because the extrapolation formulae checked quite well with the laboratory measurements of the decay of fission products.

The trouble with doing this is that if there is some element such as aluminum in the soil, it would absorb an enormous number of neutrons from the initial bomb burst and then give off, for some minutes, very intense gamma rays. In an hour or two all of the aluminum would decay and so people entering the area many hours later would not even realize that the phenomenon had occurred. However, any attempts to alleviate radiation problems in the first few minutes after the burst, that did not take into account this un-expected phenomenon, might have been completely erroneous. I know of many other examples in which people designed systems which almost everybody agreed should be quite workable; much later somebody pointed out an important but subtle effect that had been overlooked. It is hard to believe that there are not important but subtle weapons effects or even more subtle system defects which have not yet been pointed out. The example we gave about the ex-perience of the U.S. Navy with torpedoes in the first two years of World War II illustrates how important defects can exist in "proven" systems even when there are not any serious environmental strains. It is clear that the unfamiliar environmental strains of the postattack environment will cause some unexpected failures and degradations —the only question is how important will they be, particularly if the enemy is clever enough to deliberately exploit the existence of an effect we have not sufficiently prepared for.

One of the oddities I have run into in making presentations on the possibility of fighting and recuperating from wars is that most people find it very hard to believe that there will be any difficulty in the operation of SAC and easy to believe that the recuperation of society will meet unexpected and impossible difficulties. They persist in both of these beliefs even though SAC is an almost split-second operation, and there is no time to make last-minute adjustments or repairs, while in the recuperation of society, the pressure of time is much less critical. If we have sufficient inventories and food sup-plies, we could take our time about recovering. With the proper preparations we will have many months, if not years, available to make postwar adjustments and to react to the changed environment. Nevertheless, in discussing *recuperation of society,* someone is always asking: What about the problems that you have failed to analyze? These same people often find it hard to believe that a similar difficulty can occur in the much more critical split-second operation of a retaliatory force.

In 1956 it became quite clear that as soon as both sides had enough bombs an all-out war would be short. Even without the strangling effect of fallout, it was then easy to show, just by the use of blast effects alone, that one can eliminate a nation's war mobilization base. Rather interestingly, this judgment is by no means as widely accepted in 1956 by "official" experts in the government as by lay people outside. Many who adopted that point of view were thought to be idiosyncratic, fanatics, or air power enthusiasts. However, while the question of a war mobilization base was still controversial when one's enemy had 20 KT or 200 KT bombs, as soon as he had 2,000 KT bombs and higher, and also considering the delivery and defense systems that were available to both sides in 1956, the war (postattack) mobilization base is really no longer controversial; it is dead. Even the "broken-back" war is quite implausible by this time. The "broken-back" war notion is obsolete not only because of the possibility of mutual devastation but even more because it is so very unlikely that the forces of both sides would become attrited in even roughly the same way. One side is likely to get a rather commanding advantage and exploit this lead to force the other side to choose between surrender and the physical destruction of its capability to continue. In fact, with the 1956 state of preparations the short-term recovery of even a residual military capability after one or two large-scale thermonuclear strikes also seems improbable.

I should concede that the 1956 situation may not be quite as simple as I have indicated, since both sides probably have some limitations set by their stockpiles and operational constraints, but even if these are important in 1956, their importance will vanish very soon. Insofar as the limitations are serious, they are most likely much more serious for the Russians than for us. If our hypothetical 1956 war was long, it was probably because the Russians, by initiating a successful surprise attack, succeeded in blunting our blow before it got off the ground, using up most of their bombs or long-range bombers in the operation. There is some doubt as to whether the

Russians (then) have enough bombs or planes to do much more than this. Published Russian statements indicate that they think of bombs as rather rare and precious items; they do not have the casual attitude that the American military services have achieved toward this weapon by 1956.

It is worth noting that a large percentage of our heavy bomber force in 1956 is located in Texas, which does not yet have even a legal air defense identification zone to protect it from violation in peacetime, much less the necessary radars, fighters, and so on. While SAC is much more alert than in 1951, it will be two years until they go on a 15–30-minute ground alert. Clearly it must take them more time than that before they could get off the ground. This makes it easy for any Russian attack launched "out of the blue" to catch some large part of SAC on the ground if the attacking bombers can sneak through our warning barriers (nonexistent in Texas) without giving more than an hour or two of relatively unambiguous warning.

In 1956, the aircraft carriers on-station overseas are, generally speaking, probably not in a much better position if a strike comes out of the blue. Not only do they operate in a fairly relaxed way when at sea, but most of the time they are in port. For example, Admiral Combs testified about the locations and operating practices of our carriers as follows: [4]

ADMIRAL COMBS. The April 1 disposition would be . . . 2 were at sea in the Western Pacific; 2 were at sea off the China coast; 2 were in Japanese ports—1 at Yokosuka and 1 at Iwakuni. The 2 carriers in the Mediterranean were in port. One was in Naples and 1 in San Remo, Italy, near Nice in southern France. . . .

SENATOR JACKSON. . . . We have 2 at sea in the Western Pacific, 2 in Japanese ports, and in the Mediterranean they are both in port.

SENATOR SYMINGTON. If the Senator will yield there. Again going back to the premise of the importance of attacking the carrier if there is knowledge they are carrying hydrogen bombs, would not the carrier in port be subject to attack without the maneuverability it would have if at sea?

ADMIRAL COMBS. An attack without warning; yes sir.

SENATOR SYMINGTON. Without warning, yes.

By this time the Air Force is very conscious of the problem of ground vulnerability, and there are major attempts to reduce it by keeping more planes on alert and by filling holes in the warning network. There is also a great debate on how to combat the approach-

---

[4] U.S. Congress, Hearings of the Subcommittee on the Air Force of the Committee on Armed Service, United States Senate, 1956, Vol. II, p. 1013.

ing missile menace, but the intellectual debate does not influence procurement and deployment very much. Very few new military installations reflect in their design the fact that they may have to live in the missile age. In 1956 the simplest intellectual subtleties of Type I Deterrence are still mostly ignored. With a few exceptions, only the Air Force seems to be able to make the distinction between First Strike (Go First) and Second Strike (Damaged Retaliatory Forces). The Army and the Navy and almost everybody else fail to make the distinction, and on one occasion Admiral Combs testifies as to the character of Navy planning as follows:

SENATOR JACKSON. Following up the chairman's questions, what assumptions would you make as far as damage to your carriers goes—to your ability to strike when you have this warning?

Have you given the enemy credit at all for being able to cut the strike ability of the carriers at sea?

ADMIRAL COMBS. Not in this problem we have not. We worked the problem . . .

SENATOR JACKSON. Have you worked any problems with that assumption? It is reasonable to assume, is it not, that the enemy wants to destroy your ability to deliver atomic weapons. Is that not his primary mission, at least in the early stages of an air atomic conflict?

ADMIRAL COMBS. Yes sir.

SENATOR JACKSON. Have you made any studies on that?

ADMIRAL COMBS. There are none to my knowledge.[5]

The Army's views are described in the quotation from General Taylor early in this book (page 8). The layman and nongovernment experts also are prone to take preattack inventory comparisons seriously, though even in the bomber age there is an extremely large difference between First and Second Strike forces. It is only those who cannot make this distinction who continue to talk about "overkill" capability. As already mentioned, it is not until the "Missile Gap" begins to send chills up and down some spines that most people, including government experts, begin to understand the difference. Rather amusingly, or frighteningly, it is not until late 1959 that the distinction is widely understood and even then there are some conspicuous holdouts. For example, in 1958 and the early part of 1959 the installation of soft IRBM's in Europe, which have almost no ability to survive an attack by Soviet IRBM's and retaliate, are widely advertised as the answer to the Soviet ICBM threat. By late 1959 everybody close to the subject understands the vulnerability problems of the IRBM's, but some are still not accustomed to thinking

[5] *Ibid.*, pp. 1013–1014.

of carriers, overseas bomber bases, or any bases in the U.S. as potentially vulnerable and the possible "deterrent gap" implications of such vulnerability.

While U.S. air defense in 1956 has been enormously improved since 1951, it still has very large gaps. For example, as General Partridge, the Commanding Officer of the North American Air Defense Command, testified:

When we started out to build an air defense system, we started out to build one which would be suitable to combat the TU-4.

We now have a good system to fight the TU-4. Unfortunately, the Russians came along a little more rapidly than we had anticipated in their technical developments, and they introduced the jet bombers and the Bear more rapidly than was forecast.

As a result, we find ourselves in the years 1957, 1958, and early 1959 in not too good shape with regard to our high-altitude and our low-altitude air defense. . . .[6]

SENATOR JACKSON. What would happen if the Soviets today sent down directly over the Polar Cap 40 Bisons flying at maximum altitude? What would we do, what would happen?

GENERAL PARTRIDGE. The trick is to catch them before they get maximum altitude, if it is possible to do so.

SENATOR JACKSON. Where would we pick them up today?

GENERAL PARTRIDGE. The chances are pretty good that if they came across there, we would detect them if they came from the northeast, on that side.

SENATOR JACKSON. No; this is straight down the middle, right over the top, right down the middle. They are going to approach east of Barter Island, right down the middle.

GENERAL PARTRIDGE. I hope they will come on a day when there are condensation trails and the Ground Observer Corps of the Canadians will pick them up. This is what happened in one of the SAC exercises of recent months, and we had several hours over five hours warning simply because the aircraft had to circle up there and were detected by people on the ground.[7]

Partridge's testimony also contained some interesting details on the fallibility of intelligence estimates and the danger of tying our own programs too closely to the accuracy of these estimates.

MR. HAMILTON. Now, addressing your attention for the moment to the altitude of our present fighter planes, how does it happen, General, that we don't have a fighter plane which has an altitude sufficient to be as effective as I understand you would like it against the new Russian long-range bombers?

[6] *Ibid.,* Vol. I, pp. 252—253.
[7] *Ibid.,* p. 256.

GENERAL PARTRIDGE. This deficiency stems back to a lack of research and development in the years long since past, maybe 10 years ago. The engines we use today come from projects which were initiated, say 7 to 10 years ago.

At that time our budget was extremely small, and we had to make a decision as to whether we were going to work on all five of the engines that had to be developed, or whether we were going to concentrate on one.

I think we made the right decision. We concentrated on the turbojets . . . and we have some bombers and fighters which use those . . .[8]

SENATOR SYMINGTON. Is it a fair statement to say that what you mean by that is that we have an air defense system capable of handling the B-29 type, TU-4, but that we have been, in effect, caught short by the awareness in the last year or two of development in the Russian bombers?

GENERAL PARTRIDGE. Well, we have known about the Badger, the Bison and the Bear for a considerable period; just how long, I cannot say off-hand.

The Badger we saw first, but it was not until the air show of 1955 that the Russians began to show these larger bombers in numbers. Their rehearsals for the air show in Moscow in May of 1955 really introduced this note of urgency in getting along with the defenses against that type of aircraft. We didn't think they could bring them into production as quickly as they did.[9]

SENATOR SYMINGTON. In January of 1955, or February, you told us it was true the Communists had an intercontinental jet bomber, but that it would be several years before they would be in production on it.

But in May of that same year, they flew more in one formation than we had in our entire Air Force.[10]

The Civil Defense of the country in 1956 is in worse shape than the Air Defense. The Congressional (Holifield) Report on "Civil Defense for National Survival," July 27, 1956, comments on the testimony of Val Peterson, head of the Federal Civil Defense Agency, as follows:

A close reading of Administrator Peterson's testimony strongly suggests that he entertains great doubt about the value of civil defense planning in the face of the high-yield nuclear weapon threat. He came out early in his prepared statement with this dramatic description of his occupation: "I have been staring into hell for three years." Later on he said: "We just are not going to be prepared for that kind of a hell."

Although he has issued an impressive-sounding series of thirty-odd directives to Federal agencies to carry on postattack planning for various medical, welfare and other services, he told the subcommittee that a good deal of this was "academic."

[8] *Ibid.*, p. 274.
[9] *Ibid.*, p. 283.
[10] *Ibid.*, Vol. II, p. 1831.

He envisaged a bleak wasteland, with tens of millions of dead and injured, the desolate survivors living in the most wretched way, eating gruel, covered with rags, sleeping anywhere they can. He insisted to the subcommittee that he would not be a party to any pretense that America can, "by delegations, and by planning, and by thinking," ready itself for this holocaust by normal peacetime methods.

All remaining resources after an attack, in his view, would be commandeered and shared without owner identity in collective misery (one might say, "disaster socialism").

"If this kind of war occurs," Administrator Peterson said, ". . . life is going to be stark, elemental, brutal, filthy and miserable." He summed up the situation in this sentence: "That we are pitifully prepared and at best we will be pitifully prepared." At another point he referred to "a very nearly hopeless problem."

We noted earlier that he denied statements by Mr. Taylor of his staff and other engineering experts that a shelter program probably could save two-thirds of the people in a target area. He also stated his "contempt for anybody who attempts to minimize the sheer destructiveness and death and desolation that will befall mankind if these weapons are dropped."

The subcommittee observes that State and local civil defense organizations tend to emphasize their peacetime disaster work because they believe it conduces to greater public acceptance of civil defense. While the subcommittee sees some merit in this contention and certainly believes that the State and local civil defense units have a useful role to perform in peacetime disasters, it would be a serious mistake to suppose that a Federal civil defense agency must "sell" itself on that basis. The magnitude and complexity of civil defense against enemy-caused disaster are of quite different order.

The subcommittee is the last group to minimize or play down the horrors and the devastation of nuclear warfare. The FCDA must not fall into the error of substituting local disaster planning for a national defense plan to cope with nuclear war. The magnitude of the problems of such a war is so great when compared with even such devastating disaster as the New England floods of 1955, that we must realize the greater problem. Local disaster plans must be encouraged but never substituted for a modern national defense plan designed to give our Nation the best possible chance of survival.[11]

It should be noted that neither General Partridge nor Administrator Peterson had any vested interests in making their potential performance look poorer than it was. In both cases almost everybody could see the need for having a capability; the main worries of the critics were concentrated on sheer feasibility; the more feasible that

[11] "Civil Defense for National Survival," 24th Intermediate Report of the Committee on Government Operations, Sub-Committee on Military Operations, U.S. House of Representatives, 84th Congr., 2nd Sess., 1956, pp. 80–81.

Partridge and Peterson could make their respective objectives look, the more likely they were to get support.

One cannot help but get the impression in reading the testimony before the two committees that except for those who represented vested official interests or occasionally special military service interests, the government experts had more or less given up on the notion of surviving wars and were beginning to put all their bets on deterrence. If deterrence failed, they were either unprepared to face objectively and soberly what would happen to this country or they were prepared to admit that there would be some sort of total cataclysm. While they did not use the language of total world annihilation that many scientists were beginning to use, the government experts were not prepared to argue with any of these scientists. If they had objected to the extreme language, the most that they would have been able to come up with would have been some vague nonquantitative remark to the effect that man had survived some pretty horrible experiences in the past and they rather believed that he could survive the next war as well.

Even the Holifield Committee, which supported Civil Defense and did a rather impressive technical job of gathering together much valuable information, was almost completely preoccupied with short-term survival problems; it received no explicit testimony or comments indicating that the nation could handle the long-term economic, medical, and genetic effects. This was not their fault; no such testimony was available. No sober studies of any of these problems had been made. Under these circumstances very few Americans were likely to be interested in programs which, even if they succeeded in saving their lives, promised to either doom them to less than Chinese standards of living or a horrible death from cancer, not to speak of the even greater horrors in store for any deformed children that would be born.

The chief values that many of the 1956 witnesses gave to defense of people and property were the importance of maintaining at least a façade for political and morale purposes and the uncertainty and complexities such a defense would introduce for the enemy. However, nobody explained explicitly just how the defense of civilians and their property would complicate or make uncertain the enemy's operations against our SAC, although in 1956 almost all agreed that this would be his priority target and maybe his only one.

Such views of Americans on the hopelessness of trying to win wars if deterrence fails, were in sharp contrast to the views believed to be prevalent in 1956 among Soviet decision makers. They took Civil and Air Defense much more seriously. General Partridge testified that the Soviet Air Defense establishment had about four times the personnel of the U.S. Air Defense establishment, plus equipment of comparable quality. As far as Civil Defense was concerned, we did not know much in 1956 about Russian physical preparations; they were—and are—Russian military secrets. We do know that they made some major organizational efforts. For example, a 1959 report of the House Committee on Government Operations,[12] *Civil Defense in Western Europe and the Soviet Union,* states:

In the summer of 1955, a vast formal program was undertaken to train the entire Soviet population in the fundamentals of atomic defense. A 10 hour course was worked out, providing general information on the atomic bomb, its effects, and the methods of protection against it; it also provided some first-aid training and data on air-raid signals. The entire adult population of the Soviet Union was called upon to complete the course by the end of 1956; if Soviet claims are to be accepted, 85.5 per cent of the people did so.

Examination of the manuals that the Soviets used indicates that the content of the course was rather poor, concentrating mainly on "nominal atomic bombs," high-explosive and incendiary attacks and the like. However, the year 1958 was to see Soviet manuals published which were concerned with measures that were more appropriate to thermonuclear war; in particular, these manuals either emphasized or discussed such questions as improvised shelters, evacuation, rural (B country) civil defense, and so on. However, they still had some flaws. They were consistent with the view that there was an influential group in the Soviet Union which understood well what an effective "cheap" Civil Defense program would be. But it is presumed that they had to compromise their views with the old guard. Anyway, the Soviets were putting a major effort into understanding these problems and we were not. The House report on Civil Defense I just mentioned says about the Soviet 1958 program:

In view of the above, it may be significant that some modifications took place in Soviet civil defense plans in the early part of 1958. The fact that such a revision has taken place has not yet been formally announced— a reticence not unusual in the U.S.S.R.—and the complete picture of the

---

[12] Fifth Report of the Committee on Government Operations, House of Representatives, 86th Congr., 1st Sess., Washington, D.C., G.P.O., 1959, p. 42.

changes decided upon is still veiled in secrecy. However, several incidental statements appearing in Soviet publications within the last few months have made it possible to reconstruct at least some features of the new plans.

One important element announced was that of the evacuation of part of the population of large cities in the event of threat of aerial attack; previous plans had provided that the urban population was to remain where it was. However, the people to be evacuated are apparently to be limited to certain groups, such as children, aged persons, and invalids; most others are still to stay in the cities. The evacuees are to be taken to the country in vehicles supplied by the city civil defense organization, and the village authorities are required to provide them with food and shelter, and, when possible, to put them to useful work.

Why the Soviets plan to have the working force remain in the cities may be explained in their description of the aims of civil defense measures taken in factories and other installations: "The purpose of such measures is to prepare the installations for operation under conditions of air attack." This statement also implies that Soviet policy does not contemplate a substantial evacuation of production facilities and equipment from cities.

A second revision made in 1958 seems to be a result of the realization of the devastating effects of contemporary military weapons. Accordingly, special units were then set up in the civil defense organization to provide food, shelter, and other necessities for large groups of people made homeless in case of attack.

Information on other revisions is not as clear cut. Of possible significance may be the greater emphasis shown in recent Soviet publications on civil defense outside of large cities. Thus, in November 1958, recommendations were published concerning the construction of shelter, primarily against blast, in outlying suburbs, and a book devoted specifically to civil defense in rural areas is scheduled for publication early in 1959.

Finally the Soviets have recently been giving increased attention to measures to be taken in the event of a sudden outbreak of hostilities. Previously, a number of time-consuming civil defense measures were not to be undertaken until the Government announced an alert. However, several 1958 Soviet publications have stated that warning in case of air attack might be very short.[13]

The Russians also continued their training program. A second nationwide compulsory course was started on August 15, 1956 and is supposed to have been completed in December 1958. This course took 22 hours and included biological and chemical warfare in addition to new material on thermonuclear warfare. Before the second course was completed, a third compulsory training program was approved by the Central Committee of DOSAAF (on December 31, 1957). It was supposed to have been completed by late 1959, but it

[13] *Ibid.*, pp. 43–44.

441

seemed to be running a little behind. This course reviews the "theoretical" work of the previous courses and emphasizes the "practical" application of this theory. Every adult must take the course and pass examinations on the subjects:

1. Present-day Methods of Air Attack
2. Individual Defense Means
3. Collective Defense Means
4. Fire Prevention Methods
5. Rules for Behavior during Alert
6. First Aid
7. Liquidation of Results of Air Attack

In addition, the inhabitants of the rural regions are expected to pass a special test on veterinary aid. While only twelve hours were nominally allotted to the course, it was expected that many of the students would need more time before they could pass the examinations.

The question immediately comes up, "How serious were—and are—the Soviet leaders in their notion that it is possible to alleviate the consequences of a war?" Are all these preparations the result of bureaucratic inertia, or are they for indirect purposes such as civilian morale or the inducing of uncertainty in the enemy's mind? Or do they simply represent a belief that these preparations really do improve the nation's prospects for surviving and recuperating after a thermonuclear war—improve these chances enough to justify the material costs and the enormous organizational energy and man-hours put into programs? As far as I can tell, the Soviets were in 1956 and are today quite conscious of some (but possibly not all) of the dimensions of the destruction caused by a thermonuclear war. They had a "great national debate" on the possibility of surviving a war and concluded that they could.

The debate seems to have started in late 1953 when Malenkov began pushing a Russian version of the "Minimum Deterrence" theory. He and other highly placed people made a number of references to the inevitable collapse or destruction of all civilization that would result from a thermonuclear war. He immediately drew budgetary implications from the new viewpoint (or maybe like us, it was partly the other way around), and he argued that the Soviet Union could now afford to cut back on its program of investment in heavy industry and expand consumption, since the defense prob-

442

lem would now more or less solve itself. The happy Soviets could now concentrate on raising living standards.

That view was fought fiercely by the Army and Navy and many Communist bureaucrats, Khrushchev being the chief of these. Finally in March 1954 Malenkov was forced publicly to recant the view of world annihilation; henceforth, it was only the capitalists that would be destroyed. According to Herbert Dinerstein in his book *War and the Soviet Union*, the success of Malenkov's opponents was complete. For example, at least as far as the public literature goes, there has been no reference in any Soviet publication since March 1954 to the notion that war would bring the end of civilization, though Khrushchev himself has occasionally delivered remarks which indicated that he thought the war could be pretty horrible. Dinerstein goes on to state:

It was not until the beginning of 1955, when it became clear that Malenkov was about to be demoted, that the theory of the possible permanent deterrence of the United States was subjected to direct attack and officially designated as incorrect. The likelihood of war and the amount of Soviet defense expenditures was an important issue in Malenkov's political defeat. . . . It was not until his dismissal from the premiership that the party magazine *Kommunist* made a direct attack on his thesis concerning "the destruction of world civilization." The magazine described the thesis as essentially a capitalist trick to induce a false sense of security.[14]

Since then, while the Soviets have often used such terms as "unprecedented destruction," they seem to avoid such terms as "mutual annihilation." In his speech of January 14, 1960, Khrushchev still made the point that the Soviet Union could and would survive and rebuild after a thermonuclear war.[15]

Whatever their judgment about the effects of a thermonuclear war, the Soviets (as the above quotation indicates) noticed at the time that the theory of mutual homicide has some comforting financial and even psychological aspects, since it practically guarantees against deliberate attack. This in turn means that one can afford cheaper deterrents and in addition need not go to the expense of having a "fight-or-win-the-war" capability. It is partly because those "comforting" aspects of the mutual annihilation theory may weaken their defense effort, that they are so concerned to deny the theory.

[14] H. S. Dinerstein, *War and the Soviet Union*, New York, Praeger, 1959, p. 76.
[15] Reported in the *New York Times*, January 15, 1960.

In spite of the activity in the Soviet Union in civil defense, particularly in the field of training and improvised programs, most American observers, even skilled ones, usually reported in those years no significant civil defense activity in the Soviet Union. This was probably due to their feeling that the "moderate" programs of the Soviets would be of no value, and that the problems of thermonuclear war are such that any preparations of less than the multi-multi-billion-dollar sort would prove inadequate or frivolous. Thus they ignored the kinds of activities reported in the Soviet press and official publications as being purely *pro forma*. (Nevertheless, the Soviets seemed to be engaged in a much more substantial effort than even the program we are recommending for the United States in Appendix IV of this book.) [16]

Though in 1956 active and passive defense of our population and industry should have been an essential element of our posture, it was not. It was thought unimportant in 1951 because wars were so much more likely to be short than long that a war mobilization base was not very important; also, the Russians could not do enough damage to us with the few atomic bombs they had to jeopardize the future of the nation in a short war, or to interfere seriously with the war mobilization base if the war happened to be long. In 1956, protecting the war mobilization base was probably of less importance than it was in 1951 but for the opposite reason.

The amount of damage the Russians could do (in 1956) is beginning to be rather shocking. Furthermore, just because there are no sober studies available, we probably tend to overestimate the impact of a 1956 war. Because we lack an adequate Air Defense or even an inadequate Civil Defense, it is very likely that our Type II Deterrence would fail if our leaders made even a modestly cautious calculation of our capability to accept a Russian retaliatory blow. The quotes from Partridge and Peterson indicate that the two people (then) responsible respectively for Active and Passive Defenses of civilians do not think that their preparations will be very effective if the Soviets use any but the most stupid tactics. It should also be

[16] There may be another reason why American observers then and since ignore evidences of Soviet civil defense. This is a psychological one. Civil defense activity would indicate that the Soviets are taking the possibility of a thermonuclear war seriously, and even militarists find it hard to believe that anyone could do *that*. These observers feel that our own unwillingness to face up to the possibility of war and of alleviating the consequences, which shows up so dramatically in our preparations, must reflect a universal attitude. They therefore see it even when it does not exist.

noted that, in spite of the many billions that the Soviets have spent on air defense, the U.S. has enough power to come pretty close to annihilating the Russian nation if (after some preparation) it struck first. However, this does not mean that this SAC attack would prevent a Soviet retaliation. If the Soviet Union is alert (and the only circumstances in which we would attack the Soviet Union are ones in which the tension between the two nations would be so high that the Soviets would almost undoubtedly be alert), it is very reasonable to suppose that the bird would have flown the coop by the time the bombs began to land on Soviet territory. The Soviet "SAC" would be on its way with a major portion of its force against the United States. Even if we could survive this blow, nobody in the United States has made an analytic study showing that we could. Nobody has at his fingertips (in 1956) any arguments to use against those who in a crisis would choose appeasement rather than the possibility of the destruction of U.S. society.

The situation is probably symmetrical. It is quite likely that in a tense situation the Soviets could not strike the U.S. and expect the Soviet air defenses to stop enough of the U.S. retaliatory blow to make the resulting level of damage acceptable. This is probably true even though such a retaliatory blow would be significantly less in strength than a U.S. first strike. However, the Soviet air defense system might (in 1956) do relatively well against the kind of small attack that might be expected if the Soviets were able to find and exploit any serious weaknesses. If they could combine the attack with an evacuation of their own city populations to improvised protection (an evacuation which could be delayed until bombs had started to drop in the United States), then I have already mentioned that the attack would have to be very awry indeed if the Soviets are to suffer as many casualties as they suffered in World War II. In all likelihood it would be far less. However (given Soviet doctrine at that time), it is quite unlikely that they would be willing to accept the risks in cold blood or even the notion of a short war, no matter how slight the risks might be considered by an American doing paper and pencil studies.

The same doctrinaire restraint probably holds for their willingness to provoke us. While almost any objective observer of the American scene would be very doubtful that the Americans would be willing in cold blood to correct any Soviet provocation by attacking the Soviet Union, our strategic forces still look very impressive in 1956.

445

It is very doubtful that the Soviets would be willing to rely on the retaliatory threat of their own second strike capability to protect them from a U.S. attack touched off by a "hot blood" situation which might exist if they made an extremely provocative move. Therefore, for all practical purposes in 1956 we would probably have enough of both Type I and Type II Deterrences, even if objective calculations happened to cast some doubt on our capabilities in this field. However, if we were willing to rely on Soviet psychology, then the lack of any safety factor and our resulting dependence on Soviet responsibility, inertia, and caution make both kinds of deterrence unreliable. As I tried to point out in discussing how von Manstein persuaded Hitler to try the attack through the Ardennes Forest, it sometimes takes only one persuasive person with a bright idea, plus one gambling decision maker with authority, to result in a situation where a government might move in a direction which 99 per cent of a bureaucracy think inadvisable. Indeed, most of the bureaucracy may not even hear about the idea until it is too late to register objections.

Nevertheless, the Russians are not likely to challenge us in 1956. As is so often pointed out, a façade may sometimes be as effective as an objective capability. The Soviets are in fact probably quite convinced that we have more than enough Type I and II Deterrence. Since we too are convinced and so are our allies, the quality of either type of deterrence never comes to a test.

Admitting all of the above, it still must be conceded that in 1956 we are living dangerously—more dangerously than necessary, because nobody has tried very hard to distinguish between a façade and an objective capability. While deterrence is a psychological phenomenon, it is not true that one has it for all practical purposes, just because the enemy and others believe that he does. Psychological nonobjective capabilities are extremely unstable. They are subject to erosion by time and, equally important, to subtle tactics of the enemy or our own panic. The enemy can investigate and teach himself what capabilities we really have. He can also, by means of crises and other tactics, teach others what he has learned about our objective capabilities. One of the serious problems in psychological deterrence is that the learning is likely to be too convincing. These things are like a pendulum. If one has been successfully exaggerating his capabilities, removal of the façade is likely to result in disillusionment and a tremendous underestimation. This could be most serious. It may lead to quick diplomatic victories by the other side or it may lead to a disastrous situation arising because of overconfidence and miscalculation. The year 1961 seems, at this writing, likely to see such an overcorrection and corresponding readjustments in international life.

This readjustment is not inevitable. As we pointed out in Lecture II (page 285), there are many things other than Type II Deterrence threats which restrain a nation from provocative actions and these other things may, in fact, be effective in 1961. But there will still be an important difference between 1956 and 1961. In 1956 these other things were also acting, but people assumed that they were backed up by an objective Type II Deterrence capability. They will know that this is not so in 1961. This means that bargaining, even at courteous and ordinary diplomatic levels where there is no threat or even hint of violence, will be affected by consideration of what would happen if the bargaining broke down and violence or threats of violence came into the picture. It is important to realize that one does not have to be putting SAC on alert and evacuating cities to have the capability for initiating war or retaliating effectively after attack to affect innocuous-looking negotiations. Military power casts a very long shadow before it.

Another reason why the Soviets tend (in 1956) to be moderate in their provocations is that there are relatively few soft spots and power vacuums available to low levels of violence. In Europe for example, unlike the case in 1951, it is no longer possible to disguise an overwhelming aggressor force as the peaceful maneuvers of the normal satellite occupation troops. Whatever its weaknesses, NATO is strong enough to repel or hold up attacks by 10 or 20 divisions —even without using nuclear weapons. The situation is similar in most other parts of the world. Inadequate as they may be, the lines are being held by more than a corporal's guard. This means that the Soviets are restricted to either very low-level ambiguous challenges or outright and spectacular aggression. Our "psychological façade" is good enough to deter the latter, and nonmilitary programs are supposed to take care of the former.

Because our Type II Deterrence is intrinsically weak, blackmail is (in 1956) at least a theoretical possibility. However, it is probably not a good idea, even in theory, from the Russian's point of view. We have a fantastic Type III Deterrence capability—that is, our defense budget is around 10 per cent of our GNP. It is probable if the Russians blackmail us, even if we do not attack them, that unlike the French and British under the challenges that Hitler gave them, we would react by buying whatever military capability was needed in order for us to fight a war—rather than just be able to deter one. The Russians, on the other hand, are not yet in a position to launch any crash programs of sufficient magnitude to match ours, or to pre-empt if we are alert. It is therefore inadvisable for them to seriously provoke or alarm us, unless their immediate gains more than make up for the other effects of their provocation.

In addition to having thermonuclear bombs, both sides have, in the mid-1950's, inexpensive and flexible types of atomic bombs. They have developed and have begun to produce a spectrum of specialized weapons that can be used for specialized purposes. The availability of these bombs is so much greater than had been imagined in 1951 that we are almost justified in referring to this increased availability, alone, as a revolution. In the United States, at least, we are talking about possibly using bombs against such targets as individual tanks and companies of men. Certainly they seem usable in antisubmarine warfare against single submarines or light ships. We have also implemented plans to use atomic weapons in air defense; the MB-1, the warhead for the air-to-air rocket, has been tested and will soon be in production. Likewise, the Nike-Hercules, a ground-to-air rocket, is designed to carry atomic warheads.

The Russians do not have quite the same casual attitude toward bombs as we have, and there are remarks in Russian military literature that they would not use a bomb against a submarine because it is too expensive. Yet one can assume that in just a very short time their attitude will change—just as ours did.

The last B-47E has been produced but it is likely that some portion of this weapons system will remain around for at least ten years, maybe longer. However, we are talking about phasing out the early model B-47's; it is only these very late models which are likely to stay in the force for a long time. The B-36 is also now considered an obsolete plane and we are beginning to phase in its replacement, the B-52, and its jet tanker, the KC-135. Actually, the fourth model of the B-52, the B-52D, is now in production. In addition, such new weapons as the B-58, the Snark, the XB6M-1 or Seamaster (a Navy seaplane with about the capability of the B-47)—all go through their first flight tests. Although many people are excited about these new weapons systems, in all likelihood only very small numbers are going to be bought for at least the next few years. (The Sea-master is particularly interesting. It probably represents an attempt by the Navy to get involved in strategic warfare. There is a great deal of talk of the "enormous" advantage of having sea-based planes, although there are very few calculations actually given to show that these advantages actually exist. The whole concept finally seems to disappear, mainly because a new weapons system, the Polaris, gets the attention of the Navy. This last weapons system seems to be an exciting one to everybody.)

(Though not disclosed until a good deal later) the United States has gone to some trouble to pierce the Iron Curtain. The high-powered radar in Turkey that monitors Soviet missile firings and the U-2 high-altitude reconnaissance program are well-publicized examples of the kinds of activities that are carried on. *U.S. News & World Report* estimated that the United States has been spending about $2.5 billion annually on intelligence activities.[17] While the figure is in no sense official, it is clear that there is a lot of activity going on in this field which must be taken account of when one is considering the feasibility of Counterforce as Insurance or Credible First Strike Capabilities. It is also interesting to observe that there are some ways in which this information-gathering activity benefits the Soviets. If we did not have much information about their capability and if we were responsible about our national defense, we would have to hedge against the uncertainty by buying much larger forces. The Soviets, because of their smaller industrial base, could not engage in this game as well and the result would be a pronounced asymmetry in a much speeded-up arms race.

We have already mentioned that atomic weapons are being phased into air defense. In addition, the "Century" series of air defense fighters, the F-100, 101, 102, and 104, are also being phased in. With these fighters, the new radars, and the new capabilities of the ground environment, there is almost no question that air defense would work very effectively against World War II-type raids. Whether or not it would work well against the new jet aircraft-carrying nuclear weapons, particularly if subtle countermeasures are used, is still very controversial. However, further improvements in air defense are under way; in particular, production orders for Missile Master and Sage are given. These are the computers which,

[17] "The World's Big Spy Game: A Hot Front in the 'Cold War'?" Vol. XLVIII, No. 21 (May 23, 1960), p. 46.

among other things, will regulate the air battle use of the ground-to-air missiles and area defenses that are being produced.

In addition to having atomic-powered planes in development, we also have an atomic-powered rocket under way. These both look like very expensive programs, and as far as current concepts are concerned their military usefulness looks marginal. However, almost all the "experts" (including the author) are agreed that at least the basic hardware parts of the projects should be pushed. These mostly concern the power plant and its most basic component, the reactor. Whether or not the nuclear-powered missile or plane should be developed as a weapons system (a project which would be more expensive than the development of basic hardware alone) is indeed controversial. (It is decided not to do this.)

There is a great deal of worry in 1956 that the United States is falling behind, or at least losing its lead, in the technological race with the Russians. In part, this is attributed to a failure of such agencies as ARDC successfully to stimulate and guide research and development for strategic hardware. It is my belief that some of the criticism is justified—that ARDC could have done much better even with the insufficient funds that were available. Perhaps the most trenchant criticism that is launched at ARDC is that they are too firmly wedded to the Weapons System Concept. Under this notion most development and research is considered as part of a weapons system, and with relatively minor exceptions, only those projects are undertaken that can be justified as fitting into an approved weapons system. Under this concept the contracting officers and the company with the over-all systems contract has an almost impossible job to do. They are being asked to develop a great many improved components and to marry them together in a system under a tight time schedule. Frequently, in order to get the contract, the company has to promise an over-all performance that could only be obtained if each and every component met the most optimistic predictions of individual performance. This in turn means that it is most likely that the weapons system will not meet its schedule, since some of the components are almost certain not to meet the original optimistic prediction. While this would be a disappointment, it would not be a disaster if the weapons system were so designed as to hedge against a possibly degraded performance of initial components. Usually, though, it turns out that the system has been designed to take advantage of everything that it can. As a result, no compromises have been made for the possibility of any slippages, and instead of having a degraded performance the weapons system may have something close to a zero performance until it can be retrofitted or fixed.

There is also a bright spot in the research and development picture. Both American industry and the various research agencies of the Department of Defense have developed a technical and managerial skill and sophistication in research and development that promises much for the future. The airframe industry is a typical example of the changes that have occurred. Convair has acquired its Astronautics Division, Scientific Research Laboratory, and General Atomics; North American has Rocketdyne, Autonetics, and Atomics International; Boeing has its Development Center; Lockheed its Missile System Division; and so on.

The aircraft industry (which had grown accustomed to a situation in which one spends, for example, a couple of hundred million dollars on development and many billions on procurement) has begun (in 1956) to become accustomed to a new situation in which one may spend one or two billion dollars on development and from the same amount to twice as much on procurement before moving on to the next weapons system. In other words, the airplane manufacturing companies are no longer assemblers of aluminum parts; rather, they are now engaged in research and development as their major activity. The adjustment was very painful, but by 1956 it is clear that the industry is going to make it. Another effect of the tremendous increase in the rate of technological obsolescence and the increased cost of development is that we are going to tend to stick with the "Model T" or "Model A" revision of a new weapons system—there is much less tendency to go on to F, G, and H models.

At this point the Soviets are beginning to look very impressive. They have Badgers, Bears, Bisons, IRBM's and H-bombs, and are close to a successful test of an ICBM. These capabilities make deterrence a two-way street, but there are the usual doctrinal lags in adjusting to the new situation. Many of the policies enunciated by NATO and the U.S. involving the free use of atomic weapons in limited wars, massive retaliation to deter or correct minor provocations, and a de-emphasis on conventional high-explosive capabilities might have been appropriate to 1951 but are almost completely inappropriate to 1956. Nevertheless, an emphasis on the conventional use of nuclear weapons is the official theme. There are also many overtones of the Dulles "Massive Retaliation" philosophy of 1954 still left. In other words, most planners in the middle fifties, in laying down policies for the late fifties, tend to ignore the probable conditions of the late fifties and choose to be guided instead by concepts that would have been more appropriate to the early fifties. It is therefore not surprising that preparations for the early and mid-sixties are incomplete.

CHAPTER X

PRESENT AND FUTURE

WORLD WAR V (1961)

S.U.–U.S. Parity
Emergence of S.U. as a World Power
No Type II Deterrence Programmed
Potential Failure of Type I Deterrence

✧✧✧

TABLE 63

TECHNOLOGY, 1961

Arms Control (techniques and effects)
Experimental nuclear explosives
Satellites (Vanguard, Pioneer, Discoverer, Tiros, Transit, Notus, Mercury, Echo, Convier, Ranger, Mariner, etc.)
Soft Atlas and soft IRBM's deployed
25 psi Atlas, 100 psi Titan, BMEWS, and Polaris being phased in
Crash program on Minuteman and other second-generation missiles
B-47E, B-52G and H, B-58A or B form bulk of SAC
Airborne Command and Control
Bombers operated alert and dispersed
Sage and Missilemaster partially deployed
Bomarc A and Hawk being phased in
Nike-Hercules, F-100, 101, 102, 104 in service
Cheap civil defense?
Inexpensive, efficient, and versatile nuclear weapons
There are four nuclear countries
Goose, Navajo, Regulus II, F-108, etc., cancelled
British cancel Blue Streak (1960), Canada cancels CF-105 (1959)
Nuclear-powered plane and rocket still under development
X-15 test vehicle
Russians have . . . ?

✧✧✧

THE year 1961 will see arms control having some influence on our military posture. On October 31, 1958, the United States suspended the testing of nuclear weapons, and 1961 is likely to see the third

453

year of no U.S. weapon development testing. Thus 1961 will likely see the third year of an uninspected moratorium. In addition to all the other uncertainties, a U.S. military planner will worry about such questions as, Are the Soviets cheating? To what extent? What is the military significance? Even if a treaty is signed, it will take some time (two to five years) to install whatever inspection network is agreed upon. Once the inspection network is installed the military planner must consider such questions as the performance of seismographs, the ability to hide a nuclear test behind the sun, the lead time from a hidden cache of weapons to a capability in-being, the possibility that maintenance difficulties are due to sabotage, and so forth.

From the viewpoint of deterring cheating and making more certain and dramatic our response if we happen to detect cheating by clandestine intelligence, it would have been much better if the U.S. government had clearly stated that the test ban would be officially uninspected for three or four years. It would also have been a very good precedent if we had insisted on getting long lead-time items (like the buildings that house the monitoring stations) started immediately, even while negotiations were going on. Most important of all, it would have been of real value to have had in existence in 1958 an experienced organization of "hiders and finders" [1] with practical and theoretical experience on the problems. We still have no such organization, and 1961 is likely to see us entering arms control conferences uneducated and unprepared.

The test-suspension negotiations at Geneva illustrate the importance of doing our homework. In July and August of 1958 the Western and Eastern experts agreed at Geneva, after a short, hectic conference (at which most of the technical facts were worked out in long evening sessions) that about 180 stations around the world (about 21 in the Soviet Union) would suffice to pick up illegal explosions greater than 5 KT in yield. Within months, on the basis of new data and experiments, the Western experts decided they had

---

[1] Amrom Katz's term. He has suggested that we set up two organizations and turn over a large area—like the state of Texas—to them and let these two organizations play seriously various kinds of Arms Control games. We would thus build up some intellectual and experimental capital, on which our negotiators and planners could draw. The "hiders" organization has another value, one which would all by itself justify the expense of the organization. It could create a credible capability for evading an Arms Control agreement. Fred Iklé has pointed out the value of creating such possibilities. Raising the apprehension among Soviet planners that we might cheat should make them much more interested in reliable inspection procedures.

been off by at least a factor of four. A few months later, several ingenious schemes (testing in big holes or outer space) were worked out to evade the proposed inspection system almost completely as far as kiloton-type tests were concerned. While these schemes take some lead time to put in, this lead time is comparable to the time which will elapse between mid-59 and the final installation of any control system approved in 1960 or 1961.

From the viewpoint of Arms Control, one of the most interesting innovations of 1961 should be the possibility of the experimental use of nuclear explosives in one or more peacetime applications. In May 1959 the Atomic Energy Commission sponsored the Second Plowshare Symposium on Industrial and Scientific Uses of Nuclear Explosions. At an earlier symposium there had been much interest in the subject, but nobody expected anything to happen very soon. In the second one, many of the ideas had had time to mature. There were about fifty papers presented on various aspects of nuclear explosives. The suggestions for peaceful uses of nuclear explosives included: artificial harbors, sea-level ship canals, underground oil storage, power, isotope production, geothermal steam plants, salt water distillation, improvement of underground water supplies, mining, shale oil production, meteorological experiments, and other scientific experiments.

The length of the list should not be surprising. Nuclear explosives are a uniquely concentrated but very simple and relatively cheap source of power, heat, and pressure, as well as of neutrons and other radiation. Once they become even slightly available, many people will look for and find applications for these new devices which in turn will make them even more available. In fact, the terms on which they are available at this writing were spelled out by AEC at the Second Plowshare Symposium as follows: roughly a half million dollars for small explosives in the low kiloton region to perhaps a million dollars in the low megaton region. The AEC is careful to note that the above charges are for small quantities.

While no single suggestion at the 1959 symposium looked earthshaking, most experts believe that a number of the ideas discussed could be in programs by the mid-sixties. (A project to dig an artificial harbor in Alaska is definitely programmed at this writing.) Since some of the individual projects promised to use hundreds or even thousands of bombs, it is possible that even a private international market of buyers and sellers of nuclear explosives will eventually spring up. This would be particularly likely if there is technological progress in the design of very simple bombs made of readily available materials. Once there develops a legitimate market for nuclear explosives, then in the absence of controls, many nations will manufacture them for sale or peaceful use, if not by 1970, then by 1980. However, unless one of these nations is very irresponsible, there should be a fair degree of voluntary control over the distribution of these devices.

I will discuss later some of the problems that might arise as a result of the possible dissemination of nuclear weapons. I should point out, though, that at the present writing it is somewhat unlikely that nuclear explosives will be as successful as I have indicated they might be. As Lewis Bohn has forcibly pointed out to me, the above discussion mirrors almost exactly the early (incorrect) postwar expectations on the speed of development of nuclear reactors and the consequent strategic and control problems. The Baruch plan for the control of nuclear weapons was preoccupied with this much overestimated problem.

I believe that a much better economic and technical case can be made for the use of nuclear explosives than could be made for the early postwar reactors. In addition, there is a much smaller distance between a nuclear explosive and a bomb than between a reactor and a bomb. In the first case the distinction is often semantic; in the second case we may need a major chemical industry. This is one place where an attempt to raise the standard of living may result in a drastic lowering of these standards.[2] I therefore believe that if nuclear explosives do not present a problem it is likely to be because of legal, social, and political obstacles to this development. If this is correct, then those who want to see this development controlled should probably give a vote of thanks to such disrespectful people as Khrushchev and some of the "peace groups" for helping to create

[2] Dr. Harold Brown (Director, Lawrence Radiation Laboratory, Livermore) after reading the manuscript in June 1960 pointed out to me that the above discussion makes its points with too great assurance. He suggests that we may be giving up substantial gains if we restrict the peaceful use of nuclear explosives. What we will not get might even have been substantial enough to make a sizeable contribution to solving the economic problems discussed later in this chapter. We might even eat our cake and have it too, either by designing only peaceful nuclear devices which cannot be used as weapons or by restricting the use of nuclear explosives to channels which we think are safe—for example, to U.N. auspices. Finally, Dr. Brown points out that there is much controversy over whether the world or democracy would become less secure if there were a widespread distribution of nuclear weapons. Society is complicated; and while many people find it difficult to visualize the conduct of international relations in a nuclear-armed world, human society has adjusted to even larger changes than this in the past and may adjust again. Rather than fight

the social, legal, and political barriers. It has been rumored that Khrushchev would like to receive the Nobel Peace Prize, but 1961 seems much too soon for this judgment. However if, in fact, the Soviets and the U.S. do negotiate a successful ban on nuclear tests, and if the Soviets do not cheat, and lastly if the benefits which many expect to accrue from such a ban do accrue, then I personally feel that most of the above will have been the result of Khrushchev's initiative and he may be a logical candidate for Mr. Nobel's accolade.

The year 1961 should see something which was scarcely visualized in 1956, a number of satellites in orbit. One of the major activities of the Department of Defense or the Space Agency will be the problem of space surveillance; we will almost undoubtedly try to keep track of all the objects that are in the skies (assuming that nobody goes to a lot of trouble of putting up an extremely large number of small radar reflectors with the idea of saturating the system). Indicative of the new state of affairs is the Navy's Dark Fence project. This project, on February 2, 1960, detected a previously unknown satellite. By February 23, a somewhat embarrassed Department of Defense decided that the intruder was our own Discoverer 5 which had, unknown to us, gone into orbit. It would have been difficult to convince anybody in 1956 that by 1960 we would be losing satellites and then finding them. The chief military use of satellites in the early and mid-sixties will probably be in such fields as prewar reconnaissance, weather prediction, tactical warning, communication, postattack damage assessment, and possibly tactical identification of hostile ICBM bases and Polaris submarines by the radiation emitted by missiles (during the initial phase of their flight). One of the most interesting applications may be available in 1961 or

---

"Progress," one might wish to spend his time learning how to live with it. In particular, it might be tragic to evade facing inevitable future problems by encouraging wishful thinking on the possibility of preventing them from arising at all. For example, almost none of the common suggestions for preventing the diffusion of nuclear weapons are likely to change the policies of nations we worry a great deal about (such as China), unless such nations prove more cooperative than can reasonably be expected.

Harold Brown's points may turn out to have merit. In any question as complex as that under discussion, one must, in the long run, depend on informed judgment and intuition in addition to rigorous analysis. For whatever it is worth, the author of this book views the spread of nuclear weapons with the gravest apprehension. Some of the reasons for this feeling are given on pages 491 to 494. While I agree with the notion that we will not be able to control the diffusion of weapons over the next 50 years by the kinds of social, legal, and political barriers which have been erected against Project Plowshare, and which are likely to be erected by normal negotiations, such barriers can effect 5-, 10-, and 20-year delays. It is simply my judgment that if we can buy such time, it is worth buying. We will then be better able to anticipate problems and set up arrangements ahead of time.

1962. This is the Navy's Transit program that will enable a ship (or Polaris submarine) to determine its location within a small fraction of a mile, thus eliminating or reducing a major problem of ocean-based strategic missiles. If the reconnaissance satellites work out well they may eliminate or reduce one of the most important asymmetries between the U.S. and the S.U.—the Iron Curtain. They could conceivably even be of value in localizing some of the mobile or portable systems. In addition, such programs as MIDAS (infrared detecting satellite) could be of great value in giving warning of a surprise ICBM attack. Unfortunately, it is somewhat unlikely that any of the satellite systems will be, militarily speaking, reliably operable in 1961. But another 1956 gleam in the eye, ballistic missiles, will be in operating units. There will be some soft Atlas sites available, and some initial hard sites of 25 psi or higher may be coming in. Three or four Polaris submarines will be going through the operational suitability testing stage. Some Titans at around 100 psi may also be available or en route.

This small number of missiles will of course be supplemented by quite a force of manned bombers that will have in their bombbays a great deal more megatons than the missiles have in their warheads. The bombers will include a number of B-47E's (and maybe even some of the earlier models). It is likely that the last B-52 will have been produced. This will be the "H" model version or even a later one. I have already discussed the significance of these improvements in negating even an improved Soviet local defense.

Even if their defenses are thus degraded the Soviets still have to maintain them because the B-52's capability (if it gets a free ride) to carry many weapons and deliver them accurately makes them a dreadful threat in certain important situations in this time period. In 1961 missiles will not be as threatening since they will be expensive, or at least few in number, and may have relatively low accuracy and reliability and will be able to destroy only one target per missile launched.

Some of the bombers will be on 15-minute ground alert (an incredible operation by 1956 standards and one which the author of this book predicted could not be done). The Ballistic Missile Early Warning System (BMEWS), which is supposed to supply the 15-minute warning, is scheduled to arrive at just about this time; but in all probability this early capability will be incomplete or somewhat unreliable or subject to degradation by enemy action, so that we will not be able to depend on it for reliable warning. However, there will be a newly installed bomb alarm system to give instantaneous warning of any bombs dropped on any NATO bases. This means that in normal times our bombers on ground alert will complicate the enemy's attack by requiring him to be closely coordinated. Yet it may not complicate his attack to the point of infeasibility.

The bombers can be made very much more useful if they can be kept airborne or put into hard shelters or operated more dispersed, or all three. Whether any of these will be carried through adequately by 1961 seems to be quite doubtful. Unless the bombers are sheltered, put on airborne alert, or provided with reliable warning, it is the few hard missile bases plus a very small number of Polaris submarines which will provide the bulk of our reliable "strike second" Type I Deterrence in 1961.

There is one other comment I should make about the 1961 manned bombers. In all probability their penetration aids will be limited to what they can carry with them. The U.S. program of ground-launched decoys (Goose) was cancelled in 1959; presumably none of these will be available to us. As far as is publicly known, the Soviets do not have any such program either. As I mentioned in Lecture II, for some ten years air defense planning, preparations, and programs have been bedeviled by the spectre of the enemy using hundreds or thousands of ground-launched decoys. However, there is no evidence that either the United States or the Russians have ever had such devices.

The supersonic B-58 should be in full production (assuming it gets a production order) and some of them will probably already be phased into the force. The land-based IRBM's, which caused such a flurry of interest in 1958, will have been re-evaluated by 1961. Everyone will now be aware that soft overseas-based IRBM's have a major defect. Even though their vulnerability to Soviet IRBM's escaped most "expert" and almost all public notice in 1958 and 1959, it would have done no good to refrain from "rocking the boat" in those years. By the time they are emplaced all know of their second strike weakness, and their possible usefulness as a first strike weapon looks like a disability to most observers.

It was announced in 1959 that the new North American Air Defense Command combat operations center, which will have overall responsibility for the conduct of air defense, will be put deep underground. (This decision is typical of the increased importance of protective construction in the missile age. Having a headquarters that can survive is important to the performance of every kind of strategic force, and we can expect a number of crash programs in research and development in this field.) Active defense has many new capabilities. Among these are weapons such as Bomarc, Nike-Hercules, and Hawk, and elaborate computer facilities such as Sage and Missile Master. Old jet fighters have been replaced with new supersonic ones. In spite of this progress many critics are saying "too little and too late," and advocates of Finite Deterrence are pressing for major cancellations as an alternative toward greater efforts. The greatest uncertainty of the value of active defense will revolve around the question of whether the Soviets or the Americans have put in cheap but effective complementary civil defense programs (see Appendix IV) and the ability of the air defense to survive attack by missiles. (Neither problem was scarcely considered in 1956.)

The experience of the SAGE system is indicative of the difficulties that a complicated weapons system can undergo. The system was started in 1955 and the 1961-fiscal-year budget called for the completion of twenty-two direction centers, three combat centers and eight hardened super-combat centers. The super-combat centers had been added very late in the program to take account of the fact that in the missile race it was very important to have the air defense able to resist missile attacks. By 1961 it had been decided that SAGE-type air defense was beginning to become obsolete and the fiscal 1961 budget was changed to drop the hardened combat centers, a frank admission that no attempt would be made to protect this part of the defense against missile attacks. Partly the decision reflects budgeting opposition to the cost of the needed changes, partly it reflects a seeming change in the Soviet threat from bombers to missiles, but mostly the decision reflects the growing influence of the Finite Deterrence philosophy and the waning of the Counterforce as Insurance and Credible First Strike positions.

By 1961 there should be in the stockpiles of both the United States and the Soviet Union inexpensive and versatile bombs. These will have about the same relationship to the bombs of the mid-1950's as the modern motor car has to Henry Ford's Model T. The bombs will be available for any use, in such forms as ICBM warheads, air-to-air rockets, tactical fighter bombers, atomic cannons, depth

460

bombs, suitcases, and so forth. However, for the first time the developments in weapons will be outclassed by developments in other areas. All countries will realize that the crucial element in making a nation a nuclear power is possessing a weapon system and not just some warheads. In particular, all strategists will be aware of the distinction between first and second strike weapon systems and the difficulty a nation has in obtaining the latter.

The difficulty, risk, and expense of the technological race will be highlighted by cutbacks, slowdowns, and cancellations of such weapons systems as Nike-Zeus, Regulus, F-108, Bomarc, Jupiter, Thor, B-58, Nike-Hercules, and the B-70. It is of course nothing new to have a project cancelled, but there is one major difference between the kind of thing which is happening in 1961 and the kind of thing which happened say in 1951, and to some extent in 1956. It used to be true, for example, that we had to develop four or five fighters for every one that was procured in quantity, so the Air Force had a large competitive menu to pick from. It was all right to do this as long at it cost 100 million dollars or so to develop a fighter. By 1956 this cost had increased by a factor of almost 5, and the number of fighters that were being developed, as compared to the number that were procured was cut by quite a bit. By 1961 the cost of developing a fighter like the F-108 had begun to run into billions of dollars and so, at most, one fighter was programmed to be developed, and this program was in fact cancelled. This meant the whole gender was cancelled.

Similarly, for a long-range missile, the cost to develop an ICBM runs into the multiple billions. If a small force, say less than 500, is procured, development cost will about equal the procurement (though not the installation and operating) cost, and if we develop two competing missiles we may literally find that the expense of developing competitors forces us to cut our force by an appreciable amount.

The difficulties of keeping up in the technological race were reflected in the experience of the British and the Canadians. The British cancelled their Blue Streak project after spending almost a quarter billion dollars on it and the Canadians cancelled the CF-105 fighter project after spending close to a half billion dollars. It is quite clear that both of these nations will have to depend on the United States to develop major strategic weapons. The difficulty in the development of weapon systems affected France, which turned out not to be a nuclear power, although it had tested two nuclear

461

weapons. It was only a nuclear country. Their inability to make the club is highlighted by the fact that they were not invited to the Geneva negotiations for control of nuclear weapons. In fact, Secretary Gates in an interview stated that U.S. law forbids the transfer of any U.S. secret information to a foreign power that has not itself achieved any competency in the nuclear field and that as far as he (Secretary Gates) was concerned, competency was defined as being about equal to the British.

One of the most interesting and controversial 1961 projects will be the X-15 test vehicle—a device which will carry a man well over a hundred thousand feet and with speeds several times the speed of sound. It is a precursor to the hypersonic Dynasoar vehicle (expected around 1965). Nobody knows where it will fit in the military system, but few doubt it will find a place (and almost nobody argues with the necessity for at least the development program).

The nuclear-powered plane will not have been flown by 1961, although substantially more than a billion dollars will have been spent in research and development in the preceding decade. Even if one does fly in the next few years, it will likely be only a test model which may or may not be a useful military prototype. This is not to say that the project is not extremely valuable. I believe it might turn out to be very important, and that development should be pushed more vigorously than it has been. I mention the difficulties only to illustrate again how expensive research and development is today and the kinds of gambles that must be taken almost decades in advance of the payoff. A project for an atomic rocket will also be in the mill. Current estimates are that a flyable prototype may be achieved by 1965, although most people think it is likely to take somewhat longer. In any case, we will have spent more than a quarter of a billion dollars on this project by 1965, again without having any firm military requirements in view.

Let us examine one of the more menacing (but by no means the most menacing) possibilities for the 1961 strategic situation. It is difficult to compare today the strengths of two nations, but an enormous change will have occurred since 1956. Perhaps it will be as great as Khrushchev implies when he says, "a fundamental shift has taken place in the balance of power between socialist and capitalist states. . . . The distribution of forces in the international arena insures a preponderance of the peace-loving state." [3] Whether

---

[3] Speech of January 14, 1960. Quoted in *The Official Army Information Digest* (U.S. Army, Pentagon) June 1960, Vol. 15, No. 6, page 33.

Khrushchev is right or not about the Communist bloc having preponderance, in some over-all sense, the Soviets will almost undoubtedly have achieved a kind of psychological and military parity with
the United States. We will still be able to deliver enormously greater
megatonnage to the Soviet Union in a peacetime environment, but
the reader should have gathered by now that this is no criterion
for either Type I or Type II Deterrence. The United States may be
particularly weak in the latter. In fact, given the possible Soviet
lead in missiles, their interest in cheap but useful civil defense programs, and a sober attitude toward the risks of war and peace, the
Soviets are likely to have much more Type II Deterrence than we
have. What is more, everybody will know it. We will know it; our
allies will know it; the neutrals will know it; and the Russians will
know it. Because we may have so little Type II Deterrence, it will
not be necessary for the Russians to threaten or blackmail our allies;
the threat will be automatic and dominate even "friendly" negotiations. Similarly, because the Soviets will probably have "adequate"
Type I Deterrence we may not be able to use credible counter blackmail threats or even exert much aggressive pressure in a crisis.
*Therefore, by 1961 the defense of the West could take a different
form.* Europe will no longer be defended by the threat of immediate
nuclear retaliation either local or massive, but by Type III Deterrence plus whatever caution, good sense, and good will the Soviets
choose to show.

The Soviets may exhibit all of these qualities in some degree or
other. As Khrushchev has proudly announced, "We are getting
richer and when a person has more to eat he gets more democratic."
While the increasing "bourgeoisation" of large segments of Soviet
society should improve their international manners, it will still be
clear to all that however the next crisis is touched off, the Soviets
do not have to back down because of fear of an attack by the United
States—but we may. (I am assuming here that we have not put in
a civil defense program, repaired holes in our air defense, and expanded our offense, and that, in terms of a Credible First Strike
Capability, the Soviets have done these things.)

This would be a startling change in the military situation, and
it could produce startling changes in the international situation.
Just as in 1936 when the Belgians and the Dutch saw that they
could no longer rely on the British for their defense and therefore
shifted into a policy of neutralism, it is possible that many small
and medium nations will begin going in that direction. (Small and

463

medium nations are sometimes acutely conscious of their security needs. Once it becomes clear that the umbrella of the Strategic Air Command no longer protects them, they will begin to ask themselves what other arrangements they can make.) Equally possible, particularly if the Soviets are moderately but not excessively truculent, the Western European nations may rearm, form tighter alliances (possibly even moving toward a United States of Europe), or make some vigorous (or despairing?) attempts at arms control, collective security, and world government. If there is sufficient time for them to react, the Western Europeans may by themselves provide the wherewithal with which to restore the strategic balance. Figure 6 gives some comparisons of the potential power the Western European Union (EEC plus Great Britain) could muster as compared to the United States and the Soviet Union. While the use of such simple indicators as are used in Figure 6 can be misleading, the bars do indicate that, given the necessary resolve and organizing ability, the Europeans could play again the role in world affairs that their numbers, knowledge, experience, wealth, and technology would suggest as being appropriate.

The year 1961 should see another big change, which stems from the S.U.–U.S. parity and the inadequacies of U.S. Type II and III Deterrence but is in addition to these. This change is the emergence of the Soviet Union as a World Power that feels very much at home in every corner of the globe. I mentioned in discussing World War III (1951) that much of our international difficulties stemmed from the fact that the Soviets had become an important European and Asiatic power as a result of World War II. Their becoming a World Power is likely to have even more far-reaching effects. It could mean, for example, the penetration by peaceful and subversive means of Africa and the Western Hemisphere. Sometimes people misunderstand the impact of such terms as "parity" and "World Power." They seem to think of them as a score in some interesting but irrelevant game. It is not at all like that. Soviet successes and achievements—the growth of the Soviet "presence"—could well mean that the West has to move into a smaller house—that our children will not be as well fed. (I am speaking halfway between literally and figuratively.)

In discussing World Wars V through VIII, I will on the whole assume, aside from the technological revolutions, continuations of current conditions. Even for World War V, this may be unreasonable or inconsistent. For example, the weakening or disappearance of Type II Deterrence and the emergence of the Soviet Union as a

World Power must almost inevitably change the whole character of the defense of the West. Many experts think that NATO is passing through "a crisis of confidence." [4] By 1961 this crisis should have

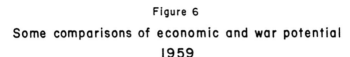

Figure 6
Some comparisons of economic and war potential
1959

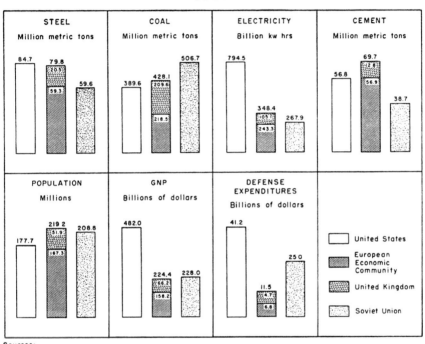

Sources:

1. Production and population of E.E.C., U.K., and U.S.: *Monthly Bulletin of Statistics*, May, 1960
2. GNP for E.E.C. and U.S.: United Nations Statistical Office
3. Soviet production and population: *Narodnoe Khoziaistvo SSSR V 1958 Godu (The National Economy of the USSR in 1958)* Moscow: 1959 put out by the Central Statistical Administration
4. Soviet GNP and Defense Expenditures: Doris Ikle, Cost Analysis Department, The RAND Corporation
5. U.S. Defense Expenditures: *The Budget of the U.S. Government, 1960*

matured. The eventual effect of this "crisis of confidence" might be to disintegrate the alliance, change it to a supranational organization, or force the creation of large limited or "independent deterrent" forces. The crisis might just bring deep feelings of insecurity (probably partially suppressed, but ready to emerge at the first hint of a crisis), or it might bring the initiation of a crash program

[4] See "The Strained Alliance," in *NATO and American Security*, ed. by Klaus Knorr, Princeton University Press, Princeton, N.J., 1959, pp. 3–10.

to restore Type II Deterrence, or something equally dramatic that is not in any of today's programs. *It is impossible at this moment to foretell what will come.* The only thing that seems relatively certain is that there will be some dramatic political or physical changes.

Similarly, in the arms control area, I will assume that the current precarious status continues. In what follows I will assume that there are no explicit agreements that are especially successful in retarding the spread of technology and that at the same time there are no incidents or forces that violently affect the current implicit agreements and practices. It should be realized that the effect of current implicit agreements is large.

Before World War II it was possible for almost any nation or even powerful private group to buy openly or clandestinely any kind of arms that it desired. One could not always get the latest model tanks or planes, but some reasonably modern ones were available at a price, even though the terms of trade at which they were available might be relatively onerous. This is not true today. Both the Soviet and the Western blocs keep a relatively tight control on the distribution of arms, and such neutrals as Sweden and Switzerland are careful not to rock any boats. There is even a tight control of the so-called "Nth-country" problem. (Even though both Sweden and Switzerland have in principle authorized their departments of defense to obtain nuclear weapons, both nations have refused to appropriate the necessary funds. The French have a program to obtain such arms, but their program seems to be addressed to the prestige of being an atomic power rather than achieving much objective capability. However, the enlargement of the nuclear list to include France may still turn out to be a major spur to other powers.)

The nuclear arms situation could have been different. If, for example, we were still in the era of the big independent private munitions maker, I would have expected that by 1961 the South Africans or somebody would have a uranium-diffusion plant financed by European capital and designed by European technicians. The ostensible purpose of this plant would be to refine uranium for nuclear reactors, but it would, on the side, either openly or clandestinely also produce weapon-grade uranium for sale. (Its major profits might come from this "side" activity.) It is clear that there are powerful sanctions operating to prevent this kind of thing from happening. Nuclear explosives are just not being treated like a "more powerful explosive." However, it is by no means clear that such sanctions will operate throughout the entire 1960 time period. In fact, if the Chinese test a bomb, or if any of the four present nuclear countries use nuclear weapons in a limited war, one could expect many more countries to feel under an extreme pressure to obtain their own nuclear arms. However, in spite of these possibilities, I will ignore the effect of dramatic stabilizing or destabilizing changes in the discussion of World Wars V through VIII.

A war caused by accident or miscalculation, or by unauthorized behavior, is a possibility in 1961. Both sides will likely have their bombers on extreme alert, and missiles, possibly with hair-trigger buttons (and safeties), will also be in the force. The probability of accident should, however, be quite low, much lower than it may become in later years, partly because, as I have already mentioned, the buttons will not normally be kept connected and partly because there just will not be very many of them.

The important tactical problem will, in 1961, not only involve pure plane attacks but pure missile attacks and combined missile, plane, and submarine attacks (though in all likelihood the strategic submarine will not yet be of great importance). Let us consider some features of a simple *pure missile attack*, though the reader is cautioned that the combined attacks are possible and introduce complexities in the analysis.

As we mentioned in Lecture II, the missile attack is a problem in engineering and physics in a way that no other military action has ever been. It is so calculable that if we let our guard drop it is quite possible that a modestly gambling or irresponsible decision maker on the other side might exploit a "temporary weakness" in the coldest of cold-blooded manners. This is particularly true because missiles in 1961 are likely to be an order of magnitude better performers than any sober analyst would have predicted in 1956. Their accuracy is phenomenal by 1956 standards, and their reliability is also likely to be much better than the early expectations.

Figure 7 shows the Russian requirements for numbers of missiles as compared to their single-shot probabilities and the amounts of retaliation they are willing to accept if we assume some fifty home bases for SAC bombers in the United States. In 1961 it is quite probable that the Soviets will have hundreds of missiles, so the only question will be what is the single-shot probability of these missiles, how much of SAC is in the air, and will that portion of SAC on 15-

467

minute ground alert receive adequate warning. The BMEWS will just be coming into service in 1961 and so may not be working reliably for some interval. We have already discussed some of the potential weaknesses of "warning" as a sole protection.

Figure 7

Missiles required to attack a 50-point target system

Almost nothing has been published in the unclassified field on what the CEP's and yields of Soviet missiles might be, so we must leave it to the reader to judge whether he thinks the Soviets might attain the technological capabilities suggested by Figure 8 as neces-

The Russians must meet basic requirements to get our bombers, and they must add whatever they need to get the missile bases. Otherwise they must be willing to accept whatever damage the small number of missiles we will have in 1961 will do. So far as any of our soft, concentrated, Atlas bases are concerned, these should not add much to Soviet requirements. The hard and/or dispersed missile bases may or may not be a different story by then. Everything will depend on the relation between the yield and CEP of the Soviet missiles and the hardness of the U.S. bases. Figure 7 indicates what combinations of yield and CEP the Soviets must attain in order to get a 50 per cent chance of destroying 4, 25, and 100 psi bases respectively in a single shot. (If one missile has a 50 per cent chance of destroying a base, then it only takes 4 missiles to have a 95 per cent chance of destroying the base.)

Almost nothing has been published in the unclassified field on what the CEP's and yields of Soviet missiles might be, so we must leave it to the reader to judge whether he thinks the Soviets might attain the technological capabilities suggested by Figure 8 as necessary for them if they are to be able to destroy the hard missile bases.[5]

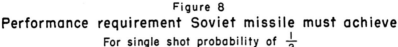

Figure 8
Performance requirement Soviet missile must achieve
For single shot probability of $\frac{1}{2}$

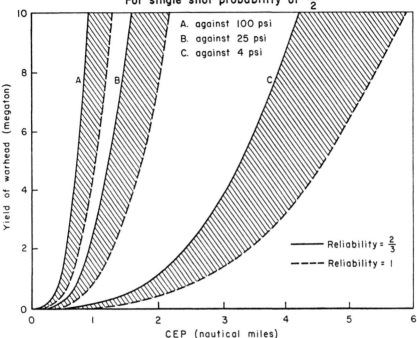

A. against 100 psi
B. against 25 psi
C. against 4 psi

Reliability $= \frac{2}{3}$

Reliability $= 1$

CEP (nautical miles)

As already mentioned, we will also have some Polaris submarines in 1961. These will be relatively new and untried, and most important of all, very few in number. Even if the program does not slip, their net destructive capability may not be very impressive in 1961. In addition, we have already suggested that the Polaris system may or may not have some vulnerabilities *as a system,* depending on what arrangements have been made to hinder peacetime attacks or surveillance and to insure adequate command and control and resistance against postattack blackmail tactics. The possible weakness of Type I Deterrence just described has aroused much concern. Except among a small number of Europeans, the even more startling

[5] It has been suggested that U.S. missiles have a CEP of between one and two miles. See, for example, the President's State of the Union address of January 7, 1960, reprinted in the *New York Times,* January 8, 1960.

disappearance of Type II Deterrence has aroused little attention.

One of the big changes in Western doctrine between hypothetical World War V of 1961 and real World Wars I and II and hypothetical World Wars III and IV is that a new type of *defensive mentality* will likely now be the official point of view. The change has been so gradual from the previous overemphasis on the offense, that few people will have noticed the change or recognized its consequences. I pointed out earlier that it is probably perfectly proper to coin a name for that new doctrine which argues that all of our strategic and most of our tactical military problems can be solved by our buying a Homicide Pact Machine. It is a new kind of "Maginot mentality." The heart of the notion of being Maginot-minded is that one does not examine his preparedness posture carefully to see whether or not (a) it can be degraded or nullified by actions of the enemy; or (b) whether it handles sufficiently well the range of strategic situations that can occur; it depends on a single panacea.

It certainly ought to be clear by this point that a total reliance on being willing to commit suicide cannot be even a moderately reliable deterrent against almost all "ambiguous" and most "non-ambiguous" challenges, including ultimatums against allies or "peacetime" attacks on our own military system; neither does it insure against irrational behavior by the enemy. It is also clear that just because we have put all our bets on the notion that Type I Deterrence will work that we are fearful to examine carefully the quality of our Type I Deterrence. As soon as one examines soberly our current (1960) and programmed postures and dependence on vague notions of deterrence, one would, I think, find it almost intolerable to live with the hope that a Homicide Pact Machine would work and prove satisfactory. However, even those who are unwilling to examine carefully the basic differences between Type I and Type II Deterrence should notice that a low-quality Type I Deterrent can run into troubles. Only one who is bemused with this new kind of "Maginot-mindedness" will not notice that, even if the Soviets do not attack, our negotiators are likely to be so fearful of provoking them that Soviet negotiators will be able to achieve most of what they want by diplomatic means, simply because we do not have adequate Type I Deterrence. If there are any slippages in our program or unexpected successes on the part of the Soviets, then we will have a low-quality Type I Deterrent.

Of course, most people will believe that whatever weaknesses we may have in 1961 will disappear in a few years because new technological developments have made Type I Deterrence very easy, and the notion that Type I Deterrence is all we need as far as our strategic forces go may still persist (unless the Soviets have gone to some trouble to dispel it). This view is set forth (somewhat more carefully and competently than is usual) in a report by the Special Project Committee on Security through Arms Control of the National Planning Association.[6] Consider the following excerpt:

1. *Deterrent strategy and the adequacy of present nuclear weapons.* The U.S. has a counter-force strategy as well as a retaliator strategy to deal with a direct Russian nuclear attack. (That is, in the event of war, we plan to destroy Russian striking forces in addition to cities.) While the counter-force element of our grand strategy has been valid for the 1950's when Russia has had relatively few and vulnerable intercontinental weapons of mass destruction, it has serious disadvantages for the missile age:

(a) It demands an accelerated arms race, with the U.S. striving for overwhelming qualitative and quantitative superiority over Russia's numerous and increasingly invulnerable forces. U.S. superiority is particularly necessary for successful counterforce action, because the U.S. presumes Russia to be the potential aggressor, and therefore the U.S. needs additional numbers to absorb the first blow, as well as superior numbers and capabilities to "win" militarily.

(b) It demands an instant response and therefore tempts preemptive action. Thus, it promotes tension, heightens the dangers of accidental war, and continuously risks world disaster.

(c) Our will to use this retaliatory force, if necessary, may become eroded through contemplation of the enormity of the resulting human catastrophe. Thus, our deterrent might be dangerously weakened.

A purely retaliatory strategy against key Russian industrial complexes can by itself soon provide adequate deterrence against a Russian attack against the U.S. as it can be based on essentially invulnerable retaliatory forces, such as small, dispersed, underground, or mobile missiles. Further, a retaliatory policy, devoid of counter-force ambitions and secure with invulnerable bases, would offer significant opportunities:

(a) Relatively small numbers of weapons systems are required, because the targets are key Russian industrial centers, which are vulnerable and few in number compared with military targets.

(b) Reaction can be delayed and yet our retaliatory capacity can still survive. This could provide time for identification and evaluation of an accident or a fanatical act; it could even provide time for evacuation of enemy cities so that our retaliatory could be against material resources rather than civilian populations.

(c) Hundreds of kilotons will probably suffice for each of these strategic weapons, making multimegaton explosions unnecessary, and thus minimizing radioactive debris.

(d) Military resources can be made available to meet pressing needs

* *1970 without Arms Control,* Washington, National Planning Association, 1958.

471

for deterrent forces to counter massed conventional attack or limited aggression. The counter-force strategy is now the doctrinal source of the arms race, demanding big bombs to make up for bombing errors and to kill with certainty small and elusive targets. It also demands smaller packaging to permit more accurate and swift delivery systems. It requires virtually indefinite testing. However, a purely retaliatory strategy vis-a-vis Russia requires only "a sufficiency"—enough destruction to deter Russia from direct nuclear attack on the U.S. will be able to use deterrent forces (when necessary) and the credibility of the retaliatory deterrent can be maintained. The Polaris and Minute Man rocket weapons now being developed will provide the U.S. with an adequate and invulnerable retaliatory force for this purpose.[7]

It might also turn out that the above views, which were quite common from 1957 to 1960, will be passé by 1961. People may understand that in addition to having stability against accident and surprise attack, *one needs stability against provocation and objective capabilities to alleviate the consequences of a failure of deterrence.* The Soviets may go to some trouble to educate us in the importance of these concepts. In fact, by 1961 almost all military planners may understand the importance of being able to accept *retaliatory* blows in the sense of being able to distinguish among 2,000,000, 5,000,000, 20,000,000, 50,000,000, and 100,000,000 U.S. or Soviet deaths. It may be apparent to everybody that we will be in a period (which may last only a few years or may last much longer) in which there is an enormous difference in the bargaining ability of a country which has made the modest preparations (in 1959–60) that enable it to put its population in a place of safety on 24 to 48 hours notice, and a country which has not made these preparations. Furthermore, it may be that no amount of earnest endeavor in 1961 will make up for inaction in 1959–60. This difference may be particularly apparent if, as I have suggested, the Russians have developed this capability and we have not.

If this last statement turns out to be correct, then the United States must be prepared, at the choice of the Soviet Union, to face an erosion of its position, an erosion much more precipitous and

[7] Similar views on "Finite Deterrence" have been expressed by many people: "Finite Deterrence Controlled Retaliation" by Commander P. H. Backus, USN, Prize Essay, 1959, *U.S. Naval Institute Proceedings*, Vol. 85 (March 1959); "The Problem of Accidental War" by Richard S. Leghorn (Colonel, Air Force Reserve), *Bulletin of the Atomic Scientists*, Vol. XIV (June 1958), pp. 205–209; "Deterrence and Defense" by George W. Rathjens, Jr., *ibid.*, pp. 225–228.

dangerous than any which is achieved by a series of successful ambiguous challenges. Soviet challenges thus need not be ambiguous.

The situation need not be so asymmetrical or dangerous. If we or both sides do in fact have some Credible First Strike Capability (including at least modest civil defense programs), then the situation will be very close to the position the world was in before World War I (or to the symmetrical situation described on pages 141 to 144). It was then true that the country which mobilized first and attacked, or which won the first large battle, could hope to win the war in a short time.

Meanwhile, the country which was slow in mobilization or which lost the first battle could at most hope to stalemate the war and drag it out. If the war were dragged out enough, both sides "lost." In spite of these calculations, even if one side thought it could win the war it tended to be wary of risking either war *or extreme provocation.*

The main difference between 1914 and 1961 would be that minutes and hours will take the place of days and years, and that the stakes and risks are much larger also. Even "winning a short war" may involve suffering millions of casualties, billions of dollars of property damage, and a somewhat more radioactive environment. "Winning a long war" would be worse still. However, even though the outcome of a "long" war will probably be closer to a mutual disaster, even in this case the disaster should not be total for the victor. The victor's position after a "long" war should be comparable to or better than the one we discussed in Lecture I in connection with the "early" or "small" war.

In 1961, because of the strategic instability and shifting balance of power, situations could easily arise in which there is enormous push and pull between Type I and Type II Deterrence. In addition, there will be pressures on the principal antagonists inducing them to settle their differences one way or another, pressures other than just the fact that they have been provoked or that their will has been thwarted.

In 1961 it will be clear to almost all of the important decision makers that technological-change years 1965, 1969, and 1973 are on their way—that all the widely advertised problems of a world without arms control may actually occur. They will realize the extreme importance of either cooperating seriously with or eliminating the opposition. In particular, it should by then be possible to estimate more accurately both the day when there will be widespread diffusion of nuclear weapons and corresponding weapon delivery systems and the possibility for successful arms control. If we have been careless about our defense, there may be circumstances under which our elimination may look to the Soviets like far and away safer and more reliable than cooperation.

In any case, 1961 is likely to be a year of decision. Not only will the previously mentioned "deterrent gaps" and "crisis of confidence" in NATO have matured and maybe passed, but the pressure on all to make arms control and other agreements should be large enough that if both sides are even remotely willing to have such agreements, some kinds should be made and implemented. Our ability to understand the implications of various arrangements will, of course, depend on whether the proper studies have been made and careful proposals prepared and analyzed. While there is today much interest in these problems, it is still quite likely that the necessary homework will not have been done. At least, it is by no means an assured fact that it will be done. Almost every conference to date has revealed evidence of startlingly inadequate preparation on both sides.

In addition to not doing enough homework, most 1961 Arms Controllers are likely to have too narrow a view to do an adequate job of design or analysis. While the "official" groups tend to be excessively devoted to the short term, most of the unofficial groups on the outside are overextended. With the exception of test ban proposals there is almost no detailed technical work or study being done on interim, medium-term arrangements, or on the phases that will have to be gone through before we can arrive at any worth while long-term solutions. It is almost as large a mistake in this field to be premature as to be laggard. One can run unnecessary risks by trying to do too much as well as by not trying enough. However, on the whole, I would prefer to see some pressure on the West to run risks by trying to do too much, rather than to play too cautious a role, since the biases the other way are extremely large. For this reason even ill-considered pressures by "peace" groups can still have a good effect. However, to the extent that they make their programs consistent with objective military problems, they are much more likely to exert a strong and beneficial influence.

WORLD WAR VI (1965)
Prematureness of Minimum Deterrence
Possibility of Soviet Strategic Superiority

I have predicted that by 1965 those U.S. and NATO planners who had bet on Minimum or even Finite Deterrence as the proper strategic approach should have seen their hopes thwarted. Unless international relations have been notably smooth between this writing and 1965, even the most obtuse will realize that the Minuteman and Polaris systems, weapons with relatively small (and possibly inaccurate) warheads, which many people have considered as the sole answer to this strategic problem, will have shown some incapacity for handling the Type I Deterrence problem *cheaply and reliably,* and a complete incapacity for the Type II Deterrence problem, at least if bought on the scale that was envisaged in 1959–60. In 1965 even nonmilitary decision makers should be sufficiently educated in the strategic calculus to realize both of these points. Some of the enthusiasts will grasp only that there is still some kind of "deterrent gap." They will only say that the concept was not sufficiently supported—not that they were premature or narrow in their original recommendations. To some extent they will be right—but the heart of the "Minimum Deterrence" argument all along was that Type I Deterrence is easy and cheap, and that Type I Deterrence plus Limited War Capabilities is all that is needed. As always, this failure may not show up in an attack; signs of an excessive caution in international negotiations will suffice. I am not saying that the weapons most often suggested for Finite Deterrence (Polaris and Minuteman) are intrinsically incapable of providing a good Type I Deterrent. I am simply saying that they cannot do the job cheaply and reliably, at least not in the early sixties. It takes more technology than we see available now to make Type I Deterrence cheap and reliable. Still, even "small" Polaris and Minuteman forces should be effective enough to deter the Soviets if relations are not too strained. However, the disappearance of U.S. Type II Deterrence (engendered by programs scheduled, ca. 1960) may cause the Soviets to overestimate psychologically their own Type I Deterrence. This makes it quite plausible that the Soviets will assay some challenges which could get out of hand. It is also quite possible that the Soviets will not overestimate; that these challenges will not raise the question of

475

Central War, but only the possibility of a series of Munichs. Independently of any international crisis, the general pressure on all nations to control the spread of armaments and the technological race could put pressures on the Soviets to try to establish a world hegemony, pressures which the threat of the Minimum Deterrence forces might not be able to balk. All of the above will put pressure on Japan, India, and most of all, Europe, to get their own "independent nuclear deterrents." However, unless there has been a crash program, these will be in the initial phases in 1965. Their development may also be slowed or prevented by a growing pressure to prevent the diffusion of nuclear weapon systems.

The above problems could be complicated to the point where the West invites a total defeat, if the Soviets happen to achieve overwhelming strategic superiority. In spite of all theories of Minimum and Finite Deterrence, this could easily happen. For example, if

✧✧✧

TABLE 64

TECHNOLOGY, 1965

"Independent" nuclear deterrents being phased in

Inexpensive reliable research missile (+ Commercial nuclear explosives?)

Limits of bomb technology (if testing is continued)

Minuteman B and Polaris C

Second-generation Atlas and Titan

BMEWS-B? Midas? SAMOS

Protected B-52G and H, B-47E, B-58

Skybolt (Airborne ballistic missile)

Super guidance

SAGE B, Bomarc B and C, Nike-Zeus A and B, Hawk B, F-108, B-58B, B-70, Dynasoar technologically possible but may be cancelled

Antiradiation drugs

Exotic fuels

Nuclear-powered airplane? Rocket?

Experimental climate control

Bacteriological and chemical warfare

Astronautics

✧✧✧

476

there were a relaxation of tension or even if there were not, the Soviet defense budget in 1965 could easily be twice ours. This would probably do the trick. Or in our preoccupation with psychological rather than objective capabilities we could easily allow some serious holes to develop. This would be especially serious if the Soviets feel great pressure to achieve a world hegemony before even a slowed down arms race makes the world dangerous for everybody. They might easily feel that it was just common sense or a "historical necessity" to use their strategic superiority, either by negotiation or force, to put an end to the arms race.

From the alliance point of view, one of the most important changes is likely to be the creation of "independent" nuclear deterrents in Europe. The reason for the quotation marks is because it is most likely that these deterrents will, in practice, rely on the existence of a U.S. deterrent for much of their effectiveness. I have already discussed (pages 283–284) that a small country may not realize much Type I Deterrence from the installation of some soft, concentrated IRBM's, but that if it hardens and disperses these IRBM's their effectiveness for Type I Deterrence is much enhanced even though the Soviets might still be able to destroy these dispersed and hardened bases in their first strike. In the second case the small nation is forcing the Soviets to use large-yield ground-burst thermonuclear bombs which will do a great deal of by-product damage. In effect, the small nation is using its own and neighboring countries' cities and population as hostages to deter the Soviets from a disarming attack, depending on Soviet reluctance to destroy these nonmilitary targets. While the policy may be effective, it still has a superficial absurdity and callousness about it which may reflect an inherent weakness that will show up in a crisis.

Even if the Europeans should obtain some second strike capability—perhaps through the use of mobile or concealed IRBM'S (the mobility might be by air, barge, train, truck, or submarine)—unless they procure a much greater firepower than they are likely to do, they will still be dependent on the U.S. deterrent. This is so not only because their system may have all of the potential inadequacies of mobile systems listed in Table 41 on page 265, but also because of the disparity of the threat which the Soviet Union can make to them as compared to the other way round.

These "independent" nuclear deterrents may still make sense even though they depend physically on the U.S. deterrent, since they make the reaction of the U.S. deterrent more credible. Even if the U.S. did not retaliate instantly against the Soviets as a result of a major Soviet provocation in Europe, the Soviets would still have to envision the Americans evacuating their cities (even against the will of the American government), putting their strategic forces on extreme alert, and probably taking various kinds of limited measures which could easily escalate. It is difficult to imagine a Soviet government willing to take this kind of risk, unless the United States had gone to some trouble to acquire an extreme Finite Deterrent posture that did not even with weeks of warning have any Credible First Strike Capability—that is, did not have the capability to limit damage by a Soviet retaliating strike to less than, say, 50 million Americans killed and the destruction of the A country. While there are influential advocates in the United States for programs that could lead to exactly that sort of Finite Deterrent posture, it is unlikely that these adherents of pure Finite Deterrence will have that much influence. Therefore the independent nuclear deterrent gives the Europeans a sort of "trigger" to the American SAC which is both different from the usual trigger that is discussed—an attempt by the European country to start a war by catalysis—and more reliable also. There are also dangers in having "independent" European deterrents, one of which is that they would encourage the growth of a Finite Deterrent philosophy in the United States, making the American SAC much harder to trigger. They may also discourage the NATO countries from procuring adequate conventional forces. Another possible weakness is the creating of opportunities for the Soviet to act as agents provocateurs. Another problem—particularly if the independent deterrents are national rather than NATO—is the subsequent pressure toward the diffusion of nuclear weapons systems everywhere and the corresponding Nth-country problems.

The most exciting developments of World War VI will have occurred in the new missiles and satellites first seen in World War V. In addition to the military program, missiles and satellites will be widely used in scientific research; any country hoping to have a high-altitude research program or wishing to put up a satellite or two for prestige should be able to buy some model missiles on the open market at a cost of less than a million dollars apiece—very likely much less. While not as efficient as military missiles at military missions, they will go from here to there. In the absence of any ICBM defense, this may give any country with access to nuclear warheads a partial "strategic capability." Thus the year 1965 could see the beginning or return of an era in which any country with some technology or funds can have a modest strategic capability (assuming of course that the bombs are available). While this strategic capability will likely be of the go-first variety, it could easily have a very big effect on some international situations. It will also begin to complicate the accident problem to the point where quick-reaction retaliation schemes will be completely infeasible.

The bombs may be available in 1965. Unless research is slowed down, nuclear weapons will not be inexpensive—they will be cheap. There should be some models available which can just about be manufactured by any high-quality ordnance manufacturer. (Other models will require every resource of technology.) Presumably, the designs of those bombs which are easily made will still be classified, and the materials restricted. It should be another five or ten years before this knowledge gets widely disseminated, and it may be even longer before the materials become generally available.

The two most likely reasons why bombs may start to become widely available and the current implicit arms control agreement on the distribution of nuclear weapons breaks down completely are because of the use of nuclear weapons in a Limited War or because current programs, looking toward the peaceful exploitation of nuclear explosives, have matured to a point where the commercial use begins to be economically irresistible. For example, I mentioned earlier that the cheapest artificial source of kilowatt hours available to man is a thermonuclear bomb. The problem is to harness this source of energy. By 1965 many people will have studied what is involved in doing this. If their research is successful, and there are no successful political, legal, or social obstacles, nuclear explosions may start to yield important peacetime applications. In any case, it is almost certain that somebody will succeed on a small scale in finding uses for nuclear explosives.

Unless tests are suspended or controlled, then in addition to being able to produce bombs by 1965 we should have approached the limits of bomb technology at least in terms of KT per pound and in terms of radioactivity per pound. This is not to say that the bombs will not be improved even more after 1965; it is only to conjecture that we could reach the point in the mid-60's where spectacular improvements will depend on a really new idea and not just on an improvement in or variation of existing ideas. Even if this book were a classified document, it would be impossible to predict what these limits of technology will involve. In theory it is possible to get about 9 KT per pound out of uranium and perhaps 3 or 4 times as much per pound from fusion reactions. This does not mean that we will get a megaton in fifty or a hundred pounds. It is quite likely that we will be hitting some bounds that are much above these theoretical limits. Whether we will attain 1 per cent, 10 per cent, or 50 per cent of theoretical efficiency is impossible to say at this time. However, whatever the limits are, we are likely to have begun to approach them by 1965. (Assuming, of course, a vigorous continuation of nuclear testing. A ban or even some controls would presumably slow down technological progress.)

There should be by 1965 a great deal of progress in other aspects of military hardware. An improved Minuteman ought to be coming in around 1965 or even a bit earlier, and a much improved form of Polaris should also be available. Large missiles of the Atlas-Titan variety, with storable liquid propellants and greatly improved payload, operating, and range characteristics will be available. Our Ballistic Missile Early Warning System (BMEWS) should have had at least one retrofit; it would not be surprising if a brand new warning system had been procured. Warning systems against ballistic missile attacks may depend not only on radar but may also use infrared, various types of electrical signals, acoustical noise, or optical observation. Such 1961 systems as SAGE, Nike-Zeus, and Hawk should be available in either improved or retrofitted models. There are possibilities that advanced bombers such as the B-70 and the nuclear airplanes may be flying, or may even be in process of being phased into the force; however, because these systems are very expensive and their military usefulness at present seems marginal, it is somewhat unlikely that they will by then be carried to the point of an operational weapons system.

In addition to the missiles, there should be a lot of manned vehicles still in the strategic force—the familiar B-47E, B-52G and H, and the B-58. These will be protected by some combination of alert, mobility, and shelter. The shelters will have to be hard enough so that it is possible to have microscopic dispersal against most weapons on a single airbase. This means that, while any single shelter could be destroyed by an accurate missile, it would take many missiles, even with relatively large-yield warheads, to destroy all the planes on a single base. The capability of the manned bomber should be further increased by the addition of 1,000 mile range Air Launched Ballistic Missiles (ALBM's). These will give the B-52 a better target coverage from outside the Soviet Union than the early Polaris submarine missile has.

Even though we have protected missiles and planes, surprise attacks out of the blue will still be a problem, though hopefully not as serious as in the early sixties. That is, even the cheaper Finite Deterrents should be good enough to prevent an attack by a cautious and unpressured opponent, though this is not necessarily going to be true. For example, just having a lot of weapons dispersed to a lot of points may not do the trick. Figure 9 shows that having a

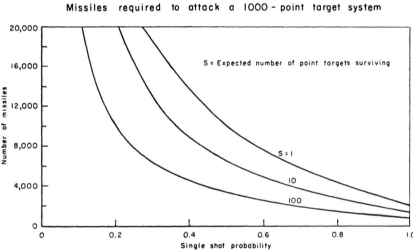

Figure 9

Missiles required to attack a 1000 - point target system

retaliatory capability distributed over a thousand fixed points, such as some proposals for Minuteman, may not be sufficient to deter a determined enemy. Depending on the average retaliation the attacker is willing to accept (the curves on Figure 9 assume 1, 10, and 100 points survive attack) and on his single shot probability of kill, the attacker may need from one to tens of thousands of missiles, but if he can get a high single shot probability, it is more likely to be closer to one than to ten thousand relatively inexpensive "go first" missiles. The systems will have to be alert, hard, or concealed in order

481

to be able to survive. It should be noted that the easiest way to get concealment, by simple unprotected mobility, may not be sufficient in itself. As explained on page 268 these mobile missiles will also have to have at least moderate hardness plus arrangements to keep the system operable as a system if they are to survive. Figure 10 shows, as a function of yield, the single shot probability of kill an attacker could attain against typical targets.

Figure 10

Probability of survival versus yield of missile warhead

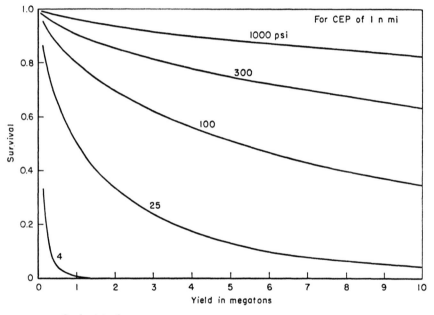

Basic data from:

Brode, H. L., *Ground Support Systems Weapons Effects*, The RAND Corporation, Paper P-1951, page 46, 31 March 1960.

The curves assume 100 per cent reliability in the attacking missile and a CEP of 1 mile. To correct for the first assumption the reader need just multiply the probability of kill by the reliability of the attacking missile. The effect of the second assumption can be estimated by noting that the efficiency of a ballistic missile goes as the square of its CEP. For a two-mile CEP it would take four missiles to achieve the same kill probability, while for ½ mile CEP it would only take one-fourth as many missiles, and so on. Figure 10 indicates that for a one mile CEP, there is much benefit to be achieved by the defense if it builds harder shelters and by the offense if it goes to higher yields. In fact, in the higher overpressure regions (greater than 30 psi) the increase in shelter hardness is exactly compensated if the offense increases the megatons in its warhead by the same factor. The above statement will not have anywhere as much force if, as some scientists believe is inevitable, there are further significant breakthroughs in guidance and the locations of the missile sites are accurately known. However, even then the defender can, by hardening, prevent the attacker from going to cheap missiles carrying very small warheads.

There should also be some breakthroughs in the art of defense by 1965. These improvements will not only occur in traditional fields but on other aspects of war as described in Table 4 (Complete Description of a Thermonuclear War). For example, drugs might be available that could increase, by some reasonably large factor, the ability of human beings to accept the short-range effects of radiation. Whether this increase will be large enough to alleviate in a significant way the larger amounts of radiation the enemy can put on our country, or that we can put on his, is hard to predict.

Exotic fuels for bombers and missiles, fuels with a much higher specific impulse or energy per pound than the traditional petroleum products are almost available today. While in 1965 they may prove to be expensive or awkward to handle, they should still make the corresponding missile systems either much cheaper or enable smaller missiles or bombers to carry an order of magnitude larger loads. These fuels may or may not be commercially available to each and every country to power the cheap reliable "research" missiles. If these other countries can, in fact, get access to super-fuels, their strategic capability would become an order of magnitude more threatening.

Some form of climate- and weather control should be more available in 1965. The Argus effect that has been receiving much prominence at this writing is an example of a current ability at a kind of weather control. Project Plowshare has made some systematic studies on the use of nuclear explosives to modify both weather and climate. In the fifth volume of the *Proceedings of the Second Plowshare Sym-*

posium (UCRL-5679), J. W. Reed speculates on the possibility that we will be able to control hurricanes by the use of 20 MT clean (relatively nonradioactive) bombs, and L. Machta discusses several suggestions on modifying climate (either increasing or decreasing the average temperature) by injecting suitable numbers and sizes of dust particles into the stratosphere through the use of nuclear explosions. He also discusses a suggestion of H. Wexler's to heat the Polar areas by creating a heat-conserving blanket of ice crystals in the troposphere. The ice crystals are created by exploding about "ten clean 10-megaton devices" at optimum depths and places in the ocean. Some years back von Neumann suggested that one could melt the ice packs by spreading a radiation absorber such as lampblack on top of the snow and ice. Other types of weather control might be coming in about this time, particularly if meteorology gets the expected impetus from the use of observation satellites to gather data and the use of high-speed computers to increase our ability to understand and predict. It is quite possible weather control could be used as a weapon. For example, some countries might be tempted to use the differential effects of dropping temperature as a weapon in a cold or mildly heated war. The Russians and the Canadians might be particularly vulnerable to this technique. The Russians, of course, can retaliate. They might do something like melting the polar ice caps or diverting the Gulf Stream, or something equally nasty. Although these two suggestions do not seem too likely, offhand, I would not make any bets.

One of the most startling things that ever happened to me occurred in 1950 when I served on a Technical Advisory Board studying nuclear-powered airplanes. I then first came in contact with the philosophy which is willing to ask any question and tackle any problem. After study, people generally conclude that certain things are feasible but not practical because they cost a little bit too much. And I really mean just about "any" proposal. Henry Kissinger remarks in his book of a few years ago, *Nuclear Weapons and Foreign Policy,* that the fires of Prometheus had then been unleashed. This is an understatement of the things that are now technologically feasible but that "cost a little too much." I have not seen any figures, but I surmise that relatively thin margins of cost prevent us from doing such extraordinary projects as melting ice caps and diverting ocean currents.

The coming crisis in technology was described by the late John von Neumann in an article entitled "Can We Survive Technology?" [8] To quote von Neumann: " 'The great globe itself' is in a rapidly maturing crisis—a crisis attributable to the fact that the environment in which technological progress must occur has become both undersized and underorganized. . . .

"In the first half of this century the accelerating Industrial Revolution encountered an absolute limitation—not on technological progress as such, but on an essential safety factor. This safety factor . . . was essentially a matter of geographical and political lebensraum: an ever broader geographical scope for technological activities, combined with an ever broader political integration of the world. Within this expanding framework it was possible to accommodate the major tensions created by technological progress.

"Now this safety mechanism is being sharply inhibited; literally and figuratively, we are running out of room. At long last, we begin to feel the effects of the finite, actual size of the earth in a critical way.

"Thus the crisis does not arise from accidental events or human errors. It is inherent in technology's relation to geography on the one hand and to political organization on the other. . . . In the years between now and 1980 the crisis will probably develop far beyond all earlier patterns. When or how it will end—or to what state of affairs it will yield—nobody can say."

The next two items on the list are Bacteriological and Chemical Warfare. In one sense, they do not belong in the 1965 technology, since they have been in existence for some years. There is today much discussion of the possibilities here, but it is hard to believe that bacteriological and chemical warfare could compete on a cost-efficiency basis with nuclear weapons, except possibly in specialized applications. It is not clear, however, that if one develops new methods or capabilities which lead to a tremendous increase in efficiency that this comparison might not be reversed, at least for small nations that did not have the resources to get into the strategic field via the nuclear weapon system route. I could be referring to *very* small nations here.

Much more important, the comparison with nuclear weapons may be misleading. It might be more appropriate to compare certain types of bacteriological and chemical warfare with nonnuclear weapons. I am thinking here of a possible use in a war or area where we do not wish to use nuclear weapons for political reasons, or be-

[8] *Fortune*, June 1955.

cause we do not want to set a precedent, or possibly because they have been banned by agreement. Offhand, it might not seem reasonable that bacteriological and chemical weapons might be acceptable when nuclear neutron weapons are not, but this might be true of specialized bacteriological or chemical weapons that could be used to enfeeble temporarily or otherwise impair the efficiency of the enemy's civilians or soldiers. The classical use of tear gas in civilian disturbances has exactly this character of being a much more acceptable weapon than ordinary bullets. In fact, it is conceivable that one might develop an effective capability of just having psychological effects on the enemy. For example, if one gave tranquilizers to the enemy soldiers in large amounts they might become unfit for military duty. It is not at all inconceivable that if the North Koreans invaded South Korea again in 1965 we would be able to keep all of North Korea continuously saturated with chemicals or organisms that reduced the efficiency of the exposed inhabitants markedly but did not injure them permanently.

The last subject I have in Table 64 is Astronautics. From the military point of view, the importance of Space Warfare may have been overplayed. It is very easy to make the obvious Mahan analogy on "control of the sea" and talk blithely and superficially of "control of space." The analogy was never really accurate even for control of the air, and, at least in the sixties, it seems to be completely misleading for space. But as we mentioned in the 1961 discussion, satellites should be very valuable in navigation, communication, warning, reconnaissance, targeting, weather prediction, and so on. One of the biggest contributions astronautics will make should be to the development of the military technology of large, low-CEP rockets and associated equipment, and to reliability in general. Unlike military programs, space programs are not psychological. If they do not work objectively, it is noticed. Therefore it is very likely that equipment developed for space will be reliable at least in peacetime. It is also worth saying that despite many misleading remarks to the effect that powerful rockets are not useful for military purposes but only for space, there do seem to be many military advantages in having large rockets: to carry greater yields, to use special trajectories, to carry countermeasures, and even to carry multiple warheads, for example.

By 1965 we may also be faced with important changes in the political arena. The last five years or so has seen the alliance of Japan and Germany with their former enemies, the penetration of the Middle East, Africa, and South America by the Soviet Union, and the creation of the European Economic Community. Equally startling changes could occur again. The obvious possibilities are comprehensive arms control agreements, a United States–Soviet *détente*, the formation of a strong United Europe; the political federation of the European Economic Community; a strong Southeast Asiatic organization; a Pan Arabic union; the desertion of a major ally to the Communist bloc; the loss of Southeast or Southwest Asia or Northeast Africa; the breakup of the NATO alliance; a split between China and Russia; a major penetration of Africa or South America by the Soviets; a breakup of the Soviet satellite empire; a change in the form of the Soviet government; a Communist revolution in a major state. While any particular one of the above events is quite improbable, it is not improbable that at least one of them or something like one of them will occur.

By 1965 we should pretty well know if we are going to have an arms control agreement or not. That is, without arms control some points of no return on the distribution of technology and equipment will be approached or will have been passed. However, the S.U.–U.S. competition, in particular Soviet Union blackmail, assuming that they are still on bad terms with us and aggressively-minded, will probably be the largest problem, rather than the Nth-country problem or other aspects of the arms race. If we have bought only a Minimum Deterrence and inadequate Limited War forces, it may be more than a problem; it may be an accomplished fact.

Chinese blackmail in 1965 or soon after is also a possibility. In the absence of effective arms control agreements they are likely to have a rather impressive strategic capability. While it should not be large enough to allow them to strike the United States and accept our retaliation, it should be large enough to destroy, say, 10 or 20 U.S. cities on a first strike. This should provide them with some Type II Deterrence against U.S. nuclear threats in Asia. Their potential strategic threat is especially troubling because the Chinese Communists seem to have more will and resolve than can be found in any other country. It might make a great deal of sense for the United States to develop and install an active defense system that is effective against airborne and missile threats from third powers such as China. Such a system may be almost essential by the late sixties, and we will need it installed by 1965 if it is to be reliable by then. The system may also have some real value against accidentally fired weapons and against Soviet retaliatory blows or late strikes—even if it is not very effective against a Soviet first strike using modern equipment that presumably will not be technologically or physically available to the Chinese.

Civil defense will still clearly be in the picture in 1965, although cheap programs may well be obsolete; again, there may be an important asymmetry between the United States and Russia. It is quite possible that the Russians would have put in a reasonable program by this time, and it is very unlikely that we will have. These Soviet programs should be especially effective if we have gone overboard on Minimum Deterrence. The technology of air defense should have been improved to the point where it could present a serious threat to the manned bomber, but it will still be very expensive to procure and maintain an adequate system. It will probably pay each side to keep at least a modest number of manned bombers to force their opponent to spend a great deal on air defense. Of course, if there are third powers around with even a modestly impressive strategic air force, it will not be as necessary for the Soviet Union and the United States to keep up a manned bomber threat to force their opponents into large expenditures for air defense.

WORLD WAR VII (1969)

Possibility of Reliable Finite Deterrence
Arms Control or "?"
Emergence of "Third" Power?
The World is ⅓ Rich, ⅓ Aspiring, and ⅓ Desperate

Let us now look at hypothetical World War VII, almost ten years and several technological revolutions from now. We must for that day seriously consider the possibility of unexpected scientific and technical breakthroughs in addition to extrapolations of current systems and ideas. It is impossible to limit or describe in advance what breakthrough might occur, but it is possible to discuss some possibilities currently being studied which might be called breakthroughs, if successful. This method of trying to estimate the total impact of technological progress is likely to involve some large underestimates of the total change, since one can almost guarantee that some startling developments will occur in unexpected areas. I will try to make up for this by some judicious exaggeration in the areas I will discuss. I believe the use of such exaggeration will give a better "feel" for the over-all possibilities than a more sober discussion of the few items I will consider.

❖❖❖

TABLE 65
TECHNOLOGY, 1969

(Extrapolations and Breakthroughs)

Advanced satellites and primitive space ships
Cheap simple bombs
Cheap simple missiles
Controlled thermonuclear reaction
Other sources of cheap neutrons
Other sources of nuclear fuels
Californium bullets
Reliable sensors
Super calculators
Cheap calories
Cheap, fast transportation for Limited War
Ground effect machines
Reliable command and control
Medical progress
Advanced materials
Disguised warfare
Doomsday Machines

❖❖❖

While the above developments are assigned to the year 1969, the reader should not take the assignment seriously. It would be better to think of them as examples of the kinds of changes that the seventies or late sixties could bring.

Assuming that the frantic competition in space between the Soviet Union and the United States continues, the year 1969 is likely to see some sophisticated space technology. It will, of course, be much cheaper to put large masses into orbit. It used to cost the Vanguard program $1,000,000 per pound of payload; the Atlas and Titan boosters will do it for about $1,000 per pound; and 1969 should see something in the neighborhood of $10 per pound. Maximum loads should be measured in the hundreds or thousands of tons rather than hundreds or thousands of pounds. There will very likely have been a landing and take-off from the moon by a manned vehicle.

There will almost undoubtedly be a lot of very sophisticated satellites in orbit, including some with crews. I would not even want to hazard a guess on the military significance of all this, but it would not surprise me if it just meant more and better of the early 60's type of capability for warning, communication, and observation, with the possible addition of some active defense and offense roles.

There will be more than just the two big powers in the missile and space business. When we enter the 1970 period, at least the most advanced nations will know in theory how to make simple bombs and missiles, and in the absence of explicit or implicit controls will be making them in practice. For this reason, I have put cheap, simple bombs and cheap, simple missiles near the top of the 1969 list because, even with arms control and certainly without, these are likely to be the most characteristic features of the late 1960 or the early 1970 period. This may or may not present the most important (and dramatic) problem. It will depend on which countries actually have weapons in their stockpiles, the explicit and implicit controls, and the state of international relations.

Under current programs, 1969 may be a little early for the diffusion of these devices to other than "advanced" nations. It is very difficult to predict the rate at which the technology, materials, and information will be disseminated. Even without explicit controls, it might be the mid-1970's or even a later period before they become cheap and simple for the majority of "developed" nations. But there are many things that could accelerate this dissemination process: the use of nuclear weapons in Limited War; successful programs for the peaceful uses of nuclear explosives in the mid-1960's might at least make nuclear "devices" widely available; the deliberate diffusion of nuclear technology by either the United States or the Soviet Union to enough allies so that there are no secrets any more; a breakthrough in technology or materials; and so forth.

As an example of this last possibility, consider the fusion reactor. It is somewhat improbable that this device will be practical by 1969. In fact, most of my colleagues who are working on this project are somewhat doubtful about any real success before the year 2000. In a way, though, this is a pessimistic attitude. I would conjecture that we, the British, and the Soviets will spend altogether more than a billion dollars, perhaps two or three billion, on this project in the next decade. It is a little startling that so many experts view the notion of even a qualified success dimly.

Let us, however, go ahead and outrage the experts by assuming not a qualified, but an outstanding success—such a success that even relatively primitive nations will find it possible either to build or buy a fusion reactor and thereby to acquire a virtually unlimited source of cheap power. This spectacular gift of technology has one minor defect (or virtue, depending on how you look at it): it gives off neutrons very copiously, so copiously that it may not be exaggerating to state that the neutrons are for all practical purposes free.

Free neutrons would mean that many kinds of nuclear fuels would also be free, or at least very cheap. With these nuclear fuels and the kind of technology that is likely to be available in 1969, it may literally turn out that a Hottentot, an educated and technical Hottentot it is true, but still one who is a member of a relatively primitive society, would be able to make bombs. This would raise forcefully the question of the illegal or uncontrolled dissemination of bombs. (One can today buy machine guns, artillery, tanks, and fighter aircraft on the gray market.) Thus the 1969 equivalent of the Malayan guerrillas or the Algerian rebels or the Puerto Rican nationalists, or even less official groups such as gangsters and wealthy dilettantes, might be able to obtain bombs.

Even if the controlled thermonuclear reaction does not prove to be a success by 1969, there are other possibilities for the cheap production of neutrons. For example, many of the commercial uses of nuclear devices would release neutrons as a by-product. This could lead to either the clandestine or open production of weapon-grade nuclear fuels. There are also possibilities that simple and inexpensive methods for producing weapon-grade nuclear fuels will be developed. It is also possible that we and others will learn how to make bombs using only or mostly materials already widely available, such as deuterium and lithium. (The much publicized small "clean" bomb would probably use such materials.) In a word, 1969 (though more likely 1979) may see the introduction of the widely advertised era of the conventional nuclear bomb in which (in the absence of adequate controls) any "legitimate" nation can get some models and some illegitimate groups or governments may also get access to nuclear weapons, but presumably under more onerous conditions than those to which legitimate purchasers are subject.

We may be too frightened of the possible consequences of the widespread diffusion of weapons. It is quite clear that if one gave the Egyptians and Israelis atomic weapons, one is likely to find both nations acting much more cautiously than they act today, simply because the consequences of "irresponsibility" are so much more disastrous. (On the other hand, even a greatly increased sense of responsibility may only mean that instead of falling upon each other the week after they come into possession of these weapons, the attack may be deferred for a year or two.) In addition, a war between Israel and Egypt would not be a world disaster but a local disaster—one which might, in fact, have some "beneficial" aspects, since it would make other nations even more conscious of the danger of these weapons and probably lead to international arrangements to control them.

Almost any sober analysis indicates that it is somewhat harder for Nth countries to cause a cataclysm than is often believed.[9] It is difficult to imagine that China or France, for example, could in the next decade obtain a large enough strategic force to strain seriously United States Type I Deterrence (although the situation in the 1970's and 1980's could become quite awkward). It is even difficult to imagine one of these nations being able to start an accidental war if the Soviets and the United States have made sensible plans to prevent this eventuality, and it is a little difficult to understand why they would want to start one, unless they were in some kind of a crisis that could be helped by such an action. In this last case, the Soviets and the United States would be likely to be on their guard. Most important of all, it is going to be difficult to get nations to make the necessary concessions until the dangers are both more apparent and more pressing than they are today.

All of the above may be true, but I believe that we should still try to make international arrangements *before* the weapons have been distributed rather than *afterward*. While it is quite possible that many laymen overestimate the immediate impact that the widespread dispersion of weapons will have, I strongly suspect that the sober analysts underestimate both the immediate and long-term problems. I will list ten such problems here. It would not be very difficult to list many more.

In a nuclear world the "small powers" would have vis-à-vis one another:

    1. greater opportunities for blackmail and mischief-making;

    2. greater accident proneness;

---

[9] See Fred C. Iklé, *Nth Countries and Disarmament*, P-1956, The RAND Corporation, April 1960, for more discussion of this important problem

3. an increased capability for "local" Munichs, Pearl Harbors, and blitzkriegs;

4. pressures to pre-empt because of points 1, 2, and 3 above;

5. a tendency to neglect conventional capabilities because of an over-reliance on nuclear capabilities;

6. internal (civil war, *coup d'état*, irresponsibility, etc.) and external (arms race, fear of fear, etc.) political problems;

7. the creation of a situation in which the diffusion of nuclear weapons to really irresponsible organizations is facilitated.

Nuclear diffusion would also:

8. complicate future problems of control, by making such control involve the small powers having to accept an obvious reduction in their sovereignty (i.e., they give something up rather than simply abstain);

9. give the Soviet Union or other large power many opportunities to act as agent-provocateur; and

10. create the capability and therefore the pressure for many nations to make a crisis serious or to exploit an on-going crisis (catalytic war or escalation).

In short, the diffusion of nuclear weapons may or may not increase the number of crises, but it will almost undoubtedly tend to increase the seriousness and the grim potentialities of any crisis or even misunderstandings which do occur, plus increasing enormously the importance of having responsible and competent governments everywhere.

The widespread possession of nuclear weapons and delivery systems strikes many observers as similar to a situation that the physicist would describe as "semistable equilibrium." For example, imagine a ball balanced on top of a small cup so that small movements of the ball can be tolerated but not large ones. If this ball and the cup are isolated, it might sit there on top of its cup forever, but if it is submitted to the vagaries and chances of a sufficiently uncontrolled environment one can guarantee that sooner or later it will fall. This can be true even though every "reasonable" analysis of the situation that looks at probable or plausible disturbances showed that the forces were in close enough balance so the ball should stay where it is. It takes an improbable or implausible force to topple the ball. But some improbable and implausible events will occur and, barring a secular change in the situation, almost with certainty the ball will eventually fall. While the analogy may simultaneously be both apt and misleading, many who have thought about this problem have come to the conclusion that reliable stability can only come through an international agency with an effective monopoly of force, or total disarmament.

For many reasons, I do not believe that the twentieth century will see a disarmed world, but it may see a world government or the equivalent. Until that day arrives, it will be of great value to try to keep, indeed *make*, the problem of national security intellectually and diplomatically simple, and the diffusion of nuclear weapons would seem to go exactly the wrong way. The two-power case seems both intellectually and practically more controllable than the Nth-power case. The diffusion of nuclear weapons not only complicates the over-all analytic problem, but the stakes at risk if events go badly would seem to be less in the two-power than in the Nth case.

The next item on the list is the Californium bullet. Californium is an artificial element that can be made by bombarding uranium with very intense neutron sources. While I do not know what it would cost to manufacture, it is undoubtedly very expensive. However, it is at least conceivable that this element or something with similar properties could be manufactured inexpensively and in quantity in 1969 or a later time period. Anyway, practical or not, it illustrates a possibility. Californium is a fissionable element that fissions much more efficiently than any of the uranium or plutonium isotopes. It produces 3½ neutrons per fission. This large number of neutrons means that a very small amount of Californium could be made into a critical mass, say an amount about the size of a bullet; that is, the nuclear rifle or pistol could be made into a reality. Therefore, if the costs of Californium could be reduced, it might be possible to make bullets which would be subcritical in their normal state, but which would become critical when hitting their target, because of compression on impact or because some neutron-absorbing element was removed. At that point the bullet might explode with a force equivalent to, say, 10 tons of TNT. Even the atomic six-gun is conceivable. The idea is, of course, impractical today, but it does indicate the kinds of things that are technologically feasible. (It is also impractical for another reason—the half-life of Californium is only a few days, so one would have to use it almost as fast as it was manufactured.)

The next item on the 1969 list is reliable sensors. By this I mean some method of identifying and tracking hostile objects that are approaching or are over one's territory. Radar is supposed to do this but, unfortunately, it is not reliable. It has many inadequacies that result in the enemy's being able to spoof, saturate, or in other ways evade the radar networks.

It is not generally realized that the usual remark, "in the air and missile age the offense has an intrinsic advantage over the defense," is only true, if at all, because our sensors are not reliable. It really is possible today to destroy any enemy object, destroy it reliably in a way that has not been possible in the past, if you know where this object is. The trouble is that the enemy goes to a great deal of trouble to prevent you from knowing where his weapons are. If you do not know where his weapons are, then all the weapons in the world, even though they may be incredibly efficient, will not do much good. A breakthrough in this field comparable to the invention of radar in 1935 might well make all forms of air offense incredibly costly. We might even argue that we were back in a situation similar to World War I, where the defense seemed to be intrinsically superior to the offense during most of the war.

One possibility for obtaining reliable sensors is to develop much better methods of receiving information; almost as important might be the development of much better methods of processing information. The futuristic computers, next on the list, might well give us the possibility of keeping track of everything that is picked up by radar in such historical detail and of treating this information with such elaborate mathematical methods that it might be the equivalent of a partial breakthrough in the sensor field.

Some of these futuristic computers will, in all likelihood, have multimillion word memories, fractional microsecond multiplication times, self-programming capabilities, marvelously elaborate and flexible kinds of input and output, such as being able to read and write books, interpret pictures, and so on. They really will begin to justify the notion of artificial brains.

The next 1969 item is the possibility of cheap calories. There are many ways that one might think of getting cheap calories. Some involve the application of the cheap power already discussed, using either direct synthesis of organic material, the application of hydroponics, or more conventionally by the extensive use of irrigation and fertilizers. These possibilities are of more importance to the Soviets and the underdeveloped nations than to us. At the present time, slightly more than one-third of the Soviet Union's man-hours and more than three-fourths of the Chinese man-hours are devoted to agriculture. The equivalent burden on the United States represents less than 10 per cent of our work force. If the Soviet Union or China could relieve themselves of this enormous burden of providing calories for their population they could increase fantastically the energy they could apply to industrial expansion and military products. The same breakthrough would scarcely affect the United States. While it might turn out to be easy to synthesize or produce "fuel" carbohydrates, it is likely to be hard to do the same for the U.S. diet, which emphasizes taste and variety.

It is difficult to estimate what the military and civilian impact of such possibilities as cheap calories or cheap power will be. For example, there might be an explosive unleashing of human energy in the underdeveloped nations. One of the major problems of these underdeveloped nations is malnutrition. The solution of this problem does not mean that they will be content to be without all the other things that make life worth living. Just the opposite is likely to be true. With their vigor increased by adequate nutrition and their time and energy no longer preoccupied with naked survival problems, the revolution of rising expectations is likely to become even more critical. In addition, these underdeveloped nations will now have the knowledge and resources they need to develop the military technology they may consider important for obtaining these other items. I am not saying they will not channel their excess energies into constructive paths. I am simply saying that to some of these nations the most constructive paths may appear to be in the direction of obtaining significant military capabilities and then using them. Once the basic nutrition and power problems are solved, one can expect increased pressure on all resources which cannot be produced by simply using unskilled manpower or cheap power, simply because people's aspirations will be increased, not to speak of the population explosion.

It is important to note that in addition to benefits, even peaceful technological innovations can cause problems. It would be most surprising if they did not. But even if one could argue that the effect of the new technology resulted in a net loss to our competitive position vis-à-vis the Soviets, it would still not necessarily be a major argument against helping the underdeveloped nations. Very few Americans or Europeans would be willing to distribute opium to the underdeveloped nations even if a very persuasive argument were made that such a distribution would greatly alleviate some of the problems caused by unrest. Similarly, one should be loath to withhold the more beneficial and constructive aspects of technology just because such progress may create problems for us. With the possible exception of military technology, the answer is not to try to eliminate or hinder progress, but to try to perceive these problems and make preparations to try to handle or alleviate them.

Even if we do not develop cheap calories, it is still likely that the problem of the underdeveloped nations will be at the center of the stage—possibly even swamping the Soviet-American rivalry. This could occur simply because of the division of the world's population into have's and have not's. About one-third of the world's citizens (North America, Europe, U.S.S.R., Australia, etc.) will, by 1969, be guaranteed a rather plush cradle to the grave minimum standard of living independent of any inheritance, ability, or worth. Another one-third or so will be on the way up the economic ladder. There will be a last third which, under current programs, will either stagnate or be just as likely to have gone down the economic ladder as well as up. In addition, tension between the have's and have not's may build up simply because the world in 1969 will be even smaller than it was in 1959. The rich and the poor will be closer neighbors. Not only will mass transportation and communication be much more available, but one form of communication—world-wide TV, through the use of satellites and cheap battery-operated TV sets—will be making its impact felt.

There is probably nothing like a news-type TV program to provide vicarious experience. One can imagine this one-third underprivileged portion of the world watching with increasing jealousy and anger the other one-third, where just being a citizen entitles one to an adequate standard of living. Very likely these people will be told by the West, "If you work hard and we help you your grandchildren will live as we live." The communists (or at least the Chinese) will be telling them (inaccurately and with disregard for their own rural slums), "If you adopt our system you can have these things within a decade." If these same people, despite their general poverty, have access to weapons, it seems to me quite clear that there will be an explosive situation. Any proposals for arms control and demilitarization must take account of the potentialities of this situation.

It might be appropriate at this point to digress into the role that communist ideology might play. Before World War II, the major appeal of communism was a tender one. The communists tried to create an image of being interested in the troubles of the poor and of being more sympathetic and kind than the hard-hearted and callous capitalists who were willing to extort any sacrifice from the oppressed. Today the appeal is almost the exact opposite. The communist attraction now is that they are a dedicated group who get things done. Only by going communist it is argued can the necessary discipline and sacrifice needed for economic development be obtained. Unless the West can also promise the underdeveloped areas some mechanism for rapid progress in the future this appeal is likely to be even more powerful than it has been. The great difficulty that the communists have had is that even naïve people have recognized that if a nation goes communist it is likely to give up its independence. This consideration has acted as a powerful brake on the expansion of communist parties. If the Soviets play their cards better, and exploit the example of China, Yugoslavia, and even Poland and Finland, and in addition relax their controls on the satellites, they will be a much more attractive neighbor, but at the same time a much more formidable opponent.

There are other important possibilities that belong in the category of extrapolations rather than breakthroughs. For example, the late sixties or early seventies should see the development of cheap, fast transportation by both air and sea. The latter could be in the form of nuclear-powered submarines or turbojet-propelled hydrofoils, both of which would go very fast (around 100 miles an hour) without spending much energy in eliminating the wave resistance that plagues normal surface shipping that tries to go fast. In cooperation with air transportation and improvements in communication, this progress could eliminate or reduce the geographical constraints that currently determine much of the strategy and tactics of limited wars. It may literally turn out that for the technically advanced nations almost any place in the globe is as accessible as any other place in the globe. Another important development—at least for high-explosive-type limited wars—would be the perfection of simple guided rockets for infantry-type soldiers or antitank weapons. These are likely to eliminate some of the advantages that elite armored divisions have and enable relatively lightly trained, immobile, but determined, citizen divisions to hold ground against attacks by mechanized divisions.

Other important developments should occur in manned satellites. These may prove less useful as offensive carriers than for reconnaissance, tactical warning, observation, and possibly even active defense. In other words, just as fast transportation eliminates the enormous asymmetry created by geography, in the limited war area the manned and other satellites may eliminate the enormous asymmetry in strategic warfare caused by the Iron Curtain. Both countries may, indeed, become open books from the sky. While this does not eliminate the possibilities of concealment, it should alleviate some of the asymmetries.

By 1969, the enormous difficulty of the mid-1960's in Command and Control should have been eliminated or reduced. This will be partly through technological progress and partly by people simply worrying about the problems and doing the right things. Here again, the satellites may play an important role.

The next item on the list is medical progress. This could be militarily significant. First of all, it could alleviate greatly our lingering problem of radioactivity. Research in genetics is less than a hundred years old, and it is quite possible that even the next ten or fifteen years will see spectacular improvements in our knowledge and capabilities. It is, in pure theory, conceivable that we will be to some extent designing our children rather than depending on the haphazard methods of the past. There would then be no long-term genetics problem. By 1969 some forms of cancer may have yielded to research, and therefore our postwar bone cancer and leukemia problems may have partially disappeared. Most likely a practical contraceptive pill will have been invented; that would sharply alleviate future population pressures. On the other side of the picture, medical improvements may decrease the death rate and thus increase the population pressures, which in turn could greatly affect international stability.

The next item on the list is materials. There are very many ways in which a breakthrough here can make enormous differences in our or the enemy's capability. Some of these breakthroughs should really be put under the head of the technological extrapolation. For example, if one could increase the operating temperatures of engines, either conventional or nuclear, by about 1,000° Fahrenheit, this would be a startling increase in efficiency. In the nuclear power field, for example, such an engine might power a plane for unlimited ranges at supersonic velocities. Other places where material developments are important are in the re-entry body of an ICBM, the reduction of structural weight in missiles and planes, improvements in solid state electronics, and so forth.

The last two items in Table 65 are probably the most important, even if not very probable. Foremost are Doomsday Machines. I am not predicting that they will be built; I have already indicated my opinion to be the opposite. It is most unlikely that either the Soviet Union or the U.S. would build such machines. However, by the late sixties or early seventies their theory should be well understood. Furthermore, there is always the possibility that a breakthrough in this field will make it possible to build a cheap machine. This raises the awful spectre of one of the less responsible powers building such a device.

Lastly, there is the possibility of disguised warfare. As man gets more and more control over his environment, war could be fought in subtle fashions. We have already made glancing references to the possibility of changing the temperature, rainfall, weather, inducing artificial earthquakes, and the like. Certain types of bacteriological and chemical warfare might be developed, and used so subtly that the nation under attack will not know it is being attacked. The possibility of debilitating a nation over a period of years to reduce its competitive capabilities is not out of the question.

Let us consider some of the historical themes of World War VII. Partly because of the possibility of Doomsday Machines and partly because of the likelihood of improvements of command and control and partly because of ordinary technological development and greater understanding of the problem, there is a real possibility that both the S.U. and the U.S. will be able to build reliable Finite Deterrent systems, reliable at least against a direct surprise attack. This is particularly likely to be true if neither side has engaged in extensive civil defense programs so that quite modest offensive capabilities could, even in a retaliatory blow, come close to destroying a country. One possible effect of this, if the tensions continued, would be to shift the battlefield to disguised warfare and limited warfare fields. Another possibility is emphasis on Controlled War and Controlled Reprisal. The third possibility is a complete elimination by the United States of any serious attempts to maintain Type II Deterrence. One likely result of this last would be the widespread distribution of nuclear deterrents to other nations so that they could protect themselves without relying on the U.S. SAC.

This brings up the second historical theme, which is the fact that by the late sixties or early seventies we should know what the program for arms control will be. In discussing the cheap, simple bomb and the cheap, simple missile, and the effects of cheap neutrons, I have already mentioned that an uncontrolled world would be a very strange place indeed. It should be clear to the reader at this point that the existence of an uncontrolled arms race, particularly one joined in by many nations, represents a very serious danger to both the U.S. and the S.U., a danger so large that they might be forced to combine together to eliminate it. Or one of these nations, most likely the Soviet Union, might try by unilateral and violent action to eliminate the arms race. It might take a rather effective Finite Deterrence to deter such a nation from doing so because the alternative (the uncontrolled arms race) could look more threatening than the retaliation from a Minimum Deterrent force.

The world of the early 1970's is likely to be complicated in another way. In all likelihood the world will still be—militarily speaking—bipolar, but barring arms control limitations, there will be third powers around with more than a nominal strategic capability. While the outstanding possibilities are a politically unified European Economic Community or an industrialized China there are other possibilities such as a unified Germany, a remilitarized Japan, or a militarized India. Even such nations as England, France, Germany, Italy, Brazil, Indonesia, and so on could have a respectable military capability, but the two most significant possibilities are the European Economic Community and China. I have already made some comments on the potentialities of the European Economic Community, so I will close this section on World War VII by discussing some of the possibilities for China.

Figure 11 gives a comparison of the rate of growth of the Soviet Union from 1930 to 1939 and China from 1950 to 1959. This chart shows clearly that China is growing quite rapidly, probably more rapidly than the Soviet Union at a corresponding point in its development. The reason for this great rate of growth seems to be mainly due to help from other communist regimes, a large work force, a rapid and successful imposition of tight discipline on this labor force, and ability to exploit the advanced technology of the fifties. Assuming that both the chart and the analysis are correct, there is some reason for believing that the above factors will continue to be operative, and by 1969 China should be about where the Soviet

501

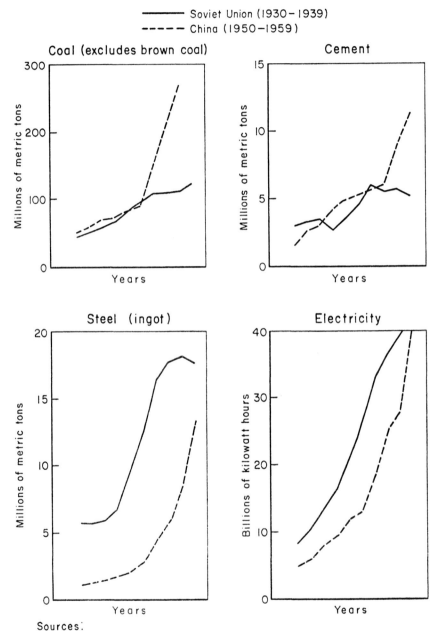

Figure II

A comparison of the growth of China
and the early Soviet Union

——— Soviet Union (1930–1939)
- - - - - China (1950–1959)

Coal (excludes brown coal)

Cement

Steel (ingot)

Electricity

Sources:
Soviet Union data: *Narodone Khoziaistvo USSR V 1958 Godu (The National Economy of the USSR in 1958)* Moscow: 1959. China data: The international edition of the *New York Times, February 1, 1960*

Union was in the mid- or late fifties as far as basic industries are concerned. It will presumably take somewhat longer to catch up in other industrial fields that use the most advanced and sophisticated technology, but by 1969 China should have gone some distance there too. In fact, given the seemingly greater adaptability of

◆◇

Figure 12
Comparisons of some Asiatic powers
1959

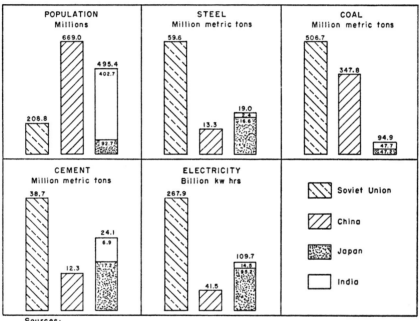

Sources:
Monthly Bulletin of Statistics, May 1960
The international edition of the *New York Times*, Feb. 1, 1960

◆◇

the average 1960 Chinese citizen to the needs of a modern industrial society—as opposed to the relative unadaptability of the typical Soviet citizen in 1930—one could expect the Chinese to be spectacularly successful in over-all output, but they are still likely to have incredible rural slums. Figure 12 gives a comparison of the Soviet Union and China today. India and Japan have been added to the chart to indicate where China's chief Asiatic rivals are. An alliance between these nations seems clearly indicated.

This capability in industry will be reflected in increased military capability. It is currently believed that the Chinese have a professional army of between 2.5 and 5,000,000 men and are training a militia of 10 to 20,000,000 (including women). While little is known about the quality of the latter, the former is clearly a competent and professional force. It is clear that as soon as the Chinese develop adequate logistics and lines of communication, they will be a most formidable threat to all contiguous areas. In any case, they are a much more formidable force even now than they were in Korea in 1951, where they gave a very good account of themselves. This does not mean that defense of all countries contiguous to China is hopeless, but it does mean that it will be hopeless in some areas and difficult in all. Unless an area is adequately occupied by trained and properly equipped troops, the Chinese will be able to take it at will and, further, they will be able to attack or threaten many areas simultaneously. On the other hand, any military operations that they conduct must be conducted subject to the risk that they might touch off an all-out strategic war with the United States, or in some cases with the Soviet Union. This will be an ever present factor in Chinese calculations, since it is most unlikely that the Chinese will be able to challenge U.S. or Soviet Type I Deterrence, while it is quite possible that both of these countries will still have a Credible First Strike Capability against China. It is, however, most unlikely that either country would be willing, under most provocations, to use its Credible First Strike Capability since the result of even a victorious exchange between one of these countries and China might not only result in very high levels of damage for the victor, but leave the victor with a sadly reduced economic and military capability vis-à-vis its main opponent. Also, as I have already discussed, the Chinese could so base their missiles as to use their own population as hostages to deter an all-out strike. Under these circumstances, if the Chinese feel aggressive, they will be in a very good position to indulge their feelings. It is also very likely that they will feel aggressive. The Chinese stopped their birth control campaign in 1958. This probably represents—whether wittingly or not is unknown— a decision to keep the majority of the population at subsistence or very low standards, so that their added population will be of economic value to them. It is most unlikely therefore that the Chinese will soon feel the softening effects of an increasing bourgeoisation or contacts with noncommunists. They are unlikely to allow the latter, since such contacts would both disclose the grimmer aspects

504

of the society to international scrutiny and weaken the discipline of the members. It is also most unlikely that the Soviets will be able to act as a strong restraining influence, for if they antagonize their erstwhile allies, these allies may follow in Tito's footsteps and either become neutral or join the West. It is, however, likely that we will regard the Soviets as a sometime responsible partner in re-straining the Chinese. It is presumably of the utmost importance for us to restrain the Chinese from using destructive nuclear weap-ons, since (as described on pages 542–543) a controlled and sym-metrical use of nuclear weapons is more likely to favor the Chinese than us. If we have to restrain them militarily it will have to be by a combination of conventional power plus Type II Deterrence to keep the war limited, or the use of Controlled Reprisal. We will presuma-bly have to exploit to the limit the apparent current advantage of the defense over the offense in conventional warfare and possibly the counterbalancing military power of a militarized India, a remili-tarized Japan, and an armed and vigorous SEATO. All this will likely take more preparations than are going to be available. We should start now the research and development, the training pro-grams, and the political and economic preparations that will be useful. Otherwise we are likely to lose a large part of Asia if the Chinese decide to be aggressive.

WORLD WAR VIII (1973)

Thirteen Years of Progress (or 50,000 Buttons)

We have discussed under World War VII some technological possibilities that have thus far more or less heralded their way. If we now consider a hypothetical World War VIII in the early 1970's, the possibilities are both less predictable and more dramatic. Instead of trying to prophesy specifics, let us try to get a slight feel for how much change the next thirteen years might bring by looking at what has happened in the last thirteen years. Table 66 indicates the basic ideas.

The first two entries in the table are not technological, but they are of the utmost significance; they may dominate all else. It is gen-erally believed that since 1947 the Soviets have managed to close quite a bit of the industrial and technological gap between them-selves and the United States. It is difficult to be quantitative here, because even if we had complete and accurate information about all the components, there are theoretical problems in comparing

TABLE 66
THIRTEEN YEARS OF PROGRESS

	1947	1960	1973
S.U. GNP/U.S. GNP	.2–.3	.3–.5	.5–1
Nth Country	1	4	?
Manned Offensive Vehicle	B-29	B-52G	Dynasoar, B-70++, Manned Satellite, Spaceship?
Weapons Carried by Above	20 KT	20 MT	BT? Specialized Weapons
Manned Defensive Vehicle	F-51	F-102	Satellite, F-108++
Armament of Above	Unguided Rockets, Guns	MB-1, Guided Rockets	MB-X, Intelligent Rockets
Surface-to-Air Missile	90 MM	Nike-Bomarc-Hawk	AICBM, Super Antiaircraft
Surface-to-Surface Missile	V-2	Atlas	?
Data Processing	Human	FSQ7	Super Brain
Bacteriological Warfare	—	?	?
Chemical Warfare	Nerve Gas	Psychogenics	?
X		?	?

two such different economies. For example, as shown in Figure 14 if we take the GNP of the Soviet Union and put it in United States prices it adds up to a much larger per cent of the U.S. GNP than if we do it the other way and put the U.S. GNP in terms of Soviet prices. The disparity between the two comparisons is so large because so much of the U.S. output is made up of consumption items and services which are relatively cheap in the United States and relatively expensive in the Soviet Union. The practice seems to be to take a geometrical mean between the two comparisons and it is probable that the CIA estimates given in Figure 13 and Figure 14 are obtained in this way. It is probably as reasonable an

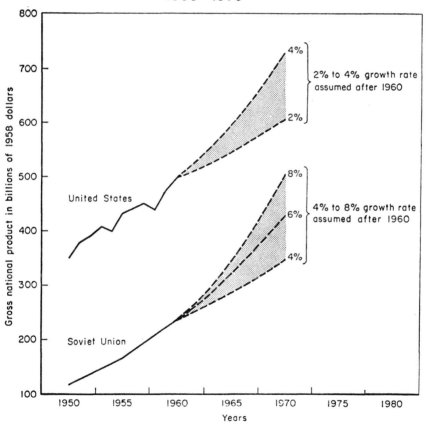

Figure 13

A comparison of the estimated growth of the Soviet and United States economies 1950—1970

Sources:

Soviet Manpower 1960—1970, Central Intelligence Agency, May 1960

Income and Output, U.S. Dept of Commerce, Nov 1958

Survey of Current Business, U.S. Dept of Commerce, Feb 1960

approximation as can be obtained. One can thus estimate that in 1947 the Soviet economy was about one-quarter as big as the U.S. economy. By 1960 it had increased relative to the U.S. economy to be about 40 per cent as large, and by 1970 it is expected that the Soviet economy will be about 75 per cent as large as the U.S. economy. While many experts believe that the above comparison exaggerates the gross national product of the Soviet Union, it may also underestimate one of the most important aspects of production in the Soviet Union. Figure 14 illustrates the potentialities of the Soviet economy.

❖❖

Figure 14

Comparison of select capital and consumer goods

1959

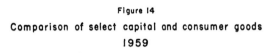

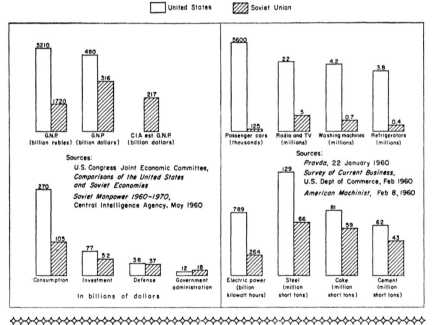

In components of production that are most essential to either military power or capital investment, the Soviets are, in 1960, quite close to being equal to the United States. It is also believed that the Soviet military establishment, if priced in U.S. terms, would cost us about what we ourselves are spending today on our own military forces—or even more. However, if the U.S. military budget were priced in rubles it would probably be larger than the Soviet budget.

But in terms of "firepower" and general over-all military capability, the Soviets seem to be on a parity with the U.S. today, even though the economy which supports their budget appears to be only 40 per cent of the United States economy. It is also believed that the Soviet *industrial* base is increasing at least twice as fast as the *industrial* base of the United States. Therefore, it is probably not an unreasonable conjecture that the Soviet industrial output in 1973 should climb to something between 60 and 100 per cent of that of the United States, where this .6 to 1.0 figure probably even underestimates those industrial products which count, as far as military end items or basic capital investment are concerned. However, the over-all GNP comparison may not be as favorable to the Soviets. I do not imply that the Soviets will not also have a quite large consumer goods output. I am simply saying that, given the unreliability of the basic data, it is very hard to estimate that aspect of the Soviet economy and that the assumptions on consumer goods may be irrelevant to our consideration.

If current tendencies continue (including the percentage of each nation's GNP allocated to military products being unchanged), we can expect the Soviets to have a military establishment which in U.S. dollars and terms is two or three times as large as the U.S. military establishment. Despite all "balance-of-terror" and "nuclear-sufficiency" themes this could be a very significant thing. I do not believe that the current trends will continue to that extent, either because the Soviets will relax, the U.S. will buckle down, some combination of these events will occur, or we will have a disaster. However, it is always of interest to extrapolate current trends to see what could happen.

The diffusion of nuclear weapons is the next big unknown. In 1947 only one country had nuclear weapons. In 1960 four countries had nuclear weapons. In 1973 it is impossible to tell how many will. With current trends it should be something between five and ten nations by then, though it might easily be as low as two and as large as twenty. The reason that it may be as low as two is that the British Labour Party's suggestion that Britain take the lead toward formation of a nonnuclear club might be accepted. In any case, the current pressures toward preventing the spread of arms is likely to increase. Currently known foreign programs indicate that relatively few nations are really trying to develop bombs. On the other hand, if a few more nations get bombs, say Germany and China, the pressure on the nonnuclear powers to follow suit would get to be rather large. Possibly even more important, if the United States or Russia uses nuclear weapons in a limited war, then unless this event itself causes a revulsion, the pressures might get very strong, so that every nation that has the capability either to manufacture or buy weapons or cajole them from allies will, in fact, do one or more of these three things. Also, the technology of some models of nuclear weapons may get very simple, both as to the availability of the special materials of which they are made and the actual difficulty of manufacturing. I have already pointed out several ways this could occur.

The other entries in Table 66, while more prosaic, are still quite startling when projected to 1973. The change from the B-29 to the B-52G is a bigger change than those which occurred from the beginning of World War II to the end of World War II. The future promises to be even more startling. We may be going from subsonic speeds to supersonic and hypersonic, from intercontinental ranges to world-circling, from air-breathing propulsion to rocket, from 50,-000 feet to outer space. We will be at least two generations past the B-70 and the Dynasoar. On the other hand, because of the growth of missiles, one can probably think of the manned vehicle in the 1973 period as being obsolete as the backbone of a strategic force. It will have only specialized jobs to do.

Weapons changes are also likely to be startling. The revolution from 20 KT to 20 MT is in some ways more earth-shaking than the initial revolution from 20 ton to 20 KT. While most of the weapons developments will occur in the area of cheapness, flexibility, and specialization, there may also be increases in size. The extrapolation to begaton-type weapons may turn out to be even more revolutionary than the first 20 ton to 20 KT jump, for even sober experts may now begin to talk about cheap Doomsday Machines as a possibility. As I have already stated, it is my belief that neither the U.S. nor the Soviet Union will manufacture any Doomsday Machines, but this will be a political, economic, and moral choice and not one dictated by technology. (I should also add that I hold this belief only moderately firmly.) The year 1973 may be a bit early to see the possibility that any of twenty nations will have the capability to manufacture Doomsday Machines, but we have been surprised before at the rate of technological development.

The manned interceptor also shows some startling possibilities in terms of extrapolations. One does not know how big a role it will play, given the introduction of guided missiles in offense and defense. Whatever its role, it is likely to have a rather impressive armament, at least if it is nuclear. The change from HVAR (high velocity aerial rockets) to the MB-1 (air defense rocket carrying a low-yield atomic bomb) means that the interceptor has an appreciable, if not 100 per cent, kill probability against anything at which it gets a good chance to fire. In fact, the technology of small, light weapons should be so fully developed that one would not be at all surprised if a 1973 fighter could not carry some quite large-yield weapons—and many of them. But there may not be any targets in the air for them to shoot at.

The surface-to-air missiles will also have had a startling development by 1973. These can now be made effective enough to have a 100 per cent kill probability against identifiable bomber targets. Any enemy using bombers must use some sort of deception tactics to get through if the defense is properly prepared. But the major threat is now missiles; attacking these may be beyond the capabilities of the defense. It is also most unlikely that flexible enough defensive missiles will be developed to use against both missiles and the air-breathing threat at all altitudes. If we are still in the defense business we will need several complementary systems. These defenses are likely to include something equivalent to coast artillery to be used against Polaris-type submarines and other seagoing threats. This same coastal defense missile may be useful against some kinds of air-breathing or other missile threats. There may or may not be special missile defenses for light attacks (i.e., China, or accidents), the defense of hard targets (deep underground headquarters), and other specialized tasks.

An equally startling revolution will have occurred in the field of data processing. The capacity of high-speed computer FSQ-7 (used in the SAGE data-processing system) compared to the manual system is today really fantastic, but for a whole series of reasons there has not been a corresponding increase in the effectiveness of area air defense. This has caused some disillusionment among the more sanguine proponents of centralized data processing, but this disappointment may be premature. Data processing, or at least handling information and data at high speed, may not only be improved as an aid to active defense, but it may in the future also turn out to be as important in Command and Control for the strategic forces as for the air defense force. The improvements will probably include some very flexible computers capable of almost

511

human initiative and perception plus some very effective man-machine combinations. This may result in very complex systems and some new types of vulnerability and accident proneness, as we have already discussed.

Finally, the surface-to-surface missile will probably represent the most important equipment-type changes by 1973. The fantastic development of this, matched by corresponding developments in the warheads, is the current great revolution in warfare. These first models are in the Model T stage, and impressive development lies in the future. Improvements are possible in many directions—smaller and cheaper missiles, simpler and more inexpensive maintenance, greater capability for dispersal, concealment, and mobility, sophisticated penetration aids, multiple warheads, midcourse or terminal guidance, and so on.

Let us consider now what the forces might look like in the mid-1970's, and for definiteness we will pick the year 1975. It is obviously impossible even remotely to predict any specifics fifteen years from now, and I will not attempt to do so. I will also make little attempt to take account of technological breakthroughs. Instead, I will conjecture what a reasonable allocation might be for either the United States or the Soviet Union, if they continue or increase their growth rate and spend about the same percentage as they do now on military products. Figure 15 shows how military spending could go over the years, assuming it starts at $45 billion in 1961 and grows at a fixed percentage each year. I will assume that each nation is on the 5 per cent curve and spends the money on the "classical" kind of military products I have been discussing. I pointed out earlier that we have been spending about 11 per cent of our GNP on defense in recent years (it has ranged from 9 to 13). Assuming that the GNP increases by about 4 or 5 per cent a year, which is a little bit higher than the 4 per cent rate we have had recently and quite a bit higher than the historic 3 per cent rates—but which is still a rate we are likely to attain (given the enormous interest and attention that has recently been forced on methods of increasing our GNP to compete with the Russians), the fifteen years from 1961 to 1975 should see us spending a little less than a trillion dollars on defense and the year 1975 should see us reaching a military budget of about 100 billion dollars. The same figures are probably low for the Russians, given the current estimated rate at which their GNP increases and the percentage they are likely to spend on defense. However, we are doing this estimating so roughly there is really no point in dif-

512

Figure 15

Possible expenditures for national security
1961–1975

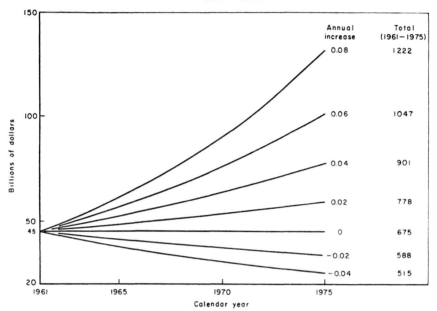

TABLE 67

A POSSIBLE 1975 MILITARY POSTURE FOR U.S. OR S.U.
(billions of dollars)

	Cumulative Budget (1961–1975)	1975 Budget
Specialized local war capability	250	25
Land-based strategic missiles	200	20
Active defense and warning	150	15
Nonmilitary defense	150	10
Seagoing missiles	100	10
Defense against sea threats	75	15
Manned vehicles	75	5
TOTAL	1,000	100

ferentiating between the U.S. and the S.U. budgets. The reader
can easily make any corrections he cares to for variations on our
assumptions.

513

The first item in Table 67 is specialized local war capability. I have avoided the words "Limited War" *because it is part of the argument of these lectures that in the future the 'Central War may have important limitations and the "Limited War" may involve strategic capabilities—for example, destruction by or of Polaris submarines at sea.* I have assumed that about one-fourth of the budget would go into local war capabilities. The $25 billion being spent in 1975 seems superficially to be about five times the current Army budget for tactical war forces, but this figure is supposed to include air, naval, and logistic support, some foreign aid, and so forth. It therefore is more like a doubling, and this may be too small. One would expect the Russians to have more money to spend on military products, and much of their extra money might go into tactical budgets —unless their ideas change (as indicated by Khrushchev in his speech of January 14, 1960; however, the Chinese may pick up the gauntlet). But one can also hope that our allies will have taken over a much larger portion of the burden of furnishing this particular capability than they do today.

I have assumed next that we have spent about $200 billion during the 1961–1975 time period on land-based strategic missiles and that the 1975 budget for this item is about $20 billion. Taking into account that the missiles might become more expensive because they have become more complex (if, for example, the other side has an AICBM or passive defense which requires superior missiles), and also taking into account that they could get very much cheaper (if there is no AICBM so that their performance can stay fixed, then improved technology should make them much cheaper), then we can argue that the budgets allotted would buy something between 5,000 and 100,000 missiles—let us call it about 20,000 for each of us. Presumably, neutrals will also have about 5,000 or 10,000. (These are likely to be much cheaper or less sophisticated than ours, and they might or might not be able to negate the AICBM and passive defenses of the larger nations with any reliability. It is a completely open question.)

Give or take a factor of 5, there are quite likely to be about 50,000 ready missiles in the world in 1975, each with its own button. Whether the missiles are kept alert or not is hard to conjecture. It is very possible that unless a nation is prepared to fire rapidly it may, even possessing 20,000 missiles, be unacceptably vulnerable to a surprise attack. On the other hand, the thought of having 50,000 alert missiles is a bit frightening. This is true particularly since many

514

of them may be in the hands of "less responsible" powers than we. It is difficult to believe that under these circumstances an occasional button will not get pressed. However, as I have already pointed out, one button being pressed does not necessarily lead to immediate all-out war, although it increases the risk. We may just be going to live in a world in which every now and then a city or town is destroyed or damaged as a result of blackmail, unauthorized behavior, or an accident.

Another big uncertainty concerns the spectrum of technological possibilities. There may be special missiles that are very, very hard and extremely alert, just for the retaliatory mission. If they can be made hard enough it is possible that they can also be left unalert so as to reduce operating costs and keep down the chance of accidents. Both sides may buy special vulnerable but cheap "go first" forces which will not even be kept alert. These would have a capability for going on alert and threatening the enemy à la Type II Deterrence. There may be very special, extremely large missiles which might not be guided but would carry extremely large warheads to be used as a terror weapon for retaliation or blackmail purposes. These could be designed to exploit either thermal or radioactivity effects as well as blast. With the civil defense program we are going to discuss later on, you could probably make arrangements to handle extremely large threats where "handle" means that most of the population can survive and recuperate in less than a generation to reasonable standards of living. On the other hand, not only would the experience itself be quite severe, but the fact that you think you can handle the problems is something you will "know" only by theory backed up by specialized experiments. The system itself will have never been tried, so the uncertainty in itself may be frightening enough to be a pretty good Type I Deterrence, one which would work under most circumstances. There may be very special missiles, possibly with quite small and clean warheads. Their use would be for the purpose of limited "nuclear retaliation" where this might be directed against "sanitary" economic or military targets. One would guess that if limited nuclear retaliation were ever taken seriously, something in the low KT range would be all that one would want to use, particularly if extreme accuracy and reliability were achieved. All in all, there should be in 1975 very many specialized missiles for specialized purposes; there will probably be more different missile models than we have plane types today.

The next item is nonmilitary defense, on which we assume $150

515

billion has been spent by the federal government. In considering what this would buy, one could also expect that another $50 to $100 billion or so would have been spent by sources outside the government, particularly if the proposed War Damage Equalization Corporation (Appendix II) subsequently comes into existence.

I have further assumed that from 1961 to 1975 we have spent fifteen times as much on civil defense as was being spent during 1975 itself. This means that I have assumed that civil defense expenditures hit a peak much earlier than 1975, presumably around 1967–1968; otherwise, there would have been a long interim period when we would not have been able to fight wars or resist blackmail.

Table 68 below indicates what we might buy for about 200 billion dollars (150 billion from the federal government and 50 from private sources).

TABLE 68

AN ADEQUATE CIVIL DEFENSE PROGRAM
(billions of dollars)

1. Personnel shelters	80
2. Industrial shelters	30
3. Food stockpiles	25
4. Evacuation, warning, dispersal, etc.	15
5. Maintenance and resupply	15
6. Cadres and personnel	15
7. Inventories, spare parts, etc.	10
8. Miscellaneous	10
	200

Because the thought of expensive civil defense programs is new to most people, I would like to give a "descriptive" breakdown of some of the above figures to show what might be bought with $200 billion.

Let us consider the personnel shelters first. We might buy about 50 million very high-quality spaces for concentrated city areas at $700 per space. These could be, for example, about 1,000 feet underground, with quick closing, 1,000 psi doors at the surface. These doors provide interim protection while people walk down to depth. At depth, they can probably take direct hits of "small" bombs (say less than 5 MT) and may even take "near" misses of "large" bombs. In a detailed study of Manhattan Island it was decided that such a system could be built with doors within 2,000 feet (about 5 minutes fast walking time) of everybody on the Island for something between $500 and $900 per shelter space.

There might be another 50 million spaces at $400 per space for medium and small cities and the suburbs of large cities. The basic shelter for the rest of the country (100 million spaces) might cost about $200 per space. There would be about 50–100 psi community shelters holding a few hundred people plus small individual family shelters which would probably be about 5–10 psi. Finally, we would spend about $5 billion subsidizing and outfitting mines to provide excess space for the evacuation of city people if there is time to do this (about 1 billion square feet outfitted and about 4 billion square feet to be used if there are about 3 or 4 months available). These subsidized mines would also provide additional postwar radiation-protected working and living space.

For $30 billion we might adequately protect an economic and industrial core, which could be used to provide a base for rebuilding the country even if just about every aboveground plant were destroyed. This means if the aboveground damage is in any way reasonably limited, the economic development of the community should be set back less than a generation—most likely very much less. It is assumed that a $30-billion subsidy will buy a couple of billion square feet of immediately usable factory space underground plus partial plants which could be finished rapidly. This would, in effect, protect between a fourth and a half of our current industrial capacity. If properly selected, this should be more than enough industrial capability to provide reasonable postwar living standards in a few years—even if everything aboveground is destroyed.

The $25 billion for food should buy about a three-year food supply, broken down as follows:

100 days processed shelter rations for 200 million shelter spaces at 50 cents per day per person = 10 billion dollars
300 days semiprocessed rations for 200 million people at 20 cents per day per person = 12 billion dollars
8 billion dollars for protecting and augmenting existing unprocessed food supplies and carryover crops to give about an additional two-year ration for 200 million people.

These food stocks would be supplemented by existing commercial and home stocks, which could do much to increase the palatability and variety of the postattack diet.

While the estimates just given for points 1 to 3 are very rough, they are based on a good deal of work. The $65 billion allocated to points 4 to 8 in Table 68 are the roughest kinds of guesses and I will not discuss them further here. The above program could probably perform very well, particularly if there were even a little warning. Even if there were no corresponding military effort, it would take a major effort on the part of the enemy to destroy the system. With the addition of a competent active offense and defense system, the civil defense system probably cannot be destroyed without the attacker using weapons that either are or come perilously close to being Doomsday Machines.

Usually when I discuss expensive programs that involve elaborate shelters, I find that people are appalled at the idea of living underground for such lengthy periods as posed here. *It should be remembered that the program is not being set up in the expectation that it will be so used, even if we have a war; rather it is intended to limit the amount of damage actually done by a war, and to increase the capability of the United States to withstand blackmail tactics.* That is, even if the worst comes and a war actually occurs, in all likelihood the war will be fought much more carefully than the preparations of the program indicate. Most of the aboveground wealth of the country will survive the war. This aboveground wealth is not really a military target and the enemy would presumably destroy it only if he is stupid, or if he is trying to blackmail us and we refuse to make appropriate concessions. If, instead of annihilation threats, he can only threaten to make us uncomfortable, this makes his threat much weaker. He is much less likely to try the threat or to carry it through if he tries it, since our own retaliation is likely to be severe. If the preparations have *not* been made, on the other hand, he must at least try the threat and the possibility that he will carry it through is, paradoxically, higher. All of the above remarks are symmetrical. In fact, it is much more probable that the Soviets will put in an elaborate program than that we will. Thus they will get any benefits in bargaining or alleviating the consequences of a war that can be gotten through such programs.

We have allocated $150 billion to active defense and warning, about one-third of which might go into defense against ballistic missiles, one-third into defense against manned bombers, and one-third into the parts of the system which are common to the two missions.

The reason for the relatively small amount for ballistic-missile defense is that it seems improbable that it will ever work very well against a determined Soviet Union first strike. The idea here is that we spend enough to make the other side work hard, plus spending for specialized purposes such as defending hard SAC bases; most important of all, we spend enough to have a capability against the enemy's residual force (the force he has left after he has been firing a while or after we have hit him). It is also important to have a capability to exploit any technological breakthroughs in the art of defense. Since we cannot build defense systems in less than ten years, it is necessary to keep a base maintained at all times. Lastly, it may also turn out that while it is infeasible to have an adequate AICBM capability against the threat posed by a large country, it may be and even should be possible to have a capability against smaller countries. Whether the Chinese would be included in the category "a small country" is difficult even to conjecture.

I have allocated about $100 billion for seagoing missiles. This will most likely be spent on Polaris-type systems. Taking account of the fact that submarines can get either less or more expensive than they are today, and making some wild guesses, this is something between 500 and 5,000 submarines. We would assume that the cheaper ones would carry something between 10 to 50 missiles apiece; the more expensive ones would carry 10 to 100. Then we would have something between 5,000 and 50,000 missiles at sea. We should have about the fourth- or fifth-generation Polaris missile in 1973, though in all likelihood the early submarines will still be on active duty, though retrofitted.

We have allocated only $75 billion for defense against sea threats, although we assume that the annual rate in 1975 is rather high— $10 billion. The reason for the rather small accumulative amount is the guess that we get into this business rather late, say post-1965.

It is quite likely that the defense against sea threats will be composed of three parts. First, there will be an area defense system. I am using the term "area defense" in the specialized sense of being able to destroy or deny an entire area. For example, one could think of mining the ocean bottoms, at least in deep water, with very large bombs, 10's or 100's of megatons in yield. Such bombs will presumably be quite inexpensive in the early 1970's, and one may be able to surround them with some kind of neutron absorbers that capture most of the neutrons and alleviate the effects of the radioactive by-products. At the outbreak of the war we could simply destroy all shipping in 10, 20, or even 50 million square miles of ocean. The same objective might be accomplished by having missiles carrying very large warheads based on the seacoast that could be fired at the outbreak of the war. These could be fired according to some barrage doctrine to cover an area more or less uniformly. This system may have several advantages over the mine system in that it is less prone to accident and sabotage and probably more flexible in operation. For example, it could be combined with an area-sensing system which can reliably track hostile submarines by having an enormous number of high-powered active and passive sensing devices. It might be efficient to do this, since it would then be possible to aim the missiles rather than just shoot them to cover an area. Whether it is more efficient or not depends on the relative costs of missiles and sensing devices.

The second part of this system for use against seagoing threats (which may overlap with the first part) would be a capability for attriting the enemy's Polaris-type submarines in peacetime. It is not at all unlikely that we will see some limited naval conflicts in this era.

The last part, and probably the most difficult, will be the capability to try to destroy the enemy's submarines as individual submarines (rather than on an area basis) either before, during, or after the first day of the war.

The final item in the budget is the manned vehicle. I here assume that the annual budget will have decreased over the years down to about one-half of today's bomber budget, although in the 14-year period I have allowed a fairly large sum, $75 billion.

This allotment assumes that the forces are kept roughly at current strength but are not fully or rapidly modernized. It is possible that many of the planes would be the same as we have today. At least, there should be a lot of B-52G's and H's around in this time period. If the other side does not have an air defense system with a large capability, such B-52's present a very serious threat. We have pointed out that they can today carry many small bombs and deliver these weapons with pinpoint accuracy. In the future, because bombs will be both cheaper and lighter, the word "many" may mean 10's or even 100's of bombs. This could be a quite destructive weapon system if the other side were not fully prepared. Therefore, even a small amount spent on manned bombers should be enough to force one's enemy into an expensive air defense system or to give up the capability of being able to fight wars. It is possible that the ICBM defense will also defend against manned bombers. Yet I doubt that the overlap between the two systems will be complete—for example, the low-altitude problem for manned bombers is likely to be unique.

In addition to improved B-52's (and Bears and Bisons) in 1975, there may be, for example, bombers of an advanced type—nuclear powered, supersonic all the way, or even hypersonic. There will certainly be some manned satellites, some of which could carry bombs. It is practically impossible to decide what manned vehicles of one sort or another will be useful, though I think it is quite likely that they will compose only a small portion of the force. However, despite much current belief, it is most unlikely that manned vehicles will be completely phased out of the force.

This, then, is one possible picture of the world in 1975. Whether the future will turn out as indicated depends to some extent on what turns in public policy we and others decide on between 1960 and that day. While many will think of it as an overarmed world, and while I probably have painted it in somewhat more intense colors than the most sober analysis would predict, it is also quite possible that I have underestimated the amount of resources and technological ingenuity the Soviets and the Americans will devote to the arms race in the next decade or two. In fact, barring controls, I have almost unquestionably underestimated the technological race. I have also tried to make clear that it takes two to not have the kind of arms race described. If only one withdraws, then that one will be in a serious position of inferiority. On the other hand, there are few who would believe that the kind of world just described could be stable for very long.

Even in this relatively lengthy discussion I have scarcely been able to touch upon, much less describe, the complexities of the technological arms race and the stability of the United States–Soviet balance of power. In particular, I have left out almost all discussion of the technology of Limited War. I have tried to point out that technological progress is so rapid that there are almost bound to be doctrinal lags. These doctrinal lags will in themselves be dangerous; leading to important gaps in our preparations, the waste of badly needed resources on obsolete concepts, the neglect of possible strengths, the overuse of especially glamorous tools, and, possibly most important of all, heightened possibilities of serious miscalculations or accidents because we have not had time to understand and make provisions for the requirements of the newly installed systems. To the extent that arms control measures are supposed to alleviate dangers or costs by allowing the current "balance of power" status and military competition to be conducted, by agreement, at cheaper or safer levels, or to the extent that one hopes to increase each state's objective capability of preventing surprise attack or other disaster, this inability to understand "the military problems" introduces almost intolerable complications. (The reason for the adverb "almost" is that we have these complications, whether or not we have arms control.) I have discussed, but much too lightly, the even more complex problem of the conduct of international relations in a world in which force is both becoming increasingly more available and increasingly less usable, a problem that is complicated by the spectacular increase in the number of sovereign nations,[10] by increased nationalism, militarism, and "ambitions" in these new nations and governments, and by the revolution of rising expectations. While the military balance of power will affect these problems, unless the balance becomes very lopsided it will not dominate them. However, the problems may dominate attempts to control or ameliorate military power. Any attempts to control the arms race must be able to live with all the stresses and strains that the above problems will create. It is most unlikely that all of these problems will be solved in an atmosphere of good will and common fellowship, or by the use of *ad hoc* committees and intuitive judgments derived from experience in almost irrelevant situations. I will try in Chapter XI to summarize the complexity and scope of the military problems and in Chapter XII the necessity for a deliberate and conscious attempt to cope with all aspects of the problem in a comprehensive fashion.

[10] There were approximately fifty sovereign nations in 1946; there are now about a hundred.

RECAPITULATION

The Richness and Urgency of the Military Problem

DELIBERATE thermonuclear war and Hitler-type challenges are so nightmarish that most people consider them (illogically) unreal and improbable—if not paranoiac delusions. The resources that are being put into countering these possibilities seem vast. Many contend that the United States has been concentrating too much effort on central war and the strategic forces. Some say the "real" problems facing the nation are in areas represented by limited war (conventional or nuclear), Soviet subversion, Soviet economic offensive, and disparities between Soviet and U.S. rates of economic growth. Others call attention to the widespread poverty in the world, the need for foreign aid, the animosity of many underdeveloped countries toward the West, the instability of the NATO alliance, deficiencies in education, the disruptive effect of increasing chauvinism, nationalism in the new states, and so forth. We do have all these problems and even more. It will be important to put more of our material and intellectual resources into solving such problems than we have been doing. But there remains another problem, the most serious of all for the West. *The problem of sheer survival*—not that we will be nibbled to death or subverted into ineffectuality, but that we will be annihilated in a blow or two, or blackmailed into accepting a series of Munichs because too many may now consider the thought of going to war to defend justice, obligations, rights, or positions bizarre or fanciful. Unless current attitudes and programs are changed, it is going to take more money, thought, and luck to meet these military problems than are likely to be available.

Let us summarize briefly a major portion of the lectures by examining some of the major military-type problems that we will have to worry about in the 1960–1975 time period. These are listed in a rough order of priority on Table 69.

The first prototype situation is Armageddon—a final battle between "good" and "evil" in which civilization itself will receive an enormous setback no matter who wins the battle or, even more finally, a battle in which human life will be wiped out. As I pointed out in discussing the Doomsday Machine, this will not always be a completely academic notion. While it does not seem technically feasible today, unless R&D is controlled, it most likely will be technically feasible in 10 to 20 years. A central problem of arms control—perhaps *the* central problem—is to delay the day when Doomsday Machines or near equivalents become practical, and when and if Doomsday Machines or near equivalents are feasible to see to it that none are built. In the long run there is presumably no question

✧✧

TABLE 69

HISTORICAL PROTOTYPES

1. Armageddon	6. Hacha
2. Camlan	7. Rotterdam
3. 1871–1914	8. Berlin
4. Pearl Harbor	9. Korea
5. Munich	10. Reichstag Fire

✧✧

that Armageddon is the major issue. To say that this catastrophe must be avoided, no matter what compromises this entails, seems to be a humorous or stupid understatement. Unfortunately, there seems to be no practical way to eliminate this possibility entirely. The best available policy seems to be one that would involve some world supervision of permissible weapon systems.

Here is a common U.S.–S.U. problem that is obviously clear-cut. Yet if we overestimate the imminence and magnitude of this danger, we face the problem of defeatism and apathy with regard to National Defense plus the possibility that the Soviets will be tempted to manipulate our fears and maybe even the problem itself for their own advantage. We should not facilitate their use of such a strategy. We should not pose the alternatives as being: (1) immediate unilateral surrender, or (2) immediate preventive war, or (3) inevitable world annihilation. If these were the only alternatives almost everyone in the West would choose number one (although some in the communist bloc might choose number two).[1] I would conjecture that the net practical effect of posing the problem in such a

---

[1] In his speech accepting the Nobel Prize for Literature in December 1950, William Faulkner expressed both the views and the kind of defeatism it can lead to as follows: "Our tragedy today is a general and universal physical fear so long sustained by now that we can even bear it. There are no longer problems of the spirit. There is only the question: When will I be blown up? Because of this, the young man or woman writing today has forgotten the problems of the human heart in conflict with itself which

524

way is not to encourage feasible and useful proposals to control the
arms race; instead, it increases the probability of a Pearl Harbor,
a Munich, or a mutually devastating war. It is dangerous to put
tempting strategies before an opponent. The temptation may cause
him not only to exploit the feasible possibilities but to overreach or
overextend himself.

Our emphasis clearly must be on balanced and achievable goals
and on means appropriate to them. Thus we must stress objective
military capabilities, genuine arms control agreements, and international arrangements which are not a disguised form of unilateral
surrender. This will involve some hard bargaining and risky tactics,
but barring some unforeseen good or bad luck, this seems to be
the only practical approach—*competent military preparations plus
tough-minded but genuine bargaining.* There is doubt in my mind
whether the West can measure up to the demands of the situation.

Second to the Armageddon problem, but included in it, is the
Camlan problem—the possibility that a war will be touched off by
an accident or misunderstanding. (I really had to stretch to find a
historical analogy to modern radar networks and super-alert quick-
reaction forces.) Camlan refers, of course, to the last battle of King
Arthur. It seems that King Arthur's son, Mordred, revolted against
his father. After some fighting the two contenders met, with all
their troops, on the field of Camlan to negotiate. Both sides were
fully armed and desperately suspicious that the other side was going
to try some ruse or stratagem. The negotiations were going along
smoothly until one of the knights was stung by an asp and drew his
sword to kill the reptile. The others saw the sword being drawn
and immediately fell upon each other. A tremendous slaughter ensued. The chronicle *Morte d'Arthur* is quite specific about the point
that the slaughter was excessive chiefly because the battle took
place without preparations and premeditation. When the battle was
over everybody except King Arthur, Mordred, and a couple of
knights lay dead.

It is difficult to overemphasize this problem, but some experts seem
to have succeeded in doing so. Some of the main support for the
pure Finite Deterrence strategy has come from people who have
become too obsessed with the possibility of an accident or miscalculation, which is caused by an overtense or overalert SAC. These

---

alone can make good writing because only that is worth writing about, worth the
agony and the sweat."

experts feel that it is essential for us to adopt slow-reacting systems, and they want us to reassure the enemy that there are no circumstances that would cause us to strike first. If this is done, the enemy can be less tense and rely on slow-reacting systems.[2] The Finite Deterrent system that has no Counterforce as Insurance Capability makes this possible because, short of an ultimate and total provocation, it is not a rational system. Firing it would result in self-destruction. The enemy can therefore rely on our being cautious. In a curious and characteristic way, even experts often assume the relaxation to be symmetrical. Finite Deterrence advocates sometimes become too relaxed and overlook essential details—almost like the full-fledged members of the Minimum Deterrence school. Many of the more passionate devotees of Finite Deterrence believe, consciously or unconsciously, that they have abolished war. If they lacked this belief they would almost have to be advocates of Counterforce as Insurance, even if they did not want to carry their preparations to the Credible First Strike stage. (Compared to the alleviation possible by even modest Counterforce as Insurance, any destabilizing effects seem small.) Some believers in Finite Deterrence pay little attention to such details as the problem of making and communicating the fire order, or the ability of the enemy to disarm the system by peacetime violence or by postattack blackmail—they assume that these events will not occur. In their drive to avoid any possibility of accident they not only accept serious or crippling compromises on all other objectives, they compromise their own objective as well. Many of the advocates of Finite Deterrence are suggesting, whether they realize it or not, what really amounts to a subtle form of unilateral disarmament.

We must consider next the complex problem of maintaining the peace and conducting international bargaining in a balance-of-power system. The current "balance of terror" can be looked upon as an intensification of the balance-of-power system. It will be recalled that before World War I the "balance of power" was supposed to make war unprofitable, or at least so risky that a potential aggressor would choose compromise to risking all. The problem is increased today because over a period of time the successful working of such a system tends to create instabilities. This complex problem, which I have called the "1871–1914" problem, is summarized briefly on pages

[2] See page 471.

368 to 370, where the following analogies between 1914 and 196X are discussed:

1. Pre-emption important (First Strike similar to mobilization)
2. Need for quick victory
3. War planning both rigid and narrowly professional
4. Tendency to excessively firm positions in a crisis
5. Increasingly widespread ignorance of the technical side of war
6. Crises tend to induce excessive physical and mental strain in crucial individuals
7. Small powers can manipulate the rivalry of large powers

The ultimate solution to the Armageddon, Camlan, and 1871–1914 problems is some form of arms control and rule of law, possibly under a world government. While we should work toward this goal, I do not believe that hysteria or one-sided propaganda insisting that the West go in for excessive accommodation or unilateral disarmament is likely to advance it in any practical way.

This book has intentionally been preoccupied with the next three problems on my chart—Pearl Harbor, Munich, and Hacha. This will distress many who consider these three problems less important than the first three. In the long run I would tend to agree with them, but the long run is determined by the short run. If the history of the Decline of the West has to be written in the year 1980, it is more likely to be occasioned by our inability to meet the problems listed under points 4, 5, and 6, rather than as the result of a catastrophe such as our problems 1, 2, and 3 or the several problems indicated in the first paragraph of this chapter. Our incapacity, if it comes, is quite likely to derive from ineptitude and apathy on our part; it may also grow out of an overconcentration—especially an intellectual overconcentration—on nonmilitary problems or on problems 1, 2, and 3.

As for the Pearl Harbor threat, I have urged here the need for an *objective retaliatory capability* and decried the tendency to rely on façades. For the Munich and Hacha threats, I have argued that we need a combination of Type II and Type III Deterrence, where the Type III Deterrence should include at least limited war forces (possibly stationed in threatened countries) and Preattack Mobilization Bases. Type II Deterrence is distasteful to many people because it may encourage a particularly dangerous type of arms race and it may also tend to destabilize Type I Deterrence. For these reasons one does wish to rely as little as possible on Type II Deterrence. Yet it is hard for me to believe that we can dispense with it totally or rely on an uncontrolled, and possibly uncontrollable, "residual fear of war." I have suggested that the main destabilizing effect of Type II Deterrence can be handled in part by not keeping the first strike forces on alert. In ordinary circumstances the existence of a non-alert Credible First Strike Capability would not put the other side under much pressure to start a pre-emptive or preventive war. Those circumstances in which it does put pressure on the enemy are exactly the circumstances under which we would feel it essential to be able to threaten him, even if it should be destabilizing for us to do so. It is to be hoped that the other problems of Type II Deterrence can be controlled by agreement and by the pressure toward self-restraint that results when one's opponent has sufficient Type II and Type III Deterrence.

The next four problems on Table 69 lack the importance of those that have gone before, but they are still of great importance, because the most probable military operations and challenges are likely to be preoccupied with them. They also require Type II and III Deterrence. Rotterdam is intended to illustrate the notion that it may pay an aggressor deliberately to damage or destroy a country in order to demonstrate to other countries that he is willing to destroy them also. Because of the potential profit accruing from enhancing his ability to coerce, he is willing to accept whatever military risks and adverse public opinion that may ensue from such an action. To give an extreme example of where it could be useful, this tactic would be an effective counter to a U.S. strategy which involved possible use of limited nuclear retaliation to protect "third" areas. Once the Soviets have acquired the reputation of being willing to lose a city as the price of getting their way, other countries would have to negotiate and compromise ahead of time even if the United States promised to retaliate for any damage the Soviets did to them. It is no compensatory relief to these countries to know that the U.S. will destroy a Soviet city or fight an inconclusive limited war every time they lose one of their capitals.

Berlin illustrates one of our more significant situations, significant in the sense of a balance between frequency and importance. Situations will arise in which the other side will have some legitimate-sounding but controversial claims. If we should give in to those claims under duress we would be creating precedents that might be destructive to our over-all position, precedents that would encourage our enemies and demoralize our friends. If we are in a position where we cannot depend on local forces to protect us and the issue does not justify the threat of all-out war, our only course is to warn the other side that his forcing the issue will mean such a deterioration in international relations that he would regret his action. In such a situation, the Preattack Mobilization Base could play a central role.

Korea illustrates another theme of this book: that we must be willing to fight wars on a local and limited basis. A myth has grown up in the United States that Korea is an example of a U.S. "defeat." From many standpoints, this is not so. We gained a great deal from our Korean experience. We built on our Preattack Mobilization Base; we displayed military firmness; and we provided an example of how to fight a "limited" war. Conflicting estimations of the success of our efforts in Korea are due to the fact that Americans never accepted their necessity, perhaps because of a weakness in explanation—or possibly more fundamental reasons. As a result, there was a tremendous animosity aroused against those responsible for waging the war. I do not know if it is possible to explain to a democratic public the rationality and necessity for being willing to fight limited wars. If it is not possible, I predict a very dim future for democracy in our troubled era.

The Reichstag Fire occurred in Germany in 1934 when a half-witted communist youth burned down the Reichstag. It is not known whether or not a Nazi acting as a double agent induced him to do it, though many believe this to be true. It is almost irrelevant whether this happened or not. The Nazis used this act by a single communist as an excuse to institute a reign of terror against all domestic communists; they expelled the communist deputies from Parliament, and they used the resulting Nazi majority to institute a dictatorship for Hitler.[3]

Even ruthless nations find it advantageous to create an incident such as the Reichstag Fire to justify aggression. Almost anybody will resist to the limit an outright cynical attempt at blackmail. But

[3] Another example of the Reichstag Fire type of problem could have been the sinking of the battleship Maine off Havana in 1898. In this case it really is not known whether or not the battleship accidentally struck a Spanish mine, whether some Spaniards somehow arranged the sinking, or whether, odd as it sounds, some Americans trying to involve us in a war did it. Perhaps it must be listed as an unexplained accident. Whatever the reason, the incident clearly played an important role among the causes of the ensuing war with Spain.

if one can persuade himself that the other side's current demands have some legitimacy (or that the other side thinks they are legitimate, so there is some reason to hope that future demands will have this legitimacy restraint), one is much more willing to negotiate current demands in a reasonable manner. In such a situation, the essence of reasonableness is compromise. This means that whenever the other side can create an incident that puts it in a position to make a reasonable demand, it has assured itself at least a minor gain.

At some time in the future the Soviets could deliberately detonate a nuclear weapon on NATO territory in such a manner as to appear that one of our weapons had accidentally exploded. It would be even more serviceable to them if they could get a saboteur to shoot a NATO or European atomic weapon at one of the Soviet satellites or perhaps the Soviet heartland. Their extreme demands would then appear to be justified. For example, if the weapon came from West Germany, the Soviets could say that the West Germans had thereby shown that they could not responsibly have weapons. They could claim that the carelessness or maliciousness of the Germans in shooting a missile justified their total destruction. However, asserting that they are a "moderate" and "reasonable" government, all they would insist on is that the Germans give up all their atomic weapons and, further, allow about 1,000 or 2,000 Soviet inspectors into the country to guarantee that no atomic weapons remained. The first demand may seem to be quite reasonable. The second is obviously outrageous when imposed unilaterally, but even that might be considered negotiable in some strategic or political situations.

The Soviets do not need to create a Reichstag Fire incident. If they wait long enough, some exploitable incident will occur naturally. Whether the incident is natural or contrived, they can make some impressive gains unless we are in a position to cope with their demands. In trying to estimate the ability of either the alliance or the United States to be resolutely firm in some future crisis, we must take account of the likelihood that there may be some ambiguity in the degree and justice of the challenge. This ambiguity will create divisions, some urging that the Soviets have a legitimate complaint and others pointing out that an alliance which is leaning over backward to meet "legitimate complaints" of its opponent will necessarily fail in its purpose of protecting its members. This controversy will set practical limits to the risks and costs that some members will be willing to incur. It is also most important that alliance capabilities be good enough and the alliance ties strong enough so that the alliance will be able to withstand strains caused by Soviet exploitation of incidents.

The prototype situations I have just discussed make overlapping and conflicting demands on our military and nonmilitary capabilities. Almost all will agree, I think, that the first three are of immense importance, but the last seven are by no means negligible. They must be handled, even though handling them will raise some conflicts with the first three. No satisfactory solution to *all* the problems can be found by relying on a single, simple strategy; the richness and variety of the possible challenges create a requirement for multiple and flexible capabilities. One hopes the acquisition of adequate Limited War capabilities and Preattack Mobilization Bases will mitigate the conflicting demands to a point where whatever problems remain can be handled by some combination of General War capabilities, unilateral and multilateral Arms Control measures, and various regional and international arrangements.

The Conflicting Objectives

It might be appropriate at this time to summarize the main conclusions somewhat more generally and abstractly than by the use of historical prototypes. Basically, we have three major military objectives in national security, as shown on Table 70.

The most important of these objectives is generally thought to be the desire for military stability. (I use the term stability because it gives the connotation of looking at the problem from the viewpoint of both the Soviets and the Americans.) The stability that is desired is a complicated thing, it is not necessarily a continuation of the status quo, but only a desire that the status quo not be changed by the use or threat of the opponent's military power. There are three kinds of stability that are desired; as always, they conflict with each other. The first corresponds to Type I Deterrence. We have mentioned many times that the balance of terror is indeed delicate, that it is far from automatic, and that it is not a simple philosophical consequence of the existence of thermonuclear weapons. There are many reasons for this instability. While these reasons change with time, Type I Deterrence is quite likely to remain unstable in the foreseeable future. The major reason for the current instability is

531

that our main deterrent—B-47's and B-52's—operates in so concentrated a manner that one weapon carrier on the offense can, if it gets through to its target, destroy many weapon carriers on the ground. Thus the defender has two possible countermeasures. He

◇◇

TABLE 70
THE CONFLICTING OBJECTIVES

I. Stability Against
    A. Surprise Attack
        1. First strike advantage
        2. Technological progress
        3. Apathy (inertia)
    B. Unpremeditated War
        1. Accidental war
        2. Catalytic war
        3. Escalation
        4. Arms control
        5. Technological progress
    C. Provocation
        1. Type III Deterrence
        2. Residual fear of war *vs.* Type II Deterrence
        3. Credible Capability will decrease with time
II. Limited Consequences if Stability Fails
    A. Need more than Finite Deterrence plus
       Limited War plus Arms Control
    B. Arms Control
    C. Apathy (psychological denial)
III. Constraints
    A. Political
    B. Economic
    C. Intellectual

◇◇

can either detect the attacker's vehicles in time for his vehicles to escape, or he must shoot enough of them down so that the net trade turns out more evenly.

Changing technology and the institution of protective measures could make important changes in the strategic equation in future years. It is even possible that trades will be reversed—that the offense will have to use up more military resources in its attack than it destroys. For example, if ICBM's are so dispersed and hardened that each of an attacker's ICBM's could destroy at most only one missile, it is clear that the attacker will usually have to shoot many ICBM's in order to have a reasonable probability of destroying at least one of the defender's ICBM's. The trades in numbers would then be against the attacker. However, I pointed out in Lecture II that this lopsided trade is not necessarily true if one compares *resources*. Because the defender's retaliatory system needs some expensive combination of *alert, hardness, dispersal,* and *concealment,* it costs more for him to increase the number of target points than it does for the attacker to increase appropriately the number of offensive missiles. While the attacker also needs a retaliatory capability, he can buy a special kind of offensive force which, while not very useful for retaliation, may be more effective dollar for dollar on the attack than the defender's retaliatory force is on the defense. In any case, the attacker has many advantages that are independent of the straightforward exchange between attacking and defending vehicles.

Let me summarize again why Type I Deterrence is difficult to assure, and why the advantages to the side that strikes first seem so great now and through the foreseeable future.

The attack can be launched in a peaceful environment at a time of the attacker's choosing. It can be carefully planned, with follow-up waves for insurance. With a large force, the attacker can afford to hit his opponent's defenses. His arrangements for Command and Control are intact. His forces can be carefully coordinated. His air defenses can be alerted and warned on the probable arrival time of the retaliatory blow. There are many situations, either before or after the attack, in which the attacker will be able to activate his civil defense plans. Because he has the initiative the attacker can look for weak spots in the defense and design his attack to exploit these weak spots. In addition, he can predict the outcome of the first strike much better than can the defender, and he can make his later plans accordingly.

By way of contrast, the side being struck must retaliate with a damaged force that must operate in a strange wartime environment. The survivors are the only ones able to retaliate. To the extent that unexpected weapons effects or other unexpected phenomena degrade operations, it is the defender who will be seriously affected. It is his country which experiences the wartime environment, not that of the attacker. Command and Control are likely to be degraded to the vanishing point. The defender's forces may be on only a normal peacetime state of alert. The defense does not know where or when the attack is coming. Lastly, the retaliating force of the defender is not likely to have extra firepower available for destroying the opponent's defenses—one means of facilitating an offense.

Let it be remembered that the surviving forces must be able to respond before being destroyed by follow-up waves of the attack. This means that the commanders who make the decision to respond must themselves survive; they must somehow be able to receive information, evaluate it quickly and accurately, and communicate their decisions to their forces *before* these follow-up waves arrive. The surviving forces must be coordinated; then they can concentrate on important targets and penetrate defenses. They must attack against the alerted active defenses (which are waiting for them), and they must overcome the enemy's passive defenses. These asymmetries between the attacker and defender may be increased by some order of magnitude through the judicious use of postattack blackmail by the attacker.

This problem of finding and correcting subtle (and hypothetical) weaknesses is, of course, compounded by the rapid rate of technological advance—a rate that seems much faster than our cultural absorption rate. It is difficult to study seriously what one must do to counter new measures until they have been around awhile. By that time it is too late to develop, proof-test, and install a countermeasure, because the technological race has set up some new problems. In this measure, countermeasure, and counter-countermeasure situation, the measure taken must be comprehensive since the defensive retaliation seems to rely on a very long chain, of which it is literally true, in many cases, that the whole is as strong as the weakest link. In such a rapidly changing situation there are intrinsic psychological, tactical, and development advantages to the offense that must be added to the old ones. The effect of these intrinsic advantages has been greatly magnified, not only because people are slow to react until they see clearly what it is they should react against, but also because of the doctrine (previously discussed) which favors the offense over the defense. These two psychological antipathies, one against reacting at all and one against being defensive-minded, are the major reasons for the unnecessary distance by which defense has lagged behind offense. However, even an enthusiastic pursuing of defensive problems might fail to solve them reliably. The aggressor has to find only *one crucial weakness;* the defender has to find all of them, and in advance.

The existence of subtle problems previously overlooked is not the only reason why it is improbable that our complex retaliatory systems would work right the first time. There is also the customary reason that exists in any large, complicated organization, one which includes complex man-machine combinations. Training under extremely realistic conditions (or even experience in the real thing) is essential if the organization is to work *reliably.* The defender will not only fail to get this realistic training, but the system will have been damaged in crucial spots before it is called upon to retaliate (excepting quick-reaction systems). This puts additional demands on the skill of the personnel they may not be able to meet. I am always amazed at the surprise experts and laymen express when possible faults in military preparations are exposed. *Most people find it very hard to believe that it is possible to spend billions of dollars on a system that has a serious inadequacy.* This may be because most of their standards are set by peacetime experience.

During peacetime, if there is something wrong with the system you notice it and correct it. Peacetime systems tend not to have any glaring inadequacies (in peacetime), which causes a misleading feeling of comfort. Unfortunately, the system has to fail only once. In fact, once is too often. The failure is noticed much too late. For this reason the fact that the system seems to be working in peacetime is not very reassuring except to the unthinking—or those who *want* to be pleasantly complacent. The tendency toward complacency is reinforced by the use of loose language—for example, "annihilating retaliation," "mutual homicide," and so on.

This tendency for our peacetime military systems, regardless of cost, to have serious or fatal wartime defects is compounded by the fact that designers and planners are among those who find it difficult to take seriously wartime performance. Some of the problems to which this gives rise are discussed in Appendix III.

This technical apathy is increased by the general lack of enthusiasm in the West for playing military games. If the Russians keep their capabilities secret and increase or change their program, it is likely that we will not react adequately—even if we get moderately good intelligence. *Barring a crisis, our country is very loath to spend money on military goods. I make this statement fully aware that we are currently budgeting a great deal of money—about 45 billion dollars annually—for national security.*

Remember that we came to spend the present annual amount only under the extreme pressure of the attack on Korea, plus a rather widespread belief in government circles that World War III was on its way. As soon as the Korean War ended and the immediate fear of all-out war decreased, pressure to reduce the budget increased markedly. That pressure proved moderately successful; the budget went down slightly in the face of further inflation and increasingly expensive weapons systems. It is clear that this pressure for decreased budgets would have been even more successful had it not been for the widely publicized Soviet progress in the long-range bomber and missile field and the Hungarian, Suez, and later Berlin crises.

It took a combination of all these things—lead-time and procurement lags, crises, threats, and loss of prestige—to maintain the defense budget. Unless the Russians are equally obliging in the future in embarrassing those in our country who would decrease national defense budgets, it is clear that we will not be able to meet any increased threats of the future, and we may not even be able to maintain our current capabilities. Nor are we likely to meet adequately the expensive challenge of Soviet technological progress.

The most important mitigating factor helping Type I Deterrence is the enormous uncertainties and immediate risks that any power considering initiation of a war must face no matter how sound his paper plans. While this is indeed a potent stabilizing influence, it may collapse in certain crisis situations (or even in a noncrisis situation), particularly if someone gets in charge who is so logical that he believes and is willing to act on the basis of logical calculations. The same is true if the decision maker is so irresponsible that he is willing to gamble all, or if he is so ignorant that he does not understand the uncertainties. (It is not at all clear that some leaders of this type could not get into high positions in Russia.)

I have been discussing the instability of deterrence in the face of a deliberate act on the part of the aggressor. On top of this must be added, unfortunately, instability due to the possibility of accident, miscalculation, sabotage, agents provocateurs, or the acts of mentally unbalanced individuals, or other kinds of unpremeditated war such as the catalytic, escalation, and reciprocal fear of surprise attack. I think very few in 1950 would have been willing to predict that we would come to live in a world with 50,000 or even 5,000 buttons and never have a few of them pushed. Today, some believe it is possible, partly because experience has shown that such a situation is safer than we would have predicted, but mostly because they have to believe it or be very unhappy about the immediate future.

The uncertainties and risks of the future are increased by the mounting race of technological progress. It is not at all unlikely that there may be some invention or discovery which cannot be handled even momentarily in our present international society. Progress is so fast, the problems are so unprecedented, and the lead times for cultural assimilation so long, that it is difficult to believe that we will understand our systems well enough to prevent accidents, miscalculations, or the need for dangerous improvisation in a crisis or unexpected contingency.

All these factors indicate that we must take seriously the problem of alleviating mutual danger by international agreement and arms control. We must be willing to do this even though we may thereby run great risks, since the alternative, an uncontrolled situation, probably involves greater risks.

The third stability problem concerns the probable future decrease in the strength of our Type II and Type III Deterrence. On the basis of current programs, I have predicted that we will lose our Type II Deterrence by hypothetical World War V (1961). We will lose it in 1961 because we have not bought enough of the right kinds of offensive forces; we have neglected instituting even a cheap civil defense program; and we have not been vigorous enough in fixing the holes in our air defense system. However, even if we had done all those things, we might still be lacking as credible a Type II Deterrent as we should have. The uncertainties mentioned before, which automatically deter any attacker, mean that our Type II Deterrence is not even as effective as paper calculations might indicate. Even decision makers who are not worried about the annihilation of civilization may worry about receiving an unacceptable level of damage to their own country (although droves of analysts tell them this probably will not happen). In any case, even with the best possible preparations, unless the opponent is quite careless, the predicted levels of damage will still be very high by peacetime or classical wartime standards. However, there is an enormous difference between having a façade and not having one. And there are feasible programs that would give us much more than the façade of being able to use nuclear retaliation as a last resort with the hope of regulating the other side's behavior. I find it somehow very hard to believe that our reliance on self-restraint by the Soviets will continue to work, particularly since I suspect the Russians will asymmetrically buy a capability to win and terminate wars, while we will try to depend on some form of a Minimum Type I Deterrent plus inadequate Limited War forces.

If we have procured only a Minimum Deterrent, it will be unsafe for us to strain our Type I Deterrence by initiating or threatening to initiate extremely "provocative" acts. *That tactic will be open only to the Soviets.* Under current programs, they alone are likely to be in a position to regulate the conditions under which an exchange of provocations might take place. A vigorous "limited" defense by us of a position that the Soviets believe they are entitled to may be looked upon by them and even by us as an extreme provocation; without an adequate Type I Deterrent it would prove dangerous even to try such a defense. Even a residual Type II Deterrent could be destabilizing.

It might be advantageous at this time to look at some of the alternatives to Type II Deterrence for handling threats other than direct massive attacks on the United States.

There are, of course, many proposals designed to handle the Type II Deterrence problem. It is difficult to analyze the potential relationships of these proposals to each other and in company with the kinds of military and passive defense capabilities I argue may be important to us in the future. Almost none of the proposals has been analyzed quantitatively, and some of them do not seem to be susceptible to such analysis. Such alternatives must, of course, be balanced somewhat subjectively. Preferences formed among them tend to express personal tastes rather than the results of careful calculation. But the fact that one set of alternatives is more difficult to analyze than another does not make the problem of choice less real. I have, for example, based part of my argument for Type II Deterrence upon an unquantitative appraisal of the extent to which such capabilities will aid the international policy and posture of the United States. It is therefore important to ask if there are better ways to achieve the same objective. I cannot pretend to give even a superficial answer here, let alone an analysis, but I shall comment briefly on some of the alternative proposals. I have mentioned some of them before, but for the sake of completeness, I shall at least list them briefly again.

Alternatives to Credible First Strike Forces for the Deterrence of Extreme Provocations

1. Threat of mutual homicide. For the most part, this has been the program for the defense of Europe and, to some extent, of the peripheral areas. As applied to the peripheral area, I think we must all agree that this reliance is a curious form of wishful thinking, but perhaps it deserves to be examined for Europe.

As I have frequently mentioned, it must be plain to the Soviets that even today sudden and serious attack on any of the NATO nations still promises bombs on Moscow in hours or less. Even a small probability of this should be enough to deter Russia from such action under almost any reasonable circumstance.

Will this effective deterrence continue for the next five or ten—or even for the next one or two—years in the face of the spectacularly growing Russian power to retaliate. As evidenced by editorials in European newspapers and by scholarly articles in the United States, experts and politicians are fast losing faith that the United States will commit suicide to save or avenge Berlin, Athens, Rome, or Paris—much less Belgrade or Vienna. Once this doubt becomes widespread, and once people everywhere seriously ask themselves, Can we depend on the United States to commit or risk committing suicide?, *the force of deterrence is undermined.* A reasonable person (and even more a group) seldom considers deliberately sacrificing himself utterly except for the immediate defense of his own family, comrades, or nation. Therefore, the immediate answer of the skeptics will almost certainly be, "We don't know." This will soon be followed by, "We can't."

There is another weakness of the pure deterrence policy (apart from its increasing noncredibility). Even if there were some way to commit the United States irrevocably and publicly to defend or avenge Europe by an all-out attack, this would not necessarily be a good policy. Before binding itself to a potential suicidal strategy, any nation should ask if it is committing itself to attack in a future situation that is likely to arise in spite of the commitment. A pure deterrence strategy, one that is likely to drag us into total war some-time in the next 10 or 20 years, fails utterly in its aim of deterrence. It is intolerable.

Here is my main objection to *mutual homicide* as a sane defense of peripheral areas. No matter what the United States or Russia does, important threats in these areas seem sure to occur. To arrange things so that the inevitable materialization of a minor threat would trip off an all-out World War would be to involve ourselves in a trap.

The same danger as this applies to the defense of all of Europe by pure deterrence, although some think the danger may be endur-able because a large war is so much less probable. But improbable does not mean impossible. Even though it is hard to imagine a large war in Europe at this writing, history has challenged our imagina-tion before. While it is difficult to conjecture specifically and plaus-ibly how it will come (see pages 136–137 for some suggestions) it *is* probable that in the next 10 to 20 years large-scale violence will occur in Europe. When this happens, the United States probably will prefer to handle the crisis on a limited war basis, if possible, rather than trigger off World War III. *In any case, the United States surely cannot be content to have the push button operate auto-matically or even semiautomatically, unless we and the Europeans have a good possibility of surviving the war.*

This consideration brings us naturally to our second topic: Would it be better to spend money on a Limited War Capability to the exclusion of a Credible First Strike Capability?

2. *Limited war capability.* I am much attracted by this alterna-tive; certainly, I definitely favor spending some money on a limited war capability. I am more extreme than some proponents of limited war, however, in that I favor having a high-explosive (HE) capa-bility, even though it threatens to be expensive. The controversy be-tween HE and nuclear weapons for limited war is peripheral to the Central War question being discussed here, but some points of con-tact between the two topics will be discussed briefly.

One of the advantages of limiting small wars to HE is that a vio-lation of the rule is so clear-cut, so unambiguous. There is a genuine distinction between nuclear and chemical explosions. The fact that very low-yield nuclear weapons could be developed which would render this distinction fuzzy and vague does not change this. Even though such devices seem to be very useful from the narrow mili-tary point of view, the breaking of the precedent would seem to me

540

to be of much more significance than the advantages to be gained. Thus the main reason for developing such small weapons is probably to blot out the distinction. But no dividing line other than nuclear–nonnuclear is anywhere near as well defined. It is this that makes it so important that it not be eliminated.

The limiting line must not only be very well defined, it must seem reasonable. Most important of all, the line must seem "acceptable," separating "tolerable" from "intolerable." Most of the world (apparently including Russia) seems to consider the use of nuclear weapons a drastic measure. The only people who do not are some of the professional students of war—in the services and out—who have been trying to talk each other into accepting the idea of using nuclear weapons routinely. I myself have had some contact with their proselytizing program. Their story seems to go like this:

A says to B sometime in 1953 (when the Korean War is safely over), "A nuclear weapon is just another weapon like any other—only larger." B says, "I agree." Neither really believed this in 1953. But such conversations have been going on repeatedly in the years that have followed, until both participants are beginning to believe it (but not quite). However, except for our two participants and people who accept government pronouncements at face value, almost everyone, I feel sure, agrees that the use of nuclear weapons is a very eventful act. Because nuclear weapons are unambiguous and also eventful, it is possible to draw a line at this point. One can also argue that it would be very useful for the United States to draw a line here.

Some advocates of limited war in which nuclear weapons would be used have carried their idea to its logical conclusion. For them, whether a nuclear weapon should be used or not depends only upon its *cost* (which is of the order of a fraction of a million dollars) and on how its use (by us, at least) accords with whatever political limitations are in force. Those who do not go as far as this nevertheless recognize that if one side uses nuclear weapons then the other must too, until their use will become relatively common. For example, the Egyptians or the Malayan guerrillas might even come to get their hands on a few small weapons. In fact, under the circumstances envisaged, nuclear weapons might become an article of commerce. South Africa, for example, has plenty of uranium and might be willing to supply raw materials or finished weapons to all on a commercial basis. They would undoubtedly be severely criticized for doing this, but it would not bother a country already the recipient of much criticism because of its internal policies.

Before committing ourselves to the acceptance of the idea of limited atomic war, we should ask what will happen in the long run if nuclear weapons are made easily available for war and if they are lightly used. Clearly, at least in peripheral war, the availability of nuclear weapons will put a premium on:

1. Blackmail
2. Surprise
3. Concealment
4. Nondependence on logistics
5. Very many and highly dispersed bases
6. Willingness to accept high per cent of casualties in a few exposed units as opposed to a smaller per cent of more units.

I submit that these six desiderata for successful limited nuclear war are also six of our most important weaknesses. For example, if nuclear weapons are to be used against us in an Asian conflict, it is hard to believe that we will be able to retain our Japanese or Philippine bases. In short, it is probably a technological and military mistake for us to countenance or to encourage the use of nuclear weapons as part of the waging of most limited wars. The kind of war we are most competent to fight and in which we have a technological and economic superiority is the high-explosives (HE) war.

In addition, modern developments in the conventional field seem to favor the defense over the offense. Current ground-to-air missiles such as Nike-Hercules, Hawk, and Bomarc should be able to inflict attrition rates of at least 10 to 50 per cent, even if restricted to the use of HE warheads. Five to ten per cent is enough to make conventional World War II-type air raids prohibitive.

The same advantage to the defense seems to be true for infantry and tank attacks. The use of minefields, antitank missiles, and modern fortification seem to give the defense a large edge. This edge is as likely as not to be increased by further developments. This means that if we can force the attacker to restrict himself to conventional weapons and we have properly trained and equipped defenders we can probably hold the line, even in the face of a numerically superior enemy. In addition, if we have the proper kind of preattack mobilization base, in *the long run* we can deliver more tons of ammunition and supplies to almost any spot on the earth's surface than the enemy can. If we wish to make the proper preparations we can probably do it in *the short run* too.

The argument on the need for Counterforce as Insurance or Type II Deterrence is influenced by whether we prefer our limited war to be nuclear or conventional. Once we have decided on a limitation on war techniques, whether it involves nuclear or only HE weapons, the pressing problem is to keep the enemy from evading this limitation. In the HE situation, I think that the Soviets would be glad to accept the limitation both because they have some common interests with us in limiting the use of nuclear weapons and because the breaking of the precedent would be quite provoking. If this is so, enforcement need not be so critical. While it is important to have a sanction available, it need not be as effective as in the atomic case. In the atomic warfare case, I feel that ability to insure effective enforcement is crucial. In addition, I feel that waging "Limited" nuclear wars is a most dangerous way to live. To the extent that this is true, we need a damage-limiting and war-fighting capability just for insurance. In any case, since an effective Type II Deterrent could play a central role in supporting the limitations, *I feel that Type II Deterrence is a complement rather than an alternative to a limited war capability.*

3. *Buttressing NATO, SEATO, and other alliances.* The NATO countries possess enough resources and population that they should be able, with a vigorous effort, to take care of many of their own defense problems without the aid of the United States. The main and probably overwhelming obstacle seems to be lack of motivation on the part of their citizens and governments.

Perhaps instead of spending for a counterforce capability, the same kind of money put into NATO would tend to solve the European part of our defense problem. In addition, large sums for SEATO and other alliances might be effective against both subversion and threats from neighboring communist countries. Insofar as the above applies to conventional capabilities, I agree—but with the proviso that the United States have the ability to limit the limited war.

One serious idea for defending Europe, advanced by some, is to give the European and/or Asiatic nations their own independent nuclear capability. They would then have the potential, alone or *en bloc*, of inflicting at least a moderate amount of damage on Russia if the Russians provoke them too far. Since the gains to the Soviets from any aggression would be limited, the prospect of even moderate damage may deter Russia. Of course, if Russia is depending on any kind of domino effects (to push one is to see all fall flat), she may think of the stakes as being all of Europe. She may be willing to accept a small risk of being struck by any one country's nuclear force.

If nuclear sharing means that every European country would come to be on its own (or even if Europe goes on its own as a unit), nuclear sharing may not be effective against Russian blackmail. This is partly because such a distribution of weapons to independent governments is likely to weaken the NATO alliance. Then there would be the vulnerability of European forces due to the difficulty of securing early warning, the close proximity of Russian offensive forces, and the devastating power of modern weapons. These all make it difficult for any European country or the whole continent to have a force which has an appreciable probability of surviving, as a system, a Russian attack and then being able *to strike back.* (I include most if not all mobile *systems* likely to be on European soil or water in this statement.) Since this will be clear, the Europeans will not have a very reliable Type I Deterrence. However, people are looking for ingenious solutions of this difficulty. Success might crown their efforts. Polaris-type or other mobile systems may help, although they may have some system weaknesses. In any case, to reduce vulnerability will alleviate but will not eliminate the blackmail and war-of-nerves problems.

On the other hand, the indicated vulnerability of European forces to Soviet attack does not settle the issue. Suppose, for example, the forces were so located (and they can be) that it would take a major thermonuclear blow to destroy them. Such a Russian blow, particularly if it came as a surprise against even one country, might be so provocative as to entail for the Russians a serious risk that our SAC (or even other European countries) would attack them. Even if we did nothing to reduce the vulnerability of our civilians, this risk might be intolerably high. If we had any kind of a Credible First Strike Capability the risk to the Soviets would almost unquestionably be too high.

If we or the Europeans do not get a Credible First Strike Capability, then it is most unlikely that just American nuclear sharing with European nations will prevent a Russia playing her cards cleverly from subjecting these countries to intense pressures. For example, if the Soviets choose to attack with either HE weapons or small atomic weapons, it would be unrealistic to think of any of these countries retaliating with an all-out strategic attack on Russia. Any such attack would guarantee a devastating Soviet counterattack with total annihilation of the country involved.

Who really believes that any country would, in fact, wipe itself out completely in order to protect itself from the Russians? I have already made the point that while "rationality of irrationality" strategies can make some sense, they should not be pushed too far. They are no substitute for Counterforce as Insurance or Credible First Strike Capabilities. Here, as elsewhere, an astute blackmailer can probably wipe out any gains to be achieved by using extreme "rationality of irrationality" strategies. We cannot export backbone.

It is hard for me to believe that it will actually be feasible to shift to other nations the burden of deterring and controlling Russian militarism. If the United States, which is acknowledged to be the strongest power today, has difficulty in meeting Russian challenges, how much more difficulty will these other nations have—even if they double or triple their military strength? It is desirable to strengthen our allies. It does not seem feasible to strengthen them enough, however, so that the United States can ignore the necessity of having SAC available as a possible last-ditch sanction to limit possible Soviet tactics.

In addition, I believe that there is one other basic objection to a nuclear-sharing strategy. The diffusion of weapons may greatly increase our problems in the late 60's and 70's. (One should distinguish here between the possibility of placing weapons under some Central European control, such as the WEU or the European Community or NATO, and the giving of nuclear capability to separate countries. This latter is not only likely to accelerate all kinds of control and safety problems, but it could fractionate the alliance.) Most important of all, as has happened in England and the United States, the acquisition of nuclear weapons could lead to the neglect of conventional capabilities. In addition, even though European capabilities may depend in a subtle way on U.S. Type II Deterrence to be effective, the connection may be too subtle to notice in peacetime and thus lead to a neglect of such capabilities.

4. *Limited or controlled nuclear retaliation.* I have referred several times to the possibility of limited or controlled nuclear retaliation. This is the extreme end of Type III Deterrence, an end which merges

into Type II Deterrence. It is a logically conceivable strategy if one really does have a reliable "balance of terror." However, if things ever came to the point where we really were trying to punish the Soviets by taking out one or two of their cities in retaliation for something they had done in Western Europe or Asia or Africa, we would probably have come pretty close to the limit. I have mentioned many times the unsatisfactory nature of this kind of strategy from the viewpoint of the countries that are being defended and internal political reactions in a democracy. It should be unnecessary to mention that this kind of thing also strains one's Type I Deterrence, very likely straining it past the breaking point. I probably would not be discussing it at all except that *the notion of "controlled" nuclear retaliation has a tremendous fascination for intellectuals and others interested in the use of force in foreign policy in the environment created by even a superficial balance of terror.* Retaliation at much lower levels than the destruction of large cities is also conceivable. It is easy to imagine reprisals against military targets such as ships at sea, or early-warning stations, or even isolated military bases. Even more, one could conceive of economic, political, and social sanctions, including such semimilitary instruments as blockades. Technological progress is likely to bring some brand new possibilities for this type of warfare. Some of these may merge in degree of violence with the destruction of cities but be politically more innocuous because of not involving such concentrated and dramatic damage. I am thinking here, for example, of such things as changing the level of the oceans, the temperature of the earth, the amount of rainfall, or the use of debilitating drugs or germs as a "hot" cold-war weapon. It is quite clear that such possibilities should and will be investigated, but I think that it is equally clear that we are interested in preserving precedents as to what is acceptable behavior and should defer using such "weapons" as long as possible. However, we may be forced into this type of warfare if we and the Soviets both choose Finite Deterrence postures and international relations deteriorate to 1936–1939 levels of behavior. However, both sides must have chosen Finite Deterrence. Suppose the Soviets have chosen the Credible First Strike Strategy and have completed their preparations. Suppose further that we have a Finite Deterrent that can deter the Soviets if they are only moderately provoked, but which might fail if they were provoked in an extreme way. Then the use of controlled nuclear retaliation and many lesser forms of violence would be out of the question. Let us now consider our Type III Deterrence.

We may lose a major element of our Type III Deterrence—large Preattack Mobilization Base—partly because we are not likely to procure military systems which can be rapidly expanded, and partly because, given the greater willingness of the Soviets to work and to allocate resources to the production of military goods, it seems almost impossible to believe that in the long run we will have a significant capability to threaten them, asymmetrically, by an accelerated arms race. It is most likely that we will not be able to match Russian strength appropriately even if their GNP is lower. This is because they seem likely to be more willing, even in a tense period, to allocate a larger percentage of their resources to military products than we will be. In addition, as already discussed, Soviet GNP is increasing faster than ours. This last is a problem of some importance. The United States is currently such a prosperous country that I think we would be satisfied with our present average of 3 per cent a year if we had no problem of competition with the Soviets. However, we do have such a problem. It may well turn out to be absolutely essential for us to dedicate real effort to seeing that the economic basis for long-run competition with the Russians (or more generally the competition of the East versus the West and not just the United States versus the Soviets) is not seriously loaded against us by the other side having greater access to relevant resources. Among other things, we must be strong enough to hope to meet all possible threats. Advancing the rate at which our GNP increases may not necessarily be a major effort. It may mean a slowdown in our consumer goods increases, particularly that part of our conspicuous consumption devoted to leisure hours. Such a program may even have some positive values in itself. In many ways it might be desirable for Americans to reverse current trends and to begin extolling the old virtues of hard work, thrift, and so forth.

The composition of this increased GNP needs to be discussed. First and foremost, it is important to have the total GNP, irrespective of composition, large enough to support the taxes necessary for increasing the military establishment and other national security programs, if such increases turn out to be necessary. For this single purpose we do not really care what the GNP is composed of—that is, it could be bowling alleys, swimming pools, beauty parlors, and the like. We are simply asking the economy to be able to bear the tax burden. We will then spend these tax revenues for things we vitally need. The economy should automatically adjust to producing the right military products simply because we are buying them. But, there is a less important objective (though one still important enough to make it worthy of specialized attention). This objective is to design the economy so that it can quickly expand its production of military goods. Under these circumstances we ought to care very much about the composition of the GNP. Studies should be undertaken to decide which sectors should be encouraged and what compromises should be made to make the economy "militarily strong." Unless such programs are carried through, that part of our Type III Deterrence due to our large Preattack Mobilization Base is likely to deteriorate. Some will still remain because even the threat of a symmetrical but accelerated arms race which is dangerous to both sides could play a role in deterring the Soviets. The rationality of irrationality strategies could play a role here.

In addition to trying to get stability against surprise attack, unpremeditated war, and provocation, we must envisage and prepare for the possibility that one or more of these stabilities will fail. For stability against surprise attack this means having some Counterforce as Insurance; for the stability against unpremeditated war, some ability to terminate the war before the two sides have wiped each other out (the Counterforce as Insurance should include a capability for negotiation and bargaining, possibly including some measures for communication and verification); and for a possible failure of stability against provocation, we need, in addition to Arms Control measures and a Limited War capability, some combination of a Preattack Mobilization Base with some degree of Credible First Strike Capability, if we are to handle the complete range of problems.

It seems to me to be clearly wishful thinking to have zero or inadequate capability against a failure of any one of the stabilities. The most controversial capability is the Credible First Strike Capability or even a Preattack Mobilization Base for such a capability. Some experts do not believe that we need more than a Limited War capability plus something called the residual fear of war. The belief is that both provocation and limited war will be self-limiting because of a fear of escalation and that this residual fear of escalation is of about the right amount to prevent serious transgressions, and that we would not wish to interfere with the "natural" level by instituting conscious or explicit programs. My own opinion is just the opposite. I feel that the fear of natural escalation is an extremely poor way to control provocation both because it will not deter when there are great pressures, and because it is dangerous to leave the possibility of escalation uncontrolled. A Credible First Strike Capability should succeed in deterring many crises from occurring. If they occur anyway, it should put pressure on both sides to settle the crises and, failing a settlement, give one a capability to fight and terminate a controlled war, hopefully at much lower levels of damage than are usually envisaged. I suspect that the main reason why there has been a neglect of the kind of capability that could be classed as a war-fighting capability as opposed to a war-deterring capability has to do with the phenomenon of psychological denial —a refusal to admit that such events can occur, not because there is good evidence that they cannot occur but simply because most people, including professional students of war, feel that if deterrence fails there is nothing that can be done to alleviate the consequences and further that nothing is gained by considering the situation seriously. At least one's peace of mind is preserved if he refuses to look this horrible possibility in the face.

The third class of objectives on Table 70 is different in character from the first two. They are more in the nature of ground rules than objectives. They are the constraints under which we must solve our problem. We must choose solutions which can be politically carried through, which can be supported with the resources that are available and, most of all, which do not set excessive demands on our intellectual capabilities. While there is a tendency to stress the political and economic difficulties of measures that are recommended or discussed, it is my personal belief that we tend to exaggerate these difficulties; that when a good case can be made that will survive scrutiny by skeptical or even hostile audiences, it is much easier to get a measure adopted than is often thought. The main reason why people do not seem to adopt the obvious solution is that upon analysis the obvious benefits often disappear into a maze of bewildering and conflicting contradictions, and that the situation is not as simple as the naïve advocate would have it be.

Every senior man in Washington or other allied capital must have at least five people a day come into his office with *the* solution to his problem, and since almost all of these solutions have incompatible premises, it is quite likely that four of the five people are wrong, and very possibly all five are. The problem is to devise solutions which will withstand analysis (and hopefully actual experience). I do not have the space in this book to discuss how in fact to design "good" systems and how to test these designs (though I have made many methodological comments already which give the most important principles). I just wish to emphasize that it is often possible to have a good case but it is very rare to find such a case being made. One of the reasons for this rarity is that it is almost impossible for any individual to do a comprehensive analysis by himself. An individual can think up bright ideas, have good insight and a sound judgment, but he cannot put together the kind of complete and detailed story in support of over-all recommendations that is necessary if he is to be able to answer the most obvious questions that will come up.

One of the most obvious and startling things about the approach in the West, and most likely in the East as well, to these complicated and technical problems, is that there are very few organizations available in which a study of a comprehensive program can be made, and almost none of these organizations exist outside of the Department of Defense in the United States. Yet the security problem is much too broad to be treated from a narrow military point of view. Unless other organizations and other governments set up the institutions they need in order to examine and devise solutions to their security problems, it is most unlikely that any blueprint will be drawn up that will help to get us out of the mess we are in. This does not mean that we will not get out of the mess, because there is always the possibility that muddling through or sheer statesmanship will work, but I find these last two quite implausible without at least an assist from systematic professional work.

CHAPTER XII

THE PROBLEM MUST BE TAKEN SERIOUSLY

We Need Better Planning and Analysis

I WANT TO BEGIN my concluding chapter by repeating the opening words of the book: "On July 16, 1960 the world entered the sixteenth year of the nuclear era. Yet we are increasingly aware that after living with nuclear bombs for fifteen years we still have a great deal to learn about the possible effects of a nuclear war. We have even more to learn about conducting international relations in a world in which force tends to be both increasingly more available and increasingly more dangerous to use, and therefore in practice increasingly unusable. As a result of this continuous secular change in the basic structure of the international situation, foreign and defense policies formulated early in the nuclear era badly need review and reformulation."

Every sophisticated reader knows that thermonuclear war and international relations are such complicated subjects that the above paragraph would be pertinent even if a major effort to study the national security problem in full depth and scope had already been made with marked success. No matter how successful analysis and study had been in the fifteen years between the first explosion at Alamogordo and its anniversary on July 16, 1960 there would have been important areas in which more work needed to be done. This work, when accomplished, would influence policy. But the above paragraph is written in a quite different spirit, one of both sorrow and frustration at the small amount of work that has been done and the shallowness with which most of it has been pursued. When I look back at some of my own work I am appalled by the academic character of much of it. My only consolation is that on the whole my professional colleagues have often done as badly as I, while many "lay" analysts have done much worse.

It is difficult for people to face up to the problems. A child should be able to make the distinctions in Table 3 of Chapter I, Tragic but Distinguishable Postwar States, but few adults seem to be able to do this. Even some experts insist on talking as if the only choices available were immediate surrender, immediate preventive war, or eventual world annihilation. *This is certainly not the case now and, with luck and skill, never will be the case.* Furthermore, consider the distinction between deterrence Types I, II, and III. I have been using this terminology and making these distinctions since 1955. It is interesting that while many authors made similar distinctions, it was very difficult for me to get most of my peers to recognize the importance of making these distinctions, much less letting them influence the design of a weapon system. Some even denied that the distinctions existed. The year 1955 was the year of the Summit and the smiling Russian; this meant to most of my civilian colleagues that subversion, not violence, was the problem. Most of those few who worried about violence were unable to distinguish among moderate, major, or total provocations (*that is,* they either believed in massive retaliation for anything or they belonged to the Minimum Deterrence school and worried only about self-limiting Limited Wars). By the end of 1956, after the Suez and Hungarian crises, it became much easier to explain the difference, and by 1958, after Sputnik and Berlin had shaken everybody's complacency, it became almost unnecessary to explain the difference. However, it should be clear that on crucial notions such as the three types of deterrence or the nature of the immediate and long-term choices available to us, it will be disastrous to depend on the Soviets or on events to educate us. The necessary programs that exploit the "subtle" differences have too long a lead time to allow us to indulge in that kind of sloppy thinking.

Or consider the eminently important problem of fallout. There is tremendous interest both in and out of the government on studying the peacetime problems that result from nuclear tests. The Atomic Energy Commission alone spends between $20 and $30 million a year studying this problem. There is relatively little interest, either inside or outside of government, on the wartime aspects of fallout. I would guess that less than 5 per cent of the sum that is spent on the peacetime problem of fallout is spent on the special problems connected with war, even though these wartime problems are more critical and difficult. Outside government the amount of thinking, analysis, and discussion of the wartime problems is minute compared to that given the peacetime problem.

To take another example, I believe that until the RAND civil defense study of 1957, no one had seriously studied how long it would take to recuperate from the effects of a thermonuclear war. There had been many studies on the problem of war production and the destruction of "war value added" by manufacturing. Rather remarkably, these studies were done in contexts which usually conceded that postattack war production was probably not a very important matter for research. These studies still evaded the obviously important problem of postwar recuperation. While, admittedly, the RAND study was not profound compared with the difficulty of the problem, this just sharpens the point I am trying to make: that in the year 1957, 12 years after Hiroshima, this problem was so unstudied, that a first cut could be of tremendous interest and have a great impact.

I believe the basic reason for this lack of study of many important problems is less irresponsibility or incompetency than the enormous psychological difficulty which everybody has of coming to grips with the concept of thermonuclear war as a disaster that may be experienced and recovered from. It seems to be much better to deter the event. Peace seems so desirable and war so ridiculous. Everybody prefers to spend his time thinking about the prevention of war by deterrence or negotiation. Not only do they spend little or no time on what the war itself might be like or on the problem of recovering from a war, they usually indulge in wishful thinking, since deterrence or negotiation is after all a psychological rather than an objective thing. But there is an enormous difference between creating a psychological façade and an objective capability in practice if not in theory. For deterrence, the differences show up in equipment, deployment, training, and operating practices. For negotiation, the differences show up in a refusal to face what can happen if the other side decides to misbehave or in the things we must do ourselves if negotiations are to be successful enough to make a significant change in the situation.

The concentration on psychology and wishful thinking shows up in peculiar ways in our studies. For example, I mentioned in Lecture II the difficulty that many analysts have in considering the possibility of an evacuation by the Soviet Union in a tense period followed by an ultimatum or quasi-ultimatum. This is a very plausible possibility. Yet it is almost never studied. The Soviets tested nuclear weapons in 1949, yet we still have not bothered to acquire even inexpensive evacuation capabilities. Even though the most unsophisticated should be able to realize that there is an enormous difference in the ability of a nation to conduct international negotiations and stand up to threats if it can put its people in a place of safety in 24 or 48 hours than if it cannot do this, many experts have neglected the importance of evacuation. In spite of so clear and practical a problem, we have completely bemused ourselves with "How does one escape the 15-minute threat?" or with the impossibility of doing this. It is not that this latter threat is unimportant; it is simply that it cannot be handled except by deterrence or by trying to persuade the enemy to be rational even if he goes to war. It is my belief, in any case, that situations in which evacuation is feasible are more important than the surprise attack out of the blue with a major effort directed at cities.

I discussed at some length under the heading Why Don't We Care? many reasons why government experts and others with responsibility have been apathetic toward such important problems as these. Most of the reasons can be lumped under the idea that the people involved are just not serious about the problem of thermonuclear war. In many cases, they are close to the frivolous and use desperate or "subtle" arguments to avoid facing the problem directly.

It is the official view to take the military problems seriously. Every year NATO or other official agencies put out a paper that starts with a remark like this: "The Free World faces the mounting challenge of international communism backed by Soviet power. Only last month in Moscow the communist rulers again gave clear warning of their determination to press on to domination over the entire world, if possible by subversion, if necessary by violence. . . ." [1] If one added explicitly the words "Pearl Harbor," "blackmail," and "Hitler-type terror tactics," one would get a fairly good view of the official position.

So far as feasible possibilities are concerned, I suspect that the official view is a reasonably good basis on which to do military planning. It is probably a little, but not very, pessimistic as a prediction of what the Russians actually will do if we allow a posture to develop that would tempt them. There are nonmilitary restraints on their behavior that may work, but it is hard to believe that these are reliable. The unofficial view held by almost all "thinking" people dismisses many of the official spectres as fantasies. Here is a typical and relatively sober example:

In a paper that specifically quotes and challenges the official view

[1] "Declaration of Principle," NATO Conference, Paris, December, 1957.

expressed above, the distinguished military analyst, Walter Millis, summarized approvingly the prevailing "intellectual" position.

Three propositions would probably be accepted today by most Americans:

That neither of the super-powers can today destroy the other, or even impose crippling restrictions on the other's freedom of action, without itself being blown to fragments in the process;

That serious conflicts between them must therefore be resolved by some process of accommodation or negotiation;

That fruitful negotiation is all but impossible in an atmosphere of war psychosis, enflamed by exaggerated suspicions and unnecessary fears.

These propositions imply no approval of Soviet aims. They merely reflect the factual situation. It is evident that this situation is leading to increasing, if less complete, agreement among Americans to some further propositions: One—that the dangers to this country of a sudden Soviet sneak attack have been exaggerated out of all relation to reality. . . .[2]

It should be noted that even though the above view is not the official one as expressed in formal documents, it approached being a universal unofficial view among those American experts without vested service interests. Until recently, it was shared by almost all knowledgeable and intellectual Europeans, who often decried what they called the American "Pearl Harbor" and "Munich" mentality. As a result, even though the unofficial and official views were almost diametrically opposed, in day-to-day concrete policy decisions it was often the *un*official view that carried the day. It is of such stuff that "Pearl Harbors" and "Munichs" are made.

One way in which the intellectual quality of the work in this field could be improved would be if the critics were both more discerning and more savage. It would be well for us to be contemptuous of those who measure Type I Deterrence by preattack inventory of forces and who cannot distinguish between first strike and second strike forces. Equally undeserving of respect are "experts" who do not distinguish between the three types of deterrence, between the use of credible and silly threats, between "bankruptcy" and a reduction in standards of living, between sober and reliable measures versus desperate gambles or uncalculated "calculated risks," be-

[2] Reprinted in *Foreign Policy and the Free Society*, Walter Millis and John Courtney Murray, S.J., The Fund for the Republic, Oceana Publications, New York, 1958, p. 6.

tween deterrence by assumption or deterrence by objectively capable systems, and so on.

We should be equally critical of all who oversimplify in a dangerous or idiosyncratic way. I tried to make clear that in treating over-all national security problems, one may wish to be more sophisticated than I have been; yet one can scarcely afford to simplify much more. At the minimum one has to consider all of the things that are listed in Table 28 (Peacetime Objectives), Table 30 (Wartime Objectives), and Table 33 (Eight Basic Situations). Insofar as one tries to propose comprehensive solutions, he must be this complicated. Specialists who are trying to solve only specialized problems need not try to solve as global a set of problems as these, but I earnestly suggest consulting the above tables as a sort of checklist for any who would urge us to go to pure Polaris or pure Minuteman systems or various forms of near-Doomsday Machines and Homicide Pacts for "*the* solution." I will include in the category of idiosyncratic proposals sweeping reforms in the national or international order as a complete substitute for the possession of military power. Such proposals will undoubtedly be an essential supplement and complement, but for at least the next decade or two, we are going to need large and competent military establishments.

We Must Be More Sober about Deterrence

In spite of our reliance on the idea that deterrence will work, we usually do not analyze carefully the basic concepts behind such a policy. Neither do we make sober evaluation of our capability to carry through such a policy. This somewhat lackadaisical interest in bedrock concepts is probably related to a subconscious fear that our foundations cannot stand close examination.

In this book I have tried to make two separate major points on the subject of Type I Deterrence. This is the first: *Reliable deterrence of a war is much more difficult than has been supposed in the past.* And the other is: *The quality of our deterrence can make a great deal of difference in our position and policy.* The resulting view is in sharp contrast to the common, though unofficial, dogma that insofar as war is initiated as a rational act or policy the most primitive deterrence capability will be sufficient; further, that since war, if it comes, will be both irrationally initiated and overwhelming, no Deterrence or Counterforce as Insurance Capability can make much difference. I have argued that this is not so; that high-quality deterrence capabilities do in fact influence both rational and irrational actions in very important ways; and that a failure of deterrence can be alleviated.

In addition, to evaluate the effectiveness of our deterrent it is not enough to ask a common question: Will our deterrence tend to prevent a responsible and cautious Soviet decision maker from risking all by attacking us by surprise and in cold blood, that is, "out of the blue," when his alternative seems to be a stable and secure peace in which he seems to be getting all his desires? One question is insufficient. Most people, the author of this book included, seem to agree that such prevention may be relatively easy to achieve. Even a frown or hard word might deter such an enemy. But there is still a vastly important issue left. Is our deterrent powerful enough to withstand all the stresses and strains of the cold war, all the sudden and unexpected changes, the possible accidents and miscalculations, the satellite revolts, the limited wars, the crises in Berlin and elsewhere, the optimists, gamblers, or logicians who believe in paper plans, the reciprocal fear of surprise attack, and any other kind of tense or unstable situations? We must always remember that the historical stream has a disconcerting habit of being richer and more imaginative than any scholar. *At the minimum, an adequate deterrent for the United States must provide an objective basis for a Soviet calculation that would persuade them that, no matter how skillful or ingenious they were, an attack on the United States would lead to a very high risk if not certainty of large-scale destruction to Soviet civil society and military forces.*

Very few of the "military experts" who speak so reassuringly of capabilities for "annihilating retaliation" or who say that all we have to fear is "war by miscalculation or accident" have ever actually seen and studied a calculation which took account of even a few of the complexities just summarized. Much less have they taken into consideration all of them. Nor do they seem to have considered seriously the kinds of crises which can arise to strain our Type I Deterrence, even if we try to avoid such crises. It is a sobering thought that if we are even a little careless the enemy may go to war by "calculation" rather than by miscalculation. Even if he were momentarily deterred for fear that his calculation were wrong, it would be a vastly dangerous way to live. It would be a dangerous mistake to try to calculate the minimal force required to deter in some *ideal* circumstance; it would be even worse to depend on the "psychology" of the S.U. decision makers. Instead of these slender straws, our posture should provide insurance against unforeseen contingencies. The stakes are large. The cost of insurance is small by comparison with the price of miscalculation. It would be reckless and irresponsible not to take an all-encompassing view.

Type I Deterrence is far from being enough. Deterrence may fail despite our best efforts. Even seemingly adequate deterrence measures may fail. No matter how threatening our retaliatory force may be, war can still occur for any of the following reasons:

1. Accidental triggering of either alert force or both of them;
2. Miscalculation by one side of the opponent's intentions;
3. Irrational or pathological actions; illogical or irresponsible gambling; and,
4. If the leaders of the Soviet Union are presented with a situation in which they feel that, dangerous as war is, it is more dangerous for them to stay at peace;
5. Escalation or catalysis.

It should also be pointed out that war-initiating action under 2, 3, and 4 may be much more likely to come from the Soviet Union or from a China armed with nuclear weapons than those who have adopted the mutual annihilation view believe. (Neither of these powers seems to have accepted apocalyptic views of war.) In any case, inadequate deterrent measures might fail under still other circumstances.

Thermonuclear war seems so horrible that it is difficult for most people to imagine that such events can—and do—occur. People have a belief, conscious or unconscious, that an all-out war is impossible—*inconceivable* would be a more accurate word. Peace-loving people believe, in effect, that the invention of fission and fusion bombs has abolished war. (One only wishes he could agree.) They believe this because they desperately want to believe it. I suspect that any moderately prudent man who examined the situation objectively would conclude that it is extremely optimistic to ignore the possibility of war or threat of war; at the same time this moderately prudent man might ignore many things which are possible but extremely unlikely—that is to say, the possibilities we are talking about are not "worst cases" which only pedants or narrow professionals worry about.

We should also remember that historically we did not acquire this large military establishment to deter a direct attack on the United States, but to defend Europe and Asia. Even if we have adequate Type I Deterrence and Counterforce as Insurance we still need Type II and Type III Deterrence. Even if one accepts the balance-of-terror theory and believes that we do not have to worry about a deliberate Soviet attack on the United States, we are still faced with important strategic problems. In 1914 and 1939 it was the British who came to feel they had to declare war—not the Germans. The Germans would have been delighted to see the British sit the war out. Such a circumstance might arise again. If the balance of terror were totally reliable we would be as likely to be deterred from striking the Soviets as they would be from striking us. We must still be able to fight and survive wars just as long as it is possible to have such a capability. Not only is it prudent to take out insurance against a war occurring unintentionally, but we must also be able to stand up to the threat of fighting or, credibly, to threaten to initiate a war ourselves—unpleasant though this sounds and is. We must at least make it risky for the enemy to force us into situations in which we must choose between fighting and appeasing. We must have an "alternative to peace," so long as there is no world government and it is technologically and economically possible to have such an alternative. This "alternative to peace" must include a general war capability as well as a limited war capability.

Under current programs the United States may in a few years find itself unwilling to accept a Soviet retaliatory blow, no matter what the provocation. To get into such a situation would be equivalent to disowning our alliance obligations by signing what would amount to a nonaggression treaty with the Soviets—a nonaggression treaty with almost 200 million American hostages to guarantee performance. Before drifting into such an "alliance," we should ask ourselves: What does it mean to live with this nonaggression treaty? Can we prevent it from being "signed"? Can we delay its "ratification"? Those who would rely on limited means to control possible Soviet provocations must ask themselves the question, What keeps the enemy's counteraction to acceptable limits if there are no credible Type II Deterrence capabilities?

Those who think of very limited capabilities or mutual-homicide threats either separately or in combination as being sufficient to meet our Type II Deterrence problems are ignoring the dynamics of bargaining and conflict situations. When two men or two nations are arguing over something that both feel to be important it is common for things to get out of control, for prestige to become committed, and for threats and counterthreats and actions and counteractions to increase in almost limitless intensity—that is, unless there are internal or external sanctions to set and enforce limits.

These remarks will distress all who very properly view the thought of fighting a war with so much horror they feel uneasy at having even a high-quality deterrent force, much less a credible capability for initiating, fighting, and terminating all kinds of wars. I can sympathize with this attitude. But I believe it borders on the irresponsible.

The threat of force has long been an important regulatory factor in international affairs; one cannot remove or greatly weaken this threat without expecting all kinds of unforeseen changes—not all of them necessarily for the better. It is true that many of the measures that preserve our ability to fight and survive wars may turn out to be temporary expedients. They may not solve our long-run security problems. But this hardly means they are not important. You cannot reach 1970 or 1975 if you do not successfully pass through 1960 and 1965. If we neglect our short-term problems, we are bound to run serious risks of a disastrous deterioration in the international situation or in our own posture. This in turn may make it impossible to arrive at a reasonable, stable state.

In fact, insofar as the balance-of-terror theory is correct, if any nation actually becomes militarily provocative, then no matter what our previous threats have been we must meet that behavior by using limited means, or we will simply allow that nation to get away with whatever it is trying to do. The aggressor will realize this too, and he will gain confidence from the realization. For this reason any attempt to use threats of mutual homicide to control an aggressor's behavior (short of trying to deter him from an attack on one's own country) is ill-advised. Even if one intends his threat seriously, it will still not be credible to the enemy or ally—particularly if the challenge is ambiguous in any way. If this view of the mutual homicide threat is correct, then we need other external controls to coerce the Soviets in any conflicts that may arise. To depend on their exercising internal controls when there is a conspicuous gap in the range of our capabilities seems to me to be wishful thinking. To be able to take only very limited action or steps leading to mutual annihilation does leave a conspicuous gap which the Soviets may try to exploit—either in a crisis or even in cold blood.

There is another problem that arises if we should not have the ability to fight and survive a war. Insofar as the mutual homicide view is not correct and only one of us believes that it is, or insofar as it should prove correct but one or both of us have not fully assimilated the meaning of this notion, we are still likely to stumble into war as the result of miscalculation—much as World War I started. In either case, it seems to be very dangerous to assume away some of our most important military problems by placing excessive faith in the quality and capabilities of existing and programmed Type I Deterrence forces and the range of situations that such forces will be able to handle, arguing that the important problems now lie in the nonmilitary or limited war arenas and saying that other preparations can be neglected.

It is of some importance to comprehend the complete range of our military problems before they reach the crisis stage—in some cases years before they reach that stage. I mentioned in the Preface that this book is dedicated to an attempt to anticipate such crises and, more importantly, to create an intellectual environment in which potential and hypothetical crises are seriously and critically examined while there is still time to program corrective measures.

I have conceded that as technology advances it is quite possible that technical validity may be given the common picture of a war in which both sides can easily be destroyed—irrespective of the preparations that are made before the war. Doomsday Machines may be built (but it is most unlikely that they will be connected up to a high-speed computer). Even then, unless we are willing to surrender we must at least make preparations to fight wars carefully. If a war occurs it might be the desire of both parties to fight it "carefully." Even the façade of being able and willing, under duress, to fight a war might produce enough uncertainty in a potential aggressor's mind of our intentions or behavior that he would not be able to afford to make the most unambiguous and provocative types of challenges.

Many people seem to have adopted the following rather curious set of views. They are perfectly willing to concede that if there were no H-bombs or atomic bombs in the world we might then expect the Russians to behave very badly; they admit that we or our allies might then be called upon to use violence in order to restrain

Russian behavior. Many of these same people believe that the chance of being called on to use violence somehow gets smaller as the credibility that it will be used gets smaller. This belief is based upon a notion (imprecisely formulated, but influential) that the risks of violence are symmetrical and that the Russians will inevitably be deterred from misbehaving. This does not take into account the fact that over the years both nations are going to learn that acts of provocation get safer and safer. (The nations will learn it even more than did the Europeans from 1871 to 1914, because there will exist a theory that this is, after all, a correct view of the world.)

Many people think it important to emphasize the horror and impracticability of thermonuclear war. Then they instill a sense of urgency that we must settle our survival problem by peaceful means. Temptation will be removed from any adventurers. But a problem immediately arises. If this program of deterrence-by-exaggeration is to be successful, it must be mutual and reliable. If the West alone is subjected to a continuous barrage of the automatic mutual annihilation theory, this cannot help but tempt us to drop our guard. Insofar as the mutual annihilation theory is correct—and understood to be so by both sides—this is not serious; but insofar as the theory is not correct, it can be dreadfully dangerous for us to be negligent. In addition, as I keep pointing out, mutual belief in the automatic annihilation theory is an open invitation to Munich-type blackmail. Therefore, to the extent that the theory may not be true, we should avoid deliberately weakening ourselves to the point where we cannot withstand such tactics.

We must take the military problem seriously, treating it as a military problem rather than one whose primary importance lies in the prewar impact on budgets, foreign relations, domestic politics, international prestige, the business cycle, and the like—that is, we must begin thinking of thermonuclear war as something which may have to be fought or deterred by an objective capability, rather than as a sort of nightmare which is banished by the possession in peacetime of a system which can deliver bombs (the Minimum Deterrence position). It is almost incredibly difficult for even planners and experts to do so. Most of us simply do not believe in war, or at least in *deliberate* thermonuclear war, and most people also find it hard to worry concretely about accidents and miscalculations. However, it is my belief that our almost complete reliance on deterrence working is probably an example of frivolity or wishful thinking.

In any geographical area where it became known that there was one chance in a hundred of a hurricane or an earthquake, one would find that many concessions would be made, affecting almost all activities, to meet the risk presented by these potential hurricanes and earthquakes. Inhabitants take out insurance; they build their houses to make them more resistant; they build special cellars; they put up warning systems. All these things are done without any notion of deterring this hypothetical event, but in the hope of actually alleviating it and being in a reasonable position after the situation has occurred. Some will try various forms of prayer or incantation to deter or avert, but even the most religious or superstitious will know that such preparations are incomplete. While one can presumably put more faith in the notion of deterrence in the military field, even an imprudent person should be unwilling to place all bets on deterrence working, so long as there are reasonable ways to hedge the bet. The race with the enemy involves much more than prestige and a sort of polite make-believe bluffing. The competition is deadly serious, simply because the equipment that is being bought may be used, and because it makes a world of difference how it is used.

Even those who are bemused with the intellectual simplicity and logic of pure deterrence as a solution to our military problems and have very few qualms about our current position should be willing to hedge their bets by buying what I have called a Preattack Mobilization Base. This would enable our country to obtain very rapidly the capabilities it will need if the international situation ever deteriorates. Very few—even of the more optimistic—would be willing to depend upon our current posture (or our future posture as indicated by current programs) as an adequate means of handling a Hitler-type of opponent. But even Hitler took about four or five years to move from relatively innocuous challenges to ones that put the issue of major appeasement or fighting a war squarely up to his opponents. It is not likely that we will again have four or five years of relatively unambiguous warning. But if the international situation does take a serious turn for the worse we may have one or two years, and it would seem to be simple prudence to have the capability to use such warning. I have already discussed the possibility that having this capability could in itself have a decided deterring effect on potential Hitlers or other types of gamblers. Many suggestions in Lecture I are partly or wholly concerned with preparations for a part of such a Preattack Mobilization Base. It is hard for me to believe that any person who takes a serious long-range view would be unwilling to see our government spend hundreds of millions of dollars a year on such preparations for survival. The future peaceful course of international relations is just not that certain. However, the Preattack Mobilization Base should not be relied on for Type I Deterrence except to provide additional insurance.

It should supplement our Type II Deterrence and our capability to fight either limited or general wars. Type I Deterrence is too important to depend on strategic warning or on wishful thinking.

We Must Be Willing To Allocate the Necessary Resources

Once one accepts the view that nations are not inevitably annihilated in a war and that the "automatic overkill" theory is premature, if not wrong, he accepts the idea that there are significant differences between victory, stalemate, and defeat. Once we believe that deterrence can be strained or can fail, we must also believe that such differences ought to affect both our preparations and how we fight our wars.

If the overkill theory is wrong, we can talk about higher and lower quality military systems. We can say that we really can buy more insurance and capabilities by spending money or doing things more intelligently. We can understand that we may be running serious risks by cutting budgets, being inefficient, or failing to react sufficiently to changes in the threat.

It is impossible for me to believe that we can meet our current military problems satisfactorily without increasing the national budget by 10 to 20 per cent. It may seem implausible on the face of it, that a change of 15 per cent or so would change the character of the situation from unsatisfactory to satisfactory. While 15 per cent could make a large difference, it should not make that much difference. Yet it does, and the reason is not hard to see. The claims of the newer (and often most important) problems that have just emerged or been recognized cannot be met adequately and rapidly by scaling down the older systems and shifting resources. In this fight between the emergencies created as changing technology affects older postures, we are occasionally going to meet crises with an expanding budget or we are not really going to meet them. While it is important to shift resources, this shifting cannot always be accomplished rapidly enough. This stems only partly from political reasons; we often do not know enough about these problems to make such drastic changes safely. In fact, given the probable increase in GNP in both nations and the increased rate at which technology is moving, it may be necessary even in the presence of comprehensive arms control measures to continue to increase military budgets every year.

It is extremely annoying to members of Congress and to others to see additional money allocated to defense when they are morally certain there is a lot of fat in the existing defense budget. They feel that if the new money is not allocated the three service chiefs will find the resources they need by cutting the fat; if they cannot, it "serves them right" not to get the money.

There are several things wrong with this view. The first is that it is more than the Department of Defense that is "served right"; it may turn out to be the country that gets it in the neck. The second is that it is quite clear that there is going to have to be a lot of fat in the Department of Defense, some of which is not really fat but only seems to be. (See discussion on pages 160 to 162 under heading Not Look or Be Too Expensive.)

I am not trying to say that if we were all-wise or all-powerful we could actually solve our military problems at the current budget levels. I am merely suggesting that since there are places in our over-all security posture that seem to be desperately underfinanced, we ought to take money away from other places where the situation is less desperate, arriving at a better, though still unsatisfactory, result. I believe that after we have done this we could still justify a fairly large increase in the budget. But suppose the over-all military budget were ideally satisfactory. It still does not seem wise to accept large risks just because we cannot, for political and practical reasons, shift resources rapidly enough.

In this argument between the claims of national security and all the other claims on our resources, I find it hair-raising that we should be taking not mild "calculated risks" but something close to desperate gambles on the accuracy of estimates of Soviet and United States lead times or on even closer estimates of the kind of behavior that the Soviets may choose to indulge in. At least we should not be taking desperate chances because other claims on our resources are said to be so pressing. One has only to look around the United States to see how improbable it is that such a position could be tenable. We not only have unutilized resources, but it is clear that the country is allocating resources lavishly, even frivolously, on unprecedentedly high standards of living.

A common fear, that raising our expenditures by some significant amount would just help the communists by weakening us economically, is probably baseless if we exercise reasonable prudence in how we raise the money. Lenin is often quoted to the effect that it would be a good Soviet strategy to force the United States to bankrupt itself by overspending on military items. The quotation seems to be erroneous; a careful search of Soviet literature and all the known writings of Lenin has failed to disclose the existence of any remark of that type.[3] In fact, Marxist beliefs tend to go in the other direction. They argue that large military expenditures are essential to the capitalist nations to maintain their prosperity. This view is also held by many non-Marxist opponents and even by some adherents of capitalism. I do not believe that spending money on munitions is a good way to maintain prosperity. I believe the opposite; that except for idiosyncracies of the business cycle, such expenditures tend to reduce our current standard of living and our rate of economic growth. But I also believe that, if necessary, we can afford such expenditures.

I do not think we should become a militaristic society, nor do I believe that serious questions with regard to the long-run effects of inflation and the demoralizing and dislocating effects of high taxes are not important. But even if the defense budget climbs to somewhat higher levels we should be able to handle inflationary pressures and the impact of the new taxes, at the same time preserving what will look to all the world, including us, like a predominantly civilian and rather comfortable society. We are still not at the stage of making really hard economic choices.

We have no right to be indignant if it turns out that we cannot eat our cake and have it too. Security may come at a higher price than we have been accustomed to paying. It may, for example, include a willingness to incur casualties in limited wars just to improve our bargaining position moderately. This is a high price to pay. However, the monetary part of the price for security still runs low, so low in terms of percentage of our gross national product, that a responsible policy probably would not require a cutback in

[3] Private communication by Roger Hilsman, Deputy Director, Legislative Reference Service, Library of Congress.

current standards of living—just a cutback in the rate at which they *increase*. If we include in this concept of security an increase in the rate of capital investment, then in the long run it might even mean an increase in our standard of living, though it may involve some reduction in the consumption of consumer goods for the next decade or so.

Some time ago I had occasion to attend some meetings of one of those committees of distinguished citizens called together for the purpose of evaluating certain government programs. The first question that one of the more senior members of the committee asked was how long the country could go on spending 10 per cent of its gross national product for national security. I found this an almost incredibly naïve and selfish question. It is my belief, shared by competent colleagues, that if this country can reach the year 1975 while spending only 10 or even 15 per cent of its GNP on national security we will be lucky indeed. Never has a nation lived so well as this one. To plead poverty is singularly unattractive.

I have already made the point that even if quite elaborate and successful arms control measures ensue, it will not be safe in the short run for us to reduce budgets by very much if at all. The only effect such measures would have on a responsible United States government would be to prevent an increase in the budget or to keep the increases to a smaller rate. I consider this latter to be the most likely result of a responsible reaction to most worthwhile arms control agreements.

The continual analogies that are made as to how money that goes down the "rathole" of national security could, in a more reasonable world, be spent on schools, roads, hospitals, scientific research, foreign aid and so on, strike me as a dangerous kind of wishful thinking. Even fanatic proponents of the reform of our society rarely argue that the adoption of their measures would result in elimination or major reduction in the budget items for law enforcement. It is hard to see why we should begrudge the costs required to encourage proper international behavior more than we begrudge budgets for the much simpler problem of proper domestic behavior. To go back to my original analogy of people living in hurricane country, they do not bewail the money they spend on protection against hurricanes; it is simply a fact of life. They can, if they choose, move to another state or country where there are no hurricanes. Presumably they prefer living in the hurricane country and accepting the cost. To some extent, we have similar choices. We could certainly cut our national security expenses, at least temporarily, if we wished to "accommodate" ourselves to the Soviets as they are and will be. By temporarily, I mean just a few years. Some believe we might obtain a few decades. I do not care to guess.

I believe that in any world short of Utopia—and I am not willing to include in this term worlds greatly improved over our current one—we will have an important and expensive national security problem. It is not that our other problems are not important; it is only that it is a combination of irresponsibility and wishful thinking to look to large cutbacks in the national security program as a source of such funds.

We Must Take Seriously
the Consequences of Growth in Soviet Power

It is difficult and even impossible for most Americans to believe that they have an enemy. This is particularly true of intellectuals and "men of good will." The view that "the United States has trapped itself in a rigid position by fixing on a baseless stereotype of the Soviets as implacable, malevolent enemies bound and determined to fight out a protracted conflict over centuries" is not the picture that most Americans actually hold. Except in periods of actual strain or crisis they tend to believe otherwise: that all sane men are reasonable and it ought to be easy to clear up this misunderstanding by a few meetings and agreements (that is, they believe in what the psychiatrist calls a "self-fulfilling prophesy" in the sense that "good will generates good will," rather than the usual worry that "suspicion and hostility generate suspicion and hostility"). However, it should not be necessary to think of the Soviets as compulsively hostile to recognize that they represent, and in all likelihood will continue to represent, a vast danger. I concede that, aside from the ideological differences and the problem of security itself, there do not seem to be any other objective quarrels between the United States and Russia that justify the risks and costs to which we subject each other. It is probably true that the major thing that the Soviet Union and the United States have to fear from each other is fear itself. (I am postulating some enormously optimistic assumptions. One is that the Soviets would ultimately be willing to give up any hope of world domination to be achieved by the use of military force. Another is that they would give up their curious notion that the only satisfactory *status quo* is a situation in which the Soviet World increases every year and the Free World decreases, and that all kinds of subversive and violent activities are a normal part of this peacetime *status quo*. On the other hand, our understandable hope that one day the satellite nations will be liberated does not look to the Soviets like a reasonable acceptance of the *status quo*.)

Aside from the caveats given above about Soviet and United States expectations and hopes, and the problem of security itself, both the Soviet Union and the United States are *status quo* powers. In this respect the situation is quite different from what it was in World War I; then all the great powers competed in trying to carve out empires for themselves, both inside and outside Europe. It is even different from what it was before World War II, when there were strong "revisionist" powers determined to upset the Treaty of Versailles and even more. Today, a normal increase of two or three years in the gross national product of either Soviet Russia or the United States is of greater significance militarily and economically than sizeable additions or subtractions of territory (for example, East Germany). This means that we can afford to be relaxed about changes in our respective "spheres of influence." But even if it were conceded that all we have to fear is fear, this would not imply that the problem is simple. Nor can the problem be eliminated during the next decade or so by any kind of arrangements that appear practical. It is only to say that there do not seem to be any fundamental blocks to making things more manageable and safer than the current arrangement, which involves an almost uncontrolled arms race ameliorated by some implicit (and vague) agreements and by some unilateral actions.

But even if we arrive at some arms control agreements that eliminate the most dangerous aspects of the competition, we will still need the use or threat of use of force to regulate the (hopefully) small number of minor clashes that will occur even in the best regulated worlds. After all, even if we temporarily eliminated rivalry and settled all current problems, unless both countries are willing to adopt extremely high standards of behavior, standards that are quite likely unrealistically high, there would still be minor clashes between them. And minor clashes have an unfortunate after effect unless they are settled. They tend to be dynamic, leading to major ones almost as a by-product. While many people are suggesting various versions of a "rule by law" to prevent minor clashes from becoming major ones, I am not very hopeful that we can succeed totally. Such efforts are to be encouraged—in fact they are indispensable—but they can alleviate the problem only to the point where inevitable conflicts of interest can be handled, not eliminated. We will still need a "balance of terror" or other military sanctions to persuade those who would be tempted to use violence to use other machinery instead. If the balance is to be stable and not subject to being overturned by minor changes in tactics, posture, technological innovation, or cheating on arms control agreements, it will have to be based on a massive program. If the settlements are to reflect our views or interests, then we must be able to exert effectively an influence comparable to or superior to the Soviets.

It is also quite clear that there is a more fundamental problem than the current one between the Soviet Union and the United States that may soon color all our thoughts and actions and that may take the place of imperialism or revisionism in making things unstable. This problem is particularly likely to move to the center of the stage if the United States and the Soviet Union settle their differences. This problem is the clash between the starving and the well-fed, between those who hunger for all the basic human needs and those who, relatively speaking, are well supplied with the resources needed to satisfy these needs. Given the "revolution of rising expectations," increasingly widespread industrialism, and increasing military technology that is likely to be widely available in the future, this seems to be a problem which, even with the utmost cooperation by the United States and Russia, is unlikely to be alleviated without bloodshed of some sort.

I know of no population expert who is very hopeful, for example, that the world will see much less than an increase of two or three billion people in the next fifty years. I know of no experts who think that even with some startling technological innovations and the investment of much more capital into increasing productivity than is likely to be the case that these people can be born and live without increasing the total amount of human misery in some inordinate fashion. This population pressure will almost automatically create a strained international situation that could react against the friendliest agreement between the United States and Russia and cause it to collapse; or it might go the other way—it might create pressures for the "have's" to unite against the "have not's." Anyway, it is unlikely that the problem will be settled in any kind of satisfactory way unless the West is and appears to be so militarily, economically, and politically competent that the Soviets realize there is no point in fishing in troubled waters—the gains are all to be made by cooperation and agreement.

This means that we must have a competent and flexible military posture and be willing to use it to influence events if challenged. This does not mean continuous recourse to "brinkmanship" or to threats of massive retaliation, but only intervening when necessary —as we intervened in Korea. Lebanon and Indochina may also be examples. Such intervention must be achieved without interfering with legitimate political and even revolutionary developments and with due regard for the niceties and the wishes and feelings of our allies, neutrals, and perhaps even the Soviets, but we should not collapse on an important issue just because there is criticism at home or abroad. The need for intervention may well be decreased if we have the capacity and resolve to do it.

We have already suffered one series of disasters that might have been partly avoidable if we had been more responsible and aware of the consequences of the growth of Soviet power. To a large extent, the extremely critical nature of our future Type II and Type III Deterrence problems stems as much from the loss of China and Eastern Europe as from advances in technology and the general growth of internal Russian power.

At the risk of stirring up a hornet's nest, I would like to make some comments on the loss of both of these areas, not to criticize what has been done in the past but to point out the need and necessity for making hard decisions. If the reader does not agree with the implied criticism of the policies, he can take the analogy as apocryphal rather than real.

The loss of China and Eastern Europe seems to be at least partly related to the fact that toward the end of World War II the peoples of the West almost *unanimously* refused to take the future military problem seriously. In a helter-skelter demobilization plus concessions and policies designed to demonstrate the spirit of good will they gave up most of their bargaining ability vis-à-vis the Soviets. A fairly prevalent—almost uniform—U.S. attitude in 1943 on the future problem of containing the Russians was expressed in an American planning paper for the 1943 Quebec Conference which stated: "Russia's postwar position in Europe will be a dominant one. With Germany crushed there is no power in Europe to oppose her tremendous military forces. The conclusion to the foregoing is obvious. . . ." [4]

While a conclusion (that if there is a power vacuum the Russians will occupy it and if we do not want them to occupy it we had better not let the power vacuum exist) does seem obvious today, this was not in fact the conclusion drawn by the American planners in 1943. They argued that Soviet dominance meant we must do as little as possible that could be construed as being hostile or suspicious by the Russians—even if some believed it could be justified as a legitimate self-defense activity. They argued that if we behaved toward the Russians with the utmost correctness, they would naturally also behave toward us with the utmost correctness; then we would get along just fine (non-self-fulfilled prophesy). This theory existed in spite of the fact that at various points in U.S. and British history one can find many examples where, when we had the power to do something very advantageous, we went ahead and did it, even without worrying on occasions too much about the feelings of those who were powerless to stop us. I believe a very convincing case can be made that if we had held only a moderately more realistic attitude, our position in East Europe today would be much better and Europe itself would not be in such a precarious strategic situation.

Colleagues tell me it is also quite possible that we lost China unnecessarily. While this proposition is more controversial than the previous one, they argue plausibly that the critical problems the Chinese faced in 1947 and 1948 were inflation and corruption, the latter being of special importance in the Army. The morale of the soldiers was disastrously impaired, not only because they were unpaid for months at a time, but in addition they believed that senior officers and politicians were embezzling their pay funds. Many of these same soldiers fought extremely well in Burma and other places when their finances, logistics, technical services, and some of the training were in American hands. These colleagues believe that if we had sent a relatively small number of enlisted men and officers, some number in the neighborhood of 10 to 20 thousand, to handle the problems of logistics, technical services, and finance for the Chinese Army, added some air support, and finally some additional financial aid to the Chinese economy (about on the scale of our aid to Korea, Formosa, etc.), it would have been quite possible for

[4] Herbert Agar, *Price of Power: America since 1945*, University of Chicago Press, 1957.

Nationalist China to have survived the Chinese communist attack. Even in retrospect it is hard to judge the soundness of this proposition. While such proposals as these were considered, I do not believe they were considered seriously, mostly because it was thought that aid would be needed on a much more massive scale. Partly it was because it would have been politically and internationally embarrassing to "intervene" in the "internal" affairs of China, and partly because nobody really understood how effectively the communists would organize China. The nature of the problems that could result from our unwillingness to intervene to this extent was not anticipated.

It is clear that if we had intervened in China our government would have been the target of extreme and vitriolic criticism from domestic and foreign critics. In addition, one politically sensitive incident after another would have occurred, incidents that might have been costly to the prestige of both the country and the party in power. Even if the intervention were completely successful, it would be attacked by many as a failure, since very few, if any, of the critics would balance the real and obvious costs of intervention against the then hypothetical problems that would have occurred in the absence of the hated intervention policy. It is typical of this kind of situation, especially in a democracy, that the consequences of the loss of China would not be fully or maybe even seriously explored, with the obvious and immediate risks and costs of intervention balanced against the less immediate, and hypothetical long-run, risks and costs of not intervening. It is much simpler from the political point of view under such circumstances if one just lets the Chinese communists take over.

We Must Take Seriously
the Problem of Reaching 1975

Since it now seems most unlikely that the Soviet menace will go away of itself, and since we have eschewed preventive war as a possibility, we must seek the solution to our problems along the path of some degree of coexistence or collaboration. To do this effectively we must appear extremely competent to the Soviet leaders. They must feel that we are putting adequate attention and resources into meeting our military, political, and economic problems. This is not a question of attempting to bargain from strength, but one of looking so invulnerable to blackmail and aggressive tactics that Soviet leaders will feel it is worthwhile to make agreements and foolish not to. We must look much more dangerous as an opponent than as a collaborator, even an uneasy collaborator.

I have the impression that up to about 1956–57 the average senior Russian had an enormous respect for U.S. planners and decision makers—which they now (in 1960) have begun to lose. Many of their comments on remarks made by some of our military and political leaders are contemptuous. While most of the time these "contemptuous" Russians are obviously just trying to make some cheap propaganda, recently a number of their remarks have been technically sound. Under these circumstances their pretense of contempt for our ineptitude can easily turn into the real thing. This could be a most dangerous and ominous development. In the precarious present and the even more precarious future it would be well to go to some trouble not only *to be* competent as an antagonist to the Russians, but *to look* competent.

Ideally, winning the cold war would mean the establishment of peaceful, democratic, and prosperous nations everywhere and the complete elimination of all international conflicts of greater significance than those that, for example, occasionally plague U.S.–British relations. No sober student of the international scene visualizes anything of this sort occurring. Even a more limited objective— the attainment of a physical security that is independent of Soviet rationality and responsibility—is probably unattainable. There is no acceptable way to protect ourselves from a psychotic Soviet decision maker who launches a surprise attack without making rational calculations.

But the situation is worse than this. It is most unlikely that the world can live with an uncontrolled arms race lasting for several decades. It is not that we could not match Soviet expenditures; it is simply that as technology advances and as weapons become more powerful and more diverse, it is most likely that there will have to be at least implicit agreements on their use, distribution, and character if we are not to run unacceptably high risks of unauthorized or irresponsible behavior. No matter how antagonistic the Soviets feel toward us, they have common interests with us in this field. This does not mean that they will not try to exploit the common danger to obtain unilateral advantages; it simply means that there is an important area for bargaining here, one that we must fully exploit.

I mentioned earlier that we could fruitfully describe our problem as being in three parts: that of satisfactorily reaching 1961, of reaching 1965, and finally, of reaching 1975. This is a graphic way of speaking, and it also emphasizes the important aspect that *some short-term measures may compete with medium-term measures, and that both the short- and medium-term measures may compete with long-term measures.* We must take these clashes seriously. As an example of some of the clashes, I think that the current belief that our short-term strategic problems would be alleviated if we proved willing to use nuclear weapons in such contingencies as a Chinese attack on Formosa is correct. I also believe that our medium-term Type I Deterrence problems might be alleviated if we encourage the growth of an "independent" nuclear capability among our allies. But both of these "strategic choices" are likely to increase our 1975 problem. It is by no means too early now to consider the 1975 problem as already being in a critical phase.

There is some pressure of time on us to work out these medium- and long-range problems soon. Waiting can be dangerous. In our present international society, it is not at all unlikely that there could be some invention or scientific discovery or crisis that could not be handled even momentarily. It is difficult to believe that muddling through will work indefinitely.

I am not using the term "muddling through" in a derogatory sense. As I understand it, the behavior described by this term means to wait until one can see the problem clearly and then adopt a pragmatic and undogmatic approach in working out methods of solving it after it has been clearly formulated. The alternative would be to try to anticipate troubles so far in advance that the suggested cures are likely to be worse than the problems.

I believe that this is, on the whole, quite a good way to do things. It has been true in the past that intellectuals (who do like to anticipate trouble in advance) have not been good at suggesting adequate solutions for the poorly understood and badly posed problems of the future. In a distressingly high percentage of the cases their solutions would have caused more trouble than the problems themselves. But I believe that if we cannot anticipate these problems and prepare solutions before they reach the crisis stage, we are not going to solve them. (Friends who are even more dubious about some outspoken intellectuals than I am, tell me that if this is true it is just another way of saying that we will not solve our problems. I am more hopeful than this, partly because I see some possibilities that more serious planning will come about by the institution of some of the measures suggested in Appendix I, and that other fruitful action based on facing the facts may yet come before it is too late.)

In any case we must do homework. We must know what we are trying to achieve, the kinds of concessions that we can afford to give, and the kinds of concessions that we insist on getting from the Soviets. All of this will require, among other things, much higher quality preparations for negotiations than have been customary.

We must also take seriously the problem of alleviating the conflict by arms control and international agreement. We do not have unlimited time. Our problems are being increased rapidly by many things, including the mounting rate of technological progress, the "revolution of rising expectations," increasing nationalism, and an increasing diffusion of the newer military technologies. If we are to anticipate, ward off, and prepare for crisis and trouble, if we are to design for safer and better security systems, if we are to control our destiny, we will need much better mechanisms than we have had for forward thinking, for imaginative research into problems of strategy and foreign policy, and for anticipating future technical and military developments and planning to meet them.

These mechanisms can be made available. The tools actually or potentially available to the analyst, planner, and decision maker, both organizational and technical, are many times better than anything we have had before. It is just barely possible that with determined efforts by large numbers of responsible people we can achieve enough to make a significant difference. The survival of our civilization may depend on our making this effort.

PART II

APPENDICES

INTRODUCTION

WHILE there are many implicit and even a few explicit suggestions on policy in the preceding lectures, I have tried on the whole to avoid making recommendations. The purpose of these lectures has been to expose problems and to pose relevant questions sharply and precisely. I will now make some specific suggestions. In doing so I will avoid the subject of weapons systems, partly because the rationale, justification, and caveats for specific suggestions involving numbers cannot be made without getting into classified data. The reason for this is that the evaluation of any specific course of action depends on having access to estimates of such secret data as the costs and performance of both the enemy's systems and our own. For example, if the enemy can increase the accuracy of his first strike missiles, we may wish to switch from a system operating on hard, fixed, and known bases to one which uses mobile or hidden bases; if the enemy builds stronger shelters to protect his forces or people against our ICBM's, we could consider going the other way—reallocating some resources from a mobile system to a fixed system, but one that would be more accurate and could carry larger warheads.

Instead of discussing force size, composition, or deployment, I am going to offer in the second part of this book some suggestions on long-range matters which I feel might make a significant difference in our capability in the 1960–75 period. Almost all of these matters were first covered by me in various formal or informal documents written in recent years. Some of these may seem at first glance too specialized to belong in this book, but I will try to show why I consider them fundamental and important. I have by no means covered the range of national security problems, but I do believe that these composite suggestions comprise important steps in the right direction.

I

IMPROVE POLICY FORMULATION *

I would like to start this chapter on policy formulation with a quotation from Alexis de Tocqueville's *Democracy in America:* [1]

It is therefore very difficult to ascertain, at present, what degree of sagacity the American democracy will display in the conduct of the foreign policy of the country; upon this point its adversaries as well as its friends must suspend their judgment. As for myself, I do not hesitate to say that it is especially in the conduct of their foreign relations that democracies appear to me decidedly inferior to other governments. Experience, instruction, and habit almost always succeed in creating in a democracy a homely species of practical wisdom and that science of the petty occurrences of life which is called good sense. Good sense may suffice to direct the ordinary course of society; and among a people whose education is completed, the advantages of democratic liberty in the internal affairs of the country may more than compensate for the evils inherent in a democratic government. But it is not always so in the relations with foreign nations.

Foreign politics demand scarcely any of those qualities which are peculiar to a democracy; they require, on the contrary, the perfect use of almost all those in which it is deficient. Democracy is favorable to the increase of the internal resources of a state; it diffuses wealth and comfort, promotes public spirit, and fortifies the respect for law in all classes of society: all these are advantages which have only an indirect influence over the relations which one people bears to another. But a democracy can only with great difficulty regulate the details of an important undertaking, persevere in a fixed design, and work out its execution in spite of serious obstacles. It cannot combine its measures with secrecy or await their consequences with patience. These are qualities which more especially belong to an individual or an aristocracy; and they are precisely the qualities by which a nation, like an individual, attains a dominant position.

If, on the contrary, we observe the natural defects of aristocracy, we shall

* In 1959 I joined for a time an informal group in Washington that met to discuss various methods of improving policy making in the government. Some of what I have to say in this chapter—including some of the language—has come out of these informal discussions, although I take complete responsibility for the formulation, presentation, and emphasis. Some members of the group are staff members of various governmental agencies, and it would be inappropriate to list them here. However, the following can be mentioned: Roger Hilsman, Library of Congress; James E. King, Jr., Washington Center of Foreign Policy Research; H. Field Haviland and Charles A. H. Thomson, then of the Brookings Institution and now of The RAND Corporation; Evron Kirkpatrick, American Political Science Association; Jeffrey C. Kitchen and George Tanham, The RAND Corporation; Joseph Slater, the Ford Foundation; Ernest W. Lefever, Foreign Policy Consultant to Senator Humphrey; Colgate Prentice, Office of Vice President Nixon. Roger Hilsman's interpretation of the discussion, "Planning for National Security: A Proposal," appeared in the *Bulletin of the Atomic Scientists,* Vol. XVI (March 1960), pp. 93–96.

[1] The original edition was published in 1835. A paperback edition, edited by Phillips Bradley, was published by Vintage Books, New York, 1954; in that edition this passage may be found in Vol. I, pp. 243–245.

find that, comparatively speaking, they do not injure the direction of the external affairs of the state. The capital fault of which aristocracies may be accused is that they work for themselves and not for the people. In foreign politics it is rare for the interest of the aristocracy to be distinct from that of the people.

. . . . Almost all the nations that have exercised a powerful influence upon the destinies of the world, by conceiving, following out, and executing vast designs, from the Romans to the English, have been governed by aristocratic institutions. Nor will this be a subject of wonder when we recollect that nothing in the world is so conservative in its views as an aristocracy. The mass of the people may be led astray by ignorance or passion; the mind of a king may be biased and made to vacillate in his designs, and, besides, a king is not immortal. But an aristocratic body is too numerous to be led astray by intrigue, and yet not numerous enough to yield readily to the intoxication of unreflecting passion. An aristocracy is a firm and enlightened body that never dies.

The second paragraph of this quotation is one of the most widely quoted passages of a widely quoted book; unfortunately, it may have lost some of its impact since 1835 through repetition. Today, however, foreign and long-term military policy involves issues of survival in an unprecedented fashion. The quote should be freshened up to become the warning it was intended to be. I chose to quote from de Tocqueville at length because I believe he describes the core of our problem as well as anybody has. It is very difficult to believe that we can muddle through the next ten or twenty years in the characteristic fashion of a democracy.

Even though de Tocqueville has indicated that the contrary is true, a pragmatic muddling through policy has often been a better guide than the use of theoretical long-range planning, even in foreign policy. However, given the pace of technology and the catastrophe-prone way in which problems come up today, particularly in the military and foreign policy fields, it just does not seem credible that muddling through will be a satisfactory approach to the future.

One does not have to be of a partisan or critical nature to feel uneasy about our current methods of forming and carrying out policy or to realize that they show many of the weaknesses indicated by de Tocqueville. While I would conjecture that, on the whole, policy-making machinery today is much better than it has ever been, it nevertheless seems to be seriously inadequate to the needs.

It may be that it takes a democracy about a generation to make fundamental changes in foreign policy and military policy. It seems most implausible that there will be that kind of time available to us. Therefore it is essential to make whatever changes may be necessary in our current machinery to expedite the introduction of sober, well-conceived, and thoroughly reviewed innovations, and it is equally important to have the same kind of continuity for approved policies that de Tocqueville claims is the special virtue of aristocratic governments.

So far as minor tinkering with the structure of government is concerned, there are at least two ideas which would seem to be valuable in improving policy making in this way. One would be to attach to the head administrator in a number of parts of the government (including the President of the United States, the chiefs of various services, and the heads of many of the departments and executive agencies of the government) a long-range and medium-range policy planning group, which would not be deluged by the immediate cares of the day. Rather, it would have a chance to "think big" about its organization and its place in the over-all scheme of things—with particular emphasis though perhaps not sole concentration on National Security Problems. The second idea would be to set up a special organization dedicated to long-range studies in the National Security Field. It would not be the main purpose of this latter organization to collate ideas or to coordinate proposals, but rather to add to the intellectual capital available—to produce ideas for others to collate and coordinate.

I would like to discuss the first proposal in detail only for the President's office, though much of what I have to say would carry over to other agencies.

At the present time, on paper at least, the President seems to have some fairly good machinery available for formulating and executing policy. For the over-all problems of the government he has the Cabinet to advise him. For the special problems of National Security, he has the National Security Council (NSC), whose purpose is to provide a synthesis of U.S. policy in this field. Its statutory members are the Vice President, the head of the Office of Civil and Defense Mobilization, the head of the Department of Defense, and the Secretary of State. Various other government officials attend the Council meeting if the occasion warrants or because they are regularly invited. The "regular participant members" are the Director of the Budget Bureau and the Secretary of the Treasury.

In addition to its members, the National Security Council has three suborganizations to help it. First, there is the Central Intelligence Agency to supply it with fundamental data; second, the Operations Coordinating Board sees to it that government policies are carried out at all levels; and finally, the National Security Council Planning Board does staff work and planning. The latter is composed mainly of delegates from various parts of the government. These delegates are supposed to speak for themselves, but in practice they seem to show a departmental point of view. My suggestion is to introduce some simple reforms into the Planning Board which might greatly improve its performance.

The National Security Council Planning Board is headed by the President's assistant for national security. He has relatively little authority. Most papers that come from the NSC are coordinated—that is, each separate department of the government is responsible for the section to which its expertness applies. While it considers the advice and comments of other departments, it writes its section of the policy paper from a departmental (i.e., often a vested interest or doctrinal) point of view.

The President's assistant for national security affairs should be given the right to draft and release his own papers from his special vantage with an over-all point of view, and he should have the right, at his discretion, to omit criticisms or comments from other departments (though if he is wise he will normally pass these along at least as addenda). In a sense, he should be an Assistant President for planning National Security Affairs. In line with his increased responsibilities, he should have a special senior staff (a National Policy Planning Staff) of from ten to twenty additional people whose sole job would be to advise him on major issues. The other representatives on the Planning Board should be formally recognized as being what they are—representatives of their agencies. It is not the purpose of the suggestion to eliminate the role of the NSC as a sort of internal forum for arranging political compromises among the different departments of the executive side of government, but to give it a "party leader" who has sufficient authority to get a major program through. In some ways this should strengthen its role as a forum and legislature for the executive department of government. Although the suggestion may strike many as a relatively minor one, I believe that with the proper person as the President's assistant, it would make an enormous difference in the conduct of our affairs—it would create a bureaucracy with a vested interest in innovation and comprehensive programs as its major function.

While coordination among equals and close equals is a good way to run the government so far as it has to meet accustomed problems or implement well-understood policies, it seems wholly inadequate for the innovation of new policies to meet the unprecedented challenges of technology and foreign policy that face us. There is an enormous value to having the formulation of a new policy to meet a new challenge come out of one man's brain, insofar as one man properly advised can grasp the problem. It is difficult to imagine any committee of equals producing a well-articulated, consistent and yet broad (in the sense of contingency analysis) original program. This would be true even if the committee were dedicated to its task, and under current conditions we do not really have even a committee dedicated to the "whole problem" approach.

This seems true despite the many efforts, such as those of the State Department Policy Planning Staff and the National Security Council Staff, to establish within the Executive Branch such a group or groups. While the reasons for the failure of such a group to materialize are numerous and varied, the principal ones are: the tendency to establish separate institutional arrangements for the consideration of foreign and domestic policy; resistance by some officials to the establishment of a staff agency which might undercut or override their own proposals; philosophical opposition to the introduction of a broadly based and truly national (as distinct from agency) point of view; difficulty in finding a responsible sponsor or head through whom staff views could be made known at the national level; and the tendency of such planning offices as were established to become involved in operational matters. Whatever the causes for this failure, the lack of a National Policy Planning Staff and of ways whereby the advice of such a staff could be made known at an appropriate national level have handicapped the policy makers in reaching decisions on complex and difficult national issues and have prevented even a pretense of long-range, over-all planning.

If the National Policy Planning Staff is to provide meaningful advice on the whole spectrum of national policy, it must be large enough to contain people with knowledge of the various areas of governmental concern (political, military, economic, social, etc.), some with experience in one or more of the agencies of the government, some without such previous experience. It should also be small enough to encourage cohesion of view and to prevent compartmentalization. These two requirements, taken together, indicate that the staff should be composed of about twenty to thirty people with broad background and experience in and out of government, rather than a lifetime of service with one department or in one field.

The staff must also be nonpartisan in the bureaucratic as well as the political sense of that word. This is why its members should be placed on the permanent payroll of a Presidential office—as distinct from an agency. Provision should be made, quite informally, for helping or permitting members of this staff to move on to other jobs, in and out of government, so that staff members may gain additional and varied experience and so that the group will not "go stale." If the members are as competent and as carefully selected as is envisaged, this should present no problem. (Other agencies, both public and private, will be clamoring for their services.)

Placing this group within the Office of the President should help to make it effective, as well as nonpartisan. While there are arguments for placing such a staff directly under the President as an independent entity, I believe it is better to tie it to the NSC staff structure and to make the Special Assistant to the President for National Security Affairs its head. This would ensure that the group has a direct and logical channel to the President through the Special Assistant to the President for National Security Affairs and yet also make it possible for the responsible departmental officials to have full opportunity to deal with the products of the group.

To place the National Policy Planning Staff above the Special Assistant for National Security Affairs would court creating new competitive relations; to place it below would minimize its importance. However, giving the Special Assistant the job of head of the National Policy Planning Staff, as proposed here, requires that his position and charter be strengthened as suggested. Such a strengthened position would mean that the Special Assistant should have the personal confidence of the President and, as distinguished from the staff, he will probably have a political coloration. He should truly be an Assistant President for National Security Affairs.

The primary purpose of the National Policy Planning Staff would be, as its name implies, to develop and analyze major policy alternatives, with particular attention to long-range and time-phased national security planning. Within this framework would be developed the regional, departmental, and national functional policy papers.

The term "national security" can and must be interpreted broadly if

583

the work of this staff is to have any real meaning. For example, U.S. agricultural policy affects not only the domestic economy but foreign economies, our relations with other countries, and the resources which we may have available to implement our foreign policy. While the Planning Staff should not be concerned with domestic affairs in detail, it should include people knowledgeable in the major domestic fields and should consider the effect on foreign policy of decisions taken with regard to domestic affairs. It should also be responsible for recommending broad fiscal, resource, and other domestic policies that would have major impact on our ability to implement national security policy.

Its work would fall into four fields:

(1) Preparing policy papers for consideration by the NSC mechanism;

(2) Developing policy alternatives and analyzing them in terms of feasibility-costs-risks-benefits;

(3) Studying major national security trends and significant developments, and suggesting ways in which to prepare for future eventualities (perhaps the most important function);

(4) Surveying national security policy for gaps and for troublesome areas.

It should be noted that the work of this staff would be limited to policy *planning;* it is not designed to undertake policy coordination and has only a small role in the evaluation of achievements.

While this chapter does not make any specific proposals for either *policy coordination* or *evaluation,* it is recognized that they are functions essential to the planning process and need attention and possibly major improvement if the purposes and intent of the National Security Act are to be fulfilled. By their nature they also require focus in the Office of the President, where existing mechanisms can be strengthened and expanded. While such a National Policy Planning Staff should be kept informed of progress in implementing national policy, it should not itself engage in this process. Its duty through the Special Assistant for National Security Affairs would be to provide the President on a national basis with the best staff advice possible, and to leave to the President or to those policy-making officials whom he designates, responsibility for accepting, rejecting, or promoting its views and findings.

In any case, the opposition to centralized direction by a civilian "general staff" is so intense and far-reaching as virtually to preclude the immediate establishment of any organization with more functions than has already been allotted to the suggested ones. There is no necessity to tie relatively simple and almost noncontroversial reforms in policy formulation to far-reaching and controversial reforms in the Executive Branch and in Administration.

As previously indicated, some of the personnel of the Policy Planning Staff may come from other government agencies, but should not remain associated with them. Such a staff should obviously maintain liaison with policy-planning elements elsewhere in the Executive Office and in the operating departments of the government, as well as with intelligence staffs. Particular care would have to be taken to establish close working relationships among the Policy Planning Staff, the NSC mechanism, and those elements concerned with the preparation and implementation of plans and programs and with the process of evaluation.

The National Policy Planning Staff would also require detailed studies on major political, military, and other matters that it could not undertake with its own staff resources. It would have to be able to call upon and have close relationships with the National Security Research Organization (NSRO) discussed below. Its members should also have access to and, to the extent compatible with security, participate in the projects of private study groups such as the Council on Foreign Relations, various international centers, and so forth (with their permission, of course).

I would like now to discuss the second proposal to improve policy making. One of the points which should have been sensed by the reader is that useful studies can and must be made, and that much light can be shed on many of the problems of national security by systematic large-scale research. Contrariwise, it should be clear that an important number of these problems would be beyond any individual, even if he had full access to and the cooperation of all the relevant government departments. These problems require an inter-disciplinary team working together over long periods of time. The emphasis here is on the word "team" rather than, for example, "committee." The notion of the inter-disciplinary approach has been so abused that disillusionment with its value has become common. This is particularly true of the form in which it is often utilized—as sort of a part-time committee of equals where the emphasis is on voting rather than on investigation, invention, and integration. The success or failure of such committees not only depends a great deal on the abilities of various individuals to work closely together on a voluntary basis (a quality not too common in the academic field), but fundamentally on the problem's being intrinsically simple and all information available. (The only thing lacking might be one man who has familiarity with all aspects of the problem.)

What I have in mind, however, is something quite different. I am thinking of an organization in which it is possible to organize temporary teams, perhaps for three weeks to three years, that would have one and not over two project leaders on whom the responsibility for the quality of the study is firmly saddled. These project leaders should have the authority and a capability to call on a wide range of full- and part-time help in addition to their team members. The skills of the team plus the full-time help ought to cover all the important disciplines that affect the study. They need to be supplemented by frequent use of consultants, partly with the idea of playing experts against each other and partly with the idea of getting all the information that is available. (The notion of playing experts against each other may strike some as rather crude, but experience has shown that it is unwise and even dangerous to accept verbatim the opinions of a single expert.)

585

Another important characteristic such a project must have is flexibility, a willingness to shift points of view and techniques and even major objectives. This means a willingness to discard months or even years of work if the study discloses that past approaches were inappropriate. It means an atmosphere in which this discarding is almost penalty-free. (The step might even be encouraged!) It also means the ability on the part of the project leader to get new people on the team as needed and release some of the other members when they are not needed. All of this implies that the project has to be a small part of a large organization whose existence does not depend on the success of any single project and from which people can be drawn and to which people can be released rather easily. To maintain the project's quality, the environment should also include responsible "loyal and disloyal" critics, as well as advisors and consultants.

Such an environment would require an organization with between one hundred and one thousand staff members. If one combines this with the notion that the project leader must be independent and able to mold the study as he sees fit, I think the statement can fairly be made that no activity such as this now exists on the national level. For example, there is literally no organization working for the national government that could supply the proper staff to document and amplify the three lectures in the first part of this book, although there are many organizations working for the three service branches that conceivably could do this job.

The idea of doing such long-range research is not new. It is now conventional for the military to plan five, ten, and even fifteen years ahead. This planning or analysis is done in detail when possible, in broad brush when it is not. The plans or views that are developed must often be scrapped as the uncertain future emerges, but good or bad it is at least essential to do the analysis. Even a poor analysis is better than none not only because the analysis itself is educational, but because it is better for an agency to have an explicit set of views as to what its functions, responsibilities, problems, and environment are going to be than to have nothing at all for internal and external critics and collaborators to judge and to react against, and with which alternative proposals and views can be compared.

The military use a number of techniques and agencies for their basic planning and analysis. While many of these have not lived up to their expectations, in almost all cases people feel that the cure comes from more and better rather than from less—at least on those problems for which over-all planning seems appropriate. There has been some criticism, almost certainly justified, that planning and analysis is sometimes confused with an attempt to achieve an impossible degree of coordination and detailed prediction, resulting in a stifling of ideas and an undue complexity in projects, but the need for long-range analysis of the proper sort is not disputed.

Aside from the three services, about the only other place which carries on such analysis is the Office of Secretary of Defense. However, most of those in OSD who are actually spending much time on long-range problems are located in such agencies as Weapons Systems Evaluation Group, Research and Engineering, Advanced Research Projects Agency, and so on. Because of their location, their attention is often restricted to relatively parochial subjects and almost always directed to the purely "hardware" aspects of the future; they do not engage in truly "national" studies. Actually, the three services do much more long-range thinking than OSD. Each of the services has "loyal" operations analysis groups, such as the Headquarters Operations Analysis Group in the Air Force and the Operations Evaluation Group in the Navy. In addition, the Army and the Air Force also have large, competent, and influential scientific advisory boards that have direct access to the corresponding chief of staff. These boards have permanent secretariats and civilian and military directors. They are composed of both "hard" and "soft" scientists from outside the government who spend a good deal of time in evaluating current and future trends and in suggesting new ideas. All of these are in addition to numerous committees and staffs, both military and civilian, that try to plan ahead.

In spite of the elaborate in-house capabilities, the Army and Air Force still contract out with private agencies to do the special kind of long-range planning and the analyses that we have been discussing. The Army's contracts are with the Operations Research Office (Johns Hopkins), Stanford Research Institute, and others. The Air Force contracts are with The RAND Corporation, Anser, Institute of Air Weapons Research, Mitre Corporation, and others.

The RAND Corporation, with which I have been for some years, is the largest and possibly the most prestigious of these organizations. It has over 900 employees, approximately two-thirds of whom have technical backgrounds. Its Air Force budget runs to some $13,000,000 annually. In spite of its size and expense the RAND Corporation has no formal staff responsibilities. Only a small percentage of the studies undertaken at the organization are created "to order" and must meet deadlines imposed from outside. In essence, RAND researchers have access to every level and every part of the Air Force, yet nobody has to act on their advice and they do not (usually) have to research exactly what outsiders think they want at the moment. RAND's Military Advisory Group is formally charged with the duty of advising the Air Staff on how best to make use of the resources of talent in the corporation.

It was a great shock to me to discover that there is very little comparable activity on the civilian side of the federal government (or in the military or civilian side of allied and neutral governments). In fact, it might be fair to say that there is no full-time, independent planning or analysis of the larger problems. There are frequent committees, which sometimes perform a valuable service, but their charter only runs for a few months. They generally serve only as a filter and clearing house for already existing ideas; rarely if ever do they add to our intellectual capital. Equally important, the committees just write their report and then disband; therefore, in the important sense of not being responsible for defending their recommendations in detail or advising on implementation, they can justly be charged with being "irresponsible" or at least "unresponsible." In any case, they are under no pressure to supply adequate documentation or to differentiate between judgment and analysis. As a result, important issues are sometimes decided or analyzed almost on a "frivolous" basis.

The permanent staffs, almost without exception, have their time taken up by the day-to-day jobs of administration, coordination, and liaison, and by the annual budget and other crises. This over-concern with immediate problems is true of the current NSC organization. In any case, the more complicated problems cannot be handled either by individuals or by part-time intragovernmental committees, even if they were to have the time and talent. I mentioned in Lecture III that every study with which I am familiar that has resulted in new views or the production of orienting "philosophy" has taken more than two years to complete and has required a team of disciplined and interested technical and nontechnical people. In fact, I have found that operations analysis organizations with hundreds of members, many of them of almost extraordinary competence, are just able, working full-time, to keep abreast of current military developments; only rarely do they successfully initiate detailed long-range planning. In these relatively few successful studies it was also necessary to have, in addition to the team members, access to competing expert consultants who took an interest in the project and were not bound by special loyalties. It should be clear that even the talented individual in or out of government will have difficulty in doing an equivalent project on his own.

I am not trying to say that the above approach automatically produces acceptable work; often it does not, and I have written elsewhere on some of the reasons why it does not.[2] I am saying that there does not seem to be any other environment than that supplied by the relatively large independent planning organization in which it is possible even to hope to treat certain complicated problems with any completeness—problems that must be treated if we are to try to anticipate events and supply our decision makers with the basic knowledge they have to have.

It seems to me of the highest importance that we create a National Security Research Organization whose major purpose will be to house large study projects. Such an organization could do many things, any one of which might have a large enough impact to easily justify its existence, but its *raison d'être* should be the large study.

Let us now consider some of the other functions of such an organization. First, it could house independent scholars, technicians, and experts who are working by themselves on either narrow problems or the most global aspects of world affairs. It could only help both the independent work and the in-house projects to have systematic interaction, advice, and criticism. Second, the NSRO could do a certain amount of what I would

[2] H. Kahn and I. Mann, *The Techniques of Systems Analysis*, RM-1829-1, December 3, 1956 (Revised June 1957); and *Ten Common Pitfalls*, RM-1937, July 17, 1957.

IMPROVE POLICY FORMULATION

call loyal analysis for the government—that is, analysis to the order of some governmental agency.

Such agency work would increase the prestige of the organization because this agency would be more likely to appreciate the skills and techniques of the organization and would also tend to identify itself with the organization. This, in turn, would make more palatable the organization's independence—even to those officials who are dubious about long-range and large-scope studies that might cut across bureaucratic lines. It should be clear, however, that doing loyal studies or analyses to order must always be kept a secondary function, even if this can only be done by occasionally antagonizing senior government officials and departments whose pet projects have been turned down. This is necessary to protect not only the intellectual independence of the organization, but its resources as well.

In practice it is difficult to prevent demands on the time and resources of such an organization from becoming inordinate—in fact, it is clear that the better the organization is, the more demands will be made and the more difficult it will be to protect the independent scholarship and free study that are important parts of its activities.

The NSRO could also act as a high-level training center for selected people in and out of the government through formal lectures, short or long courses, or, better, by having people actually spend a year or two with the organization either as working members, or with some liaison assignments relevant to their previous work. If this were done, the organization could diffuse a larger and more expert point of view toward crucial questions in all parts of the government and academic worlds. It might even be desirable to have "trainees" from the "outside" world—that is, the political, business, and professional worlds.

In addition, NSRO might spawn new organizations to handle specialized tasks of various sorts. The most natural way that this would occur would be when a project became permanent and large. It would then be transferred to another organization or a new organization would be set up; probably with some transfer of personnel. The original organization, of course, would not normally undertake such large permanent obligations, particularly if they involved operating responsibilities. Otherwise, we would have the familiar problem of the tail wagging the dog.

NSRO could act in lieu of or as a supplement to an in-house staff for any department of the government—but always on a restricted and temporary basis. Doing this would create two familiar problems. First, the personnel involved would tend to lose their independence and would not be able to serve the department in the way we originally conceived. Second, if the organization had easy access to decision makers, it might be forced to give up some of its informality and independence. For NSRO to do its work, its staff would have to be allowed the freedom to make mistakes and blunders. But no responsible organization could allow that much freedom to its employees if they were regularly influencing major decisions. It would have to monitor, regulate, and referee the work much more closely, which in turn would stifle the mechanisms on which we would be depending for the major product.

No one should be required to coordinate with the long-range planning organization, although their comments on a restricted number of staff papers may be requested. In particular, the organization should not be required to give opinions on all important issues. It is absolutely necessary for the staff of this agency to be able individually and collectively to suspend judgment or even to withdraw into academic isolation on issues on which it does not feel competent.

The staff itself must be the final judge of what it considers to be subject to research. While it should generally set itself the widest practical goals, the qualification "practical" is an important one. For example, the organization might well try to study the impact on consumers, taxpayers, and the general price level of trying to get a six per cent annual increase in GNP, but it could scarcely come up with a conclusion that the sacrifices and risks are or are not worthwhile. It can only describe them. To give another example, it can try to decide whether giving our overseas allies IRBM's will really give them an independent nuclear deterrent, but the problem of whether it would be *desirable* to give them an independent nuclear deterrent may not be as researchable, though the staff could clearly make relevant comments on this issue.

To summarize, such an organization has many needs that are hard to supply—financial stability, flexible hiring policies, and incredibly elastic working conditions; access to all kinds of proprietory and secret information; independence of individual projects to the point where it is almost the rule that many project leaders will make fools of themselves; protection against crash programs and too many urgent requests for help; and so on. There are also some things it does *not* need—immediate and sympathetic access to the highest levels of policy making, for example.

While it is often desirable to have the researchers present their ideas directly, it is usually helpful rather than harmful to let them do a little fighting to get them presented. Regular governmental staffs should have all the opportunity they need for review and criticism of studies before they go to the top levels. In addition, to the extent that they wish, these staffs should be allowed and encouraged to incorporate ideas in their own programs on the staff and working level rather than have the suggestions come down from on high. This sometimes leads to morale problems with those of the original researchers who come from an academic tradition in which each man owns and presents his own ideas, but a sympathetic and knowledgeable management should have no trouble in handling these problems.

Some desirable characteristics that NSRO should have (some of which have already been mentioned) include:

1. It should not be monolithic. All reports, except for formal organizational recommendations, should be signed by the researchers themselves. There should be review within the organization, but if an author insists

on being in error, he should have the privilege. Others should have the corresponding privilege of objecting or of amplifying by including signed notes, marginalia, and appendices in any controversial reports.

2. It should be allowed to fund its obligations as it goes along, so that it can, for example, make what amounts to tenure appointments. If possible, funds appropriated for special studies should be given on a "No year" basis.

3. In order to allow it to establish close working relations with government and with private organizations, it should be allowed to send and receive liaison people, transfer money, give and take dollar-a-year contracts, certify a "need-to-know" for its employees, consultants and liaison personnel, and so on.

4. It should be allowed to subcontract work to private and public agencies for research, development, and analysis. So long as the contract is small, say less than $100,000, no question of duplication of an existing agency's function should be allowed to arise.

5. It should have some mechanism for setting up independent organizations to take over desirable projects, especially those which start small but later become too large to keep conveniently within the organizational setup. Giving birth to new organizations should be one of its major functions.

6. It should be allowed to receive proprietary and sensitive information which it will not divulge to anyone without the written permission of the supplier of the information.

7. NSRO should be a quasi-independent organization with a Congressional charter, an endowment sufficient to enable it to live partly off the income, and the right to request annual or special appropriations. Its director and most of its trustees or policy-making officials should not be members of government; however, the Executive Branch should be represented on its board of trustees. It should be affiliated with and responsive to the Executive Office of the President and should be a research arm of the National Policy Planning Staff already described. While the bulk of its work should be self-generated, some of its projects would come from the Executive Office in the form of suggestions or assignments from the President, the National Security Council, the National Policy Planning Staff, or other Executive Office elements concerned with national policy.

8. The sphere of interest of NSRO would be primarily in national security affairs. However, this concept should include the study of domestic programs and policies having impact on national security. Its sphere of interest should include the social as well as the physical sciences; indeed, problems in the political-military-economic field are as important as, and perhaps knottier than, those in the technological and scientific areas.

The following are suggested as illustrative of the kinds of areas that might be examined:

a. All aspects of arms control.

b. Policy implications of the arms race and technological progress.

591

c. Long-range policy with respect to the communist bloc.

d. A viable strategy for NATO in the nuclear age.

e. Aid to underdeveloped nations.

f. Cultural penetration as an instrument of U.S. foreign policy.

g. The use of agricultural surpluses in foreign aid programs.

h. Prospects and techniques for an effective air defense.

i. Alternative mixes of offensive weapons systems.

j. Problems of taxation, inflation, and economic growth and stability.

9. As a supporting element of the Executive Office, NSRO ought to receive the assistance of all other government agencies in obtaining the necessary data, personnel, and access to information. In some instances, particularly in the beginning, Presidential authority may be needed for this purpose; however, as the organization proves itself it may be anticipated that access and assistance will be readily available on the working level. Liaison offices or senior points of contact in the major agencies will facilitate these efforts.

10. The interchanges of information with and the use of personnel from private colleges, institutions, and study groups at home and abroad should be a matter of routine. Only by such interchanges can NSRO keep abreast of what is being done outside the government and tap the talents and the energies of individuals serving in private capacities, without disrupting the work of the institutions to which they belong. It might be well to establish a permanent contractual arrangement with selected universities and institutions so that they can have a voice in the direction of effort and could coordinate the use of their resources in support of NSRO. Whatever method is used, it can only help NSRO to carry out its assigned responsibilities if it serves as a link between governmental and nongovernmental activities.

An important element of this link would be a liberal policy for the open publication of material. This can also serve as a means of disseminating information and of arousing public interest and concern with the problems facing government. While many of the studies that NSRO undertakes (especially those requested by the Office of the President) will be of a classified nature, every effort should be made to publish as much of the material as possible, subject only to normal security clearances and to a liberal interpretation of the client relationship that NSRO will have with the Office of the President. In particular, material which dissents from approved programs and policies should not be restricted routinely on that basis alone.

In order to stimulate thinking about the organization, I would like to close this chapter with some specific organizational suggestions, presenting items without much discussion. They are offered to give the reader an idea of what the organizational structure might be.

A. Board of Trustees (BOT)

1. Composition: six from academic or professional life, six from "public affairs," three from industry, three from governmental or political life, three from its organizational management.

2. Self-perpetuating, but the President or Congress might have veto rights.
3. Should have enough salary to justify part-time participation in the corporation's affairs.
4. Full semiannual meetings and more frequent meetings of subcommittees.
5. Mediates between NSRO and EAG (Executive Advisory Group, described later).
6. Mediates between Management Committee and NABS's Director.
7. Reviews programs.
8. Makes basic decisions.
9. Handles all the normal functions of a board of trustees.

B. Executive Advisory Group
1. May be required by statute or just by contract.
2. Should have about twenty-five full members, about fifty auditors.
3. Allocation of full members: headed by President's Assistant for National Security Affairs, two from OCDM, two from DOD, three from the services (one from each), two from the State Department, eight from other members of the cabinet, one from FRB, one from AEC, one from NASA, one from BOB, one from NAS, one from CIA, one from CEA, one from Vice-President's office.
4. Each full member is allowed to bring one auditor to meetings. In addition, auditors should be invited from such other agencies as seems appropriate.
5. Should have full-time secretariat whose head (and maybe sole member) is on NSC Planning Board and is chosen by the President's Assistant for National Security.
6. Should have the right to suggest specific studies. In case of controversy, the trustees should mediate.
7. Major functions:
   a. Advises government on how to use NSRO;
   b. Hears formal briefings from NSRO about once or twice a year;
   c. Provides two-way channel for information and flow of ideas;
   d. Formally advises trustees of their evaluation of how NSRO is functioning;
   e. Advises on level of NSRO budget and any basic changes in function;
   f. Mediates between Legislative Advisory Group and the Executive Advisory Group or NSRO;
   g. Determines which of the briefings the Legislative Advisory Group is to hear;
   h. Advises other executive agencies to hear briefings and sometimes asks these other agencies to take a formal position on these briefings.

C. Legislative Advisory Group
  1. May be statutory or just "courtesy."
  2. Full members are appointed by Majority and Minority Leaders of Congress.
  3. Auditor members should include Congressional staff.
  4. Has no normative or regulatory functions.
  5. Has full-time secretariat, hired by NSRO or some part of Executive Office. This should reduce the problem of unauthorized leaks to members of Congress or their staffs.
  6. The secretariat and Legislative Advisory Group briefings should provide the major channel through which information is fed to Congress. Unlike the Executive agencies, Congressional staffs should not have direct working relations with NSRO, although authorized information-gathering would be encouraged.
  7. Specific requests for studies or sensitive information by members of Congress should be discouraged, although not forbidden. Possibly these should be filtered through the Executive Advisory Group. There should be at least informal liaison with the Legislative Reference Service of the Library of Congress.
D. Internal Organization of NSRO
  1. Possibly six semi-independent functional divisions:
     a. Technology;
     b. Social Science (including foreign policy, economics, geography, and history);
     c. Physical Science (including mathematics);
     d. Strategic Analysis (coordinates research in strategy and tries to furnish leadership for certain kinds of projects);
     e. Operations (studies costs, operations, legal questions, administrative efficiency, etc.);
     f. Services (security, guards, publications, personnel, etc.).
  2. The heads of the divisions shall form a management committee to advise the Director on fundamental policies. In case of disagreement, the Director can choose to have his own views prevail, but the trustees shall then be informed of the dispute and its disposition.
  3. While each division will be allowed (within its budgetary limits) to hire consultants and employees with skills that would naturally lie in another division, the excessive use of this privilege should be discouraged.
  4. Projects should normally be organized across divisional lines. Project leaders can come from any of the divisions.

The reason for suggesting three such groups as the Board of Trustees, the Executive Advisory Group, and the Legislative Advisory Group is that while the NSRO will be formally a creature of the Executive, one would like it to have a semi-independent existence and exert part of its influence by educating senior people in and out of government. I conjecture that the formal structure just suggested could go a great distance in facilitating this activity. We are preparing for large, important, influential, and responsible captive and critical audiences for our findings.

When the NSRO builds up its competency and prestige it could do other things along this line. It might be quite reasonable for the trustees and legislative advisors, in particular, to play a rather special role in trying to raise the general intellectual level of discussion on national security affairs. In addition, the NSRO might issue signed reports in the same way the National Academy of Sciences, the National Planning Association, or the Committee for Economic Development do. Some of these reports to the general public would really be the result of an informed intuition rather than an analysis. While not directly related to studies, such reports could be very useful. These should be signed by members of the Board of Trustees as semipersonal documents. Such reports should, of course, be sharply differentiated from the direct output of the analytical side of the organization.

The eventual hope is to have decision makers so competent and so well informed (a sort of intellectual pressure group for long-range thinking) that we have some of the benefits of an "aristocracy" in treating long-range programs without the well-known disadvantages of aristocracy. In other words, we should go to great lengths to make the proper arrangements so that the de Tocqueville quotation which started this chapter does not apply to our democracy.

There are many reasons for having independent functional divisions rather than organizing on a project basis. Experience has shown that it is almost impossible to hire really first-rate technical and scientific people except into a division which is a natural professional home. Few good mathematicians, for example, would be willing to tie themselves to a permanent nonmathematical project, but quite a number would join a Math division which looks and acts a great deal like an academic mathematics department, and then work part- or full-time on a number of projects, as their interests and the work load dictate.

I would also like to mention the extreme importance of being able to organize new projects easily and being able to release to a pool people no longer needed. A functional organization is very suitable for this purpose.

The reason we are having a special strategic analysis division in which we could put many of the senior project leaders has to do partly with the extreme desirability of having such people working closely together (in the sense of interaction and information rather than coordination) and partly for preventing a stratification and a hardening in the informal organizational structure by breaking up some of the lines from project leaders to team. Experience has shown that first-rate project leaders tend to be very competitive as individuals. If left in their separate divisions there is a tendency for them to try to hoard the resources most easily available to them, and not to make available to project leaders in other divisions the resources that they may need. The competition also tends to lead to a lack of communication and cooperation between project leaders in different divisions. I believe that putting the senior people in a single division and having them report to a single head should help overcome all these possible drawbacks. Lastly, the breaking up of some of the authority lines which were established when these project leaders were in divisions is important to give young people a chance to grow.

II

PROPOSAL FOR A WAR DAMAGE
EQUALIZATION CORPORATION

As soon as one takes seriously the possibility of war and the necessity of recuperation from war several financial problems become immediately apparent. They include:

1. The need to start rather expensive long-range programs with great rapidity;
2. The desirability of accumulating specialized stockpiles for recuperation purposes after a surprise attack and for use as a Preattack Mobilization Base for an emergency military and civil defense program for use when international relations deteriorate;
3. The unlikelihood of being able to finance routinely the first two items above as part of the federal budget; this should be true even if the nation becomes civil defense conscious, since shelter programs are likely, as much for political as strategic reasons, to have first claim on the resources allocated to civil defense.
4. The need for such postattack financial measures as compensation, stabilization, rehabilitation and continued operation of going corporate enterprises that will become legally insolvent or will have lost their legal management;
5. The desirability of arranging a portion of postattack compensation and rehabilitation in accordance with some sort of insurance-type principle;
6. The desirability of having some of the risks of war damage reflected in the peacetime practices of the civilian economy.

I suggest that all of the above objectives, and others, will best be met by setting up a single government corporation, to be called provisionally the War Damage Equalization Corporation (WDEC). This chapter discusses some of the characteristics that such a corporation might have and some of the arguments for and against its establishment.

There are three primary methods available to the government for financing long-range nonmilitary defense programs intended to decrease our vulnerability to enemy attack and to help prepare for national recuperation from a war. The most obvious is to use taxes. Thus the cost of such programs would be included in the regular federal budget. However, from a political standpoint it seems unlikely that we could finance long-term programs this way. (Even pressing short-term problems are often inadequately financed by this method.) Of course, we could assign higher priorities to some of these long-range problems than to immediate problems, but Americans tend to over-discount unpleasant aspects of the future. Even if there were no political problems, it might still be desirable to raise a large percentage of the funds for long-range nonmilitary defense programs outside the federal budget.

A second possible way to raise the necessary money would be to institute some sort of compulsory insurance scheme. One could argue that since the major purpose of these measures is *to restore prewar society*, those who have large economic stakes in our peacetime society ought to be asked to contribute much more toward preparing for the economic part of this rehabilitation than those with less at stake. Thus the contribution ought to be *proportional to wealth at risk* rather than to the classical graduated income tax or the straight property tax.

Compulsory insurance has a number of very attractive features to it. It would raise the most political problems, no doubt, but it would solve participation and equity problems, for coverage would be complete. It would not be necessary to compromise details of the plan in order to make certain promises which might be a handicap to recuperation in the postwar world. Compulsory insurance would also intensify various advantageous side effects. (Discriminatory rates could help bring dispersion of industry, for example.) But on practical, political, and theoretical grounds I prefer a voluntary insurance scheme as the method of raising the money.

The notion of having the United States government sell or make available some kind of insurance to compensate its citizens for damage they may suffer as a result of a war may not appeal to most people, at least on first thought. The writer has found that nearly everybody agrees in principle (after much discussion) that some sort of compensation should be made available, and that the details need to be made clear well in advance so that people can plan. There is also agreement that compensation should be tied to some sort of insurance principle. There are, of course, great differences of opinion on the form this insurance should take. I propose here a fairly specific voluntary scheme without implying that every aspect of the proposal has been carefully thought through. I quite frankly hope to arouse discussion on the matter. It will be recognized that any such scheme is very complicated. Some months of investigation and discussion would be needed to firm up a rounded proposition.[1]

I propose that the federal government offer to sell insurance to individuals and corporations that would compensate them for any losses they suffer as a result of enemy action. This compensation should be in terms of dollars numerically equivalent to the prewar value of the property (the way a normal insurance company would compensate), or a variable number of dollars as set by a postwar equalization commission (to allow for inflation). This equalization commission would set a rate of indemnification in accordance with certain equalization principles to be discussed later.

---

[1] For discussion of war damage insurance from a somewhat different perspective, see two papers by Jack Hirschleifer: "War Damage Insurance," *Review of Economics* and *Statistics*, Vol. No. 35 (May 1953), pp. 144–153; and "Compensation for War Damage: An Economic View," *Columbia Law Review*, Vol. 55 (February 1955), pp. 180–194.

In no case, however, should the rate set by the postwar commission be less than the face value of the policy.

A possible set of rates charged by the corporation might be .1 per cent, .3 per cent, or .5 per cent, according to the risk class.[2] It is hoped that the discriminatory rates will have at least a mild effect in reducing industrial vulnerability. These rates are slightly less than fire insurance rates for masonry buildings and about a half or a third of those for frame houses. They are analogous to the rates charged in World War II by the government's War Damage Insurance Corporation, which had a very respectable volume of business. With such rates and reasonably extensive participation, the government corporation might collect from $1 to $5 billion a year. Additional sums could be gathered by direct insurance on lives or by the reinsurance of current life insurance. (At a cost of, say, 10 per cent of the premium, this could raise close to $1 billion.) By reinsuring workmen's compensation other sums could be raised. If it were desired to speed the program for obtaining the recuperation capability and the Pre-attack Mobilization Base, additional money might be raised by letting the equalization commission sell bonds to be paid off from the premiums it collects in the future.

To give the program an initial impetus and to discourage latecomers and opportunists, it is suggested that in the first two or three years participants get full protection immediately. From that time on (except for new construction and bona fide new purchases) it might take two years of premium buying before full coverage was granted to new customers. The latter might be allowed one-third coverage in the first year and two-thirds in the second.

It is suggested that a government corporation to be called the War Damage Equalization Corporation (WDEC) be set up to administer the scheme. (The word "Insurance" has been deliberately left out of the title because the scheme is nonacturial.)

Any future war disaster is almost certain to entail large-scale inflation. WDEC should protect the insured against some of the effects of this inflation. The equalization principle that should guide WDEC is that the insured should not be protected against all loss, but that his loss should approximate the average loss suffered by the country.

It would be improper to promise to pay the insurees 100 cents on each dollar of face value in real terms. This flows from the fact that payments to be made will come not from a reserve,[3] but from some sort of tax on the

[2] The suggested rates are arbitrary. The guiding criterion in setting rates is to maximize revenue and, to a lesser extent, to minimize problems of public acceptance. Whether the suggested rates do this is anybody's guess. As pointed out later, the actuarial situation has been almost ignored.

[3] There is an important caveat to be made here. If the government has a Preattack Mobilization Base and recuperation capability, it will own valuable disposable assets which can be used to pay off the insurees. To simplify the example, the role played by these assets is ignored. In practice, they would allow either increased payments or smaller capital levees or both.

remaining wealth of the country. For example, if 100 per cent of the country had been insured and half of the country had been destroyed, then any attempt to pay off 100 cents on the dollar would result in taking away all the property owned by people who had not been touched and giving it to the people who had. This would shift unfairly the entire cost of the war. A far more reasonable thing to do would be to equalize the loss.

Therefore, if a country suffered 50 per cent damage, the insuree might receive fifty cents in real dollars on each dollar of face value. In postwar money that would probably be more than 100 cents per prewar dollar of coverage because of inflation. There is a small possibility that any postwar inflation would be less than that assumed; then payment at face value would comprise more than the equalized loss. It is felt that this risk is negligible in the absence of the present scheme. It is probably even theoretically impossible (given the probable levels of damage) if the scheme exists.

Let me hasten to add that the numbers used above are illustrative only. In the near future, if we take adequate active and passive defense measures, we could expect that the level of damage would be less than one-third of the total national wealth, under some circumstances much less. Even this high level of damage does not mean that the government will automatically be forced to take one-third of the property value from people who have not been damaged. First, the actual payments that the government will have to make should be substantially less than the face value of the damage. (There will be many kinds of damage that have not been covered by the insurance.) Second, if some of the other programs I recommend are carried through, the government will automatically become the owner of certain well-protected resources that will be extremely valuable in the postwar world. The sale of these resources should raise some of the funds needed to pay off the insurees. Perhaps some property in the postwar environment will come into government hands through lack of legitimate surviving claimants. Advance legislation restricting inheritance to named beneficiaries of a will or close relatives might guarantee that this would be the case.

A fairly large amount will remain to be paid off. This residual amount should presumably be raised by some kind of net worth tax. (I am informed that some, if not all, forms of net worth taxes might be unconstitutional. If this turns out to be the case, alternatives would have to be worked out.)

Some Possible Benefits of WDEC

I would like now to discuss some of the possible benefits to be realized from this scheme as outlined here.

1. There is a market and need for this insurance.

The first reaction of many to a proposal like this is that if it is *voluntary* people will not buy. This reaction, although very common, may be misleading from a market research point of view. There is much evidence that there are ample people and organizations glad to buy insurance to get the program going. Once it operates in even a moderate way there will be reasons for expecting wide-scale participation after a time.

Probably the most ready customers for war damage insurance will be financial institutions that have to have it in order to be solvent, at least on paper, if war occurs. If one has a fiduciary responsibility toward money, he does not ask the question that is most often posed, "Will there be a reasonable and livable postwar world?" Rather, he inquires, "Can I pay off the depositors?" It is not the banker's job to ask if, *in his judgment,* life will go on; it is his job to see to it that if war comes his fiscal responsibilities will be discharged in the postwar world. It is for the benefit of these financial institutions that we make it a condition on WDEC that it pay at least the face value of the policy.

As an aid to starting the program, it might be wise to let financial institutions insure their currently outstanding loans at a bargain rate—say, at one-half or one-third of the normal rates. Once they got into the program, they would pass on future costs to their customers.

The potential class of immediate customers is actually much wider than just financial institutions. In World War II, with essentially no selling campaign, the government collected $260 million in payments for $114 billion worth of insurance. The rates varied from .1 to .3 per cent, according to the class of property covered. Possibly even more indicative of the widespread interest in war damage insurance are the responses to hearings before a subcommittee of the Committee on Banking and Currency of the United States Senate in 1952. Almost all the nongovernment witnesses were in favor of some sort of insurance scheme. The fact that so many people would like to have insurance-type protection against war damage is a major argument in favor of a War Damage Equalization Corporation. There seems to be a definite need that only the federal government can fill. The existence of this need makes the desirability of some form of voluntary federal war damage insurance almost noncontroversial. It is worth emphasizing this point.

For many reasons, the average person does not take kindly to the idea of selling damage insurance in time of peace. However, the possibility of war does exist. If we take this possibility seriously we should make appropriate preparations. If we believe that we should prepare now to restore in the postwar world a reasonable facsimile of society, these preparations should include the possibility of protecting ourselves as individuals from some of the economic consequences of a war. It was true in both World War I and World War II that as soon as the war started there was an immediate demand for war damage insurance. The government met the need. At the start of the Korean War, Congress held the hearings I just mentioned but the war ended before anything developed on the legislative stage. Today it would clearly be much too late to make any such preparation after the war or the crisis had started. It therefore seems appropriate to make such preparations in a period of peace. Indeed, in the absence of preparation and adequate records, it will probably be impossible in the confusion of the postwar world to even determine who owns what, much less what compensation any individual is entitled to. Since it is impossible for private companies to satisfy the legitimate need for protection, such needs can only be supplied by government. Even those who think war unlikely or who consider civil defense of little value should let people who want insurance buy it.

2. It raises revenue for passive defense purposes.

WDEC will perform a real service for those who want protection against the risks of war. More than this, however, it may raise money that could be used to finance long-term programs in the passive defense field—programs that could give interesting capabilities in the middle and late 1960's and the early 1970's. This is an aspect of particular interest to me. These capabilities, while relatively inexpensive if obtained as a result of a long-term program, are very expensive in time and resources on a crash basis. They will improve our chance of recuperation, even if a war begins before we can put in a crash program of preparation.

One is entitled to ask the question, Why should such a corporation put its money into passive defense programs? The reason, I think, is evident. It would clearly be a violation of its fiduciary responsibilities for WDEC to put its money into the normal type of reserve. A collection of bonds is exactly the wrong kind of resource for the postwar world. Any payoff to the corporate beneficiaries would have to come from the wealth that survived the war, whether owned by the government or private parties. It should be the purpose of the corporation to spend its funds to increase the wealth that survives the war, and I suspect that it would be almost (but not completely) irrelevant to the corporation whether this wealth were private or public.

It would also be undesirable for WDEC to use most of its funds to pay for a major portion of the cost of a personnel shelter program. Yet, it would certainly be reasonable for it to expend a portion of its funds for the survival of its customers. Probably the corporation should spend no money in the personnel protection field except where it can do so with a great deal of leverage. For example, it might undertake preliminary design and engineering of shelter projects so that other organizations would be able to carry out the program more efficiently than if this paperwork were not done. It might even match the cost of shelters, on a two-, three-, or four-way split with federal, state, local, and private individuals, but its contribution should presumably, in all cases, be significantly less than one-half the total cost of the project.

There are important exceptions to the policy of avoiding the personnel shelter field. If one looks at how the corporation ought to spend its money, he notices that it could make important contributions to the personnel shelter field in three ways. First, the corporation ought to create and improve a lot of underground space by a subsidized mine program. The main function of this space would be to give protection for industry in the prewar period and stockpiles and radiation-protected housing and working space in the postwar period. But all of the space would be available *on a few hours warning* for notably adequate protection of population. A WDEC organized in 1961 might have one or two billion square feet by 1966. This would be adequate to shelter under austere conditions up to 100 million people in a strategic evacuation. Second, the industrial shelters to be encouraged by the corporation should be designed to be potentially useful as personnel protection. Third, the corporation ought to stockpile the materials that the government would need if it ever went into a crash program of shelter construction. These materials would be very useful in a reconstruction effort if war should come before a crash program could be instituted.

3. It is relatively riskless for the government.

One of the major reasons why one can urge the government to set up a WDEC is that in some sense the creation of this organization does not increase inordinately the financial obligations of the government. Every knowledgeable person with whom I have discussed this question agrees that if the government survives a war, it will be forced to compensate most citizens for their losses. Of course, a ceiling would be put on the compensation (as was done in the Philippines compensation in the last war, where losses were compensated "in full" up to $500, and to the extent of 52.5 per cent of amounts over $500, where the $500 was in terms of prewar value. Because of the postwar inflation, replacement costs turned out to be triple original costs). In selling the insurance the government has automatically obligated itself to pay the equalized losses of even its largest customers. I feel, however, that this partial restoration of the prewar pattern of property rights is a gain, not a loss; in any case it is a relatively small additional obligation when compared to the obligation of reimbursing the mass of U.S. citizens, particularly if this obligation is undertaken without any advance preparation.

4. There are educational aspects.

As previously mentioned, the discriminatory rates are low, so low that the direct economic incentive to relocate and protect is probably small. The psychological impact may be much larger. First, and probably most important, it forces attention on the postwar world in a constructive way. One of the real problems of passive defense is that most people's imaginations stop with the concept of war and refuse even to consider the possibility of a postwar world.

There is another important educational effect. Many insurance agents have observed that people will not build very often in high fire-rate areas. This is not so much because the cost of the high rates are themselves a real bar, but because they do not want their building to burn down even if they are reimbursed. Almost all property owners would prefer to have their property intact, rather than have destruction of their property result in a valid paper claim on WDEC. (Once it is brought home to them that there is a great and inescapable risk in doing some of the things they are doing while omitting other actions, they may well change their activities.)

A general relocating effect brought about by discriminatory rates is much more palatable politically than action directives to individual companies could even be. Thus if the government should tell the Lockheed Aircraft Corporation (as it once did) that it cannot build a plant in a certain area, it aggravates both the corporation and the local Congressman. If, on the other hand, the government says that any company that builds "safely" or in relatively safe areas (or both) will be benefited by a reduction in insurance rates or by the payment of a premium by WDEC, it does not irritate any particular corporation very much and it bothers the Congressman from a nonsafe area much less, though undoubtedly he will be irritated. It is not unprecedented for the government to favor certain regions. While there has usually been grumbling in the regions that were not so favored, the grumbling has not been as intense as for a region which is singled out for disfavor.

5. It may create some dispersal and hardening.

While the economic impact of the suggested discriminatory rates is not very large, it may be large enough to influence the new location or construction and maybe even the relocation or reconstruction of marginal concerns and activities. By "marginal" I mean that large costs are not involved; the firms are easily persuaded to change from risky locations and risky-type construction to less risky locations and construction. It is difficult to guess the magnitude of this effect, but it should be large enough to decrease vulnerability appreciably.

6. It has important stabilizing and rehabilitating functions.

To some people, the major advantage of such schemes as this is that it makes explicit preparations in advance for the restoration of property rights and activities. There are many ways of doing this. But it is important to realize that no matter what preparations have or have not been made the government would still have the responsibility for assuring the financial viability of the economy. In short, it would see to it that undamaged banks, other financial institutions, and critical businesses would not be forced to halt operations because of paper insolvency or lack of credit. While the WDEC is only one way of making explicit preparations for doing this, it should have its job greatly simplified because both the physical and financial basis for maintaining economic momentum will have been increased as a result of its actions. It is also likely to do a good professional job of preparing because this will be one of its major functions.

This proposal clearly has advantages. It also has defects.

1. It complicates recuperation.

The scheme may complicate recuperation processes in at least two ways. First, those who have not been insured may raise objections against the idea of the government's using any of its scarce resources to pay off those who hold policies. These objections may be somewhat mollified if the government or WDEC gives a limited amount of free or quite inexpensive insurance to everybody. Then there will be relatively little total destitution, and all will have at least a small stake in the prewar pattern of property rights.

Another way the existence of WDEC might complicate the recuperation effort is that in its attempt to pay off its obligations, the government may well put resources in the hands of the wrong people. I feel intuitively that the details of the plan can be so arranged that this effect can also be moderated. However, nobody has looked at the problem in any detail. In advance of a detailed study it is difficult to judge how serious this complication will be compared to the gain of having greater resources.

2. The scheme is nonactuarial.

The proposed scheme is nonactuarial, and many knowledgeable people feel that the rates are far too low for the possible gains that the insurees would have. Others (mostly those who doubt the *existence* of a postwar world or the possibility of even a technical win by the U.S.) feel the exact opposite—the rates are too high. For purposes of illustration let me assume some numbers and then estimate the payoff. There is, say, one chance in thirty per year of war. There is perhaps one chance in two of one's property being destroyed in that war. Also, the probability of a postwar payment and its utility is about one-half. (Actually, of course, the net probability and utility of the postwar payment may be greater than it was prewar rather than less).[4] Then the expected value of the dollar of coverage is $\frac{1}{30} \times \frac{1}{2} \times \frac{1}{3}$, or $\frac{1}{120}$. If the scheme were fully actuarial, the premiums would normally be higher than the expected value. This could make them around 1 per cent or more. However, I have suggested an average rate of around .3 per cent, undercharging people by about a factor of three (according to this calculation).

One could use less pessimistic assumptions and not make the overpayment look so bad. I feel, however, that one would be equally justified in making more pessimistic assumptions and make the underpayment look outrageous. In any case, the actuarial or nonactuarial aspects of the situation are not central. I am pleased that the scheme might give a bargain to the policyholders, since I feel that any postwar world they might be "enjoying" would be largely due to their foresight. The funds spent by WDEC

[4] This one-half is supposed to include the possibility of repudiation of WDEC's obligation because of defeat or other events, as well as adjustment for inflation or the changed utility of money.

could play a major and even an overriding role in making possible a quick recuperation in the postwar world. From the social point of view, it would thus be a very good thing for society to encourage people to invest in this enterprise. Since the investment would be open to all who own property, owners who did not take advantage of their opportunity would have little valid complaint. Those who did not own property might have a valid complaint, but probably not, since the claims would be paid off by a non-recurring (and therefore probably nonshiftable) tax on property.

It is possible, of course, that even if their complaints were not valid the malcontents or the destitute or even more likely, those who are being taxed, would still have enough influence to prevent the assumed payments.[5] Naturally, I would hope this would not happen. The possibility of this depends partly on whether the United States manages to preserve its courts and legal processes. Partly it depends on whether we adopt an attitude common to some undeveloped nations who find it impossible to attract foreign investment because whenever the investments are successful the country gets incensed at the large profits, confiscating them. As a result, these countries find that they cannot get socially worthwhile and potentially profitable projects going. Whether this sort of thing happens in the United States depends not only on postwar ideology and morale but also on the extent to which the insurance has been sold in the prewar world. That is, if the majority of the populace is covered, one can assume that they share an interest in making WDEC pay off. In this field, as in many other fields, nothing succeeds like success.

There is another aspect of the nonactuarial character of WDEC that deserves discussion. If one believes that the actuarial rates are much higher than the suggested ones, he is in effect subsidizing people and wealth to stay in target areas. For example, if a plant is in a target area and has, say, one chance in fifty of being destroyed in a war, the owner of that plant, if he is sensible, should move it to a less risky area. WDEC may induce him not to move by offering him such cheap insurance that the financial risk of his staying in a target area has been negated. However, as a practical matter this effect is probably small. Except in very isolated instances it should be of no consequence. For some obscure reason, people do not seem to have taken account of the possibility that war will decide where they should live and invest their money. Therefore, any move in the direction of taking account of this risk is good. Rather than cause a regression, institution of even these low rates should cause a significant improvement. If it does not, it would mean that people have become conscious of the risks of war, and the corporation could probably raise its rates.

---

[5] Sidney Winter suggests to me that I may be asking for civil war or at least serious political strain if we put a capital levy on those who have been lucky. I would think not if the bill were presented soon after the cataclysm when altruistic feelings are likely to be at a peak, and if in addition the payments were spread over a long time. However, the two if's are important and the first one in particular requires elaborate prewar preparation.

3. The scheme penalizes the wrong people.

It is possible to make a case to the effect that the wrong people are bearing the burden. Even the voluntary WDEC has some effect akin to a property tax. And it has discriminatory rates. One could argue that it is not up to any particular private citizen whose property happens to be at risk to bear the costs, but that it is the duty of the federal government or of the community as a whole. While I believe this is in some sense correct, I also believe there is no reason why the federal government should subsidize bad patterns that increase the risks incurred by a war. In other words, any costs created by the risk of war should be borne in such a way that risks are decreased, not increased.

There is another and more subtle sense in which discriminatory rates penalize the wrong people. I have argued that people who have property in target areas should pay higher rates. Since most people live close to their property, it is these who are most likely to be killed in a war. They will hardly benefit from the survival of the rest of the postwar world. On the other hand, the people in nontarget areas who pay lower rates are the ones who, on the average, are most likely to survive. These will benefit from the preparations that have been made to facilitate occupation.

These objections might be more germane if the rates were noticably more discriminatory than the ones I have suggested. I do not believe that any case can be made, however, at the low level of discrimination suggested. The extra likelihood that owners in target areas will have their property destroyed should more than make up for the possibility that the owners themselves will be killed.

4. Misallocates resources.

Probably the most frequent objection raised (by people in the planning field at least) is that it is wrong to marry the revenues of this corporation to the passive defense program. To put it differently, it may be wrong to delimit the extent of the passive defense program by the revenues raised by the corporation. This objection could have force. First, more revenue might come to be raised by this corporation from the private sector of the economy than ought to be spent on passive defense. In judgment, it should be remembered that the alternative is not to spend this money on, say reducing the vulnerability of SAC, or on a limited war capability, or more education, or any of the other activities that have such a vociferous claim on the government's purse. The alternative use of this money is that it be spent in the private sector of the economy or on passive defense measures. I believe that a good case can be made that the private sector can and should afford the extra expense for this purpose.

WDEC, of course, has a marginal effect. It makes it harder for the government to raise money by additional taxes because every time the private sector has to bear increased costs, it has less left over to pay taxes. This effect is likely to be only marginal—if it exists at all.

One could also argue that WDEC would misallocate resources by not spending enough. The counter argument would be that there is no objection to the government adding directly to the funds of WDEC. Of course, it might happen that if WDEC did not exist the government would have raised by conventional taxes even more money for a long-range program than the joint WDEC-federal program does. This is so unlikely politically that it scarcely deserves consideration. I have already suggested that WDEC undertake only small responsibilities in the short-range field where the government might be willing to spend money of its own.

5. Forecloses alternatives.

A possible major objection to WDEC is that there may be alternative institutional arrangements which are better—for example, the raising of money by taxes or by compulsory insurance comes immediately to mind. It seems improbable that the government would use either of these methods to raise money for any long-range program. In addition, there are important reasons (of a doctrinaire and ideological type) for preferring voluntary schemes to compulsory ones whenever possible. Therefore, I have no hesitancy in suggesting a voluntary WDEC program. After the program is started, if we decide that other institutional arrangements should be made, we can change the enabling legislation. I find very weak any objections based on the notion that somebody will discover or put forth a better scheme. There is a pressing need for the immediate institution of the kind of programs that WDEC can design and finance.

Some Facts on Insurance

Fire insurance rates vary greatly because of differences in the risk of the property being insured as well as the degree of protection provided by the area in which the property is located.

Occupied residential houses are rated according to their location and whether the house is of frame or masonry construction. Table 1 provides some examples of this variation in California. Every community in the nation is rated by the Fire Rating Bureau according to the danger of fire inherent in the topography, the efficiency of the fire and police departments, and other pertinent considerations, and the rates are determined accordingly. These ratings are constantly reviewed. They range from 2 to 10. Thus insurance for a masonry house in San Francisco which has a 2 rating would be $.23 on $100, while the same house in Mono County with a 10 rating would be $.60 on $100.

A much wider range than this exists for commercial enterprises. An oil refinery may have to pay $7 per $100, an amusement park $3, and a beauty shop $2. Since the rates for commercial enterprises are determined individually, the above illustrations are of limited value. (The reluctance of the Rating Bureau to quote insurance rates for commercial enterprises makes it difficult to obtain more illustrations.)

◇◇

TABLE 1

COMPARISON OF INSURANCE RATES ON RESIDENTIAL HOUSES OF SELECTED TOWNS IN CALIFORNIA

Town, Locality or Fire Protection District	Masonry Rate Per $100	Frame Rate Per $100
Alhambra	.248	.74
Disneyland	.318	.95
Apple Valley F.P.D.	.550	1.66
Beaumont	.530	1.57
Beverly Hills	.280	.90
Culver City	.274	.82
Hermosa Beach	.407	1.21
Inglewood	.274	.82
Laguna Beach	.357	1.06
Los Angeles City		
Central Area	.248	.74
Costal Area I	.274	.82
II	.302	.90
III	.471	1.40
San Fernando Valley I	.274	.82
II	.318	.95
Mono County	.600	1.80
Redondo Beach	.318	.95
San Diego I	.270	.86
II	.274	.82
III	.302	.90
IV	.530	1.57
Santa Monica I	.270	.78
II	.274	.82

◇◇

The premiums paid for life and fire insurance in the largest metropolitan areas, in all metropolitan areas, and in the total U. S. are presented in Table 2. This information is listed by metropolitan area, by county, and by state in the source cited. No information was found for the value of assets covered by fire insurance in metropolitan areas, but a rough estimate may be obtained from the premium data.

Workmen's compensation premiums in 1955 amounted to $1,197,053,000 in the United States, of which $992,794,000 or 83% was paid in the 262 metropolitan areas which account for 84% of total private employment.

Table 3 provides some examples of the variation to be found in the rates for workmen's compensation insurance for different types of occupations as well as in different states. The former reflects variations

609

APPENDIX II

TABLE 2

PREMIUMS OF LIFE AND FIRE INSURANCE, 1955
(millions)

	Total Population	Life Premiums		
		Ordinary	Industrial	Group
17 Metropolitan Areas [a]	52.8	2,556	452	483
262 Metropolitan Areas [b]	108.8	4,637	957	872
National	165.9	6,046	1,437	1,078

Total National Premiums = $8,564 millions

	Fire and Extended Coverage			
	Residential	Mercantile	Industrial	Total
17 Metropolitan Areas	301	248	218	767
262 Metropolitan Areas	625	524	457	1,605
National	934	748	592	2,274

[a] Metropolitan areas with a population of over a million.
[b] All recognized and "potential" areas. The former are the 168 areas designated by the federal government's Committee on Metropolitan Areas, all of which contain a city with 50,000 or more. The latter are 94 areas in which the city population is only 35,000 or more, but which have the other characteristics of metropolitan life.
SOURCE: "County Patterns of Insurance Sales," *Spectator*, 1957.

in the risk found in industries, while the latter is largely due to differences in the extent of the coverage offered in the various states.

TABLE 3

COMPARISON OF MANUAL RATES OF
WORKMEN'S COMPENSATION

Manual Rate for Each Code Number [a]

State	1421	2222	2585	5183	7219	8050
Alabama	$1.65	.30	.50	.78	1.85	.21
California	6.19	1.21	1.46	1.70	3.00	.57
Illinois	2.36	.50	.90	1.41	1.65	.38
Kansas	2.07	.39	.74	1.30	2.22	.27
Massachusetts	6.58	1.33	1.64	2.15	4.03	.93
Michigan	2.05	.36	.73	1.26	1.73	.31
New York	6.82	1.94	2.29	3.99	5.84	1.31
Tennessee	2.39	.47	.66	.98	1.39	.23

(*table continues on next page*)

Manual Rate for Each Code Number

State	1421	2222	2585	5183	7219	8050
Texas	5.60	1.20	1.17	2.23	5.79	.52
Wisconsin	3.16	.60	1.03	1.76	2.81	.43

ª Per income of $100 a week.

Code:

1421–Blast-furnace operation
2222–Cotton spinning and weaving
2585–Laundries
5183–Plumbing
7219–Truckmen
8050–Five-and-ten cent stores
SOURCE: Somers and Somers, *Workmen's Compensation*, New York, Wiley, 1954, p. 115.

❖❖

It is not widely realized that the U. S. government held a substantial program of all war damage insurance in World War II. Two aspects of the program are summarized in Tables 4 and 5.

❖❖

TABLE 4

DISTRIBUTION OF LIABILITY BY CLASSES
(MARCH 31, 1944)

Class	Amount of Risk	Per Cent of Total
Mfg. plants, piers, warehouses, etc.	$ 27,214,087,000	23.9
Apartment houses, hotels, offices, mercantile establishments, and other buildings not used for manufacturing	25,275,523,000	22.1
Dwellings and contents	24,580,648,000	21.4
Registered mail and express	21,369,816,000	19.0
Churches, hospitals, educational institutions, and public buildings	5,496,560,000	4.7
Publicly and privately owned utilities	4,606,461,000	4.0
Other property	3,721,505,000	3.3
Transit risks	1,752,585,000	1.6
	$114,017,194,000	100.0

SOURCE: *War Damage Indemnity*, United States Chamber of Commerce, September 1950, p. 17.

❖❖

611

TABLE 5

GEOGRAPHICAL DISTRIBUTION OF POLICIES
(MARCH 31, 1944)

	No. of Policies Issued	Per Cent of Total in Continental U.S.	Amount of Liability	Per Cent of Total in Continental U.S.
Continental U.S.				
Atlantic Coast States	5,285,891	61.4	$ 70,500,906,000	64.8
Pacific Coast States	2,071,682	24.0	16,120,358,000	14.9
North Central States	845,567	9.7	15,761,527,000	14.5
Gulf States	236,048	2.6	2,993,973,000	2.7
Other States	195,904	2.3	3,320,120,000	3.1
	8,635,092	100.0	$108,696,884,000	100.0
Territories	58,459		947,760,000	
	8,693,551		$109,644,644,000	
Blanked and Floater Policies	60,180		4,372,550,000	
	8,753,731		$114,017,194,000	

SOURCE: *War Damage Indemnity*, United States Chamber of Commerce, September 1950, p. 16; and *Encyclopedia Americana*.

III

THE SPECIAL IMPORTANCE OF
INSTALLATIONS *

A Curious Gap

ONE military area in which we do not seem to take sufficient account of the possibility of war is in the *structures* that we build. It has not been the custom in this country even in the design of purely military installations to take account of the fact that they could need protection —either from fallout or blast—if they are to be used during the war or in the postwar period.

It has been announced that the government has some underground headquarters and that it is going to build more (that is, headquarters for the North American Air Defense Command and some of the future SAGE Air Defense Control Centers). It has been further announced that the ICBM installations are to be built hard. So far as I know, these are the only installations that have ever been publicly announced as hard, or built to survive attack. We not only do not have enough current capability, we are not carrying on much research either.

I have mentioned that in World War II the military dropped most of their historic reluctance to accept technological and scientific innovations. Since that time there has been no other group in America more enthusiastic in its support of research and development. The Department of Defense spends annually almost $6 billion—or almost one out of every seven dollars that it is given—on research and development. This is a fantastic sum of money to spend; yet it will undoubtedly increase in the future. With all this expenditure, however, some vital fields for research are not having sufficient attention paid to them.

If I were asked to pick a large basic area that is not being investigated enough, an area most likely to return the greatest profit per dollar spent, I would choose basic studies in reducing the vulnerability of various types of fixed and mobile installations and their contents. The next most profitable area, I would argue, is in applied research in the same field. There seem to be several cases where we are likely to spend a few hundred million to a billion dollars on certain specialized installations—where it

---

* Most of the material contained in this chapter was presented in a talk I gave to a protective construction conference held at The RAND Corporation in Santa Monica, California. The audience was composed of technical personnel, mostly from civil, mechanical, and electrical engineering fields, and of staff representatives of several relevant departments of the government. Though the talk was rather specialized, it is of some value to indicate some of the problems that come up in working with technical people and technical advisors in a rapidly changing technological situation. The comments were made in the context of installation problems; yet they have a much wider relevance, although I should add that the problems discussed are particularly acute in the installation field.

would not be at all surprising if we could not cut the cost by a large amount, or get greatly improved performance with the same money, if we had spent only a few million dollars more on research and development.

These problems have been underemphasized in an atmosphere in which almost all research and development is encouraged. Why is this? It stems in part from the fact that the whole field does not seem to be "romantic," and therefore does not receive the necessary financial and administrative support, and in part from being dominated by certain relatively unimaginative engineering groups (as compared to the aeronautical and electronic engineers). I hope the remarks I have to make will not alienate my many friends in the architect-engineering and allied professions, but it seems to be true that of all the engineering professions this is, on the whole, the least technical. Possibly for that reason, it is the one least affected by the rapid advances of the last twenty years. There are almost no large companies who find it profitable to push the state of the art. With a few exceptions, the temperament and talents of the professionals do not lie in the direction of basic research and technical innovation. What research the private companies and academic institutions do carry out tends to be in fields remote from military application and is restricted to relatively narrow extensions of current practice. These difficulties in getting technological innovation are multiplied by the conservative character of the officials who make the decisions and give guidance. Many of them are very competent, and almost all are responsible, but they just do not have a research or innovator attitude. What is even more important, they do not take *war* seriously.

Today almost everybody realizes that we must emphasize measures designed to insure the survival of our strategic forces after a surprise attack. This is so even if it means serious budgetary and operational compromises with what our offensive capability would be if it did not have to be protected from the enemy's strike. There is still much controversy about the qualitative and quantitative aspects of these defensive measures, but whatever measures are finally adopted will result in requirements for new and more elaborate installations. As a result, many informed people think there is likely to be a major increase, possibly a doubling, in the military construction program of the Department of Defense in the next few years. This will provide alert, protected and dispersed facilities for missiles and planes and for both offense and defense. In spite of this clear understanding on the future, most of these new installations are likely to be designed on a crash basis. We can presume bad design.

The Problem of Innovation

There are many reasons why designs are likely to be inadequate. A high proportion of these new installations will be of novel design, sometimes embodying new or esoteric principles. If the designer of these installations is to do a good or even a barely adequate job, he is likely to find his reserves of experience, knowledge, ingenuity, and technique strained to the limits. Unless he is willing to "go to school" again and work with strange and sometimes demanding collaborators, he will find the technological job well beyond him.

If past history is any guide, many designers, technical advisors, and some staffs are going to resist both the new technology and the rapid introduction of innovation. Since policy is not supposed to be made at this level, it can be expected that people will disclaim responsibility with some such remark as, "We just receive orders and carry them out." In practice, life is not like that. Whatever the organizational chart may say, much policy is made at the technician and lower staff levels. Policy filters upward and often changes in the process of filtering, but many major decisions have already been made before the filtering process starts. This is not formally or legally the case, but it is so nevertheless.

Many technicians like to think that all they do is explore the alternatives available to the policy maker and describe these in some appropriate level of detail. After this the policy maker chooses which alternative he likes best. However, it is much too difficult and time-consuming for the average staff or engineering firm to explore very many alternatives. After a preliminary (often a *very* preliminary) examination, the staff will generally decide on one or two alternatives as the right ones to explore. They will then present these alternatives to the policy people either to accept or reject. The choice on which alternatives are worth exploring will be based partly on guidance available from the top. It will depend in part on the conscious and subconscious view the "technical" explorers have of what is important and what is not. And the background and experience of the available designers will play a central role. The trouble with this way of choosing which alternatives to explore is that guidance from the top turns out to be circular. It is strongly influenced by the views of the people being guided. Important or unimportant comes to be judged more in terms of the day-to-day peacetime and bureaucratic context than by performance during an unreal and hypothetical war of the future. Therefore, only solutions which seem reasonable and safe are considered, and "reasonable" and "safe" are defined, naturally, by peacetime standards —not by wartime standards. Finally, in a rapidly changing technology, the background and experience of the most readily available designers may not be even remotely appropriate.

Because the most important decisions may be made by default rather than by conscious choice, few if any of the people involved will even realize that a decision has been made. In addition, because the busy policy makers lack technical background, presentations made to them tend to be short and superficial. Therefore, a lot of important decisions are inevitably made in the process of deciding what packages to present for acceptance or rejection. For all these reasons, it would be worthwhile to make a major effort to improve the interaction of technique and policy in the installation field, to improve the technical capability of the professionals, and to reduce the lead time for the introduction of innovations.

This problem of getting first-rate work done on the new problems that face us in the protective construction field has not been entirely ignored. However, the two methods used by the government have not been spectacularly successful despite evidence that some aspects will remain useful approaches for the future. The first method was an ever increasing tendency (which reached nearly 100 per cent in the Air Force) to give the more complicated projects to new firms with a Mechanical Engineering or other background rather than to use the older Architect-Engineer concerns. While this seems to guarantee that one gets young people with new ideas and persons with more appropriate technical backgrounds than can be found in the older firms, it also means that the new firms are inexperienced in some older skills and tend to do rather badly in parts of the project which fall within more conventional bailiwicks. In at least one case, there was insistence on specifications which required extraordinarily expensive and unnecessary machine tooling of structural steel members to close tolerances. In another case, very elaborate newly invented mechanical devices were specified when minor modifications of inexpensive and reliable on-the-shelf items would have done just as well. The chief cure for this difficulty would simply seem to be higher standards on the part of the government monitors, forcing these new concerns to hire people or go into joint ventures with those holding the appropriate classical skills.

In the long run, it will be necessary for members of one profession or the other to educate themselves in all relevant aspects of the new and old technologies. The problem is not very different from that faced by those who developed radar technology during and after World War II. It was found almost impossible to use people from the electrical engineering profession, particularly those who had more or less specialized in the power field. They were bewildered by the new concepts. For example, I can remember once trying to explain to a puzzled engineer how a wave guide could carry power without a return circuit. Much of the design was in the hands of physicists and very young electrical engineers, neither of whom had any experience in designing equipment that could be easily produced and maintained. These initial hurdles were overcome by close collaboration and on-the-job education. Today we have many people who have learned all aspects of radar technology. Some of these people call themselves electrical engineers and others call themselves physicists, but fundamentally they have a new profession. *The same thing must be done in the protective construction field.*

The second method the government has used is to establish various kinds of monitoring and advisory committees. While such committees can play a useful role, they can be abused. For example, a part-time committee without actual responsibility for a project is almost completely ineffective in the crucial areas of innovating and inventing. By the nature of events, this failure does not show up unless we contrast it with the work of the rather small number of firms that have in fact been ingenious and original. The advisory or monitoring committee works out especially badly if the firms which are being monitored or advised use the assistance of the committee as an excuse for giving up in-house responsibility and capability for the more technical aspects of the problem; that is, instead of hiring full-time, first-rate (or even second-rate) people who are competent in the new techniques and technologies, they tend to get a very superficial education in the new ideas. Whenever they get into trouble they ask their associated committee how to solve the problem. This means that only the standard textbook solutions are ever used.

The innovation problem in the installation field is fundamentally no different than the problems we face in other fields except that the lack of glamour, competition, and verve means that nobody notices the inadequacies.

The Problem of Obsolescence

As the architecture and engineering professions and the associated government agencies are currently comprised they cannot deal with the basic source of most of our difficulties. This is the rapidity of change in the art and technology of war. I have mentioned that every five years seems to bring a technological revolution. This introduces tremendous difficulties for both the planner and the designer. Lessons and techniques learned last year at bitter cost may be worthless today.

It takes about four or five years from the time we first lay down the requirements for a building until the Beneficial Occupancy Date. Most people think that a building ought to have a useful life of at least twenty years, but this is far too much to expect of any military structure in the world of today. Still, they should not be planned with the expectation that they will last less than five or ten years. This means, if my arithmetic is correct, that we should at this writing be considering the 1965–70 period the absolute minimum. If we want much more than a five-year life for our buildings, or even a little more time for thinking and research, we should be looking at the 1970–75 period also. To my knowledge, this kind of forward thinking has not been customary in the protective structure field.

If this were a classified document I could illustrate this point by giving the history of several weapons systems that became prematurely obsolete —in some cases before they had been fully procured—because the designers or planners showed insufficient foresight or imagination. Taking into account rapid changes in the art of war, it is inevitable that this should happen occasionally, but responsible designers and engineers should try to guard against it. In all too many cases planners or designers have failed to anticipate even a mild degree of technological progress. Sometimes the error has been compounded. Crash programs designed to provide a quick-fix have been underdesigned, so that even these run a risk of being obsolete before they are fully installed or procured.

Under such circumstances there is a heavy responsibility upon installation engineers and designers to work closely and sympathetically with the professional military planners and operators. In this way there can be full exploration of all problems and possibilities. It is especially important to build systems that have been designed to meet the full range of threats or that can be retrofitted or improved to meet increases or changes in the threat.

This means that those in the installation field have to be encouraged to look for new ideas and gadgets, push research and development, and take some technological gambles. It seems to be true in almost every other field of military technology that the majority of really new ideas did not originate in official requirements or in massive projects pushed by the official agencies or large companies. Instead, they came from the small percentage of successful ideas pushed by individuals or small organizations (some of them almost fanatic in character). Few of the large number of ideas generated by small outfits and individuals are successful; yet it is these few which are the base of much of our military system today.

For the *field of protective construction,* however, I think it fair to say that the profession has lagged significantly behind the need. They have not been pushing the state of the art. On the whole they have waited for leadership from government. I am sure that these last remarks will disturb friends of mine in the profession—some because they will regard the remarks as unfair, others because they know that they have a basis in fact.

Engineers and staffs were talking of design techniques that were suitable against conventional heavy explosives back when we were faced with the 20 KT bomb. By the time they had mastered the 20 KT we were facing the MT bomb carried by a bomber. Today, of course, we face the ICBM. We have people designing buildings for single-bomb drops at a time when the enemy may be intending to have thousands of ICBM's by the 1965–75 time period. People are designing buildings to survive inaccurate weapons carrying low yields, even though it is almost certain that the enemy will improve his accuracy and yield if he finds it necessary to do this in order to destroy an important target.

Possibly more difficult than the intellectual problem of planning for an uncertain world, though intertwined with it, is the psychological one of taking seriously the possible performance of these buildings in a future war. Many people seem to believe (or they act as if they believe) that preparation for war is a sort of Alice-in-Wonderland activity that is almost unrelated to any real eventuality. I have said much about the reality of the threat of thermonuclear war and the need for seriously preparing, not only to *deter* a war, but to be able to *fight* one. It is most important that all the technical people who work on installations problems be conscious of these ideas, or of some equivalent set they find more palatable.

Like many in our nation, designers of military structures do not always take war seriously. If one puts up a building in peacetime and it operates reasonably well, the fact that it would not perform in wartime may never be noticed. At the most, it is only noticed once. One goes to sleep at night and the building is still there when one wakes up the next day. Thus are created illusions of permanence. The fact that there are inadequacies in the design of the building from the viewpoint of its wartime performance is not as apparent as some trivial inadequacy that shows up in day-to-day performance.

If, for example, there are not enough toilets, everybody notices and complains. While quite different things are important in a war, you are not normally fighting a war. Thus there is an almost overwhelming tendency to compromise the design (particularly where there is uncertainty) in favor of better peacetime performance or lower costs. The wartime performance can "safely" be neglected. No designer would take one chance in ten that his building would fall down in peacetime, but he will cheerfully take the bigger chance that during the lifetime of the building it will prove to be a total failure in wartime. ("Total failure" is defined as the ability of the enemy to destroy the building at trivial military cost.) It seems necessary to make a war seem more real before the requirements for living in a war can be made to seem worth being worried about. The academic and the hypothetical will then be moved to one side.

The Mathematics of Survival

It might be appropriate, at this point, to make some comments about operational requirements. The word "operational" does not refer to such things as how the doors open and close, but rather to the military function of protective construction in a war. I am going to restrict my comments to some of the operational aspects of a special kind of installation—the hard shelter whose job it is to protect a plane or missile. I am going to start with an elementary discussion of the relationships between the size of the enemy's bombs, the accuracy of his aim, and the degree of protection we need.

Shelters can play two quite different roles. They can make it harder for the enemy to destroy any particular target or they can limit the damage to a small area or part of the target. In the first role, one can consider the entire protected complex to be concentrated at a single point. The enemy's bomb is then assumed to have the following character: If it lands beyond a certain distance (called the lethal radius) the target survives untouched. If the bomb lands closer to the target than the lethal radius the target is assumed to be totally destroyed. The use of such concepts as point targets and lethal radii are mathematical idealizations that introduce inaccuracies into the analysis, but for our purposes these concepts will be satisfactory. I want to introduce one more concept, the circular probable error, usually and illogically abbreviated CEP. The CEP is a measure of delivery accuracy. It is the radius of a circle about the target point within which, on the average, half of the bombs will fall.

619

The other half, on the average, fall outside. Denoting the lethal radius by R and the CEP by C, we can write down a simple formula for the probability that a target point will survive an attack of n bombs.

$$S = (\tfrac{1}{2})^{\left(\frac{nR^2}{C^2}\right)} \tag{1}$$

The effect of hardening is to decrease the lethal radius R. An approximate formula for the lethal radius of a megaton weapon against hard targets (greater than about 30 psi) is given by:

$$R = \left(\frac{46W}{P-15}\right)^{\tfrac{1}{3}} \tag{2}$$

where W is the yield of the attacking weapon in megatons, P is the equivalent static resistance of target in psi and R is the lethal radius in miles.

If we substitute from Equation 2 into Equation 1 we get approximately

$$S = (\tfrac{1}{2})^E$$

where

$$E = \frac{10nW^{\tfrac{2}{3}}}{C^2(P-15)^{\tfrac{2}{3}}} \tag{3}$$

I have reduced the numerical value of the exponent (E) slightly, partly to take into account certain experimental weapons effects that do not show up in idealized calculations and partly to make the numerical coefficient come out an even 10.

Roughly speaking, when the E is of the order of 1, the system is probably not an ideal one from either the enemy's point of view or ours. From our point of view we have been one-half destroyed while from the enemy's point of view one-half of us survives his attack. Therefore, the exponent equal to 1 represents an interesting value to both sides. One question we can ask is, How large an attack must the enemy make (i.e., how many bombs must be dropped) if he is to make (E) equal to 1? This is given by setting E in Equation 4 equal to 1 and solving for n. We get

$$n = \frac{C^2(P-15)^{\tfrac{2}{3}}}{10W^{\tfrac{2}{3}}} \tag{4}$$

Let us for the moment assume that P is 231 (to make $P-15$ a perfect cube). Then $(P-15)^{\tfrac{2}{3}} = 36$ and

$$n = 3.6\frac{C^2}{W^{\tfrac{2}{3}}} \tag{5}$$

For manned bombers C is supposed to be substantially less than a mile. Even if it were as large as one mile the enemy would only have to carry about 7 MT to get a 50 per cent chance of destroying our 231 psi shelters. It will certainly be feasible for him to carry such loads in the time period we are talking about (1960–1970). Furthermore, even if we raised the resistance of the shelters by a factor of about 4 (which seems to be about the current *technical* limit for a B-52 shelter) the enemy might still get by with only one bomb, either by increasing his yield by the same factor of 4 or by cutting his CEP to one-half mile. Either of these might be feasible in the indicated time period. At first sight, therefore, shelters seem to hold little promise as a defense against manned bombers. (We will have some qualifying remarks to make about this later.)

The same kind of analysis might make shelters look much better against the ICBM, at least during the early part of this time period. The reason is that W is expected to be smaller and C to be larger for the ICBM than for the bomber. While we do not know what the CEP or yield of the Russian ICBM will be, few seem to think that it will be as good as a bomber's. Most technical people think it will be much less and that the ICBM's performance will remain less than the bomber's for some time. If one assumes that the ICBM has half the accuracy of our assumed bomber and substitutes two miles in the formula, one finds that n must be approximately 4 to cause 50 per cent damage. If we substitute 5 miles, it takes about twenty-five bombs to cause 50 per cent damage. Shelters now become a potentially fruitful possibility.

Any way of preventing the enemy's bombs from landing close to a shelter can make a hard shelter very useful. The most obvious way of doing this is to keep the enemy uncertain by a few miles of the exact location of the shelter. While it is often said that this tactic is available to the Soviets but not to us, this just seems another example of our unwillingness to take the problem seriously. If we apply both money and administrative talent to the problem it should be possible to keep the *exact* location of most hardened installations secret. For example, we could locate missiles in large government reservations where the exact records of the location of each missile were kept separate at each reservation and no master list made. In order to prevent clandestine observers from disclosing the location we could plan a lot of decoy installations or camouflage the actual installations, or do both. As for keeping things classified during construction, we could use more cleared people and let fewer outsiders know what is happening. All of these seem feasible if we are willing to subject ourselves to moderate expense and trouble. As an example of the frivolous type of objection that is raised to this kind of proposal, consider the idea that we will not be able to prevent private flyers from going over these areas. While they are a very important group politically, they also happen to be a rather patriotic group. Patriotic or not, if we take the issue seriously we can ban them and make the ban stick.

There are also special possibilities for active defense against missiles if we are only trying to shoot down those missiles that have trajectories which indicate landings close to the target point. This makes it very much more difficult for the enemy to saturate and to spoof. Insofar as the enemy uses terminal guidance, rather simple jamming techniques may be effective in causing CEP's of the order of a few miles. This is another field where we are sadly wanting in research. Still, some work has been done.

Let us now look at the second role shelters can play. Even if the CEP of the enemy were so small that he could depend on hitting anything he aimed at, we might still want to use shelters. Hardening of this kind reduces the lethal radius of the enemy's weapon and usually, therefore, the cost of dispersal. For example, against an unhardened bomber base or ICBM installation, a one-megaton bomb is likely to have a lethal radius of five miles or more. If the same base is hardened to about 35 psi, the lethal radius of the same weapon is cut to about a mile. Even if the enemy had zero CEP and perfectly reliable weapons, so that he could always destroy whatever he aimed at, we could still force him to use *many* one-megaton weapons by separating the installations. While unhardened installations would have to be about ten miles apart, if they were hardened the distance would be (for a one-megaton weapon) only about two miles. Those knowledgeable on the operation of airplane and missile bases will know that dispersal tends to be expensive. It could easily be worthwhile to spend some money on hardening in order to decrease the degree of dispersal required.

This kind of dispersal (where a single base is spread out) is called microscopic dispersal. It is to be compared with what is called macroscopic dispersal, where the target points are separated by extremely large distances so that each point will unquestionably be a separate target. In the latter case, these points must be operated as separate bases. This further increases costs and complicates the peacetime operation.

Contingency Design

Let me digress to give a qualitative picture of how one decides how hard he should make his shelters. This is an oversimplified version of an analysis made by RAND and others. Let us start with a certain sum of money to be allocated between the offensive part of a weapons system and/or its protection—with particular emphasis on protection by shelters. Assume that we judge the effectiveness of our force by the amount of damage that it is to do to the enemy. The question then is: What percentage of the money should be spent on shelters and what percentage on the offensive system, that is, on the bomb carriers and associated equipment?

At least two cases require attention: first, when our offensive carriers get off before the enemy's bombs have landed, and second, when they do not. The first case corresponds to our starting the war, thus preempting or at least getting some kind of warning. The second case (when we do not succeed in launching our attack before his bombs land) is considered, for a whole series of reasons, to be the most important in the ICBM era.

Figure 1 summarizes a typical analysis for the two cases under some appropriate assumptions. In the "we strike first" (or "we get off before") case it is obviously wasteful to spend money on protective construction. If we get off before the bombs land our offensive forces do not need any protection (unless, of course, we wish to protect facilities for use in a

❖❖

Figure I

Simplified analysis of the value of protective construction

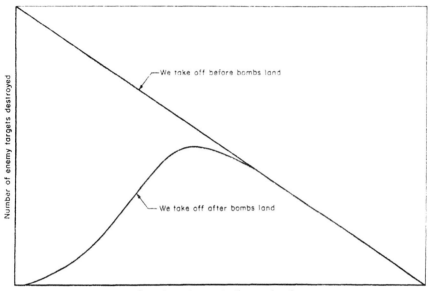

❖❖

possible second strike). In the "we strike after bombs land" case, it is disastrous not to have hardening or to have only moderate amounts. The value of hardening increases quite sharply after a certain minimal level, rises to a peak, and then decreases relatively slowly.

The reason for the rather small payoff from moderate amounts of hardening and the sudden increase once a threshold is passed is found in Equation 3, which shows that the hardening term $(P\text{-}15)$ appears in the denominator of an exponent. It is the nature of such a formula that, for any reasonable relation between the level of protection and its cost, the over-all system performance will have the behavior we have just discussed. The reason why the two curves join is obvious. If you overharden a great deal, it does not make any difference whether you strike first or second—the enemy cannot touch you. The reason you go down to zero eventually is that if you spend everything on hardening you have nothing left for attacking.

It has been found that such simple curves are useful, but that they can be very misleading; the problem must be analyzed in a more sophisticated way. Recommendations based on any analyses made with a single set of assumptions might be completely changed if the assumptions were changed. In an analysis there are always uncertainties and controversies, but there are sensible ways to treat such uncertainties. Contrary to much popular opinion, the results of a "good" analysis are not arbitrary. For our purpose, we need only take the first step toward a sophisticated analysis and look at what might happen if, in addition to using the "best" assumptions, we also looked at pessimistic and optimistic ones.

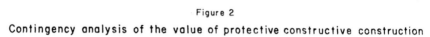

Figure 2

Contingency analysis of the value of protective constructive construction

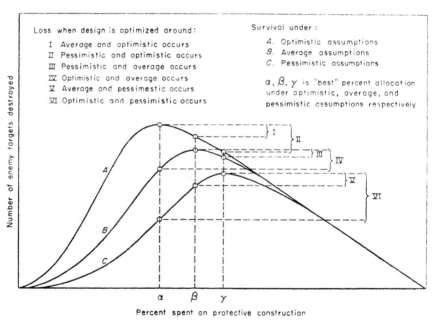

Percent spent on protective construction

Figure 2 shows hypothetical results of a contingency analysis for a "you strike after bombs land" case, giving the three sets of assumptions: pessimistic, best guess, and optimistic. One important thing to notice is that in this case, the losses are much worse if one uses the best guess. Analysis seems to indicate that it is a disaster not to harden enough and only moderately wasteful to harden too much. Both statements are to be taken within reason, of course.

When one talks about hardening he should generally also talk about an insurance factor; that is, one should not ask what is the minimum capability that the enemy is likely to have: rather, what is the maximum? This procedure may seem to involve unnecessary expense. While hardening programs for a strategic air force look expensive in an absolute sense (since they are in the billions of dollars), they are inexpensive relative to the cost of the total weapons system. Still, a billion dollars more or less remains a lot of money, especially if it is to be spent for such unromantic things as concrete, reinforcing steel, and holes in the ground. Moreover, the things the extra money buys do not show up in a glamorous way. Hardening of installations is a far cry from thinking of the arms race in terms of national prestige and international relations. In this area we must not be afraid of being called "Maginot-minded." We simply must ask: What happens if the enemy hits us? To shirk an answer is to increase our danger beyond reasonable limits.

IV

A PROPOSED CIVIL DEFENSE PROGRAM *

I URGE that the federal government allocate a minimum of $500 million over and above the current budget (about $50,000,000 per year) for expenditure in one or two years to achieve five objectives in the civil defense area. These objectives are:

1. The creation of capabilities—incomplete but worthwhile—by strengthening and changing the focus of current civil defense programs. There should be the creation of feasible *evacuation measures, improvisation of fallout protection, provision for control of damage, and modest preparations for recuperation.* Given these other measures, there ought to be the institution of vigorous programs of education and technical assistance for private organizations, key individuals, and the general public.

Inexpensive measures might save from twenty to fifty million lives! Contingent damage to property would be limited. Our ability to recuperate would be markedly improved. And an environment in which private citizens could do sensible things on their own to increase their chances of survival would be created. Are these things worth the effort? Anybody who can make the distinctions in Table 3, Tragic but Distinguishable Postwar States, will think they are.

2. There needs to be research and development on many aspects of the art of nonmilitary defense. Unlike R&D on military matters, nonmilitary defense has received comparatively little money and effort (except the efforts of a few dedicated and hard-working officials and volunteers in our cities). Imaginative research could not only result in large improvements in the effectiveness of defense measures, but it would inevitably uncover many unsuspected problems. After an attack these would surely pose many unpleasant surprises. Even the small RAND study indicated that a modest but properly directed research effort would pay enormous dividends.

3. Accompanying the research and development work should come a vigorous effort on the systems design of various combinations of military

* Most of the material in this section derives from The RAND Corporation Research Memorandum RM-2206-RC, "Some Specific Suggestions for Obtaining Early Nonmilitary Defense Capabilities and Initiating Long-range Programs," by Herman Kahn, et al. That report was originally prepared in 1957, and was circulated in a limited fashion to various individuals for information and comment. Minor modifications have been made in the material to correspond to some changes in my viewpoint, but from a research standpoint there has been no thorough-going revision. The dollar recommendations may be considered as quantitative expressions of intuitive judgments; still, I probably have substantially more justification for my estimates than do many official proposals in this field. These things are inevitably uncertain. For reasonable programs, the over-all performance variations accompanying minor changes in allocations are so small that as a researcher, citizen, voter, and taxpayer, I am prepared to defend the numerical recommendations—even if as an analyst I have to concede that there is incomplete documentation.

626

and nonmilitary defense. This effort should produce specifications, including phasing, for many alternative programs. These specifications should be of sufficient detail to permit their costing and performance to be calculated over time and under many circumstances. Paper planning and design should be undertaken for a number of the alternatives so that any program finally adopted would be less costly and have its lead time reduced (perhaps by three to five years over conventional methods of proceeding).

4. While it is now technically feasible to start a large-scale program of nonmilitary defense, there are many uncertainties and gaps in our knowledge. After the second and third objectives have been accomplished, the proper balance between military and nonmilitary expenditures can be studied. The government could then make wiser decisions, and some of our past and present difficulties resulting from a combination of ignorance and uncertainty would be eliminated or decreased. (The decision to go ahead or *not to go ahead* with a multibillion-dollar program should not be made until objectives 2 and 3 have been carried out. But objectives 2 and 3 should be pursued vigorously so as not to delay this important decision unnecessarily.)

5. There seem to be many possibilities for inexpensive preparatory actions that could result in the creation of important capabilities in the years 1960–70. Irrespective of any decision to go or not go into a multibillion-dollar program, these possibilities should be studied; if and when such actions are found desirable they should be put into practice.

A possible allocation for the additional $500 million to be spent on civil defense might go as follows:

1. Radiation Meters	$100,000,000 + [1]
2. Utilization of Existing Structures for Fallout Protection	150,000,000 +
3. Preliminary Research and Development of a Spectrum of Shelter Programs	75,000,000
4. Movement, Damage Control, and Anti-contamination, etc.	75,000,000 +
5. Systems Studies and Planning	10,000,000
6. Other Research and Development	20,000,000
7. Prototype Shelters	30,000,000
8. Education and Technical Assistance	25,000,000
9. Miscellaneous	15,000,000
	$500,000,000 +

The above program can be divided conceptually into a short-range program for capabilities-in-being and a preparatory program for the more distant future. However, there is much overlap and joint use in the two programs; therefore I do not budget them separately.

[1] Federal share of expenditures; the + after these numbers indicates that they might well be supplemented by state, city, and private funds stimulated by the program.

About 60 to 70 per cent of the $500 million would be spent for capabilities useful if a war started in the immediate future. Because the possible gains are so large it should be unnecessary to have to justify spending such a small sum of money except to indicate that the gains are plausible, even though there are some natural uncertainties about the final results. Three hundred million dollars is a very small sum to spend to try to make the difference between a relatively expeditious recovery for the survivors of a war and slow—or no—recovery; to buy the kinds of capabilities that would determine whether or not the Russians might be able to blackmail us; and to save tens of millions of lives.

About 30 to 40 per cent of the $500 million in our proposed budget, or less than $200 million, is allocated to research, analysis, development, planning, and design for a spectrum of civil defense programs. This may seem to be a great deal of money to spend on producing pieces of paper and prototypes. *But I believe that $200 million is a reasonable sum of money to spend on finding out how best to secure the lives and property of the nation.* I would regard the proposed research program as a mandatory condition to any decision to spend large sums on passive defense itself. And this research ought to be undertaken before continuing our lethargy any further.

Is $200 million an unreasonably large sum? Compared to past research budgets for FCDA and OCDM of less than 1 per cent of this amount, $200 million seems outrageously large. Yet it once cost from $50 to $100 million to develop an engine for a military airplane, $100 to $200 million to develop an interceptor aircraft, and $500 million to $1 billion to develop an intercontinental bomber. These dollar figures should now be multiplied by about five. The Atlas and Titan development programs cost between $1 and $2 billion. The Department of Defense spends more than $5 billion every year on military research and development. A complete nonmilitary defense program is at least as complicated and valuable as an old-style interceptor aircraft, and to begrudge spending $200 million because we have refused to come to grips with this problem in the past is simply to repeat the old error.

Perhaps $200 million is too little to be spending on long-range programs. Some people suggest the immediate initiation of large-scale passive defense programs that would cost in the neighborhood of $25 billion. It is improbable that very large sums could be spent *efficiently* on construction in the next year or two. If the attempt were made without a prior program of the sort we are suggesting, it is almost certain that not only would the wrong sorts of personal protection be procured, but there would also be major, and maybe disastrous, inadequacies and lacunae in the over-all program. From a sophisticated and hard-headed point of view, the main justification for the large program would be that this is the most practical way to get the small program. I have two objections to this "real politics" approach. It is expensive. Doing the small program for its own sake, rather than as a by-product of a large program, means that we will do it better, concentrating attention on the main issues of

What, How, and When (rather than have everybody's time and attention taken up with a large program of construction).

Certain inexpensive or flexible measures, a Preattack Mobilization Base for civil defense for example, might accompany and be based on the results of the research program. Procurement of materials likely to cause bottlenecks in a larger program—corrugated, reinforcing and structural steel, cement, and other building materials—would not only prevent a lag in the completion date of even the largest later programs but would put us in a position to initiate a crash program in one or two years if the international situation deteriorated.

To repeat: a decision to go ahead or *not go ahead* on a multibillion-dollar program *should be made separately from and subsequent to the completion of the proposed $200-million research program.*

Still addressing myself for the moment to the proponents of large programs, there is at least one good reason why the government may now be loath to make a commitment for shelters. The shelter program itself has been looked at in only a superficial way, and many of the problems associated with preserving a civilization and a standard of living have not been looked at even superficially. While The RAND Corporation study I directed tried to look at these over-all problems and concentrated on the question, How does the country look five or ten years after the war as a function of our preparations?, we scarcely scratched the surface. We believe we have shown that it is plausible that in the immediate future with inexpensive measures the United States could be an acceptable place to live even a year after the war. However, we concede that the uncertainties are large enough to raise the question of sheer survival, and the problem gets more severe in the later time periods.

Until the feasibility of recovery and other long-term problems and their solutions are settled, it will be hard to arouse real interest in attempts to alleviate the consequence of war. But it is possible to settle these questions relatively inexpensively and at the same time to avoid delaying the completion date for a full program for the immediate acquisition of moderate capabilities. The $200,000,000 of the proposed civil defense budget should be spent on what might be termed a cheap Preattack Mobilization Base: the time-consuming preliminary phases of research, development, analysis, planning, and design portions for a major civil defense program.

The preliminary activity should not be restricted to any prechosen program. The scale of the final program will presumably be determined by the results of these investigations and the international situation at the time. It should not be fixed prematurely. It is also most important to consider explicitly time periods in the late 1960's and early 1970's. Unless we start work soon on the long-range programs needed to ameliorate the effects of the potentially very destructive attacks of this time period, we will find that we have irrevocably lost many valuable opportunities to guide economic growth into the proper channels.

The goal here in allocating funds to projects is not that every dollar be spent economically, but rather to give every subject adequate coverage. While we were generous, we tried to refrain from padding. Although our figure of $200 million is only approximate, it may be low if an adequate job of research, development, systems analysis, planning, and design is to be undertaken. Many of the potential civil defense programs are so expensive that it is worthwhile to spend money speculatively if there is any chance at all that the over-all program would be helped by even a small percentage. This is one reason why the aim should not be to see that every dime is spent in full knowledge that it will result in a successful project, but rather to see that all possibly fruitful avenues are explored. Otherwise, there may be disastrous inadequacies or even complete lacunae in the program that is finally adopted.

Such a many-sided program of study, planning, and innovation requires a strong *monitoring effort* of a sort that is not common in most government agencies. This effort has to be much more than the ordinary R&D administration. The monitors must maintain a close and continuous observation of all the programs and constantly evaluate their direction and results. While they should be able to suggest the termination of fruitless research activity, their main purpose should be to encourage the expansion of promising effort. Most important, they must be alert to identify gaps and inadequacies in the programs and to suggest remedial action.

Because of their crucial role, the monitors must obviously be exceptionally competent and well-informed leaders. However, the monitors do not need and should not have the authority to orient all programs toward predetermined objectives. Experience has shown that attempts to over-coordinate programs tend to create inflexibility and to stifle new, unproven ideas or independent approaches. Hence, the monitors should act as an advisory group rather than as a "research czar." But they must have the authority to make suggestions and offer criticism at all levels and to have the right to contact the researchers or planners in the field.

The monitoring group could be located in the independent long-range planning organization, mentioned in Appendix I, and act for the various government agencies that will be principally concerned with the non-military defense effort, or it could be a special group in OCDM or under the Presidential Assistant for National Security Affairs. In order to maintain a good feel for the program as a whole and to foresee future requirements, the monitors should be closely associated with the systems analysis and operations research program. Perhaps they should also have direct access to funds for small studies or pilot projects.

The Full Program [2]

A general description of the $500,000,000 program will make clearer what I have in mind. Somewhat more detail can be found in the previously

---

[2] Something like this program is now being done by OCDM, but on about $1/10$ to $1/20$ of the suggested scale.

mentioned RAND Corporation Report, RM 2206-RC, on deposit in major libraries.

1. Radiation Meters ($100,000,000)

Our program calls for $2 million for dose-rate meters (at about $20 a meter), $10 million for self-reading dosimeters (at about $5 a meter, including an allowance for chargers), and $20 to $50 million for very simple dosimeters (at about $1 to $2 a meter).

A portion, but not all, of the meters would be distributed before hostilities. The rest would not be distributed until a "National Emergency" occurred or until the postattack period. They should be stored with this in mind. In the case of the simple dosimeter, it may be cheaper and just as satisfactory to create a protected, standby manufacturing capacity. The final distribution of meters might go somewhat as follows: 500,000 dose-rate or survey meters to the large shelters (capable of sheltering more than, say, 50 persons); 1,000,000 to outdoor workers of various types, such as farmers, prospectors, foresters, construction workers, and so on; 250,000 to individuals and organizations in various towns and cities; and 250,000 to the working teams discussed below under item 4.

The self-reading dosimeters would be distributed approximately as follows: 2,500,000 to the work parties (discussed under No. 4 below); 2,500,000 to shelters, schools, and other places; and 5,000,000 to the people who work out-of-doors in possibly uncontrolled environments. The $1 to $2 dosimeters would be issued to everybody who is in an even moderately hot area and is not working under completely controlled conditions. The total budget allocated above is more than $100 million, but we think the number of meters suggested could be obtained and distributed if the government were to allocate only that amount. The rest of the cost could be handled by "stimulated" expenditures for meters by local governments, private groups, and individuals following federal guidance.

2. Utilization of Existing Structures for Fallout Protection ($150,000,000)

About $50 million would be spent on identifying, counting, and labeling the various structures that either provide valuable levels of fallout protection as they now stand or can easily be modified to do so. The rest of the money would be spent for such supplies as radios, minimal toilet equipment (even things as primitive as buckets), and possibly minimum food supplies (candy bars, multipurpose foods, and such). Materials for improving the protection of the shelter would be needed. The survey should discover places that can be used as improvised fallout shelters with various amounts of advance warning—one hour, two hours, four hours, eight hours, sixteen hours, two days, two weeks, and even longer. Detailed plans would reveal the different kinds of improvisations that are possible as a function of the available time.

3. Preliminary Phase (including Research and Development) of a Spectrum of Shelter Programs ($75,000,000)

An apparently short-sighted thing that OCDM did in the late 1950's, I think, was to reduce its expenditures on the study of blast shelters. This was done partly because of a lack of funds but mostly because it was not part of the current "National Shelter Policy" to have blast shelters. As I have tried to stress in this book, we just do not know today what we will want five or ten years from now; current programs and requirements should not over-influence current research and development. We should not prejudge these unknown future desires of ours by failing to undertake inexpensive preliminary work on many more things than we expect to procure. It is only by having a broad base of research and development that we can expect to understand our problems and be in a position to have a flexible procurement policy.

These last remarks have special point for research and development and even preliminary programming in the shelter field. It is clear that if the international situation had already deteriorated to the point where we felt there was a high probability that we would have to fight a war, we would now be instituting a very luxurious shelter system, indeed. It may turn out that, given the possibilities for weapons development, a pure fallout system will not be adequate in the late 1960's and early 1970's. Thus the shelter studies should investigate the many different levels of protection that would be compatible with programs costing as little as $2 or $3 billion—or as much as $200 billion.

A possible allocation for the $75,000,000 I have suggested for shelters would be as follows:

Theoretical work in the response of structures	$ 1,000,000
Theoretical work in design	1,000,000
Basic designs	3,000,000
Experimental testing	15,000,000
Detailed study of:	
10 large cities	10,000,000
10 medium cities	5,000,000
10 towns and rural areas	5,000,000
Study of geology and underground possibilities	10,000,000
Study of nonpersonnel shelters	10,000,000
Special equipment	10,000,000
Miscellaneous	5,000,000
	$75,000,000

4. Movement, Damage Control, Anticontamination ($75,000,000)

The two main things we should hope to provide under this category are the capability to evacuate to improvised protection and the creation of a core of "reservists" that would be organized to facilitate the evacuation, and the improvisation of shelters pre- or postattack. The latter would also be useful during the immediate postattack and longer run rescue, decontamination, debris clearing, continuity of government, housing, and repair problems. There are at least five million people in the United States who have the proper skills for such work. We should sign up 200,000 of these people as part-time but paid cadres and as many others as possible as unpaid part-time cadres or just available volunteers. The 200,000 people might go through a one-week or two-week training course every year. In wartime, or in a tense preattack situation, we should plan to expand them by a factor of 5 to 20. Such an organization would probably cost about $500 per man per year, or about $100 million per year for 200,000 people. However, it would be practically impossible to spend more than $25 to $50 million in the first year or two when this group is being organized, and this is the amount in our budget. This cadre might be supplemented (or replaced) by the military reserves.

Another $25 to $50 million would go for all the measures that are needed to create different kinds of potentially useful evacuation capabilities. What money is left, probably around $10 to $30 million, would be used to study and implement the damage-control measures that will be necessary to limit the bonus damage when cities, factories, and homes are abandoned, to control fires, and to provide some additional protection for some government or crucial commercial stocks. This last figure is very definitely an allotment and not an estimate.

5. Systems Studies and Planning ($10,000,000)

The program described to this point has been composed mainly of interim measures intended to fill the gap until we can decide what our long-range plans should be.

Among the first things to be studied and planned for are the different kinds of nonmilitary defense systems needed for various situations, and how we can build large degrees of flexibility into our programs. We must design systems that will put us in a position where we can exploit favorable circumstances and hedge against unfavorable ones. Probably the worst defect of civil defense planning today is that it tends to concentrate on a single set of assumptions and circumstances; concentration is on a surprise attack directed at civilians. This set happens to be the most difficult to handle. As a result, civil defense recommendations have not been tested against a large number of possibilities. For example, as soon as one takes seriously the possibility of a *tense situation*, one gets interested in evacuation. Proposed plans should not only consider a large range of circumstances, they should also consider phasing problems. Then we will get early capabilities and still be able to accommodate growth in the future—particularly growth required by either unexpectedly large threats or higher standards. Some of the situations that might be studied are:

a. Movement of the population to shelters, considering warnings of minutes, or of 1 to 3 hours, and 10 to 20 hours; partial strategic evacuation during an ordinary crisis and almost complete strategic evacuation during tense situations.

b. The various attack-response patterns suggested in the lectures.

c. Enemy tactics corresponding to three possible enemy target objectives: military, population, and recuperation—or mixtures of these three.

d. Civil defense postures as influenced or determined by many things. Among these are variations in our own or enemy objectives, budget levels and allocations, disarmament, degrees of tension, changes in NATO, Chinese developments, other Russian satellite developments, and so on.

e. Other strategic and tactical considerations. For example, the study of sneak attacks and other unconventional tactics or weapons. Re-attacks, and various ways that war can be terminated, might also be subjected to analysis.

f. World-wide planning.

g. Basic technical uncertainties to be studied and allowed for include the performance and effects of weapons, carriers, air defense systems, medical unknowns, and so on.

In addition, all studies should be conducted with an eye to understanding and exploiting interactions between military and nonmilitary defenses. Some areas in which these interactions occur, and some proposed research projects, are:

a. The circumstances in which wars can start should be examined to determine what roles can be played by augmentation abilities brought into play in tense situations, on D-day, or even after D-day. For the civil defense Preattack Mobilization Base the study of the conflicting and complementary requirements for the corresponding military prewar mobilization capability is important. Lastly (and most important) we must re-examine the requirements for civil defense in different kinds of long (2–30 days) war situations.

b. Civil defense contributes to the over-all problem by reducing the job of air defense and air offense to manageable proportions. Thus large military budgets are made more acceptable. (Fighting and winning a war takes more military power than is needed for pure deterrence.) Use of nuclear weapons in air defense is made safer and more flexible. Important elements of our air defense and air offense capabilities are protected as a by-product of civil defense preparations.

c. On the military side, air defense provides warning, increases the enemy's raid-size requirements (even for minimum-objective attacks), forces him to use expensive carriers and tactics, cuts down his force, and decreases his bombing accuracy. Air defense may provide time against ICBM attacks by killing the first few missiles so that people can get into shelters.

d. Air offense (and effective active and passive defense) forces the enemy to buy expensive defenses to counter the U.S. Credible First Strike Capability. Air offense also draws his attacks (particularly his first strike) away from population and recuperation targets, ends the war quickly either by destroying the enemy or forcing him to negotiate, and complicates the enemy's job by being dispersed, hard, and alert.

It might be appropriate at this point to comment on some of the characteristics of *good analyses and plans*, particularly the treatment of uncertainty. The worst mistake made in civil defense planning in the past has been to overemphasize a simple or a small number of contingencies and assumptions as opposed to the many cases I have suggested for study. The following lengthy quotation is from a report by Irwin Mann and myself and will therefore appear as ordinary text.[3]

An item of equipment cannot be fully analyzed in isolation; frequently its interaction with the entire environment, including other equipment, has to be considered. The art of systems analysis is born of this fact; systems demand analysis *as systems*.

Systems are analyzed with the intention of describing, evaluating, improving, and comparing with other systems. In the early days many people naïvely thought that this last meant picking a single definite quantitative measure of effectiveness, finding a best set of assumptions, and then using modern mathematics and high-speed computers to carry out the computations. Often their professional bias led them to believe that the central issues revolved around what kind of mathematics to use and how to use the computer.

With some exceptions, the early picture was illusory. First, there is the trivial point that even modern techniques are not usually powerful enough to treat even simple practical problems without great simplification and idealization. The ability and knowledge necessary to do this simplification and idealization is not always standard equipment of scientists and mathematicians or even of their practical military collaborators.

Much more important, the concept of a simple optimizing calculation ignores the central role of uncertainty. The uncertainty arises not only because we do not actually know what we have (much less what the enemy has) or what is going to happen, but also because we cannot agree on what we are trying to do.

In practice, three kinds of uncertainty can be distinguished:
1. Statistical Uncertainty
2. Real Uncertainty
3. Uncertainty about the Enemy's Actions

We will mention each of these uncertainties in turn.

Statistical Uncertainty. This is the kind of uncertainty that pertains to fluctuation phenomena and random variables. It is the uncertainty associated with "honest" gambling devices. There are almost no conceptual difficulties in treating it—it merely makes the problems *computationally* more complicated.

Real Uncertainty. This is the uncertainty that arises from the fact that people believe different assumptions, have different tastes (and therefore

[3] Herman Kahn and Irwin Mann, *Techniques of Systems Analysis*, The RAND Corporation, Research Memorandum RM-1829-1, June 1957.

objectives), and are (more often than not) ignorant. It has been argued by scholars that any single individual can, perhaps, treat this uncertainty as being identical to the statistical uncertainty mentioned above, but it is in general impossible for a group to do this in any satisfactory way.[4] For example, it is possible for individuals to assign subjectively evaluated numbers to such things as the probability of war or the probability of success of a research program, but there is typically no way of getting a useful consensus on these numbers. Usually, the best that can be done is to set limits between which most reasonable people agree the probabilities lie.

The fact that people have different objectives has almost the same conceptual effect on the design of a socially satisfactory system as the disagreement about empirical assumptions. People value differently, for example, deterring a war as opposed to winning it or alleviating its consequences, if deterrence fails; they ascribe different values to human lives (some even differentiate between different categories of human lives, such as civilian and military, or friendly, neutral, and enemy), future preparedness vs. present, preparedness vs. current standard of living, aggressive vs. defensive policies, etc. Our category, "Real Uncertainty," covers differences in objectives as well as differences in assumptions.

The treatment of real uncertainty is somewhat controversial, but we believe actually fairly well understood, practically. It is handled mainly by what we call, "Contingency Design."

Uncertainty Due to Enemy Reaction. This uncertainty is a curious and baffling mixture of statistical and real uncertainty, complicated by the fact that we are playing a non-zero-sum game.[5] It is often very difficult to treat satisfactorily. A reasonable guiding principle seems to be (at least for a rich country), to compromise designs so as to be prepared for the possibility that the enemy is bright, knowledgeable, and malevolent, and yet be able to exploit the situation if the enemy fails in any of these qualities.

To be specific: To assume that the enemy is bright means giving him the freedom (for the purpose of analysis) to use the resources he has in the way that is best for him, even if you do not think he is smart enough to do so.

To assume that he is knowledgeable means giving the enemy credit for knowing your weaknesses if he could have found out about them by using reasonable effort. You should be willing to do this even though you yourself have just learned about these weaknesses.

To assume that the enemy is malevolent means that you will at least look at the case where the enemy does what is worst for you—even though it may not be rational for him to do this. This is sometimes an awful pros-

---

[4] See the discussion on committees on pages 120–124.

[5] The terminology "non-zero-sum game," refers to any conflict situation where there are gains to be achieved if the contenders cooperate. Among other things, this introduces the possibilities of implicit or explicit bargaining between the two contenders. Many of our concepts of deterrence come out of the notion that the game we are playing with Russia is non-zero-sum.

pect and, in addition, plainly pessimistic, so one may wish to design against a "rational" rather than a malevolent enemy; but as much as possible, one should carry some insurance against the latter possibility. (The quotation from *Techniques of Systems Analysis* ends here.)

6. Other Research and Development ($20,000,000)

This is for miscellaneous research in the medical, biological, food, agricultural, anticontamination, and fallout areas. The AEC currently spends about the allotted sum every year to study the inherently simpler problem of peacetime fallout from tests. The equally important special wartime problems are mostly being neglected.

7. Prototype Shelters ($20,000,000)

I would suggest building about 10 million dollars' worth of large shelters which, if economically feasible, might include some peacetime functions. In addition to customary shelters, this program should include more elaborate shelters and high over-pressure shelters. The other $10 million should go for private family-type shelters, running an average of, say, $1,000 apiece. This should enable us to build 10,000 shelters, or one for every 20,000 people. This means that every town in the United States would have one or more prototype shelters for people to see and examine.

8. Education and Technical Assistance ($25,000,000)

It is one of the major objectives of the above program to create an environment in which private citizens and organizations can do sensible things on their own.

I feel that at least part of the present apathy in the United States is due to ignorance of what can be done. It is also due to doubt that *anything* can be done. This apathy is intensified by the regrettable inadequacy of official pamphlets. The problem does not result from security restrictions or inadequate releases of information. The official studies behind the pamphlets are inadequate. Better studies and more definitive government programs are needed. Realistic long-range planning, such as we are proposing, would go far toward restoring public confidence in the merits of government plans and suggestions. Even more effectively, the institution of the "cheap" program, which depends mainly on improvised fallout shelters, would encourage many to build more adequate shelters of their own. As long as there is no reasonable over-all program, few will undertake private actions.

In addition to general information, the government should offer to share some of the private expenses. However, because of the small size of the program, the government should not contribute anything toward private projects unless it gets a great deal of leverage for its money. One of the easiest ways to get such leverage would be for the government to spend small sums of money on the preliminary phases of the private projects—that is, it should be willing to go to a private company with a complete set of blueprints showing that company what it would have to do if it participated in a serious way in such a program. This would enable the company, without spending any of its own money or much energy, to get specific ideas of the cost and performance of its own program. It would help eliminate the inertia that might otherwise prevent companies from initiating action. The government should do similar things for private persons, not only by furnishing complete blueprints for either the modification of existing buildings, or for the incorporation of protection in new buildings, but also by offering technical assistance in the design and treatment of special problems. It should also furnish free technical services to architects, engineers, and others.

In addition to helping private companies and individuals, the government should try to elicit as much help from the nongovernmental part of our society as it can. For example, once the research program has provided some indication of what a reasonable passive defense program should involve, the government should enlist the help of private professional groups to expedite some of the necessary intellectual and technical developments. Some of the organizations whose aid might be solicited include:

American Society for Civil Engineers
American Concrete Institute
American Bar Association
American Medical Association
American Institute of Architects
National Planning Association
Committee for Economic Development
Chambers of Commerce
National Bureau of Economic Research
American Association of Railroads
American Society for Testing of Materials
American Society for Mechanical Engineers
American Society for Electrical Engineers
American Society for Heating and Ventilating
National Association of Manufacturers

In the past, private groups have sometimes put time and energy into studies for the government, but a lack of adequate orientation has often meant that their studies were obsolete before they were published. It is important, both for the morale of the participants and the usefulness of their product, that realistic environments and planning assumptions be given to such groups. For example, the American Society of Civil Engineers (ASCE) was once reported to be considering a standard for the protection of buildings in large cities, on the order of 5 to 10 psi. Such buildings might not be useless in some situations, but they would certainly be useless if bombs dropped nearby. I would propose that a much more useful activity for the ASCE would be to look at joint-use blast and thermal resistant construction for small cities and rural areas rather than for large cities. An even more useful thing, and one which we would urge be done with a high priority, would be to look at the possibilities for joint-use fallout protection to be used with varying amounts (minutes, hours, or days) of warning. Thus buildings might be built to use sandbags or fillable shutters that could be put up at the last moment. There are many ways to construct buildings that would provide existing or improvisatorial protection. The possibilities are so promising that an appreciable portion of an expensive fallout program might be saved (though only a *portion*). It is clear there are many other examples where private organizations could be useful. Universities and foundations, for example, could make major research contributions. I include "education" in the total program, because when one improvises from existing assets it is important for many people to understand reasonably well what they should do. The government, unfortunately, has a tendency to try to depend upon education and paper plans to do everything, rather than to spend even small sums for capabilities that would make the educational program realistic and useful. Let us agree right now that our society cannot be preserved in a war by individual action supplemented by no more than government pamphlets and paper plans. I suspect that the major educational impact will come, not from the formal program of information or propaganda, but from the impact of reasonably large government resources allotted to a program that government is willing to *defend* intellectually. Then some will understand that the program is a serious effort, one that you do not have to be a "crackpot" or "wishful thinker" to join in! Conversely, if the government tries to accomplish this program by education alone, if it is unwilling itself to invest a few hundred million dollars (and thereby shows that it has little confidence in the effort) then we should not be surprised *if the program fails completely.*

It may turn out that the government does not wish to engage in a program as ambitious as the one described, modest as it may seem to many of us in the planning field. We suggest that the government try to do at least the following:

1. Reorient government planning, both military and nonmilitary, to the proper kind of short and long wars; in particular, make explicit preparations for improvising preattack and postattack capabilities.

2. Reorient current stockpile programs to contribute to postwar survival recuperation.

3. Reorient and strengthen civil defense programs to pay particular attention to those situations in which their capability is most applicable rather than try to handle all problems across-the-board.

4. Broaden the current programs of research, development, and systems analysis to consider in more detail the problems involved in recuperation and in the postwar period generally.

639

5. Study and propose legislation in some form similar to that of my proposed War Damage Equalization Corporation.

6. Initiate research on the use of mines as personnel and industrial shelters.

7. Initiate a program of technical education and assistance to orient and encourage private planning and research.

8. Do much more long-range planning in the field of nonmilitary defense and independent and dependent groups. In particular, we suggest that OCDM or the Executive Department establish a *permanent* independent long-range planning organization of the same type as RAND, ORO, SRI, or the like.

As a civil defense program this cannot be expected to solve all our problems. But it will be a vast improvement over what we now have. It would unquestionably strengthen the nation for some of the trials that may lie ahead.

V

SOME QUESTIONS AND ANSWERS

Introduction

IT is the purpose of this section to give my reaction at this writing to some of the objections and questions which have been raised at the talks I have given on the subject of this book. The subjects of the questions are listed below:

1. The calculated "costs" for a Credible First Strike are unacceptable.
2. We will not accept the possibility of uncalculable risks.
3. The program does not cover an interesting range of situations.
4. It is dangerous to dispel current illusions.
5. There are better alternatives.
6. The Preattack Mobilization Base is politically infeasible.
7. The U.S. will not survive the postwar competition.
8. Morale problems will make reconstruction impossible.
9. Counterforce as Insurance or Credible First Strike accentuates crisis.
10. Credible First Strike increases probability of surprise attack.
11. Credible First Strike is warlike and provokes S.U.
12. Credible First Strike converts peripheral war into central war.
13. Addresses the wrong problems.
14. Evacuation means war.
15. People will not accept the government's leadership.
16. An S.U. ultimatum ruins us.
17. The enemy can double-cross us.
18. System gives S.U. strategic warning.
19. The system leaves out world-wide claims on recuperation.
20. Undisciplined populations cannot evacuate.
21. Advance planning is useless.
22. Shelters are psychologically unsound.
23. Civil Defense causes an Arms Race.

1. *Objection:* "The U.S. would never deliberately risk a war which might result in the calculated losses envisaged by this program, the destruction of many American cities, and something like five to thirty million dead— all with at best only a reasonable expectation of recuperation."

Answer: No American can say definitively what the U.S. will actually do. Neither can our potential enemies, wherein lies much of the practical power of a good deterrence program. The best that any Credible First Strike Capability can do is to make it rational (or not wildly irrational) for the U.S. to go to war as an alternative to tolerating extreme provocations. The word "rational" means that five or ten years after the war is over the country will not look back on the war as a mistake. (The Soviet

641

Union, for example, undoubtedly feels that the cost of victory in World War II—20 to 30 million dead and one-third of its wealth destroyed—was preferable to domination by Nazi Germany. Similarly, it should be *credible,* that we will go to war if the President and the enemy both see plainly that going to war is rational. One can almost hear the President saying to his advisors, "How can I go to war—almost all American cities will be destroyed?" And the answer ought to be, in essence, "That's not entirely fatal, we've built some spares." Under these circumstances, the enemy cannot *rely* on the U.S. not going to war when provoked beyond endurance. The object, of course, is to get most of what we want (including encouragement and support for our allies) by deterring the enemy from inordinately provocative tactics; we want to *avoid* actually going to war.

Insofar as the enemy is willing to gamble that the U.S. will not go to war because it lacks an adequate civil or air defense program, war is brought nearer. He is obviously more willing to gamble if the urban U.S., lacking preparations, is open to total annihilation. A parallel analysis holds for the conviction of the world, friends and enemies alike, that the U.S. would support her allies in a crisis.

2. *Objection:* "The estimated damage said to be within the enemy's power is appalling. Even greater damage is possible because of possible miscalculation or, more insidiously, because of possible optimistic assumptions about enemy or U.S. capabilities. Thus, the U.S. will lack confidence in any calculations that purport to show we have a Credible First Strike Capability. The enemy will note this lack of confidence, so any Credible First Strike program is practically worthless. Without confidence we are as paralyzed as if the program did not exist."

Answer: First, the U.S. is more vulnerable to blackmail without the façade of a Credible First Strike Capability. Second, recall the asymmetry between the enemy and us. The enemy has the incentive to be a little cautious in his calculations. He admittedly knows whether he has any supersecret or unallowed-for capabilities. But it is perilous and maybe unreasonable for him not to disclose them *to us* at this juncture. Even if he does have some secret weapons, such capabilities are almost of necessity revolutionary and untried, and therefore usually doubtful. In any case, even if he has confidence in his new weapon, as long as we do not know about it, he must impute to us the same kind of estimates that we have actually made. We can only conjecture the enemy's capabilities. To this extent, a Credible First Strike Capability is like any other military system. But not having such a capability is also dangerous. One can but design against the known dangers (leaning over backwards to use assumptions that favor the enemy where this does not result in unrealistic requirements) and trust that the enemy does not have some Buck Rogers death ray.

Admittedly, the counterforce ability can only alleviate and not eliminate uncertainty about how much damage the enemy can do. We live in an uncertain and dangerous time. There is an important consolation:

civil defense programs can be designed so that the results of an attack are not very sensitive to *most* of the assumptions. For example, ordinarily doubling the number of megatons delivered less than doubles the number of casualties, instead of annihilating us.

There is an important difference between the programs which occur as a result of the crash phase of the Preattack Mobilization Base and ordinary capabilities-in-being. The crash program which looks only a few years ahead is naturally relatively reliable. An ordinary program which looks to 1970 cannot expect in advance to be this reliable. Thus, while in 1970 we should know whether our program is adequate, there cannot be a firm assurance in 1960 that what we are doing will not be obsolete by 1970. However, in this respect civil defense seems more rather than less stable than other military systems. The fact that the Preattack Mobilization Base is designed around the immediate future (with some attention to legacy values, of course) makes its operation much more reliable than ordinary programs. In fact, it might be sensible to do a full program by a series of Preattack Mobilization Bases followed by crash programs. There would be wastage and obsolescence, but this might be more than counterbalanced by the possibility of better planning.

3. *Objection:* "It is an important claim that a Credible First Strike Capability will deter the Russians from provocative actions and, failing to deter against Type II provocations, will facilitate corrective action. But the increased capability is actually too small to be worthwhile, because possible Soviet provocations will be too innocuous to be affected by such a capability or will be self-limiting because of a 'residual fear of war.' The program undoubtedly makes a marginal, but only a marginal, difference since it is designed for such improbable events."

Answer: Insofar as the international political situation involves opposition against a living, thinking enemy, if you leave yourself open to any particular form of attack you encourage *that* form. Any defense of particular areas predicated on a threat of mutual suicide or self-limiting limited wars makes one highly vulnerable to a serious war of nerves. Of course, such a war of nerves is slightly risky for the enemy, but so long as this kind of blackmail holds forth big payoffs for him, we are in effect inviting him to go ahead and try. Thereby we increase the *probability* of a crisis. The enemy can do much to minimize his already small risks. For example, he can raise the U.S. to a peak of tension, drop it, raise it, drop it, in the manner of Hitler during the Munich period (see Chapter VIII), always leaving open lines of retreat. He can actually test experimentally how much he can push the U.S. around, by initially pushing us around for small "gains."

Another point. Certain psychological types are born to exploit the current stalemate. There is the type who dwells on the weaknesses of his enemy and cannot see his own. This is exemplified by some military people who are over-indoctrinated in the offensive spirit. Then there are fanatics and reckless gamblers. The recommended program is to some extent a hedge against the contingency that any of these dangerous irresponsibles come to power in Russia. However, one does not have to envision desperate international crises to see the value of the program. Merely creating the possibility of going into high gear under the Preattack Mobilization Base or initiating some fairly drastic action once we have an effective Credible First Strike inhibits even minor provocations. This is because minor provocations sometimes lower our reaction threshold significantly. Lowering our reaction threshold hurts the enemy by limiting his future possibilities of action and in general making it clear that he is living dangerously. In short, the angrier he gets us this time, the less it takes to rouse us next time. Therefore, it is of some value to him not to aggravate us in even relatively minor ways if it is conceivable that great anger at a later date will be dangerous to him.

Finally, the Credible First Strike is not offered as an alternative to, but a complement to, our peripheral capabilities, conventional military power, and NATO. The only serious hope for conventional or limited atomic capability is that Russia, too, limits herself; the Credible First Strike Capability is the kind of thing that forces her to do so.

4. *Objection:* "Shelter programs threaten to have exactly the wrong effect. Instead of putting backbone into our leaders, it may so terrify the people that they will implore their leaders to appease the enemy, for the terrible meaning of thermonuclear war would be brought home to the people either when the shelters were being built or later, and even more harshly, during a crisis or evacuation. In this respect, mere discussion of the need for civil defense can be harmful."

Answer: It is true that a large civil defense effort would impress the nation with the serious implications of the international situation, and this might lead to public pressures for additional caution; too much caution could, of course, be harmful. Nonetheless, U.S. foreign policy would suffer less from such accentuated public awareness of the risks of total war than it would from the sudden realization in time of crisis that the country has no chances of survival should deterrence fail. In the crisis itself citizens, and particularly the leaders of a country, would have to face up to the unpleasant facts. Terror is not to be averted by the government doing nothing until it is suddenly presented with some horrible alternatives. The enemy can cure us of wishful thinking if he desires. After very few cycles of scaring us, relaxing us, scaring us, relaxing us, we will be as scared as we can get. The real answer to the objection is that since the program is directed against very violent or provocative enemy behavior, this behavior itself will arouse much more terror than will the mere building of shelters or the making of serious plans.

The initial reaction to the program may depend on how it is presented. The major emphasis ought to be on its deterrence value and on the extra insurance if deterrence fails. We do not really expect to have to use the system. Still, it is vital the people realize that the system may possibly be used even though the existence of the program makes war or serious crises less likely. Thus, the program will be realistic.

5. *Objection:* "Other methods of spending the same money will do the job better; for example, a bigger army, expanded SAC, nuclear sharing, foreign aid (economic or military)."

Answer: Discussed in Chapter XI, pages 539 to 546.

6. *Objection:* "The Preattack Mobilization Base concept is unrealistic because the U.S. would never spend the large sum envisaged no matter what the stimulus. Such things are not done in peacetime by a democracy. The only realistic possibilities are to surrender, to appease, or to engage in a limited or general war. An in-between move, such as a peacetime full or partial mobilization, is so patently ridiculous politically that the enemy can rely on our not carrying it through even under extreme provocation."

Answer: It is difficult in times of relative peace, when the nation is arguing vehemently about varying the budget by a few billion dollars, to take seriously proposals that involve a great many billions. But, as we all know, the total military expenditure can be enormous during a war. If in 1960 the nation were spending the same per cent of its gross national product on defense as in 1944, it would be spending more than $200 billion per year. And I have already pointed out that the nation has also spent spectacularly on occasions other than all-out war. Recent history is especially rich in occasions on which the nation has taken drastic steps when these seemed necessary for survival. Consider the period from 1935 to 1939. In 1935 we passed the Neutrality Act and in 1937 strengthened it. Probably most people (including experts) would have predicted on the basis of this and other evidence, that the U.S. would not soon do anything really belligerent in peacetime. But, as a result of the fall of France in 1939, we increased our military budget by 50 per cent; in 1940 we instituted our first peacetime draft; and in 1941, in spite of an explicit promise made to the draftees, we kept them in service an extra year.

Our reaction to Korea apparently would not have been anticipated by many sociologists or political scientists studying American temper. It was formerly characteristic of the U.S. that when it went to war, it did so wholeheartedly or scarcely at all. The Civil War and the First and Second World Wars exemplify the first reaction, and the Mexican and Spanish Wars the second. But Korea seemed to call for and get a different reaction. We fought in Korea in a limited but vigorous fashion and as a backup increased our military establishment fivefold, most of the extra force being kept in reserve. Evidently the American democracy can take strong action if the need seems clear. Its capacity to do so will be increased by sound and early planning. As a final example of our ability to take unprecedented, though in this case moderate, action when necessary, note that the U.S. reinstated a peacetime draft in 1946 after cancelling the wartime draft.

7. *Objection:* "It is pointless to fight a war even if victory is achieved, since the country will be so debilitated that any third- or fourth-rate power could take it over. Therefore, even though a reasonably adequate

Counterforce as Insurance program might save lives, we would not emerge as an independent country, even if technically winning the war."

Answer: Saving lives is in itself a reasonable objective; but the program is intended to be much more than a reduction in the number of immediate casualties. If the U.S. does win the war promptly, it will have had an infuriating experience that is likely to create a problem quite the opposite of that envisaged by this objection. The country will be very well sheltered, having lost all of its soft spots. It will be in a "mean temper," having just fought a war to save the world. It will be in no mood to be pushed around by other countries. It will have a large strategic air force because a properly defended air force cannot be thrown away in a single strike or two. Far from being weak or vulnerable, the U.S. might be able to "take over the world"—even though such a goal is utterly inconsistent with our political institutions and values. The least the U.S. could expect, and insist on, is that the rest of the world help, not hinder, her reconstruction effort and cooperate in organizing the peace.

8. *Objection:* "Even though the physical basis for reconstruction survives the war, the psychological, political, and social aspects might not be conducive to great postwar effort. Possibly, for instance, the population will be totally apathetic toward, or even vindictive against, the old government for having brought about such a disaster. Strife might arise between those whose property has been destroyed and those whose property has not. These and other problems could lead to paralyzing conflicts."

Answer: Assuming the program works no worse than calculations indicate, we can fairly hope for exactly the opposite effect. According to many historical examples, there may be a trend toward conservatism and an overriding drive to rebuild all that has been destroyed. The government will be able to give an honest account if its reasons for going to war, one that will calm the ire of the populace. The nation has destroyed the enemy that had to be destroyed. It did so with fewer casualties than many expected. More important, the government has a feasible and credible plan for reconstruction. In short, all of our troubles were foreseen, evaluated, and found to be worth the cost.

Now, given that a reasonable program is presented, the people will probably rally round and work for it. If our War Damage Equalization Corporation is in effect, a large portion of those who have lost property will have a real interest in government stability.

Nonetheless, there might be serious long-term effects on our political and economic institutions. We can well imagine, for example, the creation of a type of economic organization in the U.S. that would be very weak in international competition or incompatible with our current political and social ideals. But, equally well, we can imagine a renewed vigor among the population with a zealous, almost religious, dedication to reconstruction, exemplified by a 50- to 60-hour work week. Clearly, the question of what kind of political and economic institutions we could have in the postwar period is not independent of the planning that has been done—which is another pressing argument for better planning.

9. *Objection:* "The system cannot bear a prolonged crisis, so the U.S. will either have to attack or back down; at least it must rescind the evacuation order."

Answer: On the contrary, a civil defense shelter system can be designed to bear a prolonged crisis. As much as possible, the evacuation shelters should be located near reasonably comfortable housing. (Families may, of course, have to double up and then some.) The 20 to 30 million people left in cities to operate essential services should have especially designed shelters of much greater than average strength.

The evacuation itself can take place in stages. We could, for example, first evacuate women and children and whatever workers are most dispensable. This is likely to have only a moderate effect on the gross national product. The people left in the cities can still get protection by moderate overcrowding of the urban shelters. There will usually be adequate shelter within a matter of minutes, particularly if the urban workers are willing to relocate for the emergency.

I concede that the government will be under enormous pressure to do something drastic. In most situations, this will be a gain rather than a loss, for the bargaining ability of the enemy is hurt by the evident inflexibility to which our government is subjected.

10. *Objection:* "If the system is actually effective, or rather, if the S.U. believes it is, then instead of committing an extreme provocation, the S.U. will be forced to attack the U.S. directly."

Answer: Insofar as the S.U. *really* wants to commit the extreme provocation, it will indeed be forced to attack the U.S. This possibility has to be handled by making our retaliatory capability plainly adequate. This should restrain the Russians, since they must now choose between either giving up their local aggression or accepting retaliation. They should choose the former, and they probably will. If the Soviet leadership at the time is so irrational as to choose "suicide," then probably the defense program does not make much difference in precipitating the war, but it does reduce our casualties.

11. *Objection:* "The civil defense program is itself highly provocative and will either make it harder to get along with the S.U. or induce them to pre-empt."

Answer: As far as the S.U. pre-empting is concerned, we have the same answer as in item 10 above. Instituting the civil defense system by itself is (logically or illogically) no more provocative than most current recommendations for reducing our vulnerability. In terms of getting along with the S.U., the whole purpose of the system is to enable the U.S. to take much firmer positions. Whether this is good or bad depends on matters not discussed here, except insofar as I have already said why it is good to have the *ability*, or at least the *seeming ability*, to take firm stands whether or not one actually does take them.

12. *Objection:* "Credible First Strike may convert peripheral war into central war."

Answer: Insofar as the civil defense program gives us the ability to convert *at our discretion,* it should be a good thing. In my own mind, a so-called limited war involving the U.S.S.R. and, say, Japan might be one we would not want to fight on Japanese territory. And we might want very much to win it, too. One could argue that it is dangerous to have a capability of this type. We might misuse it and accidentally or purposely convert a relatively unimportant peripheral war into a general holocaust. There is at least a modicum of truth in this.

If having a good civil or air defense capability tempts the U.S. to try to make deterrence do too much by excessive commitments to take drastic action, then we automatically are assuming some big risks. All of the standard remarks on the "rationality of irrationality" apply here, only now there is an appreciable chance that the irrationality is not so bizarre. As a matter of fact, we conjecture that the real difficulty is exactly of the opposite sort as expressed in objections 1 through 4, above.

13. *Objection:* "The real danger is not extremely provocative actions but political subversion, both here and abroad, now complicated because these defense measures will have bankrupted the nation."

Answer: The improbability of bankruptcy has been discussed elsewhere. The main part of the objection is irrelevant, since the defense program is not put forward to deal with political subversion. Other activities that compete with defense for funds are similar in this respect. The problems against which defense is directed are vital; that is, they cannot be ignored. It does not refute defense to say that other problems are vital too—or even more vital. It is interesting to see that what effect adequate defense programs have on the subversion problem seems to be beneficial. A reasonable defense posture helps, because the enemy then does not have quite as much freedom of action. The U.S. defense posture should also have an antisubversive effect on the rest of the world by making it credible that the U.S. will defend them when the chips are down. Furthermore, a strong posture will, so we hope, make possible a "counter-subversion," or even stronger foreign policy by a toughened U.S. (should that seem desirable).

14. *Objection:* "The decision to evacuate is really a decision to go to war, and is therefore irrevocable."

Answer: If true and clear to the enemy, this is extremely serious, because he will be impelled to strike at the U.S. during the evacuation (not to kill civilians, who are not really a military target, but to get in the first blow). If true but unappreciated, or not quite accepted by the enemy, the objection has much less force. Since we assume adequate Type I Deterrence, he may desire to take the risk that it is not true. (However, see objection 18 on strategic warning.) *But, I maintain that evacuation is not tantamount to a decision to go to war.* The U.S. should go to great pains to make this clear. We should make any evacuation as undramatic as possible. Now imagine us evacuated. In this circumstance both we and the enemy realize that even if the U.S. should strike first to avoid being struck, we are likely to lose many if not most of our cities anyway—and much more besides. Surely we would be likely to negotiate rather than go to war. The enemy should, and probably can, be made to understand this. His willingness to rely on our limited aims will then be overriding, since his alternative (a surprise attack) has, we assume, been made very unpalatable by our strong, protected SAC.

It is clear that the enemy cannot risk stimulating the U.S. to evacuate two or three times a year. But it is perfectly conceivable to us that the U.S. might have to evacuate two or three times every decade, though some of my colleagues find even this to be risky from the viewpoint of the enemy. They expect that he would behave himself for quite some time after the first evacuation.

15. *Objection:* "The experts or the policy makers might support the decision to mobilize or to evacuate, but the public would not go along. At best, this means an unwilling and uncooperative populace, with the eventual political extinction of the current administration and, at worst, a complete paralysis of the government."

Answer: It is hard to predict popular reactions even to situations that, unlike this one, are known in detail. Yet many things will make it easy for the government to carry out the program if convinced of its essential rightness:

   a. Aside from possibly subtle psychological or sociological effects, the program is rational. It has, compared with other current military programs, high reliability. Thus the government can have more than usual confidence in its calculations—a confidence very likely to be communicated to the people.

   b. The shelters themselves will be sturdy-looking. Insofar as people evaluate their performance in terms of standard or "reasonable" attacks they will in fact be extremely sturdy, so there should be relatively little "debunking by experts."

   c. The passive defense program should be somewhat over-designed so as to meet a situation in which the enemy is (in the military sense) irrationally trying to maximize damage to civilians and industry. Most of the experts and laymen should be more (rather than less) sanguine than I, in my professional conservatism, have been about the outcome of the war. Such persons of pollyanna viewpoint may neutralize to some extent the viewers-with-alarm.

   d. In any situation calling for the mobilization or evacuation program, we can expect some previous education of the people to the hard facts of life, and therefore a willingness to face up to the responsibilities. We repeat, the U.S. has today a military draft that is a direct result of the experiences of the last 20 years. Desperate conditions demand desperate living. We did not choose this world; we just live in it.

   e. The ultimate political effects of the government's actions will depend to some extent on the results obtained. Thus, insofar as the program succeeds in deterring the enemy, this success should redound to the credit of the government.

16. *Objection:* "The enemy can prevent us from evacuating by threatening that if we evacuate, he will attack."

Answer: It is hard to believe that such an ultimatum would not be considered by the U.S. an act of war. It is therefore a bad, an almost incredibly bad, form of pre-empting. All the arguments under objections 10, 11, and 14 against pre-empting apply here with doubled force.

Even aside from this argument, the ultimatum has at most limited feasibility. Even if we did not go to war, the government could scarcely prevent the civilians from evacuating the cities on their own. Also, since an adequate system should have an appreciable capability even with minutes of warning, it would then be physically impossible for the enemy to implement his ultimatum effectively. Hopefully, even in the ICBM era his own decisional and organizational delays will prevent him from attacking on our signal to take shelter. Thus, we will have much more than minutes.

17. *Objection:* "The enemy can circumvent the evacuation by pretending to give in and then attack our cities as soon as our civilians return."

Answer: The above objection implicitly, and erroneously, assumes that civilians are a rational military target. We are evacuating to prevent the enemy from using our civilians as hostages or to keep him from hurting them just because it is easy to do so. It is hard to believe that he would go through complicated, dangerous, and sophisticated moves to destroy a nonmilitary target. Finally, all the arguments against the enemy's pre-empting still hold in this case.

18. *Objection:* "The system gives the S.U. strategic warning."

Answer: There is obviously no necessity for this to happen, since we can if we wish ignore the system in a given action. As a matter of fact, in the manned-bomber era, there is really no necessity to warn the enemy at all because it takes about 8 hours flying time (after normal tactical warning) for him to get bombs to the target. To this must be added some time for decision and organization. Even in the ICBM era, in the unlikely eventuality that we wanted to attack first out of the blue, the "adequate" system would still have considerable value, for we now get 10 to 30 minutes warning.

19. *Objection:* "What's the point of our doing this thing when it forces us to destroy a Russia which we will then only have to rebuild?"

Answer: In this form, the question is beneath anyone's notice. However, one might well ask if there would not be serious competing demands for scarce resources by Europe and Asia, demands so large that our recuperation program would be jeopardized. Depending on the war, this could happen. However, we would expect that those areas that had been hard hit and that did not have an adequate shelter program would have lost more people than resources. Those areas which have had adequate shelter programs also should have prepared to stockpile at least survival rations.

20. *Objection:* "Populations are so undisciplined that even if it is physically possible to do the evacuation operations, it is socially impossible.

From 30 to 60 million people simply cannot be moved around the country to places where they ought to be unless the operation is practiced many times."

Answer: We have examples to the contrary from natural disasters and wartime experiences in other countries, notably Britain and Germany. We agree that it is probably infeasible to train the whole population, but it is feasible to train cadres. This should be sufficient, since most people can be expected to follow reasonable-sounding orders. In rapid, tactical evacuation, the ordinary police plus special traffic controls may suffice to guide the population to the right areas. In addition, everybody who is at home or at work will have been given a map of his proper evacuation route. Most people, we hope, will have been anxious enough to look at the document or study it in peacetime. Some will even reconnoitre in advance. Most important of all, the usual picture of blind, self-destructive panic does not seem to occur except in such situations as an overt danger and a narrow escape route. If you can see the danger, the evacuation is too late anyway.

21. *Objection:* "Expensive advance plans of the Preattack Mobilization Base type are useless because they are invariably discarded or forgotten when the emergency arises. The actual response will be improvised, muddled, and probably stupid."

Answer: The reaction to a crisis is not independent of advance plans and programs. Having a good plan should appreciably improve the probability of using it. There is, of course, no guarantee that the country will in fact use the planned measures. Use of the plans and preparations will have become the rational actions for the country, so the enemy must at least take them seriously. This is a large part of the case for having such preparations.

22. *Objection:* "Shelters are psychologically unsound for Americans. They will lead to defeatism, apathy, and cowardice. Americans have never dug holes in the ground. There is no reason why they should now. What we need is more courage, morale, and discipline."

Answer: I am sure that sophisticated readers will find it hard to believe that the above objection is actually made, but I would say it is the most common of all. About the only thing one can say in answer is that in comparing the damage done in a war to a normal population with civil defense or one which has high courage, morale, and discipline but no civil defense measures, we find that the latter population does very badly. I believe that this difference in the effects of war should reflect itself in our peacetime practices.

23. *Objection:* There is between the United States and the Soviet Union an implicit agreement not to disturb the balance of terror by instituting any serious Counterforce as Insurance or Credible First Strike programs. This is most easily seen by the complete absence on either side of adequate civil defense programs. The institution of a civil defense program would break this implicit agreement and institute an arms race which would be more dangerous than the current situation.

Answer: I believe that the above is a quite reasonable objection to the immediate institution of crash programs of the 20–30 billion dollar level, although even here I would not believe the objection is necessarily overriding. However, I would give it sufficient weight so that I would hesitate to institute such a program today. On the other hand, we believe the Soviets already have programs involving a greater level of effort than that recommended in Appendix IV. Also, it is hard for me to believe that, valuable as the program in Appendix IV is, it would be more than a minor perturbation in the arms race. I would concede at most, that after the program in Appendix IV was carried out, one might hesitate in activating the Preattack Mobilization Base if Soviet behavior were reasonable and rather institute the larger programs on a stretched out basis or even hold them in abeyance.

·

INDEX

A and B countries, analogy with World War I, 350; concept of, 77–79, 306. *See also* Recuperation

Accidental war—"Accidental": 190, 205–210; Camlan analogy, 525–526; and deterrence, 157, 159, 183, 209, 217; fear of, can handicap, 209, 256, 269, 361; generates requirement for Counterforce as Insurance, 18, 526, 558; may give tactical warning, 106; miscalculation, 227–229; mutually undesirable, 225. "Non-accidental": 190, 216–217, 259; probability of, 33–34; problem begins acute stage in 1961, 467; reciprocal fear of surprise attack, 16, 158–159; serious problem, 349, 467; should be terminated rapidly, 182, 187; some scenarios, 228; stability against, 187–188, 256, 259–269. *See also* Arms control, Catalytic war, Escalation Finite Deterrence, Military stability, Multistable Deterrence, Self-fulfilling prophecy, World War I

Active defense, against second order threats, 303–304, 519; in 1973, 518–521; "leakproof," 38. *See also* Air defense, Anti-ICBM

Active deterrence, *see* Type II Deterrence

AEC, *see* Atomic Energy Commission

Air defense, 4, 100–109; against second order threats, 303–304, 519; against small attacks, 107–108; against V-2 (World War II), 382–383; analysis of, 329–330, 345; can help recuperation, 108–109; contributions to nonmilitary defense, 102; gaps in 1956, 436; German (World War II), 329–330; in U.S.S.R., 99; new capabilities (1961), 460; and Preattack Mobilization Base, 26; to prevent a "free ride," 102–103, 274–275; to protect strategic forces, 271–273; for warning, 103–107. *See also* Active defense, Semi-automatic ground environment

Air Force Magazine, 101n

Air Launched Ballistic Missiles (ALBM), 481

Air Materiel Command (AMC), 427

Air Research and Development Command (ARDC), 427, 450

Aircraft carriers, vulnerability of, 434

ALBM, *see* Air Launched Ballistic Missiles

Alert, air borne, 200, 459; innovation of ground, 458; intermittent, 181; as reaction, 257–258; and Type II Deterrence, 288. *See also* Ballistic Missile Early Warning System, Self-fulfilling prophecy, Warning

Allies, and Berlin, 222; nuclear sharing, 544–545; safety of, 30–31, 138–139, 155–156, 159, 178–179; support for, 543, 199–200, 543. *See also* Blackmail, "Hague Convention," Independent nuclear deterrents, Limited war, North Atlantic Treaty Organization, Resources

AMC, *see* Air Materiel Command

American Civil War, casualties, 169

Analysis, *see* Planning and analysis

Analytic Services Incorporated (ANSER), 587

ANSER, *see* Analytic Services Incorporated

Anti-ICBM, 519; for hard buildings, 270. *See also* Active defense, Nike-Zeus, Warning

Anticontamination, after early attack, 60–62; after late attack, 61–62; research on, 61–62, 632–633; of strontium-90, 68–89

ARDC, *see* Air Research and Development Command·

Argus effect, 483

Arms control, 4; and blackmail, 239; central problem of, 524; cheating in, 246, 254, 390; and clandestine intelligence, 247–248, 389–390; and communicating with enemy, 182, 238–239; difficulties, 230–231; difficulties in (1951), 425; and disarmament, 224, 232; discussion of, 223–255; of Doomsday Machines, 147–151, 524; during hostilities, 239; easily compatible with Minimum Deterrence, 11–12, 249; and false preemption, 228; first step argument, 233, 393; forced by public opinion, 243, 390–392; forced by technology, 223–224, 252, 484–485, 537, 574; "games," 454n; and how wars start, 226–231; implicit, 240, 252, 308, 466–467; implicit ban on use of nuclear weapons,

653

Bornet, Vaughn D., xiii
Bowen, William, xii
Boyd, William B., 348n
Bradley, Phillips, 579n
Brennan, Donald G., xii
Brinkmanship, 571
British Labour Party, suggestion for non-nuclear club, 235, 509
British Medical Journal, 53n
Brodie, Bernard, v, xi, xii, 169
Broken-back war, 433
Brown, Harold, 456n
Bryant, Peter, 228
Budget, need to raise, 564–568; studies for fixed, 341–343. *See also* Resources
Buildings, *see* Structures, Installations
Bulletin of the Atomic Scientists, 53n
Bush, Vannevar, 320, 380, 386
Buzzard, Rear Admiral Sir Anthony, 243

Calculated win, concept of, 307–308; and deterrence, 557–558; if missile gap, 194–195, 467–469; possibility of, 230; *vs.* imponderables, 191–192, 196–199
Californium bullet, 494
Cancer, 24, 53; "no threshold" theory of, 71
Carbon-14 (C-14); discussion of, 72–74
Carrier, Joseph M., Jr., xii
Catalytic war, discussion of, 231. *See also* Accidental war, China, Nth countries
Center of International Studies, Princeton University, v, viii, xi, xii
Central Intelligence Agency (CIA), 581
Central war, possible limitations to, 514. *See also* Controlled reprisal, Controlled war, Thermonuclear war
Century series fighters, 449
CEP, *see* Circular probable error
Cesium-137 (Cs-137), 57, 70n; as external gamma source, 62; and potassium, 70n; and weapons testing, 24
China, 6, 26, 509; blackmail by, 151–152, 284–285, 504–505; and controlled reprisals, 289, 505; defense against, 303–304, 511, 519; and Doomsday Machine, 151; growth rate of, 502–505; ICBM in, 284–285; loss of, 571–573; in 1960, 503; in 1969, 501–505; in 1973, 514, 519; and nuclear war, 229–230; opportunities for mischief, 492
Churchill, Winston S., 367, 371–375, 377, 394, 396
CIA, *see* Central Intelligence Agency
Circular probable error (CEP), of ballistic missiles, 468–469 and note; defined, 619

Civil defense, an adequate program, 515–518; analysis of various programs, 114–116; anticontamination research, 632–633; breakdown of minimum program costs, 627–628; cooperation of organizations, 638; costs for research on, 628–629; defense of, 639; discussion of, 626–640; education of public, 637; effectiveness of measures, 113–114; and Finite Deterrence, 17; a $500 million proposal, 626; improvisation of existing structures for, 631; interaction of military and nonmilitary defenses, 634; lead time, 26, 628–629; a minimum government effort summarized, 639–640; miscellaneous research and development, 637; monitoring of research and development, 630; objections to suggested program, 650–651; objectives of small program, 626–627; prototype shelters, 637; radiation meters, 85, 631; RAND report discussed, 114–116, 552–553, 626n; reducing lead time, 632; studies and planning, 633–634; uncertainties, 635–637. *See also* Anticontamination, Evacuation, Fallout, Postwar conditions, Postwar environment, Radiation, Recuperation
Civil defense in U.S.S.R., U.S. views of, 444. *See also* U.S.S.R., Civil defense
Civil Defense in Western Europe and the Soviet Union, 440
Clark, Grenville, 6n
Clark, Paul G., xii
Coercion, 302. *See also* Bargaining, Blackmail, Deterrence, Postattack blackmail, Ultimatums
Coker, Joseph D., xii
Cold war, and appeal of Communism, 497–498; and arms control, 223–224; and cheap calories, 497; and satellite television, 497
Combs, Vice Admiral Thomas S., USN, 434
Command and Control, 4; an Achilles' heel, 301–302; and accidental war, 188, 269; air defense can help, 108–109; difficulties in 1960's, 499; need for centralized control, 187–188; need for postattack, 163, 171, 174, 182; President's role, 187–189; protected by intrawar deterrence, 270–271. *See also* War fighting, War plans
Computers, 495, 511
Communism, appeal of, 497–498; and deterrence, 157–159
Concealment, 263–264

* The Federal Civilian Defense Administration and The Office of Defense Mobilization were combined into a single agency, Office of Civilian and Defense Mobilization, in August 1958.

INDEX

State Department Policy Planning Staff, 582
Stewart, A., 53n
Stockpiling, bombs, 460; since Korea, 344. *See also* Preattack Mobilization Base
Strategic Air Command (SAC), base location policy, 58, 173, 279, 422, 434; can be deterred, 27–30, 32–34, 35–36, 37; composition of:
in 1951, 421–422; in 1956, 448–449; in 1961, 458–459; in 1965, 480–481; in 1969, 490, 500; in 1973, 506, 510, 512, 514–515, 519, 520–521
draws attack, 103–104, 114; fail-safe for, 205, 206, 209; false alarm, 205–208, 209, 422n; must have acceptable image, 148–149, 155–160 (*see also* Alliance policy, Self-fulfilling prophecy); political worth of, 447; provoking to U.S.S.R., 157; unready in 1948, 422; Stalin underestimated, 425; vulnerability of:
analogy to British fleet, 373; in 1951, 420–421, 422–424, 425–426; in 1956, 429–430, 434–436; in 1961, 458–459, 467–469; in 1965, 480–482; in 1969, 500; in 1973, 512.
See also Alert, Atlas, B-36, B-47, B-52, B-58, Command and Control, Controlled war, Deterrence, Doctrinal lag, Minuteman, Missile gap, Mobile systems, National strategy, Polaris, Seamaster, Shelters, Snark, Titan, U.S.S.R., Vulnerability, War plans
Strategic forces, peacetime objectives, 127; wartime objectives, 162–189. *See also* National strategy, Strategic Air Command
Strategy, proper objective of, 163; *vs.* justice, 395. *See also* National strategy
Strontium-90 (Sr-90), 72; and cancer, 65; chemistry of, 70–71; contamination of large areas by, 65–66; current contamination, 64–65; decontamination and alleviation, 68, 69, 72; fatalities from, 63–64; in food, 66–69; General White on, 23–24; and leukemia, 63; Libby on, 23; need for study of, 70–71; permissible levels of, 64–65 and note; safety standards for, 69–72; unit defined, 64; and weapons testing, 24, 391
Strope, Walmer E., xii
SU, *see* U.S.S.R.
Submarines, costs for nuclear, 265; defective U.S. torpedoes (World War II), 385; defense against (World War I),

355–356; depth bombs against, 327, 356, 448; role in (World War I), 354–355; search for (World War II), 381–382
Sullivan, Charles, xii
Summaries, conflicting objectives, 345–346, 523–531, 531–550; historical prototypes, 523–531; Lectures I and II, 295–308; national security problem, 345–346. *See also* Civil defense, Installations, Policy formulation, War Damage Equalization Corporation, World Wars I–VIII
Surrender studies, need for, 174. *See also* Controlled war, Negotiation, Postattack blackmail
Symington, Stuart, 24, 437
Systems analysis, viii; for civil defense, 633; and contingency planning, 122–124; techniques of, ix note. *See also* Planning and analysis, Policy formulation, The RAND Corporation

TAC, *see* Tactical Air Command
Tactical Air Command (TAC), a use of, 106n
Tanham, George K., 579n
Tanks, 352
Taylor, Benjamin C., xii
Taylor, General Maxwell, USA (Ret.), 8n
Technological race, causes doctrinal lag, 418–419, 521–522, 534; current skill of industry, 451; difficulties of third powers, 461–462; military planner, 125, 421; predicting, 314–315, 420, 456, 488–489; problem of untested weapon systems, 430–432; weakness of ARDC system concept, 450. *See also* Arms race, Doctrinal lag, Lead time, Postattack environment, Research and Development
Teller, Edward, 23–24
Test suspension, 244; effect of cheating in, 244n, 245 and note; effect of evasion, 244–245; example of inadequate preparation, 453–455; Khrushchev and, 456–457; U.S.S.R. and U.S. attitudes toward, 252–254
Thermonuclear bombs, consequences of, 429; effects of, 429–432. *See also* Nuclear weapons
Thermonuclear war, "accidental" accident, 205–210; after an alert, 210–218; a civil defense program and, 626–640; complete description of, 22–24, 35–36,

665